THE GREENWOOD ENCYCLOPEDIA OF
Women's Issues
WORLDWIDE

Editor-in-Chief and Volume Editor

Lynn Walter
University of Wisconsin–Green
Bay

Contributors

Rasa Alisauskiene
Vilnius University, Lithuania

Aida Bagić
Centre for Women's Studies,
Zagreb, Croatia

Jasna Bakšić-Muftić
Law University of Sarajevo,
Bosnia and Herzegovina

Kathryn Bishop-Sanchez
University of Wisconsin–Madison

Alexis Bushnell
University of Iowa, Iowa City

Jill M. Bystydzienski
Iowa State University, Ames

Joy Charnley
University of Strathclyde, Centre
for Swiss Cultural Studies,
Glasgow, Scotland

Lilijana Cickaric
Institute of Social Sciences,
Belgrade, Serbia

JosAnn Cutajar
Junior College, University of
Malta, Commission for the
Advancement of Women within
the Ministry for Social Policy

Daina Stukuls Eglitis
George Washington University,
Washington, D.C.

Torgerdur Einarsdóttir
University of Iceland, Reykjavík

Tahire Erman
University of Bilkent, Ankara,
Turkey

Marianne A. Ferber
University of Illinois at Urbana-
Champaign

Elena Gapova
European Humanities University,
Minsk, Belarus

Kristen Ghodsee
Bowdoin College, Brunswick,
Maine

Ain Haas
Indiana University, Indianapolis

Linda Haas
Indiana University, Indianapolis

Vicki L. Hesli
University of Iowa, Iowa City

Armine Ishkanian
University of California, Berkeley

Nino Javakhishvili
Tbilisi State University, Georgia

Edgar Kaskla
California State University, Long
Beach

Lela Khomeriki
International Center for Civic
Culture, Tbilisi, Georgia

Anne Kovalainen
Turku School of Economics
and Business Administration,
Finland

Elizabeth L. Krause
University of Massachusetts
Amherst

Anu Laas
Tartu University, Estonia

Maria Pantelidou Maloutas
University of Athens, Greece

Eva Martínez-Hernández
University of the Basque
Country, Bilbao, Spain

Beáta Nagy
Budapest University of Economic
Sciences and Public
Administration, Hungary

Carol Nechemias
Pennsylvania State University
Harrisburg

Gillian Pascall
University of Nottingham,
United Kingdom

Livia Popescu
Babes-Bolyai University, Cluj,
Romania

Phyllis Hutton Raabe
University of New Orleans,
Louisiana

Deborah Reed-Danahay
University of Texas at Arlington

Galina Schneider
Washington, D.C.

Benjamin F. Shearer
Independent Scholar

Lyudmyla Smolyar
Odessa State Academy of Food
Technology, Odessa Scientific
Center of Women's Studies,
Ukraine; Gender Council of the
Ministry on Family and Youth;
UN Gender in Development
Program; and "Woman and
Societies" International
Renaissance Foundation

Elizabeth A. Throop
McKendree College, Lebanon,
Illinois

Eileen Trzcinski
Wayne State University, Detroit,
Michigan

Sharon L. Wolchik
George Washington University,
Washington, D.C.

Alison E. Woodward
Vesalius College and the Center
for Women's Studies, Free
University of Brussels, Belgium

Antonia Young
Bradford University, United
Kingdom; and Colgate
University, Hamilton, New York

CONTENTS

CONTENTS

*The Six-Volume Comprehensive Index begins on
page 569 of the final volume, Sub-Saharan Africa*

SET FOREWORD

The Greenwood Encyclopedia of Women's Issues Worldwide is a six-volume set presenting authoritative, comprehensive, and current data on a broad range of contemporary women's issues in more than 130 countries around the world. Each volume covers a major populated world region: Asia and Oceania, Central and South America, Europe, the Middle East and North Africa, North America and the Caribbean, and Sub-Saharan Africa. Volumes are organized by chapters, with each focusing on a specific country or group of countries or islands, following a broad outline of topics—education, employment and the economy, family and sexuality, health, politics and law, religion and spirituality, and violence. Under these topics, contributors were asked to consider a range of contemporary issues from illiteracy and wage discrepancies to unequal familial roles and political participation and to highlight issues of special concern to women in the country. In this way, the set provides a global perspective on women's issues, ensures breadth and depth of issue coverage, and facilitates cross-national comparison.

Along with locating women's agenda in specific national and historical contexts, each chapter looks at the cultural differences among women as well as the significance of class, religion, sexuality, and race on their lives. And, as women's movements and their non-governmental organizations (NGOs) are among the most worldwide forms of civic participation, their effectiveness in addressing women's issues is also examined. In addition to focusing on national and local organizations, many authors also highlight the major role the United Nations has played in addressing women's issues nationally and in supporting women's networks globally and point to the importance of its 1979 Convention on the Elimination of All Forms of Discrimination Against Women (CEDAW), which is still the most comprehensive international agreement on the rights of women.

Contributors were chosen for their expertise on women's issues in the country or area about which they write. Each contributor provides an authoritative resource guide with suggested reading, web sites, films/videos, and organizations as well as a selected bibliography and extensive references. The chapters and resource guides are designed for students, scholars, and engaged citizens to study contemporary women's issues in depth in specific countries and from a global perspective.

This ambitious project has been made possible by the work of many scholars who contributed their knowledge and commitment. I want to thank all of them and especially the other volume editors, Manisha Desai, Cheryl Toronto Kalny, Amy Lind, Bahira Sherif-Trask, and Aili Mari Tripp. Thanks also to Christine Marra of Marrathon Productions and Wendi Schnaufer of Greenwood Publishing Group for their editorial assistance.

As I read the many chapters of this series what struck me most was the sheer force and determination of the many women and men who are seeking solutions to the problems of inequality and poverty, discrimination, and injustice that lie at the root of women's experiences worldwide. I hope this series will further their vision.

Lynn Walter, Editor-in-Chief

USER'S GUIDE

The Greenwood Encyclopedia of Women's Issues Worldwide is a six-volume set covering the world's most populated regions:

Asia and Oceania

Central and South America

Europe

The Middle East and North Africa

North America and the Caribbean

Sub-Saharan Africa

All volumes contain an introduction from the editor in chief that overviews women's issues today around the world and introduces the set. Each volume editor broadly characterizes contemporary women's issues in the particular region(s). The volumes are divided into chapters, ordered alphabetically by country name. A few chapters treat several countries (e.g., Tajikistan, Kazakhstan, Turkmenistan, and Kyrgyzstan, which are grouped together as Central Asia) or a group of islands (e.g., the Netherland Antilles).

The comprehensive coverage facilitates comparisons between nations and among regions. The following is an outline showing the sections of each chapter. In rare instances where information was not available or applicable for a particular country, sections were omitted.

Profile of [the Nation]

A paragraph on the land, people(s), form of government, economy, and demographic statistics on female/male population, infant mortality, maternal mortality, total fertility, and life expectancy.

Overview of Women's Issues

A brief introduction to the major issues to be covered, giving the reader a sense of the state of women's lives in the country.

Education

Opportunities

Literacy

Employment and the Economy

Job/Career Opportunities

Unemployment

Pay

Working Conditions

    Sexual Harassment

Support for Mothers/Caretakers

    Maternal Leave

    Daycare

    Family and Medical Leave

Inheritance and Property Rights

Social/Government Programs

    Sustainable Development

    Welfare

Family and Sexuality

Gender Roles

Marriage

Reproduction

    Sex Education

    Contraception and Abortion

    Teen Pregnancy

Health

Health Care Access

Diseases and Disorders

    AIDS

    Eating Disorders

    Nutrition

    Cancer

    Depression

    Mental Illness

Politics and Law

A regional map is in the inside cover of each volume. Additionally, each chapter has an accompanying country or mini-region map. Each volume has an index consisting of subject and person entries; a comprehensive set index is included at the end of the Sub-Saharan Africa volume.

INTRODUCTION

Beginning in the late 1960s, various women's movements throughout Western Europe were pursuing an agenda that identified women as political actors with common interests and issues. At that time, the European Union (EU) had six members and, at the insistence of France, a policy requiring equal pay for women; and in the Soviet Union, East Germany, and other Eastern bloc countries, women's emancipation was official state policy.

In the intervening thirty-five years, as the European Union expanded to fifteen members, its gender equality policies developed well beyond equal pay to cover all facets of working women's lives. The globalization of European economies advanced—increasing competition; putting pressure on wages, benefits, and public sector spending; and challenging the ability of national governments to act independently to address women's issues. The Soviet Union collapsed; and the Russian Federation, the newly independent states, and the former Eastern bloc countries in Central and Eastern Europe have experienced rough transitions to democracy and capitalism. War in the Balkans, corruption, increased unemployment, and cutbacks in social programs that support women and children are some of the serious obstacles they have encountered on this path.

These dramatic realignments place women's issues in the context of a new Europe and in the framework of new strategic questions: How will access to quality education, health care, and social security be maintained or improved in this more competitive globalizing economy? Especially in the new democracies, how will diverse groups of women represent their interests at the level of the state and of Europe? How will better economic opportunities be created for women, children, and men in the less prosperous regions of Europe? How will contemporary women's issues be addressed in ways that ensure a democratic, just, and equitable future for the coming generations?

The Greenwood Encyclopedia of Women's Issues Worldwide: Europe addresses these and other questions with current data and authoritative analyses of a broad range of women's issues in thirty-nine European countries, of which eleven—Estonia, France, Germany, The Republic of Ireland, Italy, Poland, Russia, Spain, Sweden, Turkey, and the United Kingdom—are presented in more detailed contexts. Of the thirty-nine countries, fourteen—Austria, Belgium, Denmark, Finland, France, Germany, Greece, The Republic of Ireland, Italy, The Netherlands, Portugal, Spain, Sweden, and the United Kingdom—are members of the European Union, and eleven more—Bulgaria, The Czech Republic, Estonia, Hungary, Latvia, Lithuania, Malta, Poland, Romania, Slovakia, and Turkey—are knocking on the EU's door. Of the Western European countries, only Switzerland, Norway, and Iceland are the EU holdouts, although the latter two are both NATO members. Russia and the post-Soviet countries of Albania, Armenia, Belarus, Georgia, and the Ukraine; and the Yugoslav successor states of Bosnia and Herzegovina, Croatia, Kosovo,[1] Macedonia, and Serbia and Montenegro currently lie outside the institutions of an expanding European Union. However, their geographic and cultural proximity along with their interests in migration issues, developing markets, and political stability bind the futures of East and West together.

COMPARATIVE PERSPECTIVES ON WOMEN'S ISSUES

Addressing questions about women's issues that arise from the differences and commonalities among women in the new Europe requires a comparative approach. To facilitate the use of this volume for comparison across European states, each chapter follows the same broad outline of issues—education, employment and economics, family and sexuality, health, politics and law, religion, and violence. Comprehensive, in-depth, and extensive national data presented from a holistic perspective within a common framework should prove useful to those students, activists, and engaged citizens whose goals would be advanced by comparative perspectives on women's issues.[2] The authors also examine the key historical processes and contemporary practices that shape the variations in equality and well-being among women.

Conceptions of women's issues vary not only by country but also by urban/rural locations, class, ethnicity, race, sexuality, religion, and marital and family status within each state. These dimensions intersect the gender differences between women and men to create a plurality of standpoints on women's issues. This *Europe* volume examines some of these diverse perspectives on women's issues in each of the thirty-nine cases.

CHALLENGES OF THE TWENTY-FIRST CENTURY

Most women in Europe enter the twenty-first century much closer to sexual equality than their great-grandmothers were at the beginning of the twentieth.[3] Over the tumultuous century, women achieved the right to vote and to represent themselves in the judicial and political arenas, laws against sex discrimination in education and employment, access to health care and social security,[4] and publicly funded programs to help balance the responsibilities of family and the workplace.

Still, there are serious unresolved issues—among these are domestic violence, sexual harassment, and sex trafficking of women and girls across national borders into forced prostitution and pornography. Disparities in pay, the sexual division of labor in the work force and the family, as well as unequal political power are also still problems. Furthermore, not everyone enjoys the same levels of well-being and equality as the middle-class women whose movements to promote gender equality bore such abundant fruit in the nineteenth and twentieth centuries.[5] For example, Tahire Erman notes that rural women in Turkey find themselves particularly underrepresented in the centers of political decision making and disadvantaged in health, education, and employment.

The new century inherits other challenges to women's position in society. Firstly, economic policies to reduce debt and inflation have increased unemployment, created downward pressure on wages, and in some cases have led to cutbacks in social services. For instance, in the United Kingdom a series of budget cuts, which began under the government of Margaret Thatcher, have lowered the quality of health, educational, and other social services. Gillian Pascall points out that the budget reduction measures have increased social inequality and that the burdens fall hardest on women with the fewest resources. And many women in Central and Eastern Europe have experienced declining standards of living as social rights, pensions, savings, and jobs disappear in the economic depression that followed the collapse of communism.

WESTERN EUROPE

There are radically new political structures within which Western European women pursue their interests—importantly, the European Union's authority over employment laws and monetary policy. In cases like the Nordic countries of Iceland, Norway, Sweden, Finland, and Denmark, women's rights advocates have successfully exercised their national political rights to vote, form political associations, and run for political office to establish relative equality and security. Thus, some in those countries fear that the Union will weaken their national sovereignty and economic independence and thereby threaten their progress.

On the other hand, as Deborah Reed-Danahay notes for French women's organizations, the EU has its own institutional supports for women's rights. An important example is the European Commission's support of the formation of the European Women's Lobby, a network of women's organizations to exchange ideas and develop new strategies to address women's issues. Women constitute 31 percent of the members of the European Parliament, which is the most democratic and least powerful of European Union institutions. Its Committee on Women's Rights proposes equal opportunity legislation. European Union gender equality laws are focused on economic issues, including equal pay and equal treatment in the workplace as well as childcare and maternity/parental leave; they also address human rights issues such as trafficking in persons and other forms of forced prostitution.

However, the EU has taken a hands-off stance toward other issues of critical importance to women, especially ones that are considered private, family matters or national affairs.[6] Also, EU gender equity institutions are remote and difficult for grassroots groups to comprehend and utilize, and, as institutions, they are marginal to EU power structures. Thus, activists regularly criticize the "femocracies" (official gender equity bureaucracies) for being insensitive to the problems of ordinary women and for being underfunded and ineffective.

The EU in conjunction with the United Nations' Beijing Platform for Action is promoting "gender mainstreaming," a strategy to assess the impact of all public policies and institutions on gender equality. Elizabeth Throop points to Irish efforts to "mainstream equality" in its National Development Plan. It is also a priority of the newly established Ministry for Gender Equality in Denmark. Among the many countries that are also exploring the implication of gender mainstreaming is the Ukraine. Lyudmyla Smolyar affirms that Ukrainian women are eager to engage other European women in a constructive dialogue about what gender mainstreaming will mean for women.

CENTRAL AND EASTERN EUROPE

Along with facing a rise in sex trafficking, prostitution, and pornography, women in the postcommunist countries have also experienced a decline in benefits like subsidized childcare, reversals in their reproductive rights, increasing levels of violence, retreats to patriarchal family values, and a backlash against feminism. Feminism has been discredited by its association with the official state feminism of their former communist governments and by the perceived incapacity of Western feminism to meet the needs of women and men for basic and secure livelihoods. According to Daina Stukuls Eglitis, in Latvia it is women who have borne the brunt of these economic and political setbacks. Interestingly, however, she also reports that the common opinion there is that women's response to the difficulties has typically been "resolve and resolution," whereas men have more often resorted to "drinking and despair."

To counter these setbacks, women are devising strategies that do not rely upon direct access to the central government.[7] Their new social movements and autonomous women's organizations are operating within newly established freedoms of association and speech. For example, Elena Gapova points out that the decrease in women's political representation in Belarus is being countered by the rise of civil society, notably in the form of nongovernmental women's organizations (NGOs). Nino Javakhishvili and Lela Khomeriki support this point, arguing that in Georgia women's nongovernmental organizations, along with the media, must play a major role in monitoring public policy and laws on such issues as gender discrimination, trafficking, and family violence.

However, the effectiveness of new women's organizations depends largely upon their ability to appeal to ordinary women in the country. In Bulgaria, the recent economic decline has been so devastating that women see their issues as much more closely tied to those of Bulgarian men than to other European women. Kristen Ghodsee argues that along with women's rejection of Western feminism, the failure of the few Bulgarian women's organizations to appeal to average women on the basis of mutual interests with men has diminished their effectiveness as change agents.

Another problem confronting women in Russia and the other Central and Eastern European countries is the rise of violent national and religious conflicts. In Albania, Croatia, Serbia and Montenegro, Bosnia and Herzegovina, Macedonia, and Kosovo, war filled the gap left by the collapse of strong central governments and brought with it the scourges of war—killing, "ethnic cleansing,"[8] rape, torture, and other violations of human rights. And even where the transition has been a relatively peaceful one, women in Central and Eastern Europe enter "Europe" at an economic and political disadvantage relative to women in the West. They are located at the margins of the new Europe in what one Bulgarian woman dubbed its "backyard."[9]

Lastly, increasing numbers of Central and Eastern European women have immigrated to the West from poverty and strife toward what they hope will be jobs, prosperity, and peace. In Western Europe, the immigration of lower-income populations has led to expressed concerns about increased crime rates and to nationalist reactions against immigrant groups. The disadvantages faced by immigrant women—whether from Central and Eastern Europe, Turkey, or developing countries—make it clear that not all women share the same perspectives. In France, for example, Deborah Reed-Danahay notes that immigrant women from North Africa have been the focus of national debate on whether they should be allowed to wear headscarves to public school and to practice female circumcision, both practices sanctioned by custom.

WOMEN'S RIGHTS

European women have made progress in claiming sex equality and social security as the entitlements of national citizenship and, more broadly, as human rights. Internationally, women's rights have also been conceptualized as human rights, most importantly in Convention to End All Forms of Discrimination Against Women (CEDAW), adopted by the United Nations in 1979. All of the countries covered in this volume have ratified CEDAW, except Kosovo which is not an independent state.

Following CEDAW, women's rights are conceptualized here as including *civil rights*, *political rights*, and *social rights*. In Europe many of women's basic civil rights such as personal liberty, the rights to own property and conclude valid contracts, and the right to equal justice were achieved in the nineteenth century. However, other civil rights, like women's right to control their own reproduction and sexuality, are politically charged issues in Ireland, Poland, and Turkey today. For example, Tahire Erman points out that family planning has been politicized in conflicts between Kurdish male nationalists and the patriarchal state, with the nationalists accusing the state of deliberately trying to control the Kurdish population. And although there have been strides in recognizing civil partnerships for homosexuals, nowhere do lesbian and gay partners enjoy all the legal prerogatives that attach to familial status as heterosexuals do. For example, only Denmark, Iceland, the Netherlands, and, in 2003, Sweden permit same-sex couples to adopt children.

POLITICS AND LAW

The Right to Vote

Political rights authorize women to participate fully in the decision-making processes of government and politics at all levels. In 1906, Finland, with its strong tradition of equality, became the first country in Europe to legalize votes and political office for women; and, as Anne Kovalainen points out, it is still a leader among nations in upholding women's equality. Other states in Europe granted women's right to vote and hold public offices after World War I, at the impetus of first-wave[10] feminist movements. World War II and fascist governments in Italy, Portugal, and Spain effectively postponed the practice of women's voting until 1945, 1976, and 1975, respectively. Joy Charnley notes that Switzerland was also a late adopter, having granted women's right to vote in 1971, when, some feminists there claim, the real power no longer rested in parliament.

Political Participation

Just as with civil rights, the political rights in law do not necessarily lead to equality in practice. If they did, then women's representation in European parliaments, where equal political rights are written into the law, would not average 15.1 percent and range from 4.4 percent in Turkey to a high of 45.3 percent in Sweden.

In every country, women's politics has taken the form of political party and trade union politics and parliamentary actions as well as feminist movements and autonomous women's organizations. For example, Linda Haas argues that the relatively high number of women in the Swedish parliament is, in part, the result of women threatening to form their own political party. Icelandic women went further, as Torgerdur Einarsdóttir points out, and actually formed a Women's Party, grounded in the ideas of a women's culture and maternal politics. They elected one of their own as mayor of Reykjavík and also did manage to increase the number of women in parliament. Women in Poland, whose representation declined with the collapse of communism, formed a coalition of fifty women's organizations to elect more women to parliament, as Jill Bystydzienski reports. And Tahire Erman points to the Association for the Support and Education of Women Political Candidates (KA-DER), which was established to promote women's representation in the Turkish parliament.

Sex Quotas

Eva Martínez-Hernández argues that in Spain, increases in female representation to nearly 30 percent are attributable to sex quotas on the candidates' list for the Socialist Party. The strategy of imposing sex quotas on political party candidate lists has also been used effectively in German parliamentary elections (31.2 percent). Deborah Reed-Danahay reports that in France, where women constitute 12.2 percent of the parliament, the issue of *parity* has split feminists. Some oppose this proposal to require that half of members of parliament be women on the grounds that it runs counter to notions of universal citizenship. On the other hand, proponents argue that it is necessary to address the dearth of female representatives in the centers of democratic power and influence.

SOCIAL RIGHTS

The entitlement of citizens to social security undergirds European social welfare systems. Ideally, within such systems unemployment, childhood, old age, illness, or disability should not reduce one's well-being below acceptable community standards or stand in the way of one's future capacity to thrive. The 1920s and 1930s saw the partial realization of this fundamental social right in most countries through programs such as health insurance, unemployment and workman's compensation, old-age pensions, mothers' pensions, and disability pensions. These early forms of social security were tied to the recipient's relationship to the labor force. Their establishment was the result of a historic compromise between employer associations and organized labor to stabilize wages, quiet labor unrest, increase demand, promote full employment, and raise Europe out of economic depression.

William Beveridge's 1942 report on ways to address "Want, Disease, Ignorance, Squalor and Idleness" in the UK epitomized the immediate postwar social welfare programs in Western Europe, as Gillian Pascall notes in her chapter.[11] Although the former Soviet bloc countries saw women's full employment in a communist economy as the path to women's equality, policies in Western Europe were congruent with Beveridge's assumption that a man should earn a "family wage" that supported his family while his wife stayed at home as a full-time mother and homemaker. This model of the ideal family was reinforced by (1) concerns about low birthrates during the Depression, which spurred discussion about how to support families and (2) concerns about the needs of children, which, presumably, were best met by stay-at-home mothers. The idea that children's welfare was best insured by full-time mothers was one of the pillars supporting what were referred to as "mothers' pensions," paid to widowed, divorced, and single mothers to support their children without being in the labor force.

Employed Mothers and Childcare

Overcoming the devastation of war and depression, Western European economies grew rapidly in the 1960s through the mid-1970s. The economic boom increased demand for labor—two sources of which were married women with children and foreign *guest workers*.[12] Whether immigrants or married women were drawn most heavily into the labor market depended upon how strong the cultural commitment was to a male-breadwinner/female-caregiver model of the family. For example, Eileen Trzcinski (see Table 15.1) notes that in Germany married women's labor force participation rates were much higher in East Germany, while West Germany preferred immigrant workers.

The economic expansion, the need for more workers, and the concern for the welfare of children all contributed to changes in post–World War II social policies, especially regarding employed mothers. Since then, programs supporting mothers' labor force participation, such as paid maternity and parental leave, family allowances, publicly funded childcare, early childhood education, and after-school programs, have all been part of the social welfare mix.[13] National variations in the length of maternity leave, the level at which a parent on leave is reimbursed for her lost wages, the size of family allowances, and the availability of publicly funded childcare are described in the chapters in this volume.

In all countries, women make decisions about education, occupations, employment, marriage, and the number and spacing of their children based in part on the availability and quality of such programs. For example, Elizabeth Krause outlines some of the everyday ways that Italian women resist the opposition to the remedies designed to promote gender equity. She recounts that women in a Sicilian factory reportedly agreed to take turns becoming pregnant, hoping thereby to avoid their employer's resistance to officially mandated maternity leave.

Social Welfare Programs

Contemporary social policy analysts have examined the relationship between states' welfare policies and their national political economies—communist, social democratic, liberal, or conservative.[14] Their analyses have been criticized for understating the significance of gender and family as factors shaping welfare policy.[15] Among the early critics, Jane Lewis (1992, 1997) links variations in welfare systems to the strength of a country's commitment to maintaining a male-breadwinner family. Ireland, the UK, and Germany fit what Lewis labeled "strong male-breadwinner states." France represents her "modified male-breadwinner" model, and Sweden is a case of her "weak male-breadwinner" state.[16]

The ideals of a "strong male-breadwinner state" are expressed in the Irish Constitution, which affirms, "The State shall . . . endeavour to ensure that mothers shall not be obliged by economic necessity to engage in labour to the neglect of their duties in the home" (quoted by Elizabeth Throop). The French "modified male-breadwinner state" is pro-natalist (i.e., favoring policies to increase the number of children being born), encouraging women to have children through payments per child in the form of family allowances as well as parental education and upbringing allowances. On the other hand, it also strongly supports public daycare, as Deborah Reed-Danahay reports. A "weak male-breadwinner state," Sweden has taken a universalistic approach to social welfare through its efforts to eliminate gender roles. Linda Haas cites a recent Swedish government report calling for "social parity" in the form of "equal access to education and opportunities to advance personal ambitions, interests and talents, shared responsibility for home and children, and freedom from gender-related violence."

The Work of Caring

Publicly funded childcare and maternity leaves have made it easier for women in Europe to be both paid employees and familial caregivers. However, governments have been less able and more reluctant to address the inequalities in family responsibilities, skirting the problem of employed women's *double shift*—in the workplace and in the home. The association of women with caregiving roles in the family is reflected in caregiving work in the labor force. Thus, women face a highly sex-segregated labor market and a family system in which caregiving is considered largely their responsibility in both spheres.[17]

Programs promoting sexual equality in care work are countered by values supporting male authority and female dependence within the family and society. Even in the case of Sweden, where there has been a great deal of public attention paid to eliminating gender roles in the family, Linda Haas notes that shared responsibility for childcare is not yet a reality. Women also differ among themselves on the ideal conception of gender and family relations. For example, many middle- and lower-income women in Turkey see being a housewife and full-time mother as a prestigious status, one that demonstrates that a woman's husband's income is high enough to support her. However, as Tahire Erman also notes, such attitudes make it easier for employers to avoid providing childcare and maternity leave to their young female employees.

FAMILY AND SEXUALITY

Second-wave women's movements that arose in Western Europe in the 1960s and 1970s challenged traditional notions of marriage and family.[18] They pointed out that the supposedly personal aspects of women's lives such as care work, reproduction, sexuality, fertility, motherhood, family relations, and domestic violence raised political issues with societal implications. For example, Maria Pantelidou Maloutas states that in Greece, fundamental change means addressing the issues of the male-dominated family, where childcare and housework are considered women's work, and challenging the "naturalness" of gender stereotypes. JosAnn Cutajar makes a similar argument about women in Malta.

Among these "personal" issues, sexuality has been politicized in a number of ways, for example, with demands for reproductive rights and also for the cultural and legal establishment of lesbian, gay, bisexual, and transgendered rights. Laws to permit lesbian and gay partners to form legal unions have now been enacted in many European countries. Eileen Trzcinski reports that in 2001 Germany provided for the recognition of homosexuality as "another form of sexual orientation alongside heterosexuality. . . . As such, it is an integral part of human identity," which makes it a protected identity under the section of the German Constitution providing for freedom of activity. Catholic Poland, Italy, Spain, and Ireland and Islamic Turkey are more conservative in their conceptions of sexuality. For example, the new Polish Constitution explicitly "protects motherhood and marriage as a union of a man and a woman" (quoted by Jill Bystydzienski). Similarly, most Central and Eastern European countries either have not considered the issue of homosexual rights or have explicitly rejected them. However, Aida Bagić reports that in June 2002, Zagreb, Croatia, celebrated its first Gay Pride rally.

Reproduction

Abortion

In the Soviet era, abortion was freely available and frequently used as a form of birth control. That is still the case in most Central and Eastern European countries, Albania and Poland being the exceptions. In Western Europe, women's movements made control of one's own body and reproduction a priority. They succeeded in changing policies throughout Protestant Europe and in Turkey and Italy. Today Italian law is typical in permitting abortion through the first twelve weeks of pregnancy for "medical, psychological, and social reasons."

Because Catholicism was associated with the repressive Franco regime, its hold on Spanish values has been undermined. Eva Martínez-Hernández points out that the regime circumscribed women's life and forbade any discussion of sexuality or birth control to the extent that the progress made by women in the rest of Europe did not begin in Spain until the 1980s. In 1985 an absolute ban on abortion was lifted, and it was legalized in three circumstances—to save the mother's life, to end pregnancy from rape, or to abort a deformed fetus. In Poland, Catholic resistance to communism enhanced its message of conservative family values. From 1956, abortion was available on demand in Poland. Indeed, women from Western Europe who, prior to the 1960s, faced stricter anti-abortion laws would travel to Poland to get abortions. However, as Jill Bystydzienski notes, in 1993, the postcommunist parliament passed a law banning abortion except under similar conditions as apply in Spain. The Irish Constitution prohibits abortion, but it is available in the UK. Although anti-abortion campaigners tried unsuccessfully to restrict pregnant Irish women from traveling to England, nearly 6,000 of them obtained abortions there in 1998 alone, according to data reported by Elizabeth Throop.

Fertility

As they were during the Depression, low birth rates are once again a concern in Europe. Except for Turkey and Albania, all are below population replacement rates in total fertility. Recent concerns over the low fertility rates in Germany (1.4 total fertility) and Italy (1.2 total fertility) and what this means for future economic growth and for the ability of governments to support social programs for the elderly are clear examples of the intersection of private and public issues. Eileen Trzcinski reports that in Germany they are rethinking their strong male-breadwinner model of the family and trying to devise ways for both men and women to combine wage-earning and caregiving work. For Italy, the low birth rate has placed women "on the hot spot." That is, there have been pressures from the media and the political sphere to redefine women as primarily mothers. Elizabeth Krause also points out that the new opportunities for women in Italy have not necessarily made family relations more egalitarian.

VIOLENCE

In addition to the violence directed against women of other ethnic and religious communities that accompanied the breakup of the former Yugoslavia, the stresses of war increased the level of violence against women and girls within the family and community. In the case of Serbia and Montenegro, Lilijana Cickaric argues that the ideologies of nationalism and traditionalism have negatively impacted cultural perceptions of domestic violence. And the market freedoms that have come with Central and Eastern European independence from the Soviet Union have permitted the proliferation of prostitution and pornography. Ain Haas speculates that in Estonia, increases in sexual assaults and eating disorders may be tied, in part, to these exploitative sexual practices.

Unfortunately, in many cases the issue of domestic violence illustrates that the practical realization and the enforcement of women's rights do not necessarily follow from their mere existence in the law. Domestic violence has been notoriously difficult to address through legislation, because of the presumed privacy of the family, the male-dominated structures of justice systems, and the inadequacy of legal remedies in preventing domestic violence as opposed to prosecuting it after the fact. As Livia Popescu notes for Romania, women's economic dependence upon their perpetrators combined with the lack of shelters make it much less likely that women will attempt to use the law to end the abuse.

For this reason, feminists have advocated and established shelters for abused women and their children, at first without government support. Addressing violence against women in Germany, Eileen Trzcinski emphasizes, took the development of shelters and changes in cultural attitudes, supported by European Union policy initiatives. Like the women's centers established elsewhere in Europe, Women's Aid and Rape Crisis Centres in the UK have operated outside of the formal institutions of government with ideals of "mutual support rather than charity, self-determination rather than hierarchy, and open access rather than bureaucratic gatekeeping." Gillian Pascall notes that they have also connected the need of women for domestic violence shelter to national housing policy.

Despite changing cultural attitudes and increasing state support for women's movement policy initiatives, violence against women remains a very serious problem. Nevertheless, a reason for optimism about ending it is the 1993 United Nations Declaration on the Elimination of Violence against Women. This important international declaration recognizes that human rights are being violated *within the family* and calls for UN and national-level cooperation with grassroots groups working to end violence against women. Implementing a global strategy to address a problem not long ago considered to be a purely private matter requires that we see both its worldwide scope and its local and national dimensions.

OUTLOOK FOR THE TWENTY-FIRST CENTURY

This volume on women's issues in Europe is one of the six-volume set on contemporary women's issues worldwide. It reflects the reality that women's lives are shaped not only by conditions in their own countries but also by the state of the world. Links forged by shared environment, globalization, international relations, United Nations gender equality and development programs, and women's nongovernmental organizations connect their futures. Women in Development Europe (WIDE), a network of nongovernmental development organizations and human rights activists, epitomizes the ways women are working together internationally to create "a world based on gender equality and justice." Students, scholars, and engaged citizens who share their visions have broken down barriers of stereotypes and discrimination, crossed boundaries of conflict and difference, and challenged entrenched power to improve the lives of women and men. We hope they will find this work useful to that end.

NOTES

1. Kosovo's permanent status remains unclear. It is presently under the jurisdiction of the UN.

2. This volume is part of a six-volume set, *The Greenwood Encyclopedia of Women's Issues Worldwide*, which covers women's issues in Sub-Saharan Africa, Asia and Oceania, Europe, the Middle East and North Africa, North America and the Caribbean, and Central and South America. All of the volumes follow this same broad issues outline, although the subtopics may vary according to national conditions.

3. The twentieth century, with two World Wars, the Holocaust, Stalinist purges, and the recent "ethnic cleansing" in Bosnia and Kosovo was one of devastating loss of life, property, and human dignity for women, children, and men. At any one point in time and in any one place, such tragic histories have overwhelmed impulses toward equality and justice, suppressing human rights in general and women's rights in particular.

4. The term "social security" is used here in its most general sense—public programs to insure that people who are unable to support themselves do not fall below community standards in their standard of living and their future capacity to thrive.

5. Karen Offen, *European Feminisms, 1700–1950* (Stanford, CA: Stanford University Press, 2000).

6. Madeleine Shea, "The European Union," in *Women's Rights: A Global View*, ed. Lynn Walter (Westport, CT: Greenwood Press), 85–98.

7. Tanya Renne, *Ana's Land: Sisterhood in Eastern Europe* (Boulder, CO: Westview Press, 1997).

8. "Ethnic cleansing" is a euphemism for removal of a specific ethnic population from a territory by forced removal, terror, or genocide.

9. Barbara Einhorn and Jeanne Gregory, "Introduction: The Idea of Europe," *The European Journal of Women's Studies 5*, no. 3–4 (1998): 293–96.

10. The women's movements that began in the nineteenth or early twentieth centuries to promote women's rights, including the suffrage movements for the right to vote, are labeled "first-wave" movements. The "second-wave" began in the late 1960s and 1970s to address more deeply engrained cultural attitudes and gender stereotypes, and today's feminism is often labeled "third-wave."

11. O'Connor, Orloff, and Shaver (1999, 57) note that the Beveridge Report was also a model for social policy in the Commonwealth countries of Canada and Australia.

12. Many of the guest workers came from Turkey and are attracted to Western Europe by its greater job opportunities and higher wages.

13. Although the International Labor Organization (ILO) called for maternity leave benefits as early as 1919, it was not until larger numbers of middle-income married women with children began to join the labor force that paid maternity leave benefits became a widespread and commonly accepted practice. The earlier forms were proposed in the context of debates over protective labor legislation limiting the hours and types of work that women were allowed to do, especially pregnant women and mothers.

14. Gøsta Esping-Andersen (1990) divides welfare regimes into "social democratic," "conservative-corporatist," and "liberal." The "social democratic" regime, typified by Sweden, is one in which there are universal citizenship rights to social security; the "conservative-corporatist" regime is characterized by the idea that social rights should be based upon one's class and status and supports the traditionally gendered family. This type includes Germany, France, and Italy. The UK represents the "liberal" regime where governmental support is distributed only as a social safety net after the family and the market have failed to provide the social minimum.

15. The term "welfare" covers all of the many governmental programs designed to redistribute risk and social security. These programs include but are not limited to national health care, old-age pensions, unemployment and workman's compensation, public education, childcare, maternity benefits, and parental leave. See also Diane Sainsbury, ed., *Gendering Welfare States* (London: Sage Publications, 1994) on the significance of gender for welfare state regimes.

16. Linda Haas uses the term "dual-breadwinner" to describe the Swedish model, a term that implies more equality than Lewis's term "weak male-breadwinner."

17. Eileen Drew, Ruth Emerek, and Evelyn Mahon, eds., *Women, Work and the Family in Europe* (London: Routledge, 1998); Madonna Harrington Meyer, *Care Work: Gender, Labor and the Welfare State* (New York: Routledge, 2000).

18. See Monica Threlfall, ed., *Mapping the Women's Movement: Feminist Politics and Social Transformation in the North* (London: Verso, 1996) for case studies of women's movements in Europe.

RESOURCE GUIDE

Web Sites

European Database: Women in Decision-making, www.db-decision.de/index_E.htm.

Gender Equality (a European Union site), europa.eu.int/comm/employment_social/equ_opp/index_en.htm.

Genderstats (a World Bank site), genderstats.worldbank.org/.

International Information Centre and Archives for the Women's Movement, www.iiav.nl/eng/index.html.

Inter-parliamentary Union (current national and regional data on women in parliaments worldwide), www.ipu.org.

OECD DAC (Organisation of Economic Cooperation and Development Assistance Committee) Gender Equality Group, www.oecd.org/dac/Gender/index.htm.

Regional Women's Directory Database, www.zinfo.hr/indoc/IndocHomeW.htm.

The State of the World Population 2000 (a United Nations site), www.unfpa.org/swp/2000/english/index.html.

Women's Studies EuroMap, women-www.uia.ac.be/women/index.html.

Organizations

Committee on Women's Rights
Web site: www.europarl.eu.int/committees/femm_home.htm

The European Union
Web site: europa.eu.int/

The European Women's Lobby
18 Rue Hydraulique
B-1210 Bruxelles, Belgium
Phone: 32-2-217-90-20
Fax: 32-2-2-219-84 51
Email: ewl@womenlobby.org
Web site: www.womenlobby.org/

Karat (Coalition for Gender Equality)
ul. Karmelicka 16 m. 13
00-163 Warsaw, Poland
Phone/Fax: (4822) 636-83-07
Email: karat@zigzag.pl
Web site: www.karat.org/links/pages/

A coalition of women's non-governmental organizations in Central and Eastern European (CEE) and Commonwealth of Independent States (CIS) countries.

Network of East-West Women
1761 S Street NW, Suite LL-12
Washington, DC 20009
Phone: 1 (202) 299-9001
Fax: 1 (202) 299-9003
Web site: www.neww.org/

WIDE, the Women in Development Europe
10 Rue de la Science
1000 Brussels, Belgium
Phone: 32-2-545.90.70
Fax: 32-2-512-73-42
Email: wide@gn.apc.org
Web site: www.eurosur.org/wide/

SELECTED BIBLIOGRAPHY

Drew, Eileen, Ruth Emerek, and Evelyn Mahon, eds. *Women, Work and the Family in Europe*. London: Routledge, 1998.

Einhorn, Barbara, and Jeanne Gregory. "Introduction: The Idea of Europe." *The European Journal of Women's Studies* 5, no. 3–4 (1998): 293–96.

Elman, R. Amy, ed. *Sexual Politics and the European Union*. Providence: Berghahn Books, 1996.

Esping-Andersen, Gøsta. *The Three Worlds of Welfare Capitalism*. Princeton, NJ: Princeton University Press, 1992.

Lewis, Jane. "Gender and the Development of Welfare Regimes." *Journal of European Social Policy* 2, no. 3 (1992): 159–73.

———. "Gender and Welfare Regimes: Further Thoughts." *Social Politics* (Summer 1997): 160–77.

Meyer, Madonna Harrington, ed. *Care Work: Gender, Labor and the Welfare State*. New York: Routledge, 2000.

O'Connor, Julia S., Ann Shola Orloff, and Sheila Shaver. *States, Markets, Families: Gender, Liberalism and Social Policy in Australia, Canada, Great Britain and the United States*. Cambridge: Cambridge University Press, 1999.

Offen, Karen. *European Feminisms, 1700–1950*. Stanford, CA: Stanford University Press, 2000.

Renne, Tanya. *Ana's Land: Sisterhood in Eastern Europe*. Boulder, CO: Westview Press, 1997.

Rossilli, Mariagrazia, ed. *Gender Policies in the European Union*. New York: Peter Lang, 2000.

Sainsbury, Diane, ed. *Gendering Welfare States*. London: Sage Publications, 1994.

Shea, Madeleine. "The European Union." In *Women's Rights: A Global View*, edited by Lynn Walter, 85–98. Westport, CT: Greenwood Press, 2001.

Threlfall, Monica, ed. *Mapping the Women's Movement: Feminist Politics and Social Transformation in the North*. London: Verso, 1996.

Walter, Lynn. "The Future of Social Welfare in Denmark." In *Speaking Out: Women Poverty and Public Policy*, edited by Katherine A. Rhoades and Anne Statham, 119–28. Madison, WI: University of Wisconsin System Women's Studies Librarian, 1998.

———. "Denmark: Women's Rights and Women's Welfare." In *Women's Rights, A Global View*, edited by Lynn Walter, 57–70. Westport, CT: Greenwood Press, 2001.

I

ALBANIA

Antonia Young

PROFILE OF ALBANIA

Albania has an area of 28,748 square kilometers,[1] 75 percent of which is mountainous, and 30 percent of the country rises to over 1,000 meters above sea level. It has a western coastline of 362 kilometers along the Adriatic Sea. Twenty-four percent of the land is arable and 36 percent forested. Albania's neighboring countries are Montenegro to the north, Kosovo[2] and Macedonia to the east, Greece to the south, and Italy, less than eighty kilometers across the Adriatic, to the west.

Albania has a population of approximately 3.4 million, with a density of 115 people per square kilometer, almost one third of whom are now estimated to live in the capital, Tirana. Up to 1990, 64 percent of the population was rural and only 300,000 were living in the capital. The sex ratio at birth is 1.08 male/female; the annual birthrate has now declined to 19.01 per 1,000; the annual death rate is 6.5 deaths per 1,000. Infant mortality is 35.7 deaths per 1,000 live births. Maternal death rate is 40.6 per 100,000. Female life expectancy at birth is 74.87 years. The fertility rate has declined from seven children per woman in 1960 to 2.32 in 2002. Fertility is about 25 percent higher in rural than in ur-

ban areas. Population growth, which was at 2 percent under communist rule, is now down to 0.88 percent, making Albania the only European country with a positive population growth rate. One third of the population is under fifteen years of age.

Albania was the last Balkan country to free itself from Ottoman rule and the last European country to break from communism, becoming, in 1992, a unitary multiparty, democratic, parliamentary republic sometimes known as an "emerging democracy." In its transition from totalitarianism to authoritarianism under the leadership of Sali Berisha as president until the change of regime in 1997, Albania's government became based on the separation and balance of legislative, executive, and judicial powers. The country is administered in twelve regions, sixty-five municipalities, and 309 communes.

Albania, the most isolated of former communist countries, is extremely poor. For example, the infrastructure is in shambles and has received little attention in the last decade. Hundreds of thousands of imported vehicles now navigate substandard roads. Many villages are inaccessible by vehicle, and many more accessible only for six months of the year when snow or mudslides have been cleared. The whole country suffers frequent water and electricity cuts, often for hours or even days at a time, especially in winter.

OVERVIEW OF WOMEN'S ISSUES

In communist times (up to 1990), there was an attempt to equalize the working lives of Albanians: women were expected to work in agricultural and manufacturing cooperatives. However, this actually increased their already heavy workload as no compensation was allowed them at home where they still were responsible for all domestic chores and childrearing. With the fall of communism, many women were actually relieved to be able to return to working only in the home; however, this reconfirmed patriarchal traditions, and many then found that they no longer had the choice of employment. Some issues that are discussed by Western women (e.g., sexual harassment or lesbian motherhood) are barely considered in Albania.

One of the major issues for the Albanian women's movement is the demand for separate nuclear family living space, in contrast to the strong tradition for new wives being brought, as the most junior member, into their husband's family's home, there to perform the domestic chores for the whole extended family. A further demand is for women to have at least an equal share in family decision making, especially concerning the upbringing of their own children. This will be discussed later in the section on gender roles.

EDUCATION

Opportunities

Enver Hoxha's strict communist dictatorship (1945–1985) achieved considerable success in the area of education. Prior to World War II, all university students had to study abroad. Albania's first university was founded in 1957 in Tirana, the capital, and there are now four more—in Elbasan, Shkodra, Gjirokastër, and Vlorë. However, access to a university education was limited under communism to those whose families had "correct" political behavior. Now university entrance is greatly facilitated by bribes. As of 1990, primary schools accommodated all children for the eight-year compulsory period from ages six to fourteen. In 1998 gross primary school enrollment was 97 percent for girls, 95 percent for boys; secondary school was 84 percent for boys and 72 percent for girls.

With the fall of communism, school attendance has declined due to a number of factors. There is the increased need for poor families to supplement their income from their children's employment. Many girls of secondary school age are kept at home by families because of new fears both for their safety and for their reputations in view of the longer journeys to school. Young girls are in very real danger of being abducted and taken out of the country for prostitution. There is another group of hundreds, maybe even thousands, of girls in the north who are kept out of school due to restrictions imposed by blood feuds. Besides the difficulties faced in getting children to school, there are also problems in staffing schools with professionally trained teachers due in part to the very low pay, which in turn makes migration or emigration a more attractive option than remaining in country. Funding of the education sector averages only about 9 percent of the annual budget.

Literacy

Prior to the Second World War, the literacy rate in Albania was only around 5 percent. By 1990, Albania's literacy rate had increased to 93 percent both for women and men.

EMPLOYMENT AND THE ECONOMY

The per capita gross domestic product (GDP) is $1,867, the growth rate is 7.3 percent, and inflation is 3.1 percent. Albania ranks with Romania and Moldova as amongst the poorest European countries.

Job/Career Opportunities

Under communism, Albanian women's rate of participation in the work force was one of the highest in Europe (83–94 percent), but during the

Elderly women spin and knit outside with boy, Permet, Albania. Photo © TRIP/E. Parker.

transition from state socialism women were the first to lose their jobs. The unemployment rate is extremely hard to gauge; estimates vary between 16 percent and 80 percent, and it is considered far higher for women than for men. There has been a slight improvement in recent years.

In urban areas the major concerns of women in the shift from communism relate to employment, where despite enlightened government legislation attempting to combat this problem, women are overrepresented in lower-paying jobs in educational, administrative, and secretarial work. For instance, women make up 80 percent of schoolteachers, but most school directors are men. Although women often choose journalism as a profession, most are not well paid and men still dominate high-level positions in the media. The number of women in foreign service has increased, with forty in the ministry of foreign affairs and twenty in the embassies.[3]

Pay

Although the Labour Code prohibits discrimination in the workplace, the average salaries of women in all sectors and at all levels are about 80–85 percent that of men.

Working Conditions

Sexual Harassment

The 1995 Labour Code recognizes sexual harassment, but retribution for the offense is extremely rare.

Support for Mothers/Caretakers

Migration of men from the rural areas in search of work abroad makes them frequently unable to send remittances or even to return to their families left behind. This has seriously affected their wives, who are left stranded to take care of both elderly parents and children.

Maternal Leave

Pregnant women are prohibited by law from undertaking night shifts. Legally, a woman is entitled to 365 days of paid maternity leave with 80 percent pay, social insurance, and a guaranteed right to return to her position. In reality, this is rarely the case.

Inheritance and Property Rights

Land privatization has been implemented in most areas but lacks standardization in method and legality. Although women have an equal legal right to inheritance and property ownership (first established in Albania in 1928 and reaffirmed in 1993), in practice it is usually men who hold the ownership, especially in the rural areas where few women know their rights or how to claim them and fewer still would dare to try, especially when facing the improbability of success.

Although women theoretically have access to credit, since their names are rarely attached to property or businesses in reality few have such access.

The effects of Westernization are bringing enormous changes to Tirana and to a lesser extent to other towns, thus increasing the contrast between urban and rural life. Traditionally, families without a male head could allocate one of their women to change gender and become the household head with all the rights of a man. In the long term, there is optimism that as the rule of law is strengthened, and as the functioning of democracy improves, women, especially those involved in energetic nongovernmental organizations (NGOs), will achieve some of their demands.

Social/Government Programs

Sustainable Development

Transition from totalitarian communism to an open-market economy has been difficult. It was exacerbated first by a severe depression accompanying the end of the centrally planned system. The next obstacle, in 1996, was inflationary pressure attempting to counteract a budget deficit exceeding 12 percent of the GDP. The drastic collapse of financial pyramid schemes in 1997 resulted in economic disaster, whereby an estimated one third of the population lost major portions of their assets, misplaced in the fraudulent programs. Gradual improvement has been recorded since that date, although there remain serious economic pressures causing widespread uncertainty and insecurity, especially for the elderly. Remittances from abroad throughout the last decade of the twentieth century substantially supplemented the GDP, helping to offset the large foreign trade deficit. Overall credit given to the private sector was a mere 3 percent of the GDP in the first years of the twenty-first century.

Welfare

Under communism, the welfare regime, though very rudimentary, nevertheless provided a greatly improved situation to that before World War II. Current assets do not equal needs, and, despite laws making provisions for those in greatest need, there is considerable corruption whereby those in the position to authorize welfare payments frequently take advantage of the situation and demand a fee before making the authorization.

FAMILY AND SEXUALITY

Gender Roles

Gender roles are clearly delineated, especially in rural areas. However, the Albanian words are identical for the terms granddaughter/niece, grandson/nephew, sister/cousin, and brother/cousin—in traditional large families, such distinctions were irrelevant.

Traditionally men control all family decisions, even concerning the upbringing of their own children. A widowed, and especially a divorced, mother has no rights to take her children, particularly sons, with her if she returns to her birth family. It is out of the question that she should set up any alternative home. Such traditions as these are changing in the urban areas through women's efforts.

There is extreme discrimination against women participating in sports. Very few facilities are available to women, and there is little encouragement even in primary school.

Marriage

Traditionally marriages were always arranged by parents, usually through a broker. Arranged marriages are still commonly practiced, though some of the more educated young people in the larger towns are making their own choices of partner. Religious marriage ceremonies have no legal standing but are frequently performed. There were attempts to eradicate arranged marriages under communism when stable relationships were encouraged, to the point where serious efforts were made concerning attempts at reconciliation between couples experiencing marriage difficulties. More drastically, when there was a marriage breakdown, divorcées could lose their jobs or even be sent to a "reeducation" location (e.g., forced mine labor).

Traditional law forbidding marriage between cousins even to the seventh generation is still generally observed, accounting for the preference for men to marry women from outside their own village or area. Intermarriage between Albanians and Serbs is extremely rare. The Family Code of 1992 defines the minimum age for marriage to be sixteen for women and eighteen for men. In urban areas, there is a gradual reassessment of the needs of marriage, away from the view that a man marries in order to bring a strong young worker into his birth family; however, few Albanian marriages would be viewed by Westerners as equal partnerships. Albanians might well counter this by questioning the validity of Western marriages, whose partners may be apart for months at a time, and by pointing out that far more Western marriages end in divorce than Albanian ones. The number of marriages has declined throughout the 1990s, possibly reflecting the impact of economic uncertainty and also due to the migration of more young men than young women. The number of divorces has also declined, but it has been suggested that because women are burdened with greater financial dependence on their husbands, they have less freedom to break away from bad relationships. Evidence points to the fact that single-parent families exist almost exclusively due to the migration or death of the other parent.

Reproduction

Sex Education

Since 1994 there has been a legal provision countrywide for sex education for all children aged fourteen and older consisting of nine hours of information on the prevention of HIV/AIDS and STDs. The first family planning project was started in 1992 with the goal to inform the population about contraceptive use.

Contraception and Abortion

Contraception and abortion were both illegal under communism (the population grew threefold between 1950 and 1990). The reason contraception and abortion were illegal was the desire of the Hoxha regime to increase the labor force by increasing the population. Throughout the 1990s there have been various agencies attempting to provide information and education on these issues, but results have been varied, and they are least effective in the Catholic north. These issues were barely discussed before the mid-1990s and are still taboo in the rural areas. Pre- and extramarital relationships, single parenthood, and lesbianism are all issues for which discussion is confined mostly to the capital city.

The 1977 Albanian Penal Code punished abortion as both a crime and a misdemeanor, although by 1991 it became legal under certain circumstances, that include receiving mandatory counseling. The contraceptive prevalence for any method (traditional, medical, barrier, or natural) is estimated at 11 percent of couples, and that for modern methods is estimated at 8.3 percent. The current use of contraception was reported by 58 percent of married or partnered women. The most popular method is withdrawal, which is used by 33 percent of married women. Although the Albanian

Family Planning Association was founded in 1993, abortion is one of the most important methods of managing fertility in Albania. Legally, men have no say in a woman's decision on abortion. Many women resort to abortion, but due to a lack of available resources and the expense to the individuals, they must choose illegal procedures. It is estimated that for every three births there are two abortions.[4]

Teen Pregnancy

There is a noticeable lack of any kind of reproductive or health advice center for adolescents. The high rate of births to teenagers (34 per 1,000 to women aged 15–19 years) is apparently accounted for by the custom of marriage at an early age and is therefore not perceived as a problem. Illegitimate births are kept to a minimum due to several factors including a high degree of family and social control, young age at marriage, and strong religious condemnation. These all combine to ensure that opportunities for teenage sexual liaisons are minimal, especially in rural areas.

HEALTH

Health Care Access

Under communism, health care was equally provided to all (with the exception of those thousands exiled or imprisoned as "enemies of the state"). Since communism's fall, the need for health care greatly exceeds its availability. Of the unemployed, 37 percent have no health coverage and cannot afford to seek any form of medical treatment.

Since 1990 international investment has provided facilities in some areas. Between 1990 and 1995, public expenditure on health was 2.7 percent of the GDP. By 1996 there were 137 women's counseling centers and twenty-eight district maternity hospitals; however, corruption and theft have prevented fair access to these. Those who can afford it prefer to receive major medical attention abroad.

Diseases and Disorders

Amongst the female population aged 14–18 years, 32 percent are cigarette smokers (compared to 57 percent among males of the same age), whereas alcohol consumption is predominantly a male phenomenon. Production, traffic, and use of drugs have spread rapidly in Albania. The problem is exacerbated by the fact that 65 percent of the population is under thirty years old. The ratio of male drug users to female ones is at least 4:1. As many as 70 percent of users are from educated families. A 1990 survey among adults aged 25 and above indicated that nearly half of the male population of Albania smoked, but only 7.9 percent of females. In 1992, the age-standardized death rate from lung cancer was 20/100,000 for males and 7/100,000 for females.[5]

AIDS

AIDS was first identified in Albania in 1991. Since that date, numbers of cases have been slowly rising. Thirty-eight cases were reported between 1993 and 1998; seven of which ended in death. The adult prevalence rate is less than 0.01 percent (1999); people living with HIV/AIDS equals less than 100 as of 2000; and deaths from HIV/AIDS totaled less than 100 in 1999, affecting no children under fourteen. In 2002, the number of drug users in Albania was some 25,000 to 30,000, of which 5,000 were women. The number of women infected by HIV/AIDS in 2002 was ten.[6] Since 2000, there has been legal provision for free treatment for HIV/AIDS; syphilis, which was discovered again in 1995; and gonorrhea. It is questionable as to whether all those in need would know, or dare to find out, how to acquire the treatment.

Eating Disorders

Eating disorders have not been considered a problem in Albania. Until the 1990s, all but the top-ranking communist officials were severely underfed. Within two years, it was possible to observe the whole nation putting on weight, with little attention to diet. By 1995 it was possible to observe an occasional overweight person, but there are still very few who are obese.

Cancer

Much work has to be done to heighten awareness of the high incidence of breast and uterine cancer. The Council of Ministers' Decision no. 397 of 1999 prohibits the promotion, advertising, and distribution in health centers of products that replace breast milk.

Depression

Findings in a recent study reveal that one in every four women suffers from depression, caused by unemployment, poverty, and abuse and beating by her spouse.[7]

POLITICS AND LAW

Suffrage

There is universal—and compulsory—suffrage at age eighteen for all citizens.

Political Participation

Despite some encouragement for women to participate in government at either the local or national level, few women have been appointed to high ministerial positions. The 1997 Assembly contained 7.3 percent women deputies; of the nineteen cabinet members, two were women. Women are also very poorly represented on local election committees, if at all.

Women's Rights

Urban women are asserting women's rights as they challenge firmly entrenched traditions. In 1997, a Sub-Commission for Youth and Women, developed from the earlier parliamentary Women's Group, encouraged the activity of several forums for women of the political parties, but despite their worthy aims the resulting benefits to women, especially in the rural areas, have been few. Women's rights are considerably limited, especially in northern Albania where traditional law, known as the *Kanun* (a set of traditional laws, codified in the fifteenth century and committed to print at the beginning of the twentieth century) assigns women to the ownership of men with no rights of their own. Article 31 of the published *Kanun* states, "A woman is known as a sack, made to endure as long as she lives in her husband's house. . . ." (Other aspects of the *Kanun* are, however, exemplary and prove Albania's long legal tradition.)[8]

Feminist Movements

Albania played an important role in the Fourth World Conference on Women in Beijing (1995). Approximately 25 Albanian women participated in meetings focused on gender issues and in activities ranging from family planning to leadership, legal protection and counseling, sensitization on gender discrimination, and domestic violence.

The NGO Women's Advocacy Center, founded in 1997, provides free legal services, particularly in cases of divorce, separation, alimony, child custody, and paternity. Their first center for abused women was opened in 1998.

Lesbian Rights

Same-sex relationships were criminalized until June 1995, although the law was primarily directed at men. There is little tolerance for homosexuality, but the legal age of sexual consent is eighteen for homosexual men and fourteen for lesbians and heterosexuals. Prejudice against homosexuality makes it difficult to make contact with concerned groups. One group founded in the mid-1990s is *Shoqata Gay Albania* (Gay Albania Society).

Military Service

Women are no longer required to perform military service, which they had been prior to 1990.

RELIGION AND SPIRITUALITY

Due to previous Ottoman influence, approximately 70 percent of the population are Muslim. Twenty percent of the population are Albanian Orthodox, who live mostly in the south, and 10 percent are Catholic, residing mostly in the north.

Women's Roles

Women have a subordinate role in religion, although they make up the majority of observers in all faiths.

Rituals and Religious Practices

Everyone in Albania can nominally say to which of the three main religious faiths their family belonged in the past. Approximate percentages of the population remain 70 percent Muslim, 20 percent Orthodox (mostly in southern Albania) and 10 percent Catholic, although the majority would not now claim to be religious, although the percentages remain approximately the same. The Muslim religion, as practiced in Albania, cooperates with the other religions and does not ban girls from education.[9]

Historically, members of all faiths in Albania have been very tolerant and free in sharing religious practices with one another. Even Hoxha (in confirming his atheist state) used Vasko Pasha's well-known phrase, "The religion of Albanians is Albanianism." From 1967 to 1990, Albania operated as an atheist state. Hoxha forbade any religious rites from being performed, inflicting years of hard labor, torture, and even death to those who flouted his declaration. He commanded the closure of all 2,169 religious institutions and turned them to other uses or had them destroyed.

There is greater religious participation in rural areas where patriarchal traditions are deeply entrenched and strongly affect most people's lives. Outside influences put great pressure on the population to convert. About sixty minor religions have tried to claim converts, with a total success rate of about 1 percent of the population. Although common, religious marriage ceremonies have no legal standing.

VIOLENCE

Domestic Violence

The Criminal Code of Albania of the early 1990s has no specific provisions for dealing with domestic violence, though a death threat could bring imprisonment of up to one year to the violator and a sentence of 10–20 years to a convicted murderer. However, such a conviction could only follow a series of almost impossible demands from the violated, with no governmental support. There are no official statistics for domestic violence, and it has been estimated that although up to 65 percent of married women suffer it to some degree, only 5 percent of incidents are ever reported. Work is being done to help the many women who suffer, but there are very few shelters, and these operate only in the larger towns.[10]

Rape/Sexual Assault

Rape is a punishable offense, with imprisonment for up to fifteen years if the victim is under thirteen. Reflexions, founded in 1995, was one of the first organizations to focus on the protection of abused women.

Trafficking in Women and Children

Trafficking in women and children is a serious problem in Albania. Children and adolescents are at considerable risk of either being kidnapped or lured by promises of jobs or comfortable marriages. Divorced women have proved to be highly vulnerable, especially those with children to maintain and with this hope of a chance to emigrate to escape their "shame" since they are often stigmatized and not welcomed even by close relatives. An estimated 30,000 Albanian women are currently working abroad as prostitutes, half of them in Italy. They cannot afford to live on their own, and their chances of remarriage in Albania are minimal. Prostitution is illegal in Albania, and prostitutes are punished rather than the clients.[11] Albania is used as a conduit for women trafficked from Bulgaria, Moldova, Romania, Russia, and Ukraine and usually taken on to Italy or Greece. A government-funded center for the treatment of trafficking victims was established in 2002 in Vlorë (the port town most easily accessible to reach Italy) with a 30-person capacity. That year, 196 cases of women trafficked for prostitution were recorded.[12]

War and Military Repression

Albania has so far avoided war in its break from communism. Many of the deaths of approximately 2,000 killed in 1997 resulted from random shooting at the hands of young people who had suddenly acquired arms when military arms depots were opened up under a state of anarchy during that time. It was estimated at the time that every male from the age of ten upwards had at least one firearm and ample ammunition. There has been some success with ongoing initiatives in all towns to collect and dispose of arms.

A further major problem concerning violence in Albania is the revival of blood feuds, mainly in northern Albania, where it has been estimated that as many as 5,000 have been killed since 1990. This also leads to the traditional "closing" of the home of the killer, who may expect that any male from his family will be the object of the next blood feud killing. When homes are "closed," the men stay home and do not go out to work and usually the children do not attend school. Since women are never the targets of blood feuds, in these cases all agricultural work falls to the women, adding to their already arduous domestic work. There are said to be over 2,000 families involved in feuds affecting over 20,000 people.[13] There are several blood feud reconciliation groups working both to resolve the feuds and to educate people to abandon the tradition. Mediators are always men.

OUTLOOK FOR THE TWENTY-FIRST CENTURY

After two major shocks in the 1990s—first the fall of communism, and second the collapse of the pyramid schemes—life in Albania is slowly finding a more normal course. Although many people are leaving the country in search of making an easier living elsewhere, there is a new optimism within the country, and slowly international investors are returning after their rapid withdrawal in 1997. The Constitution of 1998 brings Albanian law in line with the rest of Europe. Cautious optimism suggests that in the long term, stability in Albania can be achieved. It is essential that there should be universal governmental provisions made of at least rudimentary health care and elementary education to ensure that those remaining in the rural areas develop the necessary assets for self-reliance rather than follow earlier migrants into the overcrowded towns. Albania has managed to maintain reasonable relations with its neighbors and has developed good trade relations with Montenegro, Greece, and Italy. It is the only country to fully recognize Kosovo and to accept Kosovars without visa restrictions, thus entitling their own population to a reciprocal arrangement.

NOTES

1. One kilometer equals 0.6 miles.

2. Kosovo is the current spelling for the formerly autonomous region of Serbia in Yugoslavia. Kosova is the spelling in the Albanian language. Kosovo is a term adopted by the non-partisan English-speaking world.

3. U.S. Department of State, "Albania, Country Reports on Human Rights Prac-

tices," U.S. Department of State, 2000, www.state.gov/g/drl/rls/hrrpt/2000/eur/668. htm.

4. Ines A. Murzaku and Z. Dervishi, "Values in Transition: The Divorce Dilemma among Albanian Women," *Analysis of Current Events* 14, no. 2 (May 2002): 8–11.

5. Center for Disease Control (CDC), "Tobacco or Health: A Global Status Report, Albania," CDC, 1997, www.cdc.gov/tobacco/who/albania.htm.

6. Committee on Elimination of Discrimination against Women, "Principle of Equality, Customary Law, Human Trafficking Addressed as Albania Responds to Women's Anti-discrimination Committee," January 24, 2003, www.un.org/News/Press/docs/2003/wom1381.doc.htm.

7. *Gazeta Shqiptare*, May 13, 2000, www.mondotimes.com/1/world/al or http://pages.albaniaonline.net/balkanweb/.

8. Shtjefën Gjeçov, *Kanuni i Lekë Dakagjinit* (The Code of Lekë Dukagjini), trans. Leonard Fox (New York: Gjonlekaj, 1989).

9. Committee on Elimination of Discrimination against Women, 2003.

10. Murzaku and Dervishi, 2002; Committee on Elimination of Discrimination against Women, 2003.

11. U.S. Department of State, 2000, 7.

12. Committee on Elimination of Discrimination against Women, 2003.

13. B. Jolis, "Honor Killing Makes a Comeback," *The Guardian* (August 14, 1996).

RESOURCE GUIDE

Suggested Reading

Murzaku, Ines A., and Z. Dervishi. "Values in Transition: The Divorce Dilemma among Albanian Women." *Analysis of Current Events*, 14, no. 2 (May 2000): 8–11.

Post, Susan E. Pritchett. *Women in Modern Albania*. Jefferson, NC: McFarland, 1998.

Vickers, Miranda. *The Albanians: A Modern History*. New York: I. B. Tauris, 1995.

Videos/Films

Life Sold in Side-walk. 2000. Directed by Majlinda Bregu. Produced by Tirana Women's Center.

Taboo. 2002. National Geographic. First episode in a 13-part series. Contrasts the lives of urban and rural Albanian women.

Web Sites

Network Women's Program, www.soros.org/women/html/infoservs2.htm.

Women's Information and Documentation Centre (WIDC), www.neww.org/countries/Albania/wctirana.htm or qirjaku@women-center.tirana.al.

Women's Legal Group in Albania, www.neww.org/countries/Albania/albania050696.htm.

Organizations

Albanian Women's Centre
Directors: Eglantina Gjermeni and Edliza Muhedini
P.O. Box 2418
Tirana, Albania
Phone: (++355) 223-693/243-526
Email: edgemeni@hotmail.com, tina@women-center.tirana.al, or postmaster@women
 -center.tirana.al

Independent Forum of Albanian Women
President: Diana Culi
Rr. Reshit Collaku, no. 100
Tirana, Albania
Phone: (++355) 42-47269
Fax: (++ 355) 42-28309
Email: fpgsh@ngo.org.al

International Collaboration of Women for Peace and Freedom
President: Tatjana Prifti
Rr. Naim Frasheri, p. 84, shk. 2, ap. 31
Tirana, Albania
Phone: (++355) 42-27938

Law, Business and the Rights of Rural Women
President: Amedije Daci
Rr. Shyqyri Berxolli, no. 78/1
Tirana, Albania
Phone/Fax: (++355) 42-39526

Young Intellectuals, Hope (Intelektualet e Rinj, Shprese)
President: Zenepe Dibra
L. Qemal Stafa, Rr. Daut Boriçi, 874
Shkoder, Albania
Email: IRSH@albnet.net

SELECTED BIBLIOGRAPHY

Committee on Elimination of Discrimination against Women. "Principle of Equality, Customary Law, Human Trafficking Addressed as Albania Responds to Women's Anti-discrimination Committee." www.un.org/News/Press/docs/2003/wom1381.doc.htm. January 24, 2003.

"Convention of the Elimination of all Forms of Discrimination against Women." *Initial and First Periodic Report of State Parties*. Tirana, Albania: 2002.

U.S. Department of State. "Albania: Country Reports on Human Rights Practices." U.S. Department of State, 2000. www.state.gov/g/drl/rls/hrrpt/2000/eur/668.htm.

Young, Antonia. *Albania*. World Bibliographical Series no. 94. Santa Barbara, CA: ABC-CLIO Press, 1997. Lists over 1,000 books and articles with one-paragraph annotations, mostly in English, in about sixty subject areas all relating to Albania and Kosovo.

2

ARMENIA

Armine Ishkanian

PROFILE OF ARMENIA

Armenia is a small (29,800 square kilometers),[1] landlocked, mountainous (37.2 percent of it is mountain terrain) country in Eurasia. It has a population of approximately 3.8 million (3,754,100)[2] of which 96 percent are ethnic Armenians and the remaining 4 percent are Russians, Kurds, Yezidis, Greeks, Jews, and Assyrians. Armenian, or *Hayeren*, is the official language, and the official state religion is the Armenian Apostolic Church (*Hayastaneayts Ekeghetsi*).

Armenia declared independence from the Soviet Union on September 21, 1991. Since then, it has undergone the transition to a republican form of government with executive, legislative, and judicial branches. It has also privatized most property and lands formerly owned by the state; fully liberalized prices; established banking, tax, and customs structures; and introduced the Armenian dram as the official currency.[3] Although there has been stable growth since 1993 in the trade and service sectors, the current gross domestic product (GDP) is only 40 percent of the 1989 rate. Poverty increased rapidly following independence in 1991 and by 1996, 85 percent of the families (740,000 families)

were receiving benefits from the Paros Family Benefit Program for Vulnerable Families.[4] The situation has not improved: in 2000, 55 percent were classified as poor and 22.9 percent as very poor.[5]

As a result of these dire socioeconomic conditions, there has been emigration from Armenia, a decline of the birthrate by 53 percent (11.47 births/ 1,000 people), and −.21 percent population growth since 1991. The mortality rate has fluctuated between 6.2 percent and 6.6 percent, peaking at 7.4 percent in 1993, and life expectancy is 74.4 years. Women, who on average live seven years longer than men, make up 51.5 percent of the population. The infant mortality rate has decreased in recent years to an average of 13.4 percent for girls and 17.2 percent for boys, and the average trimester figure for maternal mortality is 30.4 percent.[6]

OVERVIEW OF WOMEN'S ISSUES

When Armenia became part of the USSR in 1920, the Soviet government, in an effort to consolidate its power, began to challenge the traditional values and "break the cake of custom"[7] in order to supersede all ethnic cultural beliefs and traditions. Since the family was the focus of conservative resistance, the communists sought to "emancipate" women and develop loyalties outside the traditional patriarchal household. Arranged marriages were banned, divorce became easier to obtain, and the state provided free health care (including abortions), childcare, and even counseling for women. In the Soviet Constitution the political equality of the sexes was mandated, and women were given the same rights as men.

Young Armenian woman, Yervan. Photo © TRIP/J. Ananian.

Although women made gains in public life, attitudes about the family and women's role within the family continued in a traditional, patriarchal pattern. And, following the collapse of the Soviet Union, women suffered many setbacks in the political and economic realms. Women today are not only the majority of the unemployed and the poor, but they have also largely been left out of the government and political parties.

EDUCATION

Opportunities

Education is highly valued and women, who have traditionally had the role of preserving and transmitting Armenian culture and traditions, are the overwhelming majority of educators and comprise 82 percent of the profession. There is an eight-year system of compulsory education. In urban areas, a university degree is not only considered essential for having a better life and being a cultured (*kulturagan*)[8] person, but it is also a part of a woman's dowry. A university-educated woman is considered a more desirable spouse and mother because she will be able to better educate and discipline her children and assist her husband to advance politically. Sixty-one percent of university students in private universities and 51 percent of students in public universities are women. The ratio of women to men in the educational system only decreases at the graduate level, where 68.3 percent of graduate students are men.

Literacy

There is a 98.9 percent adult literacy rate.[9]

EMPLOYMENT AND THE ECONOMY

Job/Career Opportunities

Women, who had entered the working world in vast numbers after Soviet rule and enjoyed the benefits of a socioeconomic safety net, have suffered most from the difficult economic transition. Currently they constitute nearly 70 percent of the country's 20 percent of unemployed workers. Women are well represented in the fields of medicine, education, the arts, international relations and law, middle management, midlevel banking, economics, chemistry, biology, and marketing. Despite their educational achievements, women are underrepresented in law enforcement, the higher echelons of government, upper management, and in the business/financial sectors.

Pay

When they are employed, women's wages are generally 50 percent less than men's earnings.[10]

Working Conditions

In the post-Soviet period, the state has increasingly withdrawn from ensuring employment opportunities and enforcing existing labor laws. Private employers frequently subject women to discriminatory labor practices including firing pregnant women, avoiding hiring newly married women or women with young children, and sexually harassing female employees.[11]

Sexual Harassment

Sexual harassment is a common phenomenon. Women who are harassed rarely report these violations for fear of losing their jobs and the material benefits they reap from relationships with employers. Since independence, the Armenian courts, labor unions, and governmental agencies responsible for the implementation of labor policies have not maintained statistics on labor disputes, nor have they attempted to analyze or address the nature and causes of such problems.[12]

Support for Mothers/Caretakers

Post-Soviet structural adjustment policies have eliminated subsidies for food, utilities, transportation, and childcare programs. The lack of such services and the prevalence of unjust labor practices negatively impact working women.

Maternal Leave

According to the Labor Code, a working mother is entitled to pregnancy and maternity leave, but in reality, private employers prefer to fire pregnant women and new mothers, and state employers fail to provide paid maternity leave.

Daycare

Unlike during the Soviet era, there are now no free daycare centers, nurseries, and kindergartens.

Inheritance and Property Rights

Men and women can equally inherit land, money, and property, but given the level of poverty, only the wealthiest 5 percent of families have anything to bequeath to their children.

Social/Government Programs

Sustainable Development

In Armenia's new free-market economy, nongovernmental organizations (NGOs) are expected to share the burden with the state in providing social safety nets and welfare programs for the poor. Because NGOs rely heavily on foreign aid and this aid is not always directed at alleviating poverty, impoverishment continues to be a major problem. In 2002, the government released the Interim Poverty Reduction Strategy Paper that was developed in consultation with NGOs to systematically address poverty and to coordinate its efforts with NGOs in promoting sustainable development and economic growth.

Welfare

Due to a lack of sufficient funding, NGOs have not been able to adequately provide for the vulnerable sectors of the population, and the government, for its part, has not done enough to assist the disabled, elderly, war widows, and orphans, who are most in need.

FAMILY AND SEXUALITY

Gender Roles

Within the family, women are the primary caretakers and motherhood is seen as being sacred (*soorp*).[13] As the hearth (*odjakh*), pillar (*syun*), and lamp (*jrak*) of the family, Armenian mothers are expected to love and nurture their children and to sacrifice their needs and desires for the family. Women who are not mothers are pitied because they have not attained the highest status a woman can achieve. The gender roles and stereotypes ascribed to men and women within the family apply in the public sphere as well, where men are seen as the leaders and decision makers in the political, economic, and military realms, whereas women are expected to be the self-sacrificing nurturers and supporters of the nation (i.e., the family writ large).

Marriage

Armenians are monogamous, and there are very few arranged marriages. Most couples marry for love and although women are able to voice their marriage choices and initiate divorce, men have more control over their sexuality and marriage choices. In the Armenian Church wedding ceremony, the bride promises to be obedient (*hunazand*) to the husband, and the groom promises to protect (*der gangnel*) his bride. Rural marital relationships are patriarchal, whereas urban marriages, particularly between educated couples, tend to be more egalitarian.

Divorce, except in cases of infertility or infidelity, is avoided at all costs for the sake of the children. Women who are divorced or widowed describe themselves as *ander* (without a protector) and believe that they are easy targets for the sexual advances of other men. Very few divorcées or widows remarry, and in the few instances when they do, they tend to marry divorced men or widowers.

Reproduction

Many couples begin to have children soon after marriage. If a couple fails to have a child during the first two years after marriage, families on both sides become concerned. In rural areas and in some urban families, a couple's infertility is blamed on the wife and often leads to divorce.

Sex Education

Because sex education courses are not taught in schools and parents are ashamed to speak with their children about sex, girls and boys learn about sex from their friends and older siblings.

Contraception and Abortion

In spite of the efforts of local and international NGOs, abortion continues to be the primary method of family planning. According to a Ministry of Health survey, 51 percent of all pregnancies are terminated by abortion, and the average woman has two abortions in her lifetime. Only 3.1 percent of Armenian women use intravaginal contraception, and 1.9 percent use oral contraceptives. Reasons for this include limited access to contraceptives and a widespread perception that oral and intravaginal contraceptives lead to infertility.[14]

Teen Pregnancy

Teens that become pregnant are encouraged by their parents to marry the father of the child or to have an abortion. The number of unwed teenage mothers is miniscule because these women and their children become outcasts and are ostracized by their relatives and community.

HEALTH

Health Care Access

There has been a sharp decline in the availability of health care services as public expenditures on the health care system have decreased from 2.7 percent of GDP in 1990 to 1.4 percent in 1998. Patients are responsible for all payments, both official and unofficial (i.e., gifts and other types of bribery), to physicians. For this reason, patients only seek medical assistance in emergency situations.

The Family and Marriage Code and the 1996 law on health care and medical services ensure the reproductive rights of women and women's access to free pre- and postnatal care. Maternity and gynecological services, which are theoretically subsidized by the state, are available at twenty-two full-service hospitals, twenty-nine maternity wards, thirty-six obstetric centers, and sixty-four maternity posts across Armenia. These provisions, however, are no guarantee that women will not have to make unofficial payments or gifts to physicians and nurses in order to receive quality care.

Diseases and Disorders

AIDS

Until 1994, no cases of HIV had been registered. In 2000 there were 135 registered cases of HIV of which thirty-four were women over age twenty.[15] In 1998 the National Assembly passed a law on AIDS to initiate an HIV prevention program.

Cancer

Breast cancer is the number one cause of death among women, and nearly 650 women are diagnosed with breast cancer each year. Breast cancer, unlike other diseases, however, is now being actively addressed and treated. The Armenian American Mammography University Center, which opened on April 27, 1997, is the first health facility of its kind in the former Soviet Union dedicated to providing women from the entire region with mammography and ultrasound technology for breast cancer screening.

POLITICS AND LAW

Suffrage

Women were granted the right to vote in 1918 by the government of the first independent Republic of Armenia.

Political Participation

Armenians believe that women are not supposed to be involved or interested in politics because politics is believed to be "men's work" and inherently corrupt. There is a handful of women in the over fifty political parties, and following the May 2003 parliamentary elections, there are only six women in the 131-seat National Assembly. As of May 2003, the Minister of Culture, Sports, and Youth Affairs is a woman. All other cabinet ministers are also men. Having been squeezed out of the government, women are currently active in the NGO sector, where they lead two thirds of the over 3,000 NGOs that have emerged in the post-Soviet period.

Women's Rights

Fundamental human rights, freedoms, and equality are guaranteed by the Armenian Constitution, which was adopted in 1995. Men and women are equal under the law. These laws only exist on paper, however, and there are no enforcement mechanisms.

Feminist Movements

Given the high value that is placed on family, feminism has not been very popular; and even women who promote gender equality and criticize the government for not including women in positions of power never define themselves as "feminists." Indeed, they often take offense at being referred to as feminists. The vilification of feminism is also due to the seventy years of state opposition to feminism as a bourgeois ideology. During the 1920s, Bolshevic women leaders such as Alexandria Kollontai viewed feminism as a self-indulgent bourgeois ideology that was perpetuated by well-to-do liberal women who had no idea of the struggles faced by working class and rural women. While it was commonly accepted that women had special problems and needs, it was thought that those needs could better be resolved through Communist Party structures. This position regarding the "woman question" was maintained throughout the 70 years of Soviet rule. In Armenia feminism was and continues to be resented as an anti-family radical ideology.[16] Therefore, there has never been a feminist movement.

Lesbian Rights

Homophobia and discrimination against homosexuals is widespread, and lesbians cannot legally marry or become parents.

Military Service

Although a number of Armenian women fought and defended their homes during the Ottoman Turkish genocide of the Armenians (1915–1918) and in the Nagorno Karabagh conflict (1988–1994), men have traditionally been the warriors and military leaders in Armenian society. Although women do not currently serve in the Armenian army, they play an active role in conflict mediation and peace building through their participation in NGOs.

RELIGION AND SPIRITUALITY

Following the adoption of Christianity in 301 A.D., Armenian society became more patriarchal, and the beliefs related to Anahit, the pre-

Christian goddess of fertility, morality, and maternity, were transferred onto the Virgin Mary.[17]

Women's Roles

Today women play a marginal role in the Armenian Apostolic Church: although there are female saints, Armenians do not have any monastic orders for women nor are there any female priests.

Rituals and Religious Practices

In addition to the celebration of traditional Christian holidays such as Easter and Christmas, Armenians also have feasts celebrating the female saints Hripsime, Gayane, and Shoghakat and the Festival of the Virgin Mary and the Blessing of the Grapes. The feast of the Virgin Mary, which is celebrated on the second Sunday of August, is a harvest and fertility festival originally dedicated to the goddess Anahit.[18]

VIOLENCE

Domestic Violence

Domestic violence was not an issue that was readily identified by local women or NGOs before the arrival of Western, feminist NGOs and consultants in the 1990s. In spite of the efforts of these groups and some local women's NGOs, most Armenians continue to believe that domestic violence is a private, family matter and that government regulation will have a deleterious impact on society. Domestic violence is a problem, but it has yet to be adequately understood and addressed with locally meaningful and culturally informed measures. A number of local NGOs, including the Maternity Fund of Armenia, the Armenian Caritas, and the Akunk Center for Ethnosociological Studies are attempting to find means by which this can be achieved.

Rape/Sexual Assault

Violence against women and rape are strongly condemned in society, and the rape of adolescents and children is punished with the utmost severity. Rape of adult women, however, is more difficult to prosecute as the burden of proof rests with the woman who must prove that she did not agree to have intercourse with her attacker. For this reason, most rape cases are unreported. There were 30 reported cases of rape in Armenia in 2002. During the period of independence (1991–present) the year with the highest number of reported rape cases was 1991, when a total of 48 cases were reported to the appropriate law enforcement bodies.[19]

Trafficking in Women and Children

Trafficking in all its forms is a relatively recent but rapidly growing phenomenon. Due to the clandestine nature of trafficking, there are no reliable figures of the actual number of women and children who are trafficked. There are data on the destinations of the trafficking, according to which the overwhelming majority of Armenian women and children who are trafficked end up in the United Arab Emirates, Syria, or Turkey.[20]

OUTLOOK FOR THE TWENTY-FIRST CENTURY

Although in the post-Soviet period there has been a partial return to patriarchal beliefs, contemporary attitudes regarding gender roles are a mixture of Soviet and pre-Soviet beliefs as men and women attempt to redefine their roles within the family and in society in the context of a constantly changing socioeconomic and political climate.

NOTES

1. One kilometer equals 0.6 miles.

2. Although there are no official figures, it is commonly acknowledged by most scholars that since 1991, at least 500,000 and quite possibly as many as 1 million Armenians (out of a total population of almost 3.8 million in 1990) have left Armenia. It is difficult to estimate the actual number of people since many migrants leave Armenia through illegal means and do not register their departure with the appropriate government agencies.

3. As of May 2003, 580 dram = US$1.

4. Armenian Department of Statistics; UNDP, 2000.

5. Poverty is measured by per capita expenditures on food.

6. UNDP, 1999, 54.

7. Matossian, 1961, 35.

8. In Soviet Armenia, intellectuals, professionals, and higher party functionaries had high social status and rank because class at that time was determined according to the *kultura* model. The word *kultura* in Armenian is usually translated by the word "culture," but people tend to use it to mean "class," "sophistication," or "civilization." Access to cultural, educational, and ideological capital and resources was an important factor in determining one's class status according to the defunct *kultura* model; and in some urban circles, these factors remain important.

9. UNDP, 2000, 113.

10. Gyuzalyan, 2000, 36.

11. UNDP, 2000, 64.

12. UNDP, 1999, 37.

13. "Sacred" motherhood refers to the Armenian belief dating from Armenia's pre-Christian past when the primary deity in the pantheon was Anahit, the goddess of fertility, morality, and maternity; see Zeitlian, 1992.

14. UNDP, 1999, 55.

15. UNDP, 2000, 72.

16. Buckley, 1989.

17. Zeitlian, 1992, viii.

18. Pikichian, 2001, 217.

19. Ministry of Health, 2003, 18.
20. Atovmyan, 2001, 41.

RESOURCE GUIDE

Suggested Reading

Dudwick, Nora. "Out of the Kitchen into the Crossfire: Women in Independent Armenia." In *Post-Soviet Women: From the Baltic to Central Asia*, edited by Mary Buckley, 235–49. Cambridge: Cambridge University Press, 1997. A discussion of the impact of post-Soviet economic and political changes and events on the lives of women.

Ishkanian, Armine. *Hearths and Modernity: The Role of Women in NGOs in Post-Soviet Armenia*. Ph.D. diss., University of California, San Diego, 2000. An examination of the impact of post-Soviet socioeconomic and political changes and events on the lives of women in Armenia and how these changes and events have led to women's active participation in NGOs.

Matossian, Mary. *The Impact of Soviet Policies in Armenia*. Amsterdam: Leinden Press, 1961. Several chapters address the impact of Soviet policies on women.

Moghadam, Valentine. "Gender and Economic Reforms: A Framework for Analysis and Evidence from Central Asia, the Caucasus, and Turkey." In *Gender and Identity Construction: Women in Central Asia, the Caucasus, and Turkey*, edited by Feride Acar and Ayse Gunes-Ayata, 23–43. Boston: Brill Publishers, 2000. A discussion of the impact of neoliberal economic policies on women in the Caucasian and Central Asian states.

Zeitlian, Sona. "Nationalism and the Development of Armenian Women's Rights Movement." In *Armenian Women in a Changing World*, edited by Barbara Merguerian and Diana Jafferian, 82–93. Belmont, MA: AIWA Press, 1995. Discussion of Armenian women's experiences in the twentieth century leading up to independence.

Web Sites

Armenia 1999: Women Status Report—The Impact of Transition, www.undp.am/archive/gender/UN/undp/WSR/index.htm.

Government of Armenia Interim Poverty Reduction Paper, www.gov.am/en/gov/iprsp/.

International Organization of Migration, Irregular Migration and Smuggling of Migrants from Armenia (IOM, January 2002), www.iom.int//DOCUMENTS/PUBLICATION/EN/armenia_trafficking.pdf.

———. Trafficking in Women and Children from the Republic of Armenia: A Study for the International Organization for Migration (2001), www.iom.int/iomwebsite/Publication/ServletSearchPublication?event=detail&id=872.

Organizations

Center for Gender Studies of the Democracy Today NGO
17 Nalbandian Street, Apt. 4
Yerevan, Armenia 375001

Phone: (374-1) 56-56-80, (374-1) 58-56-92
Fax: (374-1) 56-56-80
Email: sshah@arminco.com or root@shahin.arminco.com

The Center for Gender Studies conducts research and publishes reports on contemporary issues related to Armenian women.
Hazarashen Armenian Center of Ethnological Research
Norki Massiv 7, 20/28
Yerevan, Armenia
Phone: (374-1) 58-62-28
Email: azgagir@arminco.com

Hazarashen conducts research on sustainable development, poverty, and related gender issues.

SELECTED BIBLIOGRAPHY

Atovmyan, Marat. "Issues of Prostitution and Trafficking in Women in Armenia." In *The Millennium Generation: Gender Studies*, edited by Anahit Haroutunian and Elizabeth Winship, 38–44. Yerevan, Armenia: United Nations Development Program, 2001.

Buckley, Mary. *Women and Ideology in the Soviet Union*. New York: Harvester Wheatsheaf Press, 1989.

Gyuzalyan, Hayk. "Zpaghvatzootyan Genderayin Aspektun" ("The Gender Aspect of Employment"). *At the Doorstep to the XXI Century Journal* 1, no. 1 (2000): 35–37.

Hovannisian, Richard. *Armenia on the Road to Independence*. Berkeley: University of California Press, 1967.

Ishkanian, Armine. "Surviving Post-Soviet Poverty: Experiences and Narratives of Armenian Temporary Labor Migrants in the US." *The Anthropology of East Europe Review: Central Europe, Eastern Europe, and Eurasia*, 20, no. 2: 23–30.

———"Working at the Global/Local Nexus: Challenges Facing Women in Armenia's NGO Sector." In *Women in Post-Communist Transitions*, edited by Carol Nechemias and Kathleen Kuehnast. Washington, DC: Woodrow Wilson Center Press, forthcoming.

Lapidus, Gail. "Discussant's Comments." In *Making the Transition Work for Women in Europe and Central Asia (World Bank Discussion Papers, 411)*, edited by Marnia Lazreg, 102–6. Washington, DC: World Bank Publications, 2000.

Matossian, Mary. *The Impact of Soviet Policies in Armenia*. Amsterdam: Leinden Press, 1961.

Ministry of Health of America. "The Problem of Violence in the Context of General Health Policy." Report presented by Karine Saribekian, Head of the Mother and Child Health Protection Department, April 29, 2003.

Pikichian, Hripsime. "Festival and Feast." In *Armenian Folk Arts, Culture, and Identity*, edited by Levon Abrahamian and Nancy Sweezy, 217–34. Bloomington: Indiana University Press, 2001.

United Nations Development Program (UNDP). *Armenia: Women Status Report—The Impact of Transition*. Yerevan, Armenia: UNDP Press, 1999.

———. *Armenia 2000 Human Rights and Human Development: Action for Progress Human Development Report*. Yerevan, Armenia: UNDP Press, 2000.

Zeitlian, Sona. *Hai Knotch Teruh Hai Hegahpoghagan Zharzhman Metch* (The Role of Armenian Women in the Armenian Revolutionary Movement) (In Armenian). Los Angeles: Hraztan Sarkis Zeitlian Publications.

3

AUSTRIA

Benjamin F. Shearer

PROFILE OF AUSTRIA

Once the heart of the Austro-Hungarian Empire, which was ruled from Vienna for hundreds of years by the Habsburg dynasty, the modern Republic of Austria emerged from the aftermath of World War I in 1918 as a small state. Its 32,369 square miles is two-thirds covered by the Eastern Alps, and 46 percent is heavily forested. The Danube Region lies along the Danube River, which flows for 220 miles through Austria.[1]

Following its collapse under Nazi rule, the republic was revived in 1945 under Allied occupation. The Austrian State Treaty of 1955 marked Austria's return to independence as a democratic republic. Also in 1955, Austria declared its permanent neutrality and joined the United Nations.[2] The federal president is elected for a six-year term "by the populace on the basis of an equal, direct, secret and personal ballot." The president, federal ministers, state secretaries, and members of the state governments form the executive authorities. The president appoints the chancellor and, with her or his recommendation, the other federal government ministers.[3] The Parliament consists of the *Nationalrat* and the *Bundesrat*. The *Nationalrat*, con-

vened by the president, is popularly elected on the same basis as the president and carries out federal legislative functions together with the *Bundesrat*. The *Bundesrat* is elected by the state diets on the basis of "proportional election." The state with the largest population sends twelve members to the *Bundesrat*; the others send fewer but no less than three. The party in each state having the second-largest number of members in the diet must receive at least one seat in the *Bundesrat*.[4]

Austrians enjoy a high standard of living. Austria has been a member of the European Union since 1995. Its free market economy, "with a strong emphasis on social factors favoring the economically less privileged," continues with Union membership.[5] In 2001, 69 percent of the gross domestic product (GDP) came from services, 29 percent from industry, and 2 percent from agriculture. GDP per capita was estimated at $27,000.[6] Almost two thirds of import and export trade is within the European Union, but nearly 14 percent of trade is with the emerging markets of formerly Soviet-dominated nations to the east. Labor relations have been dominated by the 1.5 million–member Austrian Trade Union Federation, which represents half of the nation's paid employees. The federation has pursued economic policies that have made it a partner with business, industry, and government in Austria's economic and social development.[7]

The total population of Austria in 2002 was estimated at 8,169,929. Of these, 88 percent were German, 2 percent were naturalized citizens, and 9.3 percent were nonnationals including Hungarians, Slovaks, Croatians, Slovenes, and Czechs. There are .95 males for each female in the total population. Life expectancy at birth was seventy-eight years overall, with male life expectancy at 74.85 years and female life expectancy at 81.31 years. Thus, in the sixty-five years and older group, there are only .62 males for each female. The total fertility rate was 1.4 and the infant mortality rate was 4.39 per 1,000 live births.[8] In 1995, the maternal mortality rate per 100,000 live births was 11.[9]

OVERVIEW OF WOMEN'S ISSUES

The small democratic Austrian state that came out of the First World War has sought its identity through the turmoil of war and foreign occupation. A classical patriarchal society was solidly ensconced and reinforced by welfare policy. Women had virtually no political or economic power and were shut out from decision-making positions. In the 1970s, as feminists began to question these old values and as women's labor force participation increased, policies gradually began to change. Austria's entry into the European Union in 1995 was, in a way, a new path to its identity. Austria would place itself and its future in an integrated Europe and accept the human rights policies of the Union as its own.

EDUCATION

Opportunities

Until 1919, the secondary education of girls took place in private and church institutions. There were no public secondary schools for girls. The goal of the 1919 law that opened boys' schools to girls was not coeducation but to conserve resources, since there was not enough money in the treasury to create a girls' system that would meet the new equality laws.[10]

During the 2000–2001 school year, there were 203,069 boys and 190,517 girls enrolled in the elementary schools. Of the 33,853 elementary school teachers, 29,591 (87.4 percent) were female. There were 138,121 boys and 125,425 girls enrolled in the secondary schools where female teachers outnumber male teachers nearly two to one (22,377 versus 11,608).[11] There are, however, dramatic differences at the third level of education. During the 1999–2000 school year, the enrollment of Austrian students in higher vocational studies, including technical education, business, tourism, and media/telecommunications, totaled 9,652, of which only 2,796 (29 percent) were female.[12] On the other hand, in that same year Austrian women students slightly outnumbered men in the universities, where there were 103,820 women and 102,439 men.[13] Yet there were 1,791 male professors and only 175 (8.9 percent) female professors, which was twice the percentage of women in 1975–1976.[14]

One of the instructional principles of the coeducational secondary system is male and female equality. In 1983, for example, industrial arts classes were opened to both sexes, and in 1987 home economics became required for boys and girls.[15] It might be argued that at least in terms of higher education outcomes, the lesson of equality is being learned. Between 1955–1956 and 1998–1999, the number of female graduates from higher vocational schools and universities went from 592 to 7,792, an increase of 1316 percent. In 1955–1956, women constituted only 20 percent of the graduates. By the 1998–1999 academic year, they were 47 percent of the graduates.[16] Even as gender segregation clearly

Teacher and students at the Vienna Conservatory of Music. Photo © Stuart Franklin/Magnum Photos.

remains in educational workplaces and educational choices, women have made great strides in advancing their own learning through higher participation rates in advanced education.

Literacy

The literacy rate is 98 percent.[17] Education has been compulsory since 1869. At that time, eight years of education were required. Today, nine years are mandated. Children aged six to ten are enrolled in elementary schools. Secondary education follows in intermediate schools or the lower levels of high schools until at least age fourteen. Students' options after compulsory schooling are entering the work force (some further polytechnic training is available) or pursuing vocational or university education. Students who earn a certificate from a general education high school may enter university. State-sponsored schools are free, with books and travel mostly covered by the state.[18]

EMPLOYMENT AND THE ECONOMY

Job/Career Opportunities

Women constituted 43 percent of the labor force in the period 1995–2000.[19] Female workers have predominated in the textile, clothing, restaurant, personal service, health, education, house rental, and household services sectors. They have been grossly underrepresented in the utilities, mining, paper, construction, metals, wood processing, and transport sectors.[20] In 1999, the average annual gross earnings of women was 60 percent of that of men. The largest pay gaps were in these sectors: financial intermediation (in which women earn 54 percent of what men earn); community, social, and personal activities (55 percent); utilities (56 percent); wholesale and retail trade (56 percent); and agriculture, hunting, and forestry (58 percent). In low-wage sectors such as restaurants and private household services, the pay gaps were relatively low (74 percent and 92 percent respectively).[21]

Pay

Several factors contribute to the overall pay differential between men and women. First, more women work part-time. In 1996, 29 percent of women workers were employed part-time whereas only 4 percent of men were. This may account for up to 15 percent of the gap. Second, men also tend to work more overtime, which is estimated to account for 5 percent of the differential. Third, women who have taken leave for family reasons earn less money over time than those who do not, whether they go to part-time work or return to full-time work. Fourth, many women are aggregated in low-pay sectors, which skews the gross data. Most importantly, however, the pay gap begins with the first job out of school, when men receive 18 percent more than the women in the same occupation.[22]

Working Conditions

The 1979 Act on Equal Treatment for Men and Women, which outlawed any kind of discrimination at work based on sex, has not succeeded in narrowing pay differentials between men and women. Exacerbating the problem is the trend toward atypical employment arrangements caused by changes in labor demand. For example, by 2001, the steadily increasing percentage of labor force working part-time reached 17.4 percent. Most of the increase was in the service sector, where women predominate.[23] Neither has women's climb up the managerial ladder been swift with equal treatment. In the period 1985–1997, only 22 percent of administrative and management workers were women.[24]

Sexual Harassment

In 1993, the Equal Treatment Act was amended to add a provision for equal pay for equal work and to criminalize sexual harassment as discriminatory. One national study found that 81 percent of women had experienced sexual harassment, defined to include sexist behavior.[25] There is evidence, however, that employers discourage women from lodging complaints or seeking compensation for damages.[26] Only 142 of the 850 cases before the Ombudsman for Equal Opportunity in 2000 were sexual harassment complaints.[27]

Support for Mothers/Caretakers

Maternal Leave

New parents enjoy certain rights and benefits by law. The maternity leave law establishes a "maternal protection period" eight weeks before and eight to sixteen weeks after giving birth, depending on the health of the mother. During this time the mother may not work, but she receives a maternity allowance from the insurance sickness fund. The amount of the allowance is determined by her average earnings during the thirteen weeks prior to leave. Pregnant women are protected from dismissal from work during pregnancy and for at least four months thereafter. The law on parental leave allows for unpaid leave up to two years. The mother must first apply for this leave with her employer, who must grant it. After three months, the mother may opt to return to work and give the remainder of the leave to the father. The father is obligated to notify his employer of his intention to take leave within four weeks after the birth of the child.

Parents adopting children may also make use of the parental leave benefits. The parent responsible for childcare may receive a special leave allowance in lieu of pay if she or he had been employed for fifty-two weeks and was subject to unemployment insurance within two years of applying. Other options are also available to new parents. Rather than taking parental leave, by agreement with the employer a male or female employee may opt to reduce working hours by at least 40 percent until the child reaches four years old. And even if the leave option has been chosen, when the child reaches one year of age, the mother may, with the employer's agreement, work part-time on maternity grounds. If the father is also using the right to work part-time option, the mother may use it until the child is two years of age. The mother may also work part-time on maternity grounds until the child reaches three years of age if only she is working part-time or if both parents are working part-time alternately.[28]

Daycare

Childcare is provided through daycare centers and crèches. In 2000–2001, 35,522 children were enrolled in the nation's 811 state-funded daycare centers, 590 crèches provided care for 11,027 children, and 219,309 children attended kindergarten. Municipalities operate 75 percent of the kindergartens. Kindergarten is optional for three-to-six-year-olds, as compulsory education begins at six. In 1999, however, 90 percent of five-year-olds were enrolled in kindergartens.[29]

Social/Government Programs

Sustainable Development

Agenda 21 is a comprehensive set of guidelines for sustainable development that was adopted by Austria and 178 other nations in 1992. A very high priority was placed on protecting and promoting human health. AIDS prevention programs have been operating since 1987. Health care and social services have been integrated in health care and social districts to reduce costs and allow people to remain near home. The Austrian Healthy Cities Network was created in 1992 with the hope of developing healthier city life and new approaches to information exchange.

Essential to successful sustainable development initiatives is the inclusion of all major groups in society. In regard to women, Austria reported that it had ratified the Convention on the Elimination of All Forms of Discrimination against Women in 1982. The proportion of women decision makers was increasing. Curricula and other educational material were being assessed, revised, and implemented to promote "dissemination of gender-relevant knowledge." Policies were being formulated and implemented to achieve equality throughout society and assure women's participation in sustainable development. And mechanisms to assess the impact of environmental policies and programs on women were to be established. Through legislation, equality had been expanded: in 1995, the Equal Treatment Act was being implemented, and violence in the family and the division of labor in the household had been addressed.[30]

Welfare

The Austrian government proudly states that its "welfare measures begin before birth and accompany an Austrian citizen throughout his or her life." The social security system provides "extensive insurance coverage in the event of accident, illness (including surgery), childbirth, spa treatment, unemployment, invalidity, old age, and pension payments for surviving spouses." Austrian workers have the legal right to five weeks of paid vacation each year, and parents receive children's allowances.[31]

The welfare system also recognizes, to a limited extent, the dual roles women play in home and work. Childrearing increases the retirement benefits for a mother or father at the maximum rate of four years per child, but raising a child does not alone entitle anyone to a pension. In fact, however, although equality policies have been put into place that ideally make men and women equal before the law, welfare policies produce "effects which preserve traditional gender roles."[32] Married women who do not work outside the home, for example, are completely dependent on their spouses for medical insurance and have no state pension eligibility regardless of the extent of their caregiving activities.

FAMILY AND SEXUALITY

Gender Roles

Until 1975, a husband had to give permission for his wife to work outside the home. The revision of the Family Act in 1975 "can be regarded as the beginning of policies supporting gender equality."[33] The father was no longer recognized by law as the head of the family. Single mothers and unmarried couples were also recognized as families eligible for social protection. Yet it was not until 1989 that rape in marriage was recognized as criminal and not until 1990 that leave for a new child included both parents. The 1995 Surname Act finally allowed married couples to keep their own names.[34] In 2002, the restriction on women working at night ended.[35]

In spite of notable and new trends in family life, traditional gender roles in the home persist as they do in the workplace. Men do not seem to be as willing as women to share household tasks. A study in 1981 found that women do more unpaid household work than men no matter what their status. Employed men spent 78 minutes per week on average doing housework, but employed women spent 239 minutes. Unemployed men spent

122 minutes on housework, and unemployed women spent 404 minutes. White-collar men spent 85 minutes a week on housework, and white-collar women spent 207 hours.[36] By the end of the 1980s, a survey found that 80 percent of married women were alone doing the laundry, 66 percent were doing the cooking, and 51 percent the cleaning. Twenty percent of men did no housework at all.[37] Throughout this time of immense social change, men still viewed themselves as breadwinners, and women, manipulated in part by welfare policies that provided full benefits only to paid workers, viewed themselves as both workers and caregivers.

Marriage

There have been dramatic changes in the family. From the 1960s to the early 1990s, fertility rates dropped to all-time lows, 20–30 percent of women decided not to have children, and twice as many married couples decided not to have children. Families got smaller and single-parent households, 90 percent of which were headed by women, grew faster than two-parent households. Marriages began a steady decline, and divorces and births outside of wedlock began a steady increase.[38] These trends only accelerated in the new century. Between 1951 and 2000, the number of marriages fell from 52,167 to 39,228 annually. Ages at marriage continued to advance. In 1951, the average age of grooms was 28.1 and of brides, 25.5. By 2000, the average age of grooms rose to 31.6 and brides, 28.9.[39] Births outside of wedlock increased from 24.8 percent in 1991 to 31.3 percent in 2000 while the number of births declined from 94,629 to 78,268.[40] The divorce rate, which had nearly tripled between 1961 and 1991 to 33.5 percent, rose to 43.1 percent in 2000.[41]

Reproduction

Sex Education

Sex education is included in the curriculum of the high schools.[42]

Contraception and Abortion

Approximately 71 percent of women between fifteen and forty-nine years of age use some kind of contraception method. Contraceptives are easily available from general practice physicians and through many of the nearly 300 family and partner counseling centers. The Ministry of Family Affairs funds family planning services.[43] The 1975 abortion law permits abortion on request before the end of the first trimester. Abortions may also be performed in the second trimester if the woman's life is in danger, if there is risk to the woman's physical health, or if the woman is under fourteen years of age. Only physicians may perform abortions.[44]

HEALTH

Health Care Access

The mandatory health insurance system covers 99 percent of the population.[45] There are nine district and nine occupational sickness funds, some of which own their own hospitals or clinics. Physicians, pharmacists, and hospitals generally contract with the sickness funds and are directly paid by them.[46]

Diseases and Disorders

Austrians generally enjoy good health and easy access to health services. Heart disease was the leading cause of death for men and women in 2000. Deaths of women from heart disease occurred at the rate of 204.3 per 100,000 women. The breast cancer death rate for women was 40.1 per 100,000 women.[47] HIV/AIDS deaths were estimated at eight in 2001.[48] Of thirty reported AIDS cases in 2001, twelve resulted from sex between men, nine from sex between men and women, and nine from injecting drug users.[49]

Austria does not have a women's health movement "in the sense of a large number of women in a political movement declaring themselves to be competent experts on their own health, developing joint projects, constituting a conscious self-help movement, [and] drawing up woman-centered strategies."[50] However, although the self-help movement is marginal, it is developing. The Women's Health Center at Graz is a member of the Network of Women's Health Centers and a good example of what can be as other women's centers come together throughout the nation. The Graz Center is an independent, nonprofit organization that is part of the international women's health movement, an advocate for women's health, and a "necessary complement and corrective to other major interest groups in the health care system (pharmaceutical industry, Board of Physicians, public insurance)." The center supports self-help groups, places women's health on the political agenda, advocates for women-friendly services, and conducts model programs. One such program was a gender health audit of six businesses and nonprofit organizations. The audit revealed, among other things, that health promotion activities did not target women and that the health and well-being of women employees was not placed in the context of "gendered working conditions." The center also provides through its web site access to numerous self-help organizations including those dealing with cancer and eating disorders.[51]

In April 2001, a women's health division was established in the Federal Ministry of Social Security and Generations. The division focuses its activities on "the networking of women's health institutions, women's health centers and experts of women's health, for discussing and developing national concepts of specific women's health programs in the field of promoting health, health supply and health research." The division also is attempting to wed the psychosocial and ethical aspects of care with the purely medical aspect of care.[52]

POLITICS AND LAW

Suffrage

Women and men who have "completed their eighteenth year before January 1 of the year of the election" are eligible to vote.[53]

Political Participation

All Austrian citizens are equal before the law, and birth, gender, status, class, or religion have no legal privileges. All Austrian citizens also have equal access to public office.[54] Yet since women were permitted to vote in 1918, their numbers in the population have never reached parity in political office. Between 1919 and 1934, the percentage of women in the National Council was between 4.2 percent and 7.3 percent.[55] By 1987, women held 11 percent of parliamentary seats. In 1995, the percentage jumped to 23 and it went up slightly in 2001 to 27. In 1998, only 25 percent of the decision-making positions in government was held by women. Women held 4 percent of the subministerial level positions.[56] In the nine state assemblies, women held only eighty-eight of 448 seats, or 19.6 percent.[57]

Women's Rights

While women continue to struggle for political power, they have not been wholly unsuccessful, the impetus for reform having been fueled also by Austria's requirement to meet European Union guidelines on women's rights. Women's organizations are vital, however, in keeping the pressure on government to enhance the role of women in society and promote women's causes. When the right-wing Freedom Party came into office in 2000, it abolished the ten-year-old Office of the Minister for Women's Affairs, evidence that the old patriarchal society still lingered.[58] The largest platform for women's rights in Austria is the Austrian Women's Ring. The nonpartisan ring has more than forty member organizations including women's organizations from churches, trade unions, and political parties, and it represents over 1 million members. Its purpose is to promote the equal treatment of men and women.[59]

Lesbian Rights

The movement for lesbian rights has not kept pace with the general movement for women's rights. The ban on male and female homosexuality was not abolished until 1971. The ban on distribution of positive information about homosexuality and gay and lesbian associations was not lifted until 1997. Same-sex partnerships or marriages are not legally recognized and, therefore, surviving partners have no legal right to inheritance as heterosexual partners would have. Gay and lesbian employees also have no right to leave for caring for a sick partner and no right to obtain dependent insurance for a partner not working. Lesbian partners are considered single women for income tax purposes, and thus are not eligible for the tax reduction that heterosexual couples receive. Same-sex couples are not permitted to adopt, nor are individuals if it is known they are homosexual.[60]

Military Service

The Defense Act on Women in the Austrian Armed Forces, which permitted women to enter the military for the first time, was passed in December 1997 and went into effect on January 1, 1998. The impetus for this legislation was not military reform but European Union requirements. Eighteen-year-old men will continue to be conscripted into the armed services, but women may join voluntarily either to become noncommissioned officers or officers. Seventy-three women currently serve in the armed forces.[61]

RELIGION AND SPIRITUALITY

Freedom of religion is a guaranteed right of all Austrian citizens. Roman Catholics comprise the largest sect at 78 percent, followed by Protestants, mostly Augsburg Confession Lutheran, at 5 percent. Of the population, 4.5 percent belongs to another religion (including Islam), and 9 percent claim no religion. The religion, if any, of the remaining 3.5 percent is unknown. Less than one third of Catholics attend church regularly.[62]

VIOLENCE

Exact data on violence against women are difficult to determine because only about 10 percent of actual cases of abuse may be reported.[63] There are, however, some data available that are indicators of an extensive problem. A 1991 study found that 10–20 percent of women living in relationships suffered physical violence. In 1994, a survey revealed that 91 percent of physicians had treated at least one woman victimized by violence.[64] Results from a 1996 survey indicated that 3.8 percent of women overall and 6.4 percent of women in urban areas were victims of sexual offenses, including sexual harassment. These were the highest percentages reported either in Europe or North America and were higher than the victimization rates for any other crimes (and overall) in Austria, perhaps because of extensive awareness projects that produce more reporting of crime.

Rapes totaled 553 for a rate per 100,000 population of 6.9, the same rate as in 1990.[65]

Domestic Violence

The first women's shelter opened in Vienna in 1978. Since then, the Autonomous Austrian Women's Shelter Network, a subsidized nonprofit organization funded also by donations and research contracts, has continued to grow and develop. In 1997, 1,030 women and 1,065 children spent a total of 96,535 nights in sixteen shelters, but 237 women and children had to be turned away for lack of space.[66] By 2000, there were eighteen shelters that housed 1,224 women and 1,214 children for 110,002 nights. In addition, 12,661 counseling sessions were provided for women not living in the shelters.[67]

Building shelters helped to fulfill some very critical immediate needs, but it did not further the ideal of eliminating violence against women. With the new insight that violence of any kind in any place against women is a violation of human rights, a number of new programs were initiated in the 1990s. A platform against domestic violence was adopted, police were placed in mandatory training programs, and information resources and training strategies were developed. By 1998, five intervention centers had been opened to meet the needs of women who may not go to counseling centers but need assistance in the case of abuse. The 1997 Law on the Protection against Violence in the Family was perhaps the crowning achievement of a working group of police, representatives of the judiciary, intervention centers, and women's shelters. This innovative law permitted police to remove a violent person, related to the victim or not, from a home at once whether or not that person owned the home. Courts could now ban a person from a home and its surrounding area with a temporary injunction of up to three months. Later legislation extended this period. In the first year after this legislation became effective, from May 1997 to April 1998, police had expelled or barred from returning to their homes 1,993 people. After two years, the number of bans or expulsions had reached 5,778. Also in that two-year period, 462 temporary injunctions were granted out of 577 filed. Wives and female partners made up over 90 percent of those requesting the injunctions.[68]

Trafficking in Women

The trafficking of women is absolutely linked to prostitution, and Austria's geographical center between Eastern and Western Europe makes such trafficking an important social issue. The numbers are unknown, but since prostitution is legal, prostitutes must be registered. Some idea of the breadth of the problem can be gleaned from data on unregistered prostitutes. In Vienna, for example, the number of illegal prostitutes had grown from 2,800 in 1990 to 4,300 in 1995 while the number of registered prostitutes had fallen from 800 to 670. As the borders of Eastern European countries formerly under Soviet domination opened, a large influx of women from those countries entered Austria. The number of trafficking cases rose from fifty in 1990 to 316 in 1994, but only half of the cases resulted in charges.[69] The government is working to curb trafficking and increase awareness of the issue. In 2000, harder sentences were created for trafficking, but in the same year, 125 complaints were filed involving illegal trafficking and ten convictions were obtained.[70]

OUTLOOK FOR THE TWENTY-FIRST CENTURY

Austria has been slow to develop policies that truly make men and women equal. There has been no movement at all to assure equality for lesbians and gays. Gender segregation exists throughout society, in the schools, in the workplace, in the home, and most certainly in politics. Traditional views of the family persist. Violence against women is an issue just recently being addressed. It is unclear in which direction future governments will go to deliver complete emancipation, but up until now, the governments seem to have been reluctant participants in changing laws and policies. The extra layer of government added by membership in the European Union should be some protection against wild sways in political policy as it concerns women's issues. But no matter what positions government may take, the trends in family, work life, and women's expectations have been clear for forty years.

The women's health movement and the self-help movement are nascent but building quickly. As these movements grow and take on more power as social partners, political power should come with it. Since the birth of the First Republic, women's voices in political matters have been muted by lack of participation, a barrier that must be overcome to assure that the many gains that have been won go on and are furthered.

NOTES

1. Republic of Austria, "Austria—The Country and Its People," www.austria.gv.at.

2. Republic of Austria, "Austria—History," www.austria.gv.at.

3. Republic of Austria, "Austria—Political System—Federal President," www.austria.gv.at.

4. Republic of Austria, "Political System—The Parliament," www.austria.gv.at.

5. Republic of Austria, "Austria—Economy," www.austria.gv.at.

6. CIA, "World Factbook 2002—Austria," www.cia.gov.

7. U.S. Department of State, Bureau of European and Eurasian Affairs, "Background Note: Austria," www.state.gov (accessed March 2002).

8. CIA, 2002.

9. UN Statistics Division, "Millennium Indicators," http://unstats.un.org.

10. Gabriella Hauch, "Rights at Last? The First Generation of Female Members of Parliament in Austria," in *Women in Austria*, ed. Günter Bischof et al., Contemporary Austrian Studies, vol. 6 (New Brunswick, NJ, and London: Transaction Publishers, 1998), 65–66.

11. Statistik Austria, *Statistisches Jahrbuch 2002*, 127.

12. Statistik Austria, 2002, 132.

13. Statistik Austria, 2002, 127.

14. Statistik Austria, 2002, 117.

15. Education International, "Summary on Education Reform—Austria," www.ei-ie.org.

16. Statistik Austria, 2002, 117.

17. CIA, 2002.

18. Republic of Austria, "Austria—Education," www.austria.gv.at.

19. UN Statistics Division, "The World's Women 2000: Trends and Statistics: Indicators of Economic Activity," http://unstats.un.org.

20. Gudrun Biffl, "Women and Their Work in the Labor Market and in the Household," in *Austrian Women in the Nineteenth and Twentieth Centuries*, ed. David F. Good et al. (Providence, RI, and Oxford: Berghahn Books, 1996), 146.

21. European Industrial Relations Observatory (EIRO) On-Line, "Austria—Gender-related Pay Differentials Examined," March 28, 2001, www.eiro.eurofound.ie.

22. EIRO, "Austria."

23. European Industrial Relations Observatory (EIRO) On-Line, "2001 Annual Review for Austria," www.eiro.eurofound.ie.

24. UN Statistics Division, 2000.

25. Greetje Timmerman and Cristien Bajema, "Sexual Harassment in Northwest Europe: A Cross-Cultural Comparison," *European Journal of Women's Studies* 6 (1999): 426–27.

26. International Women's Rights Action Watch, "Publications: Country Reports: Austria," October 5, 1999, http://iwraw.igc.org.

27. U.S. Department of State, "Austria: Country Reports on Human Rights Practices—2001," www.state.gov.

28. Europa, "Dialogue with Citizens: Austria—Parental Leave"; and Europa, "Dialogue with Citizens: Austria—Maternity or Adoption Leave," both from www.europa.eu.int.

29. Statistik Austria, 2002, 119; and European Primary Schools Association, "Primary Education in Austria," January 23, 2003, www.epsaweb.org.

30. UN, Department of Economic and Social Affairs, "Country Profile—Austria: Implementation of Agenda 21," www.un.org.

31. Republic of Austria, "Austria—Social Security," www.austria.gv.at; and "Social Security Programs throughout the World: Europe, 2002—Austria," www.ssa.gov.

32. Sieglinde Katharina Rosenberger, "Politics, Gender, and Equality," in *Women in Austria*, ed. Günter Bischof et al., Contemporary Austrian Studies, vol. 6 (New Brunswick and London: Transaction Publishers, 1998), 114–15.

33. Rosenberger, 1998, 110.

34. Rosenberger, 1998, 110–11.

35. U.S. Department of State, 2001.

36. Gudrun Biffl, 1998, 151.

37. Eric Solsten, ed., "Austria: A Country Study: Status of Women," Federal Research Division of the Library of Congress, December 1993, http://lcweb2.loc.gov.

38. Solsten, 1993.

39. Statistik Austria, *Statistisches Jahrbuch 2000*, 68.

40. Statistik Austria, 2000, 73.

41. Statistik Austria, 2000, 80.

42. Education International, "Summary on Education Reform—Austria," www. ei-ie.org.

43. International Planned Parenthood Federation, "Country Profiles: Austria," http://ippfnet.ippf.org.

44. IPPF European Network, "Abortion Legislation in Europe," January 2002, www.ippfen.org.

45. Solsten, 1993.

46. Social Security Administration, 2002.

47. Statistik Austria, 2000, 107.

48. CIA, 2002.

49. "Aids Cases by Exposure Category in Europe," www.avert.org.

50. WHNET, "The Women's Health Movement—National Report: Austria," www.gesundheit-nds.de.

51. "Women's Health Center Graz," www.fgz.co.at.

52. Bundesministerium für Soziale Sicherheit und Generationen, "Weitere Veranstaltungen zum Thema 'Frauengesundheit,' " www.bmsg.gv.at.

53. Republic of Austria, "Political System—the Parliament," www.austria.gv.at.

54. Republic of Austria, "Austria—Political System—Basic Rights and Freedoms," www.austria.gv.at.

55. Hauch, 1998, 67–68.

56. UN Statistics Division, "The World's Women 2000: Trends and Statistics—Women in Public Life," http://unstats.un.org.

57. EUROPARL, "Differential Impact of Electoral Systems on Female Political Representation," www.europarl.eu.int.

58. IWRAW, "Publications: Country Reports: Austria," www.iwraw.igc.org.

59. Austrian Women's Ring, www.frauenring.at.

60. The International Lesbian and Gay Association, "World Legal Survey: Austria," www.ilga.org.

61. Dietmar Pfarr, "Women in the Austrian Armed Forces," *Minerva: Quarterly Report on Women and the Military* 17 (31 December 1999): 13–14.

62. CIA, 2002; and Republic of Austria, "Austria—The Country and Its People."

63. U.S. Department of State, 2001.

64. Rosa Logar, "Domestic Violence Measures and Intervention Projects in Austria," Österreichische Frauenhäuser, Informationsstelle gegen Gewalt, www.aoef.at.

65. EU Accession Monitoring Program, "Austria," www.eumap.org/library.datab/Documents/1017433744.27/austria.pdf, 8.

66. Logar.

67. "Statistik der autonomen Österreichischen Frauenhäuser," Österreichische Frauenhäuser, Informationsstelle gegen Gewalt, www.aoef.at.

68. Logar.

69. International Organization for Migration, Migration Information Programme, "Trafficking in Women to Austria for Sexual Exploitation," June 1996, www.iom.int, 7, 9–10.

70. U.S. Department of State, 2001.

RESOURCE GUIDE

Suggested Reading

Bischof, Günter, et al., eds. *Women in Austria*. Contemporary Austrian Studies, vol. 6. New Brunswick, NJ, and London: Transaction Publishers, 1998.

Good, David F., et al., eds. *Austrian Women in the Nineteenth and Twentieth Centuries*. Providence, RI, and Oxford: Berghahn Books, 1996.

Solsten, Eric, ed. "Austria: A Country Study." Federal Research Division of the Library of Congress. December 1993. http://lcweb2.loc.gov.

Web Sites

Austrian Women's Ring, www.frauenring.at.
This is the site for Austria's largest women's rights group.

Government of Austria, www.austria.gv.at.
This is the main site for the government of Austria from which general information is available about the country and its government.

Österreichische Frauenhäuser, www.aoef.at.
This is the site for Austrian women's shelters.

Women's Health Center Graz, www.fgz.co.at.
This is the main site for women's health centers in Austria.

SELECTED BIBLIOGRAPHY

International Organization for Migration, Migration Information Programme. "Trafficking in Women to Austria for Sexual Exploitation." June 1996. www.iom.int.

International Women's Rights Action Watch. "Publications: Country Reports: Austria." October 5, 1999. http://iwraw.igc.org.

U.S. Department of State. "Austria: Country Reports on Human Rights Practices— 2001." www.state.gov.

WHNET. "The Women's Health Movement—National Report: Austria." www.gesundheit-nds.de.

4

BELARUS

Elena Gapova

PROFILE OF BELARUS

The geography of Belarus, one of the New Independent States (NIS) created after the disintegration of the USSR in 1991, consists of plains with significant forests and a wide lake region in the northwest. Belarus has had a long history of incorporation into empires, realignment of borders, and foreign invasions. Partial recognition of Belarusian nationhood was achieved under Soviet rule in 1921, and since 1945 Belarus has been a member of the UN. During World War II the nation lost one in four people, which is the highest proportional casualty rate in the world. Since 1991 the country entered a period of transition to a market economy and parliamentary democracy, though the Soviet legacy of social services is still very strong.

The population of the country is 9.5 million people, 53 percent of whom are women. About 81 percent of the population are Belarusians and 11 percent are Russians; other significant ethnic groups are Poles, Ukrainians, and Jews.

Current life expectancy, after a serious drop of the post-1991 period, is 73.9 for women and 62.2 for men. The infant mortality rate is 9.3 per 1,000 live births and the maternal mortality rate is 21.3 per 100,000 live births. The total fertility (average number of births per woman) is 1.2.

OVERVIEW OF WOMEN'S ISSUES

Since the 1920s, Belarusian women have been incorporated into the labor force, and after World War II they had an extensive system of social provisioning based on their work contribution. Since 1991, the country has been going through enormous transformation, which affected women both positively and negatively. Some run their own businesses or take up challenging careers, whereas for others the change to market economy, with its over 40 percent reduction in gross domestic product, has led to unemployment, loss of social security, and loss of status. The subsidized childcare and extended maternity benefits, which were possible under a centrally controlled economy, have made women "expensive" employees, which became a reason for women to be fired first and hired last.

Under socialism, women were represented in decision-making bodies in substantial numbers, which, to a large extent, were tokens of the Soviet regime. After the first free elections of 1993, their representation in the Parliament fell to 3 percent. Conservative (religious or nationalist) revivals triggered antiliberal discourse on women's roles and reproduction, and market relations paved the way for making women's sexuality a commodity, thus increasing prostitution and trafficking. On the other hand, the emergence of civil society brought about new opportunities for articulating women's interests through groups and organizations.

EDUCATION

Opportunities

Women became fully incorporated into primary, secondary, and higher education in the period between the two world wars. Later, the Soviet-standardized educational system became an important venue for preparing women for inclusion into the labor force. Currently, women are better educated than men and make up 58.4 percent of all people with university degrees and 65.8 percent of those with vocational secondary training. Seventeen percent of all women graduate from universities compared to 14 percent of men.

However, these gains are a mixed blessing. The prestige and salaries of intellectual jobs have been declining since the 1980s; thus, the better educated are not always better paid. Women and men in secondary vocational schools choose occupational training based on traditional views of division of labor, with women preferring services, light industries, office work, and auxiliary health care. Women hold 76 percent of the degrees in education but only 28 percent of the engineering degrees and 33 percent of the degrees in math and science. There are five times more female than male teachers in schools with high teaching loads, and women teachers make up a smaller portion of those with graduate degrees: 32.5 percent are "candidates of science" (the equivalent of a doctorate) but only 11.9 percent are full professors. One of the new educational gains is the emergence of gender studies as a special field; training for a master's degree is provided at the Centre for Gender Studies at European Humanities University in Minsk.

Literacy

In the 1920s, when the illiteracy rate was very high, the Soviet government embarked on the policy of "liquidation of illiteracy" through adult education classes. The literacy rate is currently 99.6 percent.

EMPLOYMENT AND THE ECONOMY

During the Soviet era, women had very high rates of labor force participation, since all able-bodied adults were expected to work. As a legacy, women still make up 52 percent of the working population.

Job/Career Opportunities

Labor force structure is undergoing a transformation. The percent of women employed in production is going down relative to men but is increasing in nonproduction (and lower-paid) branches of the economy. Women outnumber men ten times among medical personnel. There are 1.5 times more women than men in health care, social welfare, education, public services, and civil service—working in state agencies with a fixed income. Men are now moving into areas that were once female-dominated, such as finance and insurance, as these fields grow in significance in a market economy. In all occupations, women tend to occupy lower and middle positions, with men disproportionately becoming managers. In the private sector, which emerged after socialism, 9.1 percent of men had started a business of their own compared to only 2.7 percent of women. Men were able to transform the advantages they had as heads of state-run businesses into market assets. Furthermore, these official estimates disregard the informal economy, where large numbers of women are employed

Watch factory workers, Minsk, Belarus. Photo © TRIP/V. Kolpakov.

in unskilled occupations such as street vendors and home help, without any social security.

Unemployment is the phenomenon brought by the introduction of the market economy, and women were 81.4 percent of the unemployed in 1992 and 60.3 percent in 2001. The length of time women stay unemployed is also longer than it is for men. Women, because of their caretaking responsibilities, are less flexible in adapting to new situations: compared to men, they are less likely to take extra jobs, go into private business, or change occupations.

Pay

Under the Constitution, women and men get equal pay for equal work; but in fact, women's wages are 81 percent of men's. The real income difference is even bigger, since the post-Soviet market economy largely takes the form of shadow, or informal, economy. During the transition to a formal market economy, it functions as a shock absorber, providing opportunities to get extra resources. Not everybody, though, is cushioned equally: single mothers and others in a weak position have lower returns from their investments in the shadow economy than those in the stronger formal economy (e.g., those who own businesses). The opacity of the shadow market serves to veil the exploitation of women.

Working Conditions

Sexual Harassment

There is no law in Belarus regarding sexual harassment in the workplace, as the issue is an underrecognized phenomenon. Moreover, job advertisements in the market sector are often explicit about employees being of a certain sex and age and even being good-looking.

Support for Mothers/Caretakers

Belarus has a legacy from the former Soviet system of support for mothers/caretakers, which includes almost free daycare, a four-month fully paid maternity leave, and a three-year partially paid childcare leave (that can be taken by any family member). Additionally, mothers can take up to six years of unpaid leave, which is included as work time for purposes of calculating their retirement plans. Currently, this extended system is feasible in the public sector only, where leave payments are low. And since there have never been any steps to encourage men to take childcare leaves, the extended leave has become a serious obstacle to the hiring of women in the market sector.

FAMILY AND SEXUALITY

Gender Roles

Although women in Belarus have high levels of labor force participation and many are sole breadwinners, views on the division of labor in the family are rather traditional. After divorce, custody of the children is normally given to mothers; women usually "reign" in the households and make decisions on matters such as childrearing.

Reproduction

Because of the very high casualty rate in World War II, reproduction has been a matter of special concern for the nation. The one-quarter of the population lost in the war was replaced by the mid-1970s. Since early 1993, however, the mortality rate has been higher than the fertility rate: in 2001, there were 13.5 deaths and 9.4 births per 1,000 people, with a natural population decrease of –4.1. There is a largely conservative debate on women's roles and reproduction, but no steps have been taken to restrict access to abortion. In 1986 Belarus was affected by the Chernobyl nuclear reactor disaster: though the accident took place in Ukraine, Belarus received 70 percent of radioactive fallout. The fear of bearing children with genetic deviations is considered one of the reasons for the low fertility rate.

The number of births to nonmarried mothers has been growing and now constitutes 18 percent of all births. Another visible trend is the growing number of "refusnik mothers" who, as a result of unwanted pregnancies, give birth to babies and leave them in maternity hospitals to be sent to foster homes or put up for adoption. Public opinion is that this behavior is evidence of "women forgetting their natural duties."

Contraception and Abortion

Abortion was the most widely used method of fertility regulation in the former USSR. Currently, with modern contraceptives being expensive and sex education in its initial stages, it still is. There are 123 abortions per 100 births, with 26.2 percent of them in the 20–29 age group.

Teen Pregnancy

Teen pregnancy is slowly going down, though it is still one of the highest in Europe with sixty pregnancies per 1,000 women in the 15–19-year-old age group.

HEALTH

Health Care Access

Under Soviet rule, health care was universal and free of charge, though the quality of the services was not always high. Private clinics and doctors currently complement the public health care system. Women, who more often than men tend to be poor, and the elderly, of whom 67 percent are female, have no access to private health care and have to resort to state clinics, which are often underfunded.

AIDS

Currently, there are 3,587 HIV-positive people in Belarus, or 37 per 100,000 people, of whom 21 percent were infected through sexual intercourse. As the rate of prostitution rises, this number is growing.[1]

POLITICS AND LAW

Suffrage

Women in Belarus, then part of the Russian Empire, received suffrage and related political rights in 1917. All citizens have the right to vote from the age of eighteen.

Political Participation

The communist system brought many women into political positions, but as women's issues were considered a part of class issues, women could not articulate their own independent concerns. After 1991, women's representation in decision-making bodies dropped significantly. They now comprise 37 percent of officials at the local level but only 10 percent of the deputies in the House of Representatives of the National Assembly. Women comprise 30 percent of the members of the Supreme Court.

Women's Rights

Feminist Movements

The first independent postcommunist women's organization—Women's League—was registered in Belarus in 1992. Since then, several dozen women's groups, both progressive and conservative, have appeared. Women's groups address the issues of support for mothers/caretakers, reproductive health, women's political participation, and violence against women.

Lesbian Rights

Lesbian and gay rights are hardly ever mentioned among the issues of concern in the country.

RELIGION AND SPIRITUALITY

About 80 percent of believers are Russian Orthodox and 20 percent are Catholic.[2] Though women comprise most of the churchgoers, both religions are traditional and do not allow for women to be ordained. Female students are accepted to the Theology Department of European Humanities University in Minsk.

VIOLENCE

Violence against women has been recognized as an equality issue largely through the efforts of international agencies and, especially after 1995, the UN women's conference in Beijing. The issue of violence is the one in which cooperation between women's organizations and the state has been most productive. Several hotlines and shelters have been started in cities. Many cases of rape and violence, though, remain unreported: in 2001, only 313 people were convicted for rape.

OUTLOOK FOR THE TWENTY-FIRST CENTURY

Institutional and cultural shifts of the last decade produced some new opportunities for women but also deprived them of some of their resources. Their current situation is complex, and the outlook for their futures is unclear.

NOTES

1. Ministry of Health cited in Демографическая ситуация и репродуктивные права в Беларуси. Женское Независимое Демократическое Движение. Мн., 2002.

2. Ministry of Statistics and Analysis of the Republic of Belarus, www.president.gov.by/Minstat/en/main.html.

RESOURCE GUIDE

Suggested Reading

Gapova, Elena. "National Dreams and Domestic Goddesses." *Transitions* 5, no.1 (1998).
———. "On Nation, Gender and Class Formation in Belarus . . . and Elsewhere in the Post-Soviet World." *Nationalities Paper* 30, no. 4 (2002): 639–62.

————. "Reinventing Men and Women within the Belarusian Nationalist Project." In *From Gender to Nation*, edited by Julie Mostov and Rada Ivecovic, 81–98. Ravenna, Italy: Longo Editore, 2002.

————. "Women in the National Discourse in Belarus." *European Journal of Women's Studies*, 5, no. 3–4 (1998).

————. "Women's Question and National Projects in Soviet Byelorussia and Western Belarus, 1921–1939." In *Zwischen Kriegen. Nationen, Nationalismen und Geschlechterverhältnisse in Mittel-und Osteuropa, 1918–1939*, edited by Johanna Gehmacher, Elizabeth Harvey, and Sophia Kemlein. Osnabrück, Germany: fibre-Verlag, forthcoming.

United Nations Development Programme. *Women of Belarus Seen through the Era, National Report on the Status of Women*. Minsk, Belarus: UNDP, 1997.

Web Sites

Centre for Gender Studies at European Humanities University, www.gender.ehu.by. Contains information on research, teaching, and publications in the field of gender in Belarus.

Gender in Development Project, www.gender.by.

Ministry of Statistics and Analysis of the Republic of Belarus, www.president.gov.by/Minstat/en/main.html.

National Report on the Status of Women, www.un.minsk.by/wid/97/.
The most extensive publication on the Web describing Belarusian women's issues.

Svetlana Aleksievich, Belarusian woman-writer (her books based on oral history have been translated into 12 languages), alexievich.promedia.by/eng/editions.htm.

Women's Independent Democratic Movement, www.widm.org.
Offers information on the organization's projects.

Organizations

Centre for Gender Studies at European Humanities University
24, pr. Skoriny
Minsk, 220030
Belarus
Phone/Fax: (375) (17) 239 3383
Email: gender@ehu.unibel.by
Web site: www.gender.ehu.by

Focuses on research in gender and nationalism, visual arts, women, and media and has a master's program in gender studies.

Belarusian Organization of Young Christian Women
St. Krupskoi, 2, # 70
Minsk, 220018
Belarus

Phone/Fax: (375) (17) 240 3482
Email: bywca@open.by
Actively involved in work with hotlines and shelters.

SELECTED BIBLIOGRAPHY

Marples, David. *Belarus: From Soviet Rule to Nuclear Catastrophe*. New York: St. Martin's Press, 1996.

Sokolova, Galina. "The Gender Structure of Employment and Unemployment." *Belarus in the World*, no. 3 (1998): 46–49.

United Nations Development Programme. "Belarus: Choice for the Future." *National Report on Human Development*. Minsk, Belarus: UNDP, 2000.

———. *Women of Belarus Seen through the Era*. In *National Report on the Status of Women*. Minsk, Belarus: UNDP, 1997.

Vakar, Nicholas. *Byelorussia: The Making of a Nation*. Cambridge, MA: 1956.

Selected Belarusian/Russian Bibliography

Демографическая ситуация и репродуктивные права в Беларуси. Женское Независимое Демократическое Движение. Мн., 2002.

Женщины и мужчины Республики Беларусь. Статистический сборник. Мн., 2001.

Семья, женщины и дети г. Минска. Статистический сборник. Мн., 1999.

Данные переписи неселения на 16 февраля 1999г.

5

BELGIUM

Alison E. Woodward

PROFILE OF BELGIUM

Belgium is one of the most developed countries in the world. According to the United Nations Development Programme's 2002 Human Development Index, Belgium ranks fourth in the world thanks to its extensive welfare state and wealthy economy.[1] It is small, but with a population of 10,263,000 it is as densely settled as Japan ($333/k^2$).[2] Belgium has evolved into an extensively federal state with a highly complex structure. Politically this helps manage longstanding conflicts between the two major linguistic groups in the country, the Dutch-speaking Flemings (60 percent) and the French-speaking Walloons and Brussels residents (40 percent). There is also a small German-speaking minority in the country. At the heart of Europe, Belgium also plays host to the European Union institutions (Commission, Council of Ministers, and Parliament), NATO, and a number of other international organizations. It has a varied population of foreign origin who are concentrated primarily in urban areas. Today, one in ten Belgians has a foreign antecedent.[3]

Women have a slight advantage in the population statistics today, as the population is 51 percent female.[4] Belgium reflects a Northern European fertility pro-

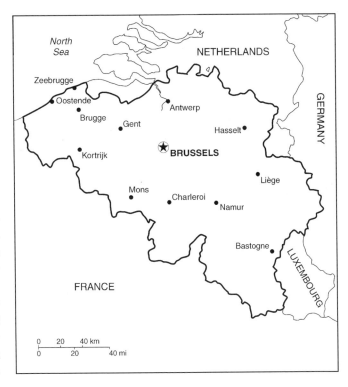

file: it has been below replacement rate since the mid 1970s, and it has stabilized at circa 1.5.[5] The infant mortality rate between 0–1 year of age is very low, at 10 per 1,000 live births[6] Maternal mortality is also low. Women can expect to live until 79, whereas male life expectancy is 72.

OVERVIEW OF WOMEN'S ISSUES

Although Belgium is highly ranked by the United Nations in terms of the general welfare of its population, the only place where it does not rank in the top ten is in the position of women. The Gender Empowerment Index of the United Nations Development Programme places Belgium at number fourteen. Great strides have been made in the last twenty-five years, but there are still a number of issues that need to be solved if Belgium is to become a beacon of gender equality among developed countries. The issues that remain problematic for women revolve around the economic and political positions of women, gender roles in the home, and questions of discrimination, sexual violence, and human trafficking. Furthermore, the changing ethnic population of Belgium poses new challenges for assuring that the entire population of women enjoys the rights guaranteed by Belgian law.

EDUCATION

Women have had a lot of catching up to do in terms of education, but recently the scales have become even, with women doing slightly better than men in secondary education and entering university at the same rate as men. All Belgians are required to complete twelve years of education.

Opportunities

Today, 66 percent of tertiary enrollments are female, or 130 women for every 100 men as of 1998.[7] Women still tend to choose specializations in the humanities rather than in the sciences. Today 10 percent more women than men are entering the academic preparatory high schools, but their presence in the vocational and technical high schools has been diminishing.[8] There seems to be a slight trend toward women achieving better results in school. In 1998 10 percent more women than men received university diplomas.[9]

Literacy

Almost all Belgians are literate, although some are not literate enough to function successfully in modern society. Eighteen percent of those aged 16–65 are functionally illiterate.[10]

EMPLOYMENT AND THE ECONOMY

Job/Career Opportunities

Thanks to increasing access to education, Belgian women are taking up their place in the world of employment. The percentage of women with a paid job has been growing with each generation. Whereas the percentage of all men who are in the employed population has shrunk slightly in the last thirty years from 54 percent of all men to 49 percent, the percentage of all women in the labor market has increased from 25 percent of all women in 1970 to 37 percent in 1998.[11] At present, women make up 42 percent of those active on the labor market (i.e., employed at least one hour a week or looking for work).[12] This is slightly below the average for the European Union.[13] The general increase in jobs in the public sector and in services since the 1970s has primarily benefited women.

It is only recently that a growing number of educated women have appeared with a vision of a life cycle including a long-term, full-time commitment to the labor force in a well-paid job. Previously, women worked until they bore children and then dropped out of the labor market almost entirely. Today almost 85 percent of women between 25 and 35 years of age are employed in Belgium, but very few women over fifty-five hold a job.

In 1998 more women (14.9 percent) were unemployed than men (9.0 percent).[14] As women studied longer, they became eligible for unemployment benefits after their studies and this has led, among other things, to an evolution in the unemployment figures of women. Women are more likely to be in part-time work and more likely to be out of the work force once they reach middle age than men. This is related to the fact that until 1996 the legal pension age for women is sixty whereas men must work until age sixty-five. It will be sixty-five as of the year 2009, thanks to the Royal Decree (K.B.) of December 23, 1996.[15]

Pay

The pay gap remains a thorny issue in Belgian gender equality debates. It formed a key theme in the Belgian presidency of the European Union in 2001. The figures reported to the UN in 1998 showed that Belgian women had an average annual income of 16,784 U.S. dollars whereas men had more than twice as much at 38,005 U.S. dollars.[16] This puts Belgium more toward the middle of the European Union in terms of pay distribution, despite the high investment in childcare. Also, the longer the career, the greater the pay gap between men and women. Belgium follows Finland, Sweden, Denmark, and united Germany in having a women's pay ratio to men of 85.72 percent for full-time workers.[17]

Working Conditions

Second-wave feminists in Belgium demanded equal conditions on the labor market. Equal pay has still not been realized. However, a number of roadblocks have been eliminated, including a long-standing discriminatory ban on night work for women.

Sexual Harassment

Both women and men do experience sexual harassment at work, and legislation has been passed to eliminate this discrimination as well. As the minister for equal opportunities has also been minister of labor, the first legal actions were taken in legislating against sexual harassment in the workplace. The law protecting employees against undesired sexual behavior was passed in 1992, and it was extended in 1999 to criminalize sexual harassment as a form of sexual discrimination.

Support for Mothers/Caretakers

There is little public debate about working mothers in Belgium. Seldom is the argument made that a working mother is bad for her children, yet it is also the case that children are inscribed in the mothers' list of responsibilities rather than being a joint concern of mother and father. Women are expected to work but are also expected to see children and their family as their most important identity. Most women work because they have to rather than because they choose to in terms of a professional vocation or because of personal development. However, increasingly the two-earner model has become a necessity for maintaining an acceptable lifestyle.[18]

Since the 1970s, an increasing number of programs enable families to combine work and childcare. For example there exists a provision of flexible leave systems that allow individuals to take career breaks without sacrificing their job seniority and position. The leaves can be used for professional development, elder care, or other family concerns.

Maternal Leave

Maternity leave has been guaranteed for fourteen weeks. This may be taken before the birth of the baby and continue after the birth with a maternity allowance and significant salary replacement. Fathers are also allowed several days of paid leave at the birth of the child.

Daycare

Support for preschool care through publicly funded crèches and tax rebates for the cost of care at recognized childcare facilities are also among the most significant programs to help employed parents as is a program of preschool care in school facilities from the age of two and a half years that is taken up by more than 95 percent of Belgian parents.

Inheritance and Property Rights

Upon marriage, unless a particular preagreement is signed, property acquired after marriage becomes joint property.

FAMILY AND SEXUALITY

Gender Roles

Belgians are fairly traditional in their beliefs about the division of labor within the family. The male breadwinner model persists even when women bring home the bread. Women carry out almost all household chores and do the majority of childcare even when they are employed.[19] Many explain the high percentage of part-time employment among women as a reflection of women's family-centeredness.

Marriage

People still get married, and unmarried cohabitation is not as frequent as in the Northern European countries. The divorce rate has been climbing while the marriage rate has been dropping. There are now slightly more divorces per year than marriages. People marry relatively late, with women entering into marriage for the first time at around twenty-six and men at twenty-eight years of age.[20]

Reproduction

Having children should be a popular sport in Belgium, as each child is greeted with a monetary child premium and families receive a supplementary child allowance for each child until the child is twenty-five or begins to earn a living. Most children are desired and obtained within wedlock. Indigenous Belgian women have children at a later age than nonindigenous women.

Young Belgians have their first sexual encounter at younger and younger ages. Almost 90 percent have lost their virginity by the age of nineteen, with boys beginning somewhat earlier than girls.[21]

Sex Education

Sex education is one of the areas where Belgium shows a less positive record in promoting gender equality. Sex education is not part of the compulsory curriculum, and it may be limited to one lecture in the sixth grade about menstruation and some discussions in the classes in ethics and religion. The coverage is spotty, and so young people report that most of their information comes from the media and friends, and seven out of ten young people report dissatisfaction with school sex education.[22] Women's groups argue that better sex education is important in reducing disease, combating sexual violence and other sexually related problems and in creating tolerance for other forms of sexuality.

Contraception and Abortion

The condom has been increasing in popularity as the contraceptive of choice among young people, but some think this may have contributed to more accidents. Since abortion was legalized in 1990, the abortion rate appears to have been climbing. The morning-after pill was liberalized in 2000, but it, too, does not seem to have reduced the number of abortions.

Teen Pregnancy

Belgium is near the middle in Europe in terms of teenage motherhood, with around 7.7 girls per thousand. This figure has been declining, and the remaining cases are due in part to insufficient knowledge about contraception and in part to the conscious wish for children among the younger wives in the immigrant populations from Turkey, South Central Europe, and North Africa.

HEALTH

Health Care Access

Health care is very good in Belgium. It is financed by contributions of employers and employees, and the benefits can be paid to dependents. Belgians have a choice of care and hospitals, and they find most of their costs reimbursed by their health insurance.

Diseases and Disorders

There are gender dimensions to health problems in Belgium. Women feel subjectively less well and report more complaints than men. The Belgian proverb is, "Women get sick and men die."

AIDS

Sexually transmitted diseases including AIDS are a continuing health problem in Belgium, which was one of the first countries to recognize a heterosexual spread of AIDS. Homosexuality in Belgium was taboo, which may have led to difficulties in public education in the early years of the HIV crisis. Belgium has longstanding ties with areas in Africa with a high rate of infection. These two factors, combined with an underdeveloped approach to sex education, have undoubtedly contributed to the spread of sexually transmitted diseases such as AIDS.

Eating Disorders

Several health problems are almost exclusively female, including eating disorders, which affect some 15 percent of Flemish women.[23] Flemish statistics indicate that more than half of the girls between eleven and eighteen think they are too fat.[24]

Cancer

Osteoporosis and breast cancer are also women's health problems. Breast cancer is the most frequent type of cancer among Belgian women. In 2001, a public health campaign began for free breast cancer screening.

POLITICS AND LAW

Suffrage

Women did not receive full suffrage until 1948, although they could be elected to national office from 1921. The suffrage issue foundered on the differences between the socialists and Catholics, in which ironically the Catholic politicians favored women's suffrage, whereas the socialists feared that women would vote more conservatively. This delayed women from getting the vote until after the Second World War. The delay led to a rather late development of political citizenship for women and a long-term lag in their participation and representation in electoral politics.

Political Participation

The stagnation in the representation of women in political decision making has led to a number of increasingly stringent measures to raise the number of women in elected posts. In 1994 a law was passed requiring that maximally two thirds of each party's electoral lists can be composed of one sex or parties lose public subsidies. The recommendation is that lists be composed of at least half of each sex and that the first two places be occupied by two different sexes. The 1994 law has gradually gone into effect and led to an equally gradual increase in women in politics.

Parity democracy (50/50) is the goal of the organized women's movement, including elected representatives, and numerous legislative initiatives

including constitutional reform are under consideration. Belgium ranks seventh in the International Parliamentary Union's classification of the representation of women in parliament. Around 35 percent of the seats in the two national chambers are held by females. Women are also part of the national government, although in a lesser proportion, and the vice prime minister is a woman. The representation of women in the regional parliaments and their governments varies widely.

Since 1996, Belgium requires a yearly report from each of the ministers to the parliament regarding the fulfillment of the obligations of the resolutions of the World Conference in Beijing. The results on equal opportunities and gender are screened by parliament and consulting committees including a group of university experts on mainstreaming. The government has approved the construction of a gender institute to guide gender equality and antidiscrimination efforts.

Belgian policewoman, Brussels. Photo © TRIP/H. Rogers.

Women's Rights

Economic issues have been important as a basis for unity in the Belgian women's movements. The country has substantial social cleavages based on differences in class, language, and religion, but the issue of the economic position of women was a common denominator. The first women's rights demands in the nineteenth and twentieth centuries centered on access to education (first entrance to university, 1880) and to the professions (first doctor, 1884). The driving forces behind these issues were women from the upper middle classes. The first women's rights organization was founded in 1892 (*League Belge du droit des femmes*). The split between Catholic and socialist standpoints is reflected in the second-wave feminist movement, which fragmented due to the abortion controversy.

Feminist Movements

Women's movements in Belgium are not always "feminist" movements. However, they have often had common causes, especially around issues of women and work. The renewed women's movement began with a strike at Herstal in 1966, which became a European cause célèbre since women in this munitions factory struck for equal pay. This strike ultimately had wider implications for the beginning of women's rights legal actions in the European Union. For Belgium, it meant the renewal of the women's movement and the fight for economic rights to property and equal pay. The movement was to remain a national movement for only a short time. The end of the 1960s saw a growing split between the French- and Dutch-speaking communities, leading to a 1968 division in the National Council of Women on linguistic grounds. An autonomous women's movement also sprung up outside such established groups as the Catholic and socialist women's organizations. The radical groups of the autonomous movement used colorful protest tactics and demonstrations to get more women's issues on the public agenda.

A number of successes in civil rights were booked. However, one of the most problematic points was the position on body and sexual rights. These were very divisive in the Belgian case. It was often impossible to organize collective actions if abortion was on the agenda. The abortion question led to a split with moderate Christian women's organizations in the mid-1970s. Only in 1990 would abortion become legal.

In the 1980s, the women's rights activists became more institutionalized thanks to the establishment of women's policy agencies at the national and regional levels and the beginning of women's studies. Courses were organized both by universities and by the autonomous women's movement. Every year since 1972, Flemish women's rights advocates and feminists organize a Women's Day on November 11. There is also a movement to make International Women's Day on March 8 a legal holiday, and there are always organized events on this day as well.

Lesbian Rights

Belgium is not a forerunner in gay rights. Homosexuality and public discussion about homosexuality have been taboo. Lesbian women have found their place in the women's movement, but at times they have also made their case with homosexual men. Real progress on gay rights only began in the 1990s.

When the Catholic parties left national government at the end of the nineties, the gay and lesbian movement was able to pursue two of its main goals, anti-discrimination legislation and permission to marry. An anti-discrimination law including discrimination on the basis of sexual preference was passed at the end of 2002. In July of 2003 marriage was opened to homosexual couples of Belgian nationality or to nationals of countries that recognize same sex marriage (de facto, the Netherlands).[25]

Women wishing to have children have been able to get in vitro fertilization help, but there is still no recognition of parental rights for the same-sex partner, either in the case of natural birth or in the case of adoption. Single parents are allowed to adopt children, however, and this has been a solution for some homosexual couples.

Military Service

Belgium has a professional army without conscriptions. Women were first allowed to join the Belgian army in 1976. Their number has steadily grown, and they constitute about 7 percent of the army. The highest proportion of women in the military is in the medical services, at 20 percent. The proportion of women has remained the same since 1980, and their mobility into higher ranks is also minimal. Women are mostly in administrative and logistic functions. Only 5 percent of women have jobs as warriors.

RELIGION AND SPIRITUALITY

Belgium is an overwhelmingly Roman Catholic country, with 75 percent of the population declared Roman Catholics. The remainder is primarily free-thinking, anticlerical, or agnostic. Less than 5 percent of the population is Protestant, Muslim, or Jewish. However, religion is not a central part of Belgian life, with only 11 percent of the population claiming to go to church on a weekly basis and an ever-falling percent making use of church rituals such as marriage and baptism.[26] However, the Roman Catholic identity proved to be a major stumbling block in reforming laws dealing with divorce, abortion and women's bodily rights, and contraception. It has also hindered sex education. A major example of the problems that the dominant belief system pose was King Baudouin's abdication for one day in connection with the passage of abortion liberalization in the 1990s. The abdication led to a constitutional crisis. Religious conflict around gender issues has also been reflected in relation to the usage of veils by young Muslim girls in schools and professional life.

Women's Roles

As women are still prohibited from the priesthood, women do not hold positions of power in religion in Belgium. However, they are important in the fabric of religious society as members of religious orders, and in assisting functions. There are some eighty religious communities of women in Flanders alone, ranging from orders of teaching sisters to contemplative orders, although a number of the orders are gradually thinning out.

VIOLENCE

Belgium established a federal office for women in the mid-1980s, and from the start, violence against women was one of its priority concerns. Police officers have received special training in dealing with rape and family violence. There is a national action plan at all levels of government of measures to fight violence against women.

Domestic Violence

Since 1997 physical violence between partners (including cohabitants) is against the law. Stalking became a criminal act in 1998. The women's movement itself has been instrumental in setting up safe houses for victims of family violence.

Rape/Sexual Assault

The government also has been instrumental in funding research to demonstrate the extent to which violence against women is an everyday problem in all walks of life. This research has been used to fuel regular public awareness-raising campaigns. The women's movement continues to demonstrate for safety at night via "Take back the night" campaigns. As everywhere in the world, there are few signs that this problem has become notably better, despite the campaigns.

Trafficking in Women and Children

Prostitution and the traffic in women are also problematic in Belgium, which is frequently seen as the hub of transactions with women in the sex industry from outside of Europe. Prostitution is legal, although living off the earnings of a prostitute is not.

The use of women in advertising is another sore point. The Flemish Ministry for Equal Opportunities helps fund a web site (Zorra) that scans advertising and posts it for discussion on gender aspects, and this has led to both complaints and awards for gender-aware advertising.

OUTLOOK FOR THE TWENTY-FIRST CENTURY

Belgium is a small, rich European country. Although the population is nominally Catholic, it is northern and secular in outlook. The position of women has been improving steadily since women were enfranchised politically in 1948. However, traditional ideas about the role of women in the family are still entrenched. Women have made few inroads into the top positions of power in the economy and politics. Violence against women and the presentation of women as sex objects in the media are still part of daily life. It is far too early to speak of a truly gender-egalitarian society.

Men are not yet partners in the gender equality project. This is still seen as a "women's problem," despite rhetoric about gender mainstreaming from European Union institutions and the Belgian government itself. Nonetheless, the pragmatic Belgian approach to the combination of work and family life and the general commitment to a welfare state guaranteeing good health care and democratic education have meant that women's opportunities for development are relatively good in comparison to almost every other country in the world. If men were to see that gender issues are also their concern, Belgium might turn into paradise for women and men alike.

NOTES

1. United Nations Development Programme (UNDP), 2002, www.undp.org/hdr2002/presskit/HDR%20PR_GEM.pdf.

2. Olivier Mouton et al., *Belgium: A State of Mind* (Tielt, Belgium: Lanoo, 2001), 41.

3. Mouton et al., 2001, 30.

4. Belgian federal government, www.belgium.fgov.be/nl.

5. Mieke Van Haegendoren, ed., *Mannen en vrouwen op de drempel van de 21ste eeuw: gebruikershandboek genderstatistieken (Men and women on the threshold of the 21st century: a user's guide to gender statistics)* (Brussels: Federaal Ministerie van Tewerkstelling en Arbeid, 2002), 25.

6. Van Haegendoren, 2001, 70.

7. UNDP, 2002.

8. Mouton et al., 2001, 74.

9. Mouton et al., 2001, 87.

10. UNDP, 2002.

11. Mieke Van Haegendoren, ed., *Mannen en vrouwen (Men and women)* (Brussels: Federaal Ministerie, 2002), 95.

12. Van Haegendoren, 2002, 98.

13. European Commission Employment and Social Affairs, *Towards a Community Strategy on Gender Equality* (Luxembourg: Office for Official Publications of the European Communities, vol. COM/2000/335 final, 2001): 14.

14. Van Haegendoren, 2002, 107.

15. C.-R. Buyck, "Een onder zoek haar de positie" ("A study of the position of women managers in small, medium, and large enterprises"), in *Faculteit Economische* (Leuven, Belgium: Katholieke Universiteit Leuven), 5.

16. UNDP, 2002.

17. 1995 data with Sweden at 88 percent. Robert Plasma, "Indicators on Gender Pay Equality," 3.

18. Bea Cantillon, *Nieuwe behoeften Naar Zekerheid* (Leuven, Belgium: Acco, 1990).

19. Ignace Glorieux, K. Copens, and Suzanne Koelet, *Vlaanderen in uren en minuten: De tijdsbesteding van de Vlamingen in 480 tabellen (Women in hours and minutes: the time use of Flemings in 480 tables)* (Brussels: VUB Press, 2002), CD-Rom.

20. Mouton et al., 2001, 88.

21. Mouton et al., 2001, 75.

22. Mouton et al., 2001, 77–78.

23. Mieke Maerten, "Vrouwen worden ziek. Mannen sterven. Gender specifieke aspecten van gezondheid en gezondheidszorg," *RoSa-factsheet*, no. 8 (March 2001), www.rosadoc.be/site (accessed September 2002).

24. Maerten, 2001, 6.

25. Joyce Leplae, "Na de wittebroodsweken van de wet: Juridische situatie van holeibi's na de goedkeuring van het homohuwelijk en de antidiscriminatiewet" ("After the honeymoon of the law, the legal situation of holebi's after the approval of homosexual marriage and the anti-discrimination law") *RoSa-factsheet*, no. 21 (January 2003), www.rosadoc.be/site/.

26. www.belgium.fgov.be/nl.

RESOURCE GUIDE

Suggested Readings

Federal Ministry of Employment and Labor Equal Opportunities Unit. *Women and Men in Belgium: Towards an Equal Society*. Brussels: Belgian Federal Ministry of Employment and Labor Equal Opportunities Unit, 2001.

Mouton, Olivier, Marie-Anne Wilssens, Frédéric Antoine, and Marc Reynebeau. *Belgium: A State of Mind*. Tielt: Lanoo, 2001.

Web Sites

Amazone, www.amazone.be.
The web site of the federally funded center for the women's movement in Brussels. The site is in three languages and provides information about equal opportunities, the women's movement, data banks on policies such as gender mainstreaming, and numerous links to sites on European women's policy as well as the most up-to-date information on Belgium's women's policy in Dutch and French.

Belgian federal government, www.belgium.fgov.be/nl.
This web site provides links to information on federal equal opportunities policies and other gender split statistics on Belgium.

Comme des femmes, www.commesdesfemmes.be.
This is the French language feminist e-magazine with editions for Swiss, French and Belgian readers.

Divazine, www.divazine.be.
This is an exciting, Dutch language, feminist-edited monthly e-magazine covering politics, culture, news and general interest topics. It presents investigative- and interview-based reporting on elections, violence, immigration and women, and other current topics.

Femistyle, www.femistyle.be.
Less openly feminist than *Divazine*, this is also an e-magazine covering topics that include emancipation issues, fashion, and lifestyle.

RoSa, www.rosadoc.be.
The web site of the Flemish women's studies documentation center. It has numerous fact sheets in English on Belgian women as well as an extensive library catalog.

Women's Studies EuroMap, www.uia.ac.be/women/.
At the heart of Europe but with limited resources, academic Belgian women have made good use of the web to reach out to other initiatives, and this site provides one of the best guides to what is happening in European women's studies, including Belgian initiatives.

Zorra, www.zorra.be.
A lively site with pictures from Belgian advertising and discussion on them. Some parts of the site, such as literature lists, are in English. Zorra is part of an international network of media watchdogs.

Videos/Films

Belgium has had several important women film directors (Chantal Akerman, Marion Hansen, and the late Nicole van Goethem among others). Their films span the genres from the avant-garde to the mainstream. There are a number of recent films that could be characterized as women's films, such as the award-winning *Rosetta* by the Dardenne brothers, which deals with the situation of a young woman in Wallonia trying to get work. The film led to a major change in job policy for young women at the federal level called the Rosetta plan.

The Documentary *Femmes-Machines* treats the women's strike at munitions factory FN-Herstal which led to the equal pay legislation of the European Union. Another film which could be seen as a women's film because of the powerful acting by two senior women stars is *Pauline and Paulette*, about two elderly sisters. As a small country, Belgium frequently participates in co-productions on films featuring strong women characters such as the Dutch director Marleen Gorris's *Antonia's Line* (1995).

Femmes-Machines. 1995. Directed by Marie-Anne Thunissen. Distributed by RTBF-Liege.
Greek Tragedy. 1985. Directed by Nicole van Goethem.
Nuit et jour. 1991. Directed by Chantal Akerman. Distributed by Facets Multimedia.
Pauline and Paulette. 2001. Directed by Lieven de Brauwer. Distributed by Cinéart/Facets Multimedia.
The Quarry. 1998. Directed by Marion Hansel. Distributed by Facets Multimedia.
Rosetta. 1999. Directed by Jean-Pierre and Luc Dardenne. Distributed by Cinélibre/Facets Multimedia.
Rosie. 1998. Directed by Patrice Troye. Distributed by Facets Multimedia.

Organizations

Amazone
Middaglijnstraat 10
B1210
Brussels, Belgium
Web site: www.amazone.be

The national center for the women's movement, which houses Sophia, the two womens' councils, and numerous other women's organizations and which organizes regular activities for women's education and development.

The Dutch-language Women's Council (Nederlandstalige Vrouwenraad)
Middaglijnstraat 10

B-1210
Brussels, Belgium
Web site: www.vrouwenraad.be

The Federal Ministry of Employment and Labor: Equal Opportunity Unit
Belliaardstraat 51
B-1040 Brussels, Belgium
Web site: www.meta.fgov.be

The Flemish Ministry of Welfare and Equal Opportunities: Equal Opportunities Unit,
  Gelijkekansen in Vlaanderen
Boudewijnlaan 30
B-1000 Brussels, Belgium
Web site: www.gelijkekansen.be

The French Community Ministry of Equal Opportunities
Direction de l'Egalité des chances
Ministere de la communauté française de Belgique
Leopoldan II,
B-1080 Brussels, Belgium
Web site: www.cfwb.be/ega/gales

The French-language Women's Council (Conseil des femmes francophones de Bel-
  gique)
Middaglijnstraat 10
B-1210 Brussels, Belgium

Research Support Point Equal Opportunities Policy
University of Antwerp
Steunpunt Gelijkekansenbeleid
Prinsstraat 13 2000
Antwerp, Belgium
Email: steunpuntgek©ua.ac.be
Web site: www.steunpuntgelijkekansen.be

Sophia
Rue de Méridien 10
B1210 Brussels, Belgium
Web site: www.sophia.be

The Belgian Coordinating network for women's studies.

Women's Coordination Committee (Flemish) (Vrouwen Overleg Komitee)
Middaglijnstraat 10
1210 Brussels, Belgium
Web site: www.amazone.be/nl_residents_vok.html

SELECTED BIBLIOGRAPHY

European Commission Employment and Social Affairs. *Towards a Community Strategy
  on Gender Equality.* Luxembourg: Office for Official Publications of the European Communities, 2001, vol. COM/2000/335 final.

Federal Ministry of Employment and Labor Equal Opportunities Unit. *Women and Men in Belgium. Towards an Equal Society.* Brussels: Belgian Federal Ministry of Employment and Labor Equal Opportunities Unit, 2001.

Plasma, Robert. "Indicators on Gender Pay Equality: The Belgian Presidency Initiative." Paper presented at the launch of program relating to the Community Framework Strategy on gender equality (2001–2005). September 13, 2001. European Parliament, Brussels.

United Nations Development Program (UNDP). 2002. www.undp.org/hdr2002/hdi.pdf.

Dutch and French Selected Bibliography

Buyck, C.-R. "Een onderzoek naar de positie van vrouwelijke kaderleden in KMO's en Grote Ondernemingen." ("A study of the position of women managers in small, medium and large enterprises"). Faculteit Economische en Toegepaste Economische Wetenschappen. Leuven, Belgium: Katholieke Universiteit Leuven, 2000.

Cantillon, Bea. *Nieuwe behoeften naar zekerheid: Vrouwen, gezin en inkomensverdeling* (*New need for security: women, family, and income distribution*). Leuven, Belgium: Acco, 1990.

Glorieux, Ignace, K. Copens, and Suzanne Koelet. *Vlaanderen in uren en minuten: de tijdsbesteding van de Vlamingen in 480 tabellen* (*Flanders in hours and minutes: the time use of Flemings in 480 tables*). Brussels: VUB Press, 2002. CD-Rom.

Leplae, Joyca. "Het basisonderwijs en het secondair onderwijs in Vlaanderen onder de genderloop" ("Elementary and secondary education in Flanders under the gender lens"). RoSa-factsheet, no. 10 (April 2001). www.rosadoc.be/site/.

———. "Na de wittebroodsweken van de wet: Juridische situatie van holebi's na de goedkeuring van het homohuwelijk en de antidiscriminatiewet" ("After the honeymoon of the law: The legal situation of holebi's after the approval of homosexual marriage and the anti-discrimination law"). RoSa-factsheet, no. 21 (January 2003). www.rosadoc.be/site/.

Maerten, Mieke. "Vrouwen worden ziek. Mannen sterven. Gender specifieke aspected van gezondheid en gezondheidszorg ("Women get sick, men die. Gender specific aspect of health and health care"). RoSa-factsheet, no. 8 (March 2001). www.rosadoc.be/site/.

Van Haegendoren, Mieke, ed. *Mannen en vrouwen op de drempel van de 21ste eeuw: Gebruikershandboek genderstatistieken* (*Men and Women on the threshold of the 21st century, a user's guide to gender statistics*). Brussels: Federaal Ministerie van Tewerkstelling en Arbeid, 2002.

Vereecken, Frank. "Vrouwen in het leger" ("Women in the army"). RoSa-factsheet, no. 7 (February 2001). www.rosadoc.be/site/ (accessed September 2002).

———. "Religieuzen in Vlaanderen" ("Religious women in Flanders"). RoSa-factsheet, no. 9 (April 2001). www.rosadoc.be/site/ (accessed September 2002).

6

BOSNIA AND HERZEGOVINA

Jasna Bakšić-Muftić

PROFILE OF BOSNIA AND HERZEGOVINA

The current situation in Bosnia and Herzegovina (BiH) has been shaped by its communist heritage as a state within the Socialist Federal Republic of Yugoslavia (1945–1992); by the war in BiH, related to its proclamation of independence and its recognition by the international community (1992–1995); and by the signing of the Dayton Peace Accord in November 1995. It is charac-
terized by a dual transition from war to peace and from a command economy and a one-party system to a market economy and political pluralism. The United Nations and its various agencies, the Council of Europe, the European Union, the Organization for Security and Cooperation in Europe, the embassies of the European Union countries and of the United States of America, and international nongovern-mental organizations (INGOs) operating in BiH all played a role in building a stable and sustainable state of BiH and a democratic society.

Ethnic and religious diversity characterize BiH. The population is 48.1 percent Bosniags, 14.3 percent Croat, and 37.1 percent Serbian. Its religions include 40

percent Muslim, 31 percent Orthodox, 15 percent Catholic, and 4 percent Protestant.[1] The remaining 10 percent are atheists and non-believers.

In 2000 the population of BiH was 3,977,000, 51 percent of which were female. Life expectancy of women was 76 and of men was 71. The infant mortality rate that year was 13 per 1,000 live births. The total fertility rate was 1.6. The maternal mortality rate was 15 per 100,000 live births in 1995.[2]

OVERVIEW OF WOMEN'S ISSUES

Part of the communist heritage is a degree of inertia that results in issues not being viewed from the perspective of gender equality. The communist ideology recognized class differences only, with all other differences (including those between men and women) subordinate to class differences. Not until the postwar period have women's issues been the subject of qualitative analysis of the hidden, but real, inequalities between men and women in BiH.

EDUCATION

Opportunities

The socialist myth of the equality of men and women, and of their enjoying equality of opportunity, has been given a jolt.[3] Statistics have shown that, despite legal requirements in regard to primary education and the official ideological stance that men and women are equal, men and women are not equal. Men in BiH have higher educational qualifications than women: there is a higher proportion of women without any education, a higher proportion of women who have completed only primary education, and a smaller proportion of women who have graduated from high school, but only a small proportion of both have university degrees, although even there men are ahead of women.

Literacy

There are no reliable statistics on the literacy rate of citizens of BiH.

EMPLOYMENT AND THE ECONOMY

Job/Career Opportunities

Women's official labor force participation is relatively low at 38 percent.[4] As a result of the differences in educational qualifications, there are also differences in employment and in the workplace where men and women both work. However, a major shift has taken place in postwar BiH regarding awareness of discrimination and the use of the term. In the prewar period the term "discrimination" was not used, since it was contrary to the ruling ideology of class equality and, thus, of the equality of men and women. Existing differences in the position of women and men were masked by the political phrase "improvement in the status of women" and the academic phrase "the humanization of relations between the sexes," which implied the recognition of the social roles of men and women, corresponding for the most part to the patriarchal matrix. The term "discrimination against women" is now a commonplace in the legal, political, and academic vocabulary and has become part of women's awareness in BiH.

Pay

Women are less well paid, and their pension qualifications are different (women can retire after fewer years in the workforce and at a younger age than men) so that women's pensions are nominally lower than those of men in BiH. If one bears in mind the difficult financial circumstances of pensioners as a whole, women pensioners are a particularly at-risk category (particularly in cases when they are living alone as a one-member household).

Working Conditions

In a study that included a question on whether the women polled had been faced with or currently experience unequal treatment during their career, 35 percent of those polled answered in the affirmative.[5] Almost 70 percent of those polled described employing women in less well paid jobs and the fact that men found it easier to gain promotion to management positions as examples of unequal treatment of men and women, while one third of those polled drew attention to the greater ease with which men could take advantage of opportunities for further education and training, and 10 percent noted that women were more likely to be fired when a crisis arose. These responses indicate a trend toward a critical view of the issue of equality and equal opportunities for women and men in BiH.

Support for Mothers/Caretakers

By way of illustration of the position of women in BiH and the obstacles to changing the current situation, one may take the views of the women themselves, as given in their responses. The patriarchal tradition and customs that determine the position of women in the family and society were cited as obstacles by 70 percent of those polled, inconsistent application of the law were cited by 32 percent, inadequate organization of public services to support the family by 37 percent, male aggressiveness by 39 percent, and the passivity and lack of interest on the part of women themselves by 38 percent of those polled.

FAMILY AND SEXUALITY

One of the results of the war in BiH is a rise in the number of female-headed households. The households of war widows have joined the more common types, such as those headed by unmarried, divorced, and widowed women. This situation should be viewed in the light of the problem of displaced persons and returnees, who are living not only away from their own homes but also outside their former economic, social, and cultural milieus. Many women in this category are also burdened by specific war traumas that make them an especially vulnerable, at-risk category of the population.

In the postwar period, female-headed households are affected not only by all the problems that the population of BiH as a whole is confronted with, but also by additional difficulties that result from gender inequalities and the unequal opportunities available to women and men. The poverty in which more than half of BiH households are living has a greater impact on female-headed households, which follow the global trend of the feminization of poverty.

Gender Roles

The revival of the patriarchal approach to women's place in society often lies concealed behind historical romanticism, nostalgia, and the call for a "return to traditional values." The starting point for this approach is the view that communism disrupted the system of values and relationships in which the man was the breadwinner and the woman was the housewife and mother; that the family suffered as a result of women going out to work and the concomitant loss of quality of life in the family; that the function of upbringing, which is primarily the woman's responsibility, was markedly weakened; and that instead of alleviating and improving their position, women's equality merely brought with it twofold obligations (at work and in the home) and had the effect of multiple degradation of women. Proponents of this theory believe that women should

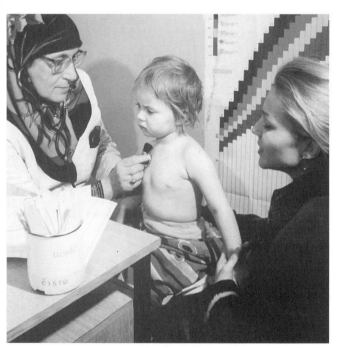

Clinic in Sarajevo, Bosnia, funded by Kuwait. Photo © TRIP/ Ibrahim.

return to the home, family, and children and should regain their dignity in the arena in which they are most respected and in the function that society values most highly—motherhood. The discourse on women's rights is a typical import of Western origin, they feel, which is inappropriate to their own culture and tradition.

Governmental bodies, with the help of foreign donors, have launched a number of projects and programs aimed at improving the position of women in BiH. However, there is opposition to the implementation of these projects, and barriers exist as a result of the patriarchal understanding of the social role of men and women or of treating the issue as unimportant compared to all the other issues faced by BiH as a society and a state. This includes the widespread view that "women's issues" are a marginal topic, socially and politically insignificant, and that addressing them is not a priority at this point in the development of BiH.

POLITICS AND LAW

Suffrage

All BiH citizens sixteen years of age, if they are employed, are able to vote. By eighteen years of age, the privilege to vote is universal.

Political Participation

Along with local women's nongovernmental organizations (NGOs), the international community in BiH exerts pressure on authorities at all levels to develop gender policies and to include the gender component within their political activities so as to take into account the interests and needs of all their citizens, male and female alike, on an equal basis. As of the November 2000 election, of the fifteen-member upper house of Parliament, none are women. In the lower house, women hold three of forty-two seats or 7.1 percent.[6]

The active involvement of the international community is for the primary aim of promoting women politically, in which the political role of women is seen as a factor for change in political relations and a bridge in the process of reintegration of the state of BiH and of society within it. The Organization of Security and Co-operation in Europe (OSCE) was influential in the adoption of interim electoral rules that decreed a quota of at least 30 percent of women candidates from each party, thereby ensuring that BiH joined global trends in this regard.

Women's Rights

The Constitution of BiH, which is an integral part of the Dayton Peace Accord, includes an article on human rights that includes a clause providing that "the enjoyment of the rights and freedoms provided for . . . shall be secured to all persons in Bosnia and Herzegovina without discrimination on any ground such as sex, race, colour, language, religion, political or other opinion, national or social origin, association with a national minority, property, birth or other status." In addition to this general clause of the Constitution of BiH, the 1979 UN Convention on the Elimination of All Forms of Discrimination against Women (CEDAW), to which BiH is a signatory, calls for similar antidiscrimination laws.

State-level bodies have been established in BiH and charged with the implementation of the policy of equality between men and women; these are the Committee for Issues of Equality between Men and Women of the Parliamentary Assembly of BiH, and at the entity level governmental bodies have been established: the Gender Centre of the Federation of BiH and the Commission for Gender Equality in Republika Srpska.

A law on sexual equality came into force in March 2003. Its purpose is to regulate, promote, and protect genuine equality between men and women in both the public and private spheres and to prevent direct and indirect discrimination on the grounds of sex. Equality is guaranteed in all fields, particularly those of education, employment, and the workplace; health and social security; the economy and public life; culture and sport; and the media, regardless of marital and family status. In addition, a growing number of gender-integrated laws are expected, along with the harmonization of laws at the state level.

However, in order to ensure that changes to the position of women in BiH become a reality, the state authorities must recognize the gender problem and have a genuine political will to enforce laws. Although the members of the BiH Parliamentary Committee for Equality Issues have been appointed, individual parliamentary deputies have a traditional view of the role of men and women in society. They see women in political life as second-rate or inferior political partners, and the very existence of the committee, like its work, is accorded little significance.

Nongovernmental organizations have an important part to play in bringing this issue onto the agenda and mobilizing society to resolve certain aspects of it. NGOs focus on various activities, from humanitarian work aimed at helping the female returnee population, women's education, strengthening the economic network of women, the political promotion of women and supporting women in political life, and work with women from minority groups to advocacy and lobbying. However, building civil society, strengthening civil initiatives, the promotion and advancement of civil values, building women's networks, and other activities in this field are relatively new phenomena, established only since the beginning of the postwar period. Therefore, the NGOs lack knowledge and experience. Furthermore, there may be conflicts of interest between donors on the one hand and genuine local needs on the other.

The position of women in BiH today cannot be defined simply, because of the existence of numerous different trends. Postwar, postcommunist

BiH is shadowed by a large number of political, cultural, and traditional myths that inhibit any overview of the true state of affairs. The issues of women's rights, equality and discrimination, women in the state, and women in society have become an interesting locus for trying out various political options and positions.

For instance, there are those for whom the rights of women are an issue that has been dealt with legally; given that the legislative equality of men and women has long since been enacted, they maintain that women have an extremely favorable position in the family and in society, and that their numbers in management positions in the business world and their involvement in political life are proportionate to their interest. To make the distinction between women's rights and rights in general, and to speak of them as a separate issue, creates an insufficiently articulated topic; rather, women's rights should not be treated separately from the general social and legal context.

Others lack interest in women's issues, because they see them as subordinate and unimportant compared to all the more pressing concerns faced by BiH as a state and society. Lack of interest is, in part, the outcome of insufficient knowledge and inadequate information on the issue. In cases of political benevolence that seek to undertake certain measures entailing the affirmation of women's rights, there is a lack of ideas on what specifically needs to be done in this regard. Lack of interest is also, in part, the consequence of inherited lack of concern for the issue. Few people have directed their research interests in this direction.

Feminist Movements

In addition to understanding this outline of social and political viewpoints on the issue of women's rights in BiH, one also needs to know that in traditional society the word "feminism" has negative connotations. To be dubbed a "feminist" implies a masculine, aggressive, problematic woman who does not fit in with her milieu and certainly who is against men, the family, and social values; feminists are socially stigmatized. This is the reason why it is rare for a women's association to describe itself as feminist. Most women activists distance themselves from the feminist approach, although this does not prevent their milieu from pejoratively dubbing women engaged in such activities, at least behind the scenes, as vulgar or sluttish. This indicates the current resistance of society toward acknowledging that there is the problem of women's rights and reexamining the reality of equality as opposed to legislative equality.

The promotion of women's associations comes down to calling for the adoption of the principle of equality between men and women not to remain solely at the level of legislative standards but to be actively applied in all aspects of life, from the family, economic, and social to the public and political. In keeping with their respective programs, various women's associations focus on humanitarian work with the target female population, human rights work, the problem of violence, education, women's employment issues, and women's cultural and artistic creativity.

RELIGION AND SPIRITUALITY

Women's Roles

The religious standpoint concerning women's place in society is an evaluation of women's rights, as well as the place and role of women in society and the state, within the context of traditional religious views. Sometimes, in the case of Islam, religious practice in Islamic countries is taken as the sole authoritative indicator. This approach entails a complete and radical reexamination of the status, rights, and position of Muslim women in particular. Given that men are the socially more powerful category, their interpretation of ideology and religion can involve their reading into it their own interests in preserving their status and their social, economic, and political positions.

VIOLENCE

Domestic Violence

The issue of domestic violence has been considered a private matter in BiH. As such, it has not been the subject of direct intervention by the state or its agencies, except in the case of criminal acts. Marriage is assumed to be a harmonious relationship between the partners, for the most part, within the context of patriarchal attitudes and values. To speak of private matters or admit to tensions is regarded as shameful.

Only in the past five years has the consideration of domestic violence as a form of violence against women become part of public discourse. Domestic violence has ceased to be a purely private, domestic problem and become a public issue largely as a result of the work of non-governmental women's organizations. This new approach to the problem of domestic violence can be seen from an analysis of current legislation in BiH and in studies conducted by NGOs.[7] Their studies demonstrate that domestic violence—psychological, physical and sexual—is present in both BiH, but that there is still a lack of awareness of domestic violence as a specific form of violence against women and insufficient support for women victims of domestic violence.

These and other studies[8] have shown that typical perpetrators are partners or husbands with secondary educations between the ages of 31 and 50. Few fit the stereotype of perpetrators as less educated, alcoholics, drug addicts, or mentally ill.

Women list mental violence as the most widespread form of violence

(43 percent), followed by physical violence (33 percent) and sexual violence (24 percent). It appears that there are no profound causal links between what prompted the violence and the violence itself.[9] As a rule it was the most trivial of incidents that prompted physical and sexual violence. The violence occurred throughout the marriage or relationship, usually daily or several times a week.

Women victims of domestic violence lack support from their immediate circles and meet with lack of understanding. They minimized the problem and share the view that the women themselves have caused tensions within the relationship and are complicit in the violence they suffer for not obeying or submitting to their husbands' or partners' wishes and desires. In conformity to patriarchal values and the attitudes, women are expected to keep quiet about the problem (since it is shameful) and to stay in the relationship (value of the institution of marriage). In most cases women victims of domestic violence do not appeal to the perpetrator's family for help; and even when they do, they usually do not get it.

Women turn for help to the police, social work centers, and health care institutions. However, these institutions have not helped women victims of violence and have not come up to their expectations for the most part. One conclusion is that the way the police operate and react is not appropriate to victims' needs, even when victims' lives are at risk.[10] In many cases the police reaction is stereotypical, blaming the women themselves for keeping quiet about the violence or claiming that there is no legal basis for them to react.

Social work centers, for the most part, are not seen as places where women can get help. Social workers in these centers expressed mistrust when victims mentioned violence, and women had the feeling they were misunderstood.[11] Also, very few women seek medical help after suffering violence, largely out of shame or because they lack the necessary funds.

A particularly significant fact highlighted by this study is the failure by women victims of violence to recognize the violence as a form of human rights violation. Only when the violence becomes more frequent do women consider themselves victims and not merely women experiencing the normal things that happen in every marriage. Their awareness of violence is usually at the point when mental violence turns into physical violence; however, if the violence is perpetrated under the influence of alcohol, a certain number of women remain convinced that it would not have happened otherwise, or that the husband's or partner's behavior would change if he just stopped drinking.

The study showed that women are aware of their legal rights, including the right to protection from violence, but also that they are not always ready to exercise those rights. Knowing their rights is related to contacting non-governmental organizations.[12]

Non-governmental organizations are an important element in the network of support and help for women victims of violence. In NGOs, women get psychological help and support, accommodation, and legal aid. Women have a positive evaluation of the work of NGOs.

OUTLOOK FOR THE TWENTY-FIRST CENTURY

At the legal level, women are in a position of equality in regard to the recognition, exercise, and enjoyment of human rights. There are state institutions responsible for the equality of men and women in both the legislature and the executive authorities. Despite this, however, inequality between men and women remains present in BiH as a result of the patriarchal culture and tradition on the one hand, and the communist ideology of class equality on the other, which masked the inequality of women and men and the lack of equal opportunities for women in society,

With regard to the approach to women and their position in society, there are various trends currently present from the revival of the patriarchal cultural matrix and sheer disregard for the issue to efforts aimed at improving the current situation.

Unlike earlier periods, women themselves are displaying more critical attitudes in regard to their position and the forms of discrimination to which they are exposed. There is a growing number of studies focusing on the female population and the various problems faced by women, activities by NGOs are in evidence, and there are more women experts in this domain who are conducting studies shedding light on the issue. However, there is still no critical mass of women in political life that would initiate genuine gender policies. The tragedy experienced by the women of BiH has compelled them to make their own decisions about their future, and the various forms of activity in which they have been involved have helped them to gain knowledge and experience in using the legal and civil opportunities available to them.

NOTES

1. All of the statistics in this paragraph are from the World Bank, "Genderstats," genderstats.worldbank.org (accessed September 30, 2002).

2. These figures are cited on U.S. State Department, "Background Notes on Bosnia and Herzegovina," www.state.gov/www/background_notes/Bosnia_0012_bgn.html (accessed September 30, 2002). This cites the Bosnia-Herzegovina Agency for Statistics December 2000 as their source.

3. According to the Gender Equality Index, BiH occupies the second-to-lowest position among the Stability Pact countries, ahead only of Moldavia and behind Slovenia, Hungary, Croatia, Bulgaria, Rumania, Macedonia, Turkey, and Albania. Among the countries of Central and Eastern Europe, BiH is in last place, behind the Czech Republic, Slovakia, and Poland. By comparison with the countries of the former Soviet Union, BiH is in seventh place, behind Lithuania, Latvia, Belorus, Russia, Armenia, and Ukraine and ahead of Moldavia, Uzbekistan, Tajikistan, Azerbaidjan, Estonia, and

others. United Nations Development Programme (UNDP), "Human Development Report" (2002), www.undp.org.

4. World Bank, 2002.

5. This pilot survey was carried out in summer 2002 (lasting from July 23 to August 1, 2002) and covered a total of 428 women. All of those polled were female members of joint households and were aged eighteen or over; they came from a total of 270 households, Dr. Nada Sofronić-Ler and Dr. Jasna Bakšić-Muftić, project designers, "Project NGO STAR."

6. Inter-parliamentary Union, www.ipu.org (accessed September 30, 2002).

7. Medika Infoteka, "(Ne) živjeti sa nasiljem-Drugi pogled 2." *Violence Against Women*, research conducted by three non-governmental women's organizations—Žene ženama, Sarajevo; Udružena žena, Banja Luka; and Medika Infoteka, Zenica—published by Information Centre for the Disabled "LOTOS" Tuzla, Banja Luka, Zenica, Sarajevo, June 2000.

8. Dr. Jasna Bakšić-Muftić, Dr. Nada Sofronić-Ler, Dr. Jasminka Gradaščević-Sijerčić, and Maida Fetahagić, MA, "Socio-economic status of women in Bosnia and Herzegovina," STAR pilot study, December 2002.

9. *Violence Against Women*, 2000, 25. Violence was prompted by:

- the vacuum cleaner being out of order,
- a badly washed saucepan,
- a meal not to the perpetrator's taste,
- the woman suggesting that they either sort out their relationship or get a divorce,
- the woman complaining that the man had bought bad apples although they had no money to spare,
- the woman told him to take his own underwear out of the cupboard,
- the woman asked him to have his drunken friend leave the apartment,
- the woman said she wanted a divorce,
- the man's friend hurt her feelings but she didn't want to apologize,
- the man had a fight with his sister,
- they stayed out shopping too long,
- the woman went to visit her sister without the man's permission.

10. *Violence Against Women*, 2000, 40. Some of the reactions from the police were:

- "they asked me why I'd had another child when my husband was like that (violent)."
- "I went to the police when I found a grenade under my husband's bed, they told me the procedure for this was very long and I'd do better to put it back where I found it. They didn't write anything down."
- "My husband attacked me in the street when we were already divorced. The police said they could do nothing. They promised to react once the property was divided, so I began proceedings, but I find it hard to believe them. When I was still married they told me they couldn't react because I was married, but even when I was divorced they still didn't help."
- "I called them when he injured me with a knife. They did nothing except report him to the magistrates' court."
- "I called them only after I'd left him, because he was still threatening me. They didn't come, they didn't protect me, but they kept calling me on the phone and inviting me for coffee."
- "They didn't do anything. The police commander even insulted me and told me I was to blame for provoking my husband."

11. *Violence Against Women*, 2000, 42. Responses from women explaining why they were not happy with the social work centers:

- "I got the impression they were blaming me for the violence, because the social worker asked what I said to him when he was ill-treating me."
- "I achieved what I wanted, which was a divorce, but I felt contemptible and humiliated."
- "I had the feeling they didn't believe anything I was saying."
- "When I said he was ill-treating me they didn't react at all. They sent us home and said we had a week to settle our differences."
- "No one believed me. Although I told them he was ill-treating the children when I wasn't there, they wrote in their opinion for the court that he was an acceptable father."
- "He threatened to kill me in front of the social worker, but she didn't react at all."
- "They didn't believe me, he came all dressed up in a suit, but after our discussion he hit me outside the center building."

12. *Violence Against Women*, 2000, 71.

RESOURCE GUIDE

Web Sites

Inter-parliamentary Union, www.ipu.org.

U.S. State Department, "Background Notes on Bosnia and Herzegovina," www.state.gov/www/background_notes/Bosnia_0012_bgn.html.

Organizations

Women to Women / Žene Ženama
St. Ante Fijamenga 14 b
71000 Sarajevo
Phone/Fax: (387) 33 645 234

Movement of mothers from enclaves Srebrenica and Žepa / Pokret majki enklava Srebrenice i Žepe
Phone: (387) 33-214-794

Women's and citizen's association providing legal support, support for refugees, and support for displaced, missing and returning people ("returnees").

ADL Barcelona
Jasminka Mujezinović
St. Bravadiluk bb, 71 000
Sarajevo
Phone/Fax: (387) 33-237-240, 236-899, 236-953
Email: adl@bih.net.ba

Citizen's association. The basic goals of ADL Barcelona are direct preparation of women's rights, direct support and protection to women victims of violence, empowerment of women in small enterprises, and reconstruction programs. Activities of ADL Barcelona are women's rights, psychosocial support, advocacy, business, media, legal support, women's health and medical support and support for refugees and displaced, missing, and returning people ("returnees").

ŽAR Sarajevo
Nermina Balhjević
St. Alipašina 9 / III
Sarajevo
Phone/Fax: (387) 33-205-010
Email: ce.zar@smartnet.ba

Citizen's organization. Its activities include education, legal support, women's rights, and advocacy.

SELECTED BIBLIOGRAPHY

Sofronić-Ler, Nada, and Jasna Bakšić Muftić. "Project NGO STAR." 2002.
United Nations Development Programme (UNDP). Human Development Report. 2002. www.undp.org/, http://hdr.undp.org/reports/view_reports.cfm?country=BIH&countryname=BOSNIA%20AND%20HERCEGOVINA.
World Bank. "Genderstats." genderstats.worldbank.org (accessed September 30, 2002).

7

BULGARIA

Kristen Ghodsee

PROFILE OF BULGARIA

The Republic of Bulgaria is a mountainous country in the very southeast corner of Europe. The Black Sea defines the eastern border. Bulgaria is a parliamentary democracy with the distinction of being the first postcommunist country to have democratically elected its former monarch as its prime minister. Bulgaria began its economic transformation from a centrally planned economy to a market economy in 1989. In 2000, it had a gross domestic product (GDP) of US$12 billion.[1]

Bulgaria had a total population of 8.2 million in 1999 with 1,052 women per 1,000 men.[2] The nation has an infant mortality rate of 15 per 1,000 live births, well below the European and Central Asian combined average of 21 per 1,000 in 1999.[3] Maternal mortality stood at 12.9 percent in the same year.[4] Bulgaria has the second-lowest fertility rate in Europe (after Lithuania) at 1.1 children per woman—well below replacement levels. Women outlive men by an average of seven years; male life expectancy in 2000 was 67.6 years compared to the female life expectancy of 74.6 years.[5]

OVERVIEW OF WOMEN'S ISSUES

Bulgarian women have long enjoyed formal legal equality with men. One of the central tenets of the previous communist regime was the absolute equality of the sexes. Although there was still a significant gendered division under the socialist system, communism went a long way in creating the institutions and mechanisms to support women's productive and reproductive roles in society. Since the end of the centrally planned economy, women in general have seen a drastic deterioration in their living standards and a concomitant resurrection of patriarchal attitudes in society. The economic and political decline in women's status, however, has been in the context of rapid and poorly managed political and economic change in the entire country—changes that have devastated both men and women.

In this context, Bulgarian women seldom separate their own problems and concerns from the problems and concerns of their male compatriots. Most women reject Western feminism, and there is little political organizing along gendered lines. The handful of women's NGOs in Bulgaria has much closer links with international feminist networks than with average Bulgarian women, and "gender problems" are rarely taken seriously either by politicians or the national media. Because of this attitude, many gender specific consequences of the post-1989 changes have remained unchallenged.

EDUCATION

Opportunities

Women have excellent educational opportunities, with female enrollments generally exceeding male enrollments at all levels. In 1999, the combined primary, secondary, and tertiary enrollment ratio was 76 percent for women compared to only 69 percent for men, meaning that women have greater access to education.[6] Women are also well represented in higher education. Of the 36,484 Bulgarians who received bachelor's or master's degrees in 1999, 64 percent were women.[7] But at the very upper echelons of the educational establishment men outnumber women—only 36 percent of the doctoral degrees awarded in 1999 were earned by women.[8]

Literacy

In 1999, Bulgaria's adult literacy rate for women was 97.7 percent, higher than that of Greece, Spain, and Portugal—all current members of the European Union.[9]

EMPLOYMENT AND THE ECONOMY

Job/Career Opportunities

Women, like men, are limited in their career opportunities by the high unemployment rates that have characterized the post-socialist period. Although the national unemployment average is approximately 18 percent, this figure hides vast regional disparities, particularly between rural and urban areas. In some parts of Bulgaria, official unemployment rates reach 40 percent,[10] with unofficial estimates putting the figure much higher. The severe contraction of employment in the public sector has not been compensated for by job creation in the private sector. Furthermore, women are at a disadvantage in finding employment in the few private sector jobs that do exist because of gender discrimination in hiring, career advancement, and remuneration, although there are some expanding sectors in the economy, such as tourism. Tourism is Bulgaria's most important "export," and women continue to be the majority of the employed workforce.[11]

Elderly vendor, Hissarya, Bulgaria. Photo © TRIP/B. Crawshaw.

Pay

The provision for equal pay for equal work for women was removed from the legal code in 1992 on the grounds that it was a vestige of communism and not suitable to a market economy. Despite such obstacles, women in 1998 made 41 percent of the earned income in the country—a figure higher than in the United States (40 percent), Canada (38 percent), France (39 percent), and the Netherlands (34 percent).[12] The percentage of administrators and managers who are women is 28.9 percent (compared to only 9.4 percent in France), as were an impressive 57 percent of professional and technical workers in 1998 (compared to 52.6 percent in the United States).

Working Conditions

Working conditions for both men and women favor employers because of the high unemployment rates throughout the country. The Bulgarian Labor Code has some protections for workers, but these protections only apply to workers with labor contracts (the paperwork required for formal employment). Because many Bulgarians are desperate to find work, they often agree to work without a contract and thus forfeit any legal protection they may have.

Sexual Harassment

Although Bulgarian patriarchal culture is ever present in the workplace, sexual harassment is technically against the law. The Penal Code provides for the protection of female employees in the workplace forced to have sexual intercourse with a man in a more senior position. There is no provision against a "hostile" work environment, and the law is only enforced in cases that show clear economic dependence. According to recent research, sexual discrimination and sexual harassment in the workplace are serious problems for women in Bulgaria.[13]

Support for Mothers/Caretakers

Maternal Leave

Due to Bulgaria's extremely low birth rate, women still enjoy relatively generous maternity leaves, though shorter than those enjoyed in previous times. Today, Bulgarian women have 135 days of paid maternity leave with the possibility of supplementary paid childcare leave until the child is two. During the first 135 days, a woman's full salary and professional status are maintained. Afterwards, a woman will receive the national minimum salary and a small child allowance, both of which are generally insignificant amounts, especially for urban women. Women may also take one year of unpaid leave until the child is three years old. The high competition for jobs, however, makes many of these legal provisions counterproductive to women who find themselves discriminated against in hiring decisions. Furthermore, legal prohibitions that protected women from particular kinds of exploitation under communism, such as a prohibition on taking business trips, often hinder women's career advancement opportunities in the market economy.

Daycare

The state no longer provides free access to childcare facilities, and most private providers are either too expensive or of very poor quality. Women often rely on the "grandma service," relying on their mothers, mothers-in-law, or other older female family members to provide childcare during working hours. Many women consider this dependency on older relatives undesirable, and it has contributed to a marked decline in birthrates since 1989.[14]

Inheritance and Property Rights

The civil law does not in any way restrict rights to property on the basis of gender. The law on inheritance dates from 1949 and allows women to own any kind of property. There are no restrictions on the inheritance rights of women. Children of a deceased person inherit in equal parts regardless of sex. In cases where there are no children, the parents of the deceased inherit in equal parts. Bulgaria also allows for communal property between spouses. In the event of a divorce, all money and property acquired during marriage must be divided equally between the husband and wife.[15]

FAMILY AND SEXUALITY

Gender Roles

Before 1989, the Bulgarian government made a conscious effort to control degrading images of women and to promote positive gender role models for women. Socialist-era propaganda often featured illustrations of men and women working together to build a bright egalitarian future. Women were portrayed as tractor drivers and factory workers in an effort to erase gendered stereotypes about women's "natural" capabilities. The official construction of gender roles changed dramatically after the collapse of the communist system. Resurgent nationalist discourses conflated women's liberation with socialism and reinforced popular beliefs that communism made women ugly and distorted their "natural" femininity.

New market dynamics that value beauty over competence for women workers further reinforce the notion that gender equality is both backward and undesirable. "Feminists" and "careerists" are imagined as unattractive and undesirable women who are angry because of their poor genetic luck. International cosmetic companies have found ravenous markets in Bulgaria, where "prettiness" can now be the difference between having work and not having work. Many employment announcements specify "attractiveness" as a job requirement. Pornography, once illegal, is now readily available and often on public display. Finally, pop stars and young actresses model feminine behaviors that emphasize sexual desirability and economic dependence on wealthy men.

Marriage

Marriage is one of the key paths to social and economic advancement for both genders. Men and women can marry freely, and individuals choose their partners without needing to obtain the official permission of their parents. Arranged marriages are not the custom, and women can delay or avoid marriage as they wish. In practice, however, it is still customary for women to marry younger—an unmarried women at age thirty was traditionally considered a spinster. Socially, delaying marriage for too long makes women seem undesirable. Additionally, most twenty-something women cannot survive independently without working. At the same time, "careerists," or women who put their careers before their family responsibilities, are stigmatized. Financial constraints and the difficulties of having families and careers force many young women to delay marriage indefinitely, despite their wishes to start a family.[16] Brides are not expected to be virgins when they marry, and women in general are sexually active before marriage. There is very little stigma attached to unmarried couples living together, and the rate of cohabitation is on the rise.[17] Children born out of wedlock enjoy the same legal rights as their legitimate brothers and sisters. Despite the flexibility of family arrangements, Bulgaria has one of the lowest fertility rates in all of Europe with only 1.1 children per woman. This has resulted in a precipitous population decline that has been sensationalized by the Bulgarian government and media. This may result in more explicit pro-natalist policies toward women's fertility in the future.[18]

Once the decision to become a wife is made, Bulgarian women enjoy many legal rights and protections. The law sets out clearly that women are not obliged to take their husband's name and that each spouse has the freedom to choose his or her profession. Men and women have equal responsibility for any children they may have, and in case of divorce women are most likely to be awarded custody. Under the centrally planned economy, child support payments were automatically deducted from a father's salary. Although many fathers are still obliged to pay child support, the new realities of a market economy make enforcement of these payments nearly impossible. Even if a woman successfully collects support payments from her spouse, the amounts are not indexed to inflation and can soon become insignificant.

Reproduction

Sex Education

There is no sex education built into the official primary or secondary school curricula, but some NGOs are pressing for its introduction.

Contraception and Abortion

During socialism, abortion was the primary means of contraception as other birth control methods were often unavailable. Other contraceptives have become more available since 1989, but today terminations still outnumber live births. Abortion remains the most popular family planning choice. Abortion has been legal since 1957, and the public accepts abortion more readily than it accepts divorce. Women must bear the cost of an abortion unless the procedure is medically necessary, the woman is a minor, or she is a victim of rape. However, abortion prices are within the reach of most women's economic means and are generally safe.

HEALTH

Health Care Access

Theoretically, all Bulgarians have access to health care. In practice, however, the strict budgetary constraints imposed on the government by the International Monetary Fund and the shrinking of state budgets have led to an erosion in health care provision. Although there are state hospitals and clinics, access to these facilities is limited by the long waiting times. Furthermore, low salaries for doctors and surgeons have contributed to a brain drain of qualified medical personnel out of the country and to increased corruption among those who stay behind. State bureaucrats and professionals at all levels ask for bribes in hard currency.[19] In some cases, doctors in hospitals refuse immediate treatment to sick patients if they cannot afford to pay a bribe. Lower-level health care personnel, such as hospital administrators, release necessary (and free) medical equipment only if presented with the proper "incentives."

The only alternative to the public health system are small private clinics where health care service is superior but significantly more expensive and beyond the means of the majority of Bulgarian women. One positive note is the provision of free prenatal care for all pregnant women. Between 1990 and 1999, 99 percent of all births were attended by skilled health care staff.[20] Women also have access to free postnatal care until they are fully recovered from labor and delivery.

Diseases and Disorders

AIDS

One study worries about an increase in sexually transmitted diseases among women sex workers.[21] Despite this, HIV/AIDS has not yet become a problem. Only .01 percent of the population in 1999 was estimated to be HIV-positive, and there were fewer than 100 HIV/AIDS deaths.[22]

Cancer

Since 1989, however, there has been an increase in the rates of breast and cervical cancer.[23] Periodic examinations for these diseases are not easily accessible and are not free of charge. The same is true for annual gynecological examinations.

POLITICS AND LAW

Suffrage

The Bulgarian Constitution guarantees universal suffrage. Although there are no exact statistical data on the percentage of women voters, the International Helsinki Federation for Human Rights (2000) asserts that women are more active than men in the electoral process.

Political Participation

In the realm of politics, Bulgarian women have both lost and gained ground since 1989. In 1988, before the fall of the Zhivkov regime, women held 21 percent of the seats in the Parliament. After the advent of free elections, this number dropped dramatically to only 8.5 percent. By 1999, this number had risen again to 11.5 percent,[24] still a substantial decline from the communist years. Barbara Einhorn has argued that, in the case of Eastern and Central Europe, this decrease in numbers should not be cause for alarm.[25] She claims that women in politics today, even in their decreased numbers, are more powerful because they can express challenging political opinions instead of silently toeing the party line. However, all politicians (both male and female) during communism were obliged to follow established party doctrine. In this respect, women are still significantly underrepresented in elected office compared to their previous record of participation, until the 2001 elections when the change in government increased women's parliamentary presense to 26.2 percent. In 2002, Bulgaria had the highest percentages of female parliamentarians in all of the former socialist countries.

Bulgaria also briefly had a female prime minister, Reneta Indjova, in 1994. Moreover, several women have held high ministerial positions in various governments, most notably Nadezhda Mihailova, the minister of foreign affairs under the Union of Democratic Forces government in power from 1997 to 2001. The political bureaucracy is also primarily made up of women. Anecdotal evidence also suggests that the local staffs of international organizations are also primarily women.[26] These few jobs are among the most desirable and pay the highest salaries in the country. The NGO sector is also largely female run. Ironically, many female leaders of the NGOs have seen their own standards of living increase through access to the international funding given to them to combat the declining living standards of Bulgarian women as a whole.

Women's Rights

Particularly troublesome is the fact that as women opted out of politics in the 1990s, there may have been fewer advocates for the large social safety net, which once supported women's double burden of obligations to her family and to the workplace, much of which has now eroded. A good example of this was a debate that raged around the issue of maternity leave. The Ministry of Labor and Social Policy wanted to preserve the generous provisions available to Bulgarian women whereas the Ministry of Finance, the World Bank, and the IMF claimed they were a "barrier to foreign investment."[27] Of course, women politicians do not necessarily promote "women's" issues or even a social agenda when they get into power—they, too, are constrained by external influences on the country's polity and economy.

Feminist Movements

It is important to note that there is no organized feminist movement. Women are largely organized around political parties or class divisions and often resist cooperating with women of different political perspectives despite their common gender.[28] If anything, there is an active sentiment against Western feminism. On some levels, this is the result of the naïveté of many women's activists from Western countries. These women usually have training and experience with gender projects in developing countries. They come to Eastern Europe expecting that women there will resemble their "Third World" sisters. But Bulgarian women are, for example, very educated and sophisticated political subjects with long and varied experience in the formal economy. Furthermore, many were previously active in communist women's organizations that once fiercely criticized what was then called "bourgeois feminism" for its complicity with capitalist exploitation. Indeed, today many Eastern European women still consider class the key variable in the discussion of oppression[29] with gender, nationality, and ethnic identity being secondary. The fundamental misunderstanding of the social and cultural legacies of Marxist-Leninism in the Bulgarian context has made it difficult for Western feminist movements to take hold among ordinary women.

Lesbian Rights

In terms of lesbian rights, there is no law expressly forbidding homosexuality unless homosexual acts are committed with a minor. Homosexual couples are generally tolerated in society, although sexuality is widely considered a private matter and there are few openly gay or lesbian organizations. In the capital, Sofia, there is a popular gay and lesbian discothèque and several bars and clubs catering to same-sex couples. Most of these spaces, however, are quite mixed in the sense that gay couples, lesbian couples, and heterosexual couples mingle freely amongst each other.[30] Transvestites are also very common in Sofia, and according to some scholars are at the very top of the gay hierarchy.[31]

RELIGION AND SPIRITUALITY

Bulgarian Orthodox Christians are 83.5 percent of the population, although over four decades of Marxist-Leninist doctrine did much to inhibit the power of the church. Bulgaria also has a large Muslim minority of 13 percent that largely corresponds with the ethnic Turkish minority. Other religious minorities include Roman Catholics, Uniate Catholics, and Jews. Historically, Bulgaria has been very tolerant of religious minorities, most famously in its protection of the Bulgarian Jews during World War II in spite of its alliance with Nazi Germany.[32]

Women's Roles

Although women have played a variety of important functions in the Eastern Church throughout its long history, like the Roman Catholic Church, Orthodoxy is firmly against the ordination of women into the priesthood.[33] Women, however, have had strong spiritual roles outside of the official confines of the church. The most famous example of a revered spiritual leader is Baba Vanga (Granny Vanga), widely believed to be a clairvoyant, prophet, and saintly woman throughout Bulgaria as well as in parts of Russia, Greece, Macedonia, and Romania. For decades Baba Vanga (who could allegedly speak with the dead) was sought out by both leaders of the Bulgarian Communist Party and foreign dignitaries such as the Indian Prime Minister Indira Gandhi.[34]

In 1967, Baba Vanga received official recognition of her special abilities by the communist government and was appointed as a research fellow at the Bulgarian Academy of Sciences. After 1989, Bulgaria's new presidents and prime ministers came to seek her counsel amidst growing interest by the Bulgarian national media. More importantly, ordinary Bulgarians considered Baba Vanga a living saint despite the strong objections of the Orthodox Church. By the mid-1990s, she had over 8,000 godchildren and had personally raised the funds necessary to consecrate her own church. So great was her influence on believers that many followers still hold that Baba Vanga sacrificed her life in 1996 to stop the war in the former Yugoslavia and contain its spread to Bulgaria and Macedonia. According to one scholar, the Dayton Accord was widely interpreted as proof of the efficacy of Vanga's spiritual intervention in material affairs.[35]

VIOLENCE

Domestic Violence

Domestic violence is a serious issue in Bulgaria.[36] Because domestic violence is considered a private matter between the families of the husband and wife, abuse is seldom reported unless it results in serious injury or death. Furthermore, the law does not prosecute for domestic violence unless the spouse is permanently injured, disfigured, or killed. Because domestic violence is underreported, it is very difficult to determine the scale of the problem. Few cases ever make it to court, and the majority of those that do are eventually abandoned.[37] Many Bulgarians also tend to "ghettoize" the issue as one that affects only Turkish and Roma (Gypsy) women in Bulgaria.

The government has no official programs in place to deal with the victims of domestic violence. This may, however, have more to do with fiscal constraints rather than a lack of concern. International women's organizations and a handful of bilateral aid organizations have made funds available for the establishment of battered women's shelters. Currently, there are several shelters and hotlines available for victims of abuse in the large cities of Sofia, Varna, and Bourgas.

Rape/Sexual Assault

Like domestic violence, rape and sexual assault are also underreported and considered to be private matters. Unlike domestic violence, however, rape and sexual assault are clearly penalized under Bulgarian law although the burden of proof lay largely with the victim. After the transition to democracy, enforcement became more lax. The lawlessness that characterized the initial transformation period led to a marked increase in the number of rapes reported to the police.[38] Although the state provides free abortions to victims of rape, there are few institutional supports available for victims of sexual violence. Again, women's nongovernmental organizations have largely taken up this cause, and there are some counseling services available.

Trafficking in Women and Children

The International Organization for Migration (IOM) estimates that over 10,000 Bulgarian women, many of them minors, were working as what they define as "sex slaves" in Western Europe in 1999.[39] The IOM has little information on who these women actually are, and the 10,000 figure is also questionable because the movement of women and children into Western Europe is often through illegal means and is difficult to trace. What is sure is that young Bulgarian women before 2001[40] were so eager to go abroad that they were often the victims of international crime syndicates. Typically, young women applied to employment "agencies" that promised to arrange legal work in Western European countries as an au pair, nanny, or nurse. The agencies arranged the visas and paid for the transportation. The women agreed to pay the money back from their future salaries. In many cases, however, the women's money and passports were confiscated on arrival, and they were forced to work as illegal prostitutes in order to pay back their debts. Few tried to escape for fear of their own lives or the lives of loved ones back in Bulgaria. Because the women and girls left the country of their own "free will," with valid visas and the appropriate documentation, it was very difficult to control this kind of activity.[41] It has also been documented that Bulgarian Roma families willingly sell their own daughters into prostitution, although once again it is difficult to know the extent of the problem.[42]

OUTLOOK FOR THE TWENTY-FIRST CENTURY

Since 1989, Bulgaria and Bulgarian women have been through a period of drastic and tumultuous change. The collapse of the socialist state and the centrally planned economy saw the end of the entitlements that once supported women's multiple roles in the family and formal economy. The transition to democracy and capitalism has given Bulgarian women both new opportunities and new challenges. As Bulgaria slowly becomes more integrated with the West, particularly through its recent membership in NATO and its aspiration to join the European Union, Bulgarian women will hopefully begin to enjoy the social, political, and economic fruits of democracy and free markets after so many years of difficult transition.

NOTES

1. World Bank, "Bulgaria at a Glance," 2002, www.worldbank.org/data (accessed September 2, 2002).

2. National Statistical Institute (NSI), *Statistical Yearbook 2002* (Sofia, Bulgaria: Author, 2001).

3. World Bank, 2002.

4. NSI, 2001.

5. NSI, 2001.

6. During the communist regime, men generally tended to pursue technical courses or manufacturing apprenticeships whereas women studied more formal subjects in high school and went on to university. Before 1989, this difference resulted in a highly gendered division of labor in which women were concentrated in lower-paid administrative and professional jobs (because communism valued manufacturing above all else). In the postcommunist period, however, women's general education has become extremely valuable in the new market economy. Furthermore, women's dominance of general education institutions continues. United Nations Development Programme (UNDP), *Human Development Report, 1999* (New York: Author, 2000).

7. NSI, 2001.

8. NSI, 2001.

9. NSI, 2001.

10. NSI, 2001.

11. Kristen Ghodsee, "State Support in the Market: Women and Tourism Employment in Post-Socialist Bulgaria," *International Journal of Politics, Culture and Society* 16, no. 3 (Spring 2003): 465–82.

12. United Nations Development Programme, *Human Development Report 1998* (New York: Author, 1999).

13. Study conducted by the Minnesota Advocates for Human Rights, *Sex Discrimination and Sexual Harassment* (Minneapolis: Author, 1999).

14. Ron Lesthaeghe and Johan Surkyn, *New Forms of Household Formation* (Brussels: Vrije Universiteit, 2002).

15. International Helsinki Federation for Human Rights, "Bulgaria," in *Women 2000* (Helsinki, Finland: Author, 2000).

16. Republic of Bulgaria, "Consideration of Reports" (New York: United Nations, 1994).

17. Lesthaeghe and Surkyn, 2002.

18. Kristen Ghodsee, "Brain Drain, Bogus Asylum Seekers, and Babies: Conflicting Discourses of Mobility and Fertility in Bulgaria and the European Union," *The Anthropology of East Europe Review* 20, no. 2 (Autumn 2002): 13–20.

19. A. Grodeland, T. Koshechkina, and W. Miller, "Foolish to Give," *Europe-Asia Studies* 50, no. 4 (June 1998).

20. World Bank, 2002.

21. K. Tchoudomirova, M. Domeika, and P.A. Mardh, "Demographic Data on Prostitutes," *International Journal on STD and AIDS* 8, no. 3 (1997): 181–91.

22. Central Intelligence Agency (CIA), "The World Factbook: Bulgaria," www.cia.gov/publications/factbook/geos/bu.html.

23. International Helsinki Federation for Human Rights, 2000.

24. Leslie Holmes, *Post-Communism: An Introduction* (Durham, NC: Duke University Press, 1997); and Women's Alliance for Development, "Women in Bulgaria 2000," www.geocities.com/woalde.

25. Barbara Einhorn, *Cinderella goes to Market* (London: Verso, 1993).

26. For instance, in 1999–2000 the office of the World Bank Resident Mission in Bulgaria employed only three men on its entire staff. The resident representative, Thomas O'Brien, was a man, but all of the high-level positions beneath him were filled by Bulgarian women.

27. Personal communication with the World Bank Resident Mission in Sofia, July 2000; and the FIAS Report, 1999.

28. Kristen Ghodsee, "Women and Economic Transition: Mobsters and Mail-Order Brides in Bulgaria," *The Center for Slavic and Eastern European Studies Newsletter* 3, no. 17 (Fall 2000): 5–8.

29. Elena Gapova, "Nation, Gender, and Class Formation in Belarus" (2002).

30. Robin Brooks, "Cross-dressing in Bulgaria," *Bad Subjects*, no. 50 (June 2000).

31. Brooks, 2000.

32. M. Lalkov, *A History of Bulgaria: An Outline* (Sofia, Bulgaria: St. Kliment Ohridski Press, 1998); and R. J. Crampton, *A Concise History of Bulgaria* (Cambridge: Cambridge University Press, 1997).

33. Valerie A. Karras, *Women in the Eastern Church* (1997).

34. Ilia Illiev, "The Social Construction of a Saintly Woman in Bulgaria," in *A*

Captured Moment in Time, vol. 10, ed. Adrianne Rubeli and Nina Vucenik (Vienna: IWM, 2000).

35. Illiev, 2000.

36. Minnesota Advocates for Human Rights, *Domestic Violence in Bulgaria* (Minneapolis: Author, 1996).

37. Minnesota Advocates for Human Rights, 1996.

38. Republic of Bulgaria, 1994.

39. International Organization for Migration (IOM) estimates (1999).

40. Prior to 2001, Bulgarians were on the Schengen blacklist and could not travel freely to the European Union. After 2001, the freedom of movement for Bulgarians may have lessened the appeal of would-be traffickers because the young women could now go abroad of their own accord.

41. For an interesting and thorough examination of the problem, see www.qweb. kvinnoforum.se/papers/traffickingreport.html for the Trafficking Report.

42. International Helsinki Federation for Human Rights, 2000.

RESOURCE GUIDE

Suggested Reading

Daskalova, Krassimira. "Women's Problems, Women's Discourses in Bulgaria." In *Reproducing Gender: Politics, Publics, and Everyday Life after Socialism*, edited by S. Gal and G. Kligman, 337–69. Princeton, NJ: Princeton University Press, 2000.

Ghodsee, Kristen. "State Support in the Market: Women and Tourism Employment in Post-Socialist Bulgaria." *International Journal of Politics, Culture and Society* 16, no. 3. Spring 2003: 465–82.

International Helsinki Federation for Human Rights. "Bulgaria." In *Women 2000: An Investigation into the Status of Women's Rights in Central and South-Eastern Europe and the Newly Independent States*. Helsinki: Author, 2001. Available online at www.ihf-hr.org/reports/women/woman_2000.pdf.

Todorova, Maria. "The Bulgarian Case: Women's Issues or Feminist Issues?" In *Gender Politics and Post-Communism: Reflections from Eastern Europe and the Former Soviet Union*, edited by Nanette Funk and Magda Mueller, 30–38. New York: Routledge, 1993.

United Nations Development Programme. *Women in Poverty*. Bulgaria: United Nations Development Programme, 1998.

Web Sites

Animus Association Foundation, www.animus.search.bg.
A women's nongovernmental organization created to help victims of violence. The team of the foundation consists of clinical psychologists, psychotherapists, and social workers.

Bulgarian Online, www.online.bg.
This is a general searchable web site in both English and Bulgarian with excellent

Internet archives. The "News and Media" section gives users access to articles about Bulgarian women from news sources around the world.

The Sofia Echo. www.sofiaecho.com.
Bulgaria's English language newspaper online. The paper is owned by a British woman with strong interests in women's issues.

Republic of Bulgaria, www.government.bg.

United Nations Development Programme, Bulgaria office, www.undp.bg.
Has excellent links to reports and statistics of the situation of women in Bulgaria.

Organizations

Bulgarian Association of University Women (BAUW)
125, "Tzarigradsko Chaussee" Blvd., Block 3, Room 418
Sofia, Bulgaria
Phone/Fax: (359) 2 70 73 42
Email: bauw@feb.uni-sofia.bg

This NGO of women with degrees in the humanities, social sciences, engineering, and science is active in advocating for women's special needs in combining work and family responsibilities. Students can join as observers.

Women's Alliance for Development
2, Neofit Rilski Street, 1000
Sofia, Bulgaria
Phone/Fax: (+359) 2 980 55 32, (+359) 2 980 59 20
Email: wad@yellowpages-bg.net
Web site: www.womenbg.org/en/

This organization's goal is the enhancement of sustainable development via working for more gender equality in access to resources, rights, decision making within the family, and socioeconomic and political aspects of society.

SELECTED BIBLIOGRAPHY

Brooks, Robin. "Cross-dressing in Bulgaria: Gay-identity, Post-Communist Fear, and Magical Love." *Bad Subjects*, no. 50 (June 2000). http://eserver.org/bs/50/brooks.html.

Central Intelligence Agency (CIA). "The World Factbook: Bulgaria." www.cia.gov/cia/publications/factbook/geos/bu.html.

Crampton, R. J. *A Concise History of Bulgaria*. Cambridge: Cambridge University Press, 1997.

Einhorn, Barbara. *Cinderella Goes to Market: Citizenship, Gender, and Women's Movements in East Central Europe*. London: Verso, 1993.

Gapova, Elena. *Nation, Gender and Class Formation in Belarus . . . and Elsewhere in the Post-Soviet World*. Paper presented at the Annual Soyuz Symposium in Ann Arbor, Michigan, in February 2002.

Ghodsee, Kristen. "Women and Economic Transition: Mobsters and Mail-Order Brides in Bulgaria." *The Center for Slavic and Eastern European Studies Newsletter*

3, no. 17 (Fall 2000): 5–8. http://ist-socrates.berkeley.edu/~csees/publications/2000_17-03.pdf.

———. "Brain Drain, Bogus Asylum Seekers, and Babies: Conflicting Discourses of Mobility and Fertility in Bulgaria and the European Union." *The Anthropology of East Europe Review* 20, no. 2 (Autumn 2002): 13–20.

Grodeland, A., T. Koshechkina, and W. Miller. "Foolish to Give and Yet More Foolish Not to Take: In-depth Interviews with Post-Communist Citizens on Their Everyday Use of Bribes and Contacts." *Europe-Asia Studies* 50, no. 4 (June 1998): 651–77.

Holmes, Leslie. *Post-Communism: An Introduction*. Durham, NC: Duke University Press, 1997.

Illiev, Ilia. "The Social Construction of a Saintly Woman in Bulgaria." In *A Captured Moment in Time: IWM Junior Visiting Fellows Conferences*, vol. 10, edited by Adrianne Rubeli and Nina Vucenik. Vienna: IWM, 2000.

International Helsinki Federation for Human Rights. "Bulgaria." In *Women 2000: An Investigation into the Status of Women's Rights in Central and South-Eastern Europe and the Newly Independent States*. Helsinki: Author, 2001. Available online at www.ihf-hr.org/reports/women/woman_2000.pdf.

Karras, Valerie A. *Women in the Eastern Church: Past, Present and Future*. Paper presented at the tenth Annual Conference of Orthodox Christian Laity at the Hellenic College and Holy Cross, Brookline, Massachusetts, in November 1997. Available online at www.voithia.org/content/qmpcwinwor3.htm.

Lalkov, M. *A History of Bulgaria: An Outline*. Sofia, Bulgaria: St. Kliment Ohridski University Press, 1998.

Lesthaeghe, Ron, and Johan Surkyn. *New Forms of Household Formation in Central and Eastern Europe: Are They Related to Newly Emerging Value Orientations?* Working Paper 2002. Brussels, Belgium: Vrije Universiteit Brussel—Interface Demography, 2002.

Minnesota Advocates for Human Rights. *Domestic Violence in Bulgaria*. Minneapolis, MN: Minnesota Advocates for Human Rights, April 1996.

———. *Sex Discrimination and Sexual Harassment in the Workplace in Bulgaria*. Minneapolis: Minnesota Advocates for Human Rights, 1999.

National Statistical Institute. *Statistical Yearbook 2000*. Sofia, Bulgaria: National Statistical Institute, 2001.

Republic of Bulgaria. "Consideration of Reports Submitted by States Parties under Article 18 of the Convention on the Elimination of All Forms of Discrimination against Women: Second and Third Periodic Reports of the States Parties." CEDAW/C/BGR/2–3. New York: United Nations, 1994.

Staikova-Alexandrova, Raia. "Bulgaria: The Present Situation of Women." In *The Impact of Economic and Political Reform on the Status of Women in Eastern Europe: Proceedings of a United Nations Regional Seminar*. New York: United Nations, 1992.

Tchoudomirova, K., M. Domeika, and P.A. Mardh. "Demographic Data on Prostitutes from Bulgaria—A Recruitment Country for International (Migratory) Prostitutes." *International Journal of STD and AIDS* 8, no. 3 (1997): 187–91.

Todorova, Maria. "The Bulgarian Case: Women's Issues or Feminist Issues?" In *Gender Politics and Post-Communism: Reflections from Eastern Europe and the Former Soviet Union*, edited by Nanette Funk and Magda Mueller, 30–38. New York: Routledge, 1993.

United Nations Development Programme. *Women in Poverty*. Sofia, Bulgaria: United Nations Development Programme, 1998.

———. *Human Development Report 1998*. New York: Author, 1999.

———. *Human Development Report 1999*. New York: Author, 2000.

———. *Human Development Report 2000*. New York: Author, 2001.

Women's Alliance for Development (WAD). "Women in Bulgaria 2000." www.geocities.com/woalde.

World Bank. "Bulgaria at a Glance." www.worldbank.org/data (accessed September 2, 2002).

———. "Bulgaria: Data Profile." www.worldbank.org/data (accessed September 2, 2002).

8

CROATIA

Aida Bagić

PROFILE OF CROATIA

The Republic of Croatia is one of the countries that emerged from the breakup of socialist Yugoslavia. Its constitution was enacted on December 22, 1990, and it was internationally recognized on January 15, 1992. Compared to other post-Yugoslav countries, Croatia is economically far better off with an estimated gross domestic product for 2001 of US$4,566 per capita.[1]

Croatia is a parliamentary democracy. In January 2000, for the first time since the introduction of a multiparty system, the government changed from the right-wing HDZ (Croatian Democratic Union) to the party coalition led by Social Democrats (a reformed communist party that introduced the multiparty system).

The decade of authoritarian rule of the Croatian Democratic Union, however, left the new government with numerous problems to be solved, ranging from mismanagement of the privatization process[2] to social policy reforms. Although the current government continues to cooperate with the International War Crimes Tribunal in The Hague, the public has only recently

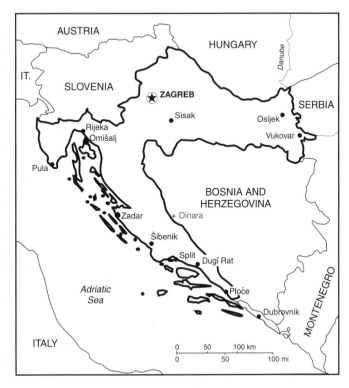

started to deal with crimes committed by Croatians during the war period between 1991 and 1995.

According to the last census, held in April 2001, Croatia has 4,437,460 inhabitants, 2,301,560 of whom are women. In 1991, out of 4,784,265 inhabitants women made up 51.5 percent of the population; today they are 52 percent.[3] This growth is sometimes explained as a consequence of the losses in population from the war and the increasing numbers of young and qualified people, more often men than women, emigrating from Croatia.

The ethnic composition in 1991 was 78 percent Croatian, 12 percent Serbian, and 10 percent Hungarian, Slovenian, Muslim, and others. In 2001, the percentage of those identifying as Croatians rose to 89.63 percent, and the percentage of all the other ethnicities had fallen to under 10 percent (4.54 percent are Serbians and all of the others are below 1 percent each). Croatia is a predominantly Catholic country (76.5 percent in 1991, 88 percent in 2001); other religions include Orthodox, Muslim, and Protestant.[4]

Women's life expectancy is 77, and men's is 67. The infant mortality rate fell from 62.9 per 1,000 live births in 1961 to 7.4 in 2000; the stillbirth rate declined from 12.7 to 5.2 during that same time. The average number of marriages in the period 1991–2000 is 35 percent lower than it was in the period 1961–1970. The average age of a mother at the birth of her first child has been slightly increasing for quite a long period. In 1961 it was 23.6, and in 2000 it was 25.6.[5] The total fertility rate was 1.4 in 2000.[6]

OVERVIEW OF WOMEN'S ISSUES

Since Croatia became an independent country, war and nationalism have been among the major factors working against the status and benefits that women gained under socialist rule. After the first democratic, multiparty elections in 1990, the percentage of women in the last session of the socialist Croatian parliament dropped from 25 percent to 4.8 percent. Although under socialism parliaments were not the real site of political decision making, this decline in women's representation was a striking marker of the new political tendencies in the new independent nation-state. Under the new circumstances of a market economy—along with the economic deterioration brought about by war years—women have had to find ways both individually and collectively to address the issues that matter to them.

In a recent opinion poll conducted in the Southeastern European countries, both men and women in Croatia identified unemployment, poverty, and corruption as the largest current problems, although not in the same order.[7] About 11 percent more women than men picked unemployment. Women also gave much more importance to "jobs for our children /unemployment of our children," family income, and abuse of narcotics and alcohol, whereas men more often saw the problems as the inadequate bureaucracy, the malfunctioning legal system, and the desire for association of the country with the European Union and/or NATO.

The largest difference between women and men in their conception of societal problems was in how they perceived domestic violence and the issue of abandoned children. The need to address the problem of domestic violence led to the emergence of a large number of women's organizations during the past decade. Its inclusion among important social issues to some extent denotes the organizations' success in raising public awareness. In Croatia, 4.1 percent of respondents found it more important than the problem of abandoned children, the country's association with the NATO and/or the EU, the low trustworthiness of the media, and ethnic confrontations.

EDUCATION

Opportunities

In 1987, 50.7 percent of university graduates were women,[8] and in 2001, they had reached 55.6 percent.[9]

Literacy

Among those ten years of age or older, 3.04 percent were illiterate according to the 1991 census. Of those, 0.51 percent were male and 2.49 percent were female. Among younger citizens, men and women are equal in literacy.[10]

EMPLOYMENT AND THE ECONOMY

Job/Career Opportunities

Women's participation in the labor force grew from 43 percent in 1991 to 45 percent in 2001. They are also 54.3 percent of the unemployed. Women are more readily laid off than men as indicated by the fact that among all the unemployed, women actually have higher educational attainments than the unemployed men. Among women over the age of forty, the loss of a job often means permanent unemployment with few governmental or job-related supports for her in her old age.[11]

In the transition to capitalism, the typical shift toward a service economy also holds true for Croatia, where 70 percent of the jobs are now in services like tourism, catering, and caretaking. The service sector, which tends to be lower paid than industrial or managerial positions, is where most women find employment, including professional careers. On the ladder of professional careers, women tend to occupy the lower ranks of pay, authority, and status. Although more and more women are employed in small business or as independent professionals, the services, especially health care and education, are dominated by women. Women are also the majority of those employed in retail trades, whether in the formal economy or in the informal sector.

Pay

Within the labor law, there is an article on equal payment for equal work of equal value. It also provides for priority in employment of the underrepresented gender. However, it has not yet had any major impact on the distribution of jobs and careers. Also, a new law promoting small businesses has a clause providing for the development of women enterprises.

Working Conditions

Besides unemployment, women face other problems in the work force and economy. Many women are employed in the informal sector of the economy, which is estimated to contribute 30 percent of the gross national product. There they have jobs with no social security benefits and, in the case of certain black market jobs, they face threats to their person.

Sexual Harassment

Younger women may confront sexual harassment or other forms of blackmail in order to get and keep their jobs. Older women face other forms of discrimination. For example, it is not uncommon for job advertisements to specify that the applicant be under the age of thirty. Also, the ads might indicate directly that the applicant should be male, or, more indirectly, specify that the applicant should be available for overtime work and travel.

During job interviews, women may be asked personal questions about whether they intend to marry or to have children, and they may be required to take pregnancy tests. Despite its illegality, they may also be forced to sign a statement agreeing not to get pregnant during their first few months of employment.

Support for Mothers/Caretakers

The socialist benefits of a relatively high standard included childcare, a network of accessible kindergartens, and other benefits for working women; free health and pension schemes; a high level of employment of women; and free education. These greatly contributed to the level of independence of women.

FAMILY AND SEXUALITY

Gender Roles

Despite the equal status of women and men in Croatian legislature, including equal access to education and employment, the traditional division of labor persists, primarily at home. According to recent research on women's position in Croatian society, hardly any household duties are equally shared by both partners: women are almost exclusively responsible for doing laundry (96 percent), ironing (96 percent), preparing meals (85 percent), and washing the dishes (81 percent), and men for light house repairs (85 percent), changing the electricity fuses (80 percent), and putting fuel in the car (72 percent). In families with children, women and men share responsibility when it comes to playing with children (62 percent of men) and taking them out (57 percent of men), as well as in helping with school work (39 percent of men), whereas women are those who are more often responsible for feeding children (68 percent) and taking care of them in case of illness (73 percent). Clearly, gender-stereotyped division of labor affects both women and men.[12]

Marriage

There are currently 1.07 million marriages in Croatia and only 30,000 of these are common-law marriages. Marriage rates declined steadily from the mid-1960s. In 2000 the marriage rate was 5 per 1,000 inhabitants, or 0.5 percent. The divorce rate per 1,000 marriages was 200.07 in 2000, 156.5 in 1999, and 163.4 in 1998.[13] Family law allows for marriage partners to keep their surnames, although many women choose to take their husband's surname or add it to their own.

Reproduction

Contraception and Abortion

During the early 1990s contraception became scarce, not always accessible, and expensive. At the same time, the conservative political trends joined by the Catholic Church often attacked the right to choice and accessibility of abortion. Thanks to the strong opposition of women's groups, abortion was never banned in Croatia, but significantly enough, it was the first medical service that became "commercialized" and thus became very expensive. Since 1991, gynecologists in public health institutions are allowed to conscientiously object to performing abortions, which causes tremendous problems for women in some provincial regions. Often, though, these very same doctors perform abortions in their private practices.

HEALTH

Health Care Access

Most Croatians do not have good information about women's health status and do not know much about the availability or lack of specific health services and treatments. There is no women's health movement to advocate for women's health. In the Women's Network of Croatia, there is only one organization, a breast cancer support group, devoted specifically to health issues.

About 25 percent of women receive Pap tests. Screening for girls under fourteen is not included under the free gynecological health services.

Diseases and Disorders

Cancer

One of the leading causes of death among Croatian women is breast cancer. However, only approximately 1 percent of women are screened for it.

POLITICS AND LAW

Suffrage

Croatian women received the right to vote in 1945, after the establishment of the socialist Yugoslavia (of which Croatia was one of the constituting republics) at the end of World War II. In the period between the two world wars, when Croatia was part of the Kingdom of Yugoslavia, there had been numerous unsuccessful initiatives advocating women's right to vote.

Political Participation

Immediately after the fall of communism, women's representation in Parliament fell to 4.8 percent, rising to about 8 percent since 1995. With the elections of 2000, generally considered the turning point in democratic processes in Croatia, 22 percent of women were elected to the Parliament. At that time, this was one of the highest proportions of women in Southern and Eastern European parliaments. The Women's Network of Croatia, as well as the Ad hoc Women's Coalition, organized before the election, played an enormous role in that change.

There are no women in the parliament's presidium; the president and all six deputy presidents are men. Women preside over six of twenty-four parliamentary committees, but they head three of four parliamentary delegations. Due to changes in the Croatian government in August 2002, the percentage of female ministers has grown from 13 percent to 16.6 percent. In the new government, out of twenty-four members of the cabinet, four are women—the vice president of government, who is also the minister of defense; the minister of tourism; the minister of justice and public administration; and the fourth, a former head of parliamentary gender equality committee, is a minister without portfolio and a secretary of the prime minister's cabinet.[14]

Electoral workers empty a ballot box for counting at a polling station in Zagreb, Croatia, January 2000. AP/Wide World Photos.

Women make up some 20 percent of deputy ministers and assistant ministers. Before new nominations were to be made, the Women's Network released a public request to increase the number of women in government. Although there is now one woman more than before, the figures do not truly reflect the level of trust that the electorate has placed in women by electing them to Parliament. There are twelve women mayors (10 percent), 12 percent of regional assemblies are women, and only some 14 percent in local self-governments are women. This is a considerable increase compared to the previous situation but still far below the expected level.

Only one woman heads a political party, but almost all parties have introduced internal quotas and the parties of the governing coalition had up to 40 percent women on their candidates' lists. All the leading parties maintain some form of women's forum. The ad hoc coalition and the Women's Network have been requesting women's quotas and the introduction of gender prospective into the electoral law since 1995. Although these requests were not fulfilled, by 1999 the "women's question" became a serious topic in mainstream politics and was particularly supported by a strong campaign organized by the Women's Network in 1999. All their efforts bore fruit during the elections of 2000.

According to the National Policy for Promotion of Gender Equality (first ratified by the Parliament in 1997), the government was obliged to increase the participation of women in all its departments and offices by 2000. Although this promise has not been fulfilled in practice, the visibility of women in various levels of government and in a few of the ministerial positions demonstrates some changes in a positive direction.

Women's Rights

On the normative and legal level, Croatia is a member and has ratified all the UN and European documents and conventions including CEDAW, its optional protocol, the European Convention on Human Rights, and other binding and nonbinding international documents related to the elimination of discrimination, improvement of status, and empowerment of women.

Since its adoption in 1991, the Croatian Constitution has contained the prohibition of sex discrimination within its antidiscrimination clause. In 2000, the clause on gender equality was added to the "highest principles of the Croatian Constitution." Nevertheless, the description and direct prohibition of gender discrimination, as proposed by CEDAW, was never discussed in the Croatian Parliament, although women's human rights groups attempted several times to introduce that clause. Its absence causes problems in introducing nondiscrimination provisions in particular laws.

However, within the last ten years, particularly within the period between 2000 and 2002, several institutional supports for gender equality and women's human rights have been established. These include the founding of the governmental Office for Gender Equality (in 1997) and the gender equality clause of the Croatian Constitution (added in 2000). Also in 2000, the Committee for Gender Equality in the Parliament was established.

National policy for the promotion of gender equality, founded on the Beijing Conference Platform and the Special Meeting of the UN General Assembly, Beijing+5, was accepted by the Parliament in 2000. It contains an action program for the period 2001–2005 that addresses education, health, violence, armed conflicts, the economy, women in the positions of power and decision making, media, and the environment.

Although it is understaffed and underfinanced, the Office for Gender Equality has been active in seeking the input of representatives from women's organizations. Importantly, for example, in preparation of the National Politics for Promotion of Gender Equality, a wide range of representatives from the women's NGOs was consulted, and almost all their suggestions were included.

Feminist Movements

Compared to other Eastern European countries, Yugoslav successor states, including Croatia, have long had relatively significant women's associations and feminist activism. In the beginnings of the war, the feminist groups helped women victims regardless of their nationality. That strategy of addressing all forms of discrimination and all types of violence has placed them in a key position to speak about a new postwar civil society.

As in other South European countries, the 1990s saw the proliferation of women's groups. The support of international donors has made it possible for ideas that have been circulating around for many years to become realities. For instance, in 1989 there was only one organization in Croatia—the SOS telephone line for women victims of domestic violence—which could be considered a women's organization providing direct help to women. Today its functions are performed by a number of women's organizations. The 2000 *Directory of Women's Groups* lists forty-nine organizations, sixteen of them located in the capital city of Zagreb. The directory includes groups with a wide variety of activities, ranging from feminist publishing and education to women's economic empowerment and lesbian issues.[15] The Women's Network of Croatia was established in 1995. It functions, mostly informally, through regular gatherings to exchange experiences. Its membership consists of more than sixty groups and organizations, including peace and human rights groups with women's issues on their agenda.[16]

Lesbian Rights

Although homosexual relations are not penalized, the dominant public attitudes toward lesbians and gays are negative. The first Gay Pride rally was held in Zagreb, the capital of Croatia, only in June 2002 (organized by the lesbian group Kontra and the gay and lesbian association Iskorak) under heavy police protection. Currently, lesbian and gay associations are lobbying for the recognition of domestic partnerships within the family law, which is supported by Social Democrats and various liberal parties but opposed by the conservative right-wing parties and the Catholic Church. A simultaneous campaign for the rights of homosexuals was organized by the lesbian organization Lori from the coastal town of Rijeka.

RELIGION AND SPIRITUALITY

Croatia is predominately Catholic, with 88 percent of Croatians declaring themselves as Roman Catholic in the last census, which was held in April 2001. Other religions include Orthodox Christianity, Muslim, and Protestant.

Although officially separated from the state, the Catholic Church has a considerable influence on everyday life, for example through challenging the legality of abortion rights and promoting motherhood as the most important role for women. In the 1990s, there were several initiatives attempting to criminalize abortion led by nationalist right-wing parties and some NGOs. The largest and strongest pro-life association in Croatia is the Croatian Movement for Population, led by a Catholic priest and supported financially by the government.

In rural areas and other areas with strong religious influences and beliefs, single mothers still face prejudice. Although this rarely amounts to public condemnation or expulsion from the family, single mothers can encounter problems because Croatia is still a mostly rural environment in which the church is "the mother and the teacher."[17]

VIOLENCE

Domestic Violence

The beginning of women's organizing in Croatia began primarily around the issues of violence against women. The very first shelter for women victims of domestic violence was opened in December 1990 by the Autonomous Women's House Zagreb (formerly Women's Aid Now). Today there are two shelters in the capital city of Zagreb and two more in smaller cities.[18]

There have also been some changes and proposed changes in the laws regarding violence. For example, spousal rape has been defined as criminal and legally equivalent to rape perpetrated by other persons. This measure is even being implemented in practice. After many years of lobbying by women's groups, the penalty and family laws finally acquired provisions against domestic violence and established the possibility of restraining orders, as well as requirements for psychological treatment for violent behavior within the family. With these changes, the prosecutor is obliged "to react in a case of heavy bodily harms inflicted within family members." Before this, it was up to the injured persons to press charges.

Rape

In 1999, there were 245 reported cases of sexual violence in Croatia; among them 100 have been reported as rape. Out of that, 115 persons have been convicted, among them 41 for rape. The most frequent punishment for rape did not exceed 3 years in prison (8 persons sentenced to 6–12 months in prison, 11 to 1–2 years, 8 to 2–3 years, 9 to 3–5 years, 4 to 5–10 years, 1 to 10 to 15 years).[19]

As of 1997, spousal rape (both in traditional marriage or common-law marriage) was criminalized and became the legal equivalent to rape perpetrated by other persons. In the case of marital rape, however, the victim herself needs to press charges against the perpetrator, whereas in other cases the charges are pressed through the official channels.

Trafficking in Women and Children

In contrast to other countries in the region, it seems that Croatia is primarily a transit country for women trafficked for sexual exploitation and only to a limited extent a destination country. Since 1999, twenty-four cases of trafficking in women have been recorded in Croatia and some twelve women from Croatia have been found in Spain, Switzerland, and Italy, the latter being the main country of destination for women who are in transit through Croatia.[20]

On the other hand, it is difficult to determine the scale of the problem since the information on trafficking is not easily available. As of May 2001, there is a national committee against trafficking in people involving both governmental and nongovernmental organizations and working on raising awareness and prevention of the problem.

War and Military Repression

According to the official estimates of the Croatian authorities, during the war period (1991–1995) some 15,500 people got killed or are reported missing and 37,000 have been wounded; the estimates on civilians killed or wounded range from 34 percent to 64 percent. There is no precise data on the number of victims on the Serbian side, although it can be estimated that it is at least the same as that on the Croatian side.[21]

Women have been affected primarily as displaced persons (at the beginning of war, within Croatia) and as refugees (Croats from Bosnia and Herzegovina and Serbs who fled from Croatia to other parts of the former Yugoslavia in the summer of 1995), as well as victims of sexual violence. In 1994, the UN Commission of Experts released a report claiming 4,500 documented cases of rape and sexual violation both in Bosnia and Herzegovina and Croatia, while at the same time giving credibility to the estimation of 20,000 women being violated that was stated in a report by the EC Investigative Mission of Experts in February 1993.[22]

Most internally displaced Croats have returned to their homes. At the end of 2002, most of the 350,000 displaced Croatian Serbs had still not returned home. Property issues remain the main obstacle to sustainable return, with thousands of returnees finding their prewar homes destroyed or occupied by others. Difficult economic situations in the areas formerly affected by war (e.g., a lack of employment opportunities and the closure of many factories) also contribute to the slow process of return.

OUTLOOK FOR THE TWENTY-FIRST CENTURY

The Republic of Croatia in the long run aspires to become a member of the European Union, and so the situation of women will very much be influenced by all the legal and economic requirements that the country needs to fulfill within the process of European integration. In this process, it will be critical for feminist and women's organizations to be strong enough to keep up the pressure from below.

NOTES

1. Croatian Bureau of Statistics, www.dzs.hr/Eng/FirstRelease/firstrelease.htm.

2. The privatization process is moving the economy from a largely socialist one to a market economy, which necessitated a shift from public to private ownership of productive resources.

3. Croatian Bureau of Statistics.

4. The results of the last census have been contested regarding ethnic composition and religious denomination since it is presumed that a large number of minority members, especially those of Serbian origin, decided to declare themselves as Croatians.

5. Croatian Bureau of Statistics.

6. World Bank, "Genderstats," http://genderstats.worldbank.org.

7. See http://idea.int/balkans/surveys.cfm.

8. Maja Vađić, "Govor brojki: Analiza statističkih podataka o zastupljenosti žena u obrazovanju," Kruh I ruže, br. 1, proljeće 1994.

9. This refers to the age group up to thirty-nine years. Among younger university graduates, there are even more women: 65 percent up to the age of twenty-four, 61.4 percent up to the age of twenty-nine, and 59 percent up to the age of thirty-four. See Večernji list www.vecernji-list.hr/SPEKTAR/2002/07/14/Pages/zene.html.

10. UNESCO, www2.unesco.org/wef/countryreports/croatia/rapport_2_2.htm.

11. Jagoda Milidrag-Smid, "The impact of privatization and structural adjustment on women's status, the example of Croatia," Znet, July 8, 2002, www.zmag.org/content/showarticle.cfm?SectionID=12&ItemID=2085.

12. Inga Tomić-Koludrović and Suzana Kunac, Rizici modernizacije. Žene u Hrvatskoj devedesetih (The Risks of Modernization: Women in Croatia in the 1990s) (Split, Croatia: Udruga građana Stope nade, 2000).

13. See the table, "Population-Basic Indicators," Croatian Bureau of Statistics, www.dzs.hr.

14. Croatian National Government, www.vlada.hr.

15. Directory can be found online at: www.zinfo.hr. Crow E-Zine also keeps a regularly updated list of women's groups and organizations.

16. Bagić, Op.cit.

17. International Helsinki Federation for Human Rights, Women 2000: An Investigation into the Status of Women's Rights in Central and South-Eastern Europe and the Newly Independent States (Vienna: International Helsinki Federation for Human Rights, 2000), www.ihf-hr.org/reports/women/croatia.pdf.

18. Karlovak and Rovinj.

19. Maja Mamula and Đurđica Kolarec, Seksualno nasilje (Sexual violence) (Zagreb, Croatia: Centar za žene žrtve rata, 2001), 43–44.

20. Barbara Limanowska, Trafficking in Human Beings in Southeastern Europe (New York: UNICEF, UNHCHR, and OSCE/ODIHR, 2002), www.unhchr.ch/women/trafficking.pdf.

21. Ozren Žunec, War in Croatia 1991–1995, Part Two: From Sarajevo Truce to Final Operations.

22. Vesna Kesić, "The Status of Rape as a War Crime in International Law: Changes Introduced after the Wars in the Former Yugoslavia and Rwanda" (masters' thesis, New School University, 2001), www.seeline-project.net/resources.htm.

RESOURCE GUIDE

Suggested Reading

Benderly, Jill. "Feminist Movements in Yugoslavia, 1978–1992." In *State–Society Relations in Yugoslavia 1945–1992*, edited by Melissa K. Bokovoy, Jill A. Irvine, and Carol S. Lilly, 183–209. London: Macmillan, 1997.

Bokovoy, Melissa K., Jill A. Irvine, and Carol S. Lilly. *State-Society Relations in Yugoslavia 1945–1992*. London: Macmillan, 1997.

Center for Reproductive Law and Policy (CRLP). *Women of the World: Laws and Policies Affecting Their Reproductive Lives*. New York: Author, 2000.

Ramet, Sabrina P., ed. *Gender and Politics in the Western Balkans: Women and Society, and Politics in Yugoslavia and the Yugoslav Successor States*. University Park: Pennsylvania State University Press, 1999.

Renne, Tanya, ed. *Ana's Land: Sisterhood in Eastern Europe*. Boulder, CO: Westview Press, 1997.

Women 2000. *An Investigation into the Status of Women's Rights in Central and South-Eastern Europe and the Newly Independent States*. Vienna: International Helsinki Federation for Human Rights, 2000. www.ihf-hr.org/reports/women/croatia.pdf.

Videos/Films

The Boy Who Rushed/Dečko kojem se žurilo. 2001. 53 minutes. 35mm. Directed by Biljana Čakić-Veselić. Produced by FACTUM. Language: Croatian (available with English subtitles). Order information: nenad.puhovski@iod.tel.hr. Phone: (+385-1) 4854 823. Fax: (+385-1) 4856 455. An intimate story of a filmmaker searching for her brother who disappeared during the recent war in Croatia. Her search becomes in many ways parallel to that of her grandmother, whose husband was killed during World War II.

Distorted Reflections/Iskrivljeni odrazi. 2000–2001. 30 minutes. Mini DV. Directed by Tatjana Božić. Produced by Fade In, B.a.B.e. Language: Croatian (available with English subtitles). Order information: babe@zamir.net. A documentary on distorted images of women in the Croatian media. Through unusual editing, the film examines stereotypes about women and split messages sent to women on a daily basis through mass media.

Fine Dead Girls/Fine mrtve djevojke. 2002. 77 minutes. Feature (cinemascope, color). Directed by Dalibor Matanić. Produced by Alka Film. Language: Croatian (available with English subtitles). Order information: www.dalibormatanic.com (Nominated for the 2002 Academy Award in the Foreign Language Film Award category). Two students in a concealed lesbian relationship face harsh prejudices of the society that surrounds them when their affiliation is discovered. Very good overview of the current problems in Croatian society.

Women's Voices: The Croatian Case. 1999. 30 minutes. PAL, Beta/VHS. Directed by Sanja Iveković. Produced by Women's Art Center—ELEKTRA. Language: English. Order information: sanjai@zamir.net. The author talks with prominent Croatian feminists, activists, and intellectuals. Their statements about the role of women in the past and present of the region and their personal experience in dealing with the "Western" perception of Eastern Europe are of utmost importance in understanding the sociopolitical situation in Croatia at the time.

Web Sites

Croatian Bureau of Statistics, www.dzs.hr/Eng/FirstRelease/firstrelease.htm.

Crow E-Zine, www.crowmagazine.com.
An Internet women's magazine published since 1998. It covers a wide variety of women's issues from a feminist perspective. Articles are published both in Croatian and in English.

The South Eastern European Women's Legal Initiative, www.seeline-project.net/reports.htm.

Organizations

B.a.B.e.
Vlaska 79/III, 10000
Zagreb, Croatia
Phone/Fax: (+385-1) 4611 686
Email: babe@zamir.net
Web site: www.babe.hr

A women's human rights group working in Croatia. The word "Babe" (pronounced *Bah-beh*) in Croatian also means "old hag." The women of B.a.B.e. want to give new meaning to this ugly name that is used against women.

Center for Women's Studies
Berislavićeva 12, 10000
Zagreb, Croatia
Phone/Fax: (++385-1) 48-72-406
Email: zenstud@zamir.net
Web site: www.zenstud.hr

Founded in 1995 by feminist scholars, activists, and artists, the Center for Women's Studies in Zagreb is an independent educational center offering a place for academic discussion on women's and feminist issues. Currently there are no women's studies programs within the Croatian regular university system, only individual courses in some social science and humanities departments. The center is involved in establishing a regular undergraduate program at the Faculty of Arts and Letters in Zagreb.

Women's Infoteka (Ženska Infoteka)
Varšavska 16, 10000
Zagreb, Croatia
Phone: (385-1) 4830 557
Fax: (385-1) 4830 552
Email: zinfo@zamir.net
Web site: www.zinfo.hr

A women's information and documentation center founded in Zagreb in December 1992 as the first of the sort in Croatia and Eastern Europe. Since 1993, it has published the feminist quarterly *Bread & Roses* in Croatian with extensive summaries in English.

SELECTED BIBLIOGRAPHY

Milidrag-Smid, Jagoda. "The impact of Privatization and Structural Adjustment on Women's Status: The Example of Croatia." *Znet*. July 8, 2002. www.zmag.org/content/showarticle.cfm?SectionID=12&ItemID=2085.

UNESCO. www2.unesco.org/wef/countryreports/croatia/rapport_2_2.htm.

World Bank. "Genderstats." http://genderstats.worldbank.org.

9

THE CZECH REPUBLIC

Marianne A. Ferber and
Phyllis Hutton Raabe

PROFILE OF THE CZECH REPUBLIC

The "Czech Lands," Bohemia, Moravia, and part of Silesia, comprised a province of the Austrian and later Austro-Hungarian Empire for three centuries after they lost their independence early in the seventeenth century. At the end of World War I, they joined with Slovakia to become Czechoslovakia,[1] only to be separated during World War II, then reunited, and then separated again in January 1993 to become the Czech Republic (CR). Surprisingly, in spite of all this turmoil, little fighting has occurred in these territories throughout this long, turbulent period.

The CR covers 78,866 square kilometers, and its population in 2000 included 4,994,000 men and 5,279,000 women.[2] Czechs comprise about 95 percent of the population, Slovaks 3 percent, Poles and Germans 0.5 percent each,[3] Roma 0.33 percent, and Hungarians 0.20 percent.

In 2000, the CR had the ninth-largest proportion of people over seventy-six years of age and the sixth-lowest proportion under fifteen among seventy-six countries. This was the result of both high life expectancy—it ranked four-teenth—and a birthrate of 9.1 live births per 1,000 midyear population—tied for the lowest.[4] The total fertility rate declined from 1.87 in 1989 to 1.16 in 1998.[5]

OVERVIEW OF WOMEN'S ISSUES

The partnership between women and men against a common enemy, initially the relatively benign Austro-Hungarian Empire and later the more malignant modern dictatorships, led women to view men as partners in a common struggle rather than as oppressors. This remains true, even though women have never achieved full equality.[6]

EDUCATION

Opportunities

In the CR, education is the responsibility of the national government. Primary grades 1–5 and secondary grades 6–9 are compulsory and are attended by almost 97 percent of children ages 6–15. After that, there is a choice of gymnasium (college preparatory), secondary vocational, or secondary technical school, then tertiary schools that offer three-year programs. The proportion of secondary school graduates in these schools is very high,[7] and the schools are generally of high quality. Among forty-two countries, Czech students ranked tenth in math and seventh in sciences in the international "Math and Science Achievement of Eighth Graders" competition, higher in both categories than the United States.[8] On the other hand, relatively few young people go to university.

Although Czech schools are not officially segregated, most girls who continue their education past secondary school go to humanities-oriented gymnasia, whereas boys go to ones that emphasize science. Similarly, although 45 percent of university students are women, they disproportionately specialize in traditional women's fields such as languages, sociology, and education.[9]

Literacy

Reflecting the overall high quality of education at all levels, the CR had a 99.9 percent literacy rate as of 1999.

EMPLOYMENT AND THE ECONOMY

Evaluations of the economy of the CR will differ considerably, depending on the emphasis placed on traditional measures of economic success as opposed to other indicators. On the one hand, per capita gross domestic product (GDP) declined from $5,620 in 1996 to $5,189 in 1999,[10] the value of the currency declined, and unemployment rose. On the other hand, indicators of well-being suggest that the CR is doing reasonably well, not only compared with other Central and Eastern European countries but also with EU and North American countries. Presumably at least in part as a result of govern-

Vegetable market, Prague, Czech Republic. Photo © TRIP/Eric Smith.

ment policies, the degree of inequality in the Czech economy remains modest compared to other Central and Eastern European countries, and even more so when compared to the United States.[11]

Job/Career Opportunities

Women in the CR have by no means achieved equality with men in the labor market.[12] Not only is there considerable occupational segregation but also women are substantially underrepresented at higher levels within occupations.[13] Women in the CR have been surprisingly complacent about, or even unaware of, their inferior position in the labor market. For instance, no less than 48 percent of women thought that their chances in the labor market were about equal with those of men.[14]

Pay

The gender earnings gap is about 25 percent, greater than in many other European and North American countries.[15]

Support for Mothers/Caretakers

Maternal Leave

The government guarantees twenty-eight weeks of maternity leave with pay and access to paid parental leave by both fathers and mothers until the child is three years old.[16] Furthermore, pregnant women or mothers of children less than three years old cannot be dismissed except when a business closes.[17]

Daycare

Daycare for infants is now very scarce, but fully 90 percent of children three to six years old are in kindergarten.[18]

Family and Medical Leave

Either parent may work part-time and flexible hours or take off seven days (single parents, thirteen days) per year to care for a sick child.

Social/Government Programs

Family-friendly programs, whether the government provides them or requires employers to do so, also improve the quality of life. Because of strong popular support (especially by women, but also by men), such programs continued even during the early years of transition when centrist and right-leaning parties were in power.

Welfare

In 1999, the government spent as much as 55 percent of its budget, and about 20 percent of GDP, on social security and welfare programs.[19] Therefore, a number of programs have come under attack[20] and more stringent requirements for some benefits have been imposed, including means testing. Also, retirement age is to rise modestly from sixty to sixty-two for men and from fifty-five to fifty-nine for women by 2006.[21]

FAMILY AND SEXUALITY

Gender Roles

Women in the CR are more inclined to view men as partners than as adversaries as the result of women's historically high status in society during their common struggles against common enemies.[22] This attitude is reinforced by the unusual combination of high esteem for women's roles both in the family and as breadwinners.[23] Most Czech women say that they derive identity from their job, would not give it up even if they did not need the income,[24] and do not agree that "being a housewife is just as fulfilling as working for pay."[25] They are clearly unwilling to choose between job and family but rather take pride in combining the two.[26]

Consequently, although they do the lion's share of household work and childcare (see Table 9.1), women's labor force participation rate in the CR

Table 9.1

Division of Household Activities (in Percentages) among Economically Active Spouses or Partners as Reported by Men and Women in the Czech Republic

Task/Sex	Usually or always the woman	Both the same	Usually or always the man
Washing clothes			
M	93.1	5.8	1.2
W	96.7	2.1	1.3
Minor repairs			
M	38.6	23.9	37.5
W	48.3	22.0	29.7
Caring for sick			
M	65.8	34.2	0.9
W	69.3	30.3	0.4
Everyday shopping			
M	63.6	32.9	3.5
W	71.3	23.2	5.5
Cooking			
M	60.3	36.2	3.5
W	65.1	32.4	2.5

Source: A. Krizková, "The Division of Labor in Czech Households in the 1990s," *Czech Sociological Review* 9, no. 1 (spring 2001): 85–98.

declined only modestly after 1989; for women between ages thirty-five and fifty-four, it remains as high as 87.9 percent.[27] In Western Europe, this rate is approached only in the Scandinavian countries, but there the proportion of women working part-time ranges from 20 percent to over 40 percent, whereas it remains well below 10 percent in the CR.[28] The main adjustment that Czech women have made to the problem of "the double burden" has been to severely reduce the number of children they have.

Marriage

During the 1990s, the divorce rate increased so much that by the middle of the decade every third marriage was expected to break up,[29] but the marriage rate at 5.2 remains about average and the very low proportion of children born to single women together with the very high proportion of pregnant brides[30] is consistent with the view that "marriage and family are still seen . . . as the most attractive option."[31]

Reproduction

Sex Education

The CR report for the period 1995–1999 on the Convention on the Elimination of All Forms of Discrimination notes that the Society for Family

Planning and Sexual Education operates a telephone advice line for family planning. Focused on methods of reliable contraceptives, it also offers help in solving more immediate and critical problems such as unwanted pregnancies and complications from abortions. Although the society is a nongovernmental organization, it receives financial support from the Ministry of Education as part of the National Health Program.

Contraception and Abortion

Abortions are legal, but minors must have parental consent.[32]

Initially, one reason for its low birthrate was that the CR, unlike a number of other Central and Eastern European countries, continues to have very liberal abortion laws. It has been estimated that in the early 1990s every third pregnancy was aborted.[33] Even the Catholic Czech Conference of Bishops accepted that "when there are 189,000 abortions performed annually, it would be impossible suddenly to reduce the number to zero."[34] Since then, the number has declined substantially, from 126,507 in 1990 to 46,022 in 1997.[35] The abortion rate (per 1,000 women) declined from 1.59 in 1988 to 0.59 in 1997,[36] and the number of abortions per 100 live births declined from 49.2 to 41.3, as fees for abortions were increased and contraception was made more readily available.[37]

Teen Pregnancy

Paralleling the general decline in total fertility from 1.87 in 1989 to 1.16 in 1998, the fertility rates of young women 17–22 years of age declined by more than half, and the already low fertility rate of girls 14 to 19 dropped even lower.[38] The out-of-wedlock birth rate remained very low,[39] while the percent of children born within eight months after marriage declined somewhat from 53 percent in 1989 to 47 percent in 1998.[40] This decline in premarital conception may be related to women's postponing of marriage and childbirth[41] as indicated by the rise in the average age of the mother at first birth from 22 to 24.[42]

HEALTH

Health Care Access

Men and women of the CR have a life expectancy of 76.7 (71.1 for men and 78.1 for women), exceeded by only thirteen countries, and the CR ranks eighth in low infant mortality at 5.6 per 1,000 as compared to 6.2 in the United States.[43] Obviously, these accomplishments must in substantial part be credited to high-quality universal health care.

Table 9.2
Development of the Incidence of Venereal Diseases and
HIV-positive Persons

	1991		1994		1997	
	Men	Women	Men	Women	Men	Women
Syphilis	111	124	172	181	234	279
Gonorrhea	4182	2964	1760	1099	662	387
Lymphogranuloma venerum	0	0	0	0	0	0
Ulcus molle	0	0	0	0	0	0
HIV-positive	11	1	30	8	49	14

Source: Second Periodical Report on the Fulfillment of the Convention on the Elimination of
All Forms of Discrimination against Women in the Czech Republic over the Period 1995
to June 1999.

Diseases and Disorders

AIDS

The growth in prostitution and sex trafficking that has occurred since
the collapse of the Soviet bloc and opening to the West has led to increases
in HIV and other sexually transmitted diseases, as indicated in Table 9.2.

POLITICS AND LAW

The CR is a democratic republic with an elected legislature, a prime
minister who is head of the government, and a president who is head of
state.[44] Left-leaning political parties are strong and soon recovered from
their low standing directly after the "velvet revolution." In 2002, perhaps
as a result of the increase in unemployment and threatened cutbacks in
social programs,[45] the Social Democratic Party received 30.7 percent of the
vote (up from 4.1 percent in 1990), which was large enough to enable it
to form the government. Even the reformed Communist Party received
18.5 percent of the vote (up from 13.2 percent in 1990). In addition, the
centrist parties are reported to have moved somewhat to the left over the
last decade.[46]

Suffrage

As a result of women's prominent role in the nineteenth-century struggle
for independence, notably in perpetuating the Czech language and establishing a Czech literature, women had a relatively favorable position in the
new country and were, without debate, accorded the right to vote and to
stand for office in 1918, when the country was founded.[47]

Political Participation

Women have been surprisingly complacent about their very low representation among elected officials at the local as well as the national levels, and for the most part they claim that they are not interested in holding political office. This is usually explained as the result of the years under communism, when their "family responsibilities" enabled them to opt out of the generally disdained party activities.

Women's Rights

Feminist Movements

As for the attitude of Czech women toward feminism, it has so far mainly ranged from indifference to hostility. This is not really surprising because feminism was reviled by communists as a bourgeois device for creating divisions within the working class and has been ridiculed by Czech men.[48] The question is how long it will be before Czech women see through these self-serving arguments from people who find it advantageous to "keep women in their place." Some insiders who have the benefit of inside observation expect feminism to gain wider acceptance. There has already been some support for what is termed "sane feminism."[49] Others expect that as the conditions women face become more like those in the West, their views are likely to become more like those in the West as well, and they will increasingly acknowledge their thus far hidden feminist convictions.[50]

Lesbian Rights

There are no restrictions on lesbian rights in the CR and little prejudice, especially in comparison to the prejudices against feminism.[51] The sexual revolution there was generated, in part, by the work of the Union of all Organizations of Homosexual Citizens (SOHO). Among its accomplishments was successfully lobbying for the lowering of the age of consent for homosexuals to fifteen in accordance with the law for heterosexuals.[52]

RELIGION AND SPIRITUALITY

Virtually all of the population is Christian,[53] 39 percent of them Catholic,[54] but in spite of the increased influence of the Catholic Church during the communist period because of its resistance to an unpopular government, the CR "might be the most secularized country in Europe."[55] This was evident in their responses to a 1994 survey: 64 percent of men and 55 percent of women responded that they had no religion, and 59 percent of men and 54 percent of women answered that they never attended religious services. Only 7 percent of men and 8 percent of women said they attended services once a week.[56]

Women's Roles

Before the fall of communism in 1989, the "underground" Catholic Church responded to the shortage of priests in Czechoslovakia by permitting some married men and even some women to be ordained. Since then, the Church has refused to confirm them as priests and offered to ordain them as deacons instead. The married men also had the option of joining the Greek Orthodox Church, whose priests are usually married.

VIOLENCE

Domestic Violence

Although there are no official statistics on the extent of the problem of domestic violence in the CR, one can safely assume that the situation is not unlike that in Western Europe. Recognition of the problem came in the 1990s with the work of nongovernmental organizations to enlighten the general public and the state authorities.[57] Today, much of the funding for these organizations comes from foreign countries.[58] In 1998, the government listed domestic violence as a priority issue in its efforts to promote gender equality. Despite its expressed priority, the state and municipal governments have done little to support women's centers, to publicize the problem, to change laws, or to assist victims. Police officers, untrained in dealing with domestic violence victims, consider it to be a mostly private problem.[59]

Rape/Sexual Assault

In a survey of sexual behavior in the CR, 11.6 percent of women reported having experienced sexually aggressive behavior, 3.4 percent of them more than once. Highlighting the problem of domestic rape, most of these experiences occurred between domestic partners, whereas only 10 percent of the assaults were committed by a stranger. Of Czech men, 4.8 percent responded positively to the question of whether they had ever forced a woman to have sexual contact. The most common form of these forced contacts was vaginal coitus. Data from this survey indicate that police assault and rape statistics seriously undercount their occurrence, since only 3.4 percent of the offenses were reported to police.[60]

Female victims of rape and other forms of violence against women are increasingly receiving assistance in connection with recently instituted programs to assist crime victims in general.[61] Sexual offender treatment programs, instituted as early as 1976, include inpatient and outpatient treatment. The relatively low recidivism rate of under 20 percent provides some evidence of their success.[62]

Trafficking in Women and Children

The sharp rise in prostitution and pornography in the CR is part of a general trend in the postcommunist period in Central and Eastern Europe.[63] While prostitution has been decriminalized; it is tied to increases in sexually transmitted diseases as well as criminal activities such as procurement, violence against women, and sex trafficking.[64]

The penal code states that the "person, who lures, hires or transports a woman abroad with the intention of using her for sexual intercourse with another person" commits the crime of trafficking in women. Sentencing is more severe if the trafficker commits the offense as a member of an organized group, against a woman under eighteen, or with intent to use the woman for prostitution.

Although trafficking in women is not statistically monitored, it is clear that Czech women are victims of this crime and that the CR is also a country of transit and destination for trafficked persons from other countries. The International Organization for Migration finds that the largest groups of forced prostitutes in Austria and the Netherlands come from the CR. Czech women are also the third-largest trafficked group in Germany. The Czech Interior Ministry says that most of the women being brought to the CR are trafficked from other Eastern European countries by organized crime groups.

Trafficked women are often enticed to leave their countries with false promises. When they arrive in the CR, they are forced into prostitution by threats and violence. The traffickers make a point of taking their documents, thus making them totally dependent on their "owners." Most prostitutes have a drug problem and nearly all are afraid of cooperating with the police. Typically, the newcomers are taken to the German border areas, where they are rotated among the Czech brothels in order to offer "fresh faces" to customers. After becoming a "used face," a woman is sold into the sex industry in Western countries.

La Strada is registered as a public nonprofit organization that focuses on prevention of prostitution, support of victims, legislation, and dissemination of information. It regards trafficking in women as a crucial human rights issue and thus a violation of women's rights. La Strada is part of an international program for prevention of trafficking in women that also operates in the Netherlands, Poland, Bulgaria, and Ukraine. La Strada began its work in the Czech Republic in 1995 as a project of the ProFem foundation (a Central European consultation center for women's projects) and was registered as an independent organization in 1998.

Publications designed for women who are potential victims of criminal activity and for groups of women at risk are published by the nongovernmental Coordinating Circle for Prevention of Violence against Women (Koordinacní kruh prevence násilí na zenách) and the ProFem Foundation. These publications include materials issued by La Strada that are aimed at prostitutes and young women of different social groups, and brochures on incest and domestic violence published by the ProFem Foundation.[65]

OUTLOOK FOR THE TWENTY-FIRST CENTURY

It has been suggested that entry into the EU, which presumably will occur in January 2004,[66] will improve the status of women in the CR because the CR will have to conform to EU laws requiring equal treatment for men and women. This includes equal access for women and men to training and promotion; prohibition of discrimination and sexual harassment; offering leave, other than for childbirth, to both parents; as well as implementing equal pay for equal work and equal pay for work of equal value. Also, employers will be required to inform workers of all legal regulations concerning unequal treatment. It is not clear, however, how much difference all this will make because the effectiveness of laws always depends on their enforcement, which appears to have been lax with respect to this type of legislation in the EU as well as in the CR.

NOTES

This is to thank Alena Heiltlinger for her assistance in making contact with Czech women, including Hana Haskova, Lois A. Herman, Mirka Holubová, Alena Krizkova, Marcela Linkova, and Linda Sokacova, who were extremely helpful in providing information that would have been difficult to obtain without them.

1. It also included the very small province of Subcarpathian Ruthenia, which at the end of World War II was ceded to the Soviet Union.

2. These figures are from the U.S. Census Bureau, *IDB Summary Demographic Data: Czech Republic* (Washington, DC: U.S. Census Bureau, 2001).

3. Almost all Germans were expelled in 1948 in retaliation for their support of the Munich agreement of 1938 when the allies ceded Sudetenland to Hitler's Germany.

4. United Nations, *Demographic Yearbook* (New York: Author, 2001), Table 1355.

5. Zdenek Pavlik et al., "Population Development in the Czech Republic." *The World's Women* (New York: Author, 2000).

6. Hana Havelková, "A Few Prefeminist Thoughts," in *Gender Politics and Post-Communism*, ed. Nanette Funk and Magda Mueller (New York: Routledge, 1993) 62–73; and Jirina Siklova, "Feminism and the Roots of Apathy," *Social Research* 64, no. 2 (1997): 258–80.

7. *Europa World Yearbook* (London: Europa, 2001).

8. *World Almanac* (New York: The World Almanac Books, 2002).

9. Jirina Siklová, "Are Women in Central and Eastern Europe Conservative?" in Funk and Mueller, 1993, 74–83.

10. European Bank for Reconstruction and Development, *Transition Report* (London: Author, 2000).

11. B. Gustafsson and M. Johanssen, "In Search of Smoking Guns," *American Sociological Review* 64, no. 4 (August 1999): 585–605.

12. It has also been noted that both violence against women and prostitution are problems that are not being adequately addressed. Hana Havelková, "Transitory and Persistent Differences," in *Transitions, Environments, Translations*, ed. Joan W. Scott et al. (New York: Routledge, 1997), 56–62; and Alena Heitlinger, "The Impact of the Transition," in Funk and Mueller, 1993, 95–108.

13. Marianne A. Ferber and Phyllis Hutton Raabe, "Women in the Czech Republic," *Journal of Politics, Culture, and Society* 16, no. 3 (spring 2003): 407–30.

14. Phyllis Hutton Raabe, "Women and Gender," *Czech Sociological Review* 7, no. 2 (fall 1990): 223–30.

15. International Labour Organization, *Yearbook of Labour Statistics* (Author, 2001).

16. Network of East-West Women, "Legal Guide" (Author, 2001).

17. Organization of Economic Cooperation and Development, *Structural Change* (Paris: Author, 1993).

18. *Europa World Yearbook*, 2001.

19. European Bank for Reconstruction and Development, 2000.

20. Milica Antic Gaber, "Politics in Transition," in Scott et al., 1998, 143–52.

21. The Economist Intelligence Unit Limited, *Country Profile* (Author, 2000–2001).

22. Jirina Siklová, "McDonalds, Terminators, Coca-Colas—and Feminism?" in *Ana's Land*, ed. Tanya Renne (Boulder, CO: Westview Press, 1997b), 76–81.

23. Phyllis Hutton Raabe, "Women, Work, and Family," *Community, Work and Family*, 1, no. 1 (1998): 51–63.

24. Siklová, 1993.

25. Raabe, 1998.

26. Havelková, 1993; and Jaroslava Stastná, "New Opportunities in the Czech Republic," *Transition* 1, no. 16 (September 8, 1995): 24–28, 61.

27. The participation rate for women sixteen years of age and over is only 64.9. This is the result of the low labor force participation of young mothers, who are not included in the labor force when they take maternity leaves and the very low retirement age. See Vera Kucharová, "Women and Employment," *Czech Sociological Review* 7, no. 2 (1999): 179–94.

28. International Labour Organization, 2001.

29. Heitlinger, 1995.

30. Ludmila Fialová and Milan Kucera report that by the mid-1990s, half of first children were the product of premarital conception. See Ludmila Fialová and Milan Kucera, "The Main Features of Population Development," *Czech Sociological Review* 5, no. 1 (spring 1997): 93–112.

31. Siklová, 1993.

32. Fialová and Kucera, 1997.

33. As Valentine Moghadam put it, "Abortion was used as a means of contraception rather than a last resort" (4). Valentine Moghadam, ed., *Democratic Reforms and Position of Women* (New York: Clarendon Press, 1993).

34. Heitlinger, 1993, 102.

35. United Nations, *Demographic Yearbook* (New York: Author, 1999).

36. Pavlík et al., 1999, Table 5.3.

37. Stastná, 1995.

38. Pavlík et al., 1999, Table 4.1 and Figure 4.2.

39. Organization for Economic Cooperation and Development, 1993.

40. Pavlík et al., 1999, Table 4.1.

41. Fialová and Kucera, 1997.

42. Pavlík et al., 1999, Figure 4.2.

43. Maternal deaths per live births is another indicator of the quality of health care, but the numbers in most CEE and economically advanced countries are so low that comparisons of rates are not useful. United Nations, 2001.

44. This is essentially a hybrid between the parliamentary system and the U.S. system, in which the president plays the pivotal role.

45. Public opinion polls suggest that it is particularly women who have resisted efforts to dismantle the welfare state that has provided substantial support for the great majority of "prime age" women who combine homemaking and full-time jobs.

46. *EIU—Country Economic News*, 2002. See also, for instance, Raabe, 1998, for evidence in social scientific surveys for family-friendly policies.

47. Another reason for this was Tomás Garrigue Masaryk, the founder and first president of Czechoslovakia. The son of serfs who became a professor at Charles University, Masaryk adopted his American wife's maiden name as his middle name and, together with her, translated John Stuart Mill's *Essay on the Subjugation of Women* into Czech.

48. Notably the famous writer Skvorecky. Also, Czech President Václav Havel termed feminism a refuge for bored housewives and dissatisfied mistresses (cited in Heitlinger, 1995).

49. Elzbieta Matynia notes that *feminism* is a pejorative term, thus some overtly support the term *sane feminism* instead. Elzbieta Matynia, "Women after Communism," *Social Research* 61, no. 2 (summer 1994): 351–77.

50. Havelková, 1996; Siklová, 1993.

51. Siklová, 1999.

52. Malinová, 1995.

53. The small minority of Jews was decimated during the German occupation.

54. *Europa World Yearbook*, 2001.

55. Dusan Luzny and Jolana Navratilová, "Religion and Secularisation in the Czech Republic," *Czech Sociological Review* 9, no. 1 (spring 2001): 85–98.

56. Cermáková and Batnár, 1994.

57. Petra Hejnová, *Survey on the Status of Women* (Prague: Gender Studies, 2000).

58. Siklová, 1999.

59. Hejnová, 2000.

60. Weiss and Zverina, 1999.

61. Havelková, 1997.

62. Weiss, 1999.

63. Heitlinger, 1995.

64. Petra Hejnová, *Survey on the Status of Women* (Prague: Gender Studies, 2000), gender.office@ecn.cz.

65. *Second Periodical Report on the Fulfillment of the Convention on the Elimination of All Forms of Discrimination against Women in the Czech Republic over the Period 1995 to June 30, 1999* (Prague: Gender Studies, 1999).

66. Network of East-West Women, 2001.

RESOURCE GUIDE

Suggested Reading

Cermáková, Marie, ed. *The Position of Czech Women in the Society of the 1990s in the Spectrum of Research*. Special issue. *Czech Sociological Review* 7, no. 2 (fall 1999). www.soc.cas.cz.

Cermáková, Marie, Hana Haskova, Alena Krizkova, Marcela Linkova, Hana Harikova, and Martina Musilova. *Relations and Changes of Gender Differences in the Czech Society in the 90's*. Prague: Institute of Sociology, Academy of Sciences of the Czech Republic, 2000. www.soc.cas.cz.

"The Czech Republic." In *Europa World Yearbook*. London: Europa Publications, 2001.

Grun, Carola, and Stephan Klasen. "Growth, Income Distribution and Well-Being in Transition Economies." *Economics of Transition* 9, no. 2 (2001): 359–94.

Hejnová, Petra. *Survey on the Status of Women*. Prague: Gender Studies, 2000. gender.office@ecn.cz.

Network of East-West Women. *Legal Guide on Women's Rights in the Czech Republic: Labor Law*. Author, 2001. www.neww.org.

Raabe, Phyllis H. "Women, Work, and Family in the Czech Republic — and Comparisons with the West." *Community, Work & Family*, 1, no. 1: 51–63.

Second Periodical Report on the Fulfillment of the Convention on the Elimination of All Forms of Discrimination against Women in the Czech Republic over the Period 1995 to June 30, 1999. Prague: Gender Studies, 1999. www.gender@ecn.cz.

Siklová, Jirina. "McDonald's, Terminators, Coca Cola Ads — and Feminism?" In *Ana's Land: Sisterhood in Eastern Europe*, edited by Tanya Renne, 76–81. Boulder, CO: Westview Press, 1997.

Web Sites

Czech Sociological Review (in English), The Institute of Sociology, Prague, www.soc.cas.cz

"Gender and Sociology," The Institute of Sociology, Prague, genderteam@soc.cas.cz.

Gender Studies, Prague, gender.office@ecn.cz.

Kosmas: Czechoslovak and Central European Journal, www.english.tamu.edu/pubs/kosmas.
Published biannually by the Czechoslovak Society of Arts and Sciences.

Organizations

There are numerous women's organizations (and related NGOs) in the Czech Republic. They range from those within the Social Democratic Party (Social Democratic Women) and some that are concerned with the environment (Prague Mothers) to others concerned with violence against women (e.g., White Safety Circle) (see *Altos and Sopranos — A Pocket Handbook of Women's Organizations*, Gender Studies Centre, 1994). For current information and addresses of Czech Republic women's organizations, contact the Gender Studies Center (gender.office@ecn.cz).

SELECTED BIBLIOGRAPHY

The Economist Intelligence Unit Limited. *EIU — Country Economic New*. 2002.

European Bank for Reconstruction and Development (EBRD). *Transition Report*. London: Author, 2000.

Ferber, Marianne A., and Phyllis Hutton Raabe. "Women in the Czech Republic: Feminism, Czech Style." *Journal of Politics, Culture and Society* 16, no. 3 (spring 2003): 407–30.

Fialová, Ludmila, and Milan Kucera. "The Main Features of Population Development in the Czech Republic during the Transformation of Society." *Czech Sociological Review* 5, no. 1 (spring 1997): 93–112.

Gaber, Milica Antic. "Politics in Transition." In *Transitions, Environments, Translations: Feminisms in International Politics*, edited by Joan W. Scott, Cora Kaplan, and Debra Keates, 143–52. New York: Routledge, 1998.

Gustafsson, B., and M. Johanssen. "In Search of Smoking Guns: What Makes Income Inequality Vary over Time in Different Countries?" *American Sociological Review* 64, no. 4 (August 1999): 585–605.

Havelková, Hana. "A Few Prefeminist Thoughts." In *Gender Politics and Post-Communism*, edited by Nanette Funk and Magda Mueller, 62–73. New York: Routledge, 1993.

———. "Abstract Citizenship? Women and Power in the Czech Republic." *Social Politics. International Studies in Gender, State & Society* 3, no. 2–3 (summer 1996): 343–60.

———. "Transitory and Persistent Differences: Feminism East and West." In *Transitions, Environments, Translations: Feminisms in International Politics*, edited by Joan W. Scott, Cora Kaplan, and Debra Keates, 56–62. New York: Routledge.

Heitlinger, Alena. "The Impact of the Transition from Communism on the Status of Women in the Czech and Slovak Republics." In *Gender Politics and Post-Communism*, edited by Nanette Funk and Magda Mueller, 95–108. London: Routledge, 1993.

———. "Women's Equality, Work, and Family in the Czech Republic." In *Family, Women, and Employment in Central-Eastern Europe*, edited by Barbara Lobodzinská, 87–99. Westport, CT: Greenwood Press, 1995.

Hejnová, Petra. *Project of International Helsinki Federation*. Edited version. Prague: Gender Studies, July 2000.

International Labour Organization (ILO). *Yearbook of Labour Statistics*. Geneva: Author, 2001.

Krizková, Alena. "The Division of Labor in Czech Households in the 1990s." *Czech Sociological Review* 7, no. 2 (1999): 205–14.

Kucharová, Vera. "Women and Employment." *Czech Sociological Review* 7, no. 2 (1999): 179–94.

Luzny, Dusan, and Jolana Navratilová. "Religion and Secularisation in the Czech Republic." *Czech Sociological Review* 9, no. 1 (spring 2001): 85–98.

Malinová, Hana. "The Recent Rise in Prostitution in the Czech Republic." *Journal of Community Health* 20 (April 1995): 213–18.

Matynia, Elzbieta. "Women after Communism: A Bitter Freedom." *Social Research* 61, no. 2 (summer 1994): 351–77.

Moghadam, Valentine, ed. *Democratic Reforms and Position of Women in Transitional Economies*. New York: Clarendon Press, 1993.

Network of East-West Women. "Legal Guide on Women's Rights in the Czech Republic: Labor Law." August 2001.

Organization for Economic Cooperation & Development. *Structural Change in Central and Eastern Europe: Labour Market and Social Policy Implications*. Paris: Author, 1993.

Pavlík, Zdenek, et al. "Population Development in the Czech Republic." Department of Geography and Geodemography, Faculty of Science, Charles University, 1999.

Raabe, Phyllis H. "Women, Work, and Family in the Czech Republic—and Comparisons with the West." *Community, Work & Family* 1, no. 1 (1998): 51–63.

———. "Women and Gender in the Czech Republic and Cross-National Comparisons." *Czech Sociological Review* 7, no. 2 (fall 1999): 223–30.

Siklová, Jirina. "Are Women in Central and Eastern Europe Conservative?" In *Gender Politics and Post-Communism*, edited by Nanette Funk and Magda Mueller, 74–83. London: Routledge, 1993.

———. "Feminism and the Roots of Apathy in the Czech Republic." *Social Research* 64, no. 2 (1997a): 258–80.

———. "McDonalds, Terminators, Coca Cola Ads—and Feminism?" In *Ana's Land. Sisterhood in Eastern Europe*, edited by Tanya Renne, 76–81. Boulder, CO: Westview Press, 1997b.

Siklová, Jirina. "Women and Human Rights in Post-Communist Countries. The Situation in the Czech Republic." In *Planning and Human Rights*, edited by Tovi Fenster, 153–676. New York: Routledge, 1999.

Stastná, Jaroslava. "New Opportunities in the Czech Republic." *Transition* 1, no. 16 (September 8, 1995): 24–28, 61.

United Nations. *Demographic Yearbook*. New York: Author, 1999.

———. *The World's Women*. New York: Author, 2000.

U.S. Census Bureau. "IDB Summary Demographic Data Czech Republic." Washington, DC: Author, 2001.

Weiss, Peter. "Assessment and Treatment of Sex Offenders in the Czech Republic and in Eastern Europe." *Journal of Interpersonal Violence* 14, no. 4 (April 1999): 411–27.

Weiss, Peter, and Jaroslav Zverina. "Experiences with Sexual Aggression within the General Population in the Czech Republic." *Archives of Sexual Behavior* 28, no. 3 (June 1999): 265–67.

10

DENMARK

Lynn Walter

PROFILE OF DENMARK

Denmark's 5.3 million inhabitants live within fifty-two kilometers of the Baltic or North Seas that moderate the climate of their northern land. The sea and the land were once their main sources of livelihood. Today, they provide employment for only the 3.3 percent of the population still earning their living directly in agriculture, forestry, or fishing, while over 70.2 percent are employed in services and 26.4 percent in industry.[1] The Kingdom of Denmark includes Greenland and the Faroe Islands, although both now have home rule. Margrethe II, the reigning constitutional monarch, has largely ceremonial functions.

Denmark is known for its strongly egalitarian and democratic political culture. Its single-chamber parliament—the Folketing—is democratically elected within a multiparty system.[2] In 2002, eight political parties were represented in the Folketing, led by the Liberal Party and Prime Minister Anders Fogh Rasmussen.

Until late into the twentieth century, modern Denmark came close to being a nation-state with a single nationality and religion. Immigrants and their descendants even today make up only

7.4 percent of the population. In 1998, Turkish residents were the largest minority group, numbering 37,500 people, and those from the Yugoslav successor states were second with 34,000.[3] Danes typically are quite secular in their outlook on life; nevertheless, 85.4 percent are members of the national church—the Lutheran Evangelical Church. The next largest religious group is Muslim—approximately 119,000 people (2 percent)—followed by Roman Catholic with 35,000.[4]

Internationally, Denmark is a member of the Nordic Council, NATO, the UN, and the European Union, but it has rejected membership in the European Monetary Union. It ranks number one among nations in the percent of gross national income devoted to development assistance—1.06 percent in 1999.[5]

Danes are supported by an extensive social welfare system in which health care, education, and social security are universal entitlements of national citizenship. Support for such programs is very high among voters, despite relatively high taxation levels. Recently, however, resistance has surfaced on the part of some citizens to providing social welfare benefits to new immigrants and refugees.

Since the life expectancy for women is 79.0 and only 74.2 for men, the population is 50.6 percent female.[6] The infant mortality rate is 4.2 per 1,000 live births in 1999, and the maternal mortality rate is 7.4 per 100,000 live births in 1996.[7] Although at 1.7 the total fertility rate falls below the population replacement level, it is, nevertheless, one of the highest among European Union countries.[8]

OVERVIEW OF WOMEN'S ISSUES

Danish women have already achieved equal legal rights in education, employment, political participation, and family relations. Combine this with a high standard of living and first-rate, publicly funded education, health, childcare, maternity leaves, and social security, as well as a relatively equitable representation in Parliament, and they must rank among the most fortunate worldwide. Even so, Danes continue to work for more gender equity in the workplace and the family, focusing on such problems as wage discrepancies, job segregation, and domestic violence; for legal rights to be fully realized; and for deep-rooted gender-discriminatory practices to be exposed and challenged.

Danish woman takes advantage of Amsterdam's White Bicycle program. Photo © Painet.

In this struggle women's solidarity is crosscut by class, ethnicity, immigrant status, and sexualities that shape their outlook. Nevertheless, since they are the majority of the employees as well as the clients of the advanced social welfare state, women share a concern that cutbacks in public sector social expenditures, whether the result of globalization, Europeanization, or economic downturn, will be especially distressing for women and may lead to retreats from their progress toward gender equity.

EDUCATION

Opportunities

All Danish children have access to free public education from the first stage of preschool to the compulsory ninth and optional tenth years, resulting in an estimated 98–99 percent literacy rate.[9] After the basic-level education, 86.5 percent of recent cohorts (those age 25–29 in 2000) decided to continue to the upper secondary–stage academic and vocational educations; 61.2 percent stopped there, and 25.3 percent went on to some form of higher education.[10] All levels are tuition free, and students over eighteen years of age are supported with a student stipend.

Access to education was one of the first issues that the Danish women's movement raised in the nineteenth century. In 1859 women gained the right to a primary education and in 1875 to attend universities;[11] and they have gradually increased their numbers in higher education. Today, at the upper secondary level, girls are more likely than boys to choose the general academic track (especially the language as opposed to the mathematics track) and to go on to higher education. Although the numbers have increased, they are less likely than men to attend upper secondary vocational schools or to attain advanced degrees that give them specific professional-level qualifications. Almost all fields in vocational and professional education are dominated by one sex or the other; among the male-dominated fields are transportation, construction, and engineering,[12] and women predominate in social services.

The second wave of the women's movement, which began in the late 1960s, questioned the practices that lead to the identification of fields of study as masculine or feminine and their impact on women's careers and wages. The rise in their awareness of gender stereotypes has contributed to more women entering male-dominated fields, though significant differences remain. The development of the field of Women's Studies was advanced by the new women's movement and continues to very actively research questions of gendered inequalities. Unfortunately, government support for a relatively new center for research on women was recently eliminated as a budget reduction measure. Women constitute only 21 percent of university teachers,[13] though their numbers are increasing among those completing doctoral degrees.[14]

Literacy

The functional literacy rate for the country is 98–99 percent.[15]

EMPLOYMENT AND THE ECONOMY

With 73.6 percent of women age 16–66 in the labor force in 2000 (compared to 81.4 percent of men), Denmark ranks with the other Nordic countries as among the highest in Europe.[16] However, the rate for ethnic minority women is much lower at 45 percent.[17] The overall unemployment rates were relatively low—5.3 percent for women and 4.2 percent for men in 2002.[18] There has been a steep decline in the percentage of women who are working part-time from 1978, when 48 percent of employed women worked part-time, to 1998, when only 17 percent were.[19] The combination of lower pay, more leaves of absence, and more part-time employment means that women, on average, also have smaller pensions than men.

Job/Career Opportunities

The labor market in Denmark is very sex-segregated: in 2000 65.3 percent of women were employed in the public sector, whereas 62.6 percent of men were employed in the private sector.[20] Within the public sector, women make up 75 percent of the municipal employees but only 10 percent of the top leaders of the municipalities, illustrating both horizontal and vertical job segregation. In skilled crafts, transportation, agriculture, fishing, and industry, men make up 68–90 percent of employees.[21] The reasons for the differences in types of employment between women and men include divergent educational tracks, the more flexible accommodation of public sector jobs to parental responsibilities, and entrenched gender stereotypes favoring male-dominated managerial positions and female caregiving.

Pay

The wage gap between women and men varies from 12 to 20 percent for the labor market as a whole,[22] with the public sector gap at 10 percent and the private sector gap at 17 percent. Much of the gendered wage gap can be attributed to lower wages in the public sector, where, on the other hand, women may benefit from higher paid leaves of absence and more flexible work schedules.[23] In the private sector, however, even after controlling for education, training, seniority, and level of position, women's wages are 12 percent lower than men's.

Working Conditions

Union density is 82 percent,[24] and wages and working conditions are usually considered bargainable issues as opposed to issues for legislative action. Thus, the Equal Pay Act (1976) and the Equal Treatment Act (1978) were not enacted until European Union rules called for all member states to do so.

Sexual Harassment

Sexual harassment, prohibited under the Equal Treatment Act and EU regulations, is one issue where the law has been used to address gender inequality in the workplace. In a 1991 study, eleven percent of Danish women reported being sexually harassed at work,[25] which is below the 40–50 percent of women in the EU as a whole.[26]

Support for Mothers/Caretakers

Maternal Leave

Since the 1960s, Denmark has encouraged married women with children to join the labor force by developing social supports for their employment, including maternity, paternity, and parental leaves and publicly funded childcare and after-school programs. As of March 27, 2002, a new law grants mothers four weeks before the birth and fourteen weeks afterwards for maternity leave, and fathers have two weeks' paternity leave. In addition, either the mother or father is entitled to thirty-two more weeks of parental leave.[27] The pay for the leave is determined by labor contract or is set at 90 percent of wages up to the maximum cash benefit of DKK3,020[28] per week in 2002.[29]

Some members of the Union of Women Workers and the Union of Commercial and Clerical Employees, both female-dominated unions, fearing that the recent extension of parental leave will lead more employers to dismiss pregnant employees, propose to strengthen the penalties against it.[30] Since only 2.15 percent of men took more than the two weeks' paternity leave in 2000,[31] members of the Women's Council[32] proposed to require fathers to take more than the two-week leave in order to spread out and thereby diminish the risk that employers would fire pregnant women. The Danish Women's Society,[33] the oldest and currently most prominent feminist organization, asks why Denmark does not establish a special fund to provide financial help to employers who face difficulties when their employees take parental leaves.

Daycare

Daycare coverage has increased from 48 percent of children ages 0–9 in 1987 to 75.4 percent in 1999—55 percent of all children ages 0–2, 90.1 percent of children ages 3–5, and 76.3 percent of children ages 6–9. Denmark is highest in childcare coverage in the EU in the ages 0–2 and 6–9.[34] Daycare is administered by local governments, and costs are subsidized on a sliding scale. Typically, families pay 30–33 percent of the cost[35] with nursery care at DKK2505 and daycare at DKK1969 in 2001.[36] Family Allowance, which goes to the family of each child under eighteen, was DKK12,010 annually per 0–2-year-olds in 2001 and somewhat lower for older children.[37] Additional child allowances go to support each child of single parents and pensioned parents.

FAMILY AND SEXUALITY

Gender Roles

From early in the twentieth century, Nordic countries took the lead in enacting less patriarchal family laws. As early as 1922 and 1925, marriage reform acts in Denmark included equal child custody rights, women's right to property accrued during a marriage, civil marriage, mutual spousal responsibility for support, spousal equality, and no-fault divorce. These reforms, however, remained grounded in the male provider/female caretaker family model.[38]

As more women joined the labor force, women and men in the household were more likely to share the housework. From 1964 when women spent 28.55 hours per week on housework to 1994 when they spent 18.47 hours, men's participation increased from 3.33 hours to 13.72 hours. The pattern repeated itself for girls and boys in the family.[39] However, women continue to do more housework and childcare than men, both at home and in the labor force, where they are the overwhelming majority of childcare workers.

Marriage

The 1960s saw married women's entry into the labor force and the introduction of the dual-earner family model. The marriage rate declined as cohabitation increased. Among 16–29 year olds, 57 percent live in "paperless marriages" (17 percent overall).[40] Marriage is also occurring later in life, at the average age of thirty-three for women and thirty-six for men.[41]

Arranged marriages are sometimes problematic for ethnic minority women brought up in Denmark but expected to marry a foreign man of their parents' choosing. The violence that sometimes occurs in such marriages may be the result of his disapproval of her Danish lifestyle, including broad acceptance of cohabitation and out-of-wedlock births.[42]

Reproduction

The percent of births outside of marriage rose from around 10 percent in the 1970s to 44.9 percent in 1999, reflecting the increase in cohabitation. The percentage of marriages ending in divorce increased from 29 percent in 1960 to 43 percent in 1983[43] and two out of three today.[44] The size of families declined. Families without children at home are 77 percent of all families, and the average household size was 2.2 in 2000.[45]

Sex Education

Sex education has been a compulsory part of primary and lower secondary curricula in public schools since 1972. Information on contraception is available through the national health care system, and local governments fund clinics run by Sex og Samfund, a nongovernmental organization (NGO) focused on family planning and reproductive health.

Contraception and Abortion

Seventy-one percent of women ages 15–49 use contraception.[46] The Danish Women's Society expressed concern over doctors prescribing birth control pills to younger girls because of its potential health risks, its failure to provide protection against sexually transmitted diseases, and its reinforcement of the idea that contraception is the girl's responsibility.[47] Doctors should instead promote condom use, they argued.

Since 1973, abortion on request has been available through the national health system in the first trimester of a woman's pregnancy. After the first trimester, a woman may have a legal abortion by appeal to a committee for specified reasons, including threats to her health, pregnancy by rape or incest, her youth or immaturity, and serious strain on her home life or other children.[48] The abortion rate has fallen from 403 per 1,000 live births in 1980 to 234 per 1,000 in 2000.[49]

Teen Pregnancy

The teen pregnancy rate in 1999 was relatively low at 7.7 live births per 1,000 women ages 15–19.[50]

HEALTH

Health Care Access

Danish residents are covered by a universal, publicly funded, national health care system.

Diseases and Disorders

The Women's Council believes that health authorities have not adequately addressed the role of environmental pollutants like dioxin in increasing cancer occurrences, threatening fertility, and contaminating breast milk.

AIDS

The incidence of AIDS is 0.26 percent for men and .07 percent for women in the 15–49 age group.[51] Sex og Samfund operates a national AIDS hotline, funded through the national health care system.[52] AIDS awareness is part of the primary and secondary school sex education curriculum.

Eating Disorders

Eating disorders have increased among young women, a trend that the Women's Council attributes to negative body images and the extreme emphasis on appearance as a measure of success.[53]

Cancer

Denmark's somewhat lower life expectancies of 79.0 for females and 74.2 for males compared to other EU countries are probably related to higher rates of smoking (27 percent of women in 1999) and related increases in lung cancer.[54] There has also been an increase in breast cancer from 1971 to 1995.[55] It is now the most common cancer among women,[56] and Denmark's is one of the highest rates in Europe.[57]

POLITICS AND LAW

Suffrage

In 1915, the first Danish women's movement of the nineteenth and early twentieth centuries celebrated the fulfillment of women's right to vote and hold political office.

Political Participation

It took the new women's movement of the 1960s and 1970s to bring women into political office in significant numbers. In the last national election in November 2001, 38 percent of the seats in Parliament went to women, the second highest in the world behind Sweden at 45.3 percent.[58] However, the number of women elected to county and municipal offices remained stagnant at 27 percent. And the new Center-Right coalition government has appointed fewer women ministers (28 percent) than the previous Social Democratic administration (45 percent).[59]

Women's Rights

The Equal Pay Act of 1976 and the Equal Treatment Act of 1978 are key equality laws. Along with the new Gender Equality Act of 2002, which consolidates other equality laws, they constitute the major uses of the law as a strategy to promote equality. The laws are focused primarily on labor force issues and secondarily on the composition of appointed public-sector commissions. One example of their impact is that under the 1978 Equal Treatment Act, women who volunteer for the armed services are not excluded from combat.[60]

During the 1970s and 1980s and into the 1990s, three political parties established sex quotas on their membership and elections lists, but since 1996 all of them have abolished that practice. Sex quotas in political parties are one example of "positive discrimination" (i.e., affirmative action), which has always been rather controversial as an equality strategy in Denmark.[61] If the government wishes to use it to address specific gendered issues by "positive" discrimination first, it must obtain special judicial dispensation from the Equal Treatment Act.

Institutional strategies to promote gender equity include the establishment of a Minister for Gender Equality in 1999; and in 2000, the Gender Equality Board, replacing the Equal Status Council with a smaller board, more narrowly focused on hearing complaints of sex discrimination. The Minister for Gender Equality has prioritized the strategy of "mainstreaming," that is, integrating the goal of gender equality into the composition of all governmental and public bodies and into all types of policy formation.

Although women make up 37.5 percent of the Danish seats in the European Parliament,[62] Danish women have had a conflicted attitude toward the impact of Denmark's membership in the European Union, fearing that it might lower the status of Danish women to the EU average.[63] Some also worry that the EU represents a decline in the sovereignty of the national government and a concomitant loss of political power for Danish women at the very moment when they have achieved the most influence on state-level policy.

Feminist Movements

Denmark has also had very important and large women's movements in both the nineteenth and twentieth centuries. The first-wave movement focused on changing discriminatory property, labor, and family laws and gaining the rights to vote and hold office. The new women's movement, which arose in the late 1960s, focused more on raising personal and political consciousness of gender stereotypes and practices and the ways these reinforce inequality. Members of the Redstockings, the main branch of the movement, were quite radical in their challenges to traditional gender roles and identities and in their critique of class as well as gender inequalities. Their movement can be credited with bringing an awareness of gender discrimination to the society as a whole. Existing women's organizations, including the Women's Council, the Danish Women's Society, and the Women Worker's Union, each have programs to encourage and train women to run for political office.[64]

Lesbian Rights

The lesbian movement arose from the Redstockings as a separate movement to work to end discrimination against lesbians and gays. As a result of their and others' work in 1987 and 1989, Denmark passed laws prohibiting discrimination on the basis of sexual orientation in public services and allowing same-sex couples to form civil "registered partnerships" with all the legal rights of married couples.

RELIGION AND SPIRITUALITY

Women's Roles

Since 1947, women have been allowed to be priests in the Lutheran Evangelical Church, the national church of Denmark. Women constituted 800 of the 2,000 priests, and the first woman became a bishop in 1995.[65]

Danes are known for their secular outlook and religious tolerance, evidenced by their collective efforts that saved the Danish Jews from the Holocaust. However, recent immigrants from Islamic countries have occasionally encountered prejudices against their cultural and religious practices. For example, some Muslim young women have won legal actions against employers who fired them for refusing to remove their headscarves.

VIOLENCE

Domestic Violence

It is known that over 4,250 women annually suffer domestic violence. This number is very likely to be low, as one study revealed that only 25 percent of the women who came to a crisis center had reported the abuse to authorities. Women from ethnic minorities are overrepresented in the centers, where they tend to stay longer and return more often. The new women's movement was a catalyst for bringing the hidden problem of domestic violence to light and offering volunteer-run women's shelters and crisis centers. The first was established in 1979, and now there are forty crisis centers around the country. Counties and municipalities are increasingly responsible for funding and operating them.[66]

Rape/Sexual Assault

In 2000 there were 2,800 reported sexual offenses, of which 497 were rapes.[67] In 1999, after several years of effort on the part of women doctors, State Hospital in Copenhagen established a special unit for caring for victims of rape and other sexual assaults, which will also collect better data on the incidents and the nature of the violence.[68]

Trafficking in Women and Children

There have been increases in trafficking of women and girls from Central and Eastern Europe for purposes of prostitution and pornography. Trafficking in people is illegal under Danish law, but adult (18+ years of age) pornography and prostitution are not. The Women's Council has challenged the distinction between forced and voluntary prostitution when it comes to addressing the problem of sex trafficking.[69]

OUTLOOK FOR THE TWENTY-FIRST CENTURY

Sex trafficking is an example of a problem emerging from the new international alignments tied to the expansion of the European Union, the collapse of the Soviet bloc, and the globalization of the economy, which make it increasingly necessary to cross the borders of nations to address women's issues effectively. The EU's placing of women's employment, gender equality, gender "mainstreaming," and social policy on its agenda is a positive sign that its economic priorities may not necessarily come at the cost of greater inequality and cutbacks in social programs. And in 2002, a few Danish women are playing a greater role than ever in defining the issues of women at the level of Europe as a whole. But how the many and diverse communities of women make their voices count in this more distant, more complex, more powerful, and less democratic Union is the challenge of the twenty-first century.

NOTES

1. Organization for Economic Cooperation and Development, *OECD in Figures* (Paris: OECD, 2002), Supplement 1.

2. Of the 179 members, 135 are elected from a party list vote in seventeen multiseat counties, forty seats go to political parties to ensure proportional representation, and two each to Greenland and the Faeroes.

3. Government of Denmark, *National Report*, Regional Population Meeting, Budapest, Hungary, 1998.

4. Denmark's National Home Page, 2002, Denmark.dk (accessed August 24, 2002).

5. OECD, 2002.

6. OECD, 2002; and Statistics Denmark, 2002, www.dst.dk/dst/dstframeset_800_en.asp.

7. Denmark.dk, 2002; Ministries of Foreign Affairs and Social Affairs, *Denmark's National Report on Follow-up to the World Summit on Children* (Copenhagen: Author, 2001).

8. Danmarks Statistik, *Statistical Yearbook* (Copenhagen: Author, 2001).

9. Ministries of Foreign Affairs and Social Affairs, 2001.

10. Eurostat, *The Social Situation in the European Union 2002* (Brussels: European Commission, 2002).

11. Vera Eckhardt, "Demokrati og indflydelse-et kvinderetsligt perspektiv," in *Kvinder, demokrati og indflydelse*, SAMKVIND, Skriftserie 19 (1995): 40–52, 41.

12. Danmarks Statistik, 2001.

13. Tanja Hansen, "Kønnet under uddannelse," 2002, www.Akademikeren.dk (accessed August 5, 2002).

14. Danmarks Statistik og Ligestillingsrådet, *Kvinder og Mænd* (Copenhagen: Danmarks Statistiks, 1999).

15. Ministries of Foreign Affairs and Social Affairs, *Denmark's National Report on Follow-up to the World Summit on Children* (Copenhagen, 2001), 33.

16. Statistics Denmark, 2002; and OECD, 2002.

17. Minister for Gender Equality, *Ministry for Gender Equality's 2002 Perspective and Action Plan* (Copenhagen: Author, 2002).

18. Eurostat, 2002.

19. Danmarks Statistik og Ligestillingsrådet, 1999.

20. Videnscenter for Ligestilling, 2002, www.vidlige.dk (accessed August 26, 2002).

21. Danmarks Statistik og Ligestillingsrådet, 1999, 45–46.

22. The range has to do with how work time is measured, either as hours of work performed or as working hours agreed upon, but not performed, due to paid leaves, vacations, and the like, and what benefits are counted in wage figures.

23. Arbejdsministret & Ligestillingsrådet, *Rapport om lønforskelle mellem kvinder og mænd i Danmark* (Copenhagen: Author, 2000).

24. European Industry Relations Observatory (EIRO), "Trade union density falls," *eiro-online*, 2002b, www.eiro.eurofound.ie/2002/01/InBrief/DK0201159N.html (accessed August 16, 2002).

25. Cristien Bajema, "Denmark," in European Commission, *Sexual Harassment in the Workplace in the European Union* (Brussels: EC, 1998), 63–67.

26. European Commission, 1998.

27. Beskæftigelses Ministeriet, "Fleksibel barselorlov," 2002b, www.bm.dk/barselorlov/default.asp.

28. DKK stands for Danish krone, the national currency. The exchange rate in US$ was 7.57 Danish krone to the dollar on August 30, 2002.

29. Beskæftigelses Ministeriet, "Dagpenge," 2002a, www.bm.dk/dagpenge/; and Ministry of Social Affairs, *Social Policy in Denmark* (Copenhagen: Author, 2001).

30. European Industry Relations Observatory (EIRO), "Increased flexibility for families 'may be a set-back for gender equality'" eiro-online, 2002a, www.eiro.eurofound.ie/2002/03/Features/DK0203102F.html (accessed August 7, 2002).

31. Videnscenter for Ligestilling, 2002.

32. First established in 1899, the Women's Council is an umbrella NGO composed of fifty-two different organizations from political parties, unions, humanitarian groups, feminist organizations, and the like whose goal is "to strengthen women's rights and influence in society and create real equality between women and men."

33. Danish Women's Society, "Velkommen til Dansk Kvindesamfund," 2002, www.kvindesamfund.dk (accessed August 30, 2002).

34. Ministry of Social Affairs, 2001; and Ministry of Foreign Affairs and Equal Status Council, *Equality in Denmark, Toward a New Milennium* (Copenhagen: Author, 1999), and Danmarks Statistik og Ligestillingsrådet, 1999.

35. Ministry of Social Affairs, 2001.

36. Danmarks Statistik, *Data on Denmark* (Copenhagen: Author, 2002).

37. Ministry of Social Affairs, 2001.

38. Bente Rosenbeck, "Modernisation of Marriage in Scandinavia." In *Women's Politics and Women in Politics*, ed. Sølvi Sogner and Gro Hagemann (Oslo: Universitetet i Bergen, Cappelen Akademisk Forlag, 2000), 69–85.

39. Ministry of Foreign Affairs and Equal Status Council, 1999.

40. Eurostat, 2002.

41. Denmark.dk, 2002.

42. Helle Nielsen, *Equality in the Twilight, Danish NGO Shadow Report Prior to Beijing + Five* (Copenhagen: Women's Council, 1999).

43. Eurostat, 2002; and Klaus Petersen, "Socialdemokrati, familiepolitik, velfærdsstat i Danmark, 1930–2000," in *The Nordic Model of Marriage and the Welfare State*, ed. Kari Melby, Anu Pilkänen, Bente Rosenbeck, and Christina Carlsson Wetterberg (Copenhagen, Nord, 2000), 207–40.

44. Denmark's Embassy, 2002, www.denmarkemb.org/her_country.html (accessed July 2, 2002).

45. Eurostat, 2002.

46. International Planned Parenthood Foundation (IPPF), 2002, www.ippf.org (accessed August 29, 2002).

47. Danish Women's Society, "Kondom eller P-piller til piger og meget unge kvinder?," press release, October 9, 2001.

48. Nell Rasmussen, "Denmark," in *Abortion in the New Europe*, ed. Bill Rolston and Anna Eggert (Westport, CT: Greenwood Press, 1994), 69–84.

49. Nordic Medico-Statistical Committee (NOMESCO), 2002, www.nom-nos.dk/NOMESCO.HTM; and United Nations Economic Commission for Europe (UNECE), 2002, www.unece.org/stats/gender/web/.

50. Ministries of Foreign Affairs and Social Affairs, 2001.

51. Ministries of Foreign Affairs and Social Affairs, 2001.

52. IPPF, 2002.

53. Nielsen, 1999.

54. Danmarks Statistik, 2001; and Government of Denmark, 1998.

55. Government of Denmark, 1998.

56. Danmarks Statistik, 2001.

57. Denmark.dk, 2002.

58. Inter-parliamentary Union (IPU), 2002, www.ipu.org.

59. Asse Rieck Sørensen, contribution to the *Newsletter of the ICW* from the Women's Council in Denmark, October 25, 2001, www.kvinderaad.dk/midt_position_paper.htm.

60. NATO, "Denmark," Committee on Women in NATO, 2001, www.nato.int/ims/2001/win/denmark.htm (accessed September 1, 2002).

61. Jacobsen, Helle, "Report from Denmark," in *European Database: Women in Decision-making*, 2002, www.db-decision.de.

62. IPU, 2002.

63. In a 1972 referendum, voters narrowly approved Denmark's entry into the European Union despite a feminist campaign against it. In another national referendum in 1992, the Danes voted by a small margin against the Maastricht treaty, which would strengthen the EU and provide for a common currency.

64. Jacobsen, 2002.

65. Kirkeministeriet, 1999, www.km.dk (accessed September 1, 2002); and Denmark.dk, 2002.

66. Tværministerielle arbejdsgruppe, "Vold mod kvinder" (Copenhagen: Tværministerielle arbejdsgruppe, 2001).

67. Danmarks Statistik, 2002.

68. Kvinderådet, 2000.

69. Nielsen, 1999.

RESOURCE GUIDE

Suggested Reading

Berquist, Christine, et al., eds. *Equal Democracies? Gender and Politics in the Nordic Countries*. Oslo: Scandinavian University Press, 1999.

Matthiessen, Poul Christian. "Family Formation in Denmark." In *Welfare Trends in the Scandinavian Countries*, edited by Erik Jorgen Hansen et al., 320–26. Armonk, NY: M.E. Sharpe, 1993.

Melby, Kari, Anu Pylkkänen, Bente Rosenbeck, and Christina Carlsson Wetterberg, eds. *The Nordic Model of Marriage and the Welfare State*. Copenhagen: Nord, 2000.

Polakow, Valerie. "Who Cares for the Children? Denmark's Unique Child-Care Model." 1997. www.pdkintl.org/kappan/kpola974.htm.

Walter, Lynn. "Denmark: Women's Rights and Women's Welfare." In *Women's Rights: A Global View*, edited by Lynn Walter, 57–70. Westport, CT: Greenwood Press, 2001.

Videos/Films

Memories of a Marriage. 1989. Directed by Kaspar Rostrup. Distributed by 1-World Films, www.1worldfilms.com/. This is the story of the lives of a working class couple.

Babette's Feast. 1987. Directed by Gabriel Axel. Distributed by 1-World Films, www.1worldfilms.com/. This is the story of two sisters living in a remote west coast of Denmark in the 19th century whose lives are changed forever by the visit of a French woman (Academy award for Best Foreign Film).

Web Sites and Organizations

The Danish National Association for Gays and Lesbians, www.lbl.dk.

The Danish National Research and Documentation Centre on Gender Equality, www.vidlige.dk.

Danish Women's Society, www.kvindesamfund.dk.

Denmark's National Home Page (English version), www.denmark.dk.

Ministry for Gender Equality, www.lige.dk.

Statistics Denmark, www.dst.dk/dst/dstframeset_800_en.asp.

The Women's Council, www.kvinderaad.dk.

SELECTED BIBLIOGRAPHY

Bajema, Cristien. "Denmark." In *Sexual Harassment in the Workplace in the European Union*, 63–67. Brussels: EC, 1998.

Bradley, David. "Family Laws and Welfare States." In *The Nordic Model of Marriage and the Welfare State*, edited by Kari Melby, Anu Pylkkänen, Bente Rosenbeck, and Christina Carlsson Wetterberg, 65–87. Copenhagen: Nordic Council of Ministers, 2000.

Danmarks Statistik. *Statistical Yearbook*. Copenhagen: Author, 2001.

———. *Data on Denmark*. Copenhagen: Author, 2002.

Denmark's Embassy. www.denmarkemb.org/her_country.html (accessed July 2, 2002).

European Commission. *Sexual Harassment in the Workplace in the European Union*. Author, 1998.

European Industry Relations Observatory. "Increased Flexibility for Families 'May Be a Set-back for Gender Equality.'" eiro-online, 2002a. www.eiro.eurofound.ie/2002/03/Features/DK0203102F.html (accessed August 7, 2002).

———. "Trade Union Density Falls." eiro-online, 2002b. www.eiro.eurofound.ie/2002/01/InBrief/DK0201159N.html (accessed August 16, 2002).

Eurostat. *The Social Situation in the European Union 2002*. European Commission, 2002.

Government of Denmark. *National Report*. Regional Population Meeting, Budapest, Hungary, 1998.

International Planned Parenthood Foundation (IPPF). 2002. www.ippf.org (accessed August 29, 2002).

Inter-parliamentary Union (IPU). 2002. www.ipu.org (accessed August 30, 2002).

Jacobsen, Helle. "Report from Denmark." *European Database: Women in Decision-making*. 2002. www.db-decision.de (accessed July 15, 2002).

Kirkeministeriet. 1999. www.km.dk (accessed September 1, 2002).

Kvinderådet. *Nyhedsbrev*, no. 31 (December 2001). www.kvinderaad.dk (accessed August 26, 2002).

Ministry for Gender Equality. *Ministry for Gender Equality's 2002 Perspective and Action Plan*. Copenhagen: Author, 2002.

Ministry of Foreign Affairs and Equal Status Council. *Equality in Denmark, Toward a New Milennium*. Copenhagen: Author, 1999.

Ministry of Foreign Affairs and Social Affairs. *Denmark's National Report on Follow-up to the World Summit on Children*. Copenhagen: Author, 2001.

Ministry of Social Affairs. *Social Policy in Denmark*. Copenhagen: Author, 2001.

Nielsen, Helle. *Equality in the Twilight: Danish NGO Shadow Report Prior to Beijing + Five*. Copenhagen: Women's Council, 1999. www.kvinderaad.dk/midt_position_paper.htm.

Nordic Medico-Statistical Committee (NOMESCO). 2002. www.nom-nos.dk/ NOMESCO.HTM (accessed August 27, 2002).

Organization for Economic Cooperation and Development. *OECD in Figures*, Supplement 1: Author, 2002.

Rasmussen, Nell. "Denmark." In *Abortion in the New Europe*, edited by Bill Rolston and Anna Eggert, 69–84. Westport, CT: Greenwood Press, 1994.

Rosenbeck, Bente. "Modernisation of Marriage in Scandinavia." In *Women's Politics and Women in Politics*, 69–85. Oslo: Universitetet i Bergen, Cappelen Akademisk Forlag, 2000.

Sørensen, Asse Rieck. Contribution to the *Newsletter of the ICW* from the Women's Council in Denmark. October 25, 2000. www.kvinderaad.dk/midt_position_ paper.htm (accessed July 24, 2002).

United Nations Economic Commission for Europe (UNECE). 2002. www.unece.org/ stats/gender/web/ (accessed August 29, 2002).

Selected Danish Bibliography

Arbejdsministret & Ligestillingsrådet. *Rapport om lønforskelle mellem kvinder og mænd i Danmark*, 2000.

Beskæftigelses Ministeriet. "Dagpenge." 2002a. www.bm.dk/dagpenge/.

———"Fleksibel barselorlov." 2002b. www.bm.dk/barselorlov/default.asp.

Danish Women's Society. "Kondom eller P-piller til piger og meget unge kvinder?" Press release. October 9, 2001.

———"Velkommen til Dansk Kvindesamfund." 2002. www.kvindesamfund.dk (accessed August 30, 2002).

Danmarks Statistik og Ligestillingsrådet. *Kvinder og Mænd*. Copenhagen: Author, 1999.

Eckhardt, Vera. "Demokrati og indflydelse-et kvinderetsligt perspektiv." In *Kvinder, demokrati og indflydelse*, SAMKVIND, Skriftserie 19 (1995): 40–52.

Hansen, Tanja. "Kønnet under uddannelse." 2002. www.Akademikeren.dk (accessed August 5, 2002).

Tværministerielle arbejdsgruppe. "Vold mod kvinder." Copenhagen: Author, 2001.

Videnscenter for Ligestilling. 2002. www.vidlige.dk (accessed August 26, 2002).

II

ESTONIA

Ain Haas, Edgar Kaskla, and Anu Laas

PROFILE OF ESTONIA

Located on the eastern shore of the Baltic Sea, Estonia has a population of 1,371,835 according to the 2000 census. The percentage of females is 53.9 percent. The population declined 12 percent between the censuses of 1989 and 2000 due to emigration and a falling birthrate. The aging of the society poses challenges for the new democracy in terms of adjusting as well as financing welfare and health care programs. The Estonian ethnic majority (65.3 percent) speaks a language related to Finnish, with traces of cultural influences from other Baltic Sea nationalities. The largest minority today is Russian (28.1 percent).

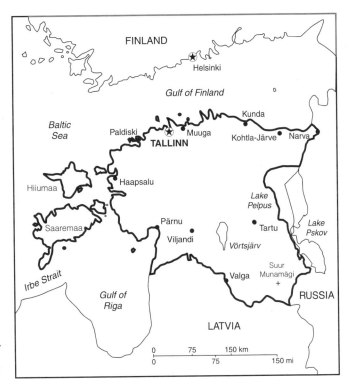

After seven centuries of rule by a succession of foreign invaders, the country had a brief period of independence between the World Wars I and II (1918–1940). Five decades of Soviet occupation followed. Estonia regained independence in 1991. The current form of government is a parliamentary democracy, with both a prime minister and a president. The period from 1991 to today is known as a period of transition. Vestiges of the Soviet system of central planning and government control of the economy are rapidly disappearing. Most enterprises are now privately owned.

Demographic statistics for 2000 show an infant mortality rate of 7.2 per 1,000 live births for females, compared to 9.5 for males. The rate of maternal deaths was 38 per 100,000 live births. In 1999, the total fertility rate (average number of live births in a woman's lifetime) was only 1.24. Life expectancy at birth was 76.1 for females and 65.2 for males in 2000.[1]

OVERVIEW OF WOMEN'S ISSUES

Three major sources of cultural influence also affect women's status today: ancestral peasant traditions, the Soviet legacy, and new Western-oriented institutions of political democracy and private enterprise. Generally, the status of women is improving, but in some areas, there is stagnation or even regression.

During the Soviet occupation, official ideology was favorable to gender equality. Women were encouraged to enter higher educational institutions and traditionally male occupations. However, women also retained primary responsibility for childcare, shopping, cooking, and housekeeping. This limited their availability for the most demanding jobs and leadership positions requiring long work hours and travel. The emergence of independent feminist organizations was discouraged, for women's liberation was expected to follow inevitably from the Communist Revolution.

In the post-Soviet era, women have continued to make gains in many areas, such as education and political participation; as the government emulates the profeminist policies of Western European countries and seeks to arrange Estonia's entry into the European Union (EU). On the other hand, women were the losers in a privatization process that favored incumbent, mostly male, executives. The new Estonian government has been relatively slow in pushing for greater gender equality. The most frequently offered excuse is that the country cannot afford such a reform until the economic transition is further along.

As in the rest of the EU, popular culture shows a fascination with beauty pageants, fashion modeling, skimpy clothing, cosmetics, Barbie dolls, and sexually explicit advertising and entertainment. Women were traditionally valued for their work, but there is an unprecedented emphasis on physical appearance today.

EDUCATION

Opportunities

Under Soviet rule, the doors to higher education opened wide for women. They comprised about two thirds of Tartu University's student body in the Soviet period.[2] New institutions of higher learning were founded, and the number of college-level students tripled in the first ten years.[3]

After the restoration of independence in 1991, dozens of new private institutions have been added, and females continue to get more education than males. In 1996, women's expected educational attainment was 13.4 years, compared to men's 12.8.[4] In 1999, 22 percent of females ages 15–74 had completed college, compared to 17 percent for males.[5] Only in vocational education institutions are females outnumbered, but their 46 percent share of enrollments in 2000 was not far from parity with males. Among those pursuing bachelor's degrees, 56 percent were female. It was 60 percent among graduate students pursuing a master's degree and 56 percent among doctoral students.[6]

Literacy

At the beginning of the interwar era of national independence, the literacy rate for the country was already very high. By the beginning of the post-Soviet period of independence, literacy was virtually universal, rounding off to 100 percent in 1994.[7] There is a minute gender difference among those ages twenty-five or more, 99.4 percent literate for women and 99.8 percent for men, but both sexes are at 99.9 percent in the 15–24 age group.[8]

EMPLOYMENT AND THE ECONOMY

In 2000, 65 percent of women and 77 percent of men ages 15–64 were in the labor force. Both figures are down 7 percent from 1990. Some of the gender gap is due to females' staying in school longer, but other reasons are the earlier retirement and longer life span of women. Soviet policy let women retire at fifty-five years, men at sixty. The new government has gradually been moving toward sixty and sixty-five, respectively, by 2003.

Clerical staff at bank, Tallinn, Estonia. Photo © TRIP/T. Noorits.

Job/Career Opportunities

At the end of the Soviet era, the unemployment rate was very low (0.7 percent in 1990), with females' rate being higher than males'. During the transition period of the 1990s, the unemployment rate rose steadily, reaching 13.9 percent among ages 15–64 in 2000. Females have generally fared better than males (12.9 percent versus 14.9 percent), which has been true since 1997. Females' average length of unemployment is shorter.

The main reason for this gender gap is the heavy male dominance of the extractive sector, especially agriculture. The decline in this sector has been dramatic, with the number of jobs down by about two thirds in the 1990s. By 2000, it included only 7.4 percent of employed persons. The more stable manufacturing/construction/mining/utilities sector had 33.5 percent, while the female-dominated service sector has grown to include 59.1 percent of employed persons.[9]

Grants are available to unemployed people to set up new businesses. In 1999, 6 percent of female and 11 percent of male employed persons were self-employed. Women's businesses tend to be smaller. About two thirds of female entrepreneurs have no employees, compared to half for males.[10]

Among the major job categories in 2000, clerks were the most likely to be female (76 percent), then the category of service/shop/market sales workers (75 percent), professionals (71 percent), technicians and associate professionals (65 percent), unskilled workers (59 percent), skilled agricultural/fishery workers (40 percent), senior officials/managers/legislators (36 percent), plant and machine operators and assemblers (25 percent), and craft and related trade workers (17 percent). Over 40 percent of the employed would have to change jobs in order to reach a 50/50 gender distribution within the categories listed above. In most of the nine categories, the percentages moved toward greater parity between the genders in 1989–2000. In leadership positions and crafts, there was regression toward greater male dominance.[11]

Pay

Although Estonian women are well educated, their potential is underutilized, and there is too low a reward for investments into women's human capital. The female–male pay differential has increased. In 1992, the year after Estonia broke away from the Soviet Union, women's hourly pay was 80 percent of men's. It dropped to 72 percent in one year, and little has changed since. In 1999, for instance, it was at 73.5 percent.[12] The discrepancy in pay is partly due to the types of jobs that women have. Traditional preconceptions still steer women into certain kinds of jobs or affect the pay level when women arrive in large numbers. For example, one study found that 66 percent of Estonians would prefer a male boss, whereas only 11 percent would prefer a female in charge.[13] Job ads often specify the gender considered appropriate for candidates. The pay level in an occupational category tends to decrease as the percentage of females increases.

Working Conditions

A 1993 study found that women workers reported less control over the timing and order of their tasks than men, but most still saw their work as interesting, satisfying, and useful. They also saw their colleagues as friends rather than rivals.[14]

The situation of women and men is quite different when it comes to occupational accidents. The injury rates were only about half as high for females as for males in 1999: 359 versus 701 per 100,000 workers. The fatality rate was 2 per 100,000 for women versus 15 for men. Both the injury and fatality rates are lower now than in the 1980s under Soviet rule.[15]

Sexual Harassment

The term "sexual harassment" is appearing with increasing frequency in media reports, which focus on matters of definition and foreign scandals or lawsuits. Victims tend to see incidents as isolated cases of the perpetrator's momentary weakness rather than as a feature of the work environment.[16] In September 2002, the Estonian legislature took under consideration a proposal from the Justice Ministry, "Equal Rights and Equal Treatment." It would ban sexual harassment, among other forms of discrimination, and hold employers responsible for ensuring it does not occur.

Support for Mothers/Caretakers

In the Soviet era, various programs were established to help women (but not men) bond with their children and to strengthen the family unit.[17] In the post-Soviet period, the basic structure of these programs has been retained, but benefits and scope of coverage have generally increased.[18]

Maternal Leave

Mothers get seventy days of fully paid leave before childbirth and fifty-six days after (plus fourteen extra days in case of complications). Those not working get the same as the minimum salary. Partially paid leave is available until the child turns three.[19] In 1999, support for the first two years after childbirth rose to 592 EEK per month, which was 13 percent of the average monthly gross pay that year; for the third year after childbirth, it was about 300 EEK.[20] Fathers and grandparents are eligible for such leave but rarely take the mother's place.[21]

Daycare

An extensive system of daycare services (kindergarten and nursery) developed under Soviet rule. Most parents had access (70 percent in 1987). The facilities were provided by the government or the workplace, with parents paying about one third of the real costs.[22] Now churches have begun to offer preschool classes and daycare facilities as well. The main problem with daycare services today is the rising cost, and outside the capital city of Tallinn it can be hard to find a facility that stays open past the rush hour. In 2000, 13 percent of one-year-olds were enrolled in some kind of preschool institution, 50 percent were enrolled at age two, 72 percent at age three, 76 percent at age four, 80 percent at age five, and 79 percent at age six.[23] Since July 2002, local governments are required to make daycare available to all. Parents must pay for food, but otherwise the care is subsidized so that parents' monthly costs cannot exceed 20 percent of the minimum salary.[24]

Family and Medical Leave

Parents get a few days of paid vacation to care for children with medical or other problems: six days annually if a child is under age three or if there are at least three children, and otherwise only three days. Also, fourteen days of unpaid leave are permitted. Modest support is provided for parents who stay home to care for a disabled child (age eighteen or under); they receive half the rate for parental leave to care for an infant.[25] There is little compensation for staying home to care for elderly, invalid, or disabled adult relatives, but assistance from visiting home care workers and daycare facilities is available.

Inheritance and Property Rights

Women got economic rights in the early 1930s due to the efforts of female lawyers.[26] In the Soviet era, property and inheritance rights for both sexes were severely restricted, as businesses were nationalized, farms collectivized, some housing confiscated, and so on. The post-Soviet government restored the earlier rights, with no sex discrimination in this regard.

Social/Government Programs

Welfare

The new government has gradually expanded welfare programs of various kinds to the extent that economic growth and increasing tax revenues allow. Avoidance of deficit spending has meant severe hardships for some groups during the transition period.

For example, pensions were really meager in the early 1990s. Pensions for retired workers have been similar for women and men: about 30 percent of the average monthly pay in 2000.[27] But women retire earlier and live longer, so low pensions are a more acute problem for them. Women also earn less than men during their work years and may withdraw from the labor force to care for children, elderly parents, and relatives, which reduces their pensions. Widow pensions do not exist.

In addition to the parental leave benefits already discussed, parents got a regular child allowance: 150 EEK a month for the first child, 224 for the second child, and to 300 for the third or subsequent child in 2000. This is equivalent to 3–6 percent of the country's average monthly pay. Single parents got a special supplement of 286 EEK, or another 6 percent.[28]

FAMILY AND SEXUALITY

Gender Roles

Women take primary responsibility for all duties related to the household, including cooking, cleaning, and childcare, whereas men are seen as the primary breadwinners. Since most women work full-time outside the home as well, they carry a dual burden.[29] The inequity is evident in the results of a 1998 study: 47 percent of men but only 31 percent of women reported having four or more hours of leisure time on weekdays, with little change since 1993.[30] Another study found 65 percent of couples quarrelling about the division of domestic chores.[31]

Men tend to be more supportive of traditional gender roles.[32] From recent observations, young men seem more inclined to share household and childcare duties, though it is still not the norm. A 1998 survey found that women and men had very similar priorities, both rating children and family above professional work in importance. However, women tended to give children and family somewhat higher importance than did men, and men ranked professional work as slightly more important than did women.[33] Yet few women would want to give up work to become a full-time housewife.[34]

Gender stereotypes are perpetuated by the primary socializing agents. Parents and teachers tend to steer boys and girls toward different kinds of toys or play. Schoolchildren hold very traditional attitudes.[35] Boys are much more conservative than girls. Boys show strong support for the idea that breadwinning is the province of males.

The traditional gender contract with a double standard regarding sexuality is quite obvious. Society tends to accept men's "higher" sexual needs and frown on women's sexual freedom. There is widespread tolerance or resignation with regard to the keeping of mistresses, especially by economically or politically prominent men.

Marriage

In late Soviet times, a housing shortage contributed to the postpone-ment of marriage, and the divorce rate rose gradually. These trends accel-erated considerably in the first years of the transitional era but abated somewhat in recent years. The new marriage rate dropped from 7.49 per 1,000 residents in 1990 to 4.01 in 2000. The average age of first marriage in 1998 was 24.3 for women and 26.5 for men, up about two years each since 1990. The total first-marriage rate for women was 0.35 in 1998.

Marriages are generally perceived to be unstable. For every 1,000 new marriages registered, there were 491 divorces in 1990 and a much higher figure of 771 in 2000.[36] After divorce, children usually remain with the mother. If the court orders alimony or child support, it is hard to ensure compliance by the former spouse or noncustodial parent. Women must seek redress from the courts, but unfamiliarity with legal procedures and the costliness of legal advice put them at a disadvantage. The same applies to their efforts to secure an equitable division of property in divorce pro-ceedings.

Reproduction

Estonia has one of the lowest birth rates in the world. In 2000, the average female was expected to have 1.24 live births in her lifetime. In 1990, it was still at the level of population replacement (2.1).[37] In the past decade, births to married couples dropped sharply, while births to the unmarried rose steadily. In 1990–2000, the percent of live births after wedlock dropped from 72.9 percent to 45.5 percent. Out-of-wedlock births grew from 17.1 percent to 36.7 percent in the category of "father identified" (which would include cohabiting couples) and from 10.0 percent to 17.8 percent in the category of "father not identified."[38]

Sex Education

Formal sex education is provided in preschools and in primary and sec-ondary schools. Family education is taught in the last grades of upper secondary schools. The Family Planning Association of Estonia, founded in 1993, has prioritized health and sex education for youth and helped design the school health education curriculum. Since 1996, information, advice, and services have been available to all, at little or no cost, through a nationwide network of family planning clinics. By 2001, seventeen clinics had been established specifically to help youths in this regard.

Contraception and Abortion

Women tend to be seen as the ones responsible for avoiding unwanted pregnancies. In the last decade, information about reproductive technologies has become more available, and contraceptives are more accessible. In the 1990s, 70 percent of sexually active women in the reproductive age group were using contraceptives.[39] Students can buy state-subsidized contraceptives. However, affordable birth control is problematic for unemployed and low-income women. In the Soviet era, abortion was the main family planning method (legal since 1955) due to the poor quality or unavailability of contraceptives. Legally induced abortions declined from 130 per 100 births in 1995 to 97 in 2000.[40]

Teen Pregnancy

In 1990, only 0.05 percent of live births were to mothers under age sixteen, quadrupling to a still very rare 0.21 percent in 2000. Females ages 16–19 accounted for 12 percent of live births in 1990 versus 10 percent in 2000. Mothers in this age group were typically married in 1990 but not in 2000 (65 percent versus 21 percent).[41]

HEALTH

Health Care Access

As a result of investments in health care during the Soviet period, Estonia is better off than most developed countries in terms of the availability of doctors, other health care personnel, and hospital beds.[42] Another legacy of the Soviet era is the high proportion of female doctors: women comprised 77 percent of all doctors in both 1991 and 1994.[43] Estonian women generally do not have a problem with doctors being uninterested in women's health issues; however, one obvious area of neglect is women's health after menopause. Estonians have traditionally viewed the biological changes of aging as a private matter and an inevitability, but information about new treatments such as hormone replacement therapy is beginning to spread, which may change attitudes about this.

Unfortunately, the Soviet system also left a legacy of inefficient management, favoritism in treatment, informal bartering with patients, neglect of preventive care, and inattention to degenerative and chronic diseases as opposed to infectious ones.[44] The shortage of pharmacies is also a problem, and the rapidly rising cost of drugs has more of an impact on women, due to the unfavorable wage difference.[45] The number of doctors has decreased somewhat in recent years, and there were only half as many hospital beds in 2000 as in 1990, but there has been a rise in other categories of health care personnel (e.g., nurses, dentists, and laboratory technicians).[46]

Most residents are covered by the national health insurance program, for which they pay 13 percent of their income. Those outside the system still receive free first aid, medical care during pregnancy, and treatment of serious infectious and malignant diseases.[47]

Diseases and Disorders

Women are slightly more likely than men to report poor health or to get sick.[48] Since women have a much longer life expectancy, 76.3 versus 65.4 years for men in 1999,[49] they are more likely to reach the advanced ages where medical problems abound.

Cardiovascular diseases are the most common cause of death for both sexes. In 2000, 62 percent of female deaths and 46 percent of male deaths were attributed to this cause.[50] The traditional diet, which includes rich dairy products, fried foods, fatty pork, and sausages, is apparently one of the reasons, but the great stresses of the Soviet occupation and the new competitive economy must also be factors.

Alcohol poisoning and drunk driving deaths rose rapidly in the mid-1990s, especially among men. Heavier drinking also figured in the marked rise of men's deaths due to falling, drowning, and homicide.[51]

AIDS

Estonia managed to avoid this plague until quite recently. The year 2000 was a turning point, when the rate of known HIV infections suddenly increased to 28.3 per 100,000 inhabitants from only 0.6 the year before.[52] The rate is still rising rapidly,[53] although few HIV-infected people have yet developed AIDS. The first major outbreak was among needle-sharing drug users in the Russian enclave of Narva, in northeast Estonia, but the problem is now clearly evident in Tallinn as well. With widespread prostitution and the surge in sexually transmitted diseases that developed in the mid-1990s,[54] it seems likely that HIV transmission through unprotected sex will increase rapidly among both men and women.

Eating Disorders

In recent years, women have made more effort than men to change to a more balanced and healthy diet.[55] The greatest change in eating habits can be seen in teenage girls and young women. They have become serious dieters in the quest to emulate fashion models and film stars. The typical eighteen-year-old girl weighed almost twelve pounds less in 1996 than her counterpart in 1989, even though there had been a slight increase in height.[56] A 1998 study found that most tenth-grade girls (56 percent) were underweight, especially in urban areas. Only 38 percent of girls versus 68 percent of boys were content with their weight, and the discontented boys tended to want to put on more weight! The girls reported feeling pressure to diet, more for reasons of appearance than good health.[57] Nevertheless, both peasant traditions and Soviet practicality have contributed to a reservoir of admiration for strong women. Estonian modeling agencies still accept a stockier build than their counterparts would in the West.[58] Anorexia and bulimia are beginning to receive some attention in the medical field and mass media; however, statistics on the extent of such disorders in the country are lacking.

Cancer

Cancer was among the many diseases that claimed more victims in the post-Soviet era.[59] Tumors are not as common among females as among males.[60] One apparent reason is that women are only half as likely to smoke (21 percent versus 52 percent daily smokers among men) or be subjected to tobacco fumes at work.[61] Yet even among women the trend is worrisome, as those under the age of fifty are twice more likely to smoke as older women.[62]

Breast cancer is the most common form among women, killing 20.2 per 100,000 in 1997. This is not far below the death rate from cardiovascular diseases (26.7), and it is close to the average for the European Union (nineteen in 1996). Cervical cancer killed 6.5 women per 100,000 in 1997, considerably higher than the EU average (2.0 in 1996).[63]

Depression

Women were twice as likely as men to report suffering weekly from depression in a 1993 study (25 percent versus 13 percent). A 1996 study found much lower rates for "significant depression," but a 2:1 difference was typical regardless of the age group.[64] Women also seemed more prone to suicidal thoughts: 35 percent of women versus 23 percent of men ever having considered it in the 1993 study.[65] On the other hand, men tend to be more closemouthed about their mental problems for fear of looking weak to others.

Men actually follow through much more often on their self-destructive impulses. The age-standardized suicide rates in 2000 were 10.12 per 100,000 for women versus 46.28 for men, with an even bigger difference a few years earlier.[66] Women's suicide rates have been fairly stable, but men's rates soared in the mid-1990s.[67]

Men also are more inclined to drown their sorrows in drink. Alcohol poisoning and drunk driving deaths rose rapidly in the mid-1990s, especially among men. Heavier drinking also figured in the marked rise of men's deaths due to falling, drowning, and homicide.[68]

POLITICS AND LAW

Suffrage

Women have had the right to vote since 1918. Even earlier, women's organizations such as the Women's Society (1906) and the Estonian

Women's University Students Society (1911) raised issues of women's equality, including the idea of equal pay for equal work. Women report somewhat less interest in politics than men do, but they actually vote more often.[69]

Political Participation

Historically, women have been underrepresented in politics. Women hold 18 percent of parliamentary seats,[70] up from 7 percent in the last Supreme Soviet of Estonia in 1990. In local government councils in 1999, women had 28 percent of the seats, up from 9 percent in 1989. The traditional notion that "politics is a man's job" is fading. A 1996 study found over 50 percent agreeing that there are not enough women in politics, compared to only 19 percent who saw underrepresentation of females as problematic in 1993.[71]

Although a woman—Lagle Parek—was a candidate for president in 1992, no other women have been seriously considered for this largely ceremonial office. Nor has there been a female prime minister or county governor, but there have been women among the cabinet ministers, reaching a peak of five out of fourteen (36 percent) in 2002. Among the most prominent women in politics are Soviet-era dissident leader and former social affairs minister Marju Lauristin, former reform minister Liia Hänni, and former Tallinn mayor Ivi Eenmaa.

Women's Rights

Women's rights have been legally protected since the first period of Estonian independence (1918–1940). The Estonian Constitution, which took effect on July 3, 1992, forbids discrimination based on nationality, race, religion, social status, culture, and sex (Article 12). The government has also signed international treaties and agreements reinforcing women's legal protection, including the International Covenant on Human Rights, European Convention on Human Rights, and Convention on Elimination of All Forms of Discrimination against Women.

Although overt discrimination is forbidden on paper, effective enforcement mechanisms remain to be developed. The problems of hidden, inadvertent, and institutional sexism also have not been addressed. This may help explain why women are somewhat more favorable toward government intervention.[72]

A number of women's organizations have been created in recent years. They provide information about issues related to women's rights, but their main focus seems to be promoting training in economics or other fields. The Estonian Entrepreneurial Women's Association, the smaller Entrepreneurial Ladies' Association, and local branches of international organizations like the *Zonta* Club, European Women's Union, and YWCA take up issues of balancing work and family obligations.

Some political parties (e.g., Moderates, *Pro Patria*, and Social Democrats) have organized separate women's groups to develop more female activists. University-based sorority groups like the Estonian Women's University Students Society, *Indla, Filiae Patriae*, and *Amicitia* can also be considered part of the network where women's issues are frequently discussed. The Women's Studies and Resource Centre at Tallinn Pedagogical University and the Unit on Gender Studies at Tartu University work at the academic level.

Feminist Movements

There is no feminist movement yet to speak of. Feminism is usually perceived as too "loud" for a culture that values reserve and softspokenness. But many of these organizations have tried to clarify the nature of feminism and to raise consciousness about the need for it.

Lesbian Rights

Lesbian rights are not discussed openly, nor do lesbian relationships have any legal status. Personal ads seeking same-sex companions appeared already in the late Soviet era in independent newspapers of the late 1980s. Society does now recognize the presence of homosexuals, and mass media coverage has generally been sympathetic in the post-Soviet era. However, recent proposals by the Gay and Lesbian Alliances for legal recognition of homosexual unions and authorization of adoption by homosexuals have drawn much public opposition and seem unlikely to pass in the legislature anytime soon. Yet the Parliament is now considering a bill that would add sexual orientation to the list of prohibited grounds for unequal treatment, which could improve the prospects for extending homosexuals' rights.

Some lesbian couples have children, but these family arrangements are generally out of public view. In a 1993 divorce case in Tallinn, the court rejected a man's contention that his ex-wife's lesbianism and her living with another woman made her unfit to have custody of their two children.[73]

Military Service

Unlike men, women do not have mandatory military service. Some women do volunteer for noncombat roles, and a handful (four so far) have served as regular soldiers. In February 2002, there were 901 women in the armed forces, of which 514 were on active duty. Of forty-two female officers, the highest rank was held by the head of the Armed Forces Health Center.

Others (some 900) serve part-time in the women's branch of the *Kait-*

seliit (Defense Union or home guard). Girls can join the *Kodutütred* (Home Daughters), boys the *Noored Kotkad* (Young Eagles). These organizations are affiliated with the Defense Union and combine scouting activities with preparation for military service.[74]

RELIGION AND SPIRITUALITY

Historically, the Lutheran Church has been dominant, with the Russian Orthodox Church a strong second. Yet the peasants were traditionally rather lukewarm in their devotion to such faiths brought by foreign conquerors. A half century of officially promoted atheism under Soviet rule and now the dominance of Western-style secularism have also undermined religious fervor. In 1934, 78 percent of the population was affiliated with the Lutheran Church, followed by 19 percent with the Russian Orthodox Church.[75] A 1999 poll revealed a large contingent of unaffiliated persons (35 percent), with the self-identified Lutheran and Orthodox groups nearly equal, at 30 percent and 28 percent respectively.[76]

Women's Roles

Women tend to rate religion more highly than men do in their list of values, and women report higher levels of trust in God and the church.[77] In the middle-aged group, the sexes are rather similar and display less religiosity than among the young or the elderly. This is perhaps because the middle aged had the most exposure to Soviet atheism.[78]

The clergy are almost all male, but women are 10 percent of the Lutheran clergy.[79] Russian Orthodox nuns outnumber monks by about 2:1.[80] Even if women do not play much of a role in leading worship services, they show a special interest in spiritual matters and help draw their spouses and children to the church. Women can also be found among astrologers, "sensitives" (clairvoyants), and others claiming occult powers.

Rituals and Religious Practices

At Lutheran services, the sexes worship together with seating in family groups. The Russian Orthodox tradition is to have separate standing sections for the men and women, and to require women to cover their heads in church.

Religious Law

Since the Constitution of 1920 established a secular state, theological considerations have not steered legislation. In the current condition of religious diversity, there is no prospect for adherents of any one faith to impose their will on others through the legal system. The churches have always reinforced patriarchal authority, but they have also served as a source of comfort and moral support to women in conflict with abusive, philandering, or heavy-drinking husbands.

VIOLENCE

In the first few years after the collapse of the Soviet Union, crime rates soared. Homicide rates reached a historic peak in 1994, but gradually subsided somewhat thereafter. Women are less likely to be killed than men. In the peak year of 1994, 10.6 females per 100,000 were victims of homicide, compared to 48.4 for men.[81] Both rates were more than twice as high as they had been in 1990, the last full year of Soviet rule.[82] There is a ratio of nine males to one female among the perpetrators of murder or attempted murder.[83]

Domestic Violence

The extent of domestic violence is unclear, as Estonians value their privacy highly and do not readily divulge their marital or relationship problems to others. Abuse within the home is usually viewed as a domestic problem to be dealt with (if at all) within the family structure, so few of these attacks are reported to authorities. The cultural acceptability of wife-beating is reportedly higher in Russian families. Family conflicts account for about 12 percent of homicide cases.[84] Females clearly outnumbered males (71 percent versus 29 percent) among the 262 victims of domestic violence who ended up in shelters or rehabilitation centers in 2000.[85] These figures may include both adults and children.

Rape/Sexual Assault

As an officially recorded crime, rape or attempted rape is very rare: it comprised only seventy-three incidents among 57,799 registered offenses of all types in 2000. The rate has moved upward since the end of the Soviet era, from 3.4 per 100,000 residents in 1990 to 5.3 in 2000.[86] Although the gender of the victims was not specified in the sources, it is likely that nearly all cases involve female victims. Most reported cases are followed by an arrest and conviction, with imprisonment being the most common sentence unless the offender is a juvenile.[87]

Could there be a connection with the boom in pornography that occurred when Soviet restrictions on publications and marketing were lifted? Images of naked women on sex magazine covers were visible for several years at almost any news kiosk, until some regulation began in 1997 out of concern for the impression made on children.[88] The pornography was overwhelmingly of the "soft" variety, however, without fixation on scenes of violence, bondage, or sadomasochism.

Trafficking in Women and Children

There are occasional reports of sexual slavery, but these are usually associated with organized crime syndicates with operations abroad. Naïve women from Estonia are lured to foreign countries with promises of well-paid, legitimate jobs, but upon arrival they find themselves held captive and forced to have sex with clients. Trafficking in children is less known, though teenage girls are sometimes caught up in this kind of racket.

Exploitation of children as prostitutes or pornography models became a source of concern in the 1990s. The authorities do not tolerate this, but several factors make it hard to control. There are many street urchins in Tallinn, whose parents (usually alcoholics or drug addicts) are unwilling to supervise them or unable to provide for them. Wealthy pedophiles from nearby Western countries visit Estonia and offer considerable financial incentives for children to succumb. The country's rapid progress in computerization means that it has become easier for pedophiles to store, copy, and distribute exploitative photos.

Proposals have been made at both city council and parliamentary levels to legalize prostitution for purposes of taxation and supervision, but they have not been adopted. The public is ambivalent. The widespread feeling that prostitutes ought to pay their share of taxes is counterbalanced by a fear of what would happen if Estonia turned into a sex tourism center. Prostitutes are more numerous now and have more venues to ply their trade: new hotels, brothels (*lõbumajad* or "fun houses"), striptease sex clubs, erotic telephone lines, and so on. Newspaper ads brazenly recruit "complex-free" (uninhibited) women willing to offer "intimate services." Anecdotal evidence from newspaper stories suggests that prostitutes typically enter the profession voluntarily and cite economic hardship as the rationale.[89]

OUTLOOK FOR THE TWENTY-FIRST CENTURY

Integration into Europe (through likely EU membership) will have paradoxical effects. For example, the messages and images conveyed via Western consumer culture promote an emphasis on the superficial sexuality of females. On the other hand, foreign grants have underwritten much of the documentation of gender inequality and the institutional change that has occurred. The rules for joining the EU heighten the sense of urgency about ensuring equal treatment for women. The Equality Bureau, established under the Social Affairs Ministry in 1996, is now part of the EU Integration Department. There is also a new Commission on Equal Rights for the Sexes, and since 1999 a legal chancellor position to serve as an ombudsman for those with complaints about sexism. If the new guarantees of equality turn out to be something of a façade, they will at least promote more open and honest discussion of women's issues.

NOTES

Linda Haas provided valuable assistance with searching the English-language literature and made helpful suggestions for revising an earlier draft of the manuscript.

1. Statistics reported above come from Eesti Statistikaamet (ESA), or Statistical Office of Estonia, *Statistical Yearbook of Estonia* (Tallinn, Estonia, 2001).

2. Karl Siilivask and Hillar Palamets, *Tartu Ülikooli ajalugu III: 1918–1982* (Tallinn, Estonia: Eesti Raamat, 1982), 206.

3. Toivo U. Raun, *Estonia and the Estonians* (Stanford, CA: Hoover Institution Press, 1991), 185.

4. Eesti Statistikaamet (ESA), *Sotsiaaltrendid* (Tallinn, Estonia, 1998), 100.

5. Eesti Statistikaamet (ESA), *Labour Force 1999* (Tallinn, Estonia, 2000), 95–96.

6. ESA, 2001, 68.

7. *The World Almanac and Book of Facts: 2002* (New York: World Almanac Books, 2002), 793.

8. United Nations, *The World's Women 2000: Trends and Statistics* (New York: Author, 2000), 107.

9. ESA, 2001, 206.

10. ESA, 2000, 47.

11. Eesti Statistikaarmet, *Estonian Labour Force Surveys 1995 and 1997: Estonian Labour Force 1989–1997*, ed. Ülle Pettai and Kaja Sõstra (Tallinn, Estonia, 1998), 89; and Sotsiaalministeerium, "Employment Action Plan for 2002," 2001 (unpublished manuscript), www.sm.ee/gopro30.

12. Eesti Statistikaamet (ESA), "Average Gross Wages Per Hour of Full Time and Part Time Employees by Occupational Groups," 2001, www.stat.ee/index.aw/section=7177 (table accessed); and Taavi Männamaa, "Palgaturu soosik meessoost tippspetsialist," *Eesti Päevaleht*, November 29, 2000.

13. Küllo Arjakas, "Naíse rolli uuenemine," *Postimees*, June 5, 1998.

14. Anu Narusk, The Estonian Family in Transition, *Nationalities Papers* 23, no. 1 (1995): 145–46.

15. Derived from tallies in (ESA), *Eesti Statistika aastaraamat* (Tallinn, Estonia, 1991), 236, 329; and ESA, 2001, 188–191, 203.

16. Pille Liimal, "Ametnikutöö käib meeste sõna järgi," *Eesti Päevaleht* (September 29, 1997), 7.

17. Ene-Margrit Tiit, "Family Policy in the Estonian SSR," in *Family Situation and Policy*, ed. Dagmar Kutsar (Tartu, Estonia: Tartu University, 1990), 22–24.

18. Narusk, 1995, 145, 148.

19. Anne Joonsaar et al., *Eesti naised muutuvas ühiskonnas* (1995), 37.

20. ESA, 2001, 169, 218.

21. Narusk, 1995, 148.

22. Tiit, 1990, 25.

23. ESA, 2001, 66.

24. Mark Malvet and Helle Niit, "Perekonda toetavad poliitikad laste riskide ärahoidjana," in *Lapsed Eestis* (United Nations Development Programme, 2000).

25. Joonsaar et al., 1995, 38.

26. Especially Vera Poska-Grünthal.

27. ESA, 2001, 166, 218.

28. ESA, 2001, 169.

29. Anu Narusk, *Argielu Eestis 1990ndatel aastatel* (Tallinn, Estonia: Tallinn Pedagogical University, 1999).

30. Malle Järve, "Gendered Leisure," in *Towards a Balanced Society*, eds. Peeter

Maimik, Kadi Mänd, and Ülle-Marike Papp (United Nations Development Programme, 2000).

31. Narusk, 1995a, 147.

32. Narusk, 1999; and Anu Laas, "Feministlik perspektiiv sotsioloogias" (master's thesis, Tartu University, 2000).

33. Narusk, "Professional and family life," in Maimik et al., 2000.

34. *Sõnumileht*, February 26, 1996.

35. Narusk, 1999.

36. ESA, 1998, *Sotsiaaltrendid*: 96–97; ESA, 1999; and ESA, 2001, 49.

37. ESA, 2001, 410; and UN, 2000, 35.

38. ESA, 1998, *Sotsiaaltrendid*, 1998, 17; and ESA, 2001, 40.

39. UN, 2000, 49.

40. Eesti Statistikaamet (ESA), *Statistical Yearbook of Estonia: 1995* (Tallinn, Estonia, 1996), 66; ESA, 2001, 44.

41. Calculated from statistics in ESA, 43 (2001), 235.

42. Taie Kaasik, Ragnar Andersson, and Lars-Gunnar Hörte, "The Effects of Political and Economic Transitions on Health and Safety in Estonia," *Social Science and Medicine* 47, no. 10 (1998): 1596.

43. Donald A. Barr and Elizabeth Heger Boyle, "Gender and Professional Purity," *Gender and Society* 15, no. 1 (1991): 33, 37; and calculated from statistics in Eesti Statistikaamet (ESA), *Mees- ja naistöötajate tunnipalgad* (Tallinn, Estonia: Author, 1995), 17.

44. R.J. Nadisauskiene and Z. Padaiga, "Changes in Women's Health in the Baltic Republics of Lithuania, Latvia, and Estonia during 1970–1997," *International Journal of Gynecology and Obstetrics* 70, no. 1 (2000): 199–206; Barr & Boyle, 2001, 30; and Mall Leinsalu, "Social Variation in Self-rated Health in Estonia," *Social Science and Medicine* 55, no. 5 (2002): 847–61.

45. Kaasik et al., eds., 1998, 1596.

46. ESA, 1998, *Sotsiaaltrendid*, 70–71; and ESA, 2001, 149–51.

47. Airi Põder and J.S. Bingham, "Sexually Transmitted Infections in Estonia," *International Journal of Sexually Transmitted Disease and AIDS* 10 (1999): 671.

48. Leinsalu, 2002.

49. ESA, 2001, 406.

50. ESA, 2001, 47.

51. Kaasik, et al., 1998, 1593; Martin McKee, Joceline Pomerleau, Aileen Robertson, Iveta Pudule, Daiga Grinberga, Kamelija Kadziauskiene, Algis Abaravicius, and Sirje Vaask, "Alcohol Consumption in the Baltic Republics," *Journal of Epidemiology and Community Health* 54, no. 5 (2000): 361–66.

52. ESA, 2001, 157.

53. Eesti Haigekassa, "Eesti Haigekassa ravikindlustatute tervise edendamise ja haiguste ennetamise prioriteetide määramise taustmaterjal," 2003, www.Haigekassa.ee/HK/Ravikindlustus/tervisedendus.

54. Põder and Bingham, 1999.

55. Andrus Lipand, "Health of Women and Men in Estonia, 1990–1998," in Maimik et al., 2000.

56. Anu Jõesaar, "Eesti tüdrukud on viimastel aastatel salenenud," *Eesti Päevaleht* (February 17, 1997): 1.

57. Eha Rüütel, "Kehakaaluga rahulolematus," *Haridus 2. Tervis* (1999), www.cs.ioc.ee~haridus/archiiv/1999/haridus2/tervis.html.

58. Jõesaar, 1997.

59. ESA, 1998, *Sotsiaaltrendid*, 67–69.

60. ESA, 2001, 48, 158.

61. Ville Helasoja et al., "Smoking and Passive Smoking in Estonia, Lithuania and Finland," *European Journal of Public Health* 11, no. 2 (2001): 208.

62. Iveta Pudule et al., "Patterns of Smoking in the Baltic Republics," *Journal of Epidemiology and Community Health* 53 (1999): 279.

63. Using age-standardized death rates. Nadisauskiene and Padaiga, 2000, 3–4.

64. Lipand, 2000.

65. Virve-Ines Laidmäe, "Health and Health-Care," in *Everyday Life and Radical and Social Changes in Estonia*, ed. Anu Narusk (Tallinn, Estonia: Estonian Academy of Sciences, 1995), 20–21; see also ESA, 1998, *Sotsiaaltrendid*, 59 and Riina Raudsik, "Depressioon," *Rae Sõnumid* (December 2001).

66. Eesti Statistikaamet, personal communication.

67. Airi Värnik, *Suicide in Estonia, 1965–1995* (Tallinn, Estonia: Estonian-Swedish Suicide Institute, 1997), 46–55.

68. Kaasik et al., 1998, 1593; McKee et al., 2000.

69. Tiina Raitviir, "Participation in Politics," in Maimik et al., 2000; and Anu Laas, *Eesti naine uuel aastatuhandel.Uurigu aruanne* (Unpublished research report, Tartu University, Estonia, 2000).

70. United Nations Development Programme, *Human Development Report 2000* (New York: Oxford University Press, 2000), 165.

71. Raitviir, 2000.

72. Svetlana Stephenson, "Public Beliefs in the Causes of Wealth and Poverty," *Social Justice Research* 13, no. 2 (2000): 97.

73. Lilian Kotter, "Estonia," in *Lesbian Motherhood in Europe*, ed. Kate Griffin and Lisa Mulholland (London: Cassell, 1997).

74. Eesti Kaitsevägi, "Kaitseväe juhataja tervitas naiskaitseväelasi," 2002, www.mil.ee.

75. Raun, 1991, 135.

76. Estonian Market and Opinion Research Center, "Milleinniumi küsitlus" (1999), www.kehrakogudus.ee/vana/stat/emor.htm (accessed on May 12, 2003).

77. Leeni Hansson, "Life Values," in Narusk, 1995, *Everyday Life*, 8, 14; and Laas, 2000, *Eesti naine*.

78. Hansson, 1995, 8, 14; and Laas, 2000, *Eesti naine*.

79. Lea Jürgenstein, "Eesti luteri kiriku naisvaimulikud," *Postimees* (September 18, 2002).

80. Kristi Malmberg, "Petseri mungad võirad Eestisse kolida," *Eesti Päevaleht*, August 13, 1996, 1; and Epp Alatalu, "Siseministeerium ootab Moskva komprommise," *Postimees*, July 17, 1997.

81. Sotsiaalministeerium, "Eesti keskkonnatervise riiklik tegevusplaan," 1999, www.tervisekaitse.ee/tkuus.php?msgid=933.

82. Kaasik et al., 1998, 1593.

83. Kriminaalpreventsiooni Nõukogu, "Aruanded kuritegevuse olukorrast," no date, http://preventsioon.just.ee/eesti/kpn/kuritegevus1995grupid.html.

84. Risto Berendson, "Aastas lisandub 200 tapjat," *Eesti Päveleht*, April 3, 1998.

85. Derived from ESA, 2001, 183.

86. Derived from Eesti Statistikaamet (ESA), *Statistical Yearbook of Estonia* (Tallinn, Estonia, 1992), 178; ESA, 2001, 33, 129; and see also ESA, 1991, 379.

87. Enn Uus, "Kohtud on olnud kurjategijasõbralikud," *Sõnumileht*, May 21, 1996: 5; and ESA, 2001: 133, 135–36.

88. Anneli Ammas, "Seksikaubandust hakatakse piirama," *Eesti Päevaleht*, May 5, 1997, 3, and Kristi Malmberg, "Riik korjab porno laste silme alt," *Eesti Päevaleht*, December 17, 1997, 3.

89. Karla Küsija, "Kaheksast hommikul kuni kuueni õhtul on kõige kuumem aeg,"

Õhtuleht, May 21, 1993, 6; August Walterhaus, "Tulin linna lõbutüdrukuks," *Pühapäe-valeht*, May 14, 1994, 15; and Baltic News Service, "Politsei kahtlustab lastehaigla majas lõbumaja," *Eesti Päevaleht*, January 27, 1997, 4.

RESOURCE GUIDE

Suggested Reading

Hansson, Leeni. "Combining Work and Family: The Case of Estonian Women." In *Reconciliation of Family and Work in Eastern European Countries*, edited by Michel E. Domsch and Désirée H. Ladwig. Frankfurt: Peter Lang, 2000.
Narusk, Anu. *The Estonian Family in Transition*. Nationalities Papers 23, no. 1 (1995).

Videos/Films

Isamaa ilu [Beauty of the Fatherland]. 2001. Directed by and screenplay by Jaak Kilmi and Andres Maimik. Produced by Anu Veermäe. Distributed by Rudolf Konimois Film. (Winner of awards at film festivals of Tallinn, Leipzig, and Amsterdam.) A 56-minute documentary on two different approaches to traditional gender-role socialization of young women, expounded by Anne Eenpalu, leader of the patriotic Kodutütred [Home Daughters], and by Tiina Jantson, organizer of beauty pageants.
Suur õde [Big Sister]. 2000. Directed by and screenplay by Andres Maimik and Jaak Kilmi. Produced by Meelis Muhu. Distributed by In-Ruum. (Winner of Estonia's Culture Capital award for young filmmakers.) A 75-minute documentary, providing a behind-the-scenes look at the political impact and media coverage of five prominent Estonian women: Culture Minister Signe Kivi, businesswoman Terje Aru, former Miss Estonia Kristiina Heinmets, dissident and later Social Affairs Minister Marju Lauristin, strike movement leader Kadi Pärnits.

Web Sites

Towards a Balanced Society: Women and Men in Estonia, www.undp.ee/gender/en.
A fine anthology of recent articles edited by Peeter Maimik et al.

The Statistical Office of Estonia (in English), http://gatekeeper.stat.ee:8000/px-web.2001/dialog/statfileri.asp.
Includes detailed sex-segregated data available starting in 1995.

"Implementation of the Convention on the Elimination of All Forms of Discrimination against Women," Ministry of Foreign Affairs, www.vm.ee/eng/kat_138/776.html.

Organizations

Estonian Women's Studies and Resource Centre of Tallinn Pedagogical University
Narva mnt. 25-410
Tallinn 10120, Estonia
Web site: www.enut.tpu.ee/inglise/index.htm

Unit on Gender Studies, Tartu University
Tiigi t. 78-214
Tartu 50410, Estonia
Web site: www.enut.tpu.ee/ing/ise/index.htm

SELECTED BIBLIOGRAPHY

Barr, Donald A., and Elizabeth Heger Boyle. "Gender and Professional Purity: Explaining Formal and Informal Work Rewards for Physicians in Estonia." *Gender and Society* 15, no. 1 (2001): 29–54.

Eesti Statistikaamet [Statistical Office of Estonia]. *Statistical Yearbook of Estonia*. Tallinn, Estonia: Author, 2001.

———. *Statistical Yearbook of Estonia*. Tallinn, Estonia: Author, 2001.

Kotter, Lilian. "Estonia." In *Lesbian Motherhood in Europe*, edited by Kate Griffin and Lisa A. Mulholland, 99–103. London: Cassell, 1997.

Kutsar, Dagmar, ed. *Family Situation and Policy*. Tartu, Estonia: Tartu University, 1990.

Nadisauskiene, R.J., and Z. Padaiga. 2000. "Changes in Women's Health in the Baltic Republics of Lithuania, Latvia, and Estonia during 1970–1997." *International Journal of Gynecology and Obstetrics* 70, no. 1 (2002): 199–206.

Narusk, Anu. "The Estonian Family in Transition." *Nationalities Papers* 23, no. 1 (1995a).

Narusk, Anu, ed. *Everyday Life and Radical Social Changes in Estonia*. Tallinn, Estonia: Estonian Academy of Sciences, 1995b.

Raun, Toivo U. *Estonia and the Estonians*. Stanford, CA: Hoover Institution Press, 1991.

Selected Estonian Bibliography

Eesti Statistikaamet [Statistical Office of Estonia]. *Sotsiaaltrendid*. Tallinn, Estonia: Author, 1998.

Joonsaar, Anne et al. *Eesti naised muutuvas ühiskonnas* (Estonian National Report prepared for the United Nations' Fourth World Women's Conference), 1995.

Laas, Anu. *Eesti naine uuel aastatuhandel. Uuringu aruanne.* Unpublished research report, Tartu University, 2000.

———. "Feministlik perspektiiv sotsioloogias." Master's thesis, Tartu University, 2000.

Narusk, Anu, ed. *Argielu Eestis 1990ndatel aastatel*. Tallinn, Estonia: Tallinn Pedagogical University, 1999.

12

FINLAND

Anne Kovalainen

PROFILE OF FINLAND

Finland, a nation with a population of approximately 5.1 million, is one of the Nordic countries and a member of the European Union. Finland is the seventh-largest country in Europe, is highly industrialized but with relatively unpolluted nature, and has one of the highest standards of living in the world. Finland has strong historical traditions in equality issues: women received the right to vote in 1906 and became eligible to stand as candidates in general elections that same year—first in all of Europe. The first women in the Parliament were elected in 1907, and in the first elections where they were able to be candidates for posts, they won nineteen out of 200 Parliament seats. The first woman government minister was elected in 1926. Today, the Finnish Parliament has seventy-four women out of 200 total members (37 percent).

Tarja Halonen was the first woman elected as president, and she will serve until March 2006. In the present government, women hold 39 percent of the ministerial posts, ranging from minister of education to minister of trade and commerce. All political parties have women in their governing bodies, and one major political party had a woman party leader Anneli Jäätteenmäki, as of 2002. She also was recently elected prime minister of the new government. The constitution of Finland calls for the promotion of equality between the sexes in social activities and in working life. The equal rights law is comprehensive, covering not only working life but also other aspects, such as governmental committees and working groups.

In addition to political power in the Parliament, municipal-level power also is important from a gender perspective. The equal division of power is not only a question of equality between genders, but it is also a question of diversity and balance in the municipal decision-making bodies. The municipalities in Finland are responsible for organizing and controlling the legislatively regulated everyday life services that are crucial for women with children and for families, such as education, social and health care services, daycare services, and elder care. Women's high activity in political life is visible also at the municipal level. The share of women in municipal governments is on average 34 percent.

This political power reflects the formal visibility of women in Finnish society: of the employed population, 47.9 percent are women. Women's employment grew rapidly with the modernization of Finnish society and with the development of its societal structure and economy from an agricultural society into a postindustrial service society.

The Finnish societal and economic structures have developed in close connection with the welfare state. This development has been the result of a corporatist policy: the tripartite negotiations between employers' associations, labor unions, and the state did for a long time include general agreements on wage structure, taxation development, social policy legislation, services development, and other societal infrastructure. The development of social services has guaranteed publicly provided childcare services and thus provided possibilities for women's participation in the labor markets. Simultaneously, large public sector employment opportunities for women have been created. The strong and salient segregation prevailing in the labor markets is at least partly strengthened by the strong public sector.

The rapid development of the Finnish economy from an agricultural economy and society during the beginning of the twentieth century into a multidimensional postindustrial service economy has taken less than 100 years. Today high-tech telecommunications corporations such as Nokia and traditional corporations such as global forest product companies create the public image for the nation-state. But at least as strongly as telecommunications mirror the present-day Finland, so also does the image of the strong Nordic welfare state: one key part of the public image comes from the strong and universal welfare state service sector, which employs a large share of women.

Finland's standard of living is high in comparison to that of many European countries. During the twentieth century, Finland's total per capita production has grown more than elevenfold, an average of some 3 percent annually. This growth has been faster than in any other European country during the same period. As a result of the high standard of living, high educational level of the population, and general well-being, it is only natural that the life expectancy at birth in 2000 for women is 81.0 years and for men 74.1 years. In a similar fashion, the infant and maternal mortality

Figure 12.1
Finnish Population by Age and by Gender, 2001

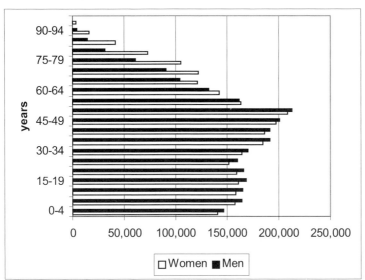

figures in Finland are among the lowest in the world. Infant mortality is 3.4 for 1,000 females and 3.8 for 1,000 males. Total fertility rate in Finland has remained under 2.0 for two decades now. The average number of children per family is 1.8 (in 1998).[1] The population in Finland is also getting older (Figure 12.1).

OVERVIEW OF WOMEN'S ISSUES

Will the strong foothold of women in public life and employment hold against the changes that are taking place in Finland due to economic restructuring and pressures coming from supranational organizations such as the EU? Finnish women bear the cultural image of being strong and independent: to have a good education, a job, and financial independence are considered to be the cornerstones of gender equality and of equal societal and citizenship positions. This cultural and societal image of strong Finnish women has its roots in the relatively late societal development from an agricultural to postindustrial society. Women's work was indispensable in agrarian communities, and the relatively low standard of living in the early decades of the twentieth century made it necessary for wives to work outside the home. Thus, Finnish women have been active in the labor markets, first in agrarian societies because of the economic necessity and later on as a natural continuation for the strong cultural pattern of working women. Gender equality thus has a long history in Finnish culture and society. The problems in gender issues in today's Finland thus are related to patterns of working life, the ability to combine work and family life, strong segregation in the economy and working life, and the questions of violence, abuse, and attitudinal sexism in society.

Despite the high standard of living, the strong differentiation prevails in society, especially in the labor markets. The existing gender differentiation known throughout the global economy comprises the social and cultural processes that overvalue male and female differences and create new divisions between women and men.[2] Gender differentiation also defines activities and work tasks as female or male, thus creating and reproducing new gendered constructions of "naturally" defined or experienced differences between genders. The rapid growth of the telecommunications industry in Finland clearly shows gendering taking place even in new industrial sectors.

Most women work in paid employment in Finland. They usually reach high, very often university, educational levels. Enrollment rate in university education in European countries is highest in Finland; close to 15 percent of the population aged 17–34 are enrolled in university education in Finland.[3] Female-dominated fields of study are many, ranging from health sciences to art and design. Despite their high education, women's salary level in 2000 was 81 percent of men's at the state employment sector, 85 percent at the municipal sector, and 83 percent at the private sector.[4] The effects of strong segregation in education are visible in the labor markets and in societal segregation in a variety of fields.

EDUCATION

Education is one of the cornerstones of Finnish society. Finland has always invested in education: the public expenditure level on educational institutions as a percentage of gross domestic product (GDP) is around 6 percent.[5] GDP is the market value of all goods and services produced in a year within a country. It is the standard measure of the overall size of the economy, and the share of educational spending relative to the GDP tells us how much of the financial resources are allocated to education within the national economy.

Preschool education in children's daycare centers and comprehensive schools takes place before their seventh birthday. All children receive a nine-year primary education, which is a universal right and without any cost to parents. Further education, either in the upper secondary general schools or in vocational schools and colleges, is also strongly subsidized, thus encouraging most young people to attend secondary education. Thirty-five percent of teenagers and young adults attend university-level education.[6]

Opportunities

The opportunities for education are many, and gender segregation is in favor of women: women enroll in university education in larger numbers than men—of university students, 55 percent are currently women and 45 percent men. Female-dominated fields of study are health sciences (92 percent of students are women), veterinary medicine (89 percent), psychology (86 percent), pharmacy (85 percent), education (83 percent), humanities (78 percent), social sciences (66 percent), art and design (64 percent), dentistry (62 percent), and medicine (61 percent). The only male-dominated field of study is engineering (81 percent male students). Mixed fields of university study are law (51 percent women students), business (54 percent), and natural sciences (55 percent).[7] The opportunities are open for women in all fields of education. However, even if the segregation would decrease further in the educational structures, diminishing segregation in the labor markets takes a relatively long time.

Literacy

According to the international PISA project, in which the reading literacy, mathematics, and natural science knowledge of fifteen-year-old schoolchildren were assessed in thirty-two countries, Finland scores first in reading abilities. However, the scoring difference between girls and boys was larger in Finland than in any other country.[8]

EMPLOYMENT AND THE ECONOMY

Finnish women have always worked. The labor force participation rate in 2001 for women was almost as high as for Finnish men. Even before the public daycare system was universally available (in the early 1970s), women's labor force participation was well over 50 percent of the adult population. When the publicly provided daycare system was introduced, women's labor force participation remained at its high level even for those women who were on maternal leave or on leave with a children's home care allowance scheme.

The Finnish economy as well as employment in Finland are, however, highly segregated according to gender. The strong segregation between women and men in employment is most visible in the division of the labor force between public and private sector: women work more at the public sector in comparison to men. Of women, 59 percent are employed in the private sector, 35 percent by local governments, and 6 percent by the central government. Of men, 83 percent are employed in the private sector, 10 percent by local governments, and 7 percent by the central government.

The Finnish economy is bipolar by structure. On the one hand, the public sector (health care, social care, elder care, childcare, education, and public administration) is responsible for a large part of the GDP and employment, especially women's employment. On the other hand, high-tech and knowledge-intensive production is the key promotion for the GDP growth. In short, the Finnish economy can be called the Nordic welfare state with a knowledge-intensive export sector.

Working life and the economy also change the ways work has been organized. Men report more stability in the workplace and also more bonuses in addition to their normal salary than women. Men also report more positively about the possibilities for career development than women throughout the years (1977–1997), irrespective of the job tasks. Women report using more computers in their work than men, and for both sexes the percentage is high: 67 percent for women and 64 percent for men.[9]

The gendering process in working life is multilayered and takes place through a variety of overlapping social processes. These processes include socialization, actions of social institutions, and a variety of interactions between individuals, groups, and norms defining and maintaining the regulative patterns for these interactions. The complexity of these processes for their part maintains the rigidity of segregation patterns in working life. The coherence of the supposed "natural" division of labor is difficult to break down, thus slowing down the process of desegregation.

Job/Career Opportunities

The high level of education does guarantee both women and men the same possibilities to enter any field they desire. However, career development does not lead to the same positions for men and for women. Over 70 percent of the employees in the public sector are women, and of those employed by municipalities, 77 percent are women. In the private sector, 39 percent of the employees are women. Partly as a consequence of the high segregation both in education and in the working life, the top positions in enterprises are very male dominated, and less than 2–3 percent of top management in companies are women. In middle and higher management, women's share is approximately 20 percent. Both horizontal and vertical segregation have taken new forms during the 1990s, but strong desegregation has not yet taken place despite changes in the economy. Segregation is even stronger in entrepreneurship, where women's entrepreneurial activities are concentrated in the female-dominated sectors.

There is also a difference between women and men in the nature of employment contracts. Although most work contracts are usually made to continue as long as both parties, employer and employee, so wish, fixed-term contracts are made for a specific time period only. This is often unfavorable for women. When the period of child home care allowance, at a maximum for three years, is over, both women and men should have the opportunity to return to their job, provided that they have a contract that has lasted longer than their childcare break. In 2001, 20 percent of women's employment contracts were fixed-term, whereas for men the share of fixed-term contracts was only 13 percent. Part-time work is not popular in Finland; 16.8 percent of women in paid employment worked part-time in 2001, whereas for men the figure is 7.1 percent.

Pay

Women get approximately 83 percent of men's salaries. Women's average salary level in 2000 is 81 percent of men's in the state employment sector, 85 percent in the municipal sector, and 83 percent in the private sector.[10] The salaries in the public sector are most often set according to job qualifications. Salaries in the private sector are more flexible in comparison to public sector ones.[11]

Working Conditions

Legislation concerning work environment and working conditions is extensive, mostly due to the strong position of labor unions. Psychological working environment and environmental production are more difficult to define. Legislation concerning bullying in the workplace exists. A variety of well-being programs, both psychologically and physically oriented, has been implemented during the last few years due to a great extent to the needs of the aging work force. Activities that maintain work ability and promote well-being are common in the Finnish workplaces, and more than two thirds of employees have access to them.

Sexual Harassment

The emergence of sexual harassment as a social problem came relatively late in Finnish society. But it is now recognized as a severely limiting condition, partly due to a few cases in which high-powered men in managerial positions were found guilty of sexual harassment. Finnish legislation on sexual harassment exists in the equality legislation. It does not explicitly differentiate between hostile or offensive work environments, but it assumes that employers will enact rules against harassment. In the present form, legislation protects employees but not customers, clients, or other persons outside of the employment contract.

Support for Mothers/Caretakers

Maternal Leave

The length of maternal and parental leave in Finland is 263 weekdays (approximately forty-four weeks). Of this leave, 105 weekdays are reserved solely for mothers (maternity allowance period), and the rest of the parental allowance period—158 weekdays—can be divided between the mother and father. Fathers are entitled to a paternity allowance period of 6–12 weekdays in connection with childbirth and to another six weekdays within their parental allowance period, but the average paternity or parental leave of fathers amounts to fifteen days.[12] That average length indicates that fathers do not very often take advantage of the possibility for parental leave.

Daycare

In 2000, 46 percent of all children under the age of six were in public or private daycare.[13] Parents with children under age three are eligible for home care allowances, that is, they are entitled to a leave of absence in order to care for their children. This new policy line was adopted in the mid-1980s—whereas in other Nordic countries, the financial support for children's public daycare is directed toward care in daycare centers and kindergartens, Finland maintains diversity in its support. The subjective right for parents to have publicly purchased childcare led to diversity in the ways the childcare was organized. The legal right to children's daycare services has been a necessity in Finland where women are actively involved in the labor market.

Daycare in Espoo, Finland. Photo © Painet.

Until the 1990s, children's daycare places increased steadily, and Finland was gradually catching up to the coverage of the daycare systems in Sweden and Denmark.[14] The 1990s recession brought a break in this development, and only during the last years of the 1990s have childcare services increased. In addition, the home care allowances and private care allowances introduced during the 1990s have increased childcare options. However, they have not increased gender equality in the sense that over 90 percent of those staying at home with their children, after parental leave, are women. However, it is important to note that women have a right to return to their old jobs after the child home care allowance period is over. The average legal allowance for child home care was approximately 350 Euro in December 2000.[15] Indeed, childcare is a public issue to a much larger extent than elderly care is. Social rights are well established, and universal principles in childcare have become stronger than they were earlier.

Family and Medical Leave

The employer has the obligation to pay salary during the sick leave of the employee. This employee right is based on employment contract legislation and collective agreements. The length of the employment relationship influences the length of the period for which salary is paid during sick leave. According to the law and many collective agreements, half of the salary is paid in employment relationships shorter than one month. After the employer's obligation to pay salary for the sick-leave period of the employee has ended, all those living permanently in Finland can get financial aid on the basis of their health insurance. In general, absenteeism from work is low in Finland. The rates are 4.6 percent for blue-collar workers and 2 percent for white-collar workers. However, absence statistics do not include sick leaves of fewer than nine days.

Inheritance and Property Rights

Both women and men have the same inheritance rights. Recently, Finland adopted legislation, in conjunction with the other Nordic countries, granting same-sex couples the right to register their relationships and to have equal rights of inheritance.

Social/Government Programs

Welfare

The welfare system in Finland is universal and includes many subjective rights for citizens. Thus, government programs specifically targeted for women and social programs for women are not that numerous, or they might be targeted to specific questions such as increasing women's entrepreneurial activities (e.g., a loan system, educational courses, and so on) or creating more after-school activities for schoolchildren. The research and development project on the reconciliation of working life and family life, and the project on the prevention of violence against women, are carried out at National Research and Development Centre for Welfare and Health (STAKES) and have been financed within the government's programs. The national Well-Being at Work Programme is a government-sponsored program that directs many of its efforts toward improving women's work situations.

FAMILY AND SEXUALITY

Gender Roles

According to time-budget studies, young families have made changes in the gender roles but fall back on the traditional, gendered division of labor at home after they have children. These studies also show that for all family types, it is the wife who works more hours per week in total. Most often in all family types, the husband works for paid work more hours per week but spends fewer hours in domestic work; thus, the total hours per week are higher for women.[16]

Marriage

The importance and role of marriage have changed over time in Finland as in many other countries. For women, their average age at their first marriage is higher than it is for first-time mothers. In 2002 the average age for tying the knot is 28.4 years for women, and for men 30.6 years. The average age for first childbirth for women is 27.6 years. These two figures tell us about the habits of cohabiting and childbirth before marriage. The nature of marriage has changed: no longer sacred by nature and more defined by habits than by its religious aspects, the wedding ceremony has become a festivity of its own. The cultural change is visible in statistics: the increase in the number of cohabiting couples occurred after 1985, and in 1999, 38.7 percent of children were born outside of marriage.

Even though there have been changes in the family structure, increases in cohabitation, and increases in the number of single mothers, the dominant family structure still seems to be the married couple, 67.8 percent of all families are married couples. The share of cohabiting couples is 18.7 percent and single mothers' share is 11.4 percent of all families. Only 2 percent of families consist of a single father and children.[17] The percentage of one-person households was highest in Finland among the fourteen EU countries. Of all households, 35 percent were one-person households.[18] Registration of same-sex couples cohabitation was made possible in Finland in 2001.

Reproduction

Sex Education

Sex education is integrated into basic education in school.

Contraception and Abortion

The most frequently used methods in contraception and family planning are pills and hormone-based IUDs (hormonal contraceptives) and IUDs and condoms (nonhormonal contraceptives). The hormonal contraceptives are available through prescription.

The abortion rate in Finland is low by international comparisons. Following the introduction of the Abortion Act in 1970, abortion numbers declined until 1995. The number of abortions performed yearly for every

1,000 females aged 15–49 rose slightly during the last two years from 8.7 in 2000 to 9.1 in 2002.[19] Abortion is permitted on both medical and on socioeconomic grounds. In over 86 percent of cases socioeconomic grounds are cited as the reason for abortion.

Teen Pregnancy

Although the abortion rate is very low, the highest number occurs among 20–24-year-olds and decreases gradually with age. Since the late 1990s, abortion numbers have been growing to some extent among teen-agers.

HEALTH

Health Care Access

Access to health care is universal and heavily compensated to all citizens. This means in practice that in the publicly provided health care system, patients do not pay the "market" price for health care. The health care system consists of public health care, where primary care and specialized health care are tightly bound together, through the gatekeeping of the primary health care doctors in the municipal health care system. Health care at work and privately paid health care are options for many, but not for all; thus, it is not a fully universal system.

Diseases and Disorders

Cancer

For women, the most common diseases are types of cancer. The cause of death for women is most often by diseases of the circulatory system or by cancer.

Depression

Depression among women has become an issue in large part because of the relatively high percentage of women taking antidepressant medication. Women appear to be more vulnerable to the effects of job insecurity, which can increase exhaustion and negatively impact both work and home lives.

POLITICS AND LAW

Suffrage

Finland became the first European nation to give women the vote in 1906.

Political Participation

Finnish women have been particularly involved with legislation concerning social issues, culture, and education. In the 1999 elections, seventy-four women were elected, or 37 percent of the members of the house (total 200 persons). Almost continuously throughout the 1990s, the speaker of parliament has been a woman. In the campaign for the presidential election in 2000, four of the candidates were women and three were men. In the recently elected government, for the first time in Finland's history half of the eighteen ministers are women. Women hold the posts of prime minister, minister of education, minister of finance, minister of cultural affairs, minister of social affairs and health, minister of health and social services, minister of labor, minister of transport and communications, and minister of foreign trade and development.

Women's Rights

The Equality Law that went into effect in 1987 committed Finland to achieving full equality for women. Finland has quota legislation, which requires that at least 40 percent of each sex should be represented in the membership of various public decision-making bodies. This has led to an increase in women's membership from 25 percent in 1980 to 48 percent in 1998.

Feminist Movements

Finland has been focused on the expansion of democracy, citizenship, and equality rather than on feminist ideas. The very early women's movement has been partly related to social classes, the early women's movements being upper class in the early nineteenth century, and then part of the labor movement and temperance movement. The feminist movement of the 1960s and 1970s had stronger and wider background in society at all levels, and the path toward equality was the key issue. The feminist activity of the 1960s and 1970s has changed today into more diversified expressions of feminism instead of a single movement.[20] By making people aware of gender inequality, such as in the disparity in wages, feminist issues have become a part of the political life and even of party politics.

Lesbian Rights

Finland's new law on same-sex-relationships, which was accepted in 2001, gives registered gay couples most of the rights of married couples but no parental rights.

RELIGION AND SPIRITUALITY

In 2000, 85 percent of the Finnish population was registered with the Evangelical-Lutheran Church of Finland. The high percentage does not indicate a strong importance of religion in everyday life but rather tells more of the habits of the heart. Other societal features point to a secularization of the society. Perhaps partly because of this, the Evangelical-Lutheran Church has developed a variety of other activities, such as national and international humanitarian and missionary work. Even if the church does not have a very visible role in the everyday life or practice of individuals, approximately 80 percent of couples are married in the church.

The roles of other churches such as the Orthodox Church and Catholic Church are minor, with less than 1.2 percent of the population belonging to these churches. Judaism and Islam are represented with over thirty other registered churches and religious communities in Finland.

Women's Roles

Women have gained the right to become clergy in the Evangelical-Lutheran Church. Finland's first women pastors were ordained in 1988. Currently the amount of women clergy in the Finnish Evangelical-Lutheran Church is 22 percent, or 720. All church posts are open to women, including that of bishop. Women's roles in the Evangelical-Lutheran Church are not without some tensions. Even if women are allowed to become pastors, some male pastors and bishops decline to work with women.

Rituals and Religious Practices

Finnish people attend church most often at Christmas and in connection with confirmations. The church reaches people most thoroughly in connection with religious rites. Even if church attendance is low, roughly 10 percent of the population attend church once a month, 80 percent of Finns are wed in the Lutheran church, and 90 percent of infants are baptized in church.

VIOLENCE

Domestic Violence

Domestic violence has been a hidden problem in Finnish society for a long time. Violence against women has been acknowledged as a serious problem only lately, and legislation has changed accordingly. Police statistics in 2000 recorded 2,876 cases of domestic violence, and the majority of victims were women. The estimates of the incoming calls to police vary between 10,000 and 12,000 annually. In 1997 the government launched a program to promote women's equality, and included in this umbrella project was one project targeting violence against women and domestic violence. It has offered support for women and created local networks that work against domestic violence.

Rape/Sexual Assault

In 2000, the number of reported sexual assaults was over 1,000. Of these, the number of reported rapes was 596. The numbers seem low in comparison to reported bodily assaults, fights, and so on (16,900 in 2000). In one-fourth of the rape cases that were reported to police in 1998, the rapist was unknown to the victim. According to research results, most often the victim knows the rapist. Rape within marriage was made criminal in 1994.[21]

OUTLOOK FOR THE TWENTY-FIRST CENTURY

Finland declared its independence on December 6, 1917, and in the winter of 1918 endured a tragic civil war. Since the days of the independence, Finnish women have declared their equality and expressed their issues in the various aspects of Finnish society. Although some topics such as equality in education and enhanced possibilities in the workplace have become relatively widespread, others remain challenges for the twenty-first century. For example, most Finnish women and men reply to the question of gender equality that women do not enjoy the same status in Finland as men. Yet, only 22 percent of women and 10 percent of men felt that the status of women was clearly inferior to that of men.[22] This contradiction is difficult to explain, but perhaps attitudes have not changed as much as they should have. Another challenging issue concerns women's abilities to reach positions of power, especially economic power, as well as top positions in all arenas.

NOTES

1. Statistics Finland, *Gender Equality Statistics* (Helsinki: Author, 2002).

2. West and Zimmerman, 1987, 137; Reskin and Padavic, 1994.

3. Organisation for Economic Cooperation and Development, *Education at a Glance*, OECD Indicators 1998 (Paris: OECD, 1998).

4. Statistics Finland, 2002.

5. OECD, 1998.

6. OECD, 1998.

7. Statistics Finland, 2002.

8. Helsingin Sanomat, *OECD Study* (Helsinki: Helsingin Sanomat, 2001).

9. Anna-Maija Lehto and Hanna Sutela, *Efficient, More Efficient, Exhausted* (Helsinki: Statistics Finland, 1998).

10. Statistics Finland, 2002.

11. Statistics Finland, *Gender Equality Statistics* (Helsinki: Author, 2001).

12. Statistics Finland, 2001.

13. Statistics Finland, 2001.

14. Teppo Kröger, "The Dilemma of Municipalities," *Journal of Social Policy* 26, no. 4 (1997).

15. Statistics Finland, 2001.

16. Statistics Finland, 1997/1998.

17. Statistics Finland, 2002.

18. According to a Eurostat study (1995).

19. Sirpa Taskinen, "Finland" in *European Observatory on Family Matters* (Brussels: European Union, 2000).

20. Solveig Bergman, *The Politics of Feminism* (Turku, Finland: Åbo Akademi University, 2002).

21. Päivi Liikamaa, "Raiskaus on edelleen vähätelty rikos. Kristiina Valkaman haastattelu," *Dialogi* 7 (2002): 12, available online at www.stakes.fi/dialogi/english/index. htm; Sirkka Perttu, Päivi Mononen-Mikkilä, Riikka Rauhala, and Päivi Särkkälä, *Päänavaus selviytymiseen* (Helsinki: National Research and Development Centre for Welfare and Health, 1999), available online at www.stakes.fi/vakivalta/text/ paanavaussuomivalmis.doc.

22. Statistics Finland, *Gender Equality Statistics* (Helsinki, 2001).

RESOURCE GUIDE

Suggested Reading

Bergman, Solveig. *The Politics of Feminism: Autonomous Feminist Movements in Finland and West Germany from the 1960s to the 1980s*. Turku, Finland: Åbo Akademi University, 2002.

Lehto, Anna-Maija, and Hanna Sutela. *Efficient, More Efficient, Exhausted: Findings of Finnish Quality of Work Life Surveys 1977–1997*. SVT. In *Labour Market*, 8. Helsinki: Statistics Finland, 1998.

Lehto, Anna-Maija, and Hanna Sutela. "Gender Equality in Working Life." In *Labor Market*, 22. Helsinki: Statistics Finland, 1999.

Rantalaiho, Liisa, and Tuula Heiskanen, eds. *Gendered Practices in Working Life*. London: Palgrave, 1997.

Riska, Elianne, and Katarina Wegar. *Women, Work and Medicine*. London: Sage, 1995.

Web Sites and Organizations

The Coalition of Finnish Women's Associations for Joint Action, www.nytkis.org/ nytkisinfoeng.html.

The coalition of the major political women's organizations in Finland and of three nonpolitical women's associations.

Ministry of Social Affairs and Health, www.vn.fi/stm/english/equality/equality_fset. htm.

The National Council of Women of Finland, www.naisjarjestojenkeskusliitto.fi/ english.html.

Over fifty member organizations representing over half a million members.

Office of the Ombudsman for Equality, the Gender Equality Unit, and the Council for Equality, www.tasa-arvo.fi/www-eng/index.html.

The ombudsman for equality works as an independent authority monitoring compliance with the Act on Equality between Women and Men. The Equality Unit prepares the government's gender equality policy. The Unit coordinates international issues.

SELECTED BIBLIOGRAPHY

Anttonen, Anneli. "The Politics of Social Care in Finland." In *Care Work: A Quest of Security*, edited by M. Daly, 143–53. Geneva: ILO, 2001.

Bergman, Solveig. *The Politics of Feminism: Autonomous Feminist Movements in Finland and West Germany from the 1960s to the 1980s*. Turku, Finland: Åbo Akademi University, 2002.

Helsingin Sanomat. *OECD Study*. Helsinki: Helsingin Sanomat, 2001.

Kröger, Teppo. "The Dilemma of Municipalities: Scandinavian Approaches to Child Day-care Provision." *Journal of Social Policy* 26 (1997): 4.

Liikamaa, Päivi. "Raiskaus on edelleen vähätelty. Kristiina Valkaman haastattelu." *Dialogi* 7 (2002): 12. www.stakes.fi/dialogi/english/index.htm.

Organization for Economic Cooperation and Development (OECD). *Education at a Glance*. OECD Indicators 1998. Paris: OECD, 1998.

Perttu, Sirkka, Päivi Mononen-Mikkilä, Riikka Rauhala, and Päivi Särkkälä. *Päänavaus selviyty miseen*. Helsinki: National Research and Development Centre for Welfare and Health, 1999. www.stakes.fi/vakivalta/text/paanavaussuomivalmis.doc.

Statistics Finland. *Gender Equality Statistics*. Helsinki: Author, 1999.

———. *Gender Equality Statistics*. Helsinki: Author, 2001.

———. *Gender Equality Statistics*. Helsinki: Author, 2002.

13

FRANCE

Deborah Reed-Danahay

PROFILE OF FRANCE

France is the largest Western European nation in surface area and is a major economic and political leader in Europe and the world. It has a democratic and highly centralized form of government. Paris is the nation's capital. The economic base depends upon industrial production and service industries, along with agriculture. France is a nation of immigrants (primarily from Portugal, Italy, Eastern Europe, and North Africa), many of whom have become citizens. The noncitizen foreign population in France was 6 percent in 1991 (comparable to that in the United States). In 1990, there were 1.6 million foreign (noncitizen) women living in France. Out of all women in France, 4.5 percent are noncitizens, less than the rate for men of 7.9 percent. Forty-eight percent of all immigrants in France are female.

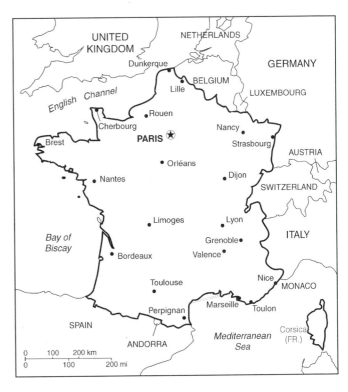

In 2001, the French population was 59,551,227. The female population is just slightly higher than the male population, with a ratio of 0.95 male/female. Approximately 80 percent of French people live in urban areas. The infant mortality rate is 4.46 deaths/1,000 live births. The fertility rate is approximately 1.7 overall and 2.8 percent for foreign women.

The life expectancy rate for those born in 2001 was 78.9, with an average of 75 for men to 83 for women.

OVERVIEW OF WOMEN'S ISSUES

The recent history of women in France has been shaped by its agricultural past, more recent trends of urbanization and industrialization, the influence of the Catholic Church, and the role of immigrants. As in most of Europe, there have been major changes associated with marriage and divorce for women, particularly since World War II. Women now marry later and divorce more frequently. France has a high rate of births out of wedlock. Today, almost half of all workers are female, and the dual-career family is the norm. Political and legal rights for women came later in France than in other European nations, and the feminist movement has struggled to overcome the inequalities among men and women. Great strides have been made, especially since the 1970s.

Two major trends from the latter half of the twentieth century affect women in France. The first trend is the growth of the European Union and its emphasis on human rights legislation. The EU has its own commissions and programs that support women's rights, and this lends support to French women's organizations. The 1997 EU Treaty of Amsterdam, the current charter of the European Union, assures women's rights among member nations—including such things as equal pay for equal work. The European Commission is currently supporting a 2001–2005 program of research and policy, "Equality of Opportunity between Men and Women," among member nations and applicants to membership in the EU. The second trend is that of the influx of immigrants, particularly from Eastern Europe and Africa. Immigrant women and their daughters have been at the center of such controversies in France as the wearing of the veil (*hajib*) to school and the practice of female excision (female genital mutilation).

EDUCATION

Opportunities

The educational system of France has long held a high reputation for excellence, particularly in secondary and higher education. There have, however, been both gender and social class inequities in this system. The opportunities for females have lagged behind those of males, and there continue to be inequalities in educational opportunity for French women. The earliest forms of primary schooling in France were in the past controlled by the Catholic Church, with girls being taught by nuns in separate schools from those of boys. France has had free and mandatory public primary schooling for males and females since the Ferry laws of 1881 and 1882. Many early schools segregated boys and girls with separate teachers, and a coeducational school was marked with the label *mixte*. Secondary schooling did not become coeducational until the 1960s.

Today, for every 100 males in higher education, there are 120 females, and girls receive university degrees at slightly higher rates than boys. It is important, however, to examine the subjects that girls study relative to boys. Young women are underrepresented in the sciences and technical subjects. They are much more prone to study literature, social sciences, and arts.

The education of Muslim immigrant girls in French schools has been at the center of debate over the wearing of the *hajib*, or scarf, to school. France has a tradition of separation of church and state, even though many Catholic schools receive state subsidies if they follow the national curriculum. In 1989 the "Affair of the Foulard (headscarf)," as it was called, provoked a major controversy in France. In a school near Paris, three North African girls were forbidden by their principal to wear the *hajib*, with the rationale that the scarf is a religious symbol and inappropriate at school. This decision was supported by the French Ministry of Culture and upheld by the French courts. There were debates on this issue among feminists, the Left and the Right, anti-immigrant groups, and others. For feminists, the issue was one of whether or not the veil represented oppression for women. For those on the Left who support the total separation of church and state in France, it was difficult to weigh the rights of immigrants against the value of religious neutrality in schools. For anti-immigrant groups on the extreme Right, the *hajib* represents encroachments upon French identity. This issue has not been completely resolved, and some school principals permit students to wear the scarf.

Literacy

France has a 99 percent literacy rate for both men and women. French women read a great deal more than do men—41 percent of women compared to 26 percent of men, for example, read at least one book per week. Women read more fiction than do men, but the reading of newspapers is about equal between the two sexes.[1]

EMPLOYMENT AND THE ECONOMY

Job/Career Opportunities

At the beginning of the twentieth century, women were just over a third of the total work force in France. There was a sharp decline of women in the work force during midcentury, but for women born in the 1950s and after, being part of the labor market is the norm. In 2000, the overall employment rate for women was 48 percent and for men 62 percent. For women between the ages of 25 and 49, the employment rate was 80 percent.

There is a high level of sex segregation in France's labor force. There are more women than men (71 percent to 47 percent) in service professions (such as primary school teachers and medical technicians). Eighty-five percent of all part-time workers in France are women. Unemployment for women is higher than for men, even when controlling for factors such as age and level of training. With the overall French unemployment rate at 10 percent in 2000, the rate for women was 11.9 percent and the rate for men was 8.5 percent.

For immigrant women in France, the opportunities for work vary considerably according to the country of origin. For example, 75 percent of Portuguese women are in the work force as compared to only 38 percent of women from Turkey. Immigrant women are also much less prone to work outside of the home if there is a child under the age of three in the household.

Pay

Despite their high levels of employment, many women are in low-paying, temporary, and part-time jobs. France passed legislation in 1972 in order to assure women equal pay with men for work of equal value. Since the 1970s, only slow progress has been made in changing the gender gap in salaries. In the private and semipublic sectors of the economy, women workers earn approximately 25 percent less than men—which is due in part to the fact that more women work in low-level types of employment and more of them work part-time. In civil service positions, there is slightly less distinction between male and female salaries, with men making a little less than 20 percent more than women. When both private and public sectors are taken together, the average female worker earns 5–15 percent less than her male counterpart, depending upon the profession.

Working Conditions

The conditions for women at work have significantly improved, in part due to legislation passed since the 1970s and 1980s. However, changing attitudes toward women and work accompany and sometimes precede legislation. It was not until 1980 that French law prohibited the dismissal of a female employee due to pregnancy. The 1983 Roudy Law, named after Yvette Roudy, then minister of women's rights, worked to ensure "equal treatment" of women in employment and at work. Companies with more than fifty employees are obligated by this law to file annual reports on employment practices with respect to gender (including such factors as training and promotion). Companies may receive state subsidies if they demonstrate exemplary employment practices that either treat women equally with men or help close gender gaps in promotions.

Sexual Harassment

Sexual harassment (*harcèlement sexuel*) in France received less attention than other aspects of working conditions for women until the 1980s, when it began to be discussed as a public policy issue. Attitudes toward consensual relationships between employees in France are generally liberal, and this is believed to be a private matter. Two feminist associations helped pressure the government to enact legislation, and they have worked to change attitudes and publicize sexual harassment at work. These organizations are European Association against Violence against Women at Work (AVFT) and League of Women's Rights (LDF). Legislation was passed in 1992 that legally defined sexual harassment and included it within the penal code. The French have adopted a narrow form of legislation, in which offenses are to be handled by management and in which only direct harassment of employees by superiors is covered. Sanctions can include up to one year in prison.

Support for Mothers/Caretakers

Most married women with children work at least part-time and are expected to also carry the burden of domestic labor and childcare in the home.

Maternal Leave

France ensures at least fourteen weeks of paid pregnancy leave for all female workers (including time before and after birth) and also mandates that this leave cannot be counted in any way against a woman's benefits or eligibility for promotion. French law also mandates that a woman must be permitted to return to the same position after such a leave.

Daycare

Women are encouraged to return to work after having a child through a program called the Return-to-Work Incentive for Women, which provides subsidies if their child is under the age of six. About 40 percent of young children under age three are in daycare. France has public daycare (*crèches*) available to working women and also subsidizes childcare in the home. Free public schooling is available in most areas starting at age two (for nursery school). Over one-third of French children are in school between the ages of two and three, and 95 percent of all three- to six-year-olds are in nursery school.

Inheritance and Property Rights

Women in France today have full legal equality with men in inheritance and property rights. Under the Napoleonic Code of the early 1800s, women's rights were fiercely eroded. A woman's property came under the direct control of her husband. The code did, however, establish equal rights of inheritance to males and females (although, after marriage, a woman lost her rights). In 1965, wives became eligible to have their own bank accounts without spousal consent. The Badinter Law of 1985 abolished all legal authority in property disposal that gave any advantage to the husband.

Social/Government Programs

Welfare

France has an elaborate social welfare program that assures minimum income and health benefits to all women. From its inception, social welfare in France has been pronatalist and profamily. Because France experienced a drop in the birthrate during World War II, it encouraged women to bear several children by providing state subsidies to families in amounts that rose with the birth of each child. France has had a "Family Code" ensuring the welfare of children and families since 1939, which was eventually blended into the social security system. The social security system, founded in 1946, is funded directly by employers and workers. A minimum level of income is assured for the unemployed and destitute under the RMI (*Revenue Minimum d'Insertion*), an unemployment assistance payment. There are several means of support to families and single mothers offered by the state. France provides Family Allowance Funds (*Caisses d'allocations familiales*) to each family in order to help with the costs of raising children. If a parent has worked for two years and stops work in order to care for a child under age three, the family will receive a Parental Education and Upbringing Allowance (*Allocation Parentele d'Education*). Stay-at-home mothers of large families receive free health insurance.

FAMILY AND SEXUALITY

Gender Roles

France's agricultural and rural past shapes the dominant model of gender roles. Peasant households traditionally had a gendered division of labor that was incorporated into community life, although husband and wife often worked together on many tasks. In general, women carried out the domestic tasks of childrearing, cooking, and housework. They were also involved in farm labor, such as harvesting and tending young animals.

With the growth of industrialization and wage labor, there was a separation of the domestic sphere of home and the workplace. Wealthier women stayed at home, overseeing the domestic duties; working-class women entered wage labor in jobs that were associated with "women's work" such as laundries, certain types of factory work, and domestic work. In bourgeois families, husbands controlled wealth and their wives had limited autonomy over their own lives or those of their children.

Eighty percent of French adults between the ages of 35 and 54 live as couples. The sexual division of labor in the average French home today is such that women, despite their high levels of employment outside of the home, do 80 percent of the domestic chores. In 60 percent of French households, men do no domestic labor at all. Of all families in France with children under the age of twenty-five, 11 percent are headed by single mothers. In nine out of ten cases, single-parent families in France are headed by mothers. Rates of

Mother shops with her children in a small village in Burgundy, France. Photo © Painet.

single mothers are much higher in urban areas and rise with the population of the city (ranging from 5.8 percent in rural areas to 14.5 percent in Paris). The standard of living is, on average, 20 percent lower for single-mother households than for two-parent households. Child support payments are never received in 30 percent of cases, although state subsidies to families can offset this to some degree.

Marriage

Marriage is both a civil and religious institution in France. Even if there is a religious ceremony, the legal marriage must take place in city hall—so that often there are two ceremonies. Women did not attain the status of full legal persons in marriage until 1965, when the French Civil Code abolished a previous law requiring a husband's consent for a woman to work, claim unemployment benefits, and open a bank account. Children are required by law to take the last name of their father if the couple is married. Since the mid-1980s, it has been legal for a child to have a hyphenated name including their father and mother's family names. Women are not required to take their husband's last name at marriage; however, in 1991 88 percent of married women had done so. After divorce, women in France are increasingly changing their names back to their maiden names.

France has seen a substantial change in marriage and divorce patterns during the past twenty years. Overall, the marriage rate is declining, and the age at marriage is rising. In total numbers, there were 39 percent fewer marriages in 1992 than there were in 1972. The divorce rate climbed from 22.5 percent in 1980 to 38.3 percent in 1996. The average age at marriage is twenty-six for women and twenty-eight for men. Most women marry within their own class milieu. Among noncitizen women in France 60 percent marry French citizens.

Cohabitation is increasingly frequent for young French men and women. More than half of all French women under the age of twenty-five who live with a partner are unmarried. A recent law permits legal unions that are not marriages for couples, lending legal status to cohabitating couples (including homosexual couples). This law, referred to as the civil solidarity pact (PACS; *pacte d'association civile et solidaire*), was passed in 1999. It is easier to dissolve than a marriage.

Reproduction

Births outside of marriage have risen from 11.4 percent of the total in 1980 to 37.6 percent in 1996. France's rate of out-of-wedlock births is second in the European Union only to that of Denmark.

Sex Education

Sex education is widely available in France, where sexual behavior is for the most part considered natural behavior even among teenagers. Concerns about contraception (in order to prevent abortions) and concerns about the health risks of sexually transmitted diseases and HIV also fuel efforts to provide adequate sex education. Families vary in how much discussion of sexual behavior occurs in the home, but there is a great deal of public information available. Sex education is taught at school and through media campaigns that, since the late 1980s, advocate safe sex and contraception. Teenagers have access to health care services for contraception (available in high schools), morning-after pills, and medical exams. French high schools sponsor free family planning clinics to teens. The MFPF (*Mouve-*

ment Français pour le Planning Familial) offers free clinics for both teen and adult women.

Contraception and Abortion

The sale of birth control and legalization of abortion came much later to France than to other European nations. The influence of the Catholic Church played a large role in this delay, while the women's movement worked to provide birth control and abortion to French women. A ban on the sale of birth control was not lifted until 1967. Contraception is now widely used in France. In 1994, of women ages 20–49 who did not wish to become pregnant, 97 percent were using birth control. The most popular form of birth control in France is the pill, followed by sterilization. Condom use among young women, particularly at the time of first sexual relations, has risen dramatically since the late 1980s when education about AIDS became widespread.

Abortion has been legal since 1975 and is now widely available to women of all ages. There are restrictions on abortion in France, however. It is easily available and free up until ten weeks, but second-trimester abortions are only available if they threaten the woman's life. In 1991, there were 18.4 abortions per 100 conceptions in France.

Teen Pregnancy

Contraception is available freely and anonymously to anyone in France, regardless of age. Unmarried minors are required, however, to have parental consent for a legal abortion. France's teen pregnancy rate is 9 per 1,000. The abortion rate for French teenagers is 7.9 per 1,000.

HEALTH

Health Care Access

France has national health care insurance, and health care is available in public and private hospitals and clinics. Ninety-nine percent of French residents are covered by health insurance of some kind. However, cutbacks in social services in France have resulted in an increasing amount of out-of-pocket medical expenses for most workers. Poor women may receive free medical care through the medical aide system. Illegal immigrants in France do not receive governmental support for health care and must rely upon charitable organizations. Services for health care are better in urban and suburban areas, leaving many rural dwellers in isolated areas with few services. Since most of the older female population lives in rural areas (where out-migration of younger people has led to an aging of the population), there is a need for services in these areas. Rural doctors do, however, still make home visits, and there is a system of visiting nurses that provide health care.

Diseases and Disorders

French women lead comparatively long and healthy lives. Female life expectancy in France is higher than in any other European nation; it was eighty-three in 2002. France also has the largest gender gap in life expectancy, with men living on average 8.5 years less than women. After age fifty-five, women outnumber men in France, and 73 percent of those over the age of eighty-five are women. Seventeen percent of all French women are aged sixty-five or older.

The leading causes of death for women in France are heart disease and cancer. French women have the second-lowest rate of cardiovascular disease in Europe, and French men have the lowest rate of European nations. This is often attributed to a combination of diet (including wine) and lifestyle—known as the "French paradox," in which despite the high incidence of cheeses and butter in the diet, there is still a relatively low level of heart disease. There is, however, an increasing amount of animal fat in the French diet, so this may change.

AIDS

AIDS, known as SIDA in France, affects more men than women. The ratio of male to female infection with HIV was 2.7 in 1993. More than half of HIV-positive women in France are aged 25–39. The proportion of women with AIDS increased from 11 percent in 1985 to 20 percent in 1993. Diagnostic tests for HIV are widely available in public clinics and centers that assure anonymity. Health insurance in France covers the cost of these tests and of treatment for all those who test positive. In general, the French have a tolerant attitude toward those with AIDS. Thanks to activist organizations, condoms are distributed in vending machines in most public places and in schools.

Cancer

One of the leading causes of death for women in France is cancer. Breast cancer is the leading cause of death by cancer for French women, followed by uterine cancer.

POLITICS AND LAW

France has a democratic government, which operates under the constitution of the Fifth Republic, established in 1958. Historically highly centralized, with Paris as its capital and cultural center, the French government began decentralization reforms in 1982. France has a president who is elected through popular vote and a prime minister, officially head of the government, who is appointed by the president. There is a bicameral parliament composed of a National Assembly and a Senate.

Suffrage

Women received the right to vote in 1944, much later than in other European nations. Universal suffrage for French males was achieved in 1848, so women had to wait almost 100 years for equality in suffrage.

Political Participation

Although historically French women voted more often for conservative political candidates, this has changed since the mid-1980s. The shift toward the left is influenced by the decline in religious participation, the rise in labor-force participation, and feminism. France has had one of the lowest rates of females elected to political office in Europe, and this fact has been referred to as "the French exception." In efforts to redress the lack of representation of women in French politics, a Secretary of State for Women's Affairs was created by the government in 1974. Journalist Françoise Giroud was the first woman in this post. Under Giroud's leadership, legislation was introduced granting women more rights in areas of employment and in marriage.

In the 1980s, a movement started to correct this historical trend, and various proposals were put forth. An influential book published in 1992, *Au Pouvoir Citoyennes: Liberté, Egalité, Parité* (Women Citizens to Power: Liberty, Equality, Parity), called for a legal change that would make female political representation mandatory. A law of parity was passed in June 2000. This law requires ballots in French local, regional, and national elections to list female as well as male candidates (with exceptions made for smaller towns or villages). In some cases, half of the candidates on a ballot must be female. The issue of parity is controversial among French feminists—with the "universalists" against such legislation and "difference" feminists, who argue that there is an "essential" difference between men and women, in favor of parity in elections.

Women's Rights

Feminist Movements

The so-called second wave of French feminism began with the women's liberation movement in the 1960s and picked up steam after May 1968, a period of rebellion among students, workers, and women. The main group of the 1970s was the Mouvement de Libération des Femmes, or MLF. The first major issue that galvanized feminist groups was the legalization of abortion. MLF was internally divided and, for the most part, did not seek to work within the system of public policy reform. Factions within MLF included a lesbian group, a psychoanalytical group, and a revolutionary group. Labor unions also began to focus on women's rights during the 1970s—including the Democratic French Confederation of Workers (CFDT), the main socialist labor union. In the late 1970s and early 1980s, the MLF splintered. Other groups such as the women's rights organization Choisir (Choose), political parties (especially the Socialist Party), as well as labor unions became prominent in political battles over women's rights. Key post-MLF groups include Association Européene contre les Violences Faites aux Femmes au Travail (AVFT) and Alliance des Femmes pour la Democratisation (AFD). New feminist groups formed by immigrant women have emerged in recent years, including Nanas Beurs, a group of young North African women. In the late twentieth century, the works of prominent French feminist theorists and writers, including Simone de Beauvoir, Hélène Cixous, Luce Iragary, and Julia Kristeva, were widely read and influenced feminist thinking throughout the West.

Lesbian Rights

Lesbians in France are legally protected from discrimination both through the French penal code, which prohibits discrimination based upon sexual orientation or "lifestyle," and labor laws that do not permit discrimination in the workplace (including in the military).

Marriage. With the new law of 1999, lesbian couples have a legal status that is available to all cohabiting couples. A lesbian couple in such a union, known as the civil solidarity pact (PACS; *pacte d'association civile et solidaire*), has the same rights of social welfare, tax, inheritance, and housing as do married couples, but the PACS is easier to dissolve.

Parenthood. In France, both single people and married couples may adopt a child, but this does not extend to those in PACS. Lesbians may adopt children as single parents, but it is often the case that declaration of homosexuality during this process may result in prohibition of the adoption by the judge. It is not possible for lesbian couples to adopt children jointly, but if one is the biological mother, the other may adopt the child. Artificial insemination in France is legally available only to married (i.e., heterosexual) couples.

Military Service

Women in the French military are all volunteers. France abolished its compulsory military service (which was strictly for males) in the late 1990s.

French women were legally permitted to serve in 1951, even though women had served unofficially since 1938. In 1972 and 1985, laws were passed to grant women equal status with men and to make sure that they are free to serve in all branches of the military (i.e., army, navy, and marines). Women are prohibited, however, from assignments such as service in the Foreign Legion, Special Forces, marine commandos, submarines, and naval aviation. The training of women is the same as that for men, and all military colleges and academies are now coeducational. Women make up 8 percent of the French military, with the highest proportion in the non-commissioned officer corps. There are two female brigadier generals.

RELIGION AND SPIRITUALITY

Religious freedom is guaranteed by the French Constitution, and the principle of separation of church and state was central to the French Revolution. The French minister of the interior is also the minister of religions, with jurisdiction over protection of the rights of religious groups to practice their religion. Neutrality in religion is an important principle for the French state, in that it seeks to preserve religious rights without preference for any particular religion, such as the dominant religion of Catholicism. Ninety percent of the population is Roman Catholic; other major religious affiliations include Muslim (3 percent), Protestant (2 percent), and Jewish (1 percent).

Women's Roles

Historically, women have been very active in church attendance. Women cannot be priests, but they frequently serve as lay persons during the Mass, giving out communion and reading Scripture. Catholic nuns played a large role in the history of education in France before they were prohibited from teaching in public schools at the start of the twentieth century. The decline in the influence of the church in France has led to a dramatic drop in religious participation, so that only 14 percent of women in France consider themselves to be practicing Catholics. However, 39 percent of women over the age of eighteen in 1993 considered themselves to be Catholic but not a "practicing" Catholic—a common distinction made in France.[2]

Historically, the role of women in the church was exemplified in figures such as Mary, the mother of Jesus (a figure of veneration and supplication), and Joan of Arc (a symbol of French identity and nationalism). Many French Catholics, particularly in rural regions, make annual pilgrimages to religious sites in veneration of the Virgin Mary—Lourdes being the most common destination.

VIOLENCE

Violence against women in France is divided by French researchers into categories such as rape, incestuous rape, domestic violence, and sexual harassment. There is a consensus that statistics on violence against women do not reflect the reality and underestimate the number of cases. There is, however, increasing attention paid to domestic violence, in particular.

Domestic Violence and Rape/Sexual Assault

A national survey (ENVEFF) was carried out in 1997 to assess violence against women. The survey found that 10 percent of women are victims of domestic violence each year (ranging from verbal insults to rape). The survey also found that young women (aged 20–24) are twice as likely to be victims of domestic violence than older women. Several women's groups, such as *SOS Femmes* (Help for Women), provide services to victims of violence. AVFT is another association that provides education and support on issues of violence against women. Changing attitudes have resulted in an increase in convictions for violence. For example, rape convictions rose 62 percent in France between 1984 and 1991.

Female Genital Mutilation

France increasingly faces issues of immigrant women and "female cutting" or female genital mutilation (FC/FGM). There are approximately 181,000 immigrants in France from sixteen countries in Africa where FC/FGM is practiced. There are no specific laws in the French penal code for these practices, which have religious bases; however, acts of mutilation toward a minor are generally prohibited, and laws about this are used to enforce sanctions against parents whose daughters have undergone FC/FGM. Both parents and providers of the procedure have been prosecuted, and since 1978 there have been twenty-five prosecutions (with sentences ranging from 1 to 5 years). There are several governmental and nongovernmental agencies working to prevent these activities among immigrants.

OUTLOOK FOR THE TWENTY-FIRST CENTURY

The French sociologist Pierre Bourdieu argued in a 1998 book that although women seem to have acquired equal rights in France, male domination persists because it is the established order of society. As with class stratification, he argues that gender stratification is tied to forms of symbolic domination. French feminists continue to fight stereotypical images of women in the media, domestic violence, and the underrepresentation of women in French politics. The new law of parity and the emphasis in the European Union on human rights should lead to improved political participation and improved living and working conditions for French women. Issues of immigrant and minority women in France will continue to become more visible as the French deal with their multicultural society in the twenty-first century, but the conditions for these women will continue to need improvement and attention. The presence of a strong and extreme right-wing, conservative element (such as the National Front) in French society threatens women's rights, and it will require vigilance to keep its influence in check.

NOTES

I would like to thank Sheri (Iasa) Duffy for her able research assistance as I prepared this chapter.

1. INSEE, *Les Femmes, Protrait Social* (Paris: Institute National de la Statistique et les Etudes Economiques, 1995), 86–87.

2. INSEE, 1995, 200–207.

RESOURCE GUIDE

Suggested Reading

Beauvoir, Simone de. *The Second Sex*. New York: Alfred A. Knopf, 1953.

Bourdieu, Pierre. *Masculine Domination*. Stanford, CA: Stanford University Press, 2001.

Gregory, Abigail, and Ursula Todd, eds. *Women in Contemporary France*. New York: Berg Publishers, 2000.

LeWita, Beatrix. *French Bourgeois Culture*. Translated by J.A. Underwood. Cambridge: Cambridge University Press, 1994.

Moi, Toril, ed. *French Feminist Thought*. Oxford: Blackwell, 1987.

Raissiguier, Catherine. *Becoming Women, Becoming Workers: Identity Formation in a French Vocational School*. Albany: State University of New York Press, 1994.

Reed-Danahay, Deborah. *Education and Identity in Rural France: The Politics of Schooling*. Cambridge: Cambridge University Press, 1996.

Rogers, Susan Carol. *Shaping Modern Times in Rural France: The Transformation and Reproduction of an Aveyronnais Community*. Princeton: Princeton University Press, 1991.

Tilly, Louise, and Joan Wallach Scott. *Women, Work and Family*. New York: Routledge, 1989.

Twomey, Lesley, ed. *Women in Contemporary Culture: Roles and Identities in France and Spain*. Portland, OR: Intellect Books, 2000.

Videos/Films

Femmes Immigrées. 1991. 29 minutes. VHS. Françoise Devinant, Jacques Durand, and Jean-Louis Jacques. Paris: CNDP. Video showing the lives of immigrant women in France.

Four French Women Tell Stories of Domestic Violence and Abuse. 60 minutes. VHS. Paris: Nausicaa Films.

Seules avec nos histories/Alone with Our Stories. 2001. Hubert Sauper, and Cecile Demur.

Web Sites

AVFT, www.avftfrance.org.
Information on sexual harassment and violence against women.

CNIDFF (National Center for Information on Women's Rights), www.infofemmes.com.

Facts on France, www.info-france-usa.org/profil/facts.
French Embassy in the U.S. web site.

Office of France's Prime Minister, www.observatoire-parite.gouv.fr/.
Monitors parity issues for women.

SOS Femmes, www.sosfemmes.com.
Site for domestic violence with resources for women suffering from domestic violence. Hotline, shelters, etc.

Organizations

Alliance des Femmes pour la Democratie (ADF)
5 rue de Lille
75007 Paris
Email: adfemmes@iway.fr

Feminist group with links to NOW; founded in the 1980s.

Association Européene Contre les Violences Faites aux Femmes au Travail (AVFT)
71 rue Saint Jacques
75005 Paris
Email: avft@avftfrance.org

Group that works against violence against women.

Choisir (Choice)
102 rue St. Dominique
75002 Paris

Women's rights group founded in the 1970s.

Coordination Française pour le Lobby Européen des Femmes (CLEF)
100 rue de Rennes
75006 Paris

The French branch of the European Lobby for Women, an NGO that works for women's rights in Europe.

Ligue des Droits de Femmes (LDF)
54 av Choisy
75013 Paris

Group founded by Simone de Beauvoir.

Mouvement Français Pour le Planning Familial (MFPF)
4 Square Saint-Irenee
75011 Paris
Phone: (33) (1) 48 07 29 10

Provides reproductive health and other counseling services for such cases as rape, female genital mutilation, and marital violence. Helps pregnant teens and immigrant women. Founded in 1920, a pioneer in advocacy of reproductive rights for French women.

Les Nana Beurs (Meufs Rebeus)
Khakija Rayass
70 rue Casteja
92100 Boulogne Billancourt
Phone: 46 21 07 29

Association of young women of North African origin.

Service des Droits des Femmes et de l'Egalite (Office for Women's Rights and Equality)
10-16 rue Brancion
75015 Paris

Part of French Ministry of Labor and Solidarity. Governmental office that promotes women's rights in France.

SELECTED BIBLIOGRAPHY

Gregory, Abigail. "Contemporary Trends in Women's Employment in France." *Modern and Contemporary France* 8, no. 2 (2000): 175–91.

Haase-Dubosc, Danielle. "Sexual Difference and Politics in France Today." *Feminist Studies* 25, no. 1 (1999): 183–211.

Hantrais, Linda. "Women, Work and Welfare in France." In *Women and Social Politics in Europe: Work, Family and the State*, edited by Jane Lewis, 116–37. Hants, England: Edward Elgar Publishing Ltd., 1993.

Holland, Alison. "Women." In *Aspects of Contemporary France*, edited by Sheila Perry, 137–52. London: Routledge, 1997.

Institute National de la Statistique et les Etudes Economiques. *Les Femmes: Portrait Social*. Paris: Institute National de la Statistique et les Etudes Economiques, 1995.

Mazur, Amy G. "Sexual Harassment, Gender Politics and Symbolic Reform." In *Chirac's Challenge: Liberalization, Europeanization and Malaise in France*, edited by John Keeler and Martin Schain, 257–78. New York: St. Martin's, 1996.

The Minerva Center. "Military Women in the NATO Armed Forces," part 4. *Minerva* 17, no. 2 (1999): 54.

Rahman, Anika, and Nahid Toubia. *Female Genital Mutilation—A Guide to Laws and Policies Worldwide*. Center for Reproductive Law and Policy. New York: St. Martin's Press, 2000.

World Health Organization (WHO). *Highlights on Health in France*. 1997. www.who.dk/document/E62011.pdf.

14

GEORGIA

Nino Javakhishvili and Lela Khomeriki

PROFILE OF GEORGIA

Georgia is one of the republics of the former Soviet Union and is now an independent state in a transitional period. It is one of the Caucasus states, along with Armenia and Azerbaijan. According to 1989 national census data, the population of Georgia is 5 million, of whom 52.2 percent are female. However, unofficial data from 2001 indicate that the population actually went down from 5 to 4 million, because the country's current poor economic condition has led to out-migration. According to the State Department of Statistics of Georgia, in the year 2000 maternal mortality was 9 per 100,000 live births, compared to 1997, when it was 35. Infant mortality was 14.9 per 1,000 live births in 2000.

Georgia is a multiethnic state. According to 1989 national census data, people from more than ninety nations live here, comprising almost 30 percent of the whole population. The remaining 70 percent are Georgian. Georgian people speak their native Georgian language, which belong to a small group of Caucasian languages with its own alphabet. Georgia is led by the president and the Parliament. It is striving to become a democracy and is introducing democratic reforms step-by-step with the support of international organizations.

OVERVIEW OF WOMEN'S ISSUES

Gender and women problems are encountered in every facet of life in the country. The traditional family model is still very strong. Negative gender stereotypes and traditions still operate in the country, with mass media and other institutes of socialization supporting their maintenance.

EDUCATION

Opportunities

On the surface, education in Georgia is the same for boys and girls. At the same time, gender analysis of textbooks and programs has not been done yet and it can be said that school education is not fully free from gender stereotypes. Educational disparity is especially vivid in rural areas and enclaves. For example, in some of the districts of East Georgia with Moslem populations, parents take their daughters out of school, believing that girls should stay home and prepare themselves for family life. Therefore, in these areas, almost always only boys are left to finish school, whereas girls have just 6–7 years of schooling. As for university education, based on 1999 data, there are slightly more girl students than boy students: 52 percent versus 48 percent.

Literacy

Ninety-nine percent of the population is literate. Of that number, literacy among males is 100 percent and among females is 98 percent.[1]

Georgian women selling gas, Svanetia. Photo © TRIP/E. Parker.

EMPLOYMENT AND THE ECONOMY

Job/Career Opportunities

Women's double burden is becoming more and more apparent as women have jobs but retain household responsibilities. There are not equal career possibilities for men and women: the glass ceiling effect is present in every state organization and in every sector such as educational, cultural, legislative, health care, and business.

Pay

The Soviet legacy lives on in work compensation. Legislatively, men and women are equally paid. However, women typically hold lower-level jobs than men. Therefore, men can earn more than 40 percent over what women do.

Working Conditions

Sexual Harassment

There are no statistical data on sexual harassment in Georgia because the Georgian mentality believes it is shameful to come forward with one's problems. However, representatives of women's organizations claim there is a certain amount of such cases in the country.

Support for Mothers/Caretakers

Rarely do political party programs include issues of support for motherhood, single mothers, or mothers with infants or many children. Although prenatal consultations and birthing are free in state clinics, these services are not of high quality.

Maternal Leave

A pregnant woman has a right to get a paid leave seventy calendar days before birth and fifty-six calendar days afterward. Women who have worked at least a year, can also receive one-half paid leave until the baby is a year and a half and unpaid leave until the baby is three years old. A mother's job is held for her and a maternal leave period is included in working years for purposes of calculating pensions and other benefits tied to the number of years employed. A father, or any other relative who takes care of a baby, can work with a flexible timetable.

Daycare

Part-time, state-supported daycare centers were well-developed in the Soviet period, but their numbers have decreased drastically. These centers are very cheap, about 15 GEL (Georgian currency, 15 GEL = 7 USD) per month. Many private daycare centers have emerged, but their services are quite expensive (50–100 USD) per month and not many families can afford it.

Inheritance and Property Rights

The main heir of family property is a man, which makes women more economically dependent.

Social/Government Programs

Although in the beginning of the 1990s, the Georgian government adopted several documents dedicated to the improvement of gender and women's issues, it did so only to be in formal compliance with the requirements of the international organizations. Government agencies responsible for equality issues have not yet been established. In 1994 Georgia endorsed the Convention to Eliminate All Forms of Discrimination against Women (CEDAW), but this fact did not get any attention from either the state or the society. Only in 1997 was the convention text published in the Georgian language. In 1995 Georgia was among the countries that agreed to develop a national plan to improve the conditions of women in order to act in accordance with the 1995 UN Women's Conference in Beijing's Platform for Action. Although Georgia did work out an action plan for 1998–2000, the most important parts of this plan—establish a women's issues department; increase women's participation in decision-making institutions; help women establish small and medium-size businesses; strengthen legislative protection mechanisms to reduce prostitution, poverty, and starvation; and include gender equality issues while working out budgetary and taxation policy—have not been realized.

FAMILY AND SEXUALITY

Gender Roles

Traditionally women's virginity is still quite strongly enforced and protected, especially outside of the capital city, Tbilisi, where more than a third of the population lives; the double standard of evaluating the morals and behavior of men and women is active.

Marriage

The average age for the first marriage for Georgian women is twenty-four years, and it is twenty-eight years for men. In 2000 Georgia adopted a law on marital contracts. Women still have serious problems in retaining family property in divorce cases. One of the most serious problems in this respect is abdication. The abdication tradition is quite strong in regions, although there are no official statistical data.

Reproduction

Sex Education

Sex education is implemented in some school programs in the Georgian capital, but religious parents do object to such education. At the same time, a Ministry of Education reform includes providing sexual education in the schools. It should be implemented countrywide in the next few years.

Contraception and Abortion

Abortion is legal in Georgia. The number of abortions is still quite high because of poor family planning education and the low rate of contraceptive use.

Teen Pregnancy

The incidence of teen pregnancy in Georgia is quite low.

POLITICS AND LAW

Despite drastic social changes, there has been no broad public discussion of gender problems and equality. Very important topics—gender equality as one of the most important components of sustainable and harmonious development of society, women's civic integration, the importance of women's new social role as decision makers, women as participants in new economic relations and democratic processes, and suffrage for women— are not being publicly debated.

Political Participation

Out of eighteen ministers, only two are women—the ministers of environmental protection and of cultural affairs. This number has not changed since 1998. At the same time, two very important state positions are held by women, speaker of the parliament and an ombudsman. Nana Devdariani is a journalist who has been ombudsman since 2000. Nino Burjanadze, a lawyer by profession, has been speaker since the autumn of 2001. However, as an MP noted, most who voted for Burjanadze to be speaker did so because they thought that as a woman she would not have further political ambitions to be the state minister or the president. No one can imagine a woman as a president in Georgia.

Women's representation is presented in Table 14.1, which shows no increase in women's low participation from 1990 to 2002. Women comprise only 14 percent of local government members countrywide. Furthermore, women's participation decreases as the government unit gets larger; plus the more recourse and power, the lower the percentage of women formally involved. Of village local councils, 15 percent of the members are women. Only 13 percent of town council members are women, and the number plummets to 9 percent for district councils. City councils number women as only 7.4 percent of their members.

Ideally, political parties should play the role of mediators between gov-

Table 14.1
Women's Representation

Year	Total number of deputies	Number of women deputies	% of women deputies (MPs)
1990	250	18	7.2
1995	250	16	6.4
1999	235	17	7.2

ernment and people—they should study needs of the population, develop programs, and then turn them into policies that result in political decisions and real action. None of the parties in Georgia is able to play this role, especially on gender issues.

Programs of political parties do not take into account women's issues. Most of them regard women's issues as not real problems and see other priorities as more urgent and serious. Until recently, only one political party had developed a gender policy. Parties do not even gather statistics on the gender of their members. Furthermore, there are almost no gender-sensitive women politicians who are motivated enough to work on gender issues and who could bring women and gender politics into Georgian political discourse. The only party that is an exception to the general pattern of neglect or avoidance of women's issues is the United Democrats (led by the former parliament speaker Zurab Jhvania), which is in the process of preparing and incorporating gender policy into its program with the help of gender and women's issues specialists and organizations.

Women's Rights

Women's and gender issues can and should be formulated, put on the agenda, and then solved either by government agencies, civic organizations, or both. However, there are no state, legal, or administrative systems through which women's rights can be implemented. There is no, or almost no, state policy regarding gender and women's issues; and there is definitely no mechanism for realizing even the existing political decisions on women and gender issues.

Feminist Movements

There are about 4,000 nongovernmental organizations (NGOs), but they cannot lobby political decision makers and they do not have tangible influence on the national government. The activities of the seventy different women's organizations have intensified in recent times: various women's organizations have completed the first stage of their development and entered a new phase. A coalition of women NGOs was established. There is an urgent need for developing strategies to address the goals of the women's movement and tactics of joint lobbying for such key issues as the increase of women's role in social and political life and equal rights policy. Correspondingly, representatives of women's organizations are more and more interested in getting deeper knowledge of gender issues in order to reach qualitatively new stages of practical activity.

In conclusion, the state ignores civic organizations and the problems they try to address. This is largely true of the mass media as well. Most editors do not want to highlight nongovernmental organizations' views of existing problems, including gender and women's issues, and most have no editorial policy on gender issues. On only two radio channels, Liberty and Green Wave, do the editors and stakeholders claim to have a clear gender policy and corresponding programs. On the other hand, civic organizations are not yet strong and powerful enough to claim their rights. Therefore, a challenge for the coming years is to end this vicious circle. There is some hope that this is possible, especially since certain prerequisites for such breakthroughs are present:

- Georgia has endorsed international conventions on women's rights and thus has taken on a commitment to international society.
- Women's organizations have entered a new phase of their development—from women's organizations to women's movements.
- Market economics and market relations have brought new roles and responsibilities to women.

OUTLOOK FOR THE TWENTY-FIRST CENTURY

The high-priority issues for the immediate future in Georgia are the development and establishment of efficient mechanisms of public monitoring of the state's commitments to women's rights, which should be done by certain nongovernmental organizations in cooperation with gender-sensitive media representatives; and the improvement of laws by bringing gender-sensitive ideas into the formation of legislation, focusing on such matters as the definition of gender discrimination, family violence, and regulations against trafficking in women and girls. These changes will be possible only if women's organizations build networks and consolidate their separate efforts into a women's movement.

NOTE

1. CIA, *World Factbook*, www.odci.gov/cia/publications/factbook/geos/gg.html#People.

RESOURCE GUIDE

Suggested Reading

Khomeriki, L. "Gender Equality Issues in Post-Soviet Georgia." In *Democracy in Georgia*, edited by George Nodia, 2003. The book is prepared by the initiative and financial support of IDEA (Stockholm, Sweden) and will be published in Georgian and English. This will be the only accessible source for readers.

Web Sites

People Harmonious Development Society, http://gains.iatp.org.ge/osgfwp.
This site is prepared and hosted by one of the local women's NGOs. Tsovinar Nazarova is the leader, and the NGO is financially supported by the Open Society—Georgia Foundation.

Women's Initiative for Equality, www.osgf.ge/wie/.
This site is prepared and hosted by one of the local women's NGOs. Lela Gaprindashvili is the leader, and the NGO is financially supported by the Open Society—Georgia Foundation.

Organizations

International Center for Civic Culture
Konstantin Kandelaki
Phone: (+995) 32 94 02 96; (+995) 32 95 38 73
Email: iccc@ip.osgf.ge

Works on democracy issues, such as local government and self-government, political parties, and gender issues.

Society of Dynamic Psychology for Development and Democracy
Nino Javakhishvili
Phone: (+995) 32 38 41 82; (+995) 32 94 38 48
Email: isr@ip.osgf.ge

Gender and women's issues, psychological and social-psychological trainings, and social research.

SELECTED BIBLIOGRAPHY

Berekashvili, N., N. Chubinidze, and L. Khomeriki. *Women Organizations in Georgia* (in Georgian and English). Tbilisi: International Center for Civic Culture, 1998.
Javakhishvili N., and I. Bregvadze. "Women Roles at a State and Family Levels." In *Exploring Gender Issues in the Caucasus Workshop Materials*, edited by Pauline M. Hallam and Barbara J. Merguerian. Yerevan, Armenia: Civic Education Project, 2000.
Javakhishvili N., and M. Nikuradze. "Efficient Highlighting of Gender Issues in Mass Media." In *Gender Policy and Mass Media*. Tbilisi: International Advisory Center for Women Education, 2002.

Khomeriki, L., and N. Javakhishvili. "Gender Dimension in Georgian Mass Media." In *Gender Policy and Mass Media*. Tbilisi: International Advisory Center for Women Education, 2002.

"Women in Political Parties." In *Georgian Political Parties, Directory 1998–1999*. Tbilisi: ICCC, 1998.

Selected Georgian Bibliography

Association of Gender Development. *Women's Condition in Georgia 2000* (in Georgian). Tbilisi.

Association of Georgian Young Lawyers. *Women Rights* (in Georgian). Tbilisi: 1999.

Gender Studies in Georgia. *Directory 1998* (in Georgian). Tbilisi.

State Statistics Department. *A Woman and a Man in Georgia: Statistical Directory 1999* (in Georgian). Tbilisi.

Surmanidze, L. *A Woman in Georgian Mentality* (in Georgian). Tbilisi: Association of Gender Development, 1998.

15

GERMANY

Eileen Trzcinski

PROFILE OF GERMANY

As defined by its constitution, Germany is a democratic and social federal state.[1] Its Basic Law is the Federal Constitution, which was ratified on May 23, 1949, and last amended on July 16, 1998. The German Democratic Republic (GDR, formerly East Germany) was reunified with the Federal Republic of Germany (FRG, formerly West Germany) on October 3, 1990. Since reunification, Germany consists of sixteen states. Germany is also one of the thirteen member states of the European Union.

There are approximately 82 million inhabitants of Germany, of whom 51.2 percent are female. The largest groups of the 7.3 million foreign residents come from Turkey (2.1 million), Serbia and Montenegro (721,000), Italy (608,000), Greece (363,000), and Poland (283,300). Over 450,000 people come from Bosnia and Herzegovina and from Croatia.[2]

Germany has one of the lowest birthrates in the world. The average fertility rate for women is 1.4 children. Life expectancy at birth is 74.4 years for males and 80.6 years for females. The death rate for children under one year per 1,000 live births is 4.5.[3] Low birthrates together with increases in life expectancy are resulting in major changes in the age distribution. Current population projections indicate

that the population in Germany will decline by more than 10 million by 2050 and that every third person will be over sixty.[4]

OVERVIEW OF WOMEN'S ISSUES

Germany has witnessed major changes as a result of reunification, the shifting demographic structure, large increases in the number of foreign residents, and its status as a full member of the European Union (EU), the economic and monetary union of Europe. In recent years, women have also made major gains in achieving educational parity with men. All of these changes are affecting women within Germany.

Despite its comprehensive social welfare system, West Germany did not develop policies that enabled women to participate equally with men in the labor market; and until recent decades, this suited the needs and preferences of women in the FRG. The picture for women from East Germany was different, however. During the existence of the GDR, they lived within a system where work and family were both equally encouraged. Hence, they found the transition to the social and economic system of the FRG difficult.

Attitudes of women in the West and East have not yet converged. However, with increasing levels of education and with pressures from the European Union, women in the West as well as those in the East are now attempting to find methods by which work at home and work in the market can be combined more easily. With its low birthrate and its anticipated need to provide increasing levels of care to an aging population, German society as a whole is attempting to find methods that allow men as well as women to participate more equally in both market and caregiving work. It is also attempting to create an environment that more easily accommodates the wide range of social and cultural attitudes that are present among German citizens as well as foreign residents.

EDUCATION

Opportunities

Women and men in Germany have equal legal access to all educational opportunities. The federal German states are independent in matters of education and culture, but each state offers a system of education divided primarily into general and vocational education. Students are required to attend nine to ten years of full-time schooling, followed by either compulsory part-time or full-time school attendance up to the age of eighteen. At the high school level, Germany offers three traditional types of schooling and a fourth model that combines features of the other three.[5] In recent years, females almost have achieved parity with males in terms of the level of qualifications they receive. Sharp distinctions still exist, however, in fields of study, with girls and women continuing to specialize in traditionally female occupations, such as nursing and teaching.

Institutions of higher education do not charge tuition. All students are entitled to educational assistance. Under the provisions of the Federal Education Assistance Act, the federal government provides all eligible students with grants and/or loans to cover basic living expenses. Historically, women have been underrepresented in institutions of higher education. Their underrepresentation increases as the level of education increases. Among current students, however, differences between men and women are rapidly narrowing. In 1998–1999, approximately 1.8 million students were enrolled at German institutions of higher education; 44.5 percent were women.

The proportion of foreign students was 9.2 percent. In the same year, the share of new entrants who were women was 48.5 percent, and the share of graduates who were women was 42.2 percent. At the highest level of academic qualification, however, the share of women was dramatically lower—only 15.3 percent of all students who attained a postdoctoral lecturing qualification were women. Differences among men and women also continue to exist in field of study. In the 1999–2000 academic year, women constituted over 80 percent of all students in colleges of education and 58 percent of all students in colleges of art. Women were, however, underrepresented at comprehensive universities where students select fields of study such as mathematics and science.[6]

Literacy

Ninety-nine percent of the population is literate.

EMPLOYMENT AND THE ECONOMY

Forty years of different economic, social, and legal conditions in the FDR and the GDR produced dramatically different patterns in how women view employment, especially while they have young children at home. One important difference is the far higher labor force participation rates for women with children in the East compared to those of the West.

Job/Career Opportunities

The 1949 Constitution of the GDR, as amended in 1968, guaranteed men and women equal rights and an equal status with regard to rights in all areas of social, state, and personal life. The right and duty to work were firmly established in law. As a result, almost every woman of working age was employed and economically independent.[7]

Women in the West have traditionally followed a pattern of employment that included a period of full-time employment after the completion of

Grocery checkout clerk, Germany. Photo © David Turnley/ CORBIS.

education, withdrawal from the labor market following childbirth, with a return to part-time work when the children entered school. Women then returned to full-time employment when their children completed school. As women in the West have achieved educational levels on a par with men, many more are now interested in maintaining stronger ties to the labor market, even when children are young. Compared with women in the East, however, their preferences tend to be for part-time rather than full-time work, particularly when their children are infants or toddlers.

For women in the West, Table 15.1 shows that 45.5 percent of all married mothers with children under age three were employed in 1998. Their labor force participation rate (a measure that includes both employed women and those actively seeking employment) was 48.2 percent. For women in the East in 1998, the employment rate for married mothers of young children was 56.8 percent, over ten percentage points higher than in the West in 1998. Among all married mothers of young children aged three and under in the East, 68.9 percent were either employed or seeking employment, with over 22.2 percent being unemployed.

Formerly, FRG law stated that a wife was entitled to employment as long as she could still fulfill her marital and familial duties. Since July 1, 1977, the law demands that each spouse, including the husband, take the interests of the other spouse and the family into account in their choice and practice of paid employment. However, the law still tended to be applied in gender-specific ways throughout the 1980s and 1990s. This lapse in implementation stems, in part, from contradictions in the Constitution between equal rights sections and those on marriage and family.

Pay

Substantial differences in wages exist for women and men in both the East and the West. The 1999 gross hourly earnings of women in production industries in the West were 24.3 percent lower than for men; gross monthly earnings of female salaried employees were 29.1 percent lower. In the East, the gaps were smaller: 19.8 percent and 25.0 percent, respectively. However, because overall wages in the East still lag about 75 percent behind those in the West, women in the West still have higher average earnings than women in the East.[8] In Germany as a whole, women constitute

Table 15.1
Rates of Employment and Labor Force Participation in Germany,
West and East, 1998, for All Women Aged 15 to 65, with Children
under 18 Years of Age

Age of Youngest Child	Germany		States in Western Germany, including West Berlin		States in Eastern Germany, including East Berlin	
	Employment Rate	Labor Market Participation Rate[1]	Employment Rate	Labor Market Participation Rate[1]	Employment Rate	Labor Market Participation Rate[1]
Married Women						
Aged under 3	46.5	50.0	45.5	48.2	56.8	68.9
Aged 3 to < 6	50.7	59.6	49.3	56.3	64.6	91.9
Aged 6 to < 10	60.6	68.9	57.4	62.4	73.3	94.9
Aged 10 to < 15	68.8	77.0	65.2	70.2	78.9	96.5
Aged 15 to < 18	69.2	76.5	66.5	70.7	77.8	94.7
Total	58.9	66.0	55.8	60.4	73.6	92.2
Single Mothers						
Aged under 3	46.1	56.9	45.1	52.7	48.3	65.8
Aged 3 to < 6	55.3	76.2	54.7	69.9	57.3	96.2
Aged 6 to < 10	64.7	84.9	65.8	79.3	62.9	96.1
Aged 10 to < 15	74.6	90.3	75.8	87.1	72.3	96.6
Aged 15 to < 18	75.3	89.0	77.7	86.6	69.5	94.6
Total	64.0	80.5	64.5	76.0	63.1	90.5

[1]Includes both employed and unemployed women.
Source: Federal Statistical Office of Germany, 1999.

80 percent of all low-wage employees, which are defined as employees working at least fifteen hours per week who earn less than 60 percent of the national median monthly wage.[9]

Overall, 87 percent of all part-time workers are women—a factor that contributes to the lower hourly wages that women earn compared with men. In 2000, 42 percent of all women in the West worked part-time compared with 23 percent in the East. Nearly two-thirds of all women who worked part-time in the West, compared with only 21 percent of women in the East, cited personal or family responsibilities as the reason for working part-time. In contrast, 52 percent of women in the East versus 8 percent of women in the West cited the lack of full-time employment as the reason for part-time work.[10]

Occupational segregation is another factor contributing to wage differentials between men and women. Of all women in wage and salary employment, 11 percent reported that they were employed as executives, with an additional 1 percent reporting that they were employed as high-level service officials. Among men, 18 percent reported that they worked as executive employees; an additional 2 percent reported work as high-level service officials.[11]

The opposite pattern holds for marginal or low-level employment (*geringfuegig Beschaeftigung*). Although women made up 44 percent of the labor force in May 2000, they held 77 percent of all marginal and low-level employment positions.[12] The greater flexibility offered by low-level work, which sometimes provides a greater choice of hours worked or fewer hours per week, enables women to compensate for the lack of structural support provided for combining work and family responsibilities. Women pay a high price for this flexibility, however, through the low wages that accompany low-level, contingent employment.

Nevertheless, differences in male and female earnings are slowly diminishing. Relative to men's earnings, women's earnings in retailing increased from 74.8 percent in 1990 to 78.8 percent in 1995 and to 86.4 percent in 1999. In financial services, women's earnings relative to men's increased from 71.7 percent in 1990 to 73.4 percent in 1995 and to 74.4 percent in 1999.[13] These changes have occurred in part because more women, particularly women who are delaying childbearing or who are remaining childless throughout their careers, have patterns of labor force participation that are similar to male patterns. In addition, strides by women in achieving parity with men in terms of educational level have contributed to a narrowing of the wage differentials.

Working Conditions

At the beginning of the twenty-first century, Germany has entered a new phase of its history concerning the role of women within the family and within the marketplace. Major changes are occurring as a result of constitutional court decisions and of legislation at the federal level. In 1994, Article 3 of the Constitution was amended to include positive action by the state to ensure gender equality. Paragraph 3.2 of the Constitution now states, "Men and women have equal rights. The State ensures the implementation of equality for women and men and takes action to abolish existing discrimination."

Historically, certain protective labor laws, such as restrictions on night work and work after 5 P.M. on Sundays and holidays, applied to most women workers. However, these restrictions did not apply to occupations with high representation by women, such as work at hospitals and restaurants. In light of the nature of these bans, many feminists concluded that the protection of men from competition with women was more central to the intent of the regulations than the protection of women.[14] New judicial interpretations of the Constitution have narrowed the range of cases in which physiological differences between females and males can be used to justify differential treatment.

However, some restrictions remain. For example, pregnant women are not permitted to work overtime or on Sundays and holidays, or to perform work that routinely requires them to stand still, stretch, bend, or stoop. Mothers are prohibited from working during the eight weeks after they have given birth. They are, however, provided with full wage replacement during compulsory maternity leave.

Sexual Harassment

A vast majority of women in Germany report that they have experienced sexual harassment at the workplace. In one survey, approximately 72 percent of German women reported that they have experienced sexual harassment. Despite the existence of laws against it at the workplace, almost no women reported the sexual harassment due to fear of retaliation, including fear of dismissal.[15] In 1994, business establishments were required to provide protections against sexual harassment.

Support for Mothers/Caretakers

Article 6 of the FRG Constitution is intended to protect citizens against governmental interference in private family life. Historically, the FRG tax structure and social policy strongly promoted the heterosexual, married couple and the nuclear family, especially two-parent, one-earner families.[16] Tax and social policy disadvantaged other forms of partnerships outside legal marriage; and constitutional protection of family privacy did not apply to single mothers and their children.

Although state interference in single-parent families has lessened, single mothers are still required to provide information on the child's father before receiving child-support payments from the state. State child-support payments to never-married mothers are smaller than child-support payments required of divorced fathers. Furthermore, never-married mothers are only entitled to receive state child-support payments for children aged twelve and under, whereas the divorced father's responsibilities for his children continue until the children reach legal adulthood and up to age twenty-seven for children attending university.

The GDR Constitution placed marriage, family, and motherhood under the protection of the state, guaranteed the family social and state support, and provided special support for large families and single mothers and fathers. Under Article 20, pregnancy and maternity leaves, special medical care, material and financial support at birth, and child allowances were supported by the state.

In practice, as well as in policy and law, the position of children of single parents was equal to the position of children of married couples in the

GDR as opposed to in the FRG, where equality among children living in different family arrangements was never a goal of law or policy.[17] Indeed, in the GDR single mothers had priority for places in childcare facilities, had longer job protection following the birth of a child, and were given wage replacement during the first year of maternity leave before mothers who were married were entitled to extended paid maternity leave.

In addition, when the father did not provide child support, a woman in the GDR could receive child-maintenance payments from the state until the child reached legal adulthood; whereas in the FRG, such child-maintenance payments were limited to three years (now five years). In addition, no payments could be received for children over twelve years of age. This policy is still in force today.

After reunification, women in the East found themselves faced with a weaker set of employment and family supports. However, rather than withdrawing from the labor market, many women in the East reacted by choosing not to have children. Immediately after reunification, the number of births declined dramatically in the East—from about 216,000 births in 1986 to only 88,000 births in 1992.[18] In 1998, major differences existed in the birthrate for women in the former territory of West Germany, 49.6 births per 1,000 women, compared with women in the former territory of East Germany, 32.5 births per 1,000 women.[19] Between 1991 and 1999, the number of children aged six years or younger who were living in East Germany declined by 58.3 percent.[20]

Maternal Leave

All women are entitled to six weeks of job-protected leave immediately prior to childbirth and are required to take eight weeks of compulsory leave after childbirth. During maternity leave, women receive full-wage replacement through a combination of employer and state-provided payments.

Daycare

Parental leave and benefits are considered a central aspect of childcare policy, especially since vacancies at childcare facilities are in short supply, particularly during the first year of a child's life. German law and policy provide no guarantee of childcare during the child's first three years. In 1999, only 8.5 percent of all infants and toddlers under three years of age were in formal childcare arrangements. In the late 1990s, all children aged three and over were guaranteed a space in childcare until the child entered primary school. As a result of this legislation, the percentage of three- and four-year-olds in childcare increased from 38.9 percent to 54.3 percent during the period 1994 to 1999.[21] Despite the legal guarantee of childcare, shortages still exist. No reliable data are available, however, that provide information on the number of parents who are unable to find childcare spaces, particularly full-time childcare, for preschool age children.

Parents pay a portion of the childcare costs based on family income.[22] When children enter primary school, children are no longer guaranteed childcare spaces. After-school childcare is not widely available. A major shortage of after-school childcare makes full-time work particularly difficult for women in Germany, because the school day for children in primary school ends at 1 P.M. German policy is currently focusing more on creating incentives for employers to provide part-time work rather than on providing childcare for school-aged children or extending the school day.[23]

Family and Medical Leave

Recent changes in parental benefits and parental leave policies illustrate major shifts in German social policy. Current policies reflect a greater emphasis on providing supports that allow women to combine work and family and on encouraging greater participation by men in caregiving. Another component of contemporary German employment and family policy entails the creation of incentives to make part-time work a more lucrative employment option, both in the short and long term.[24] Current parental leave regulations also reflect this emphasis.

German law differentiates between parental leave and monetary benefits paid during the first two years of the child's life (*Erziehungsgeld*). Prior to changes implemented in 2001, parents were entitled to three years of parental leave from paid employment with a guaranteed right to return to their same jobs (*Erziehungsurlaub*). Parents could receive up to DM 600 (Deutsche marks) per month, depending upon their income, for two years (*Erziehungsgeld*). However, in order to receive these benefits, one parent had to be the primary caregiver of the child. The parent designated as the caregiver was prohibited from working more than nineteen hours per week and could not simultaneously receive unemployment benefits or unemployment assistance and parental benefits. Such a policy effectively discriminated against single mothers.

Under the new regulations, introduced on January 1, 2001, parents can choose to receive parental benefits for one year at a rate of EURO 460 per month or for two years at a rate of EURO 307 per month.[25] The benefit levels are still income-tested, with full benefits paid during the first six months to all two-parent families with annual incomes less than EURO 51,130 per year. For single parents, full benefits are paid during the first six months when annual income is less than DM 75,000. Receipt of unemployment benefits or assistance by the parent on leave no longer automatically rules out receipt of parental benefits. Both parents are also entitled to take leave simultaneously and no longer face restrictions on the number of times they can rotate leave-taking during the three-year entitlement period. Under the new as well as the old regulations, the leave-taker has a guarantee of the same or comparable job on return from leave. Employers are prohibited from terminating employees who are on leave.

The most important new provision of the law concerns the right to part-time work during leave. Under the new regulations, parents can work up to thirty hours per week without forfeiting their right to parental benefits. Equally important is the right to part-time work for all parents who choose to take leave, now referred to as "time for parents" (*Elternzeit*) instead of parental leave/vacation (*Erziehungsurlaub*). As long as an establishment employs more than fifteen workers, the parent employed there is entitled to part-time work from nineteen to thirty hours per week. That is, employers must allow parents to work part-time, if parents want to choose this option. Parents are guaranteed the right to return to full-time work at the end of *Elternzeit*.

Parents can also choose to take the third year of leave anytime before the child is nine years old. Leave to care for children between the ages of four to eight requires the approval of the employer, so the practical impact of this provision of the new regulations is likely to be limited. A final important element of the new German parental leave legislation concerns the treatment of parental leave within the pension system. Any parent on official parental leave is credited with contributions in the statutory pension insurance system.[26]

Social/Government Programs

Welfare

Germany now has a well-developed and comprehensive set of social policies that provide generous support for families and result in low rates of relative poverty for children. Historically, the German social welfare system did not focus on the provision of supports that enable women to combine market work and caregiving, particularly when children are young. Instead, it focused far more on the development of financial supports to families that were designed to enable women to withdraw from the labor force after childbirth and during the childrearing years without economic hardship for the family. Five different policies exist: parental benefits and leave and childcare policy, both of which have previously been discussed; social assistance and long-term health insurance, which are described next; and legislation on same-sex partnerships, which is discussed in the Women's Rights section. Each highlights a different element of the German social policy; each provides important provisions for women. The Constitution guarantees social assistance (*Sozialhilfe*) to all individuals who "are in need, or in danger of becoming destitute, and are unable to overcome their difficulties on their own or with the help of other people. Under such circumstances, social assistance will be granted regardless of whether the individual is responsible for his/her current situation."[27] Social assistance can entail personal noncash assistance, cash payments, and payments in kind. It is also provided as assistance for special circumstances, such as when individuals are disabled, ill, or elderly and have no access to other benefits. Of the assistance programs available to individuals within Germany, social assistance is the least generous. It often serves as a last resort for individuals who have no entitlements to pension or unemployment insurance benefits or who have exhausted their sickness benefits. Payments under this system do ensure, however, that all individuals are protected from destitution. Standard payments for the head of a household in Western Germany averaged DM 549 in 2001; payments for children in the household are between 50 and 90 percent of the payment made to the head of household. Housing and heating expenses are covered separately as long as they are reasonable. Social assistance also covers needs that arise on a less regular basis, such as clothing, household goods, and Christmas allowances. Social assistance is not time limited, but individuals are expected to take necessary steps to achieve self-sufficiency.[28]

An important feature of the social assistance program concerns the treatment of parental benefits during the first two years of a child's life. In most cases, all sources of income reduce the total amount of social assistance to which an individual is entitled. However, parental benefits, which can amount to EURO 307 to EURO 460 per month, are not deducted from social assistance payments. Nor are single mothers required to satisfy any work requirements when their children are three years old or younger.

On January 1, 2001, mandated long-term care insurance was introduced in response to the growing number of elderly people in need of long-term care. Approximately 1.92 million people in Germany require long-term care; 570,000 live in nursing homes, and relatives, neighbors, volunteers, or professional caregivers care for the rest at home. Two features of the program are especially important for women, who are the traditional caregivers of both the young and the frail elderly. First, individuals who need long-term care but who remain at home may receive home care benefits payable to the care provider, even if the provider is a close friend or relative. The amount of the benefit depends on the intensity of the care provided. Second, when an individual provides nursing care at home for another person, including a close relative, and is not employed for more than thirty hours a week, then the caregiver is covered by the statutory pension insurance system. Contributions to the pension system are made by the long-term insurance fund.[29] Hence, both parental leave and long-term care policies recognize that historically women have paid a high price when they provide care to the young and to the old. Although neither of these policies removes all of the economic disadvantages that caregivers face, each one at least provides some relief of the short- and long-term sacrifices that caregivers make.

FAMILY AND SEXUALITY

Gender Roles

From 1991 to 2000, the number of single-father families in Germany increased by 63 percent from 204,000 to 332,000. During this period, the number of single mothers with children under eighteen years of age rose to approximately 1.6 million, an increase of 31 percent from 1991.[30]

Marriage

In May 2000, 22.4 million families lived in Germany, of which 44 percent were married couples without children, 43 percent married couples with children, and 13 percent single-parent families. Since the middle of the twentieth century, the percentage of families with children has dropped in both East and West Germany. In the West, the share of married couples with children dropped from 71 percent to 57 percent. In the East, the percentage of married couples with children dropped from 64 percent to 58 percent.

Recent years have also been marked by substantial increases in the number of consensual unions and in higher divorce rates. From 1972 to 2000, the number of unmarried, cohabiting couples without children rose from 111,000 to 1.2 million in the West. The number of unmarried couples with children rose from 25,000 to 371,000. Whereas only one in five unmarried couples in the West have children, approximately one half (48.5 percent) of the 520,000 unmarried couples in the East have children.[31] Divorce law was also more lenient in the GDR than in the FRG. The primary difference was the recognition in 1955 that irreconcilable differences constituted grounds for divorce—grounds that were not recognized in the FRG until 1977.

In the former territory of the FRG, the divorce rate increased from 61.3 divorces per 10,000 marriages in 1980 to 105.7 divorces per 10,000 in 1998. Divorce rates in unified Germany increased from 80.2 per 10,000 marriages in 1993 to 102.1 per 10,000 marriages in 1998. Prior to unification, East Germany had a divorce rate that was substantially higher than the rate in the West. A number of factors accounted for this difference, including more lenient divorce laws and a relatively high degree of economic independence for East German women compared with their West German counterparts.

Reproduction

The total fertility rate within Germany is 1.4, well below population replacement levels. The average age of mothers at the birth of live-born children was 30.1 years in 1999. The average age of married mothers at the birth of their first child was 28.8 years; for unmarried mothers, the average age was 27.5 years.

Contraception and Abortion

In 2000, the official number of recorded abortions, which is considered to be an undercount, was 134,600. Among women with reported abortions, 49 percent were married; only 5 percent were minors. Abortions are legal under current German law and are covered under the German health insurance systems. However, German law requires a waiting period of three days and requires that all women must be provided with counseling before an abortion can be performed.[32] The stated intent is to assure that women are aware of their options and that women are freely choosing abortions without outside pressure.[33]

Teen Pregnancy

Births to teenage mothers represent less than 1 percent of all births.[34]

HEALTH

Health Care Access

First introduced in 1883, the German statutory health insurance scheme is one of the oldest in the world. Today Germany provides nearly universal access to health care through a multilayered system of statutory and private insurance funds. The statutory health insurance scheme covers 90 percent of the population (72 million) with an additional 9 percent covered by private insurance policies.[35] Within Germany, legislation requires that the federal government ensure that finances and services are provided in the health care sector. However, legislative and organizational authority at the state level substantially affects hospital planning and public health care. Also, the German health care system is currently facing a number of major challenges that are a result of the recent and ongoing dramatic changes in the age composition of the population. Low birthrates coupled with increases in life expectancy for both men and women have resulted in substantial increases in the proportion of the population that is elderly and in need (or in potential need) of intensive health care services.

The German health care system invests substantially in preventative care. In the early and mid-1990s, approximately 79 percent of all pregnant women received their first examination before the thirteenth week of pregnancy. Of all pregnant women, 73 percent received at least ten medical examinations during their pregnancy.[36] Public health departments conduct medical checkups of children at the start of schooling. Other programs encompass early detection measures for schoolchildren and for men and women. For example, from age thirty-six and over, all insured men and women are entitled to a health checkup every two years. Women aged twenty and over and men aged forty-five and over are entitled to examinations for the early detection of cancer. In 1998, 48 percent of insured women took part in an early detection examination.

The German health insurance system also provides sickness benefits at a rate of up to 90 percent of take-home pay. Sickness benefits can be claimed for seventy-eight weeks in a given three-year period. Sickness benefits may also be used to care for sick children—ten days per year for each child under twelve years for each parent, up to a maximum of twenty-five days per year per parent or twenty days per year for each child for single parents, with a maximum of fifty days per year. Also included are home help and nursing care, including home nursing care for women after childbirth.

Diseases and Disorders

Within Germany, smoking and alcoholism represent health risks to a significant proportion of the population. Survey results from the 1999 national microcensus indicate that 28 percent of all citizens aged fifteen years or older self-reported that they were smokers. Although the percentage of smokers has declined for some groups, such as 20–24-year-old males, the percentage of women who smoke rose consistently throughout the early and mid-1990s. Alcoholism represents the second most common addiction problem after smoking.[37] In 1995, approximately 16 percent of men and 10 percent of women were consuming alcohol on a daily basis in excess of the amount considered dangerous to health in the long run (more than forty grams of alcohol per day for men and twenty grams of alcohol for women).

As members of a rich postindustrial society, German men and women primarily suffer from cardiovascular diseases and cancer, which also constitute the leading causes of death for both men and women. But other causes of death for women are also common, such as diseases of the circulatory system, including heart attacks and strokes. The mortality rate in the East is over 40 percent higher than in the West. This differential is explained primarily by differences in risk factors such as high blood pressure, heavy tobacco and alcohol consumption, as well as diabetes.[38]

AIDS

Within Germany, 15,682 AIDS cases were registered between 1982 and 1996. In the mid-1990s, approximately 2,000 new cases were registered each year. Of the infected persons 17 percent were women, of whom 46 percent were known to be intravenous drug users.

Eating Disorders

Although Germany's generally positive attitude to health does not necessarily lead to healthy behavior, compared with women in other countries in the European Union, German women are least likely to be either severely underweight (1.9 percent of all women) or severely overweight (3.8 percent). Statistics for the European Union as a whole indicate that 3.0 percent of all women are severely underweight, and 6.9 percent of all women are severely overweight.[39]

Cancer

For women, breast cancer is the most common cause of death by cancer (17,600 cases in 1999).

Depression

According to the Health Report for Germany,[40] approximately 6 percent of the population suffers from depression; however, women suffer from depression more than twice as much as men.

POLITICS AND LAW

Suffrage

German women gained the right to vote in 1918. The fight for suffrage was embedded within a broader movement for social justice that began in Germany in the nineteenth century. This movement encompassed measures to fight poverty and to improve the economic and social well-being of working-class women and middle-class women who were single and unable to find work. At the same time, bourgeois women were demanding access to education, to the labor market, and to equal participation in public life.

In 1891, the Social Democrats (SPD) were the first political party in Germany to advocate for equal rights for women to vote and to stand for political office. Associations of working-class women cooperated more closely with the SPD and other social democratic parties, whereas middle-class groups joined together into their own umbrella organization, the Federal Organization of German Women (BDF). Eventually coalitions between radical factions of the BDF with socialist and social-democratic women resulted in universal suffrage for German women. When the SPD and the second social democratic party (USPD) formed the first government of the new German Republic in 1918, women's suffrage was introduced into the Constitution.

Political Participation

At the federal level, the most important legislative body is the Bundestag, the Lower House of Parliament. In recent years, women have made substantial progress in obtaining more representation in the Bundestag. In 2000, women held 31.2 percent of the seats and 35.0 percent of the positions in national government. In 2001, women headed six of the thirteen federal ministries, including the Federal Ministry of Justice, the Federal Ministry of Health, and the Federal Ministry of Education and Research.[41] A number of factors account for the growing representation of women in politics. These factors include the system of proportional representation used in federal elections; a 1994 amendment to the German Constitution regarding equal rights, and initiatives for greater representation of women developed by German political parties.

The 656 members of Parliament are elected under a mixed system of proportional representation.[42] Half of the members are elected with a direct, simple majority from single-seat constituencies and the other 328 members are elected according to closed party lists in each of the sixteen multiseat German states. In an analysis of the advantages of the proportional system as opposed to the simple majority system, the directorate-general for research of the Women's Rights Series of the European Parliament explains this process as follows:

> The majoritarian system is seen to be unfair to women because with such an electoral practice, the success of the party depends heavily on the single candidate it selects. This candidate will have been selected on tightly defined criteria, as part of what makes a "successful" nominee; the selection process has been criticised for the emphasis given to "male" characteristics. . . . However, in proportional systems, the selection of candidates for the party list depends on other factors in addition to a candidate's personal appeal. The most important of these is the party's wish to appeal to as many voters as possible, which includes listing female candidates, as the absence of or small number of women on a national electoral list could be a negative factor for some of the electorate.[43]

The German experience supports this analysis. In Germany, most women in parliament are elected via the party lists rather than through the direct constituency vote.

Within Germany, the political parties have played a major role in increasing women in politics by their inclusion of women in the party lists and through the appointment of women to important decision-making positions at the state and federal level. The Green Party first introduced a strict system of gender quotas in 1980, whereby the party included a 50 percent quota in their party statutes. In 1988, the Social Democrats amended their statutes to include a flexible system of quotas that stipulated that at least one third of all candidates in internal party elections be women. For election lists, a goal of 40 percent women was set for 1998. Even the more conservative Christian Democratic Party (CDU) introduced a target goal of 30 percent female representation in party functions and election lists. Although the parties vary in whether they have met their own quotas, the party statutes have contributed to increasing the representation of women in national and state level politics.[44]

Women's Rights

The German Constitution also plays a significant role in supporting the involvement of women in politics. From its inception, the German Constitution guaranteed equal rights between women and men. Article 3 of the Constitution includes the guarantee that all people are equal before the law (Paragraph 1), the guarantee of equal rights for men and women, and the prohibition of discrimination on the basis of sex. However, as previously noted, conflicts between the equal rights clause and protection for families limited the full implementation of effective equal rights for women in practice. In 1994, Article 3 of the Constitution was amended to include positive action by the state to ensure gender equality. Paragraph 3.2 of the Constitution now states, "Men and women have equal rights. The State ensures the implementation of equality for women and men and takes action to abolish existing discrimination."

The Federal Ministry for Family Affairs, Senior Citizens, Women and Youth is the ministry responsible for overseeing women's issues, including initiating and monitoring state actions to ensure equal rights and to abolish discrimination. First established in 1953 as the Federal Ministry of Youth, Family, Women and Health, the role of the ministry has expanded substantially beyond its initial task of developing and implementing strategies to increase the birthrate with a limited view of women's affairs as exclusively family issues. Today its role includes the screening of legislative drafts for gender impact before the bills enter the legislative process.

Most federal states in Germany have passed their own equality legislation, which often include stronger provisions to promote gender equality than federal law. These state equality provisions can include mechanisms such as quotas with specified goals and timetables for achieving a higher level of equal opportunities. The federal government also funds a permanent infrastructure for women's associations at the state level, the German Women's Council (*Deutscher Frauenrat*). A prominent role for this organization includes lobbying and advocating for women in decision making.

Feminist Movements

Germany has a long and well-established feminist movement that dates back to the nineteenth century. More recently, the historical division of

Germany into East and West resulted in two very different feminist movements. After reunification, the sharply separate experiences of women in the West and the East regarding employment, family life, and political participation impeded the ability of feminists from the two parts of Germany to merge into a successful alliance. Some of these tensions may be rooted "in the different structures of state policy in the two postwar Germanies and the resulting differences in women's experiences and collective identities."[45]

Women in West Germany developed a feminist perspective that was formed in an environment where private patriarchy was the norm. Women in East Germany, in contrast, struggled to develop a feminist agenda in an environment where public patriarchy dominated their lives. Hence women in the West developed a subjective identity based primarily on their roles as mothers and wives, whereas women in the East developed an identity based primarily on their roles as mothers and workers. Under these two systems, women in the West depended more directly on individual men for their economic survival, whereas women in the East depended more directly on the state and were relatively free from economic dependence on individual men. A specific example of differences in perspectives can be seen in how women address work and childrearing. Feminists in West Germany are more likely to demand compensation for women who withdraw from the labor market or who work part-time hours when their children are young. Feminists in East Germany are more likely to demand social supports that enable women to work full-time during the years when their children are young.

Lesbian Rights

On August 1, 2001, Germany implemented legislation aimed at breaking down discrimination against gay and lesbian couples. Publications issued by the Federal Ministry of Justice (2001) concerning the legislation explain that the legislation provides recognition for other ways of life and that homosexuality requires recognition under the German Constitution:

> Homosexuality is neither a disease nor immoral behavior; nor is it unnatural or the expression of criminal attitudes or conduct. Rather, it is another form of sexual orientation alongside heterosexuality.
>   As such, it is an integral part of human identity and is therefore covered by the right to respect for human dignity contained in Article 1 of the Basic Law (German Constitution) and the individual's right to freedom of activity in Article 2 of the Basic Law.[46]

Marriage. Work commissioned by the Ministry of Justice focused on the extent of discrimination against gay and lesbian individuals and couples within Germany.[47] Part of the intent of the law is to create an environment that will help to eliminate the societal discrimination faced by gays and lesbians. The law provides for the creation of registered partnerships that allow partners to have a number of rights and responsibilities, including but not limited to:

- maintenance obligations and rights in an existing partnership;
- limited parental responsibility granted to the partner;
- inclusion of the partner in health insurance and nursing care;
- statutory right of inheritance; and
- the right of a foreign partner to join his or her partner in Germany and the right of foreign partners to naturalization.

Parenthood. The Federal Ministry of Justice's clarification of the difference between registered partnerships and marriage illustrates contemporary German legal thought on marriage and family. The following quotation further demonstrates how German interpretations of family have expanded over time:

One of the reasons marriage enjoys special protection under Article 6 of the Basic Law is precisely because of joint children of the marriage. Registered partnerships are different in this respect. . . .

Whilst it is true that traditionally, a family is understood to comprise two parents and their natural children, single parents and their children, as well as parents with stepchildren, foster children or adopted children also constitute a family, enjoying the protection of the state. A parent's sexual orientation is of no relevance in this respect. In plain terms this means that gays and lesbians who have their own natural or adopted children also enjoy the special protection granted by Article 6 of the Basic Law. It is already possible now for an unmarried man or a woman to adopt a child when the usual requirements of adoption law, especially those relating to the child's well-being, are fulfilled.[48]

RELIGION AND SPIRITUALITY

The German Constitution states that no individual may be discriminated against or favored due to their sex, faith, or religious opinions. However, women's roles in official religious activities are determined by the hierarchy, traditions, and rules and regulations of the churches that dominate within the country. In 1999, about one-third of the German population was Catholic; approximately the same percentage was affiliated with the established Protestant (Evangelical) Church. In addition, 1.9 million Muslims live within Germany. In recent years, the number of Jewish people in Germany has increased to about 67,000, primarily as a result of immigration from countries in Eastern Europe. Many other religious groups also practice within Germany, such as Buddhists, Quakers, and Bah'ai.[49]

Recent controversies concerning freedom of religion have focused on the Church of Scientology,[50] which is not recognized as a religion within Germany, and on practices of individuals who practice Islam, where the controversy centers on the definition of political versus religious practices and beliefs. In one case, a state court ruled that the wearing of a veil by a Muslim woman represented an expression of political beliefs rather than religious beliefs. Hence the court ruled that the state school was justified in refusing to hire the woman, if she continued to wear the veil, on the grounds that she represented a poor role model for students. Her wearing of the veil was viewed as a political statement regarding the position of women in society rather than as a requirement of religious law or belief. It must be noted, however, that this case was decided in Baden-Württemberg, which is historically one of the more conservative states in Germany.

Women's Roles

Although Germany has no official state church, some churches may obtain special status as corporate bodies under public law. In cases when a particular religious denomination is granted special status as a corporate body, it is supported by taxes rather than through direct contribution from church members. All individuals who are registered members of a state-recognized church pay between 8 and 9 percent of their income tax to the church of their choice.

These monies are used by the churches to support a wide range of social services, including hospitals, nursing homes, schools, facilities for the handicapped, daycare centers, and the like. Because women tend to dominate occupations in the public welfare and social service sector, churches provide a major avenue of employment for women.

Rituals and Religious Practices

Although most German women and men are affiliated with a church, regular participation in church activities is rare. Even among registered Catholics, for whom Catholic law demands weekly Sunday attendance at mass, only 19 percent attended mass regularly in 1993.[51] Among registered Protestants, 4 percent reported regular church attendance in the mid-1990s. In addition, social activities rarely center around the church.

VIOLENCE

In Germany, as in most Western industrialized countries, major efforts to recognize, define, and eliminate violence against women began in the 1970s. Today efforts to eliminate violence against women within Germany are undertaken by nonprofit organizations for women as well as by government initiatives at the federal and state levels. Many of the projects are also part of a broader campaign within the European Union to coordinate initiatives and projects in the member countries. The primary goal of this campaign is to place violence against women high on the political agenda within the European Union.[52] Its major objectives are to foster cooperation and coordination among the member states, to support nongovernmental organizations (NGOs) active in the field, to improve the available information on violence against women, to encourage preventative measures, and to provide protection for victims. Germany has shown a high level of support for this campaign. The Action Plan recognizes violence against women as encompassing a wide range of potential and actual violence, including domestic violence, sexual abuse of children, sexual harassment, and trafficking in women.

Germany initiated projects to address violence against women immediately following the International Year of Women in 1975, during which time daily violence against women emerged as an important topic of discussion and action. Initial efforts focused on domestic violence and on the establishment of shelters for women. The first German shelter for victims of domestic violence opened in 1976 as a pilot project in Berlin, with joint financing from the federal government and the Berlin Senate. Other shelters were operated as pilot projects in more rural areas. In the following decades, this narrow emphasis on domestic violence and shelters gave way to a far more comprehensive understanding of the extent of violence against women and of the need to develop legal measures and programs that targeted the perpetrators as well as the victims.[53]

Hence in the 1980s and 1990s, violence against women was seen to include sexual violence against women, sexual abuse of children, sexual harassment, sexual abuse in therapeutic relationships, and violence against older women, foreign women, and women who are disabled. Laws passed during this period dealt with issues such as rape in marriage and sexual harassment at the workplace. Criminal law provisions contained in the German Penal Code were modified to cover domestic violence.

Domestic Violence

Within Germany, statistics concerning the extent of violence against women are collected to monitor the success of legal and programmatic efforts to fight violence.[54] Husbands, partners, acquaintances, and relatives inflict two-thirds of all violence against women. Violence occurs or has occurred in one in three partnerships in Germany.

In July 1997, marital rape was classified as a prosecutable crime. More recent legislation enacted in March 2000 has centered on ensuring that victims of domestic violence have the right to remain in their own homes and apartments. The perpetrator loses the right to enter the house or apartment either on a temporary or permanent basis, depending on the circumstances. The law contains explicit provisions that prohibit the perpetrator from contacting, harassing, and coming within the proximity of the victim.[55] More than 400 shelters for women exist overall in unified Germany, with more than 100 in the East. Yearly more than 40,000 women use these shelters, many of which offer comprehensive services to help women deal with the violence and to leave the violent partnership permanently.

In 2001, federal law was modified to lower the waiting period for foreign women from four to two years for gaining the right to receive residency independent of their husband's right to residency. In addition, foreign women now have the right to obtain residency in their own name immediately upon separation from their husband on account of domestic violence.[56]

Current initiatives also view the effort to stop violence against children as a critical part of stopping violence against women in the long term. More than 100,000 cases of sexual abuse against children are reported annually in Germany. Seventy percent of the perpetrators are well known to the victim; 75 percent of the victims are girls. Reports of sexual abuse against children occur in all social classes and age groups. In many instances, the abuse has continued for several years.

Since November 2000, children have the right to an upbringing free from violence under the civil code (*Recht auf gewaltfreie Erzeihung*). Implementation of the civil code centers on the provision of materials and other support for parents and children to prevent the use of violence against children rather than centering on prosecution of parents. Other more serious forms of child abuse and neglect are covered under a different set of laws. Based on a growing body of research concerning the link between violence against children and future domestic violence, the establishment of every child's right to a nonviolent upbringing is viewed as a critical preventive element to stop violence.[57]

The current action plan of the federal government targets prevention, legislation, cooperation among institution and projects, networking of assistance services, working with perpetrators, awareness building among experts and the public at large, and international cooperation.[58] As part of this plan, the federal government convened a joint federal and state working group to coordinate law and policy that fall under the jurisdiction of the states.

The emphasis on working with perpetrators represents a shift from earlier efforts that focused almost exclusively on women and/or on criminal proceedings against perpetrators that could result in fines and/or prison sentences. The law currently in force provides the option of the imposition of a suspended sentence for the perpetrator along with mandatory attendance in a violence-prevention training course aimed at changing behavior. These courses were initially developed within the framework of the Berlin Crisis Intervention Project to Fight Domestic Abuse.

Since laws alone have little impact if they are not enforced consistently or understood by the public at large, awareness-building efforts in Germany are now designed to provide special guidelines and instructions for enforcement officials and others who provide services to victims of domestic violence on how to handle specific circumstances surrounding domestic violence. In order to raise awareness among the public at large, the federal government provides direct support to conduct studies concerning domestic violence, to publish results from these studies, and to develop brochures. It routinely holds conferences of experts and conducts educational campaigns to combat violence.

German criminal law allows victims of crime to apply for compensation. Women who have suffered impairments to their health as a result of domestic violence are eligible to file claims. Part of the awareness campaign includes information on how victims of domestic violence can apply for assistance under the Victims of Violent Crime Act.

Trafficking in Women and Children

Trafficking in women and prostitution tourism are growing problems within Germany. In 1999, police took 1,300 women into custody who were known victims of trafficking. Although the actual number of female victims is known to be much higher, no reliable estimates exist. Most victims are citizens of Eastern European countries, including Poland, Ukraine, the Czech Republic, Lithuania, Russia, and Romania.

In cities with significant foreign populations, foreign women are far overrepresented in the use of shelters. For example, approximately 145,000 immigrant women live in Berlin, which has a population of over 3 million people. However, 50 to 65 percent of the women who use shelters in Berlin are non-German citizens. Legal efforts to deal with trafficking in women have centered on allowing women who are victims to stay in Germany in order to testify in criminal proceedings without facing immediate deportation.

OUTLOOK FOR THE TWENTY-FIRST CENTURY

As Germany enters the twenty-first century, its laws and policies are changing to reflect the 1994 amendment to German Basic Law: "Men and women have equal rights. The State ensures the implementation of equality for women and men and takes action to abolish existing discrimination."

Many of the policies described indicate that Germany is attempting to redesign its laws and policies to achieve this constitutional ideal. Its approach is a comprehensive one that spans many dimensions of women's lives. Women in Germany already have access to an excellent social welfare system and to a high standard of living relative to many other women throughout the world. Although Germany faces many challenges in achieving equality for the increasing diversity of women within its borders, the outlook for women living in Germany in the twenty-first century is positive.

NOTES

1. The "social" federal state is one in which Germany's Federal Constitution guarantees the protection of human and civil rights. Federal Statistical Office of Germany (FSOG), *Employment, Wages, and Salaries*, press release (Wiesbaden: Statistisches Bundesamt, 2001).

2. Federal Statistical Office of Germany, *Federal Republic of Germany: Figures and Facts* (Wiesbaden: Statistisches Bundesamt, 2000).

3. Federal Statistical Office of Germany, *Causes of Death, Infant Mortality, and Abortions: Figures and Facts* (Wiesbaden: Statistisches Bundesamt, 2000); and FSOG, 2000, *Federal*.

4. Federal Statistical Office of Germany, *Immer weniger kinder suchen Ostereier*, press release, April 19, 2000.

5. The Gymnasium is the academic track; students who successfully complete this track receive the Abitur diploma, which qualifies them for entrance into university. Realschule is defined as a commercial high school; it awards diplomas that qualify students for admission to business and technical colleges. Hauptschule is general high school and provides vocational-oriented training. Students who complete general high school are qualified to enter three-year apprenticeship programs for technical and clerical professions. The fourth model, the comprehensive schools (Gesamtschulen), offers a combination of academic, commercial, and vocational programs.

6. Federal Statistical Office of Germany, *Institutions of Higher Education: Figures and Facts* (Wiesbaden: Statistisches Bundesamt, 1999).

7. S. Berghahn, "Frauen, Recht and Laenger Atem," in *Frauen in Deutschland 1945–1992*, ed. G. Helwig and H. Nickel (Berlin: Bundeszentrale für Politische Bildung, 1993), 71–138; and S. Berghahn and A. Fritzsche, *Frauenrecht in ost und west Deutschland* (Berlin: Basisdruck, 1991).

8. FSOG, 2001.

9. E. Marlier and S. Ponthieux, "Low-wage Employees in EU Countries," *Statistics in Focus, Population and Social Conditions, Theme 3–November 2000* (Luxembourg: Eurostat, 2000).

10. FSOG, 2001; and Federal Statistical Office of Germany, *Leben und Arbeiten in Deutschland* (Wiesbaden: Statistisches Bundesamt, 2001).

11. FSOG, 2001, *Leben*.

12. FSOG, 2001, *Leben*.

13. S. Clarke, "Earnings of Men and Women in the EU" (Luxembourg: Eurostat, 2001).

14. Eileen Trzcinski, "Gender and German Unification," *Affilia* 13, no. 1 (1998): 69–101; Berghahn, 1993; and Berghahn and Fritzsche, 1991.

15. Federal Ministry for Family Affairs, Senior Citizens, Women and Youth, *Schutz vor Gewalt gegen Frauen* (Berlin: Author, 2001).

16. Berghahn, 1993; and F. Maier, "Geschlecterverhaeltnisse der DDR im Umbruch," *Zeitschrift für Soziale reform* 37, no. 11–12 (1991): 641–62.

17. Berghahn, 1993; and Berghahn and Fritzsche, 1991.

18. Federal Statistical Office of Germany, *Zur wirschaftlichen und sozialen Lage in den neuen Bundeslandern (Economic and Social Conditions in the New German States)* (Vierteljahreszeitschrift, Wiesbaden: Statistisches Bundesamt, March).

19. Federal Statistical Office of Germany, *Statistisches Jahrbuch 2000 für die Bundesrepublik Deutschland* (Wiesbaden: Statistisches Bundesamt, 2001).

20. Federal Statistical Office of Germany, *134, 600 Schwangerschaftsabbrueche im Jahr 2000*, press release, April 5, 2001; and FSOG, 2000, *Federal*.

21. FSOG, 2001, *Causes of Death*.

22. Federal Ministry for Family Affairs, Senior Citizens, Women, and Youth, *Staatliche Hilfen für familien* (Berlin: Author, 2001).

23. Federal Ministry of Labour and Social Affairs, *Teilzeit-alles, was Recht ist* (Bonn: Bundesministerium für Arbeit und Sozialordnung, 2001).

24. Federal Ministry of Labour and Social Affairs, 2001, *Teilzeit*.

25. Federal Ministry for Family Affairs, Senior Citizens, Women and Youth, 2000, *Teilzeit*, and 2000, *Staatliche*.

26. Federal Ministry of Labour and Social Affairs 2001.

27. Federal Ministry of Labour and Social Affairs 2001.

28. For example, individuals who are able to work are obliged to accept any reasonable offer of employment. This requirement does not, however, apply in all cases, and it specifically excludes individuals caring for a very young, sick, or disabled child from the work requirement.

29. Federal Ministry of Labour and Social Affairs, *Social Security at a Glance* (in German) (Bonn: Bundesministerium für Arbeit und Sozialordnung, 2001).

30. FSOG, 2000, "134, 600," and 2000, *Federal*.

31. FSOG, 2000, *Federal*.

32. A detailed discussion of the history of abortion law and debate in both the FRG and the GDR can be found in M. Marx Ferree, W.A. Gansom, J. Gerhards, and D. Rucht, *Shaping Abortion Discourse* (Cambridge: Cambridge University Press, 2002).

33. FSOG, 2001, "134, 600."

34. FSOG, 2000, *Federal*.

35. Federal Ministry for Labour and Social Affairs, 2001, *Social Security*.

36. Federal Statistical Office of Germany, *Health Report for Germany* (Wiesbaden: Statistisches Bundesamt, 1998).

37. FSOG, 1998.

38. FSOG, 2000, *Employment*.

39. Eurostat, *Key Data on Health 2000* (Luxembourg: Author, 2000).

40. FSOG, 1998.

41. A. Seeland, *Country Report Germany: Women in Decision-making* (European Database, 2001) (Berlin: Frauen Computer Centrum), www.db-decision.de.

42. Under a system of proportional representation, political groups receive seats in proportion to their electoral strength. Political parties put forth lists of candidates. The number of candidates from each party who are seated in Parliament depends on the proportion of total votes received by the party. Proportional representation systems were first introduced in 1889 in Belgium as an electoral method designed to compensate for shortcomings of a simple majority vote system, in which the candidate with the most votes is elected.

43. Directorate-General for Research, European Parliament, *Differential Impact of Electoral Systems*, Women's Rights Series (Luxembourg: European Parliament, 1997), 6.

44. Seeland, 2001.

45. Myra Marx Ferree (1995, 10) has written extensively on the development of feminism in East and West Germany prior to and following reunification and on the source and nature of the difficulties feminists encountered as they attempted to form effective coalitions. Part of these difficulties stemmed from the different life experiences of women in the East and the West. A detailed discussion of the economic and social differences that shaped the experiences of women in the East and West during the two periods can be found in E. Trzcinski (1998, 2000).

46. Federal Ministry of Justice, *Legislation on Same Sex Partnerships* (Berlin: Author, 2001), 1.

47. H.P. Buba and L.A. Vaskovics, *Benachteiligung gleichgeschlechtich orientierter Personen und Paare* (Berlin: Federal Ministry of Justice, 2000).

48. Federal Ministry of Justice, 2001, 3.

49. Federal Statistical Office of Germany, 2000, *Federal*.

50. U.S. Department of State, *Annual Report on International Religious Freedom: Germany* (Washington, DC: Author, 2000).

51. German Information Center, "Religion and Church and State in Germany" (New York: Author, 2000).

52. European's Women's Lobby 2001. *Unveiling the hidden data on domestic violence in the European Union* (Brussels: European Women's Lobby) and European Commission, *Breaking the Silence* (Brussels: Author, 2001).

53. Federal Ministry for Family Affairs, Senior Citizens, Women and Youth, 2001.

54. Any international or temporal comparison of statistics measuring violence against women must, however, be interpreted with great caution. Major cultural differences exist in how questions are framed, in the willingness of women to report violence, and in whether women themselves view specific acts as violent.

55. Federal Ministry for Family Affairs, Senior Citizens, Women and Youth, 2001, *Chronologie der familienpolitischen Entscheidungen* (Berlin: Author, 2001).

56. Federal Ministry for Family Affairs, Senior Citizens, Women and Youth, 2001, *Chronologie*.

57. Federal Ministry for Family Affairs, Senior Citizens, Women and Youth, 2001, *Action Plan of the Federal Government to Combat Violence against Women* (Berlin: Author, 2001).

58. Federal Ministry for Family Affairs, Senior Citizens, Women and Youth, 2001, *Chronologie*.

RESOURCE GUIDE

Suggested Reading

European Commission. "Domestic violence against women: European opinion." Brussels: European Commission, 2001. http://europa.eu.int/comm/dg10/women/violence/index3_fr.html.

European Women's Lobby. *Unveiling the hidden data on domestic violence in the European Union*. Brussels: European Women's Lobby, 2001. Can be ordered at www.womenlobby.org.

Federal Ministry of Labour and Social Affairs. "Social Security at a Glance." Bonn: Bundesministerium für Arbeit und Sozialordnung, 2001. www.bma.de.

Ferree, M. Marx. "Patriarchies and Feminisms: The Two Women's Movements of Unified Germany." *Social Politics* 2, no. 1 (1995): 10–24.

James, P., ed. *Modern Germany: Politics, Society and Culture*. London: Routledge, 1998.

Mau, S. *The Moral Economy of Welfare States: Britain and Germany Compared*. London: Routledge, 2003.

Parkes, S. *Understanding Contemporary Germany*. London: Routledge, 1996.

Web Sites

All the federal ministries in Germany provide extensive information and statistics in English on a wide range of topics. The most important federal ministries for women's issues are:

Federal Ministry for Family Affairs, Senior Citizens, Women and Youth, www. bmfsfj.de.

Federal Ministry of Labor and Social Affairs, www.bma.bund.de.

Federal Ministry of Justice, www.bmj.bund.de.

Federal Statistical Office of Germany, www.statistik-bund.de.

The European Commission of the European Union, http://europa.eu.int/comm/. Publishes a wide range of articles and books that deal with all aspects of social and economic policy within current member countries and candidate countries of the European Union. Eurostat, the statistical arm of the European Commission, publishes a wide range of statistical information. Most publications are available without charge on the Internet. Books can be ordered online.

Eurostat, http://europa.eu.int/comm/eurostat.html.

The European Database: Women in Decision Making, www.db-decision.de. Compiles information and collects data on women in politics and in business.

The German Information Center, Germany On-Line, www.germany-info.org. Provides excellent links to a wide range of Internet sites on Germany and provides a good source of basic information on many aspects of German life, politics, and society.

The Organization of Economic Cooperation and Development (OECD), www.oecd. org. Publishes a wide range of books and publications that deal with social and economic policy within Germany and other countries. Many of their publications are available free of charge, and most books available for a charge can be downloaded immediately. Others can be ordered online.

Organizations

FrauenComputerZentrumBerlin (FCZB)
Women's Computer Centre Berlin
Cuvrystr. 1, 10997 Berlin, Germany
Phone: 49-030-617970-0
Web site: www.fczb.de/english/eindex4.htm

Organization provides a wide range of educational and training for women in the use of new technologies. Web site provides English version.

Gender Research Group
Dr. Ursula Pasero
Head Research Group
Breiter Weg 10, D-24105 Kiel
Phone: +49 (0)431-579 49-51
Fax: 49 (0)431-579 49-50
Email: pasero@gender.uni-kiel.de
Web site: www.gender.uni-kiel.de/zentren.htm

Provides information on research on women in Germany and links to other university-based gender research centers. Information provided in English.

German Association of Women Engineers
dib e.v.
Postfach 110 305
64218 Darmstadt
Phone: 0700/34 23 83 42
Email: info@dibev.de
Web site: www.dibev.de
Web site has English version.

Women: Frauen Seiten in Internet
Web site: www.woman.de/

Web site provides links to information and organizations for women in Germany on a wide range of women's issues. Most sites provide information in German only.

Women's Organizations in Germany
Denise Osted
Ruigezandplantsoen 4
6835 AM ARNHEM
The Netherlands
Web site: www.euronet.nl/%7Efullmoon/womlist/countries/germany.html

Dr. Osted maintains an extensive list of women's organizations listed by country. Please be advised that most web sites for women's organizations are in German only. Even in cases where English is available, the amount of information is usually quite limited in comparison with the German version.

SELECTED BIBLIOGRAPHY

Clarke, S. "Earnings of Men and Women in the EU: The Gap Narrowing but Only Slowly." *Statistics in Focus, Population and Social Conditions, Theme 3—March 2001.* Luxembourg: Eurostat, 2001.

Directorate General for Research, European Parliament. *Differential Impact of Electoral Systems on Female Political Representation. Women's Rights Series, W-10.* Luxembourg: European Parliament, 1997.

European Commission. *Breaking the Silence*. Brussels: Author, 2001.

Eurostat. *Key Data on Health 2000*. Luxembourg: Author, 2000. Can be ordered at http://europa.eu.int/comm/eurostat.html.

Federal Ministry for Family Affairs, Senior Citizens, Women and Youth. *Action Plan of the Federal Government to Combat Violence against Women*. Berlin: Author, 2001.

Federal Ministry of Justice. *Legislation on Same Sex Partnerships: The New Laws on Registered Partnerships—Legal Protection for All Ways of Life*. Berlin: Author, 2001.

Federal Ministry of Labour and Social Affairs. *Social Security at a Glance*. Bonn: Bundesministerium fuer Arbeit und Sozialordnung, 2001.

Federal Statistical Office of Germany. *Health Report for Germany*, abridged version (in English). Health Monitoring of the Federation. Wiesbaden: Statistisches Bundesamt, 1998.

———. *Geography and Climate: Figures and Facts*. Wiesbaden: Statistisches Bundesamt, 1999.

———. *Institutions of Higher Education: Figures and Facts*. Wiesbaden: Statistisches Bundesamt, 1999.

———. *School Statistics: Figures and Facts*. Wiesbaden: Statistisches Bundesamt, 1999.

———. *Causes of Death, Infant Mortality, and Abortions: Figures and Facts*. Wiesbaden: Statistisches Bundesamt, 2000.

———. *Federal Republic of Germany: Figures and Facts*. Wiesbaden: Statistisches Bundesamt, 2000.

———. *Life Expectancy Continues to Increase*. Press release, December 13, 2000. Wiesbaden: Federal Statistical Office, 2000.

———. *Population: Figures and Facts*. Wiesbaden: Statistisches Bundesamt, 2000.

———. *Population in Germany Will Decline by More than 10 Million by 2050*. Press release, July 19, 2000. Wiesbaden: Statistisches Bundesamt, 2000.

———. *Employment, Wages and Salaries, Facts and Figures*. Press releases. Wiesbaden: Statistisches Bundesamt, 2001.

Ferree, M. Marx. "Institutionalization, Identities and the Political Participation of Women in the New Federal States of Germany." In *Women and Postcommunism: Research on Russia and Eastern Europe*, edited by Metta Spencer and Barbara Wejnert, 19–34. New York: JAI Press, 1996.

Ferree, M. Marx., W.A. Gamson, J. Gerhard, and D. Rucht. *Shaping Abortion Discourse: Democracy and the Public Sphere in Germany and the United States*. Cambridge: Cambridge University Press, 2002.

German Information Center, Germany On-Line. "Religion and Church and State in Germany." New York: Author, 2001. www.germany-info.org.

Maier, F. "The Labour Market for Women and Employment Perspectives in the Aftermath of German Unification." *Cambridge Journal of Economics*, 17 (1993): 267–80.

Marlier, E., and S. Ponthieux. "Low-wage Employees in EU Countries." *Statistics in Focus, Population and Social Conditions, Theme 3–November 2000*. Luxembourg: Eurostat, 2000.

Seeland, A. *Country Report Germany: Women in Decision-making*. European Database, 2001. Berlin Fraven Computer Centrum. www.db-decision.de.

Trzcinski, E. "Gender and German Unification." *Affilia* 13, no. 1 (1998): 69–101.

———. "Family Policy in Germany: Feminist Dilemma?" *Feminist Economics*, no. 6 (2000): 1, 21–44.

U.S. Department of State, Bureau of Democracy, Human Rights and Labor. *Annual Report on International Religious Freedom: Germany*. Washington, DC: Author, 2000.

Selected German Bibliography

Berghahn, S. "Frauen, Recht and Laenger Atem: Bilanz nach ueber 40 Jahren Gleichstellungsgebot in Deutschland" ("Women and Rights: An Assessment of 40 Years of Equal Rights for Women in Germany"). In *Frauen in Deutschland 1945–1992*, edited by G. Helwig and H. Nickel, 71–138. Berlin: Bundeszentrale für Politische Bildung, 1993.

Berghahn, S., and A. Fritzsche. *Frauenrecht in ost und west Deutschland: Bilanz und Ausblick (Rights for Women in East and West Germany: Assessment and Outlook)*. Berlin: Basisdruck, 1991.

Buba, H.P., and L.A. Vaskovics. *Benachteiligung gleichgeschlechtich orientierter Personen und Paare. Studie im Aftrag des Bundesministeriums der Justiz. (Discrimination against Gay and Lesbian Individuals and Couples. Study Commissioned by the Federal Ministry of Justice)*. Berlin: Federal Ministry of Justice, 2000.

Federal Ministry for Family Affairs, Senior Citizens, Women and Youth. *Chronologie der familienpolitischen Entscheidungen seit Beginn der Legislaturperiode. Stand: 19.07.2001. (Chronology of Decisions regarding Family Politics since the Beginning of the Current Legislative Period up to 19 July 2001)*. Berlin: Author, 2001.

———. *Schutz vor Gewalt gegen Frauen (Protection against Violence against Women)*. Berlin: Author, 2001.

———. *Staatliche Hilfen fuer Familien (Types of Assistance Provided by the State to Families)*. Berlin: Author, 2001.

Federal Ministry of Labour and Social Affairs. *Teilzeit—alles, was Recht ist: Rechtlich Rahmendingungen fuer Arbeitnehmer und Arbeitgeber (Part-work—Everything that the Law Provides: Legal Conditions for Employers and Employees)*. Bonn: Bundesministerium fuer Arbeit und Sozialordnung, 2001.

Federal Statistical Office of Germany. "Immer weniger Kinder suchen Ostereier" ("Fewer and Fewer Children Are Seeking Easter Eggs"). Press release, April 19, 2000.

———. *Leben und Arbeiten in Deutschland: Ergebnisse des Mikrozensus 2000. (Life and Work in Germany: Results from the 2000 Microcensus)*. Wiesbaden: Statistisches Bundesamt, 2001.

———. "134,600 Schwangerschaftsabbrueche im Jahr 2000 in Deutschland gemeldet" ("134,600 Abortions Registered in Germany in 2000"). Press release, April 5, 2001. Wiesbaden: Statistisches Bundesamt, 2001.

———. *Statistisches Jahrbuch 2000 fuer die Bundesrepublik Deutschland (Statistical Yearbook 2000 for the Federal Republic of Germany)*. Wiesbaden: Statistisches Bundesamt, 2001.

Institut für Demoskopie Allensbach, eds. *Frauen in Deutschland: Lebensverhaeltniss, Lebensstile und Zukunftserwartungen (Women in Germany: Living Conditions, Lifestyles, and Future Expectations)*. Cologne, Germany: Bund-Verlag, 1993.

Maier, F. "Geschlechterverhaeltnisse der DDR im Umbruch—Zur Bedeutung von Arbeitsmarkt und Sozialpolitik" ("Gender Conditions in the GDR in Transition: The Meaning of Labor Market and Social Policies"). *Zeitschrift fuer Sozialreform*, 37, no. 11–12 (1991): 641–62.

16

GREECE

Maria Pantelidou Maloutas

PROFILE OF GREECE

The historical experience of Greek society, refers principally to the Ottoman rule and to the war of independence in the 1820s, as well as to the early period of Greek statehood, when the basis for the tense relationship between state and society was created.[1] The end of the first half of the twentieth century was marked by a civil war that deeply influenced Greek society and political culture, and it had lasting consequences on the political system. In 1974 Greece marked the end of a seven-year dictatorial rule, and an important liberalization of the political system started to take place.

According to the 1975 Constitution, Greece is a parliamentary republic, with a president elected in Parliament as the head of state. Executive power resides in the prime minister and his cabinet, who need a majority in the 300-seat parliament, following the elections that take place every four years, in order to form the government. The country is divided into thirteen administrative regions, headed by and appointed by the government secretary general, and there is an effort to de-

centralize government services and to facilitate the implementation of regional policies by the regions themselves.

During the last decade, the Greek economy has shown notable progress in view of the (achieved) target of participation in the third stage of the European Union (EU) in 2001. After a long period of stagnation there are important growth rates; the budget deficits have been reduced; total revenues increased; the general debt, although still among the highest in the EU, has declined; and inflation, having diminished by about ten points in less than a decade, is at the EU average today. Agriculture is still very important, since around 10 percent of the Greek gross domestic product (GDP) represents primary sector activities, compared to 15 percent for the industry, and more than 40 percent for trade though sanctioning the existence of an important trade deficit.[2] Tourism is, of course, a very important sector of the economy, and economic relations with the EU play a decisive role in the functioning and progress of the Greek economy.

The total land area is 131,957 square kilometers[3] with 15,021 kilometers of coastline. Urban areas cover 12 percent of the land, 39 percent is meadow and pasture, and 29 percent is arable. Mountains and islands characterize the landscape. According to the 2001 census, the population is 10,939,605. In the 1990s, the percentage of males grew by 7.4 percent and the female population grew only by 6 percent; but still the number of females is greater — 5,515,516 versus 5,424,089 males. Above EU averages, life expectancy is 75.3 for males and 80.5 for females, and it is higher in urban than in rural areas. Since 1998, the number of deaths has surpassed that of births, leading to a natural decrease in the population as well as its aging. However, recent data from Eurostat show an increase in the population in 2001 of 3 per 1,000 — 0.6 per 1,000 due to natural increase (9.5 per 1,000 deaths, against 10.1 per 1,000 births) and 2.4 to the arrival of economic immigrants. Total fertility is 1.38 and even lower in the greater Athens area (where more than one-third of the total population live), whereas infant mortality, around 6.7 per 1,000 in 1998, is definitely decreasing (it was 19.33 in 1978), and maternal mortality, extremely low, is among the lowest in the EU.

OVERVIEW OF WOMEN'S ISSUES

Greece is a rapidly modernizing society in which the correction of flagrant gender injustices has been identified, since the 1980s, as *one* aspect of necessary democratic changes. However, the patriarchal character of Greek society and polity remains prominent. Thus, a broad range of women's lifestyles and self-perceptions exist. The 1980s was a decade of great importance for women, following the dynamic presence of the feminist movement beginning in the mid-1970s and the socialist party's (PASOK) coming to power in 1981. Since the government wanted to harmonize its coexistence with other EU countries, important legal measures toward the equality of the sexes were taken. Nevertheless, Greek society still has a very low level, one of the lowest in the EU, of women in positions of power and decision making, which accords with the prominence of its male-centered character. Although most of the equality demands of the women's movement of the 1970s and early 1980s have more or less been satisfied, there is still much to be done to fight against women's subordinate position in every sphere of life.

EDUCATION

Opportunities

Of those obtaining a doctorate in 1997–1998, 33.5 percent were women.[4] Women are 42.2 percent of university graduates in Greece and 28.8 percent of those possessing a postgraduate degree.[5] It is notable that although the percentage of females and males in every educational level is nearly equal, at the university level women's percentage grew from 31 percent in 1970–1971 to 58.7 percent in 2000–2001.[6] Girls usually have better grades and exam scores in secondary education and therefore obtain more of the coveted university places. Nevertheless, sex segregation according to fields of study, though decreasing, still exists: women went from 6 percent of engineering students in 1971–1972 to 24.7 percent in 1997–1998 and from 28.9 percent to 46.6 percent of the medical students during the same period. However, in the humanities during the same period, women increased their percentage from 68.2 percent to 80.3 percent. These recent increases in university enrollment for women have yet to seriously challenge the predominance of men as faculty members—women are less than 10 percent of full professors in Greek universities, a percentage that nevertheless marks progress.

Since 1998, a policy has been promoted to increase the awareness of select teaching staff of primary and secondary school (more than 50 percent of whom are women) on issues related to gender discrimination. There is also an effort to create teaching materials that are nonsexist.[7] But at this moment, no important changes addressing the problem of sexism in the content of school curriculum have been instituted.

Literacy

Although the traditional lower educational level of Greek women is being seriously challenged by the recent increases in women's university enrollment, illiteracy is still a women's issue. Women account for 73.5 percent of the 617,646 persons characterized as illiterate in the Greek census.[8] Most of these women are older (one-third of illiterate women are over seventy-five), live in rural areas, and are members of ethnic minorities. In younger cohorts, illiteracy is virtually nonexistent.

EMPLOYMENT AND THE ECONOMY

Joining the European Union in 1981 marked the beginning of a process of economic and political reform and rationalization. This process was accompanied by important changes, including the decrease in the agrarian population, the development of women's employment in the wage sector, a tendency toward the lessening of gender occupational segregation, and a decline in the earning gap between men and women, all of which have had major impacts on women's lives and political perceptions.

Job/Career Opportunities

Greek women today are better represented in fields that were culturally almost closed to them in the past; new career options appear in traditional male arenas (such as the army and security forces). Nevertheless, there are significant differences between men's and women's occupational ratio, unemployment rates, career histories, professional "choices," and, most definitely, positions in decision making.

The implementation of an equal opportunities policy in employment, promoted by the EU, identified the structure of the traditional Greek family, the division of labor between members of the household, as well as underdeveloped social services as the main causes of continued gender differences in economic well-being. Of EU countries, Greece has the smallest percentage of its labor force in waged labor and the largest percentage of self-employed people. Women make up 39.2 percent of the labor force and 36.7 percent of the employed. Women's unemployment rate, 15.9 percent, is more than double that of men. In urban areas, women constitute 60.1 percent of the unemployed. It is notable that 17.1 percent of working women are university educated, compared to 13.2 percent or working men. Part-time work is not very common in Greece (4.6 percent against 18 percent EU average), but it is a women's domain, since they comprise two-thirds of the part-time employees.

Pay

Legally, there is no gender discrimination in salaries in the public or semipublic sector, but differences in salaries in the private sector always exist.

Working Conditions

Sexual Harassment

Sexual harassment in the workplace is quite extensive and is related to the profoundly male-centered character of Greek society. However, no data exist as to the size of the problem. There seems to be no specific legal provision concerning sexual harassment, which does not even exist as a term in the Greek legal code.

Support for Mothers/Caretakers

Maternal Leave

Maternal leave was increased in 1985 to sixteen weeks for public sector employees and to fifteen in the private sector. Until the child's second birthday (first birthday in the private sector), working mothers in the public sector are entitled to two hours' (one in the private sector) daily reduction of their working day, plus one hour reduction for the next two years. Instead of these reductions, in the public sector one may choose a nine-month fully paid leave. There is also in the public sector a provision for up to two years of unpaid maternal leave until the child turns six. As this kind of leave does not count toward one's pension and also puts a stop to any career strategy, it is doubtful that many women will use it.

Daycare

The insufficiency of state and community daycare facilities for preschool children and for older children after school, as well as the high cost of private centers, make it very difficult for many women with no family networks to fill the gap and to combine work with family responsibilities. These difficulties no doubt contribute to the common tendency to quit work after childbirth and to not go back.[9]

Social/Government Programs

The National Action Plan for Occupation has various provisions related to women's employment. These include measures to address unemployment, the promotion of entrepreneurship among women, programs that teach women from rural areas new skills and aptitudes, programs for re-entry into the labor market, financial assistance to employers for the employment of women, provisions for new childcare centers, and the application of EU programs. But these initiatives touch a small minority of women and are obviously not enough to solve the problem of women's unemployment and the entrenched occupational hierarchy, as well as the difficulties in combining professional and family life.

FAMILY AND SEXUALITY

The nuclear family is by far the dominant type in today's Greece.[10] Often it is surrounded by a network of close relatives ready to cover the inadequacies of the welfare system, a practice that seems to be diminishing. Single-parent families, estimated at 6 percent of all families, unmarried mothers, and alternative forms of living together are marginal.[11]

Gender Roles

Gender roles within the family, in spite of the increased participation of women in the labor market, continue to be traditional, with housework and childcare considered to be women's domain. A research project on Athenian families showed that in 31.8 percent of the households, the husband performs no household task at all, and in 30.7 percent he performs only shopping.[12]

Women prepare food for a wedding in Rhodes, Arcanghelos, Greece. Photo © Ferdinando Scianna/Magnum Photos.

The underdevelopment of public provisions for daycare for preschool children and for care of the sick, old, and disabled at home makes it very difficult for married and working women to combine different roles, since *they* have to cover the gaps of the welfare system. The low level of benefits for different kinds of families does not help the situation. Such concerns partly explain the notable difference between the economic activity rates of single women of reproductive age that are rapidly rising, and those of married women that are much lower and rather stable over time.

Marriage

According to the official statistics of 1998, 55,851 weddings took place in Greece, and the nuptial rate was 5.3 marriages per 1,000 inhabitants, still above the European average. This rate fluctuated between 7 and 8 until the 1980s. Approximately 95 percent of men and women between 45 and 49 are married, and the average age of marriage in 1998 was 30.5 for men and 26.9 for women. Of the marriages, 83.7 percent were first marriages for both.

The new Family Law of 1983 provides for equal sharing of family burdens, parental care has replaced "paternal authority," and in case of divorce both spouses are entitled to alimony. Also, divorce by mutual consent was instituted, offering a solution to some problematic cases of dissolution of marriage. Still, the divorce rate is low—0.7 per 1,000 inhabitants annually—although it has more than doubled since the 1960s.

Reproduction

Births out of marriage are rare: they comprise 3.81 per 1,000 of the total of live births in 1998, a rate that sixty years ago was only 1.3. The total of live births of the same year was 9.6 per 1,000 inhabitants, of which 99.7 percent took place in a hospital or clinic. The average age of the mother was 28.6 years, and 84.1 percent of all live births were to women between 20 and 34. The first year of marriage is the year of a child's birth for 34.2 percent of all live births that took place within marriage. Although there are a few births to teens, the more fertile group is between 25 and 29 with a rate of 89.6 per 1,000. Changes in reproductive styles that are also important socioeconomic changes are centered on the tendency toward fewer children at a younger age. However, in the greater Athens area, the average age for having children was (for both sexes together), 26.9 in 1981, 28.5 in 1991, and 29.8 in 1997.[13]

Sex Education

The Ministry of Education intermittently introduces sex information campaigns in schools.

Contraception and Abortion

According to estimations, the condom is the most widespread contraceptive method, approaching 45 percent, followed by coitus interruptus in conjunction with the rhythm method for 20–30 percent, and the pill accounts for 2 percent and the IUD for 10 percent.[14] There seems to be a wide difference between urban and rural areas as far as both the frequency of use of contraception and the types used.

Abortion, legalized in the 1980s, is a significant issue. In spite of the scarcity of statistics, which indicate that approximately 13,000 abortions were performed in 1997, it can be legitimately stated that abortion is widely used, almost as a contraceptive method, at a rate many times the official figures.[15] According to the unofficial, but accepted, estimates, 100,000 to 120,000 abortions are induced per year.[16] This number is lower than in the past due to the increased use of contraceptives (especially condoms, due to fear of AIDS). Also, teen abortions are estimated to be lower than in the past, a fact linked, according to the Ministry of Education, to its (very useful but very rare) sex information campaigns in schools.

Teen Pregnancy

Teen pregnancies are not very well documented. The official 1998 statistics indicate that births of live children occurred at a rate of 0.3 per 1,000 women of the relative age for the under 15 age group, and at a rate of 11.6 per 1,000 for the 15 to 19 age group.

HEALTH

Traditionally women have a close and multifaceted connection to health issues—as informal caretakers of the sick; as patients with specific female health issues, especially concerns related to pregnancy, childbirth, and nursing; and as main occupants of lower positions in the welfare state employed in nursing and social services. The specific health problems of women have only lately become a concern in health policies in Greece.

Health Care Access

Also, although it is undeniable that life expectancy at birth for women and men in Greece (80.5 and 75.3, respectively) indicates that the general level of health is improving, there is much to be done to modernize the national health system and make it function more smoothly, including rationalizing its administration, presenting a more friendly image, and adding more medical assistant personnel.

According to Organization for Economic Cooperation and Development data, there are 4.4 doctors per 1,000 inhabitants in Greece, one of the highest rates in the EU. However, some areas outside the major urban centers are extremely disadvantaged. For example, according to the official statistics[17] there are 2,225 obstetricians-gynecologists in public or private hospitals in Greece. Of these, 1,671 work in the greater Athens area. Some regions, like the Ionian islands or Thrace, seem very underserved (with nineteen and twenty-one, respectively).

In the Athens area, the total number of beds in private hospitals (around 8,000) is half of the total beds in public hospitals. Private maternity clinics are very popular; half of the total beds in obstetrics and gynecology belong to the private sector. In the same area, there is a total of 11,599 doctors and only 17,784 nursing personnel. The low number of nurses explains the absence of restricted visiting hours in Greek hospitals, since (female) relatives need to stay at the bedside of their sick relatives day and night.

Diseases and Disorders

The main causes of death in women appear to be circulatory diseases (56.2 percent), followed by cancer (18.2 percent), and respiratory diseases (5.5 percent). Although the number of patients discharged from hospitals in 1997 by disease[18] may not be the most reliable indicator of women's health issues, it does give some idea of the types of illnesses.

AIDS

In 1997 105 women, compared to 305 men, were discharged from hospital after being treated for AIDS. Greece participates in a number of specific European programs concerning the protection of prostitutes from AIDS (EUROPAP), its prevention in migrant prostitutes (TAMPEP), an Umbrella Network for the analysis of border issues in regard to HIV and sexually transmitted diseases, and the development of cooperative border-crossing prevention between Greece and Albania and between Greece and Bulgaria.

Eating Disorders

There are no data specific to eating disorders except for "nutritional marasmus" (progressive emaciation), which was identified for twenty-eight women and twelve men treated in hospital in 1997.

Cancer

Various programs for the prevention of specific female cancers are being promoted, often in collaboration with local authorities and various NGOs. For example, mobile units for detection of cervical cancer and for mammography reach out to women who would not otherwise be checked, and information campaigns for women are more and more widespread. But still, all these efforts reach only a small percentage of the target group. Of those patients discharged from hospital in 1997, 9,572 were discharged after treatment for breast cancer, 1,462 for cervical cancer, 1,459 for cancer of the uterus, and 3,698 for cancer of the ovaries and other uterine tumors.

Depression

There are no specific data on the extent of depression, which is probably treated privately and not in hospitals.

POLITICS AND LAW

Suffrage

Women attained the right to vote and other political rights in 1952.

Political Participation

Until 1985, Greek women followed the "traditional" voting pattern in favor of the Right and participated at very low levels or not at all in formal political activity beyond voting. In the 1985 general elections, women repaid the attention received from the socialist party, PASOK by voting massively in its favor. For the first time in Greek electoral history, a gender gap appeared in which more women than men voted in favor of PASOK in all areas: urban (+1.5 percentage points), semi-urban (+1.3 percent), and rural (+0.7 percent).[19] Women's votes accorded with PASOK's tactics (helped by EGE, its women's organization) of addressing women of all social environments. PASOK appeared to women to be willing to solve problems of legal discrimination and to offer welfare provisions, trying to prove by diverse measures like the creation of a Council for the Equality of the Sexes in 1983 (upgraded in 1985 to General Secretariat for Equality, thus sanctioning the establishment of "state feminism")[20] that it had women's issues high on its agenda. Also in the 1985 election, for the first time in Greek electoral history the vote in favor of the Right marked no real gender variation. Today there is no significant difference between women's and men's voting patterns, although a small gender gap has become a constant element.

Although women do not vote in smaller numbers than men,[21] in all other types of political activities they still show lower levels of participation. This is a generational phenomenon that is highly correlated with educational level. In fact, age is a variable of particular importance in Greek political culture, since the differences in socialization experiences from one generation to the other are very wide. In many indicators, the differences in the level of political participation between men and women in the same age group can be smaller than in different age groups of the same gender.[22] For example, young women and men (18–29) are more similar to each other than are young and old women (60+) in the frequency of newspaper reading (64.6 percent and 78.3 percent of young women and men declared frequent reading of newspapers versus 34.8 percent and 68.2 percent of the old), in the frequency of exchanging political opinions (37.5 percent and 42.9 percent of young women and men declared frequent exchange of political opinions versus 23.4 percent and 58.2 percent of the old), and in the frequency of participation in electoral campaigns (15.6 percent and 19.8

percent of young women and men declare frequent involvement in campaigns versus 8.1 percent and 23.2 percent of the old).[23]

The privatization of "women's issues" and, until the 1980s, the absolute disinterest of the political system in the reality of gender discrimination explain the very low levels of women's formal political activity.[24] Although party membership, running for public office, and entering the political elites were until recently almost exclusively male, and legitimized as such, the idea of promoting the presence of women in all elected and appointed bodies has been gaining ground. Thus, in all political parties (with the exception of the Greek Communist Party, the only party today with a woman at its head), there are gender quotas in decision-making bodies, usually set at the percentage of the party's female membership.

If voting patterns do not vary significantly by gender, in contrast, there is a massive disparity in the proportion of men and women in public office.[25] It must be underlined that today Greece presents the lowest level of female members of parliament in the EU (8.7 percent). In fifty years of political rights, only seventy-nine women have become members of parliament in Greece. Today, the Parliament is composed of twenty-six women out of 300 members. This is great progress, especially since thirty-one were actually elected, five of whom lost their seat for technical, legal reasons related to their occupations during the preelection period. Of the twenty-six remaining, twelve belong to PASOK, ten to New Democracy (Right), two to Synaspismos (Left), and two to the Communist Party. The twenty-five members of the Greek delegation to the European Parliament include today four women (16 percent).

During the last decade, the general picture of women in government is one of no more than 12 percent at best, with women being responsible or involved mostly in matters of welfare, culture, education, and justice, not considered to be crucial ministries. Today there are four women in government but only one as minister. Nevertheless, in July 2000, an "interministry committee for the equality of the sexes" was created with "mainstreaming" as its main goal.

Women politicians seem sensitized to women's issues and have called for increases in the number of women in the political elites, in accordance with the general European trend. Quotas for local election lists were thus recently approved in Parliament. The October 2002 local election was the first time that this important innovation was applied.[26] As a result, the percentage of women local councilors rose from 7 to 12 percent (the quota is applied in a system of preferential votes), while the number of women mayors rose from 14 from a total of 900 to 16. The numbers are obviously still very low. Nevertheless, it is important to note the significantly lower number of local councils with no women, which declined from 327 from a total of 900 to 116. Usually, as local councilors, women are responsible for areas that are stereotypically considered as theirs (e.g., childhood and the elderly).

Women's Rights

Although political rights were dynamically demanded during the interwar period, it was not until 1952 that women obtained full political rights. The 1975 Greek Constitution, stipulating "equality of the sexes," was followed in the 1980s by important legal measures proposed by the newly elected socialist government of PASOK: measures touching family law, divorce, abortion, employment discrimination, and facilities for employees with family responsibilities, as well as the ratification of CEDAW, the international convention for the abolition of all forms of discrimination against women.[27] In spite of their inadequacies, these measures legitimized, for the first time, the vision of a society not based on brutal gender discrimination, promoting "sex equality" to the level of a widely accepted value.

Feminist Movements

For various reasons, both internal and external, feminism is not expressed as a movement in Greece today. Apart from specific women politicians that have feminist sensitivities, feminist groups no longer function as such and women's organizations that had a massive following in the early 1980s do not really exist any more.[28] But if women's social inferiority is always apparent in Greek society, it does function in a new climate of gender awareness and of legitimization of gender "equality," created in previous decades by feminist political activity. Furthermore, scholarly thinking and writing is today influenced by feminist theory, and seminars, conferences, courses in universities, and specialized journals do exist. It seems as if a phase of feminist introspection is prevalent today, out of which new political interventions are eventually to be born.

Lesbian Rights

Lesbianism and lesbian rights do not appear as a real issue in Greek society, maybe because "sexuality without a man is not considered sexuality at all,"[29] especially in a patriarchal society. Thus, although there was a lesbian journal and a few lesbian meeting points still exist, the subject is rather ignored and nonexistent from a legal point of view.

Military Service

Women are admitted in the army in few numbers (there is a total of 6,472) and are placed in secondary positions, where they are not expected to take part in combat. Thus, their advancement is limited.

RELIGION AND SPIRITUALITY

The great majority of the population is officially registered as Orthodox Christians, and there has traditionally been a Jewish community culturally very present in Thessaloníki, Athens, and Larissa, and a Muslim minority mostly established in western Thrace, where women's position and educational levels are particularly low.

Women's Roles

The Greek Orthodox Church does not admit women, but male priests of the lower ranks can be married. Churchgoing is more common in rural than in urban areas and is traditionally a women's practice, offering them opportunities for socializing.

Rituals and Religious Practices

In 1982 civil marriage was introduced in Greece. Until then, the only possible way of getting married was the religious ceremony. Although it solved problems for couples of different religions, the way civil marriage is instituted does not offer a real choice: civil marriage takes place in often ugly city halls that do not facilitate a festive atmosphere; it is no wonder that few couples prefer it over the traditional Greek wedding. The church, which was rigorously opposed to the institution of civil marriage, considers it a sign of the failure of civil marriage that only 10 percent of all wedding ceremonies are civil.

VIOLENCE

Violence against women, as a means of social control, was confronted at a theoretical level in Greece by the autonomous feminist movement during the late 1970s. But today reliable data on all forms of violence against women are still scarce, making the extent of the problem difficult to assess and contributing to the fact that present measures to protect women are inadequate.

Domestic Violence

What is certain, by the data of the SOS telephone line,[30] is that domestic violence as well as violence against women in general are not confined to victims or offenders with specific socioeconomic profiles. Indeed, there is a relatively high frequency of it among those in the upper strata—perhaps because for women of higher educational levels, it is easier to ask for help. It is to be expected that in rural areas, where the patriarchal character of the Greek family is more pronounced and less challenged, violence against women would be more common.

Rape/Sexual Assault

After a significant debate, legislation concerning rape was reformed in 1984, a reform that only partly satisfied the women's movement. Reliable data are not easily accessible. If we take as a point of reference 1993, 270 cases of rape were reported to the police.[31] Of course, the real number must be much higher. In a research project with a sample of 1,000 students in Athens, 116 young women (11.6 percent) declared that they had been victims of rape or sexual assault.[32] Of these, only seven (6 percent) had reported it to the police. According to the official statistics of justice, in 1996 there were thirty-six sentences applied for rape in Greece.[33]

Trafficking in women took on new proportions in Greece after the massive immigration of economic refugees from Eastern Europe and the Balkans. Today trafficking refers mainly to foreign women immigrants. According to police records,[34] in 2001 the 440 known cases of trafficking were of women from Romania, Moldavia, Ukraine, Bulgaria, Belarus, Albania, Uzbekistan, and Poland. Between twenty and thirty years old, a few even younger, and often unemployed in their country, they come to Greece with the understanding that they will work as artists or baby-sitters "helped" by networks that process their illegal entry. According to certain calculations, forced prostitution has many thousands of victims and an annual rate of growth from 1990 to 2000 of between 30 percent and 115 percent.[35] In 1990, 21 percent of prostitutes could be classified as forced into prostitution, and in 2000 the percentage was 75 percent: 16,700 women out of a total of 22,200 have become prostitutes against their will.[36]

OUTLOOK FOR THE TWENTY-FIRST CENTURY

Women as citizens in Greek society and polity, although in a much better situation than they were thirty years ago, must elaborate solutions to their inferior social status and political exclusion that go to the roots of their social inferiority. Measures that attack some of the *symptoms* of oppression, while offering solutions to some women, may disguise gender inequalities that are far deeper than legal remedies alone can cure. The demand for the widest possible extension of women's presence in the public sphere is absolutely legitimate. However, it cannot create fundamental change as long as it coexists with an acceptance of the private sphere as one of men's dominance and with a tacit agreement on the "naturalness" of gender differences in roles and aptitudes. Thus, feminists must elaborate a politics that considers "more women in decision making" as *one* among other measures of women's empowerment that help undermine basic assumptions concerning the gender dichotomy. Then they will succeed in assuring an end to the sexist character of social reality and of today's "democracy" and not just in proposing new policies that just modernize traditional gender roles. To do this, women need the rebirth of a feminist movement that will take advantage of recent developments in feminist theory, and they need to be ready to face the challenges of the new century. The loss of hope in a more humane future for all, regardless of any dividing identity, and the lack of interest and respect for politics as it is today are among the most important challenges they must confront.

NOTES

1. P.N. Diamandouros, "Politics and Culture in Greece" in *Greece, 1981–1989: The Populist Decade*, ed. R. Clogg (New York: St. Martins/Macmillian, 1993), 1–21.

2. See P. Kazakos and P. Liargovas, "The Economy of Greece," in *About Greece* (Athens: Ministry for Press and Mass Media, 1999), for more data on the Greek economy.

3. One kilometer equals 0.6 miles.

4. National Statistical Service of Greece, *Statistics of Justice 1996* (in Greek) (Athens: Author, 2000), 182, 183.

5. ESYE, 2000, 153.

6. ESYE, 2000, 158.

7. See General Secretariat for Equality, *4th and 5th National Report: Greece* (Athens: Author, 2000), 109–10.

8. Data from the 1991 census, since the 2001 census is not yet made public in total.

9. C. Symeonidou, "Full and Part-time Employment of Women in Greece," in *Between Equalization and Marginalization*, eds. H. Blosfeld and C. Hakim (Oxford: Oxford University Press, 1997), 90–112.

10. Anthropological approaches to gender relations in Greek society can be of interest for the study of the family and its power structure. See P. Loizos and E. Papataxiarchis, *Contested Identities: Gender and Kinship in Modern Greece* (Princeton, NJ: Princeton University Press, 1991); and J. Dubisch, *Gender and Power in Rural Greece* (Princeton, NJ: Princeton University Press, 1986).

11. L. Maratou-Alipranti, "Single Parent Families" (in Greek), *Greek Review of Social Research* 95 (1998).

12. L. Maratou-Alipranti, *The Family in Athens: Conjugal Models and Household Practices* (in Greek) (Athens: National Center of Social Research, 1995).

13. Pandora, www.demographics.gr.

14. Pandora.

15. National Statistical Service of Greece (ESYE), *Social Welfare and Health Statistics* (in Greek) (Athens: Author, 1997), 118.

16. General Secretariat for Equality, 2000, 157.

17. ESYE, 1997, 27.

18. ESYE, 1997, 90, 92.

19. Maria Pantelidou Maloutas, "Greek Women and the Vote" (in Greek), *Greek Review of Social Research* 74 (1989).

20. Feminist activists of the autonomous groups looked with much skepticism at the institutionalization of what the governing PASOK considered to be women's interests.

21. Participation in the electoral process is compulsory in Greece.

22. Maria Pantelidou Maloutas, *Women and Politics: The Political Profile of Greek Women* (in Greek) (Athens: Gutenberg, 1992).

23. Maria Pantelidou Maloutas, *Political Behavior* (in Greek) (Athens: Sakkoulas, 1993).

24. The adjective "formal" is necessary here because, as Cram (1994, 230) notes, there is a long tradition of political participation by women in Greece "in national struggles for liberation and democracy," and on the other hand, since 1887 there has always been a women's movement when war, civil war, and dictatorship permitted it. See L. Cram, "Women's Political Participation in Greece," *Democratization* 1, no. 2 (1994), 230.

25. All data concerning women in political elites is from Maria Pantelidou Maloutas, *The Gender of Democracy: Citizenship and Gendered Subjects* (in Greek) (Athens: Savalas, 2002).

26. Pantelidou Maloutas, 2002.

27. E. Varikas, "Les femmes grecques face à la modernisation institutionelle," *Les Temps Moderne* 41 (1985): 473.

28. For the history of the women's movement in Greece after 1974, see mainly Varikas, 1985; and for a different approach, see Cram, 1994.

29. H. Psevdonymou, "Cries and Murmurs," in *Women's Greece*, edited by E. Leondidou and S. Ammer (in Greek) (Athens: Enallatikes Ekdoseis, 1992).

30. General Secretariat for Equality, *National Report of Greece* (Athens: Author, 1999), 56.

31. For which, reliable data exist. See A. Tsigris, *Rape: The Invisible Crime* (in Greek) (Athens: Sakkoulas, 1996), 347.

32. A. Tsigris, 1996, 351.

33. ESYE, 1996, 56.

34. Ministry of Public Order, seminar, June 26, 2002.

35. See G. Lazos, *Trafficking* (Athens: n.p., 2002); and G. Lazos, "Social Exclusion of the Foreign Prostitute in Contemporary Greece," in *Forms of Social Exclusion*, ed. D. Dimitriou (Athens: Alfa, 1997).

36. See G. Lazos, *The New Prostitution in Contemporary Greece* (Athens: n.p., 2002).

RESOURCE GUIDE

Suggested Reading

Cram, L. "Women's Political Participation in Greece since the Fall of the Colonels." *Democratization* 1, no. 2 (1994), 229–50. One of the rare publications on the subject in English.

Eurostat. Luxembourg. Useful data permitting the comparison of various Greek indicators to other European countries.

Laboratory of Political Communication. *About Greece*. Athens: Ministry of Press and Mass Media, 1999. An informative overview of issues.

Pantelidou Maloutas, M. "Women and Politic." In *About Greece, Laboratory of Political Communication*. Athens: Ministry of Press and Mass Media, 1999.

Symeonidou, C. "Full and Part-time Employment of Women in Greece: Trends and Relationship with Life-cycle Events." In *Between Equalization and Marginalization*, edited by H. Blossfeld and C. Hakim, 90–112. Oxford: Oxford University Press, 1997. An approach to women's lives and employment in Greece.

Web Sites

Pandora, www.demographics.gr.

Research Centre for Gender Equality, www.kethi.gr.

SELECTED BIBLIOGRAPHY

Diamandouros, P.N. "Politics and Culture in Greece." In *Greece, 1981–1989: The Populist Decade*, edited by R. Clogg, 1–21. New York: St. Martin's Press, Macmillan, 1993.

Dubisch, J. *Gender and Power in Rural Greece*. Princeton, NJ: Princeton University Press, 1986.

General Secretariat for Equality. *National Report: Greece*. For CEDAW. Athens: Author, 1999.

———. *4th and 5th National Report: Greece*. For CEDAW. Athens: Author, 2000.

Kazakos, P., and P. Liargovas. "The Economy of Greece." In *About Greece*, Laboratory of Political Communication, 160–208. Athens: Ministry of Press and Mass Media, 1999.

Lazos, G. *The New Prostitution in Contemporary Greece*. Unpublished report. Athens: n.p., 2002.

———. "Social Exclusion of the Foreign Prostitute in Contemporary Greece." In *Forms of Social Exclusion and Mechanisms of Its Reproduction*, edited by D. Dimitriou, 79–98. Athens: Alfa, 1997.

———. *Trafficking*. Unpublished report. Athens: n.p., 2002.

Loizos, P., and E. Papataxiarchis. *Contested Identities: Gender and Kinship in Modern Greece*. Princeton, NJ: Princeton University Press, 1991.

Nicolacopoulos, I., and M. Pantelidou Maloutas. *Women's Political Behaviour: Final Report*. In Greek. Athens: National Center of Social Research, 1988.

Petropulos, J.A. *Politics and Statecraft in the Kingdom of Greece 1833–1843*. Princeton, NJ: Princeton University Press, 1968.

Selected Greek and French Bibliography

Maratou-Alipranti, L. *The Family in Athens: Conjugal Models and Household Practices*. In Greek. Athens: National Center of Social Research, 1995.

———. "Single Parent Families: Recent Trends and Policy Dilemmas." In Greek. *The Greek Review of Social Research* 95 (1998): 185–208.

National Statistical Service of Greece (ESYE). *Provisional Data from the 2001 Census*. In Greek. Athens: Author, 2002.

———. *Social Welfare and Health Statistics*. In Greek. Athens: Author, 1997.

———. *Statistics of Justice, 1996*. In Greek. Athens: Author, 2000.

———. *Statistical Yearbook of Greece 2000*. In Greek. Athens: Author, 2001.

Pantelidou, Maloutas M. *The Gender of Democracy: Citizenship and Gendered Subjects*. In Greek. Athens: Savalas, 2002.

———. "Greek Women and the Vote." In Greek. *Greek Review of Social Research* 74 (1989): 3–38.

———. *Political Behaviour*. In Greek. Athens: Sakkoulas, 1993.

———. "La Présence des femmes dans la vie politique en Gréce." In *Les femmes et les hommes dans les communes d'Europe* (Pref. par. F. Gaspav). Paris: CCRE/ETUDES, 1999.

———. *Women and Politics: The Political Profile of Greek Women*. In Greek. Athens: Gutenberg, 1992.

Psevdonimou, H. "Cries and Murmurs: For the Lesbian Issue in Greece." In *Women's Greece*, edited by E. Leondidou and S. Ammer, 67–80. In Greek. Athens: Enallaktikes Ekdoseis, 1992.

Thanopoulou, M. "The Relationship between Women's Professional and Family Life: A Study of the Greek Bibliography." In Greek. *Synchrong Themata* 71–2 (1999): 171–89.

Tsiganou, J. et al. "Socially Excluded Groups in Greece: The Gender Question." Working Paper. In Greek. Athens: EKKE, 2003.

Tsigris, A. *Rape: The Invisible Crime*. In Greek. Athens: Sakkoulas, 1996.

Varikas, E. "Les femmes grecques face à la modernisation institutionnelle: Un féminisme difficile." *Les Temps Modernes* 41 (1985): 473.

17

HUNGARY

Beáta Nagy

PROFILE OF HUNGARY

After more than forty years of a socialist regime, Hungary had its first democratic election in 1990, when the country was officially named the Republic of Hungary. The Hungarian economy suffered a loss after the collapse of socialism, and this trend continued until 1994, when the economy started to recover. The total gross domestic product (GDP) was 7,098,904 million HUF[1] in 2001. The rate of unemployment is now 5.9 percent, which is relatively low in international comparison; however, the rate of economically active population aged between fifteen and seventy-four is low.[2]

Hungary has 10,043,000 inhabitants. This reflects a twenty-year-long decrease in the population from 10,709,000 in 1980, a trend that is unique in the world.[3] The number of live births per 1,000 inhabitants stabilized on the low level of 9.7; however, there has been a serious expectation that its decline would not only stop but also would reverse because the number of live births increased significantly in 2000. The main reason for the low birth rate is that women, mostly due to their jobs or higher educational levels, give birth to their first child at an older age, and this delay very often prevents them from having more children. At the same time, there is a high number of deaths (13.5) per 1,000 inhabitants. This reflects the poor health condition of the Hungarian population. The main causes of death include diseases of the circulatory system, neoplasms, and diseases of the digestive system. Due to these health problems, life expectancy of males is

extremely low at 68.15 years. This is better than it was shortly after the economic transition, when it reached only 64.53 years. (The corresponding data for women was 73.81 years in 1993 and 76.46 years in 2001.) The majority of the Hungarian population is female: 1,104 women per 1,000 men is the current sex ratio. This has been increasing in the last twenty years due to the males' lower life expectancy. Although infant mortality per 1,000 live births increased from 8.4 in 1999 to 9.2 in 2000, it is declining in the long run (in 1990, it was still 14.8).

OVERVIEW OF WOMEN'S ISSUES

Women's emancipation was a part of official party policy in the socialist period. Women were primarily targeted as a labor force, thus all welfare institutions were oriented to the achievement of this goal. The system of kindergartens, crèches, schools, dry cleaners, catering, and other services was established in order to help women be superwomen both at the workplace and at home. Although women's employment had increased and reached not only the social, but also the demographic maximum, their spouses did not share household activities. As the emancipation was organized by the Hungarian Women's Council from above and no women's movement was allowed to function, the official emancipation program did not find support in the society. Women mostly experienced the socialist emancipation as pressure and not as opportunity. Partly due to this experience, women withdrew from the labor market in large numbers after 1989. Still, many of them were able to start a career, and their male peers in economic life mostly accepted them. However, women's issues are not present in the public and political discussion. Women's situation by and large reflects what we can observe in Western societies—disadvantageous economic and social positions, underrepresentation in leading positions, and an unequal division of household duties.

EDUCATION

Opportunities

All the opportunities at every educational level are open to women. Still, there are gender-specific differences in their educational paths. Men's and women's participation in primary schools is balanced: 95 percent of the pupils finish the eighth grade of the primary school at the age of sixteen. In the school year 1999–2000, 95.9 percent of them continued their education in the same year: 25.3 percent of them at vocational schools, 39.0 percent at vocational secondary schools, and 31.6 percent at general secondary schools.[4]

Women are underrepresented at vocational schools, where they form only 36.2 percent of all apprentices. This phenomenon can be explained by the fact that these schools usually offer jobs labeled as masculine. However,

Table 17.1
Students of University and College Level Education by Fields of Study, 2000–2001

Field of Study	Total Students	Female
Engineering	42,815	10,055
Agricultural	10,821	5,947
Veterinary	928	565
Medical	7,536	4,014
Pharmaceutical	1,438	975
Sanitary	4,807	4,414
Economics	28,727	17,800
Law and state administration	10,303	6,377
Liberal arts	24,430	16,840
Natural sciences	11,537	4,877
Teachers' training (higher grade)	12,123	8,456
Teachers (higher grade)	613	575
Physical education	723	313
Teachers' training (lower grade)	8,770	7,474
Kindergarten teacher	2,107	1,957
Fine arts	3,100	1,746
Theological	3,304	1,607
Other	1,964	442
Total	176,046	94,434

Source: KSH, 2001, 230.

some female occupations can be learned at these schools as well, including shorthand, typing, and medical education. At the secondary schools pupils must take a final graduation examination. The majority (53.3 percent) of pupils in full-time education at secondary schools in 2000 were women; however, their ratio has been slightly decreasing since 1990.[5]

In higher education, women constitute the majority of students studying full-time.[6] The only field in which women are underrepresented is engineering, but their participation has increased in the last decade. Agriculture and veterinary studies, which were fields traditionally dominated by men, now have more female students. Table 17.1 shows that higher education in general is feminized, and there are some fields (e.g., teaching and health) in which women can be found almost exclusively. Feminization in itself is already a sign of underevaluation of these jobs. Besides, the Hungarian higher education has a double system with both colleges and universities. Women mostly attend colleges, which offer a less valued type of degree.

Literacy

Although there is no statistical survey on Hungarian literacy, there are indicators of poor quality in the level of some people's understanding of written text.

EMPLOYMENT AND ECONOMICS

Jobs/Career Opportunities

After the collapse of socialism, massive unemployment occurred. Almost 1 million people lost their jobs, and many of them even left the labor market altogether. Women were less affected by unemployment than men, which is a unique phenomenon. Apart from the United Kingdom, Canada, Korea, Norway, Switzerland, Sweden, and the United States, none of the Organisation for Economic Cooperation and Development (OECD) countries have seen this pattern as a stable tendency.[7] There are two reasons for women's "sheltered" position. Many women had left the labor market definitively and chose not to return. However, women who stayed in the labor force were mostly employed in the service sector, which was protected from unemployment. Table 17.2 shows the underrepresentation of women in the work force but their overrepresentation in white-collar jobs. It also provides evidence for women's underrepresentation in professional careers. Although women have the required degrees to fulfill the leading positions, they still have low numbers at that level. This can be explained by a very complex group of factors, like women's lower self-confidence, societal prejudices and discrimination,

Woman selling greens, Budapest, Hungary. Photo © TRIP/V. Schwanberg.

Table 17.2
Persons in Employment by Aggregated Major Groups of Occupation and Sex (%)

Aggregated Major Groups of Occupations	Male	Female
Leaders, intellectuals	50.7	49.3
Other nonmanual occupations	25.4	74.6
Service occupations	45.7	54.3
Agricultural occupations	74.1	25.9
Mining, manufacturing, construction occupations	77.8	22.2
Other occupations	52.8	47.2
Total	54.4	45.6

Source: KSH, 2002.

Table 17.3
Average Monthly Gross and Net Earnings of Employees by Sex, 2000 (HUF/Person)

	Gross Earnings			Net Earnings		
	Manual	Nonmanual	Together	Manual	Nonmanual	Together
Male	68,556	162,692	96,537	45,587	95,096	60,303
Female	50,224	97,827	77,736	35,651	61,423	50,546
Total	62,043	121,125	87,540	42,056	73,518	55,634

Source: KSH, 2001, 94.

women's lack of motivation, and, of course, the unbalanced division of housework.

Pay

Women earn on average 80 to 83 percent of what men earn. The difference is even higher in nonmanual jobs where women mostly fulfill routine administrative or subordinated intellectual tasks, whereas men more often have the managerial positions. (See Table 17.3.) It must be noted that the relatively high occupational segregation makes direct comparison of women's and men's earnings difficult.

According to the results of a detailed analysis, despite the economic recession, there was a narrowing wage gap between 1986 and 1996. This phenomenon can be traced back to women's improving educational and labor market experiences, since the increase of more experienced and highly educated women was faster than that of men. The change occurring in the occupational structure of economy, that is the growth of the tertiary, or service sector and the loss of industry, have contributed to women's gradually more advantageous position; however, women's work is still undervalued on the labor market.[8]

Working Conditions

Sexual Harassment

Sexual harassment is almost absent from Hungarian public discussion; however, there have been some cases that appeared in the press. Women are mostly reluctant to report on their negative experiences, since they are condemned for it and accused of being provocative in their behavior or dress. They often do not receive support from their families or their colleagues. In 2002, two cases have become known: one in a hospital in the countryside, the other in a barrack. In the latter case, the court found the officer guilty and he was moved away from his position, but shortly afterwards his punishment was considerably reduced and he was reinstated in his previous job. Although women are innocent, they are the ones who have to leave the workplace.

Support for Mothers/Caretakers

On the basis of Hungarian law, families have different forms of support related to their children. The *childcare assistance benefit*, in effect since January 1, 1999, is due by individual title, that is, every family receives it, and it is independent from income. This is a relatively small support that is paid until the children leave secondary school. *Childcare allowance and fees* are paid to the parents until the child reaches three years of age. (The childcare fee was stopped after April 1998 and then reintroduced on January 1, 2000.) As the childcare allowance is low, parents can be employed part-time after the children are eighteen months old. *Childrearing support* is a modest financial support that allows the parent—in the case of at least three children—to stay at home until the smallest child reaches eight years of age.[9] *Maternity allowance* is connected to the birth of the child, and its precondition is the regular visit of a prenatal caregiver. This is a one-time-only financial assistance.[10] Although both parents are eligible to accept the different forms of childcare, they are seen as maternal subsidies. According to the latest data, 296,000 women but only 1,000 men were absent from the labor market due to their parental obligations.[11]

Daycare

Nurseries are open for children under the age of three. Since the childcare fee is paid to parents until the child is three years of age, the number and rate of infants enrolled in nurseries are relatively low. Families living in cities have more and easier access to these institutions, whereas in villages very often they do not exist. The number of infant nurseries declined sharply after the collapse of the socialist system, because of decreasing supply and demand. Many factories abolished their childcare institutions, as they reduced their (female) work force.

Kindergartens, however, are overloaded. Most of the children of kindergarten age go to kindergarten if the institution accepts them. At many places, kindergartens refuse to admit children whose mothers are at home (either with a baby or not in the labor force). There are debates about whether kindergartens achieve their educational goals, but, as the data show, they are very popular. Surely one reason for their popularity is that they are inexpensive since most are maintained by the local government.

Table 17.4
Rate of Those Approving the Statement: "It is important to have a job, but most women desire to have a family and children."

Educational Level	Men	Women
Did not finish 8th grade	78%	83%
Finished 8th grade	77%	78%
Industrial school	72%	72%
Secondary school	61%	63%
College	68%	52%
University	45%	40%

Source: Tóth, 1995, 83.

FAMILY AND SEXUALITY

Gender Roles

Hungarian society holds very traditional attitudes concerning gender roles. Although a great percentage of women have been working over the past fifty years, people still consider men as the main breadwinners and women as housewives. There was a sharp contradiction between the reality and the attitudes in the early 1990s, when attitudes were traditional and yet women were active on the labor market. Since then, not only attitudes but also behaviors have changed back to traditional ways as large numbers of women withdrew from the labor market. Even the best-educated people share the traditional opinion on women's real task in life. The ISSP survey investigated the attitudes of the Hungarian population toward women's work and gender roles. A representative sample of the population, whose responses are listed in Table 17.4, answered the questionnaire.

The result of other investigations indicates that the positive relation toward all women's work has been declining in the late 1990s. In 1995, 73.3 percent of women still approved of women's employment, but this ratio was only 67 percent in 1999. At the same time, there has been an increase in the percent of those who would prefer to see women staying at home.[12]

Marriage

The importance of marriage has declined in the last few years. Since the 1980s the age of a person at their first marriage has increased; thus young people get married later or more often cohabitate.

Reproduction

Birth rates have decreased dramatically in forty years. In 1960, 146,461 women gave birth. Of that number, the highest rate of births (55,929) belonged to women aged 20–24, followed by those aged 25–29 (38,426). By 2000, only 97,597 live births occurred: division among age groups was highest for the 25–29-year-old age range at 35,673, followed by 20–24-year-olds (28,338), then the 30–34-year-old age group (18,525).[13] As a result of increasing cohabitation instead of marriage among couples, the number and percent of extramarital childbirths has increased from 5.5 percent in 1960 to 7.1 percent in 1980, then to 13 percent in 1990, and at present is 29 percent.[14]

Sex Education

Hungary, similarly to other East-Central European countries, has a low level of sex education. Although there have been some attempts to introduce this topic into the curriculum, there is a strong revulsion on teachers' part.

Contraception and Abortion

Contraceptives are expensive and not subsidized by the Hungarian state. In 1994 only 52 percent of *married* women were taking contraceptive pills, and another 23 percent used intra-uterine contraceptive devices.[15] The limited availability of contraceptives can partly explain the high rate of abortions.

A lack of education about sex and birth control also contributes to the high number of induced abortions per live births in Hungary. Although the number of abortions has been declining since 1970, it is still high by international standards. (There were 60.7 abortions per 100 live births in 2000 compared to the astonishing 126.7 abortions per 100 live births in 1970.)[16] The 20–24 age group has had the highest rate of induced abortion at 47,431 in 1970, dropping to 15,090 in 2000,[17] but teen pregnancy and abortion are also significant.

Teen Pregnancy

Abortions performed on teens were only 5 percent of the total abortions in 1960 but increased to approximately 12–13 percent in the 1990s. It is most frequently seen in Budapest. In contrast, the rate of live births to girls under the age of twenty has started to decline and was only 8 percent of all live births in 2000. In 1960, 1,640 girls under sixteen years of age gave birth, compared to 18,001 births to girls aged 17–19 years. By 1990, the numbers had shifted higher for girls aged sixteen and younger (2,259) and reduced for 17- to 19-year-olds (13,165). By 2000, there was a dramatic reduction in live births for the 17–19-year-old group at 6,602 and the under-16 age group had 1,197 live births.[18]

HEALTH

Health Care Access

Every Hungarian citizen paying health insurance has access to health care institutions. The inhabitants of small settlements can reach these opportunities only rarely, because the distribution of services is very uneven in Hungary. Although people can see a general practitioner, sometimes it is difficult to get to health care institutions or hospitals because of travel expenses and distances. Women are more sensitive to their health problems, which is independent of their actual health status; thus they see doctors more often then men do. Women's health status is characterized by higher morbidity, and men's by higher mortality.

Diseases and Disorders

Alcoholism is the most widespread deviant behavior in Hungarian society, damaging people's health and private relationships. More than 8 percent of the whole population is alcoholic. It is more common among men; however, women's rate among alcoholics has been on the increase. The number of male alcoholics has increased from 172,000 in 1980 to 425,000 in 1990 and continues to rise as exemplified by the 2000 rate of 624,000 male alcoholics per 1,000. Women present much lower numbers, but their rate of alcoholism is increasing consistently as well. In 1980 women numbered 52,000, rising to 163,000 in 1990 and 205,000 in 2000.[19] Most cases can be found in Budapest among people between twenty and twenty-nine years of age.

AIDS

AIDS has been widely discussed in the press since its first appearance. The number of persons infected is relatively low and stabilized at this point. In 1986, only one male was diagnosed as having AIDS. By 1987 two men and one woman died from it. The height of diagnosis and death occurred in 1996 when forty-one men and five women were confirmed, and twenty-three men and two women died. In 2000, twenty-seven people were diagnosed (twenty-five men and two women), and fifteen died from AIDS.[20]

Eating Disorders

Eating disorders are not investigated systematically in Hungary; however, it is assumed that they occur relatively often in younger cohorts. There is not any public discussion on anorexia nervosa or bulimia in Hungary.

Nutrition

Hungarian people spend 34 percent of their income on food. Traditional spicy and heavy Hungarian dishes are unhealthy. Women eat healthier than men—they eat more moderate amounts, eat more regularly and prefer healthier foods such as vegetables. Educational level and urban versus rural type of settlement define culinary customs.

Sports and recreational activities are not popular in Hungary. After finishing school, only an insignificant percentage of women spend time and energy on exercise or sports. Forty percent of women between fifteen and sixty-four say that they do not have time for regular sport activity. Unhealthy foods and the lack of exercise lead to the high incidence of diseases: 25 percent of women have high blood pressure, 7.4 percent have coronary artery disease, and 40 percent of women surveyed take medications.[21]

Cancer

Smoking is the most dangerous risk factor to women's health. In the early 1990s, 9 percent of female and 25 percent of male deaths were connected with it. In the last decade, more women started smoking at an earlier age than before; today, 37 percent of young women smoke. This increases the probability of pulmonary cancer, which is among the most common causes of death in Hungary.

Depression

Depression is more prevalent among the female population: 33 percent of women and 27 percent of men had a depressive illness in 1995. In 1998, 26 percent of women age 14–24 had depressive illness, up from 15 percent in 1995.[22]

POLITICS AND LAW

Suffrage

Women received the right to vote in 1919 during the time of the short-lived Soviet Republic, but in 1920 it was restricted to those men and women who could write and read. Then, for the first time, some groups of women were allowed to vote and run for office. As female voters helped right-wing, conservative parties into the government, feminists were extremely disappointed about the results and did not regret the new restriction in 1922, which required successful completion of the sixth grade and a minimum age of thirty years.[23] The universal right to vote came into force in 1945.

Political Participation

In the socialist period, the party politics pushed many women into the Parliament, and their participation as MPs reached more than 20 percent.

However, this did not reflect women's real position in politics, because they were mostly only "tokens." Nobody was surprised at the results of the first democratic election in 1990, when women MPs received only 7.3 percent of the parliamentary seats. This rate slightly increased to 11.1 percent in 1994, then dropped to 8.3 percent in 1998. According to the latest data, now 9.1 percent of MPs are women. The fluctuation of women's proportion in Parliament is in accordance with the leading political force: left-wing and liberal parties have both more women candidates and MPs, and in contrast, right-wing parties have fewer female members and politicians.

Women's Rights

Feminist Movements

Although the women's movement was very developed and took many forms at the beginning of the twentieth century, nongovernmental organizations (NGOs) were not allowed to function during the socialist period. In the mid-1990s, the number of women's organizations started to increase, but they are still almost invisible to society. They offer important services in relieving poverty; in the promotion of training and formal, public role taking; in providing legal aid; and in some research as well. It is very difficult for them to reach the really needy, because poor people have almost no chance of being informed about these helping organizations. Furthermore, they are marginalized and segregated in society, such that the typical middle class women, who make up the membership of these NGOs, do not have contact with them.

There are several drawbacks concerning the work of women's organizations. For instance, women's groups often focus on a very narrow, particular interest and cannot formulate questions affecting a wider public. Women's NGOs, like most other Hungarian NGOs, simply lack financial resources, which are very critical to their operations. This makes consistent, quality performance almost impossible to execute.[24] NGOs depend on both the government and other established institutions for funding, thus developing a dependent behavior and waiting for the suggestions from these institutions; as they are relatively newly founded (or refounded), these organizations also lack experience in their field of activity. Since they mostly use volunteers, professional competence is often lacking among them as well.

Lesbian Rights

In 1996, the lesbian group *Labrisz* was formed, and it was officially established in 1999. It organizes meetings for bisexual and lesbian women, tries to increase the public visibility of lesbians in society, and promotes lesbian rights by publication of handbooks on homosexuality.[25] Although homosexuality is not prohibited, it is widely disregarded in Hungarian society and lesbians meet with social prejudice all the time. Therefore, they are less willing to openly accept their sexual orientation. Lesbian women do not have the same rights as heterosexual women. (For example, they cannot marry or adopt children.)

VIOLENCE

Domestic Violence

The topic of domestic violence was not discussed in depth until the late 1990s. Sexual harassment within the family as a kind of crime was recognized only in 1997. There was considerable civil support behind this proposal, which helped put forward the bill. Public pressure was the reason that finally a section on domestic sexual harassment was added to the act. Late in 2002, protests against domestic violence have perceptibly intensified, and more and more light is being shed on domestic violence. These civil initiatives demand new regulations and measures in order to stop violence and protect victims.

OUTLOOK FOR THE TWENTY-FIRST CENTURY

In the twentieth century, Hungarian women's situation changed incredibly. Women's participation in public life increased, but they still play a marginal role in Hungarian politics. Because of their high educational level and forty-year-long socialist emancipation, women have their own experience on the labor market; however, their position is mostly disadvantageous. Hungarian people's traditional attitude concerning gender roles also hinders women's equal opportunities. Nevertheless, gradual, small changes can be observed: there is an increasing interest in studying gender studies at the universities, and new curricula have been elaborated. The number of women's nongovernmental organizations is growing, and perhaps they will influence people's ideas about changing gender roles in a changing world. The optimistic view is fueled by new developments. At the beginning of May 2003, a new ministerial position without portfolio has been created. The new Minister for Equal Opportunities focuses on the equal chances of women and men, ethnic minorities, and disabled people in society. Also, a new bill on equal opportunities and equal treatment will be submitted to Parliament in the fall of 2003.

NOTES

1. The Hungarian forint exchange rate was 247 to US$1 on October 4, 2002.
2. KSH (Hungarian Central Statistical Office), www.ksh.hu.
3. KSH, *Statistical Yearbook of Hungary 2000* (Budapest: Author, 2001).

4. KSH, 2001, 224.

5. KSH, 2001, 226.

6. Percentage of students who were women: 1990–1991: 48.8; 1998–1999: 53.2; 1999–2000: 53.6; 2000–2001: 53.6.

7. OECD, *Quarterly Labour Force Statistics*, no. 2 (1998).

8. Péter Galasi, *Nöi-férfi kereseti különbségek Magyarországon 1986–1996* (*Gender gaps in Hungary 1986–1996*) (Budapest: OMKMK, 2000).

9. Szilvia Szabó, "A nök helyzetét érintö fontosabb jogszabályokról" ("On the Most Important Regulations Effecting Women's Situation"), in (szerk.) *Vegyesváltó: Pillanatképek nökröl, férfiakról*, ed. K. Lévai, R. Kiss, and T. Gyulavári (Egyenlö Esélyek Alapítvány, 1999), 205–38.

10. Szabó, 1999.

11. Mária Frey, "Nök és férfiak a munkaeröpiacon" ("Women and Men on the Labor Market"), in *Szerepváltozások. Jelentés a nök és a férfiak helyzetéröl 2001*, ed. Ildikó Nagy, Tiborné Pongrácz, and I. Gy. Tóth (Budapest: TÁRKI—SzCsM, 2002), 17.

12. Frey, 2002.

13. KSH, 2001, 56.

14. KSH, 2001, 54.

15. *Nök és férfiak Magyarországon, 2000* (Budapest: KSH—Szociális és Családügyi Minisztérium, 2001), 54.

16. KSH, 2001, 58.

17. KSH, 2001, 58.

18. KSH, 2001, 56.

19. KSH, 2001, 194.

20. KSH, 2001, 189.

21. Péter Józan, "A nök egészségi állapotának néhány jellemzöje" ("Some characteristics of women's health"), in *Szerepváltozások. Jelentés a nök és a férfiak helyzetéröl 1999*, ed. Tiborné Pongrácz and I. Gy. Tóth (Budapest: TÁRKI—SzCsM, 1999).

22. Mária Kopp, Csilla Csoboth, and György Purebl, "Fiatal nök egészségi állapota" ("Health condition of young women"), in *Szerepváltozások. Jelentés a nök és a férfiak helyzetéröl 1999*, ed. Tiborné Pongrácz and I. Gy. Tóth (TÁRKI—SzCsM, 1999), 239–61.

23. M. Mária Kovács, "A magyar feminizmus korszakfordulója" ("Turn in Hungarian Feminism"), *Café Bábel*, no. 1–2 (1994).

24. Beáta Nagy, "Non-profit Activity for the Advocacy of Women's Equality in Hungary," paper written for the Johns Hopkins University, Institute for Policy Studies, Center for Civil Society Studies, 2001.

25. Labrisz: Lesbian Association, www.labrisz.hu/.

RESOURCE GUIDE

Suggested Reading

Fodor, Éva. "Smiling Women and Fighting Men: The Gender of the Communist Subject in State Socialist Hungary." *Gender and Society* 16, no. 2 (2002).

The Fourth and the Fifth Reports of Hungary to the UN Committee for the Elimination of all Forms of Discrimination against Women (CEDAW). Budapest: Ministry of Social and Family Affairs, 2000.

Gal, Susan, and Gail Kligman. *The Politics of Gender After Socialism: A Comparative-Historical Essay*. Princeton, NJ: Princeton University Press, 2000.

Gal, Susan, and Gail Kligman. *Reproducing Gender: Politics, Publics and Everyday Life after Socialism*. Princeton, NJ: Princeton University Press, 2000.

Lévai, K., and I. Gy. Tóth, eds. *The Changing Role of Women. Report on the Situation of Women in Hungary 1997*. Budapest: TÁRKI—Ministry of Social and Family Affair, 1999.

OSI. *Monitoring the EU Accession Process: Equal Opportunities for Women and Men*. Open Society Institute, Budapest, 2002. www.eonet.ro.

U.N. *Women's Entrepreneurship in Eastern Europe and CIS Countries*. New York: Geneva, 2003.

Videos/Films

My 20th Century. 1989. Directed by Ildiko Enyedi. Distributed by Facets Video, www.facets.org/asticat. At the turn of the 20th century, two sisters who were separated as infants find each other traveling on the Orient Express.

Web Sites

Central European University, Department of Gender Studies, www.ceu.hu/gend/gendir.html.

Hungarian Central Statistical Office, www.ksh.hu.

TÁRKI, Hungarian Gender Databank, www.tarki.hu.adatbank-h/nok/index-e.html.

Organizations

Gender and Cultural Studies Center of the Budapest University of Economic Sciences and Public Administration
1093 Budapest
Fővám tér 8
Phone: (+36-1) 217-0327
Fax: (+36-1) 217-4482
Web site: http://gender.bkae.hu

MINök, Hungarian Women on the Internet (in Hungarian)
Web site: www.minok.hu

MONA, Foundation for the Women of Hungary
1537 Budapest
P.O. Box 453/277
Hungary
Phone: (+36-1) 350-1311
Fax: (+36-1) 329-87551
Web site: www.mona-hungary.org

NANE (Women against Violence)
Web site: www.nane.hu

Network Women's Program of Open Society Institute
Web site: www.soros.org/women

SEED (Small Enterprises Economic Development)
Web site: www.vallalkozo.hu/seedcom

SELECTED BIBLIOGRAPHY

KSH. *Population Census 2001*. Budapest: Author, 2002.

———. *Statistical Yearbook of Hungary 2000*. Budapest: Author, 2001.

Nagy, Beáta. "Non-profit Activity for the Advocacy of Women's Equality in Hungary." Paper written for the Johns Hopkins University, Institute for Policy Studies, Center for Civil Society Studies, 2001.

Tóth, Olga. "Attitüdváltozások a nöi munkavállalás megítélésében" ("Changing attitudes in the evaluation of women's employment"). *Szociológiai Szemle* 1 (1995).

United Nations. *Women and Men in Europe and North America 2000*. New York: Author, 2000.

———. *Women in Transition*. Florence: UNICEF, The MONEE Project, 1999.

Selected Hungarian Bibliography

Frey, Mária. "Nök és férfiak a munkaeröpiacon" ("Women and Men on the Labor Market"). In *Szerepváltozások. Jelentés a nök és a férfiak helyzetéröl 2001*, edited by Ildikó Nagy, Tiborné Pongrácz, and I. Gy. Tóth, 9–29. Budapest: TÁRKI—SzCsM, 2002.

Galasi, Péter. *Nöi-férfi kereseti különbségek Magyarországon 1986–1996 (Gender gaps in Hungary 1986–1996)*. Budapest: OMKMK, 2000.

Józan, Péter. "A nök egészségi állapotának néhány jellemzöje" ("Some Characteristics of Women's Health"). In *Szerepváltozások. Jelentés a nök és a férfiak helyzetéröl 1999*, edited by Tiborné Pongrácz and I. Gy. Tóth, 101–115. Budapest: TÁRKI–SzCsM, 1999.

Kovács, M. Mária. "A magyar feminizmus korszakfordulója" ("Turn in Hungarian Feminism"). *Café Bábel*, no. 1–2 (1994): 179–83.

Nök és férfiak Magyarországon, 2000. Budapest: KSH—Szociális és Családügyi Minisztérium, 2001.

Szabó, Szilvia. "A nök helyzetét érintö fontosabb jogszabályokról" ("On the Most Important Regulations Effecting Women's Situation"). In *Vegyesváltó. Pillanatképek nökröl, férfiakról*, edited by K. Lévai, R. Kiss, and T. Gyulavári. Budapest: Egyenlö Esélyek Alapítvány, 1999.

Tóth, Olga. "Attitüdváltozások a nöi munkavállalás megítélésében" ("Changing Attitudes in the Evaluation of Women's Employment"). *Szociológiai Szemle* 1 (1995).

Vicsek, Lilla. "The Influence of Class Origins and Gender on Life Chances: The Case of Hungary and Top Managerial Positions." *Review of Sociology* 8, no. 1 (2002): 55–78.

Vukovich, Gabriella. "Föbb népesedési folyamatok" ("Main Demographic Processes"). In *Társadalmi Riport 2002* (Social Report 2002), edited by T. Kolosi, I. Gy. Tóth, and Gy. Vukovich, 523–48. Budapest: TÁRKI, 2002.

18

ICELAND

Torgerdur Einarsdóttir

PROFILE OF ICELAND

Iceland, a small country by all conventional standards, is a Scandinavian island, located in the North Atlantic Ocean, with a total area of 103 square kilometers.[1] In 2001, the population was approximately 286,000. The gross national product (GNP) per capita in 2001 was US$26,745.[2] The principal employment sectors in Iceland are services, which comprise 69 percent of the work force, thereof approximately 6 percent in the field of education; in industry, 23 percent; and in agriculture and fishing, 8 percent.[3]

After the period of home government in 1904–1918, Iceland became a separate state under the Danish crown, with only foreign affairs remaining under Danish control. Iceland gained full sovereignty in 1944 and the Icelandic Republic was founded. The president is elected by popular vote for a four-year term. The Icelandic Parliament has sixty-three members, and parliamentary elections are held at intervals of four years or less.

Infant mortality in Iceland is among the lowest in the world. In 2001, deaths per 1,000 in the first year was 2.7. In 2001, the total fertility rate in Iceland was 1.947, which is considerably higher than in the other Nordic

countries. In general, though, fertility rates are decreasing, from 2.169 during 1991–1995 to 2.055 in 1996–2000. At the same time, the average expected lifetime has been rapidly increasing for both men and women. For those born in 1999–2000, men can expect to live to 77.6 years old and women can expect to be 81.4 years old, and the difference between men and women has been decreasing. The demographic structure is relatively special with a rather high fertility rate and a relatively young population. In 2000, almost one out of five was below the age of fifteen (23 percent), and roughly one out of ten was older than sixty-five years (12 percent). In 1960, comparable figures were 35 percent and 8 percent, respectively.[4]

OVERVIEW OF WOMEN'S ISSUES

The situation for Icelandic women is in many ways paradoxical. They have more children than women in the other Nordic countries and their labor market participation is higher, despite underdeveloped social welfare schemes to support employed mothers. The political participation of women is also somewhat lower than in the other Nordic countries. The gender pay gap is rather high, and the gender relations are a mix of "modern" and "traditional" approaches. Icelandic women have had strong role models in the previous female president and in the previous mayor of the capital, Reykjavík. The gender discourse has been rather hostile for some years but is changing with the newly founded Feminist Association of Iceland. The media discussion on gender issues and equality issues has raised strong—and very negative—reactions. Public efforts and measures in order to strengthen the situation of women have been questioned as either "extremes" aiming not at balancing gender equality but the dominance of women, or as discrimination against men.[5]

EDUCATION

Opportunities

The 1907 Education Act made education compulsory for all children from the ages of ten to fourteen. At present, the educational level of the population is relatively high. In 2000, almost one out of five persons in the age group 25–64 had a university degree. The gender rate is similar (17 percent of the women and 19 percent of the men), although more men than women within that group had a postgraduate degree. About 30 percent have an upper secondary education; the proportion is the same for men and women. More men than women (20 percent men versus 9 percent women) have a nonuniversity tertiary education (via various vocational programs). The largest gender difference is in the group with only compulsory school education, 44 percent of which is women compared to 32 percent men.[6] Boys were more numerous than girls in schools prior to the

Education Act. Research shows that this ratio was reversed after the act was passed, and, furthermore, that girls were more successful in their studies than boys.[7]

The University of Iceland was founded in 1911, and that same year a law was enacted on women's equal access to all education and work. The first woman graduated from the University of Iceland in 1917, but after that the increase was very slow for many decades. Iceland had an explosion in education in the postwar period, somewhat later than in the other Nordic countries. But similar to many other countries, women count for the biggest part of this increase. The number of students at the upper secondary level increased three times from the mid-1960s to the mid-1970s, when one out of five students passed the matriculation examination. Women who passed the matriculation examination outnumbered men already in the mid-1970s.[8] In 2000, women numbered more than half of the students at the upper secondary level and about half of those who graduated. The number of students at the tertiary level has increased four times since 1977. Already in 1984, the proportion of men and women was the same at the tertiary level, and in 2000, women were 62 percent of the students.

Despite the leveling out of gender differences in terms of the total number of men and women in education, gender disparities in the choice of subject field remain. In that respect, Iceland follows the well-documented patterns, with women more numerous in the teaching and education sciences, social sciences, arts and humanities, and health, whereas men are in the majority in the natural sciences, computer sciences, and engineering.[9]

Literacy

Although the modern school is relatively young, the Icelandic people have historically been known for a general literacy.[10] The country's present literacy rate is 99.9 percent.[11]

EMPLOYMENT AND THE ECONOMY

Job/Career Opportunities

The labor force participation is exceptionally high, and that holds true for both men and women. In 2000, 79 percent of women and 88 percent of men ages 16–74 were active on the labor market. This high labor market participation holds true even for women with young children, as the rate exceeds 80 percent for all groups of women. Unemployment rates generally are very low, and in 2000 the rate for women was 2.5 percent against 2.0 percent for men. Another specific characteristic of the Icelandic labor market is the conspicuously long working hours. In 2000, men worked on average fifty-one hours weekly and women worked thirty-six hours. If only

Woman sorting fish, Reykjavík, Iceland. Photo © TRIP/G. Gunnarsson.

those who work full-time are taken into consideration, the average working week for men is fifty-four hours and for women is forty-four hours. In 2000, 44 percent of women worked part-time versus 11 percent of men.[12] Still another feature of the Icelandic labor market is the obvious gender segregation, both by sectors and occupations. Thus, in 2000 a vast majority of women, or 85 percent, worked within different kinds of services versus 55 percent of the men, while one third of the men worked in industry as opposed to 11 percent of the women. The gender division within occupations follows the same line. Women more rarely than men hold the highest positions in the labor market: 21 percent of the men are senior officials, managers, and professionals against 18 percent of the women. Almost half of the women (47 percent) work as clerks, in service jobs, and as shop workers, compared to 15 percent of the men.[13]

Pay

In 1992, women's average earnings were 55 percent of men's; this ratio increased to 58 percent in 2000.[14] Different amounts of hours of paid work explain a large part of the gap between men and women's average earnings. Recent surveys indicate that the adjusted gender pay gap is between 15 and 20 percent, depending on what sector is reviewed and what forms of compensation are taken into consideration. A survey from 2001 among service and sales workers found that men in full-time work earned 16 percent more than women in full-time work after accounting for occupation, working hours, and seniority.[15] Men earned about 19 percent more than women in 2000 after accounting for different hours of work.[16] In 1995, a comprehensive survey made on behalf of the Equal Status Council revealed that the difference between men and women was 11–16 percent when most factors known to affect wage formation, such as occupation, education, experience (seniority), age, working hours, and whether the job was in public and private employment were taken into consideration.[17] New research done on behalf of the Equal Status Council reveals overall gender differences in gross hourly wages at 24 percent in the public sector and 27 percent in the private sector.[18] It also indicates that the gender pay gap is not narrowing but remaining stable.

Working Conditions

Sexual Harassment

According to the current Act on Equal Status and Equal Rights of Women and Men (from 2000), employers and directors of institutions and social activities shall take special measures to prevent employees, students, and clients from being subjected to sexual harassment in the workplace, within institutions, during social activities, or within schools (Article 17). This legislation has not turned out to be effective. That is indicated by the only survey done thus far in Iceland on the extent of sexual harassment on the labor market. It was conducted in 1997 on behalf of the Equal Status Office and the Administration for Safety and Occupational Health. Although the response rate was very low (32 percent), the survey indicates that 10–30 percent of the respondents had experienced sexual harassment at their workplace.[19]

Support for Mothers/Caretakers

Maternal Leave

Birth benefits developed rather slowly during the postwar period. In 1954, state employees were entitled to three months' paid maternity leave, and a few unions successively gained similar rights. In 1975, all salaried mothers became entitled to three months' paid leave after giving birth. In the following decades, the rights to parental leave were slowly extended. In 1987, the length was extended to six months.[20]

Until 2000, Iceland had a dual system. Female civil servants retained most of their salary for six months of maternity leave, whereas male civil servants had no entitlements. Women in the private sector were entitled to maternity benefits from the State Social Security Institute for six months. These payments were a fixed amount and were, in fact, so low that they were less than most women's salaries.[21] In 1998, fathers got the rights to two weeks' paid paternity leave. In 2000, the act on parental leave was radically changed. Women and men alike now have the right to a three-month nontransferable parental leave. In the case of fathers, the law is being implemented successively over a three-year period. In addition, the parents have a three-month common right, i.e., paid leave, which they can divide according to their own wishes.

In comparison to the other Nordic countries, the Icelandic schemes have provided fewer benefits to parents both in regard to the length of parental leaves and payments given. However, at this moment no legislation exists in the Nordic countries that ensures fathers as much independent right to paternity leave as the Icelandic one does.[22]

Daycare

During the 1960s, children's daycare became an increasingly important issue in the social debate in all the Nordic countries. However, the development in Iceland was slower than in the other Nordic countries. In 1981, 14 percent of children 0–2 years old were provided daycare in Iceland (institutional or family daycare); in 1999, the comparable figure was 42 percent.[23] Also for children 3–6 years of age, the provision of public daycare was limited until the mid-1990s, with an emphasis on part-time daycare. In the city of Reykjavík, the official daycare policies until 1994 were to provide only part-time daycare for married couples.[24]

Since the 1990s, there has been an increase in daycare coverage along with a rise in full-time placements. In 1999, 91 percent of children 3–6 years old were provided some daycare provision, and 43 percent had full-time arrangements.[25] In general, as mentioned earlier, Iceland has had a relatively special pattern in this respect. Fertility rates are higher in Iceland than in the other Nordic countries, women have exceptionally high labor market participation, but daycare facilities and support to families with small children has, until very recently, been underdeveloped.

Family and Medical Leave

Iceland provides fewer benefits and services to families with children than other Nordic countries. In 1997, Iceland spent 2.4 percent of the GNP on benefits and services for families and children, whereas this support ranged from 3.5 to 3.9 in the other Nordic countries. When the different demographic structure is kept in mind, that is the relatively young age of the population, this difference becomes still more skewed.[26] These findings are confirmed by research conducted on Icelandic welfare.[27]

Inheritance and Property Rights

In 1850, a new regulation granted daughters the same inheritance rights as sons. Prior to that, daughters inherited one third and sons inherited two thirds of their parents' property. In 1861, unmarried women twenty-five years and older attained their majority for the first time. However, married women were still dependent on their husbands and were not accorded full adult legal rights. In 1900, a law was passed on the finances of couples that entitled women the full right over their own income and property.[28] According to a taxation law from 1921, which was in effect until 1978, married women were treated as appendages to their husbands. In 1978 a partially individualized taxation system was introduced with the intent of gradually making it fully individualized.[29] That has not happened, and during the current mandate period, 1999–2003, the government is giving spouses more possibilities for filing taxes jointly again.[30]

FAMILY AND SEXUALITY

Gender Roles

Women in Iceland are well educated, and they are very active on the labor market. To a large degree they work part-time, and the educational system, as well as the labor market, is highly gender segregated. In regard to gender roles, an Icelandic researcher has depicted families in Iceland as "modern traditionalists."[31] The values of Icelandic families are related to the inherited sociocultural values of the Saga Period. The myth of the "strong Icelandic woman" is reflected in everyday life. The relatively weak public family support and the rather unequal social positions of men and women bring couples into coping strategies in which the man takes on the male-breadwinner role and women the responsibility of caring, although often against her will.[32]

Iceland had a strong women's movement in the 1980s, and in 1975 the women's "Day Off" in Iceland got international media coverage. Iceland also had a female president, Vigdís Finnbogadóttir, from 1980 to 1996, who has been an important symbolic representation and role model for women in Iceland. In sharp contrast to this and the myth of strong women of the Icelandic Sagas, societal influences of women are rather limited in modern Iceland.[33]

Marriage

Marriage rates in Iceland are relatively low, as is the case in the other Nordic countries. The rates of marriage were rather high during the post-war period, with approximately 8–9 marriages per 1,000 inhabitants. After 1975 the marriage rates went down dramatically and reached its lowest rates in the mid-1990s. In recent years, the marriage frequency has risen again; and in 2001, the marriage rate was approximately 5 per 1,000 inhabitants.

Divorce rates increased successively during the postwar period. From 1975, the divorce rates have been relatively stable, with 1.9 divorces per 1,000 inhabitants. However, if divorce rates are seen in relation to marriage rates, the gap is widening. In the beginning of the 1960s, 10 percent of all marriages ended in a divorce, and this figure has increased to 40 percent in recent years. In 2001, the mean age of bridegrooms is thirty-five years and of brides thirty-two years, compared to twenty-six and twenty-four years, respectively, in 1970.[34] Merged families are also increasing. Thus, about one third of the women who got married in 1990 had been married previously.[35]

Reproduction

Sex Education

According to Icelandic law, compulsory schools are supposed to provide education about sexuality, sexual ethics, and sexual diseases and protection against them. Sex education is among the subjects for students in the tenth grade (15–16 years). The goals, as stated in the curriculum guidelines, are very general. The pupils are supposed to be aware of morality and responsibility; mutual respect and individual rights are the basis of a "sound sex identity," coupled with experience and proper conduct.[36] The implementation and success of sex education can be questioned, however, since the use of contraceptives is less common in Iceland than in the other Nordic countries. Teenage pregnancies—and teenage abortions—are also more frequent than in other Nordic countries.[37]

Contraception and Abortion

In 1975, a law was passed on contraception and abortion that made access to them easier than before. Every year, about 850 abortions are carried out in Iceland. The rate of abortions in relation to the number of women of fertile age increased during the period from 1960 to 1980.[38] However, since the 1980s, the number has stabilized at the level of approximately 12 abortions per 1,000 women of fertile age. The total number ranged from 750 to 950 during the period 1990–1996. Of those who had an abortion in 1996, approximately one third were married or cohabiting. A majority of the women, or 72 percent, had not undergone an abortion previously, and 7 percent had undergone two or more abortions.[39]

Teen Pregnancy

In Iceland, approximately 4,000 children are born yearly. The rate of relatively young and old women giving birth (15–19 years and 35–39 years) is higher than in the other Nordic countries. This has been taken as an indication that the use of contraceptives is less systematic than in the other countries.[40] Thus, 6 percent of all women giving birth in 1998 were 15–19 years old, and 21 percent were 20–24 years old. On the other hand, nearly 3 percent of the women were forty years or older.[41] The number of teenage abortions is very high. In 1996, 21 percent of all women undergoing abortions were under the age of twenty, whereas 4 percent were forty or older.

HEALTH

Health Care Access

In general, the health service in the Nordic countries is a public matter, largely financed by public spending or through compulsory health insurance schemes.[42] However, recent research indicates considerable group differences in access to primary health services in Iceland.[43] Young people seem to have less access than other groups, and low-income individuals have lower potential access to primary health care. They were also more likely to report postponement or cancellation of needed visits to the doctors. According to the study, women per se do not seem to be a vulnerable group in terms of access to primary health care. But since women in general have lower incomes than men, the lower access of low-income individuals may affect more women than men.

Diseases and Disorders

AIDS

Data on AIDS and HIV-infected people can be traced back to 1983 in Iceland. In 2002, thirty-five people had died from AIDS, fifty-two had been reported with AIDS, and 156 had been reported as HIV-infected. Men are in the majority in all these groups: they are 86 percent of those who have died from AIDS, 88 percent of those suffering from AIDS, and 79 percent of those who are HIV-infected.[44] In Iceland, most of those diagnosed with AIDS from 1999 onward are between 25 and 30 years old, and two out of three of those diagnosed from 1999 onward are heterosexual.[45] The disease seems to be transmitted differently for men and women. Having sex is infecting the majority of both men and women; however, 75 percent of HIV-positive women were infected in heterosexual intercourse, whereas 65 percent of the men were infected in homosexual intercourse. Women are also fewer (6 percent) within the group of drug users who get infected by sharing needles, versus 13 percent of the men.[46]

Cancer

Before menopause, cancer is twice as frequent among men than women. In the oldest age groups, however, cancer is more common among women.[47] The prevalence of breast cancer has been increasing in the last decades. About 150 women get breast cancer each year in Iceland. The youngest women are between twenty and thirty years old, but the incidence increases with age. Women in Iceland top the Nordic statistics as far as breast cancer is concerned. However, the treatment is getting more successful. About 47 percent of those who got breast cancer during 1956–

1965 lived for five years or longer, and currently about 74 percent can expect to live for five more years. Every year, twenty-five women are diagnosed with cervical cancer, and the likelihood of getting the disease increases with age.[48]

Depression

No gender differences are found in the overall frequency of mental diseases in Iceland, but women more often suffer from depression. From a young age, depression is more common among women than men. The incidence of depression is most often in those aged twenty to forty-five, but not around menopause as often is believed. It is estimated that, in general, approximately 20 percent of women suffer from depression some time in their lives, compared to roughly 10 percent of men.[49]

POLITICS AND LAW

Suffrage

Icelandic women reached the first stages of suffrage in the late nineteenth century. In 1882, widows and unmarried women who paid taxes got the right to vote in local elections, provided that they had reached the age of twenty-five. They did not, however, get the right to be a candidate.[50] In 1908, a new electoral regulation allowed women to run for office. In the period 1908–1926, women ran their own separate candidate lists for local and national elections, and they received a mandate in all elections except for the national elections in 1926. In the period 1982–1996, women ran women's lists again, via the Women's Party, in both local and national elections.[51] They were very successful for a certain period in the mid-1980s. In the mid-1990s, the Women's Party merged with other political parties on the Left.

Political Participation

The female portion of city and county councilors was 6 percent in 1978. The proportion of women doubled in 1982 when the Women's Party ran candidates. In 2002, the proportion of women was 31 percent, an increase of less than 1 percent yearly in the period 1986–2002.[52] In Reykjavík in 1994, the Women's Party merged into The Reykjavík Alliance and a woman from the Women's Party, Ingibjörg Sólrún Gísladóttir, was the mayor of Reykjavík until 2003. She has been a strong role model for women in Icelandic politics. The number of women in the Icelandic parliament, *Alþingi*, increased equally slowly. In 1922, the first woman was elected as a member of parliament (MP). In 1983, with the candidacy of the Women's Party, the presence of women in the Parliament increased from 5 percent to 15 percent. The rate of female MPs has increased roughly 1 percent yearly since 1983 to 35 percent in 1999.[53] However, in the national elections of 2003, the rate decreased to 30 percent.

Women's Rights

Feminist Movements

The Icelandic Women's Rights Organization was founded in 1907 by Bríet Bjarnhéðinsdóttir, one of the women behind the women's list in Reykjavík in 1908. The organization not only worked for suffrage but also for the rights of women in the broadest sense, from education to the founding of women's unions and wage struggle. The organization still exists and now operates as a nonpolitical forum for women's causes.[54]

The 1970s was the period of the Redstockings in Iceland. They started as a radical feminist movement, and during the 1970s the Redstockings managed to change dramatically the gender discourse in Iceland. They were extremely influential and affected the public agenda as well as the general opinion. However, by the beginning of the 1980s, the Redstockings had evolved into an isolated left-wing group and was replaced by a new emerging mass movement, the Women's Party. Both the Redstockings and the Women's Party were decentralized movements that challenged the patriarchal order, even though their ideology differed. The Women's Party based its ideology on women's culture and maternal politics, in contrast to the Redstockings' Marxist approach.

During the period from 1999 to 2003, no all-inclusive women's movement was operating in Iceland but many decentralized groups existed in different settings. However, in March 2003, the Feminist Association of Iceland was founded. The Association already has over 500 members, which is a very large number by Icelandic standards. The Association has been very influential during the short time it has operated and made a considerable impact on the public discussion. In February 2003, a feminist postlist was created and in the beginning of April 2003 the list had more than 500 subscribers. The debate is lively, sometimes around 80 messages per day.[55]

Lesbian Rights

In the past twenty years, the issues of gay men and lesbians have become more visible and to some extent accepted with respect to civil rights. In general, gay men and lesbians have more legal rights than in many other countries, even though equality has not been fully obtained.

In 1985, a proposition was put forth in the Parliament about investigating the legal status and social issues of gay men and lesbians. The proposition was not adopted, but when it was put forth again in 1992, it was accepted. A committee was established that included representatives from the gay and lesbian community, and it delivered a detailed report in 1994.

Marriage. The law on registered partnership entered into force on June 27, 1996. At present, eighty-one couples live in a registered partnership. However, information on the rate of female and male couples is not known.[56]

Parenthood. The law on registered homosexual partnerships is almost identical to other Nordic laws on the issue. In one respect, the Icelandic law went further than other Nordic laws, since in 2000, a law was passed that provided gay men and lesbians in registered partnership the right to step-adoptions. However, the law on registered partnership did not provide gay men and lesbians with the full right to adoptions.[57]

RELIGION AND SPIRITUALITY

The majority of the population, or 87 percent belongs to the Evangelical Lutheran Church which is the National Church of Iceland. Four percent of the people belong to the Lutheran free churches, another 4 percent belong to other religious organizations, and 5 percent belong to other churches, or are not part of any religious organization. Gender disaggregated statistics are not available on this.[58]

The Women's Church is an independent group within the Icelandic National Evangelical Lutheran Church, founded in 1993. The Women's Church bases its work on feminist theology. It holds its monthly worship service by turns in the churches put at its disposal by the congregations of the National Church.[59]

VIOLENCE

Domestic Violence

According to a national survey from 1997, 1,100 women in the 18–65 age group had been victims of domestic violence from their current or previous husband or partner during the year before the survey was conducted. The survey report states that the violence is an issue of gender power and that the relationship within the marriage often resembles relations between the strong and the weak rather than between two equal individuals. The report also revealed that about 14 percent of the women who were victims of physical violence sought support at Kvennaathvarict, the Women's Shelter.[60]

A detailed analysis of the 1,231 women who sought refuge at the Women's Shelter in Reykjavík in 1995–2000 revealed that emotional violence was the most frequent type of violence, which 75 percent of the women gave as the reason for seeking refuge at the shelter. In 50 percent of the cases, the women had been subjected to physical violence, and in 12 percent to sexual violence. In 90 percent of the cases, the perpetrator was the woman's current or previous husband. Immigrant women were highly overrepresented. About 7–15 percent of the women were immigrants, although immigrants were only 2.6 percent of the population.[61]

Rape/Sexual Assault

Accurate data on the extent of rape and sexual assault are unavailable, but the number of women seeking support at *Stígamót*, the Icelandic Counseling and Information Center for Survivors of Sexual Violence, gives an indication. During the twelve years the center has operated, 3,250 individuals have sought support. In 2001, 410 individuals sought help at the center, 225 of them for the first time. Women are 92 percent of those who seek support at the center. Those who seek support do so for several reasons, but a majority (57 percent) are victims of incest. One third seeks support after a rape.[62] An emergency ward for victims of sexual abuse has operated since 1993, first at the Hospital of Reykjavík and later at Landspitali—University Hospital. About seventy-seven individuals seek help yearly at the ward, and 88 percent of them are women under the age of twenty-five.[63]

Trafficking in Women and Children

Trafficking in women is a highly debated issue in Iceland at present. Several sex shops are operated in Reykjavík and the bigger villages, and according to *Stígamót* the trafficking of women has reached Iceland. A neoliberal ideology and free-speech discourse has made it difficult to fight the trafficking and the prostitution. Representatives of the right-wing in Iceland, who have been rather dominant in the general debate, claim that prostitution is mostly a matter of freedom of choice. Therefore, the idea of prostitution as an exploitation and violation of human rights has not been widely accepted until recently.[64]

OUTLOOK FOR THE TWENTY-FIRST CENTURY

The situation of women in Iceland is in many ways paradoxical. They are highly educated and their labor market participation is exceptionally high, but this is not reflected in their social situation, which is not as strong as their societal participation might indicate. The gender pay gap is approximately 15–20 percent and is not narrowing at the present. Gender relations in Iceland are "modern" and "traditional" at the same time. For several years, the gender discourse was rather hostile but that has changed with the founding of the Feminist Association of Iceland in 2003. In general, women in Iceland have formal and legal equality but face much hidden discrimination. The future task for women in Iceland is to identify the mechanisms behind this hidden discrimination and to develop strategies to overcome barriers to gender equality.

NOTES

1. One kilometer equals 0.6 miles.
2. Exchange rate as of September 27, 2002.
3. Statistics Iceland.
4. Statistics Iceland.
5. Einarsdóttir, 2002; Þhorgeirsdóttir, 2002.
6. Statistics Iceland.
7. Ólöf Garðarsdóttir, "Hugleiðingar um kynbundinn í fræðslu barna og unglinga á fyrri hluta 20. aldar," in *Kvennasloðir*, ed. Anna Agnarsdóttír et al. (Reykjavík: Kvennasögusafn Íslands, 2001).
8. *Konur í vísindum á Íslandi* (Reykjavík: Menntamálaráðuneytið, 2002).
9. *Konur*, 2002.
10. Jósepsson, *The Modern Icelandic School System in Historic Perspective* (Reykjavík: The National Center for Educational Materials, 1985).
11. CIA, "World Factbook: Iceland," www.odci.gov/cia/publications/factbook/geos/ic.html#Govt.
12. Statistics Iceland.
13. Statistics Iceland.
14. Statistics Iceland.
15. Ragna Benedicta Garðarsdóttir, *Launakjör félagsmanna* (Félagsvisindastofnun, Háskóla Íslands, 2002).
16. Lilja Mósesdóttir, *Evaluating Gender Equality in the Icelandic Labour Market* (in Icelandic), working paper (Reykjavík: Reykjavík University, 2001).
17. Guðbjörg Andrea Jónsdóttir, *Launamyndum og kynbundinn launamunur* (Reykjavík: Skrifstofa jafnréttismála, 1995).
18. Erling Barth, Marianne Røed, and Hege Torp, *Towards a Closing of the Gender Pay Gap. A Comparative Study of Three Occupations in Six European Countries* (Oslo: Institute for Social Research, The Norwegian Center for Gender Equality, 2002).
19. Guðbjörg Linda Rafnsdóttir and Stefanía Traustadóttir, *Kynferðisleg áreitni á vinnustöðum* (Reykjavík: Skrifstafastofa jafnréttisméla og Vinnueftirlitið, 1998).
20. Guðný Eydal, "Equal Rights to Parental Leave—The Case of Iceland," paper presented at the Fifth European Conference of Sociology, Helsinki, August–September 2001.
21. Þorgerður Einarsdottir, *Through Thick and Thin: Icelandic Men on Paternity Leave* (Reykjavík: Committee on Gender Equality, City of Reykjavík, 1998).
22. Eydal, 2001.
23. Eydal, 2001.
24. Þorgerður Einarsdóttir, "Bryddingar" (Reykjavík: Félagsvísindastofnun Háskóla Íslands og Háskólaútgáfan, 2000).
25. Statistics Iceland.
26. *Social Security in the Nordic Countries* (Copenhagen: Nordic Social Statistical Committee, 1998).
27. Eydal, 2001.

28. Elín Pálsdóttir Flygenring, "Lög og aðrar réttarheimildir er varða konur" in *Konur hvað nú?* ed. Jónína Margrét Guðnadóttir (Reykjavík, 1985).

29. Erla Þórdardóttir, "Félagslegar aðstæður kvenna," in *Konur hvað nú?* ed. Jónína Margrét Guðnadóttir (Reykjavík:, 1985).

30. Einarsdóttir, 2000.

31. Sigrún Júlíusdóttir, *Den Kapabla familjen i det isländska samhället* (in Swedish) (Göteborg, Sweden: Göteborgs Universitet, 1993).

32. Júlíusdóttir, 1993.

33. Þorgerður Einarsdóttir, "Jafnrétti án femínisma—pólitík án fræða," *Ritið* 3 (2002).

34. Statistics Iceland.

35. Einarsdóttir, 2000.

36. The National Curriculum Guide.

37. Statistics Iceland; and *Heilsufar kvenna*, April 2000.

38. *Heilsufar kvenna*, 2000.

39. *Heilbrigðisskýrslur 2002* (Reykjavík: Landlæknisembættið, 2002); Statistics Iceland.

40. *Heilsufar kvenna*, 2000.

41. *Heilbrigoisskýrslur 2002*, 2002.

42. NOMESCO, *Health Statistics in the Nordic Countries* (Nomesco, 1996).

43. Rúnar Vilhjálmsson et al., *Aðgangur að heilbríðgðisÞjónustu* (Reykjavík: Landlæknisembættið, 2001).

44. Landlæknisembættið, 2002.

45. Morgunblaðið, 2002.

46. Landlæknisembættið, 2002.

47. *Heilsufar kvenna*, 2000.

48. *Krabbameinsfélagið 2002*, 2002, www.krabb.is (accessed September 27, 2002).

49. Halldóra Ólafsdóttir, Þunglyndi hjá konum," in *Heilsufar Kvenna*, ed. Lilja Sigrún Jónsdóttir (Reykjavík: Heilbrigðis, 1998).

50. Erla Hulda Halldórsdóttir and Guðrún Dís Jónatansdóttir, eds., *Ártöl og áfangar í Sögu íslendskra kvenna* (Reykjavík: Kvennasögusafn Íslands, 1998).

51. Auður Styrkársdóttir, *From Feminism to Class Politics* (in Swedish) (Umeå, Sweden: Umeå University, 1998).

52. Einarsdóttir, 2002.

53. Einarsdóttir, 2002.

54. Sigríður Erlendsdóttir, *Veröld sem ég vil* (Reykjavík: Kvenréttindafélag Íslands, 1993).

55. Feministinn, June 29, 2003, www.feministinn.is.

56. Statistics Iceland.

57. *Samtökin 78*, 2002, www.samtokin78.is (accessed September 27, 2002).

58. Hagtídindi, 2002, 387.

59. www.Kirkjan.is/kvennakirkjan.

60. *Skýsla nefndar um orsakir, umfang og afleiðingar heimilisofbeldis og annars ofbeldis gegn konum og börnum.* Dóms- og kirkjumálaráðuneytið 1997.

61. Áslaug Einarsdóttir and Guðmundur Á. Skarphéoinsson, *Um heimilisofbeldi* (Námsritgerð: Háskóli Íslands, 2001).

62. *Stígamót, Ársskýrsla 2001* (Reykjavík, 2001).

63. *Heilsufar kvenna*, 2000.

64. *Vera, Tímarit um konur og kvenfrelsi*, no. 2, 2001; and *Vera*, no. 4, 2002.

RESOURCE GUIDE

Suggested Reading

Eydal, Guðný. "Equal Rights to Parental Leave—The Case of Iceland." Paper presented at the Fifth European Conference of Sociology, Helsinki, August 28–September 1, 2001.

Kristmundsdóttir, Sigrídur Dúna. *Doing and Becoming: Women's Movement and Women's Personhood in Iceland 1870–1990.* Reykjavík: Félagsvísindastofnun, Háskólaútgáfan, 1997.

Styrkársdóttir, Auður. *From Feminism to Class Politics: The Rise and Decline of Women's Politics in Reykjavík, 1908–1922.* Umeå, Sweden: Umeå University, Department of Political Science, 1998.

Film

The Seagull's Laughter/Mávahlátur. 2001. Directed by Agúst Gudmundsson. Produced by (IS) Ísfilm. Based on a novel by Kristín Marja Baldursdóttir.

Web Sites

The Centre for Gender Equality, www.jafnretti.is.

The Centre for Women's Studies at the University of Iceland, www.hi.is/stofn/fem/.

Gender Studies at the University of Iceland, www.felags.hi.is/page/kynjafraedi.

Vera, Tímarit um konur og kvenfrelsi, www.vera.is.
An Icelandic feminist journal.

Organizations

Bríet, félag ungra femínista (Briet, The Organisation of Young Feminists)
Ritstjórn Bríet, félag ungra femínista
Vesturgata 4b, 101
Reykjavík, Ísland
Phone: (+354) 694-9879
Email: briet@briet.is
Web site: www.briet.is

Femínistafélag Íslands (The Feminist Association of Iceland)
Kvennagarður
Laugavegi 59
101 Reykjavík
Email: feministinn@feministinn.is
Web site: www.feministinn.is

Kvenréttindafélag Íslands (The Icelandic Women's Rights Association)
Hallveigarstöðum v/ Túngötu 101
Reykjavík Ísland

Phone: (+354) 551 8156
Email: krfi@krfi.is
Web site: www.krfi.is

SELECTED BIBLIOGRAPHY

Jósepsson, Bragi. *The Modern Icelandic School System in Historic Perspective*. Reykjavík: The National Center for Educational Materials, 1985.

NOMESCO. *Health Statistics in the Nordic Countries 1996*. NOMESCO, Nordic Medico Statistical Committee, 1998.

Social Security in the Nordic Countries. Copenhagen: Nordic Social Statistical Committee, various years.

Selected Icelandic and Swedish Bibliography

"Dökkt útlit í alnæmismálum." *Morgunblaðið*, July 24, 2002.

Einarsdóttir, Áslaug, and Guðmundur Á. Skarphéðinsson. *Um heimilisofbeldi. Athugun á konum sem leita til Kvennaathvarfs og ofbeldismönnum Þeirra*. Námsritgerð: Háskóli Íslands, 2001.

Einarsdóttir, Þorgerður. *Through Thick and Thin: Icelandic Men on Paternity Leave*. Reykjavík: The Committee on Gender Equality, City of Reykjavík, 1998.

———. *Bryddingar, Um samfélagið sem mannanna verk*. Reykjavík: Félagsvísindastofnun Háskóla Íslands og Háskólaútgáfan, 2000.

———. "Jafnrétti án femínisma—pólítik án fræða. Um Þáttaskil í íslenskri jafnréttispólítík." *Ritið* 2 (2002), 9–36.

Erlendsdóttir, Sigríður Th. *Veröld sem ég vil: Saga Kvenréttindafélags Íslands 1907–1992*. Reykjavík: Kvenréttindafélag Íslands, 1993.

Flygenring, Elín Pálsdóttir. "Lög og aðrar réttarheimildir er varða konur." In *Konur hvað nú?*, edited by Jónína Margret Guðnadóttir, 29–48. 85'nefndin, samstarfsnefnd í lok kvennaáratugar SÞ og Jafnréttisráð. Reykjavík, 1985.

Garðarsdóttir, Ólöf. "Hugleiðingar um kynbundinn mun í fræslu barna og unglinga á fyrri hluta 20. aldar." In *Kvennaslóðir: Rit til heiðurs Sigríði Th. Erlendsdóttur sagnfræðingi*, edited by Anna Agnarsdóttir et al., 419–29. Reykjavík: Kvennasögusafn Íslands, 2001.

Garðarsdóttir, Ragna Benedikta. *Launakjör félagsmanna í Verslunarmannafélagi Reykjavíkur og Verslunarmannafélagi Akraness árið 2001*. Félagsvísindastofnun Háskóla Íslands, 2002.

Halldórsdóttir, Erla Hulda, and Guðrún Dís Jónatansdóttir, eds. *Ártöl og áfangar í sögu íslenskra kvenna*. Reykjavík: Kvennasögusafn Íslands, 1998.

Heilbrigðis-skýrslur 2002. Reykjavík: Landlæknisembættið, 2002.

Heilsufar kvenna: Álit og tillögur nefndar um heilsufar kvenna. Heilbrigðis- og tryggingamálaráðuneytið. April 2000.

Jónsdóttir, Guðbjörg Andrea. *Launamyndun og kynbundinn launamunur*. Reykjavík: Skrifstofa jafnréttismála, 1995.

Júlíusdóttir, Sigrún. *Den kapabla familjen i det isländska samhället. En studie i lojalitet, äktenskapsdynamik och psykosocial anpassning*. Göteborg, Sweden: Göteborgs Universitet, institutionen för Socialt arbete, 1993.

Konur í vísindum á Íslandi. Reykjavík: Menntamálaráðuneytið, 2002. 92.

Krabbameinsfélagið. 2002. www.krabb.is (accessed September 27, 2002).

"Könnun á launamun kynja." Jafnréttisráð: Nefnd um efnahagsleg völd kvenna, 2002.

Mósesdóttir, Lilja. *Evaluating Gender Equality in the Icelandic Labour Market*. Working paper. Reykjavík: Reykjavík University, 2001.

Ólafsdóttir, Halldóra. "Þunglyndi hjá konum." In *Heilsufar kvenna*, edited by Lilja Sigrún Jónsdóttir. Reykjavík: Heilbrigðis- og tryggingamálaráðuneytið, Rit 1, 1998.

Rafnsdóttir, Guðbjörg Linda, and Stefanía Traustadóttir. *Kynferðisleg áreitni á vinnustöðum*. Reykjavík: Skrifstofa jafnréttismála og Vinnueftirlitið, 1998.

Samtökin 78. www.samtokin78.is (accessed September 27, 2002).

Skýrsla nefndar um orsakir, umfang og afleiðingar heimilisofbeldis og annars ofbeldis gegn konum og börnum. Dóms- og kirkjumálaráðuneytið, February 1997.

Stígamót, Ársskýrsla 2001. Reykjavík, 2001.

Þórðardóttir, Erla. "Félagslegar aðstæður kvenna." In *Konur hvað nú?*, edited by Jónína Margrét Guðnadóttir. 85'nefndin, samstarfsnefnd í lok kvennaáratugar SÞ og Jafnréttisráð. Reykjavík, 1985.

Vera. Tímarit um konur og kvenfrelsi, no. 2 (2001), and no. 4 (2002).

Vilhjálmsson, Rúnar, Ólafur Ólafsson, Jóhann Ág. Sigurðsson, and Tryggvi Þór Herbertsson. *Aðgangur að heilbrigðisþjónustu*. Reykjavík: Landlæknisembættið, 2001.

19

THE REPUBLIC OF IRELAND

Elizabeth A. Throop

PROFILE OF THE REPUBLIC OF IRELAND

Far from being the fey, whimsical, almost otherworldly folk portrayed in literature, stage, and screen, the contemporary Irish are a sophisticated lot. In the twenty-first century, Ireland is a center of industry and services (especially tourism and software development) that provide a robust export base for its economy. In addition, the "Celtic Tiger" produces complex literature, dance, music, film, and theater while it continues to struggle with issues of reunification of the isle of Ireland. Its population is growing—3.8 million as of July 2000[1] and continues to be governed as a republic consisting of a president (Mary McAleese), prime minister (Bertie Ahern as of July 2003), and a bicameral parliament (comprised of Seanad Éireann [the senate] and Dáil Éireann [the lower house]). Ireland is also a full member of the European Union (EU). Unemployment is relatively low at about 5 percent;[2] government is concerned with job creation and training as well as increasing educational levels for all Irish people.

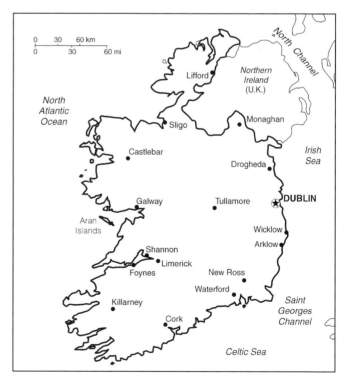

Demographically, the Irish are divided roughly in half by gender; women outnumber men, however, after age sixty-five. Infant mortality is quite low (5.62 deaths per 1,000 live births), as is maternal mortality (approximately 1 death per 10,000 patients from 1992 to 1999);[3] at the same time, the Irish population is increasing by 1.16 percent a year. As is true for many Western countries, life expectancy for the Irish is increasing: overall, an Irish person can expect to live 76.81 years; men live on average to 74.06 years, and women to 79.74 years.[4]

OVERVIEW OF WOMEN'S ISSUES

Whereas the picture painted so far of the Irish appears rosy, it also contains some dark shadings. Although the situation for women has greatly improved in Ireland in the past twenty years, many troubling issues remain. So, for example, although some newspapers report that Ireland is the "fairest place for working women,"[5] there is little to no childcare available to those working women. Birth control can sometimes be difficult for women to obtain,[6] and abortion is specifically prohibited by the Irish Constitution (8th amendment and Article 40). Women, therefore, remain unable to assert control over their sexuality. In addition, despite the lifting of the ban on married women's employment in the 1970s, only a little more than a third of Irish women work full-time,[7] which reflects, perhaps, the lack of adequate childcare. On the other hand, Irish girls and women stay in school longer than their male counterparts—but this diligence is not rewarded in employment equity as yet. Still, the Ireland of 2003 for women is a very different one than that of 1973—or of 1993, for that matter. Gender roles are being reshaped by women and by men in the Catholic Church (overwhelmingly the Irish choice for religious affiliation), in the family, in politics, in education, and in all other important social institutions in Ireland.

EDUCATION

Opportunities

Some of the gender reshaping can be seen in the arena of education. The Irish educational system is run, by and large, by the Catholic Church—the government funds free "public" education to be administered by the church. There are some nondenominational, other-denominational, and "private" schools, some of which are also government funded, but most Irish children will be educated by nuns, priests, and brothers—and successfully so, when we consider the Irish literacy rate. Irish children attend "mixed infants," a coeducational classroom for children ages 4–7; after that, most children attend same-sex schools until they attend university or trade school. Irish children may leave secondary school after passing their Junior Certificate exam (a national exam that all schoolchildren must take) at around age fifteen. Some remain in school to take their Leaving Certificate exam (another, more extensive series of national examinations) at around age seventeen. If a child is extremely lucky, she will be able to attend university, although there is room for only about 4 percent of the Irish population at the various Irish universities; admission and one's major subject are based almost solely on the results of the Leaving Certificate exam.

Over half of Irish girls take and pass the Leaving Certificate exam,[8] and, although their numbers are small, girls have the same access to university places as do boys. Indeed, girls do better in their schoolwork: "Irish women as compared to Irish men had enjoyed a disproportionate access to education, something which was relatively unusual in European terms."[9] Interestingly, more boys leave school without taking the Leaving Certificate exam. At the same time, Irish feminists argue that girls and women succeed in education only by acting like boys and men, and even then the Irish girl or woman has little access to legitimate authority.[10] Like many western countries, Ireland's commitment to gender parity in education only goes so far, and it appears only when girls and women agree to assume the behaviors and attitudes of men.

Waterford Crystal factory worker, Ireland. Photo © TRIP/J. Denham.

Still, the growing number of women's studies or feminist studies programs at all Irish universities is reason for optimism. In addition, there are a number of Irish feminist journals, scholarly works, and clearly feminist publishers (Attic Press, for instance). Although these programs, journals, and presses tend to be marginalized within the academy—again, as they are in many other western countries—the fact of their existence provides a clue to the gender reshaping taking place in Irish education.

Literacy

The Irish literacy rate is 98 percent.[11]

EMPLOYMENT AND THE ECONOMY

Job/Career Opportunities

Gender reshaping is not as evident in employment. Great strides have been made in Ireland, however, particularly in the last ten years. For example, the Irish government has made a firm commitment to "mainstreaming equality" with regard to gender issues by forming the National Development Plan (NDP) and the Gender Equality Unit of the Department of Justice, Equality and Law Reform, an effort that is aimed at bringing educational, employment, and other social policy parity for Irish women by 2006.

Pay

However, the Irish government admits that pay equity between men and women does not exist and that it requires enormous government effort to alter this condition; as a result, the government has launched programs to move toward equal pay and opportunities and, perhaps more important, has pledged to include a "gender equality perspective into all policies at all levels and at all stages"[12] by considering the differing resources available to women and men and the different kinds of lives men and women have.

Such considerations clearly are needed. Women earn 75 percent, on average, of men's wages, meaning—as in so many other western countries—that women's incomes and retirement benefits are lower than men's. Many women work in low-paying jobs, largely in the service or industrial sector, so that significant promotion to higher-paying jobs is unlikely. Also, fewer than half of all Irish women work, whether part-time or full-time,[13] and about half of Irish mothers work.[14] Yet, women retain the predominant share of responsibility for childrearing and childcare so that careers are interrupted, time on the job is interrupted, and therefore earnings and contributions to pensions are interrupted.

Support for Mothers/Caretakers

Despite its sentimental attachment to motherhood, Ireland helps mothers very little indeed. Although women are not forbidden to do paid work—as they once were upon getting married—the Irish government does not make it easy. What is most encouraging is that Ireland is facing its patriarchal past—and present—and attempting to promote legislation to allow any person, male or female, to be employed if she or he wishes to.

Maternal Leave

There are various maternal leave policies and some allowance is made by law for family leave necessities. Under the Maternity Protection Act of 1994, most employed women are provided with a minimum of fourteen weeks of maternity leave; the first 21 days are to be paid by the employer under health and safety government policies. The woman must begin her leave four weeks before the due date of her baby (Irish Department of Social and Family Affairs web site). A woman may then be entitled to receive benefits from the Irish government, through the Department of Social and Family Affairs. She will receive between €141 and €232 a week for up to eighteen weeks (less the first 21 days paid by the employer) depending on her tax contributions.[15]

Daycare

State-sponsored childcare facilities are very hard to find. Private daycare is available, but, as in so many other nations, it is expensive. The lack of adequate childcare centers discourages many women from working. At the same time, "The adherence to a concept of paid employment which is rooted in a male model, involving resistance to job sharing, no daycare facilities, and a commitment to full-time paid employment has in fact forced Irish women to choose between no paid work and full-time paid work—and they are increasing[ly] choosing the latter."[16]

Inheritance and Property Rights

Irish inheritance and property rights follow western convention. Women may inherit equally with men, women may own property, and marital property is considered joint rather than belonging solely to the husband. But as is true in many societies, women are still considered by some people to be incapable of managing monetary affairs. At the same time, however, women are, at least in part, running the Irish government. In this area, Irish law is up to date by recalling early Irish *Brehon* law, destroyed by the occupying English in the twelfth century, that allowed full inheritance rights for men and women alike.

Social/Government Programs

Welfare

Ireland, like many of its western European counterparts, has a relatively generous welfare system. Until recently, it was constructed around notions of patriarchy: this means-tested system was based on assumptions that a "normal" family consisted of a husband, his wife, and their children. Welfare benefits were understood as temporary measures that were to be considered part of the husband's contribution. Benefits were handed to men; there was a wife's benefit—considerably smaller than the husband's—and a few pence for the children. However, the wife could not receive her benefit without her husband's permission.

The "dole" has changed, however. These days, more than a dozen different means-tested programs exist to assist poor families. Categories of qualified recipients are single parents, old-age pensioners, children, widows and widowers, the unemployed, blind or disabled adults and children, and families. Other kinds of assistance include rent allowance and, in some cases, a fuel allowance. Ireland also provides entitlement programs, including a contributory pension (much like Social Security in the United States), a children's benefit, and universal health care. The Irish refer to means-tested programs as social assistance and entitlement programs as social insurance.[17] Current actual benefits paid are approximately IR£40 per week (about US$50) for a single mother and one child; Pay-Related Social Insurance (PRSI) payments, of course, will vary depending on a person's lifetime contribution.

Social insurance programs, like many other such programs, pay less money to women than they do to men. Women's work histories in Ireland, more so than in some other western countries, are spotty. Since fewer than half of all women are employed, their contributions to social insurance schemes are less than men's contributions. Because it is a contributory program rather than an entitlement or means-tested one, women's income at retirement will be less than men's—as it is also less during years of employment.

FAMILY AND SEXUALITY

Gender Roles

The Irish woman is defined almost solely as "mother." The Irish Constitution, in fact, enshrines woman as mother as it refers to the two interchangeably. That is, the Constitution sometimes uses the word "woman" to refer to females, and at other times it uses the word "mother." Articles 41.2.1 and 41.2.2, in their entirety, read as follows:

41.2.1—"In particular, the State recognizes that by her life within the home, *woman* gives to the State a support without which the common good cannot be achieved."

41.2.2—"The State shall, therefore, endeavour to ensure that *mothers* shall not be obliged by economic necessity to engage in labour to the neglect of their duties in the home." (italics added)

Much in Ireland has changed since the drafting of the Constitution, but the influence of the Irish Catholic Church in the drafting of the document in 1937 is clear.[18] The Irish still clearly believe that a woman's most important role is as a mother (and, secondarily, as a wife).

Women—mothers—are understood to be strong, stoic, and self-sacrificing in contrast to men, who are seen as weak, overemotional, and often selfish little boys. Indeed, in the mid-1990s, a popular chocolate bar was advertised on the radio by a warm female voice discussing how difficult her little boy is:

> In this spot, an Irish woman warmly talks about how irresponsible her little one is, the dreadful language he uses, and how he never goes to bed on time. But it's all worth it, she chuckles, when his "little face lights up at the sight of the candy bar." The ad ends with the woman saying, "Sometimes, though, I wonder why I married him."[19]

The gender reshaping has not yet reached that most fundamental of cultural understandings—gender itself. The traditional views of gender roles in Ireland—strong women and overemotional men—remain firmly entrenched among the Irish.

In addition, sexuality remains a very difficult issue for the Irish. In general, overt emotional expression is discouraged in Ireland; so is physical expression, particularly sexuality and especially female sexuality. Although there has been a deepening acceptance of homosexuality in Ireland, at least in Dublin (indeed, in the 1994 St. Patrick's Day parade in Dublin, three avowed homosexual groups marched proudly down the road, with no protests), any acknowledgment of physical pleasure, sexual or otherwise, is problematic to say the least. Women didn't discuss their sex lives with anyone, they said, even—or especially—with their partners. Only briefly would they say that sex is dirty, unpleasant, and uncomfortable, meant for procreation and little more.[20] Men also seemed to be very upset with any discussion of sex or sexuality.

This seems to be associated with a general distaste on the part of the Irish with any kind of physical pleasure. One does not comment on food or drink but instead consumes it quickly, without enjoying it too much and certainly without discussing it. Recipes for food are not discussed. Illness—or at least its symptoms—is not discussed. Anything having to do with the physical sensations of the body seemingly is taboo. The church counsels its flocks to concentrate on spiritual rather than corporeal matters; paying attention to physicality is a distraction, perhaps sent by the devil to lure good Catholics away from the true path.[21]

Certainly some women and men are attempting to alter some of these cultural views and acting upon, if not always overtly commenting upon, sexual issues. Yet women are still defined through their motherhood. Many men define women's careers as poor substitutes for women's "true" career, parenting. Women, in their opinion, are not fit for the cutthroat world of business—an odd perception given the general cultural belief that women are strong and rational, but men are not.

The Catholic Church, still an overwhelming influence on Irish culture, agrees that women's only work involves the family. The most recent official statement on the matter by church officials, the 1994 Catechism, declares that motherhood is the sole appropriate work for women if a calling to life as a religious sister does not appear.[22] Mothers, of course, do not ask for anything for themselves and, since "woman" and "mother" mean, at least officially, the same thing, women and women's rights have been demanded in ways rather differently than the bulk of the Western world.

Ireland, like many western countries, has its share of women who say, "I'm not a feminist, but. . . ." Irish women tend to agree that men and women should be paid the same wage for the same work, and many Irish women believe that children do just fine with a working mother.[23] There are clear feminist manifestations among Irish women; but demands for change have taken place in soft rather than strident voices. Feminists in the 1990s in Ireland, for instance, did not often aim for confrontational tactics but instead for reasoned discussion. Rather than attacking the patriarchy head on—through demands for full abortion rights, for example— Irish feminists have fought for the right to information about abortion and the right to travel freely for pregnant women, rights that had been threatened or denied until the 1990s.[24] Many Irish feminists were not comfortable with the provision of abortion; they were not sure that they supported that particular right for reproductive choice. Feminism, therefore, not too surprisingly, follows the Irish cultural gender model when attempting to make change.

And there have been changes in gender roles, despite the continual equation of women and mothers. Some fundamental alterations were just becoming evident in the mid-1990s. Although women's gender definitions have not changed all that much, men's are on the cusp of major alteration. Although there certainly are traditional men who see their roles as providing financially for the family and not much more, there is an emerging category of masculinity called by Irish folks the "new man," who is interested in sharing housework, childcare, cooking, and cleaning as well as earning. The new man is marked by his willingness to take out the children for a Sunday afternoon, walking them in the pram or taking them to the park and enjoying their company. Though no men admitted to being a new man, Irish men and women insist that there were loads of these new men around.[25] Women, however, seemed ambivalent about new men. The existence of a new man requires a new woman, one who gives up some control in the household to get some control in the world outside the household. That new woman has been slow to emerge.

Marriage

In general, Irish men and women adopt a somewhat traditional marital pattern. Although, as with so many other things, Irish marriage and family life are changing, cultural patterns die hard. In a traditional Irish marriage, men were meant to be responsible for "outside" work (taking care of crops and animal herds, if farmers; cars, jobs, garbage, and lawns, if not), while women were in charge of "inside" work (barns, housework, and childrearing, if farmers; housework, childrearing, and shopping, if not). In many traditional households, women manage the family's finances but do not often work for a wage. Women's traditional roles required a strong, stoic, self-sacrificing woman, taking care of children and men, thinking little of her own pleasures and desires. Men's traditional roles called for a hard-working, somewhat solitary, sometimes emotionally expressive husband and father.

Marriage frequently was understood as a relatively unemotional relationship. Indeed, emotional expression in general has been seen as self-indulgent and somehow too "American" to be useful for Irish marriage. Rather than focusing on how one feels, and then expressing those feelings, Irish culture—shaped heavily by the Catholic Church—regards discussions of emotion with discomfort. Intimacy, for the Irish, is not displayed through the revelation of a deeply personal inner self; to act in such a manner instead promotes distance and difference as one marks herself out as special and remarkable. Intimacy, for the Irish, seems to constitute very subtle actions of silent company and the right *not* to explain oneself.[26]

Marriage, then, has been less of a romantic venture and more one of companionship and sexuality. However, it does appear that women and men are beginning to look for what they perceive as "deeper" relationships with their partners. Although spending time alone with one's romantic partner has been relatively rare until quite recently, certainly men and women have begun engaging in couple dating behaviors rather than group outings. This may be connected not only to cultural change but also to an improving economy in Ireland: in 2003, being able to treat one's partner to a restaurant dinner is more feasible than it was in Ireland in the mid-1990s.

With a change in marital patterns come changes in rates of marital breakup. In 1995, voters passed—by one-half of a percentage point—a proposed change to the Irish Constitution to allow divorce in rather restrictive circumstances. The 15th Amendment to the Irish Constitution allows for divorce in situations in which the marital partners have lived apart for four of the last five years; the marriage cannot be repaired; financial and other provision is made for the spouses and any children; and all other conditions have been met.[27] This means, essentially, that couples wishing to divorce—and remarry—must wait five years, living separately, before being allowed to do so. In the mid-1990s, when divorce was still not legal, cultural consultants estimated the rate of legal separation, despite the lack of divorce, at about 25 percent (legal separations were allowed by law). In other words, even without legal divorce, one fourth of Irish marriages were breaking up; those in such marriages merely were not allowed to remarry. Now, of course, they can; but it is unclear whether such second marriages are taking place, given that the actual laws enacting the constitutional amendment have only been in place since 1997. Kieron Wood, an Irish barrister, estimates that 5,000 people a year are currently applying for divorce in Ireland.[28]

Reproduction

Ireland used to be known as the leader in late- or never-married adults. The average age at marriage for men in the 1940s was 33.1, and for women it was 26.1.[29] Today, the average age at marriage for men is about 28, and for women it is 26.[30] This represents a significant change in Irish culture and marriage, especially since the number of people who married in the 1940s, at least through the primary reproductive years, tended to be in the minority. In the twenty-first century, somewhere around half of adults twenty-five and over are married,[31] but as the Irish prime minister notes, "(T)here is some evidence that the marriage rate is declining, but it is too early to draw definite conclusions in this regard, because of the higher average age of marriage than was the norm in the 1960s and 1970s."[32] It is unclear exactly how many adults are married—especially given marriage breakdown.

Family size has decreased from unusually high numbers as well. The average number of children in an Irish family in 1946 was 4.25.[33] Today it is 1.9.[34] Averages can be deceptive, of course, but most Irish families in the 1990s consisted of either a single parent and one or two children, or two parents and one or two children. There are still, however, families with as many as twenty-two children.

It used to be true that unmarried mothers were the shame and the scandal of the township; these days, 25 percent of all births are to unmarried women and 33 percent of first births are to single women, and only 20 percent of these first births are to teenagers.[35] Rather than being packed away to the convent to wash floors and relinquish their babies for adoption, single women today in Ireland seem comfortable without partners. And the state does provide for its children through a relatively generous welfare program that does not punish children of single parents.

Sex Education

Irish fertility rates have certainly been reduced over the years. However, it is unlikely that this is due to effective sexual education. The official stance on sex education by the Catholic Church, which continues to control most primary and secondary education, is that the only way to appropriately express oneself sexually is within the context of marriage. The reasoning continues that, therefore, it is tempting fate to discuss sexual issues with those who are meant to be celibate—as one Irish parent said, "You don't want to be putting ideas into their little heads."

At the same time, Irish young people have access to a fair amount of information in books, electronic media, and the Internet. Although the discussion of personal sexuality remains discomfiting to many Irish people, young or old, more information regarding contraception, sexuality, and the basic physiology of sexuality is likely somewhat available. Still, Irish schools do not gladly teach sex education.[36] That being said, the Irish Department of Education has instituted the teaching of sex education in both primary and secondary schools, called "Relationships and Sexuality Education." Its purpose is to provide accurate physiological information in the context of the exploration of values and relationships.[37]

Contraception and Abortion

Women in Ireland have issues similar to women in most western countries. Access to contraception, although better than it has been even in recent history, is limited, and the Catholic Church disapproves of all contraceptive methods but the rhythm method.

Contraception is available to Irish women and men. Just about all forms that exist in Western Europe and the United States are accessible in Ireland. Although the Irish Catholic Church continues to counsel Irish women and men to use the rhythm method, a ban on the sale of contraceptives was lifted in the 1970s. Prior to that, Irish women in fact did use contraceptive pills—but the official reason was for dysmenorrhea, not birth control.[38] Other than condoms, however, few birth control methods are available over the counter.[39]

Abortion is another matter. Abortion is expressly forbidden by the Irish Constitution, in Article 40.3.3.3. Indeed, in the early 1990s, even the right for women to have access to information about abortion and abortion services provided in England was under attack; that attack was rebuffed after some difficult debate and discussion. A woman's right to travel freely was at issue: if she was pregnant and going to England, some government officials assumed she was going for an abortion and could stop her from leaving the country (since abortion was, and is, illegal in Ireland). However, ultimately the courts in Ireland decided that a woman had as much right to travel as did a man, and special amendments to the Constitution enacted in 1992 allowed women free access to travel and information regarding contraceptive and abortion methods.[40] In fact, in 1998, nearly 6,000 Irish women traveled to England or Wales to obtain an abortion.[41]

Teen Pregnancy

Despite the availability of contraception, teenagers do get pregnant in Ireland as they do everywhere else. Approximately 5 percent of all births in Ireland are to adolescents.[42] In the not so distant past, an out-of-wedlock birth was considered by most Irish to be a shameful condition, one to be hidden away. Most often, pregnant girls were sent away—sometimes it was called "visiting the auntie"—to a convent or to a relative's house far away; after birth, the girl was forced to surrender her baby for adoption and often did not return home.[43] Today, this rarely happens. Young mothers, married (if their husbands desert them) or single, are eligible for welfare benefits that allow them to live independently.[44] As in so many other societies, young Irish women today are choosing to raise their children rather than give them up for adoption; in 1998, almost 30 percent of all births were to women outside of marriage.[45]

HEALTH

Health Care Access

In general, Irish women have relatively good access to health care. Ireland provides for health care for those who cannot afford private services; no fees are charged to covered people when one uses the government health service for doctor visits and prescriptions. If a person makes more than about IR£40 per week (about US$50), copayments are required.[46] In the last decade or so, private insurance has become available, creating, in effect, a two-tiered health system—one tier is for the poor, and the better tier is for the wealthy. About 35 percent of Irish people are covered solely under the government health plan, and another 35 percent carry private insurance in addition.[47] Although numbers are not available, it appears that the remainder of the population relies solely on private health insurance.

Because of the governmental prohibition on abortion, and because of the Catholic Church's longstanding opposition to "artificial" contraception, including sterilization, women's health in Ireland is often compromised. Certainly, the days of bearing ten or more children are pretty much gone (except for some Traveler, or Irish nomadic, women),[48] showing that women are gaining some control over their fertility. At the same time, women must rely on voluntary organizations such as the Well Woman Centre in Dublin to provide reliable contraception for low or no cost. Access to a full range of medical care remains an incomplete project for Irish women.

Diseases and Disorders

Women in Ireland are most susceptible to heart disease and cancer. Moreover, the largest threat to women's health appears to be heart disease.

The overall death rate (per 100,000) from heart disease is 385.2.[49] Mary Daley argued that the stress levels of an average Irish woman in the 1980s meant that her susceptibility to heart disease was high.[50] As of 2001, heart disease accounted for 40 percent of all Irish deaths; Irish men had the highest rate of heart disease in the European Union, and Irish women had the third highest rate.[51]

Heart disease is associated with alcohol consumption as well as smoking. Women tend to drink more than is recommended. On average, and across social classes, almost 28 percent of all Irish women take more drinks in a week than is called "sensible" by health professionals—that is, fourteen units of alcohol per week for women (compared to twenty-one units for men). At the same time, women report that they eat a fairly healthy diet: only about 9 percent, on average, say that they eat fried foods more than four times per week, and about 70 percent of Irish women claim to eat four or more servings of fruit and vegetables a day.[52] Women's self-reported healthful diet is not enough to stave off heart disease and non–smoking related cancers. Perhaps the warning that Irish women's stress levels are dangerously high is to be taken seriously.

AIDS

AIDS is also affecting Irish women in a deadly way. From 1986 to 2000, 255 women have died of AIDS (701 men have died). Most of the women who have died have been 25–34 years old, and most causes of infection appear to be either through intravenous drug use or heterosexual contact.[53] Although AIDS remains a relatively minor problem so far, Irish cultural understandings until recently have not included clear discussions of birth control and disease control. The Catholic Church regards the use of condoms as a violation of church law—since it is designed in large part as "artificial" contraception—and, although more and more Irish men and women are disregarding church teachings, there remains among them a strong discomfort with discussing bodily processes.

Eating Disorders

Irish families also rarely pay attention to eating disorders. Anorexia and bulimia are relatively unknown in Ireland, although cultural consultants with daughters say that there appears to be an upswing in cases. Girls do not seem to often starve themselves or binge and purge; obesity as well is relatively rare.

Cancer

Irish women are notorious smokers of tobacco: in 1994, close to 30 percent of all Irish women smoked (the figure is almost identical for Irish men). As a result—and taking other factors into account as well—Irish women have a 35 percent risk of developing some form of cancer before seventy-five years old, and 16 percent of all female deaths in 1995 were attributable to cancers arising from smoking.[54] However, the cancer diagnosed most often for women (and for men, surprisingly) in 1995 was non-melanoma skin cancer (35 percent of all cancer cases in 1995); for women, this was followed by bowel (8.9 percent), breast (7.9 percent), and lung (7.1 percent) cancer. Cervical cancer was 4.9 percent of all new cancer diagnoses in 1995, ovarian cancer was relatively rare at 1.7 percent, and uterine (what the Irish call "womb") cancer comprised 1.1 percent of all new cancer diagnoses.[55]

Depression

Rates of depression for Irish women appear to be quite high. Although complete up-to-date statistics were unavailable at the time of writing, it appears that women are diagnosed with depression almost twice as much as men in Ireland. Irish women were diagnosed with depression on admission to an in-patient psychiatric facility 33 percent of the time in 1995; in contrast, depression was the diagnosis for men 20 percent of the time.[56] However, since men in Ireland tend to be hospitalized for psychiatric reasons more often than women, we can assume that the actual rate of depression among all Irish women is high.[57] It also is likely that women are receiving less treatment than men receive. Given the stressful lives that many Irish women lead—including trying to manage childcare, household expenses, housekeeping, shopping, a husband, and probably a part-time job—depression would seem to be a rational reaction to difficult situations.

POLITICS AND LAW

Suffrage

Although Ireland has had a poor history with regard to its treatment of women, it must be said that women in Ireland have had the vote longer than women in many western countries. Following a fight for independence from Great Britain, the Irish Free State enacted universal suffrage for all adults over twenty-one years old in 1922. However, before that, women were allowed to vote in local governmental elections (1898); in 1918, women thirty and older were allowed to vote.[58] Women also served in the Irish fight for independence, and women, albeit only a very few, were elected to the newly formed *Dáil*, or lower house.

Political Participation

Some of the most difficult situations women have had to face have involved Ireland's complicated political landscape. Although Ireland has been led by female presidents for the past decade, women remain an underrepresented group in formal politics in Ireland.

In terms of legislative and governmental representation, women currently make up 14 percent of all lower-house (*Dáil*) representatives and 18 percent of governmental ministers.[59] This actually is a reduction in representation from the early 1990s, when more women served in formal political roles than they do now. However, Irish people seem to think that there are many women politicians.[60] After all, the last two presidents have been women (Mary Robinson, now U.N. High Commissioner on Human Rights, and Mary McAleese)—but the Irish president holds little political or decision-making power.

Women's Rights

At the same time, the Irish government has decided to work on increasing parity in gender issues across many fronts. As part of the Irish Department of Justice, the Department of Equality and Law Reform concentrates on what it calls "mainstreaming equality," defined as "The (re)organization, improvement, development and evaluation of policy processes, so that a gender equality perspective is incorporated into all policies at all levels and at all stages, by the actors normally involved in policy-making."[61] This government department is attempting not only to raise the quantitative measures of women's status in employment, education, and government, but it also investigates structural and institutional sexism (among other forms of discrimination). It has set as one of its tasks the consideration of outcomes—intended and unintended—that might result from policy and program shifts.

Feminist Movements

It would be accurate to say that such a governmental department in Ireland would not have been formed without pressure from tenacious Irish feminists. There currently are hundreds of such groups in Ireland, some with a long provenance. Although Irish feminists have not argued vociferously for abortion rights, most have played important roles in fighting for the right to contraception, the right to pay equity, the right for welfare equity, and many other rights that have been denied to Irish women. Feminism came to Ireland at pretty much the same time it did to other western countries: the Women's Political Association was formed in 1971, and the Council for the Status of Women (now the National Women's Council of Ireland) emerged in 1973. Since the 1970s, various feminist groups focusing on women's health (including rape counseling services, contraception and abortion information, and accessible gynecological services), family violence, welfare reform, the formation of women's studies programs in Irish universities, lesbian (and gay) information and support groups, accessibility to psychological services, and many other issues pertinent to women have been assisting Irish women.

The Catholic Church and its various conservative lobbyists have fought consistently against many Irish feminist groups. For instance, as recently as the 1980s, a pregnant woman, apparently a cancer survivor, became ill with a recurrence of her cancer while pregnant. Her doctor refused to provide her with any treatment because it would almost certainly harm, if not destroy, the fetus she was carrying. As her condition worsened, she was given no X-rays; she was not allowed even any painkillers. The doctors and nurses insisted that she must carry the baby to full term, which she did. Both mother and child died two days after birth.[62] Although feminists invoke this story as an outrageous example of patriarchal matricide, various subterranean far-right Catholic groups (all led by men either directly or indirectly) believe that the church's prohibition on abortion and preventing harm to a fetus is absolutely and always correct. Groups such as the Society for the Protection of the Unborn Child (SPUC), the Knights of Columbanus (as distinct from the more traditional Catholic men's service organization, the Knights of Columbus), the Pro-Life Amendment Campaign (PLAC), and other shadowy groups have worked hard at convincing politicians that women's rights to reproductive control (in particular) and pay equity and other feminist issues (in general) run directly counter to all that the Catholic Church—and thus Ireland—holds dear.

However, the Irish people have taken steps toward the fuller liberation of women politically, passing referenda concerning the right to contraception, the right to information regarding abortion, the right to travel to another country to obtain an abortion, and the right to divorce. All of these rights did not exist for Irish women until the mid-to late 1980s:[63] as mentioned earlier, divorce was illegal until 1997.

Lesbian Rights

Homosexuality remains a very difficult issue for the Irish. The Catholic Church forbids homosexual behavior, although in the past few years it has allowed celibate homosexuals to be Catholic. However, the Irish appear more than a little uncomfortable with the notion of gay men and lesbians. Legislation enacted in 1992 guarantees equality for gay men and lesbians.[64] That does not mean, however, that the law is enforced or that discrimination against homosexuals does not take place. For instance, "Oasis," an Irish government web site aimed at Irish citizens, has a number of documents discussing the rights of same-sex partners in a number of arenas. Issues discussed include property rights both during and after same-sex relationships, rights to inheritance, rights to adoption and fostering for same sex couples, and other family issues. It is clear, however, that Ireland, unlike some members of the European Union, does not recognize same-sex marriages as the same legally binding relationship as heterosexual marriage. Furthermore, while a parent in a same-sex relationship who has children from a previous relationship may be awarded custody, the matter has not yet reached Irish courts as of May 2003.[65]

Military Service

Women have been part of the Irish military since 1980. At present, few women are active, full-time officers, although roughly one third of all second-line reservists are female. Approximately 500 women hold officer rank in the various branches of Irish military service. Although military service is not required of either men or women in Ireland, the military appears to be a significantly useful career choice and one that is very competitive. About 17,000 Irish men and women are currently on the waiting list to take tests for qualifying for the military. Most Irish military personnel operate as peacekeepers for the United Nations and NATO across the world (specifically in the Balkans, East Timor, and some parts of Africa), and they also assist the Irish National Police, the *Gardai Siochana*, with border patrols (the border with Northern Ireland can be difficult), prisoner transportation, protection of political prisoners, and other services. What may be most notable about the various Irish military branches is that women are entitled to serve in combat roles, as long as they can pass the appropriate physical, intellectual, and psychological tests; these tests, according to the Irish Department of Defence, are meant to be gender neutral. The Irish military has taken gender equality quite seriously and intends to continue to encourage young women to consider the military as a career.[66]

RELIGION AND SPIRITUALITY

The same cannot be said of religion and gender equity in Ireland. The Catholic Church continues to influence Irish society, and the construction of gender more particularly, to a great extent. Since over 90 percent of Irish women and men identify themselves as Catholic, understanding the church's effect on Irish society, and Irish women, is crucial. Although church control of governmental processes has waned considerably over the past decade or so, an Irish woman repeatedly encounters contradictory messages about her proper role in Irish society. The church tells her one, quite patriarchal, thing, and the media—both Irish and international—tell her something quite different.

Women's Roles

The Catholic Church's position on women's appropriate place is clear. A good Catholic woman has two roles available to her: that of a celibate religious sister (a nun) or that of a mother. Pope John Paul II specifically told Irish women, during a visit to Ireland in 1979, that women should not strive for paid work outside the home: "May Irish mothers, young women and girls not listen to those who tell them that working at a secular job, succeeding in a secular profession, is more important than the vocation of giving life and caring for this life as a mother."[67] The most recent catechism of the Catholic Church, issued in 1994, confirms this idea, indicating that motherhood—if a call to religious life does not appear—is the only worthwhile work for a woman.[68]

Rituals and Religious Practices

In the Catholic Church, seven solemn sacraments exist for practicing Catholics: baptism, first confession, first communion, confirmation, marriage, holy orders (if applicable), and last rites. All Catholics are expected to participate in these sacraments (with the exception of marriage, if one is called to a religious vocation). All sacraments must be administered by a priest of the Catholic Church. The only exception is an emergency baptism, when any practicing Catholic can baptize a dying or gravely ill baby.

In the Catholic Church, men are priests. Women are forbidden to adopt this basic, essential role in the church. The Catholic Church's view of women in the church appears to be one of paternalism and pity. Women are incapable of serving the church because the church has said that they may not. Certainly some priests disagree with the church's stance, yet the stance remains firm. Women's role in the church in Ireland is that of helper, not authority.

Women in many parishes are "allowed" to assist at mass—the fundamental worship service of the Catholic Church—either by helping people to their seats or, after appropriate training, by distributing communion to the congregation. However, they may never lead a mass, and they cannot perform the priestly ritual of transubstantiation, in which—according to Catholic belief—bread and wine are transformed into Christ's body and blood. Since transubstantiation is the centerpiece of Catholic belief, and since women are excluded from performing the ritual, it is fair to say that women's roles in Irish Catholic ritual and religious practices are minimal.

Religious Law

The Church forbids what it calls "artificial" contraception. It declares that the only allowable form of birth control is the rhythm method, in which a woman keeps track of her menstrual cycle and has sex only on what are considered "safe days." This method is notorious for its failure, of course—it results in pregnancy somewhere between 22 percent and 33 percent of the time it is used.[69]

Irish women's experiences with the church and "artificial" contraception are worth noting: a woman called a radio program whose subject was sterilization, contraception, and the Catholic Church. After six children (three of whom were conceived using the rhythm method), this woman had decided to be sterilized, and she was on the pill until the operation. She wanted to obtain absolution (forgiveness) from the parish priest following confession so she could take communion with her son at his first communion. The priest apparently "suggested a compromise solution: that she attend Confession on the Friday, did not take the pill that day, and abstained from sexual intercourse until receiving Communion with her son on the Saturday."[70] The church continues to punish women who are attempting to be good Catholics. "The distress of religious, family-oriented married women, who felt they had to alienate themselves from the sacraments to discharge what they saw as their very real responsibilities to their husbands and children," was clear from these radio programs.[71] Rather than helping Irish women sort through the minefield of sexuality and family life, the church insists on retaining quite rigid rules that few people can obey. As a result, church attendance is falling dramatically.

This means that, although the Catholic Church in Ireland attempts to influence Irish men and women with strict instructions on appropriate behavior, Irish women and men are not paying much attention (although they are not necessarily overtly protesting).[72] Still, Irish culture has been strongly shaped by the church; Irish cultural understandings regarding marriage, sexuality, and family life reflect, either in following or rebelling against, Catholic teachings.

Furthermore, the church tells its flock that marriage is permanent and monogamous. Regardless of the state of one's marriage, the church tells women (and less often men) to remain in marriage. Men who leave are not similarly punished as are women. Indeed, women were most often blamed for driving their husbands away when they were deserted.

But even if an Irish marriage is somewhat successful, how does the church tell women to behave within the marriage? What is clear is that Irish women first of all should wish for children, and many of them. If they do not want a huge family, they should abstain from sex so they do not conceive. Once the family arrives, however, a mother is meant to be self-sacrificing, stoic, strong, and nurturing. The church connects a good Irish mother with the Virgin Mary; it is not clear that the connection is quite so strong in everyday discourse, but Irish women have been shaped by this picture of the ideal mother.[73]

It appears, however, that the Irish cultural construction of mother is changing. Certainly the notion that a mother is strong, stoic, self-sacrificing, and authoritative remains. At the same time, younger women seem to be adopting a more sociable maternal style with their children, focusing on friendly and more equal relationships with their children.[74]

VIOLENCE

By and large, Ireland is not a terrifically violent place. That is to say, the homicide rate in the republic is miniscule in comparison to that of many western countries, as are the assault and rape rates. However, these numbers have been rising in the past ten years, and nonfatal violence against women has been and remains a serious problem.

Domestic Violence

As is true worldwide, women are consistently victimized by domestic abuse in Ireland. Somewhere between 18 percent and 23 percent of Irish women report that their partners have physically attacked them, and close to two thirds of Irish people know someone who has been assaulted violently by her partner.[75] In addition, two thirds of the women murdered in Ireland since 1996 were killed in their homes, and it appears that almost all of the deaths were the result of domestic abuse.[76] Private organizations exist to take hotline calls, to assist women in domestic abuse situations, and to help women bring their assailants to court. Some staunch Catholics believe that such services only encourage women to leave their husbands and to complain about such "silly little things" like emotional abuse.

Until recently, abused women were counseled by their priests to stay with their husbands and "offer it up." Women married to alcoholic men were provided with the same advice. Given that married women had few rights to independent ownership of property or wages until the last decade or so, it must be the case that the church has forced women to remain in violent and abusive marriages; the women had nowhere else to go.

Rape/Sexual Assault

There has been strong resistance to the opening of rape crisis centers as well. Various subterranean conservative Catholic groups have criticized any funding of the Irish National Rape Crisis Center, since they claim that such groups are "promoters of abortion."[77] Indeed, a full-blown constitutional crisis emerged in 1992 regarding abortion—the "Miss X" case, in which the 14-year-old victim of a rape by a friend's father was accused of being the neighborhood "bicycle." That is, some of her neighbors said that she could not have been raped, since she was known to enjoy a good "ride"—Irish slang for sexual intercourse. As is true in so many parts of the world, a woman's level of sexual activity is considered fair game for judging the truth or falsity of her claims of criminal assault. However, an accused rapist's sexual history is not relevant to an allegation of rape. The incidence of rape and sexual assault has risen in Ireland just in the past few years: rape reports have increased by 37 percent in 1998 and 1999, and sexual assault has risen by 13 percent.[78]

OUTLOOK FOR THE TWENTY-FIRST CENTURY

On the whole, Ireland is working very hard at reforming its treatment of women. The Irish government is firmly committed to altering employment, welfare, social policy, and other conditions that affect gender. There are significant changes taking place legislatively that are very encouraging. At least legally, Irish women are well on their way to full equality.

The same cannot be said with regard to women's private lives. Cultural patterns take time to change. Although superficially Ireland has shown tremendous change in the past decade, fundamental cultural understandings surrounding gender, marriage, and family life remain relatively unaltered. Women now are free to work for wages; but with little governmental support for working women, the choice remains a difficult one. Ireland is making huge efforts for gender change; it will continue to do so, but change at the personal level will take more time.

NOTES

1. Central Intelligence Agency (CIA), *World Factbook*, 2000, www.cia.gov/cia/publications/factbook/goes/ie/html.

2. CIA, 2000.

3. The Coombe Hospital, "Annual Clinical Report 1999: Maternal Mortality," 2000, www.coombe.ie./annrp99/mater.htm.

4. CIA, 2000.

5. Paul Anderson, "Ireland the Fairest Place," *Irish Times*, May 31, 2001, www.ireland.com/newspaper/breaking/2001/0308/breakings56.htm.

6. John Ardagh, *Ireland and the Irish: Portrait of a Changing Society* (London: Hamish Hamilton, 1994), 182–85.

7. Patricia Lee, "Report from Ireland from Our Transnational Partner," 2001, www.db=decision.de/Co-Re/Ireland.htm.

8. Lee, 2001.

9. Pat O'Connor, "Ireland: A Country for Women?" 2001, www.social.chass.nscu.edu/jouvert/v4i/oconn.htm.

10. O'Connor, 2001, 11.

11. CIA, 2000.

12. Irish Department of Justice, Equality, and Law Reform, "Mainstreaming Equality between Women and Men in Ireland," 2001, www.ir/gov.ie/justice/Equality/gender/NDP/gender1.htm.

13. Irish Department of Justice, 2001.

14. O'Connor, 2001, 11.

15. Irish Department of Social and Family Affairs, "Maternity Benefits," 2003, families.welfare.ie/publications/sw11.xml.

16. O'Connor, 2001, 11.

17. Irish Department of Social Welfare, 2001.

18. Elizabeth Throop, *Net Curtains and Closed Doors: Intimacy, Family, and Public Life in Dublin* (Westport, CT: Bergin & Garvey, 1999), 94–97.

19. Throop, 1999, 118.

20. Throop, 1999, 139.

21. Throop, 1999, 139.

22. *Catechism of the Catholic Church* (Chicago: Loyola University Press, 1994), §494.

23. Christopher T. Whelan and Tony Fahey, "Marriage and the Family," in *Values*

and Social Change in Ireland, ed. Christopher T. Whelan (Dublin: Gill and Macmillan, 1994), 50–59.

24. Irish Constitution, 13th and 14th Amendments, enacted in 1992.

25. Throop, 1999, 118–20.

26. Throop, 1999, 140–43.

27. Irish Constitution, Article 41.3.2.

28. Kieron Wood, "So you want an Irish divorce?" 2003, www.divorcesupport. com.

29. Patrick Clancy, "Demographic Changes and the Irish Family," in *The Changing Family*, ed. Family Studies Unit, University College Dublin (Dublin: Family Studies Unit, University College Dublin, 1984), 9.

30. Britannica, "Status of Women in Selected Countries," 2001, www.britannica. com/eb/table?eu=126552.

31. Clancy, 1984, 15.

32. Office of the Taoiseach, "Appendix 2: Statistics on Irish Women Who Have Had Abortions in England and Wales," 2001, www.irlgov.ie/taoiseach/publication/ greenpaper/appendix2.htm.

33. Clancy, 1984, 25.

34. O'Connor, 2001, 8.

35. O'Connor, 2001, 8.

36. Ardagh, 1994, 184.

37. Irish Department of Education, 2003, www.education.ie.

38. Throop, 1999, 47, n. 3.

39. Mary Daly, *Women and Poverty* (Dublin: Attic Press, 1989), 93–94.

40. 13th and 14th Amendments, Irish Constitution.

41. Office of the Taoiseach, 2001.

42. O'Connor, 2001, 8.

43. Throop, 1999, 141.

44. Paddy O'Gorman, *Queueing for a Living* (Dublin: Poolbeg, 1994).

45. Irish Department of Health, "Various Statistics Regarding AIDS, Health, and Lifestyle," 2001, www.doh.ie/statistics.

46. Irish Department of Social Welfare, 2001.

47. Irish Department of Health, 2001.

48. Irish Department of Health, 2001.

49. Britannica, 2001.

50. No recent statistics regarding women and heart disease could be found. See Mary Daly (1989, 87–88).

51. Mary B. Codd, "Fifty Years of Heart Disease in Ireland," Irish Heart Foundation, 2001, www.irishheart.ie/news/50yearsofCVD.htm.

52. Irish Department of Health, 2001.

53. Irish Department of Health, 2001.

54. Irish Department of Health, 2001.

55. Irish Department of Health, 2001.

56. Irish Department of Health, 2001.

57. Daly, 1989, 90–91.

58. Lee, 2001.

59. Lee, 2001.

60. O'Connor, 2001, 8.

61. Irish Department of Justice, 2001.

62. Emily O'Reilly, *Masterminds of the Right* (Dublin: Attic Press, 1994), 7–9.

63. O'Reilly, 1994, 7–9.

64. O'Reilly, 1994, 7–9.

65. Oasis. Web site for Irish citizens, 2003, www.oasis.gov.ie.

66. Captain Frederick O'Donovan, Irish Department of Defence, personal communication, June 29, 2001.

67. Throop, 1999, 94.

68. Throop, 1999, 94.

69. O'Reilly, 1994, 45.

70. O'Connor, 2001, 6.

71. O'Connor, 2001, 6.

72. Throop, 1999, 44–46.

73. Throop, 1999, 97.

74. Throop, 1999, 97–109.

75. Higher Education Ireland, "One in Five Irish Women Are Victims of Violence, Says Limerick Report," 2001, www.highereducationireland.com/archive/violence.html; and Women's Aid, "Irish and Worldwide Statistics on Violence against Women," 2001, www.womensaid.ie/pages/domestic/STATS.HTM.

76. Women's Aid, 2001.

77. O'Reilly, 1994, 56.

78. Women's Aid, 2001.

RESOURCE GUIDE

Suggested Reading

Beale, Jenny. *Women in Ireland: Voices of Change*. Dublin: Gill and Macmillan, 1986. A sociological analysis of women's position in 1980s Ireland based on in-depth interviews with close to thirty Irish women.

Bradley, Anthony, and Maryann Gialanella Valiulis, eds. *Gender and Sexuality in Modern Ireland*. Amherst: University of Massachusetts Press, 1997. Containing articles by many of the most respected scholars of Irish history and current society, this work explores women's position in the past and in the present.

Curtin, Chris, Pauline Jackson, and Barbara O'Connor, eds. *Gender in Irish Society*. Galway: Galway University Press, 1987. The editors of this book are among Ireland's finest scholars and have compiled a strong sociological and historical set of discussions.

Levine, June, and Lyn Madden. *Lyn: A Story of Prostitution*. Dublin: Attic Press, 1987. Based on interviews between Irish journalist Lyn Madden and a prostitute she came to know, this is a fine example of oral history and ethnography.

McCafferty, Nell. *In The Eyes of the Law*. Dublin: Poolbeg, 1987. Well-known for her feminist outlook and astute writing style, McCafferty—a journalist—points out many of the flaws in family court and other legal issues in Ireland.

O'Faolain, Nuala. *Are You Somebody? The Accidental Memoir of a Dublin Woman*. New York: Henry Holt and Company, 1996. *Irish Times* columnist's memoirs of Irish feminism and personal history.

Smyth, Ailbhe. *The Abortion Papers: Ireland*. Dublin: Attic Press, 1992. Ailbhe Smyth is one of Ireland's premier feminists.

———. *Irish Women's Studies Reader*. Dublin: Attic Press, 1993.

Videos/Films

Bogwoman. 1997. Directed by Tom Collins. The situation in Northern Ireland is shown through the view of a single mother.

Country. 2000. Directed by Kevin Liddy. Depicts the effect of an aunt who comes to take care of a motherless family in the 1970s.

Magdalene Sisters. 2002. Directed by Peter Mullan. Based on a true story of thousands of "inconvenient" Irish girls who were sent to a Catholic asylum, where they were virtually imprisoned and forced to work in a laundry to atone for their "sins" of being pregnant out of wedlock.

Web Sites

About.com, www.irishculture.about.com/library/blherstory.htm.
An accessible and well-link site on women's history in Ireland.

Irish Academic Press-Women's Studies, www.iap.ie/wmen.htm.

Melissa Thompson, www.tallgirlshorts.net/marymary/.
Prepared by Melissa Thompson, who made *Mary, Mary*, a documentary film about Irish women. Contains filming journals, full transcripts of Thompson's interviews with the women she spoke with during filming, and many other resources.

Women's Education, Research, and Resource Centre at University College Dublin, www.ucd.ie/werrc/.
Extensively linked.

Women's History Group, www.nationalarchives.ie/wh/.
Provides descriptions of thousands of print sources of information on women's history in Ireland.

Organizations

Amnesty International, Irish Section, Women's Action Network
48 Fleet Street, Dublin 2, Ireland
Phone: (+353 1) 677 6361
Fax: (+353 1) 677 6392
Email: info@amnesty.ie
Web site: www.amnesty.ie/netw/wan/wana.shtml

National Women's Council of Ireland
16–20 Cumberland St. South Dublin 2 Ireland
Phone: (+ 353 1) 661 5268/+ 353 1 661 1791
Fax: (+ 353 1) 676 0860
Email: info@nwci.ie
Web site: www.nwci.ie

One of Ireland's oldest feminist organizations.

Well Woman Centre
25 Capel Street, Dublin 1
Phone: (01) 874 9243
Fax: (01) 874 9339
Email: info@wellwomancentre.ie
Web site: www.wellwomancentre.ie

An organization that has been providing low-cost health care to Irish women for years.

SELECTED BIBLIOGRAPHY

Anderson, Paul. "Ireland the Fairest Place for Working Women, Report." *Irish Times*, May 31, 2001. www.ireland.com/newspaper/breaking/2001/0308/breaking56. htm.

Ardagh, John. *Ireland and the Irish: Portrait of a Changing Society*. London: Hamish Hamilton, 1994.

Catechism of the Catholic Church. Chicago: Loyola University Press, 1994.

Central Intelligence Agency (CIA). *World Factbook*. 2000. www.cia.gov/cia/ publications/factbook/goes/ei.html.

Clancy, Patrick. "Demographic Changes and the Irish Family." In *The Changing Family*, edited by the Family Studies Unit, Departments of Social Science, University College Dublin, 1–38. Dublin: Family Studies Unit, Departments of Social Science, University College Dublin, 1984.

Coombe Hospital. "Annual Clinical Report 1999: Maternal Mortality." 2000. www. coombe.ie/annrp99/mater.htm.

Daly, Mary. *Women and Poverty*. Dublin: Attic Press, 1989.

Higher Education Ireland. "One in Five Irish Women Are Victims of Violence, Says Limerick Report." 2001. www.highereducationireland.com/archive/Violence. html.

Irish Constitution. 2001. www.irlgov.ie/taoiseach/publication/constitution/english/ contents.htm.

Irish Department of Health. "Various Statistics regarding AIDS, Health, and Lifestyle." 2001. www.doh.ie/statistics.

Irish Department of Justice, Equality, and Law Reform. "Mainstreaming Equality between Women and Men in Ireland." 2001. www.irlgov.ie/justice/Equality/ Gender/NDP/Gender1.htm.

Irish Department of Social Welfare. "SW4—Section 1—Social Welfare—Payments Explained." 2001. www.welfare.ie/dept/booklets/sw4/sect1.htm.

Lee, Patricia. "Report from Ireland by Our Transnational Partner." European Database: Women in Decision-making. 2001. www.db-decision.de/Co-Re/Ireland. htm.

O'Connor, Pat. "Ireland: A Country for Women?" 2001. www.social.chass.ncsu.edu/ jouvert/v4i/oconn.htm.

O'Donovan, Captain Frederick. Irish Department of Defence. Personal communication, June 29, 2001.

Office of the Taoiseach. "Appendix 2: Statistics on Irish Women Who Have Had Abortions in England and Wales." 2001. www.irlgov.ie/taoiseach/publication/ greenpaper/appendix2.htm.

O'Gorman, Paddy. *Queueing for a Living*. Dublin: Poolbeg, 1994.

O'Reilly, Emily. *Masterminds of the Right*. Dublin: Attic Press, 1994.

Throop, Elizabeth. *Net Curtains and Closed Doors: Intimacy, Family, and Public Life in Dublin*. Westport, CT: Bergin & Garvey, 1999.

Whelan, Christopher T. and Tony Fahey. "Marriage and the Family." In *Values and Social Change in Ireland*, edited by Christopher T. Whelan, 45–81. Dublin: Gill and Macmillan, 1994.

Women's Aid. "Irish and Worldwide Statistics on Violence against Women." 2001. www.womensaid.ie/pages/domestic/STATS.HTM.

20

ITALY

Elizabeth L. Krause

PROFILE OF ITALY

Italy is a Mediterranean nation of 57.8 million people in a land that spans 116,320 square miles. Most Italians now live in urban centers such as Rome, Milan, Naples, Turin, Genoa, Palermo, Bologna, and Florence.[1] Mass migration from rural areas occurred after World War II, as Italians abandoned a largely agricultural way of life and embraced an industrial one. This catapulted Italy into its current position as one of the richest nations in the world. The economy, however, has developed unevenly, with the north being the richest and the south being the poorest part of the country. Central Italy is recognized for its industrial districts consisting of well-developed small and medium-sized firms, many of which are family-run. The economy's strength has relied greatly on a substantial underground economy that has functioned outside government controls, and this "hidden" labor has included a significant number of women.

Italian women have one of the lowest birthrates in the world with 9.3 births per 1,000 women, making for a total fertility rate of 1.2 births.[2] Italians also enjoy a very low infant mortality rate of 5.5 deaths per 1,000 live births.

Maternal mortality rates are among the lowest in the world; between 1990 and 1999, 7 of every 100,000 women who gave birth died in childbirth.[3] Furthermore, Italians have achieved life expectancies that rank among the longest anywhere in the world: men on average live to be 75 years old and women live on average to be 81 years old. The fact that Italian women are having small families and Italians are living longer means that Italy is an aging population. The Italian government officially views the low birth rate negatively, and this places Italian women and men of childbearing years on the hot spot. In light of contemporary population dynamics, a climate of political anxiety has emerged vis-à-vis Italy's future as a viable nation with a viable civil society. As potential reproducers, women in particular find themselves as potential targets of pronatalist policies, discourses, and moods. Alarmist reports in the media scapegoat women and attempt to narrowly define and naturalize women as biological reproducers.[4]

OVERVIEW OF WOMEN'S ISSUES

The low birthrate of Italian women is a historical trend, one that is linked to transformations in the political economy of Italy in particular and Europe in general. Women have gone from having large families in the early 1900s to very small families at the end of the 1990s.[5] Total fertility rates in Italy between 1975 and 1990 dropped from 2.18 to 1.31. These declines have also paralleled an upward shift in women's status, and women have come to achieve levels of education very similar to those of men. Women have many employment opportunities open to them in terms of careers, and the Italian government offers women a progressive maternity leave policy. Within the family, the patriarchal model has largely given way to a belief in partnership, and Italian women have access to contraception and abortion. Health care for women is state sponsored, and women have good access to affordable health care. In the realm of politics and the law, women have achieved great strides. The strides have been limited in the realm of religion, as the Catholic Church has retained its segregation of men and women who serve the church and hence its ban on women priests. Finally, violence against women in Italy exists as elsewhere, and there are ongoing struggles to address this problem.

In many ways, it sounds as though Italian women have arrived at equality and that the struggle is all but over. However, historical and ethnographic research into the everyday lives of Italian women reveals that the lived experiences of Italian women do not measure up to the hopes expressed through policies.

EDUCATION

Opportunities

By the 1970s, gender disparities in education began to disappear. The cohort of students born between 1952 and 1967 witnessed a trend in which women surpassed men in terms of university degrees (5.4 percent of the female population as compared with 5.2 percent of the male population). The same trend has occurred for high school graduates: 34.3 percent of women and 30.2 percent of men from the 1952–1967 cohort received a high school diploma. Opportunities, however, remain uneven in terms of areas of study. For example, the study of literature has become highly "feminized," whereas engineering has remained a male enclave. In the past fifty years, however, gender has been less of a deciding factor than class in terms of the possibilities for using education to improve one's life chances.[6] However, it appears that one's gender influences the chances of reducing the time it takes to finish a degree, and perhaps this has to do with the different expectations of sons as compared with daughters vis-à-vis the family.

There are more working women with a university degree than working men: about 14 percent compared to 10 percent. Perhaps working women are more qualified in terms of educational background than are working men: women who have jobs in Italy are more likely to have a high school diploma (34.7 percent) than their male counterparts (28.5 percent).[7]

Literacy

Literacy rates in Italy are hardly a concern given that 96 to 98 percent of the population is considered literate. The female literacy rate, at 96 percent, lags only slightly behind that of male literacy, at 98 percent.[8]

EMPLOYMENT AND THE ECONOMY

Job/Career Opportunities

The antidiscrimination law of 1977 (n. 903) prohibited discrimination based on sex, marital status, family situation, or pregnancy regarding access to work in all sectors and at all levels of the professional hierarchy. This law attempted to address a longstanding reality: women's participation in Italy's work force has been underrepresented, devalued, and hidden. Indeed, there is good reason to believe that women's paid economic activity has not been reliably reported in national statistics dating from the late 1800s and continuing through the present.[9]

Much of women's work has historically been hidden, and this trend continued into the late twentieth century. Numerous Italian women

Italian woman reading a newspaper at an outdoor café in Florence. Photo © Painet.

work in the "informal" sector of the economy. They often perform finishing work from their homes, and women in this sector are rarely if ever counted in labor statistics even though they may spend long hours working. These long hours result in part from the low wages they receive, particularly for piecework. These women subsist on the bottom rung of the subcontracting ladder, where they are deprived of employment benefits. Women often accept jobs as outworkers as a matter of "choice" because they can work out of their homes and hence be there when their children come home from school. Furthermore, they do enjoy at least the semblance of autonomy. However, outworkers provide an advantage to business owners because they are more flexible and less costly than regular employees.[10] As a strategy to evade an inferior status and identity, young women have sought professionalism through education, and the data suggest their education levels have surpassed men's. Yet Italian women earn only about 31 percent of their male counterparts' pay.

There is widespread popular belief that Italian women did not work "before," that now they do work, and that this conflict between work and family is to blame for the very small families now so prevalent in Italy. This popular belief is more reflective of ideas about how women are supposed to behave—idealized notions of motherhood—than how the majority of women led their lives in the past. Notions about proper roles of motherhood are also closely linked to the changes in the postwar economy, social classes, and identities. The *casalingua*, or housewife, became a symbol of prestige in the postwar era. Because women's paid labor was often done in the context of home-based workshops, it became fairly easy to erase in people's memories.

The media have perpetuated stereotypes of the historical, nonworking Italian woman and juxtaposed these against expert opinions of demographers, who depict the birthrate as a national problem. It often seems that women are being defined as the demographic scapegoats. One famous demographer went so far as to draw an analogy between anorexic teenagers who refused to eat food and Italians who refused to procreate.[11]

Italian women are joining the work force more rapidly than men, according to official statistics; however, this may actually be because as the new generation of working women increasingly becomes employed as professionals, it gives the appearance of a "massive entry" of women entering the work force. These numbers do not take account of women who have historically worked for pay in the hidden, or informal, economy.

Italian women have increasingly sought professionalization, yet they remain underrepresented in professional and technical fields. For example, whereas female administrators and managers comprise almost 54 percent of the work force, female professional and technical workers make up less than 20 percent of the work force. The glass ceiling appears to be solidly in place: the National Council for Economy and Labor (CNEL) reported that for 1998, women made up 3 percent of executives in large firms, 5 percent in mid-size firms, and 8 percent in small firms. In 1992, a law was passed to offer incentives for women entrepreneurs (law n. 215).

The *Hollywood Reporter* recognized Italian women filmmakers for breaking through barriers in filmmaking. In the 1990s, the number of women working in the film industry rose by about 30 percent, and the number of women-directed films has more than doubled. Of the ninety-nine Italian feature films produced in 1996, women directed thirteen. In 1997, Italian women formed the lobby group, Women in Audio Visuals, dedicated to promoting common interests such as cultural identity.[12]

Certain high-profile industries in Italy make for unique if not precarious opportunities for women. With Milan having topped Paris in fashion, for example, many young women head there in search of a modeling career. Italy does not have age restrictions for modeling. In March 2001, the *New York Times* reported the case of a fifteen-year-old aspiring model from Slovenia who had been drugged and raped at a Milan nightclub and the modeling agency that faced charges of abandonment of a minor.[13]

Official statistics report that unemployment hits women harder than men. Unemployment for women in 1999 was 16.8 percent as compared to 9.6 percent for men. For young adults (ages fifteen to twenty-four), unemployment reached 39 percent for women overall (66.9 percent in the south) as compared with 30.2 percent for men (53.5 percent in the south).[14]

Pay

Women's salaries in Italy are 20 percent lower than men's for comparable work, according to research conducted by the Labor Institute of the Italian General Confederation of Labor (*Confederazione Generale Italiana del Lavoro*/CGIL), or 23.5 percent lower according to research conducted by Eurostat.[15] The figures only take into account comparable work. The lower salaries for equivalent work together with the lower representation in the highest-paying professions may explain how the United Nations Development Programme in 2001 calculated women's share of earned income at 31 percent of men's. It ranked Italy twenty-sixth in its scale of gender empowerment measures: Sweden held the Number 1 spot.

Working Conditions

Sexual Harassment

The view of sexual harassment as a problem that prevents the attainment of gender parity is a highly controversial one in Italy. The courts have not consistently offered progressive rulings in this area. For example, in March 2001, Italy's highest court of appeals in Rome ruled that "a pat on a woman's bottom is not sexual harassment, provided that it is an 'isolated and impulsive act.'"[16] The high court overturned a lower court's guilty verdict against a public health agency manager accused by a woman employee. She had also claimed that the manager threatened to "damage her career if she reported the incident."

National labor unions have begun to recognize sexual harassment as a problem and have incorporated ad hoc provisions against sexual harassment in national labor contracts. These provisions appear to have served as a deterrent in the public as well as private sector. The women's hotline, *Telefono Rosa*, based in Rome, reported a decrease in workplace sexual harassment during 1997. Nevertheless, at least 728,000 women in Italy report enduring workplace harassment at least once in their lives, and some 236,000 women say they experienced it in the past three years.[17]

According to a human rights report, the Labor Ministry in December 1999, along with major trade union confederations, agreed on a workplace sexual harassment code of conduct. The code follows a 1991 EU recommendation. The intent is that it will be attached to national labor contracts in different sectors as they are negotiated.[18]

Support for Mothers/Caretakers

A woman's personal life can jeopardize her employment. For example, in one case, a male factory owner pushed out a female employee, telling her that there was no work for her. She believed that the firm had laid her off indefinitely after learning she was to be married. She was pursuing a lawsuit against the firm through the Camera di Commercio, the labor office, but the best she could hope for was one year's compensation. In another case, a young woman was "let go" when her employers caught wind of a love affair getting serious.[19]

Italian women continue to experience lives unequal to those of men. However, female employees in a Sicilian sweater factory took the matter into their own hands. Their "solution" caught the attention of high-up union officials and the international media. The women had supposedly voluntarily agreed to take turns becoming pregnant. Their idea was to avoid losing a job once they married or became pregnant. By avoiding simultaneous maternity leaves, they hoped to quell their employer's fears of a critical mass of its workers all taking maternity leave at the same time. The union, however, objected because it seemed that the employer was meddling in the personal lives of the workers.[20] A spokesperson for the union expressed the view that women should have the right to choose when they want to have a child, and that this important decision should not be determined by exigencies of production.

Maternal Leave

For at least three decades, the Italian government has recognized the importance of requiring that employers grant working women paid leave after having a baby. In theory, Italy has been very progressive in its maternity leave policies. The antidiscrimination law of 1977, for example, stipulated that men should receive equal treatment regarding missing work to care for children. In practice, however, women have often suffered from workplace discrimination once an employer learned they were getting married or expecting a child. A report on human rights noted, "Liberal maternity leave, introduced to benefit women, adds to the cost of employing them, with the result that employers sometimes find it advantageous to hire men instead."[21] A new law was passed in March 2000 to lessen the risk that love and marriage have posed for young, working women.

The preexisting maternity policy allowed women twenty weeks of leave, including eight weeks before the birth, paid at 80 percent of the salary. Women working in the public sector were offered an extra four weeks at 100 percent of earnings; after the birth, they could take another sixteen weeks of leave at 30 percent of their pay. Furthermore, once new mothers returned to work, they could reduce their workday during the child's first year by two hours without losing any pay. Under the old law, leave was granted only to the mother, who could transfer it to the father.

The new law (n. 53/2000), effective March 8, 2000, extends leave to fathers and even has incentives to encourage fathers to take at least three months in a row. Each parent can take up to six months of leave or ten months combined during the first three years of the child's life. If, however, the father takes three months in a stretch, the couple's maximum leave is extended by one month as a sort of bonus. The amount of pay is 100 percent during the first thirty days of leave. Thereafter, it is 30 percent except in low-income cases, in which it may be calculated at a higher rate. If, between the ages of three and eight years old, the child gets sick, parents get up to ten days of leave, and special leave is granted to parents of children with handicaps for up to three years. Leave applies to single parents as well as to parents who adopt babies.[22]

In extending paid leave to fathers, the new law in theory diffuses the targets of discrimination so that employers have less motivation to scapegoat women as the culprits of threatened loss of production. Indeed, the new law allows fathers potentially more leave than mothers: a maximum of seven as compared with six months.

The parental leave law of March 8, 2000, may remedy problems of workplace discrimination because of the way it includes men in the leave benefits. A thirty-two-page booklet, produced by the Provincial Commission on Equal Opportunity in Prato, Tuscany, blends humor and pragmatism as it attempts to educate citizens about the new policy: parents, whether fathers or mothers, married or unmarried, have the right to parental leave. The tension between work and family is illustrated in the booklet in a scene in which the expectant father bursts into his boss's office: "Boss! I'm expecting a baby!" "Tell your wife's employer," replies an irritated boss.

"Look, boss, with the law of 'March 8' I'm also having the baby!" The boss, pictured with a question mark, appears worried.

Of course, one is left wondering how the law will function. Will many Italian men take the parental leave they have coming to them under the new law? Although the previous maternity leave law dating from 1971 did include men, the new law includes structures and incentives for men to actually take advantage of the leave. The new law applies to both the mother and the father of a new baby, whether they work in the public or private sector. The characters in the booklet explain the way it works: "Can I take leave even if Sylvia [his expectant partner] doesn't have a job?" the "expectant" young man asks his father, who plays the role of public educator. "Certainly," the father explains. "It's a right and a responsibility for a father to be near his own children!"

The law is the realization of long-studied principles by the Italian Commission on Equal Opportunity. It was designed to foster equilibrium in terms of time demands that plague contemporary, urban society: juggling work, caretaking, and personal relations as well as family responsibilities. At the core of the law is the commitment to a structure that encourages parents to spend more time with their children. The law does this in several ways. First, it grants postpartum leave of up to six months per parent. Second, it attends to the daily needs of working parents and promotes social solidarity through up to two 2-hour "rest periods" in the middle of the working day.

Of course, there are other motivations besides economic: "Daddy!" shouts an anxiety-ridden, angry young woman pictured on the back cover of the booklet. "The psychologist told me I lacked a father figure." "It's not my fault!!" replies her balding father, sweat pouring from his head. "There was hardly anything like the law of 'March 8' in my days!"[23]

Daycare

About 92 percent of three-to-five-year-olds in Italy attended early childhood programs in 1992. Most of these programs in Italy were public. The high participation rates can be explained in part by sliding fee scales that allowed children from families of all income levels to participate and by programs that offered full-day services, which are particularly convenient for working parents.[24]

The study, commissioned for the Subcommittee on Children and Families, examined programs in Denmark, France, and Italy because of their high-quality, early-childhood care. In Italy, as well as in France and Denmark, early childhood teachers receive from 2 to 3.5 years of specialized training, and their salaries were equal to or only slightly lower than those of elementary school teachers there. The teachers were public employees and received the expected benefits: pensions, sick leave, and health care. Teacher-student ratios were the lowest in Italy, ranging from 5:1 to 7.6:1.

Approaches to caretaking emphasized balance as well as the physical, emotional, social, cognitive, and expressive skills appropriate to developmental ages.

Italy's reputation for high-quality, publicly funded daycare has resulted in a growing number of preschools in the United States being modeled after the most well-known of the Italian preschools: the Reggio-Emilia program.[25] "High quality" also refers to the food served. Local parents serve as taste-testers of the food. Eating is considered a social time and an opportunity for socialization.[26]

Family and Medical Leave

The law of March 8, 2000, also allows parents to take up to ten days off of work when their children under eight years old become sick. Special leave is also given to parents of handicapped children up to three years of age.

Inheritance and Property Rights

Italian women enjoy equal rights to inheritance and property ownership. This principle of gender equality was realized in May 1975, when legislation on family rights abolished dowry payments. This ended a practice in which individual property ownership was powerfully linked to the patriarchal family form and in which marriage was essentially an exchange between two families—or, in reality, between two male heads of family via the bride.

Social/Government Programs

Welfare and Welfare Reform

Welfare in Italy covers retirement pensions, survivors' pensions, sickness benefits, invalidity, family benefits, and unemployment benefits. In 1991, it was possible for a sixty-two-year-old to retire and receive a pension. Normal retirement age in the public sector, however, is sixty-five. In the private sector, the age is set at fifty-five for women and sixty for men. Pensions in the private sector kick in after fifteen years of contributions, and full pensions are paid after forty years. In general, pensions are calculated by years of contributions and average earnings during the previous five years. Annual ceilings apply, as do cost-of-living increases. Pensions of 60 percent are paid to survivors of insured people with five years of contributions. Surviving children are paid 20 percent each up to three children.

Sickness benefits provide 20 percent of earnings and then a generous 66.6 percent after twenty-one days if the claimant is not in the hospital. Workers whose ability to work is reduced by one third due to sickness or infirmity are eligible for an invalidity allowance. A formula based on years of insurance contributions and average earnings during the past five years is used to calculate the amount. An incapacity pension is available to workers who are permanently incapable of any work.

Family benefits, which are added to the monthly salary, are calculated according to the family income and number of children eighteen years old or younger. In 1990, for an employee earning from 1.75 to 2 million lire per month (then about US$1,050–1,200), she would qualify for a monthly benefit of 110,000 per month (about US$65). The benefit decreases as the salary increases.

Unemployment benefits equal 20 percent of the average daily wages over the previous three months but only for 180 days. The rate climbs to two thirds of the wage when unemployment is due to "redundancy" or closure.[27]

FAMILY AND SEXUALITY

In the past several decades, doctrines of the Italian state and church have claimed that they embrace an egalitarian ethic concerning women and family matters. Of course, this claim must be evaluated in the light of the Catholic Church's opposition toward any types of family planning other than the "natural," or rhythm, method. Italian women's varied experiences of family and sexuality are deeply connected to the history of the patriarchal family, on the one hand, and the legal replacement of that family form with an egalitarian model, on the other.

Gender Roles

Relations between men and women witnessed profound processes of change in the 1950s and 1960s, which then "culminated explosively in the 1970s," notes Italian social historian and feminist Luisa Passerini. Nevertheless, gender equality and egalitarian ideals have yet to be realized in practice. The reason for these ideas' explosiveness can be understood from the context in which the struggles were launched and then played out:

> The stage on which these changes took place was a country of patriarchal traditions, imbued with the Mediterranean stereotype of a privileged relationship between the mother and the male child, on which Catholicism and fascism had insistently played, in different ways, to establish their ideological domination.[28]

The doctrines adopted since the 1960s and laws passed since the 1970s can be best appreciated with a brief overview of prior church and state positions that reveal the patriarchal bent. The papal encyclical of 1930 (*Casti connubii*) naturalized the role of women as divinely responsible for the "procreation and education of offspring." The encyclical stressed the valid-ity of a gender-based hierarchy of authority within the family and went so far as to depict women's emancipation as perverting family life.[29] In the same period, fascist family laws naturalized women as reproducers for the state. Bodies were needed to populate the new Italian colonies in Africa. In 1926, the fascist government defined abortion and the spread of any birth control information as "crimes of state."[30] New civil codes between 1939 and 1942 limited women's ability to work, reinforcing regulations that forbade women from leaving the "conjugal home 'without just cause.' "[31] There is good evidence that many Italian women as well as men resisted these narrow definitions of their personhood.[32] One woman told oral his-torian Luisa Passerini that after having three children she turned to abor-tion: "I would have had more, but you didn't to spite Mussolini, you see."[33] A male worker spoke of his response to a meeting pushing the demographic campaign: "They wanted me to have children—to go home and—if you'll excuse the expression—jump on the wife. But who would be so daft? There was already so much misery, damn it! So I couldn't swallow that."[34] As a group, Sicilian artisans made the transition from large to small families during the interwar period through skillful coitus inter-ruptus. In their ethnographic research, Jane and Peter Schneider learned from informants that avoidance of conception required "skill and control on the part of the husband, and considerable cooperation and communi-cation between husband and wife, particularly if they cared (as most did) that the woman continue to experience sexual pleasure."[35]

Fascist health programs medically systematized maternity as a strategy to ensure national salvation; one effect was that breastfeeding practices were subject to intense measurements, schedules, and routines, such as the *doppia pesata*, double weighing. This practice, designed to monitor intake, required that babies be weighed before and after each feeding and that the grams be carefully recorded. When intake did not measure up to expecta-tions, women were advised to "top off," or supplement, the breast milk. Women were advised to nurse according to rigid schedules, and this further undermined milk supplies. The effects of these fascist policies have been lasting. "Fascist-era norms of scientific mothering that initially could not take hold in the face of practical considerations . . . are now observed scru-pulously."[36] The origins have been forgotten, but "parenting norms from the fascist period have become fixed in popular memory."[37]

Only beginning in the postwar period did Italian legal and religious structures begin to shift toward granting women equal rights with men. By the 1960s, papal pronouncements came to reflect the "changing needs of a changing society" and to emphasize "reciprocal love and shared com-panionship and play down the insistence on a hierarchical ranking stressed in earlier documents."[38]

Legal reform touched on the most intimate of women's issues with the introduction of the divorce bill in 1970 (law n. 898). The law persevered in a hostile environment that included a failed referendum that sought to overturn it. Repercussions were profound as this law cracked open feminist debates. The Italian state officially sought to undo the patriarchal elements of the family in 1975 with the passage of family rights legislation (law n. 151). This law promoted equality between husband and wife within the context of the family. It obliterated the official position of the husband as *capo della famiglia*, or head of household, symbolized in part by requiring women to adopt her husband's surname. It stipulated that husband and wife should mutually decide where to live after marriage and together direct family life. It no longer forced those who married foreigners to lose their Italian citizenship. It required that the husband and wife together exercise authority over children. And it insisted that couples hold property in common.[39] A document on Family Benefits and Family Policies in Europe explains, "This new family aims, at least in theory, at setting up an intense community between spouses who jointly agree upon a single family path and exercise their parental authority, while respecting the personality and bents of their children."[40] It is clear that legal reforms have challenged patriarchal rule; less clear is the effectiveness of these challenges. The author of a 2001 report on the Italian family noted that "Care of the house, children and elderly continue to be almost exclusively women's responsibility."[41] Gender equality is an expressed societal goal yet one that remains an ongoing struggle.

Marriage

Couples' crossing of the threshold into marriage has become an increasingly rare and delayed event in Italy since the mid-1970s. Between 1984 and 1994, the number of first-time marriages declined from 284,612 to 268,738. This represents a drop of 707 to 599 per 1,000 for males and from 688 to 625 for 1,000 females. The average age of first marriage, however, has continued to rise between 1984 and 1994, from 27.4 to 29.3 years for grooms and from 24.3 to 26.5 years for brides.

Divorce, meanwhile, has risen to proportions once unheard of in Italy, with about 27,500 marriages ending in divorce in 1994—a level that one divorce scholar believes will be fairly constant. Divorce remains a fairly complicated and lengthy affair; the legal waiting between separation and divorce was decreased from five to three years in 1987.[42] The quick and simple thirty-day divorce is unheard of in Italy. This kind of structural restraint favors the prolonging of the marriage institution, and it is one of several factors that leads young adults to avoid entering casually into marriage. In fact, long engagements are common and engagements lasting for as long as fifteen years are recorded.[43] Perhaps it is not surprising, then, that Italians have among the lowest divorce rates of any Europeans: In 1994, 8 per 100 marriages ended in divorce in Italy. In Austria, the rate was 34, in France 35, and in England 44.

One should not necessarily conclude that the rise in broken unions in the western world over the last thirty years indicates an increase in conjugal unhappiness and an erosion in partner rapport. Rather, broken unions signal a drastic weakening of traditional norms that subordinated couples to matrimonial bonds. They also signal a significant strengthening of new social norms of self-determination, particularly those that value individual desires over those of the couple.

Meanwhile, tying the knot has become an increasingly egalitarian affair in Italy. Consensus between the man and woman has replaced the hierarchical ideal of the marital relationship. Nevertheless, the specter of patriarchy continues to cast its shadow over the current generation. Undoubtedly, memories of old patriarchal practices in part make young lovers wary of embracing marriage, whether they do so through a civil union or church ceremony. This patriarchal structure once was such that individuals did not have the power to decide their own fate. Rather, it was decided for them, either by their parents or by the *padrone*.

In central Italy, for example, under the *mezzadria* system of sharecropping, which persisted well into the twentieth century, relationships were determined by a model of patriarchal authority: a rigid hierarchy of positions and of roles defined according to age, sex, and birth order. The social structure of agricultural families was designed to deny autonomy to the younger adult family members and to vest authority in the head of household, typically the senior male, known as the *capofamiglia*, *capoccia*, *capoccaito*, or *capo*. Parents sought to control their children's marital decisions, postmarital residence, work duties, and finances. Beside the *capofamiglia* was the *massaia*, typically his wife, who often comanaged household finances. Although she directed the household, her role ultimately affirmed patriarchal authority because of its focus on the family environment.

In the first half of the twentieth century, this rigid patriarchal family structure began to unravel. Mounting tensions led to a "peasant protest, particularly by women and youth, not so much against the countryside itself as against the rigidity of the pecking-order in the family and against their close economic dependence on its older male members."[44] For the generation that would now be of marriageable age, the challenge of replacing the patriarchal family with a democratic family remains incompletely realized. It is not an easy thing for women, who have derived much of their power as mothers through food,[45] to relinquish this realm of influence to fathers or hired caretakers or to find ways of sharing it.

Reproduction

The "logics" of a patriarchal society and of a capitalist economy have led to a portrayal of Italian women primarily in reproductive terms. The "weak" image of women contrasts with the "strong" role that women played historically in family economies.[46] In part, the trend toward very small families reflects a desire on the part of women to define themselves other than as mothers and housewives. Even though their mothers and grandmothers may have had strong identities besides family nurturers and household caretakers—say, as weavers or artisans—the fascist gender regime and the postwar political Catholic culture that followed went a long way toward making modern women feel that the moral way to define themselves was as a mother and housewife. The postwar consumer culture of central Italy meant that women became obsessed with their homes. In fact, one joke in Prato, northwest of Florence, is that you live for your house rather than having a house to live in. Prato is a place where language teachers in the mid-1990s used words like "obsession" and "fixation" to describe how women think about the condition of their homes. People there keenly remember the postwar period, when buying a refrigerator was a material acquisition with huge symbolic power that revealed to others that you were not a poor person. Such acquisitions still distance you from the "low-class folk," as does the small family.

The one-child family by 1996 had become the most "typical," with 43.8 percent of couples with children having a single child, as compared with 42.5 percent having two children and only 13.5 percent having three or more children.[47] These record-low birthrates, however, do not mean that mothering has become any less intense for Italian women. In fact, a "culture of responsibility" surrounds Italian motherhood. These motherly obligations, linked to the birth of the modern family and bourgeois notions of child-rearing,[48] mean that Italian women invest vast amounts of time and energy in educating, feeding, clothing, and nurturing children.

Sex Education

The Associazione Italiana per L'Educazione Demografica (AIED), the Italian Association of Demographic Education, offers courses to middle school students in some Italian provinces. There is also a proliferation of sex education sites written for and by Italians through the World Wide Web.[49]

Contraception and Abortion

Abortion was legalized in 1978, and contraceptive devices were made readily available in local pharmacies in the mid-1970s. With pressure from various lobbies, including the AIED, the Ministry of Health in 1976 finally overturned norms established in 1926–1927, during the height of the fascist campaign, to increase the birthrate and to eliminate birth control practices. Fascism designated abortion and also the dissemination of birth control information as crimes against the state. Women and men, however, continued to resist the fascist pronatalist campaign and to practice covert birth control.[50]

Women's right to a safe and legal abortion in 1978 (law n. 194) marked another state-level move away from patriarchy and toward women's equality. Abortion is allowed during the first twelve weeks of pregnancy for "medical, psychological, and social reasons." After the first trimester, a pregnancy can be terminated only "if there is danger to her health or a particular anomaly in the fetus."[51] Central to Italian feminist debates about abortion has been the right to sovereignty that women have over their own bodies. The arguments attributed to the legalization of abortion put an end to the "social catastrophe" of clandestine abortions, which particularly afflicted poorer and less educated women.[52]

More recently, those opposing abortion point to "diffuse female irresponsibility." Debates over abortion have increased in importance in light of a "conscientious objector" clause that allows doctors to opt out of performing abortions. Increasing numbers of doctors have declared themselves objectors, and this trend has posed a serious obstacle to obtaining legal abortions in some regions. The number of legal abortions in Italy fell between 1980 and 1990: from 220,263 in 1980, to 210,192 in 1985, and to 161,285 in 1990.[53] Presented another way, abortion rates peaked in 1983 at 16.9 abortions per 1,000 women to 9.8 per 1,000 in 1993. The age distribution of abortion rates has also shifted. In 1981, women aged 25–29 were the group to most frequently seek out an abortion; in 1991, women aged 30–34 registered the highest rates.[54]

Italy's abortion ratios (the number of abortions per 1,000 live births) are higher than those of other European countries. The abortion ratio reached a peak of 390 per 1,000 in 1984 and a low of 261 per 1,000 in 1992. For the most part, the southern regions and islands have the highest fertility rates and the lowest abortion ratios. However, official measurements do not take account of clandestine abortions, which may be performed by a physician but not reported. Clandestine practices are estimated to be the highest in the southern regions.[55]

Married women have the majority of abortions.[56] For example, in 1991 single women accounted for 38 percent of abortions and married women the remaining 62 percent. However, unmarried women more frequently terminate their pregnancies: 61 percent of conceptions among single women as compared with 15 percent of conceptions among married women are believed to be terminated. Level of education also seems to make a difference when age is also considered: among adolescents, the higher the education level, the higher the abortion rates; however, among married women aged 20–39, abortion rates declined as education increased. It has been speculated "that the choice to terminate the pregnancy may represent a symbol of emancipation among older women, for whom the family context has been characterized by the use of traditional contraceptive methods (e.g., withdrawal) and a traditional division of gender roles."[57]

Teen Pregnancy

Italy's teen pregnancy levels are among the lowest of European Union countries. The fertility rate in 1990–1995 was 9 births per 1,000 Italian girls aged 15–19. This compares with an average European Union rate of 15 per 1,000.[58] In Italy, teenagers under eighteen years old do not have ready access to abortion. Legislation requires parental consent or judicial authorization. In 1991, abortion rates among teenagers aged 15–19 remained the lowest category (4.6 per 1,000).

Teen pregnancy is not at epidemic proportions in Italy; however, this is not to say that teens are not sexually active. In fact, the years 1969–1978 are referred to as a "shock period" because of the sexual revolution that occurred. Regardless of age, place of residence, or level of instruction, young women of all cohorts demonstrated a sudden increase in the incidence of the first sexual rapport.[59]

HEALTH

Italy has a national health system as well as a separate private system. Since the early 1970s, the national system has been decentralized, with twenty regions as well as two autonomous provinces permitted to enact legislation and manage care. Regional policies are often in response to directives from the Ministry of Health. The ministry takes charge of public awareness programs and has run several such campaigns on reproductive health issues such as HIV/AIDS, breast cancer, menopause, and breastfeeding. In terms of overall reproductive and sexual health, Italy was rated first in a 2001 evaluation of 133 nations. The Sexual and Reproductive Health Risks study, authored by Population Action International (PAI) and the international relief agency CARE, assessed nations according to the following: availability of contraceptives, prenatal medical care, HIV infection rates; HIV education programs and medical care for the infected, disease-caused infertility, abortion availability, women's pregnancy-related deaths, spacing between births, and fertility rates.[60]

Health Care Access

Despite the high reproductive and sexual health rating received by Italy, the Women's Environment and Development Organization reported in 1999 that "expenditures on motherhood and family welfare are among the lowest in Europe." Furthermore, access to health care varies between the wealthier northern regions and the poorer southern regions.

Immigrant women tend to be at a disadvantage in terms of health care access, and municipalities as well as special commissions have recently initiated outreach programs to inform immigrants of their rights to seek health care: legal immigrants, that is, those with a work permit, share the same rights with Italian citizens; those without papers have free access to maternity care. Health care providers at family health-counseling centers and hospitals promise not to report illegal residents to immigration authorities.[61]

Diseases and Disorders

AIDS

The number of adults and children estimated to be living with HIV or AIDS in Italy as of 1999 is 95,000, a rate of 0.35 percent of the total population. Of those, 35,000 are women and 700 are children 0–14.[62] The Ministry of Health, with support from private groups such as clothing multinational Benetton, has sponsored several nationwide HIV/AIDS education campaigns. Regional health agencies have conducted more small-scale programs.

Eating Disorders

Approximately 230,000 women in Italy reported suffering from eating disorders as compared with 118,000 men, according to the National Conference on Mental Health in January 2001.[63]

Cancer

The National Tumor Institute's award-winning project, "Women, Illness, and Healing," since its initiation in 2000 has sought to develop a personalized treatment approach by attending to psychological, emotional, and communication exigencies. The pilot project focuses on breast-related pathologies.[64] A growing awareness of the connection between environmental toxins and cancer development has resulted in a grassroots movement to seek out locally grown foods from trustworthy "peasants" or farmers.

Depression

According to the World Health Report 2000, Italian women suffer from major depression at much higher rates than men (64 percent to 36 percent). A report from the Women's Health Prevention Center in Naples concludes that issues related to women's mental health have been overlooked as a priority problem. The authors note a "lack of attention toward women's mental health and the absence of an integrated gender approach" related to health policies, empirical research, clinical practices, prevention, and health education. The report urges that measures be taken to correct this gender gap.[65] For instance, studies of Italian women in abusive marriages have revealed that frequently the consequences of violence against women has ranged from depression to eating disorders.[66]

POLITICS AND LAW

Suffrage

Despite a strong suffrage movement in the late 1890s and numerous petitions in the early 1900s, Italian women had to wait until 1945 to exercise their voting rights. At the close of World War I, in 1919, voting rights were universally extended to males twenty-one years of age; however, women were excluded, and this exclusion was based on three justifications: lack of female military service, illiteracy, and the "lesser needs" of women.

Benito Mussolini, the fascist dictator elected in 1922, publicly expressed his support of women suffrage, and in 1925, a new law opened administrative elections to women voters. But before women could really become involved in the political process, he abolished elections altogether. With the fall of Mussolini and fascism in 1945, the right to vote was extended to all female Italian citizens. The one exception—prostitutes—was eventually abolished.

Political Participation

In 1984, a national equal opportunity commission was established, with revisions in 1988. The promotion of women's presence in local as well as provincial governments received a boost in 1993 by requiring local entities to ensure equal representation of women in elections (law n. 81). The requirements of this law were realized in some regional elections in the late 1990s, requiring that election lists include equal numbers of male and female candidates. Data from the Inter-Parliamentary Union places Italy seventy-first among 118 rankings for the number of women serving in its national parliament. As of the May 2001 elections, the Camera dei Deputati (Lower House) had women sitting in sixty-two out of 630 seats, or 9.8 percent, and in the Senato della Repubblica (Upper House) women occupied twenty-five out of 321 seats, or 7.8 percent. The deputies and senators are elected to serve five-year terms.[67]

Women's Rights

Feminist Movements

The birth of the Italian women's movement dates to July 1970, "when the manifesto of *Rivolta femminile* was posted up in the streets of Rome and Milan."[68] The manifesto rejected a definition of women in relation to men, and, as such, embraced a separatist agenda. The decade that unfolded marked Italian feminism's greatest inroads; the movement had clear agendas to legalize contraception, abortion, and divorce, and it accomplished these goals. A commitment to what has come to be known as "separate spheres feminism"[69] led to the formation of women's centers or cooperatives, which were single-gendered spaces that enabled women to relate primarily to other women and to develop *affidamento*, or trust, with older, more experienced women who served as mentors for younger women.[70] Communication and cultural practices were challenged and altered, and in the 1980s these changes led to important new policies, such as the publication of a text on nonsexist language developed by a national commission on equal opportunity. Women also became more visible through the arts, such as in literature and cinema, as well as through oral histories.[71]

At a local level, activist feminists (not necessarily associated with centers) struggle for democratic families in which men, women, and children contribute to domestic duties of cooking, cleaning, laundering, and ironing; to the nurturing of children; and to the household income when old enough to do so.

Lesbian Rights

Sexual orientation is not covered as a nondiscrimination category in the Italian Constitution, and there are no laws that protect gays and lesbians per se. However, the penal code does include related categories of gender, race, and religion. Furthermore, gay men and lesbians fired due to their sexual orientation have a good record of winning their cases; however, those fired by homophobic firms under the guise of reasons besides sexual orientation have not had legal success. Military service, required of men in Italy (though a civil service option is available to conscientious objectors), has been a cloudy issue for gays because of the issue of "sexual perversion," one of the possible reasons for being excused from service. Italy's gay and lesbian movement is working to change discriminatory law, and proposals have been introduced (in 1996 and 1999) in the Italian Parliament to ban discrimination based on sexual orientation. According to a World Legal Survey, because of the debate in Italian society about revising the Constitution, the country's gay and lesbian movement is launching a campaign to include "sexual orientation." *Arcigay* is the main gay association in Italy.[72]

Marriage. Italian law does not recognize same-sex marriage. Numerous members of parliament have presented proposals to sanction gay and lesbian unions, and their bills sought the official registration of domestic partnerships and extension of rights associated with heterosexual families. However, "None of these bills has ever been discussed in the Parliament, and they are unlikely to be discussed in the future."[73]

Parenthood. Gay and lesbian couples, as well as singles, are excluded from adopting children because Italian law allows only married couples to adopt. Granting custody to a single person is up to a judge's discretion. Medically assisted artificial insemination is not available to single women and lesbians. This status results from a 1994 internal regulation of the Professional Order of Doctors. The trend in parliament, backed by the leadership of all Italian political parties except the Rifondazione Comunista, has been to introduce bills that "limit access to medically assisted artificial insemination to married women or to unmarried women who live in a stable heterosexual relationship."[74]

Military Service

In 1981, women were legally allowed to join the ranks of state police. On September 29, 1999, the Italian Parliament gave final approval (273 to 9, lower house) to allow women to volunteer for the military. Italian men face ten months of mandatory service. Up to that point, Italy was the only NATO member that had not had women in its armed forces.

VIOLENCE

Insufficient progress has been made toward halting domestic violence against women and girls in Italy, according to a study released in 2000 by the UNICEF Innocenti Research Centre in Florence.[75] The first nationwide survey of violence, conducted by the national research institute IS-TAT, reported that at least 9.4 million women (aged 14–59) had experienced "some form of sexual violence." As of 2001, there were approximately sixty local women's associations maintaining and running shelters.[76]

Domestic Violence

There is concern that violence against women has been inadequately addressed. A 2002 study comparing battered women and children in Italy and the United States "found that family violence in Italy is a social reality at odds with the national ideology of family unity and cohesion." The ideology of "the family," indeed, may account for the "widespread neglect of the problem in Italian research circles and the media."[77]

The study, published in the *Journal of Family Violence*, was based on a sample of battered women in Rome who sought help through counselors affiliated with *Telefono Rosa*, Italy's most well-known and established hotline for victims of domestic violence The organization provides legal, psychological, and social consultation. It also organizes self-help groups as well as prevention activities to victims of sexual and domestic violence.[78] A comparative study, involving interviews with women in Italy (N = 32), Anglo women in the United States (N = 27), and Mexican immigrant women in the United States (N = 23), led researchers to conclude that "relationship violence is prevalent in Italy."[79] Several features unique to the Italian group of women as compared with the U.S. women were identified: they had fewer children, they were older, they had endured an abusive relationship longer, and they were more often married to their abusers.[80] The findings parallel results of a 1995 *Telefono Rosa* questionnaire, which included 348 respondents whose information suggested that the most likely victim of domestic violence was a married housewife between the ages of thirty-one and forty. By contrast, the battered women in an additional study were working women (62 percent, which is much higher than the official national average of 25 percent).[81] Although both studies found that alcohol had little to do with male aggression, they differed on the identification of motives that led a man to violence. The *Telefono Rosa* study attributed the aggression to "character" motives, whereas the comparative study identified male unemployment as a "distinctive feature of these families," with about one in four of the men being out of work, and hence a strong risk factor.[82]

In addition, the studies disproved a central hypothesis concerning the extended family and social support. The Italian women had on average of twelve relatives living in Rome (as compared with only three for Mexican women and 1.5 for white women living in Tucson); however, contrary to the researchers' expectations, the increased presence of extended family did not translate into increased social support. In fact, the Italian women found themselves equally socially isolated and beleaguered.

Italian women in abusive marriages revealed "acute symptoms of psychological distress."[83] The psychic consequences of violence against women ranges from depression to eating disorders.[84] Thirty-two percent of the Italian women consulted were "taking prescription mood-altering drugs through a physician." Apparently, these battered women were "seeking medication for their mental anguish and depression."[85] This finding suggests that the problem of domestic violence has largely been forced into a medical perspective—and that the victims of abuse have been pathologized. One wonders to what degree the pharmaceuticals were serving as a cover for a larger problem of abuse, as suggested in the UNICEF report.

Telefono Rosa has noted that as more females have entered into police forces, women victims of violence have increased their willingness to go to the police for help. Legislation to protect women from physical abuse was updated and strengthened in 1996, according to the Country Reports on Human Rights. Law n. 66 stipulates five to ten years of imprisonment and forbids sexual acts with minors, that is, persons under fourteen years of age.[86] Issues of women's rights related to domestic violence, sexual violence, and sexual harassment in the workplace continue to be debated.

Trafficking in Women and Children

A growing problem connected to violence relates to trafficking in immigrant women as well as girls for prostitution and forced labor. The women and girls who are trafficked for sexual exploitation tend to be vulnerable, illegal immigrants, often from Nigeria and Eastern Europe. Estimates suggest that some 20,000 women are involved in prostitution, of whom about 1,500 may be trafficked forcibly. This trend is in part reflected in shifts within Italy's prison population, a result of intensified policing of women who work in the sex trade, according to fieldwork conducted in 1997 with incarcerated African immigrant women in Rome. These women are seen as "the perpetrators of a crime, rather than victims of a larger criminal circuit."[87] Such policing strategies have broad public support, and immigrant women increasingly confront a climate of fear and anxiety toward them. Law enforcers expressed attitudes toward African women as representing "a kind of dangerous individual who was a threat to society both by committing individual crimes and by coming from culturally different and therefore dangerous nation states."[88]

The Country Report on Human Rights identified Tuscany's expanding Chinese immigrant community as a particular high risk site in trafficking children for sweatshop labor. In that community, "Children are considered to be part of the family 'production unit.'" An alliance has been made between the Chinese consulate in Florence and the local police (*carabinieri*) to persuade families to enroll their children in public schools.[89]

Italy has been among the countries to benefit from the European Commission's DAPHNE program, set up in 1997 through the European Council and European Parliament. The program is designed to deal "with human trafficking, sexual exploitation, all forms of domestic violence and abuse, as well as violence in schools and violence against minority groups and migrants." In 2000 the DAPHNE program granted the equivalent of €5 million to fight violence against women and children.[90]

OUTLOOK FOR THE TWENTY-FIRST CENTURY

One of the longstanding assumptions of research on population has been that fertility decline improves women's status. If this assumption were universally true, Italian women's record-low fertility would translate into record-high status. This is the case only if we consider the results of the Sexual and Reproductive Health Risks Study, in which Italian women were ranked at the top. But considering women's status in broader terms, the conclusion cannot be drawn that Italian women enjoy super-high status alongside their super-low fertility rates. In fact, as fertility rates fall to subreplacement levels, women's bodies and reproductive potential become sites for sneaky pronatalism. Alarmist discourses circulate about the future of the nation and warn of a population "implosion." Women, described as choosing "work and education" over family, are often the "fall guys" in this version of the story, a thinly veiled response of a less potent yet everpresent patriarchal society. Such alarmism also promotes a racial politics of birthing in which babies of immigrants are potentially valued differently than those of Italian women. Furthermore, as gender relations change and educational opportunities for women increase, the upcoming generation of Italian women and men confront new challenges for making a life, forging intimate relationships, having a career, and making a family.

The official institution of patriarchy in terms of the extended family may have given way to a more conjugal model, but patriarchy persists, though in a threatened form. Granted, increasingly rare is the extended patriarchal family and the unquestioned authority vested in the male head of household. However, public institutions are still largely run by men, women continue to earn less than their male counterparts, women are still underrepresented in government and other sectors, and women are still subject to domestic violence at troublesome though uncertain rates. Indeed, women must continually negotiate their identities and live in social worlds with power structures and sentiments that place them at a disadvantage.

The future, in terms of women's status, will likely be strongly shaped through movements in the global economy and influences of nongovernmental organizations. Numerous NGOs are engaged in the active and effective promotion of women's rights.[91] How well such organizations will be able to attend to the particular circumstances, demands, and expectations of Italian women—living in a number of different regions, often with their own sets of expectations, histories, and power structures—remains to be seen.

It has been noted that "emancipation for Italian women has been slow in coming since state formation in 1861 as compared with other European countries. . . . But those who have fought for women's equality in the family and in broader social contexts have recognized that progress for women means progress for Italian society as a whole."[92]

NOTES

Numerous intellectual and personal debts inevitably accumulate in a long-term, ongoing research project, and I appreciate the numerous friends, consultants, and colleagues who helped with various aspects of the research project on which much of this material draws. In particular, I would like to thank Giovanna Ugo for sending me material related to the parental leave policy in Prato, Enoch Page for alerting me to Asale Angel-Ajani's article on race politics in Italy, Laura McCloskey for sending me an advance version of her multiple-authored piece on domestic violence, and Lynn Walter for her conscientious editing. Research funds for ethnographic fieldwork (October 1995–August 1997) were provided by a Council for European Studies Pre-Dissertation Grant and a U.S. Fulbright Grant and Renewal. A Final Project Fund Award from The University of Arizona and a Beth Dillingham Award from the Central States Anthropological Society supported a follow-up field visit (June 1999).

1. Columbia University Press, "Italy," *The Columbia Electronic Encyclopedia*, www.columbia.edu/cu/cup/cee/cee.html; Encyclopedia.com, www.encyclopedia.com/articles/06518.html (accessed June 25, 2001); and Population Reference Bureau, "World Population Data Sheet" (2000), www.prb.org/pubs/ (accessed June 25, 2001).

2. The term "total fertility rate" refers to the average number of children born to a woman during her lifetime. See Population Reference Bureau, "World Population Data Sheet" (2000), www.prb.org (accessed February 19, 2002). An overview of demographic research can be found at the Max Planck Institute for Demographic Research, www.demogr.mpg.de/ (accessed February 19, 2002). See the country profile of the International Planned Parenthood Federation site, www.ippf.org/ (accessed February 19, 2002).

3. Not all people living in Europe benefit equally from these low maternal mortality rates. A mother who is a member of an immigrant group is much more likely to suffer from complications of pregnancy than a mother who is native-born. See "Safe Motherhood in Europe: Significant but Uneven Progress," World Health Organization, www.who.dk (accessed November 10, 2001). Development goals, gender equality, and maternal mortality rates are presented at www.developmentgoals.org (accessed November 10, 2001).

4. See in particular Michael Specter, "Population Implosion Worries a Graying Europe," *New York Times*, July 10, 1998, sec. A1.

5. Demographer Massimo Livi-Bacci (1977) mapped the onset of fertility decline in Italy's provinces. Saraceno (1996) traces out a "tentative historical and theoretical framework for understanding the decline." See Massimo Livi-Bacci, *A History of Italian Fertility* (Princeton, NJ: Princeton University Press, 1977); and Chiara Saraceno, *Sociologia della Famiglia* (Bologna, Italy: Mulino, 1996).

6. Antonio Schizzerotto, "La scuola è uguale per tutti?" In *Stato dell' Italia*, ed. Paul Ginsborg (Milan: Il Saggiatore, Bruno Mondadori, 1994), 558–62.

7. Bureau of Democracy, Human Rights, and Labor, "Italy," 2000, www.state.gov/g/drl/rls/hrrpt/2000/eur/790pf.htm.

8. "Prosperous Italy Has the Lowest Birthrate in the World," *Mother Jones* 20, no. 5 (September 1995), 50.

9. Simonetta Ortaggi Cammarossano, "Labouring Women in North and Central Italy," in *Society and Politics in the Age of the Risorgimento*, ed. John A. Davis and Paul Ginsborg (Cambridge: Cambridge University Press, 1991), 152–83.

10. V.A. Goddard, *Gender, Family and Work in Naples* (Oxford: Berg, 1996); Elizabeth L. Krause, "Natalism and Nationalism," Ph.D. diss., University of Arizona, 1999; and Sylvia Yanagisako, *Producing Culture and Capital* (Princeton, NJ: Princeton University Press, 2002).

11. Elizabeth L. Krause, "Empty Cradles," *Cultural Anthropology* 16, no. 4 (2001): 576–611 and Elizabeth Krause, *A Crisis of Births: Population Politics and Family-Making in Italy* (Belmont, CA: Wadsworth, forthcoming).

12. Giovanna Grassi, "In Italy, a Boom of their Own," *Hollywood Reporter*, no. 42 (June 10, 1997): 1–4.

13. Alessandra Stanley, "Rape of Teenager," *New York Times*, March 6, 2001, sec. A4.

14. Bureau of Democracy, Human Rights, and Labor, "Italy," 1999, www.state.gov/g/drl/hrrpt/1999/337pf.htm.

15. See Bureau of Democracy, 2000.

16. *Off Our Backs* (2001). This article, among others, was located in the excellent RDS database "Contemporary Women's Issues." Accessed June 29, 2001.

17. Bureau of Democracy, 2000.

18. See Bureau of Democracy, 2000.

19. Data from the author's field research in the Province of Prato, October 1995–August 1997 and June 1999.

20. Marta Lobato, "32 trabadores ponen," *El Mundo*, March 29, 1999, 26.

21. Bureau of Democracy, 1999.

22. Donata Gottardi, "Congeti parentali," *Guida Lavoro*, no. 30 (2000):12–15.

23. Commissione Provinciale Pari Opportunità, "Cosa dice la 'legge 8 marzo' " (Provincia di Prato: Author, 2001).

24. Parents believed that early childhood programs were good for their children, according to a 1995 report on early childhood programs.

25. Finding creative outlets to nurture the many "languages" of children is central to the Reggio approach. In fact, it received particular notoriety from a traveling art exhibit, "The 100 Languages of Children." The Reggio-Emilia programs began in the most Red zone in Italy. Italian communism of the 1970s was committed to democratic values and an ethos of quality education for all. In Italy, the vast majority of people regardless of income level take advantage of the high-quality preschools.

26. Elinor Ochs et al., "Socializing Taste," *Ethnos* 61, no. 1–2 (1996): 7–46.

27. Paula Snyder, "Italy," in The European Women's Almanac (New York: Columbia University Press, 1992), 205–17, esp. 211–12.

28. Luisa Passerini, "Gender Relations," in *Italian Cultural Studies*, ed. David Forgacs and Robert Lumley (Oxford: Oxford University Press, 1996), 145.

29. Lesley Caldwell, "Church, State, and the Family," in *Feminism and Materialism*, ed. Annette Kuhn and AnnMarie Wolpe (London: Routledge and Kegan Paul, 1978), 68–75, esp. 72, and Marzio Barbagli, "Three Household Formation Systems," in *The Family in Italy*, ed. David I. Kertzer and Richard P. Saller (New Haven, CT: Yale University Press, 1991), 250–70.

30. Victoria de Grazia, *How Fascism Ruled Women* (Berkeley: University of California Press, 1992).

31. Chiara Saraceno, "Women, Family and the Law, 1750–1942," *Journal of Family History* 15, no. 4 (1990): 427–42, esp. 440.

32. Elizabeth L. Krause, "Forward vs. Reverse Gear," *Journal of Historical Sociology* 7, no. 3 (1994).

33. Luisa Passerini, *Fascism in Popular Memory: The Cultural Experience of the Turin Working Class* (Cambridge: Cambridge University Press, 1987), 150.

34. Passerini, 1987, 151.

35. Jane C. Schneider and Peter T. Schneider, "Demographic Transition in a Sicilian Rural Town," *Journal of Family History* 9 (1984): 259. See also Schneider and Schneider, 1991. "Sex and Respectability in an Age of Fertility Decline: A Sicilian Case Study," *Social Science Medicine* 33, no. 8 (1991): 885–95. "Coitus Interruptus and Family Respectability in Catholic Europe: A Sicilian Case Study," in *Conceiving the New World Order*, eds. Faye Ginsburg and Rayna Rapp (Berkeley: University of California Press, 1995), 177–94. *Festival of the Poor: Fertility Decline and the Ideology of Class in Sicily: 1860–1980* (Tucson: University of Arizona Press, 1996).

36. Elizabeth Whitaker, *Measuring Mamma's Milk* (Ann Arbor: The University of Michigan Press, 2000), 275.

37. Whitaker, 2000, 275.

38. Caldwell, 1978, 72; and Lesley Caldwell, *Italian Family Matters* (Houndsmill, UK, and London: Macmillan, 1991).

39. Emilia Sarogni, *La Donna Italiana: Il lungo cammino v erso i diritti, 1861–1994* (Parma: Nuova Pratiche Editore, 1995), 190–91.

40. Europa, The European Observatory on the Social Situation, Demography, and Family, "Family Benefits and Family Policies in Europe: Italy," 2002, europa.eu.int/comm/employment_social/eoss/index_en.html (accessed May 25, 2003), 47.

41. Giovanni B. Sgritta, "The Situation of Families in Italy in 2001," europa.eu. int/comm/employment_social/eoss/index_en.html (accessed May 15, 2003), 2.

42. Guido Maggioni, "Le separazioni e divorzi," in *Lo stato delle famiglie in Italia*, ed. Marzio Barbagli and Chiara Saraceno (Bologna, Italy: Il Mulino, 1997), 232–47, esp. 233.

43. Data from author's field research in the Province of Prato, October 1995–August 1997 and June 1999.

44. Giacomo Becattini, "The Development of Light Industry in Tuscany: An Interpretation," in *Regional Development in a Modern European Economy*, ed. Robert Leonardi and Raffaella Y. Nanetti (London: Pinter, 1998), 77–94, esp. 83.

45. Carole M. Counihan, "Female Identity, Food, and Power," *Anthropological Quarterly* 61 (1988): 51–62.

46. Alessandra Pescarolo and Gian Bruno Ravenni, *Il Proletariato Invisible* (Milan: Franco Angeli, 1991), 33.

47. ISTAT, *Famiglia, abitazioni* (Roma: Author, 1996).

48. Marzio Barbagli, *Sotto lo stesso tetto*, 2nd ed. (Bologna, Italy: Il Mulino, 1996), 387–92; Krause, 1999; and Saraceno, 1996, 143–48.

49. Two examples are www.parmaoggi.com and www.margherita.net/sessualita (accessed November 10, 2001).

50. David Horn, *Social Bodies* (Princeton, NJ: Princeton University Press, 1994). Krause, 1994; and Passerini, 1987.

51. Women's Environment and Health Organization, "Risks, Rights and Reforms" (Author, 1999), 149.

52. Tamar Pitch, "L'aborto e la legge," in Ginsborg, 1994, 274–75, esp. 274.

53. Pitch, 1994, 274–75.

54. Silvana Salvini Bettarini and Silvana Schifini D'Andrea, "Induced Abortion in Italy," *Family Planning Perspectives* 28, no. 6 (1996): 267–70.

55. Bettarini and D'Andrea, 1996.

56. Bettarini and D'Andrea, 1996.

57. Bettarini and D'Andrea, 1996.

58. The U.S. rate is 64 births per 1,000 girls. See www.unicef.org/pon96/inbirth. htm (accessed November 10, 2001).

59. Maria Castiglioni and Gianpiero Dalla Zuanna, "L'inizio delle relazioni sessuali," in Barbagli and Saraceno, 1997, 76–85, esp. 80.

60. See www.populationaction.org/resources/publications/worldofdifference (accessed November 1, 2001).

61. Women's Environment and Development Organization, 1999.

62. "Report on the Global HIV/AIDS Epidemic—June 2000," www.unaids.org/ epidemic_update/report/#table (accessed November 1, 2001).

63. Ruggiero et al. (2001) review the history of medical knowledge of eating disorders in Italy, beginning with interpretations of starvation during the Middle Ages and ending with understandings in the present era. See Giovanni Maria Ruggiero et al., "Eating Disorders in Italy: A Historical Review," *European Eating Disorders Review* 9, no. 5 (2001): 292–300.

64. See www.istitutotumori.mi.it (accessed November 1, 2001).

65. See www.salutementaledonna.it/depression.htm (accessed November 1, 2001).

66. See www.salutementaledonna.it/depression.htm (accessed November 1, 2001).

67. See the Inter-Parliamentary Union, "Women in Parliaments," www.ipu.org/ wmn-e/world.htm (accessed February 19, 2002). The Italian Parliament can be accessed

through www.parlamento.it; the Camera dei Deputati's web site is www.camera.it/; and the Senate's web site is www.senato.it/senato.htm.

68. Passerini, 1996, 150.

69. This form of feminism is based upon the idea that men and women have or should have separate spheres of influence, power, and authority.

70. See also Lucia Chiavola Birnbaum, *Liberazione della Donna* (Middletown, CT: Wesleyan University Press, 1986); Teresa de Lauretis, "The Essence of the Triangle," *Differences* 1, no. 2 (1989); Giovanna Miceli Jeffries, ed., *Feminine Feminists* (Minneapolis: University of Minnesota Press, 1994). Sandra Kemp and Paola Bono, eds., *The Lonely Mirror* (London: Routledge, 1993).

71. Passerini, 1996, 151–52.

72. See International Lesbian and Gay Association, "World Legal Survey," www.ilga.org/Information/legal_survey/europe/italy.htm (accessed May 27, 2003). ILGA Administrative Office, 81 Kolenmarkt, B1000 Brussels, Belgium, Tel: +32-2-5022471, ilga@ilga.org.

73. Elana Biagini et al., "Equality for Lesbians and Gay Men: A Report of ILGA-Europe," June 1998, www.steff.suite.dk/report.htm#ITALY (accessed October 26, 2001).

74. See also Kate Griffin and Lisa A. Mulholland, eds., *Lesbian Motherhood in Europe* (London: Cassell, 1997), 145; and Biagini et al., 1998.

75. U.S. Department of State, International Information Programs, "U.S. Commitment to Women 2000," http://usinfo.state.gov/usa/beijing5/00060502.htm (accessed January 29, 2002).

76. See Bureau of Democracy, 2000.

77. The study (McCloskey et al., 2002) compared Italian women with Mexican immigrant and white women living in Tucson, Arizona. The U.S. women were located through battered women's shelters, an option not available to women in Rome during the data collection period of the study (1992), but were understood as "comparable in their desire and motives to seek help" (58). See Laura Ann McCloskey et al., "A Comparative Study of Battered Women," *Journal of Family Violence* 17, no. 1 (2002): 53–74.

78. The *Telefono Rosa* web site offers a range of useful information, www.show.it/tel_rosa/. The hotline number is 011 53 06 66.

79. McCloskey et al., 2002, 56.

80. McCloskey et al., 2002, 58, 67.

81. McCloskey et al., 2002, 58, 67.

82. McCloskey et al., 2002, 69.

83. McCloskey et al., 2002, 65.

84. See www.salutementaledonna.it/depression.htm (accessed November 1, 2001).

85. McCloskey et al., 2002, 66.

86. Emilia Sarogni, *La Donna Italiana* (Parma: Nuova Pratiche Editore, 1995), 190–95.

87. Asale Angel-Ajani, "Italy's Racial Cauldron," *Cultural Dynamics* 12, no. 3 (2000): 331–52, esp. 346.

88. Angel-Ajani, 2000, 344. In interviews and surveys conducted with police.

89. See Bureau of Democracy, 2000.

90. EU Institution, "The European Commission supports fight against violence to women and children," press release, http://europa.eu.int/rapid/start/ (accessed January 29, 2002).

91. See Bureau of Democracy, 2000.

92. Italian feminist scholar Emilia Sarogni (1995, 196; author's translation).

RESOURCE GUIDE

Suggested Reading

Birnbaum, Lucia Chiavola. *Liberazione della Donna: Feminism in Italy*. Middletown, CT: Wesleyan University Press, 1986.

Bull, Anna, and Paul Corner. *From Peasant to Entrepreneur: The Survival of the Family Economy in Italy*. Oxford: Berg, 1993.

Caldwell, Lesley. "Church, State, and Family: The Women's Movement in Italy." In *Feminism and Materialism*, edited by Annette Kuhn and AnnMarie Wolpe, 68–95. London: Routledge and Kegan Paul, 1978.

———. *Italian Family Matters: Women, Politics and Legal Reform*. Houndmills, UK, and London: Macmillan, 1991.

Coale, Ansley J., and Susan C. Watkins, eds. *The Decline in Fertility in Europe*. Princeton, NJ: Princeton University Press, 1986.

Counihan, Carole M. "Female Identity, Food, and Power in Contemporary Florence." *Anthropological Quarterly* 61 (1988): 51–62.

European Commission, "Family Benefits and Family Policies in Europe: Italy." European Observatory on the Social Situation, Demography, and Family, 2002. europa.eu.int/comm/employment_social/eoss/index_en.html (accessed May 25, 2003).

Grassi, Giovanna. "In Italy, A Boom of Their Own." *Hollywood Reporter*, no. 42 (June 10, 1997): 1–4.

Jeffries, Giovanna Miceli, ed. *Feminine Feminists: Cultural Practices in Italy*. Minneapolis: University of Minnesota Press, 1994.

Kemp, Sandra, and Paola Bono, eds. *The Lonely Mirror: Italian Perspectives on Feminist Theory*. London: Routledge, 1993.

Schneider, Jane C., and Peter T. Schneider. *Culture and Political Economy in Western Sicily*. New York: Academic Press, 1976.

———. "Demographic Transition in a Sicilian Rural Town." *Journal of Family History* 9 (1989): 245–73.

———. "Sex and Respectability in an Age of Fertility Decline: A Sicilian Case Study." *Social Science Medicine* 33, no. 8 (1991): 885–95.

———. "Coitus Interruptus and Family Respectability in Catholic Europe: A Sicilian Case Study." In *Conceiving the New World Order*, edited by Faye Ginsburg and Rayna Rapp. Berkeley: University of California Press, 1995.

———. *Festival of the Poor: Fertility Decline and the Ideology of Class in Sicily: 1860–1980*. Tucson: University of Arizona Press, 1996.

Sgritta, Giovanni B., "The Situation of Families in Italy in 2001." europa.eu.int/comm/employment_social/eoss/index_en.html (accessed May 15, 2003).

Snyder, Paula 1992. "Italy." In *The European Women's Almanac*, 205–17. New York: Columbia University Press, 1992.

Stanley, Alessandra. "Rape of Teenager Spotlights Fashion's Dark Side." *New York Times*, March 6, 2001, sec. A4.

Whitaker, Elizabeth Dixon. *Measuring Mamma's Milk: Fascism and the Medicalization of Maternity in Italy*. Ann Arbor: The University of Michigan Press, 2000.

Videos/Films

Caro Diario. 1995. 100 minutes. Directed by Nannie Moretti. Distributed by New Line Home Video. Italian with English Subtitles.

Ciao, professore! 1994. Directed by Lina Wertmuller. Distributed by Miramax Home Entertainment. Italian with English Subtitles.

The Garden of the Finzi-Continis. 1997. [1970]. Directed by Vittorio De Sica. Distributed by Sony Picture Classics. Italian with English Subtitles.

Nietta's Diary. 1997. 30 minutes. Directed by Romano Gabriella. Distributed by Cinenova.

A Reputation: The Rape of Artemisia Gentileschi. 1997. 30 minutes. Directed by Deborah Wignall. Produced by Films for the Humanities and Sciences.

Web Sites

European Observatory on the Social Situation, Demography and Family, europa.eu.int/comm/employment_social/eoss/index_en.html.

International Planned Parenthood Federation, www.ippf.org/.

Italian Parliament, www.parlamento.it.

The Women's Documentation Center Library in Bologna (Biblioteca delle Donne), www.women.it/bibliotecadelledonne.
Italy's primary gender research library, collects materials written by women and on women.

Women's Mental Health Prevention Centre, Naples, Italy, www.salutementaledonna.it/depression.htm.

Organizations

International Lesbian and Gay Association
81 Kolenmarkt B1000 Brussels
Belgium
Phone/Fax: +32-2-5022471
Email: ilga@ilga.org
Web site: www.ilga.org/Information/legal_survey/europe/italy.htm

Telefono Rosa
Phone: 011 53 06 66
Web site: www.show.it/tel_rosa/

SELECTED BIBLIOGRAPHY

Angel-Ajani, Asale. "Italy's Racial Cauldron: Immigration, Criminalization and the Cultural Politics of Race." *Cultural Dynamics* 12, no. 3 (2000): 331–52.

Barbagli, Marzio. "Three Household Formation Systems in Eighteenth- and Nineteenth-Century Italy." In *The Family in Italy: from Antiquity to the Present*, edited by David I. Kertzer and Richard P. Saller, 250–70. New Haven, CT: Yale University Press, 1991.

Becattini, Giacomo. "The Development of Light Industry in Tuscany: An Interpretation." In *Regional Development in a Modern European Economy: The Case of Tuscany*, edited by Robert Leonardi and Raffaella Y. Nanetti, 77–94. London: Pinter, 1998.

Bellandi, Marco, and Marco Romagnoli. "Case Study II: Prato and the Textile Industry." In *Regional Development in a Modern European Economy: The Case of Tuscany*, edited by Robert Leonardi and Raffaella Y. Nanetti, 153–79. London: Pinter, 1998.

Bettarini, Silvana Salvini, and Silvana Schifini D'Andrea. "Induced Abortion in Italy: Levels, Trends and Characteristics." *Family Planning Perspectives*, 28, no. 6 (1996): 267–70.

Biagini, Elana, Graziella Bertozzo, and Marco Ravaioli. "Equality for Lesbians and Gay Men: A Report of ILGA-Europe." June 1998. www.steff.suite.dk/report.htm#ITALY. Accessed October 26, 2001.

Bureau of Democracy, Human Rights, and Labor. Country Reports on Human Rights Practices. "Italy." www.state.gov/g/drl/rls/hrrpt/1999/337pf.htm. 1999 (accessed February 19, 2002).

———. "Italy." 2000. www.state.gov/g/drl.rls/hrrpt/2000/eur/790pf.htm (accessed February 19, 2002).

de Grazia, Victoria. *How Fascism Ruled Women: Italy, 1922–1945*. Berkeley: University of California Press, 1992.

Dei Ottati, Gabi. "Case Study I: Prato and Its Evolution in a European Context." In *Regional Development in a Modern European Economy: The Case of Tuscany*, edited by Robert Leonardi and Raffaella Y. Nanetti, 124–52. London: Pinter, 1998.

de Lauretis, Teresa. "The Essence of the Triangle or, Taking the Risk of Essentialism Seriously: Feminist Theory in Italy, the U.S., and Britain." *Differences* 1 (1989): 2.

The Economist. "Survey of the Italian Economy." *Italian Journal*, no. 1 (1988): 31–49.

EU Institution. "The European Commission Supports Fight against Violence to Women and Children." Press release. http://europa.eu.int/rapid/start/ (accessed January 29, 2002).

Goddard, V.A. *Gender, Family and Work in Naples*. Oxford: Berg, 1996.

Griffin, Kate, and Lisa A. Mulholland, eds. *Lesbian Motherhood in Europe*. London: Cassell, 1997.

Horn, David. *Social Bodies: Science, Reproduction and Italian Modernity*. Princeton, NJ: Princeton University Press, 1994.

Inter-Parliamentary Union. "Women in Parliaments." www.ipu.org/wmn-e/world.htm (accessed February 19, 2002). The Camera dei Deputati's web site is www.camera.it/; the Senate's web site is www.senato.it/senato.htm.

Kertzer, David. *Sacrificed for Honor: Italian Infant Abandonment and the Politics of Reproductive Control*. Boston: Beacon Press, 1993.

Krause, Elizabeth L. "Forward vs. Reverse Gear: The Politics of Proliferation and Resistance in the Italian Fascist State." *Journal of Historical Sociology* 7, no. 3 (1994): 261–88.

———. "Natalism and Nationalism: The Political Economy of Love, Labor and Low Fertility in Central Italy." Ph.D. diss., University of Arizona, 1999.

———. " 'Empty Cradles' and the Quiet Revolution: Demographic Discourse and Cultural Struggles of Gender, Race, and Class in Italy." *Cultural Anthropology* 16, no. 4 (2001): 576–611.

Krause, Elizabeth. *A Crisis of Births: Population Politics and Family-Making in Italy*. Belmont, CA: Wadsworth, forthcoming.

Livi-Bacci, Massimo. *A History of Italian Fertility*. Princeton, NJ: Princeton University Press, 1977.

Max Planck Institute for Demographic Research. www.demogr.mpg.de/.

McCloskey, Laura Ann, Michaela Treviso, Theresa Scioni-Bavo, and Giuliana dal Pozzo. "A Comparative Study of Battered Women and Their Children in Italy and the United States." *Journal of Family Violence* 17, no. 1 (2002): 53–74.

Ochs, Elinor, Clotilde Pontecorvo, and Alessandra Fasulo. "Socializing Taste." *Ethnos* 61, no. 1–2 (1996): 7–46.

Ortaggi Cammarosano, Simonetta. "Labouring Women in Northern and Central Italy in the Nineteenth Century." In *Society and Politics in the Age of the Risorgimento: Essays in honour of Denis Mack Smith*, edited by John A. Davis and Paul Ginsborg, 152–83. Cambridge: Cambridge University Press, 1991.

Passerini, Luisa. *Fascism in Popular Memory: The Cultural Experience of the Turin Working Class*. Cambridge: Cambridge University Press, 1987.

———. "Gender Relations." In *Italian Cultural Studies*, edited by David Forgacs and Robert Lumley, 144–59. Oxford: Oxford University Press, 1996.

Population Reference Bureau. "2000 World Population Data Sheet." www.prb.org/ pubs/ (accessed June 25, 2001).

"Prosperous Italy has the Lowest Birthrate in the World." Mother Jones 20, no. 5 (September 1995): 50.

Ruggiero, Giovanni Maria, Marcello Prandin, and Mario Mantero. "Eating Disorders in Italy: A Historical Review." *European Eating Disorders Review* 9, no. 5 (2001): 292–300.

Saraceno, Chiara. "Women, Family and the Law, 1750–1942." *Journal of Family History* 15, no. 4 (1990): 427–42.

———. "Constructing Families, Shaping Women's Lives: The Making of Italian Families Between Market Economy and State Interventions." In *The European Experience of Declining Fertility, 1850–1970: The Quiet Revolution*, edited by Louise A. Tilly, John R. Gillis, and David Levine, 251–70. Cambridge, MA: Blackwell, 1992.

Sgritta, Giovanni B. "The Situation of Families in Italy in 2001." europa.eu.int/comm/ employment_social/eoss/index_en.html (accessed May 15, 2003).

Specter, Michael. "Population Implosion Worries a Graying Europe." *New York Times*, July 10, 1998, sec. A1.

Trigilia, Carlo. "Italian Industrial Districts: Neither Myth nor Interlude." In *Industrial Districts and Local Economic Regeneration*, edited by F. Pyke and W. Sengenberger, 33–47. Geneva: International Institute for Labour Studies, 1992.

UNAIDS. "Report on the Global HIV/AIDS Epidemic—June 2000." www.unaids. org/epidemic_update/report/#table (accessed November 1, 2001).

United Nations Development Programme. "Gender Empowerment Measures." www. undp.org (accessed November 1, 2001).

UNICEF. www.unicef.org/pon96/inbirth.htm (accessed November 10, 2001).

U.S. Department of State, International Information Programs. "U.S. Commitment to Women 2000." http://usinfo.state.gov/usa/beijing5/00060502.htm (accessed January 29, 2002).

Women's Environment and Health Organization. "Risks, Rights and Reforms." New York: WEDO, 1999, 149.

World Health Organization (WHO). "Safe Motherhood in Europe: Significant but Uneven Progress." www.who.dk (accessed November 10, 2001).

Yanagisako, Sylvia. *Producing Culture and Capital: Family Firms in Italy*. Princeton, NJ: Princeton University Press, 2002.

Selected Italian Bibliography

Barbagli, Marzio. *Sotto lo stesso tetto: Mutamenti della famiglia in Italia dal XV al XX secolo*. 2nd ed. Bologna, Italy: Il Mulino, 1996.

Castiglioni, Maria, and Gianpiero Dalla Zuanna. "L'inizio delle relazioni sessuali." In *Lo stato delle famiglie in Italia*, edited by Marzio Barbagli and Chiara Saraceno, 76–85. Bologna, Italy: Il Mulino, 1997.

Commissione Provinciale Pari Opportunità. "Cosa dice la 'legge 8 marzo' sui Congedi Parentali per maternità." Provincia di Prato: Author, 2001.

Gottardi, Donata. "Congedi parentali: nuovi chiarimenti dal Ministero." *Guida al Lavoro*, Il Sole-24 Ore. no. 30 (2000): 12–15. The web site of the Ministry of Social Affairs, www.affarisociali.it/congedi (accessed July 2, 2001).

ISTAT (Istituto Naionale di Statistica). "Famiglia, abitazioni, servizi di pubblica utilità. Indagini Multiscopo sulle Famiglie Anni 1993–1994." Argomenti, no. 6. Roma: Author, 1996.

Lobato, Marta. "32 trabajadoras ponen fecha a sus embarazos para proteger sus empleos." *El Mundo*, March 29, 1999, 26.

Maggioni, Guido. "Le separazioni e i divorzi." In *Lo stato delle famiglie in Italia*, edited by Marzio Barbagli and Chiara Saraceno, 232–47. Bologna, Italy: Il Mulino, 1997.

Pescarolo, Alessandra. "I Modelli del Lavoro Femminile: Continuità e Mutamento nei Percorsi e nei Valori." Istituto Regionale per la Programmazione Economica della Toscana (IRPET). Pontassieve: Centro Stampa, 1995.

Pescarolo, Alessandra, and Gian Bruno Ravenni. *Il Proletariato Invisibile: La Manifattura della Paglia nella Toscana Mezzadrile (1820–1950)*. Milan: Franco Angeli, 1991.

Pitch, Tamar. "L'aborto e la legge." In *Stato dell'Italia*, edited by Paul Ginsborg, 274–75. Milan: Il Saggiatore, 1994.

Righi, Alessandra. "La nuzialità." In *Lo stato delle famiglie in Italia*, edited by Marzio Barbagli and Chiara Saraceno, 53–64. Bologna, Italy: Il Mulino, 1997.

Saraceno, Chiara. *Sociologia della Famiglia*. Bologna, Italy: Il Mulino, 1996.

Sarogni, Emilia. *La Donna Italiana: Il lungo cammino v erso i diritti, 1861–1994*. Parma: Nuova Pratiche Editore, 1995.

Schizzerotto, Antonio. "La scuola è uguale per tutti?" In *Stato dell' Italia*, edited by Paul Ginsborg, 558–62. Milant: Saggiatore, Bruno Mondadori, 1994.

21

KOSOVO

Antonia Young

PROFILE OF KOSOVO

Kosovo[1] and Albania contain the major parts of what was, until the end of the nineteenth century, the Albanian lands. When the Great Powers (Austro-Hungary, France, Germany, Great Britain, Italy, and Russia) met in London in 1912–1913, they drew lines on the map, thus dividing Albania from Kosovo. From that time the division of their histories grew wider, with Kosovo being incorporated into what became Yugoslavia and Albania gaining independence. This division became even more exaggerated after the Second World War, with families split over borders, unable to see one another for fifty years. Thus, despite a common history throughout five centuries under Ottoman rule and a common language, traditions, and customs, all of which are retained, the peoples of the two entities were molded under very different regimes.

Today Albania is the only country to recognize Kosovo as independent, and Kosovars are the only outsiders allowed to enter Albania free of any visa charge. However, their societies continue to receive very different treatment. Albania is a democracy whereas Kosovo is in a kind of limbo, operating under the United Nations Interim Admin-

istration Mission in Kosovo (UNMIK), which is an interim body of internationals working with the leaders of all of Kosovo's communities and under the protection of the allied NATO forces. Kosovo is divided into multinational brigade sectors, led by France, Germany, the UK, and the United States.

Kosovo, a landlocked region, has an area of 17,878 square kilometers.[2] High mountains mark the borders of Kosovo from Serbia to the east, Macedonia (FYROM) to the south, and Albania and Montenegro to the west. The central plains consist of very fertile farmlands.

Kosovo's population is approximately 2 million, over 90 percent of whom are Albanian. The remaining 8–9 percent are made up of Serbs, Roma, Turks, and Bosnians. In the Albanian population, there are 105 women to every 100 men, and there are 118 women to 100 men in the 20–49 age range, whereas in the Serb population there are 95 women to every 100 men. Since the war the capital, Prishtina, has doubled in size to about 700,000. The birthrate is now 15 per 1,000. By 2000 Kosovo had the highest infant mortality rate in Europe at 45 deaths per 1,000 live births. The maternal death rate was 30 per 100,000. Half the population is under twenty-two years of age. Life expectancy for women in Kosovo is 75 years, and for men it is 73 years.

Almost half of the population of Kosovo was expelled from their country during the 1999 war. Remarkably, 90 percent of them returned within a month of the war's end. Throughout the 1990s, increasingly fierce Serbian oppression (directed from Belgrade) was placed upon the 90 percent Albanian population of the province. During this time, young Albanian men and those in leadership roles were targeted not only for military service in other Yugoslav republics, but also for "informative talks," imprisonment, torture, and death; many others left the country.

UNMIK's objective is to establish a substantial degree of autonomy for the province, organize local administration, democratize political life, assist the return of refugees, and reconstruct the infrastructure. Kosovo has never known a multiparty government, but this is emerging despite a lack of clarity concerning exactly which body has the right to make a conclusive decision of Kosovo's permanent status.

OVERVIEW OF WOMEN'S ISSUES

For the decade prior to the war, women had become enormously active as a part of the civil resistance and peacemaking process, supporting parallel structures in health and education. They received support from international women's groups, including some countering their own government in Belgrade, as the Women in Black did. Women took charge of their lives and formed many clandestine networks for education and health clinics as well as other supportive groups. Flora Brovina, doctor and poet, devoted herself to treating patients of all ethnicities: when the war ended, she was taken as a political prisoner to Serbia where she was sentenced to twelve years' imprisonment. International outcry helped to free her just over a year later. Brovina was one of the thirty-four women candidates for parliamentary elections in 2001 and was voted into office for the Democratic Party of Kosova (PDK).

During the devastation of the 78-day war, women became hardened to situations of extreme difficulty: many were forced to leave their homes (which were often torched behind them), most were separated from their men and many from their families, many were raped, and many were killed. Women's wartime experience, along with their earlier cooperative work in dealing with an oppressive regime, served as important training for the postwar situation of reconstruction, when international nongovernmental organization (INGO) funding became available.

The difference in women's lives between those living in towns, particularly Prishtina, and those living in remote rural areas has increased since the war. Prishtina has become a cosmopolitan city, with over 1,000 NGOs. As many as 50,000 locals are employed by UNMIK and the Organization for Security and Cooperation in Europe (OSCE).

Unique to Kosovo, UNMIK established a Gender Advisory Unit in October 1999 to ensure the mainstreaming of gender issues into UNMIK's mandate, policies, and activities. This became the Office for Gender Affairs (OGA) in March 2000 with the intention of gaining the participation of local women in Kosovo's hitherto all-male consultative bodies. Although women's representation is still low, they have been included in the Gender Policy Working Group of high-level Kosovar representatives of major political parties. Additionally, the OGA put forward the Kosovo Action Plan for the Advancement of Women, outlining six priority areas: poverty reduction and economic empowerment; advances in education, science, and culture; improved health care; reduced violence against women; increased legislation and women's rights; and monitoring of implementation and gender mainstreaming. This, however, was disowned and denounced by local women who felt that "gender experts" were imposing methods and ideas upon them without sufficient consultation. OGA is both understaffed and underfunded, and thus it is ill-prepared to incorporate gender mainstreaming into the wider UNMIK intervention. The Kosova Women's Network has now sent strong advice to the women of Iraq to "raise their voice and be part of the rebuilding of their country."[3]

EDUCATION

Opportunities

Although education has always been held in high esteem in Kosovo, currently nine out of ten girls attend primary school but only one in three attends secondary school.

During the 1980s, access to education was increasingly available, and acceptance of female education even by illiterate rural families was gaining ground. A high proportion of women became doctors. In the 1990s, after the crackdown under Milošević, secondary schools were segregated by ethnicity (Serb/Albanian), teaching was in Serbian, and only Serbian history was taught.

Schools reopened in September 1999, allowing many children, even those as old as twelve years of age, their first school experience. However, several factors contribute to make school attendance difficult. A lack of transport in many areas and issues of safety still keep girls away from more distant schools. Where transport exists, it can be prohibitively expensive. Some communities resolve this problem by trying to keep open remote rural schools that UNMIK has selected for closure. In others, families opt to send their children to stay with relatives living nearer to a school, thus creating further overcrowding in badly destroyed urban living quarters. A further problem is presented in some areas where access to school is only through a different ethnic community. Also, many children are still suffering from the traumas of war and need special attention not necessarily available at school. On the positive side, there has been successful integration in several urban schools amongst Albanian, Bosnian, Roma, Egyptian, and Turkish children.

Literacy

As of 2002, approximately 10 percent of women in Kosovo are illiterate, compared to 2.3 percent of men.

EMPLOYMENT AND THE ECONOMY

Job/Career Opportunities

The Yugoslav Labour Act of 1984 is still enforced, which theoretically ensures equality of opportunities to women in the workplace. There are now several training schemes in place to provide qualifications necessary in the job market. Most of the many women's NGOs give this concern priority.

The best-paid jobs are with international bodies such as UNMIK and international aid agencies as interpreters and, for men, as drivers and guards. Curiously, it is within UNMIK and the international organizations that there is the least representation of women amongst the Kosovar employees. The Interim Administrative Council (IAC) has no women as managers or consultants on gender issues, and their department heads are predominantly men.

There are now trained women police. Eighteen percent of judges are women, and women make up less than 5 percent of lawyers who are members of the bar association. There are women working in professions in the towns where there is little family opposition to women working outside the home, although the decision to do so is likely to be strongly influenced by their husbands. Several small businesses run by women are opening, and even several women's business organizations are attracting members: one of the best known is the Women's Business Association in Gjakovë.

In the rural areas, opportunities to work outside the home are minimal due to the lack of operating markets and industry. Although few women would say they work in agriculture, many work on their family land. Only 9 percent of women own any livestock. Roma women dominated the local markets in earlier times; until recently, the question of their security has hampered this activity for them. Women in ethnic communities are the most marginalized of all. Unemployment stands at approximately 70 percent, but 37 percent of families have no employed members.

Nongovernmental organizations (NGOs) are helping women find professional fulfillment. For example, Radio TV 21 is a station that grew out of the NGO Young Women's Media Project, the goal of which was to provide independent journalism and conflict management training for women. The station staff and editorial team are now 70 percent women.

Pay

Although the Yugoslav Labour Act of 1984 is still enforced, there is no guaranteed wage equality. Salaries vary between 100 and 300 euros per month in the public sector and between 100 and 500 euros in the private sector. Employment with UNMIK and other international organizations can yield up to five times a local wage.

Although women rarely take out business loans, they may often borrow from family and friends.

Working Conditions

Sexual Harassment

Women in Kosovo experience sexual harassment, as they do in the other patriarchal regimes of the southern Balkans. Women's groups are working to combat this and the more serious widespread problem of domestic violence. Sexual harassment is not considered acceptable, and each woman's family pressure acts to keep it in check.

Support for Mothers/Caretakers

Daycare

Lack of daycare facilities is a factor cited by many women when asked what prevents them from taking employment: however, several playschools are operational, many organized by the women's group, Balkan Sunflowers.

Inheritance and Property Rights

As in Albania, although legally women have equal rights to men, customarily women have not had rights to property ownership. For example, if a woman was widowed, she would be included into her husband's family, even being expected to marry an unmarried brother if there was one (known as *levirate*). A modification of the ownership law allows a widow an equal share to her brother-in-law, but only providing that she remains in the family. Even if women knew of their state rights to inheritance, those in the rural areas would be unlikely to try to claim them and equally unlikely to succeed in such a claim. There are now several women's organizations specifically attempting to counter this problem. Only 8 percent of women in Kosovo own property at present. This situation is changing with the support of UNMIK.

There is one sphere in which women may traditionally be owners of wealth: any gold they are given is considered to be their own. It was said before the war that many women, especially in the Prizren area, owned around 5,000 euros' worth of gold, which could be used in time of great need. But most of this wealth was taken from them during the war by the Serb occupying forces.

Social/Government Programs

Sustainable Development

Kosovo was the first country to adopt the euro as its form of currency. The gross domestic product (GDP) per capita is 0.367 euros. Half the population lives in poverty, 12 percent of these in extreme poverty. Kosovo's economy has grown at about 10 percent during the past two years; this high rate of growth is partly accounted for by the fact that it is making up the losses incurred during the 1990s. An estimated US $1.2 billion, mostly from donor funding, has been invested primarily on infrastructure repairs but is likely to decline in the near future.

FAMILY AND SEXUALITY

Kosovar families traditionally are large, encompassing the extended family. In rural areas, 13 percent of families have ten or more members (compared to only 3 percent in urban areas). The family, together with the family home, holds enormous symbolic significance in a social order where territorial and kinship principles overlap and indicate the family's prestige in the community. Recent events are disrupting the pattern of rural life whereby one or two male family members became migrant workers to Germany, other Western countries, or the United States in order to support the extended family and their large home in Kosovo. This arrangement allowed the other men of the family to continue working in agriculture and local trading while caring for elderly parents, investing any surplus cash in one or more of their youngsters (preference was always given to sons).

Gender Roles

Eighty percent of mothers are the primary caretakers for their families. Gender roles in the rural areas contrast sharply with the situation in urban areas, such as Prishtina especially, and also in other towns, where the influence of the thousands of internationals is having an enormous effect in all spheres.

Marriage

Within the medical community, there is little or no recognition of the fact that a woman can be sexually active outside marriage; in the countryside, at least one case has recently been reported of a brother killing his sister when her bridegroom declared his bride not to be a virgin on the wedding day.

Traditionally, weddings are events of enormous significance, whereby two families from different villages make a strong tie, the bride moving into the bridegroom's house as a junior and subservient member. Thus, many males in a village are related to one another whereas the women have few such ties. This remains true to a lesser extent in the towns. Most weddings are formal, lengthy, and extremely lavish.

Reproduction

Sex Education

A longstanding taboo against the discussion of premarital sex and of homosexuality has prevented the introduction of sex education.

Contraception and Abortion

Until 1999 under the Serb regime, there were rigid attempts to introduce family planning as well as sterilization to the Albanian population. In opposition to such oppression, and to maintain the population under siege, neither contraception nor abortion was widely practiced. Few statistics have been available since then.

Teen Pregnancy

Teen pregnancy is virtually nonexistent in this country whose population is 90 percent Muslim. Despite rapid Westernization and an exaggerated following of fashion in Prishtina and other towns, teenage girls are closely guarded and very strictly chaperoned.

HEALTH

Health Care Access

Albanians had an extreme distrust of and little accessibility to state primary health care throughout the 1980s. By the 1990s, they had created alternative clinics. Immediately following the war, there was a focus on primary care with help from the World Health Organization (WHO), with an emphasis on "Kosovarization" to involve local administrators. The Family Medicine Training program updated the skills and practices of 100 doctors not only to practice medicine but also to train future doctors. Prishtina's University Hospital, with 2,500 beds, is one of the largest in Europe.

Diseases and Disorders

Almost all records relating to the time before the war of 1999 have been destroyed. Energy and expense since then have been focused on treating the health situation at hand rather than on providing records from such a short time period. Hence, health statistics are incomplete.

Severe health problems relate to water and air pollution, especially in the cities that are overpopulated. The problem is partly due to the return of refugees from abroad whose villages are mined or otherwise uninhabitable due to a lack of institutional services and normal infrastructure. There is a lack of education concerning the effects of garbage disposal, recycling systems, and immunization schemes.

Drug abuse is a very recent problem. The sale of heroin in Kosovo, most of it for export to other countries, is now higher than in most other European countries;[4] there is also easy availability of some addictive pharmaceutical drugs. Exact statistics are not available.

AIDS

Kosovo was relatively unaffected by HIV/AIDS until recently. The first confirmed case was registered in 1986, and forty-two further have been registered since, eleven in 2001. Recently, local NGOs have organized programs through mass media, youth magazines, and especially in youth centers to address the issues concerning protection from AIDS, as well as problems of drugs, alcohol, and smoking.

POLITICS AND LAW

As a region of Serbia, Kosovo followed Yugoslav law. Molded after 1987 by the Milošević regime, its interpretation became totally biased against Albanians. Since UNMIK took control, there has been an attempt to give police, judicial, and legal positions proportionately to the ethnic groups living in Kosovo.

Suffrage

During the 1999 war the majority of refugees were forced to hand over all identity documents to the Yugoslav military, who then destroyed them. Civil and voter registration took place following the end of the war, when over 1 million electors registered, of whom over 170,000 are non-Albanians.

Political Participation

UNMIK ensures affirmative action toward the participation of women in politics, requiring the inclusion of a woman candidate for every three on the party lists for the parliamentary elections. Of the 24.3 percent female candidates running for office in the election of October 2000, only 8.26 percent actually took office, perpetuating a self-fulfilling prophecy concerning women's ability as politicians. The results from the 2001 election show a very marked change despite the evidence that many women qualified for these positions are choosing to turn to the NGO sector, which offers better opportunities for participation and better pay.

In both the 2000 and the 2001 elections, the party (Democratic League of Kosovo, or LDK) of the nonviolent leader from the 1990s, Ibrahim Rugova, won. The 2000 election was not considered fully valid by the international community since the Serb

Kosovar Albanian woman drops her ballot in a box during municipal elections, Prishtina, October 2002. AP/Wide World Photos.

population boycotted it. However, in 2001 there was Serb participation, gaining them twenty-two seats (seven of them by women) of the 140.

Other major parties were the Democratic Party of Kosovo (PDK) and Alliance for the Future of Kosovo (AAK). Election committees throughout Kosovo were made up of approximately 70–80 percent women, many of them teachers.

Women's Rights

Groups such as the NGO Kodi in Peja/Peć provide legal advice to women, especially on domestic violence, divorce, child custody, and inheritance rights. Kodi has challenged in court the customary laws that grant men all family decision-making powers.

Military Service

Some women, especially young women, participated in the war of 1998–1999, serving with the Kosova Liberation Army (UÇK). There is now no Kosovar army. It was demilitarized, and some members became part of the Kosovo Protection Corps (KPC).

RELIGION AND SPIRITUALITY

Ninety percent of Kosovar Albanians are Muslim and ten percent are Catholic. Of the remaining 100,000 Serbs, 300,000 of whom lived in Kosovo before the war, most are Orthodox. Most of the Roma and Bosniaks are Muslims. However, Kosovo is basically a secular society. *Purdah* (the wearing of the veil by women) is rarely practiced, though many of the religious social customs are observed. No matter to which religion Kosovars belong, they identify first by ethnicity.

VIOLENCE

Domestic Violence

A recent survey found that 23 percent of women suffer domestic violence, but few would consider reporting it. In 1995, several women initiated a movement on the issue of domestic violence, urging that solutions be sought within the Albanian community rather than just blaming Serb oppression. They founded the Center for the Protection of Women and Children, gaining support from international women's movements.[5]

Rape/Sexual Assault

Cases of rape, sexual assault, and domestic violence are said to have increased in the years since the war, as is noted in most postwar societies. In the early months of 2000, babies born as a result of the thousands of wartime rapes brought shame to the mothers, some of whom committed suicide. Kosovar society is stricter than most in treating rape victims as outcasts. The same mores caused the victims themselves to hide or deny their suffering. Despite their suffering and loss of life and home, there has been little compensation to the victims.

Trafficking in Women and Children

Forced prostitution and trafficking in women and children are imposed more frequently on foreign women (from Ukraine, Bulgaria, and particularly from Moldova) than on Kosovars. The women's coalition group Kosova Women's Network, in partnership with the International Organization for Migration (IOM), provides support and shelter for women who have been trafficked to Kosovo and to those who wish to return home.

War and Military Repression

Civil wars have taken place recently in two areas close to Kosovo's boundaries: in the Preshevo Valley in Serbia and in western (especially northwestern) Macedonia. There are still 30,000 refugees and internally displaced persons in Kosovo, and there are still sporadic attacks on Serbs by extremist Albanians and vice versa. The Kosova Women's Network held a major countrywide campaign in November 2001, drawing attention to the connection between violence against women and other hate crimes.

OUTLOOK FOR THE TWENTY-FIRST CENTURY

Kosovo is in somewhat of a state of limbo, but the issues concerning its future status are under constant discussion. The desire of most of the Albanian population is for independence. Internationally it is feared that, should this be granted, it would create imbalance in the already fragile political situation of the region. Until it is resolved, there will necessarily be a feeling of uncertainty for everyone.

As many as 200,000 Serbs left immediately after the 1999 war fearing retribution for crimes inflicted or individual reprisal from extremist Albanians. The remaining 100,000 Serbs fear greater risk if NATO were to pull out. The return of Serb refugees has begun in some areas but has not been welcomed by Albanians.

The conditions for women have changed greatly since 1999. The new situation for non-Albanian women in Kosovo is somewhat precarious, although UNMIK and most of the women's organizations are at pains to try to allow them equal opportunities to those afforded Albanian women. In practical terms, this is difficult for Serbian and Roma women, who are living within protected enclaves with little access to areas outside the perimeters. Women of other minorities do not share this problem. There are currently moves to re-integrate the very controversial town of Mitrovica in the French sector where, in the previously integrated area, the north was primarily populated by Serbs and the south by Albanians. An initiative by youth groups on each side has already set up an Internet connection to assist in reaching one another.

Meanwhile life is slowly improving, houses are being rapidly rebuilt, and there is a wide availability of goods for those with the money to buy them. Much work has to be done to alleviate the extreme poverty and overcrowding for a large section of society and to give women, especially those who have lost their husbands, training and access to the workplace. It is important to revitalize industry, textile factories, local food production, and food processing plants in order to both lessen the need for imports and also reduce prices.

NOTES

1. Kosovo is the current spelling for the formerly autonomous region of Serbia in Yugoslavia. Kosova is the spelling in the Albanian language Kosovo/a is a term adopted by the non-partisan English speaking world.

2. One kilometer equals 0.6 miles.

3. Public communication from Kosova Women's Network.

4. World Health Organization, www.deploymentlink.osd.mil/du_balkans/du_balkans_tabe.htm.

5. Rachel Wareman. "No Safe Place: An Assessment of Violence against Women in Kosovo," UNIFEM, 2000.

RESOURCE GUIDE

Suggested Reading

Clark, Howard. *Kosovo: Work in Progress: Closing the Cycle of Violence*. Coventry, UK: Centre for the Study of Forgiveness and Reconciliation, 2002.

Llamazares, Monica. *The Women of Kosovo: Missing Links in a Failing Post-War Peacebuilding Process*. Master's thesis, University of Bradford, 2001.

Young, Antonia. *Women Who Become Men: Albanian Sworn Virgins*. New York: Berg Publishers, 2000. Reprint 2001.

Film/Video

Women, the Forgotten Face of War. 2002. Directed by Greta Olafsdottir and Susan Muska. Produced by Bless Bless Productions, blessbless@aol.com, www.blessblessproductions.com. Shows women's activism in Kosovo up to the war in 1999 and the aftermath and recovery. Interviews are included with well-known human rights activists and ordinary women.

Web Sites

International Organization for Migration, www.iom.ipko.org/kds/sec6-4.htm.

Albanians in Macedonia Crisis Center, Human Rights, www.alb-net.com/amcc/humanrights.htm.

Gender Equality: Legal and Institutional Framework on Women's Rights and Equal Opportunities; de Jure and de Facto Discrimination, www.womensnetwork.org/english/pdf/ihf_women.pdf.

Bay Area International Development Organizations, www.baido.org/topics/human_rights/2001/womenkosova.php.

Kosova Crisis-Women's Center—Albania, csf.colorado.edu/soc/m-fem/1999.II/msg 00032.html.

Organizations

Balkan Sunflowers, Voluntary Organisation for Social Reconstruction in the Balkans
Web site: www.ddh.nl/org/balkansunflower/
Representative for Roma women's rights in Mitrovica
Elizabeta Bajrami
Phone: (00381) 63/817-1738

Femrat ne Veprim (Women in Action)
Igbelle Hakiqi
Phone: (+381) 38-70-598

Founded in 1986, is based in Podujeva working with local and displaced women in surrounding villages, to provide a variety of training and support groups.

Kosova Women's Network
Email: info@womensnetwork.org

Made up of thirty-three women's groups throughout Kosovo with funding from the Open Society Institute. Meets in local groups in towns and villages to share strength and work on campaigns for women in education, for the economy and against violence. They put out a monthly email newsletter, *KWN Voices*.

Legjenda
Latifir Neziri
Phone/Fax: (++381) 280-82-024
Email: latifeneziri@hotmail.com

Founded in 1996 with international funding, based in Viti, and working with forty-two surrounding remote, mountainous, multiethnic villages to provide training in computer and sewing and other skills as well as psychosocial assistance.

Liria
Nazife Jonuzi
Phone: (++ 381) 28-25348

Founded in 1997, work on educating women on issues of domestic violence, trafficking, women's rights, election issues, and support programs for those suffering war trauma in Suhareka and Gjilan.

Motrat Qiriazi (the Qiriazi Sisters)
Email: motratqiriazi@ipko.org

Founded in 1989, Very active both in Kosovo and in the United States, campaigns for literacy amongst girls and women in rural areas.

SELECTED BIBLIOGRAPHY

Mertus, Julie. *Kosovo: How Myths and Truths Started a War*. Berkeley: University of California Press, 1999.

Mertus, Julie and Judy Benjamin. *War's Offensive on Women. The Humanitarian Challenge in Bosnia, Kosovo and Afghanistan*. Bloomfield, CT: Kumarian Press, 2000.

OSCE. *Report on the Gender Situation in Kosovo*. May 15, 2002.

Schwandner-Sievers, S. *Kosovo Social Assessment Report: Traditionalization—Aspirations—Frustrations—Visions*. Worldbank Report, 2000.

Wareham, Rachel. "No Safe Place: An Assessment of Violence against Women in Kosovo." UNIFEM, 2000.

22

LATVIA

Daina Stukuls Eglitis

PROFILE OF LATVIA

Latvia, a country of just under 2.4 million people,[1] is located on the Baltic Sea. Latvia's first period of independence, which lasted from 1918 to 1941, was followed by fifty years of Soviet occupation. Since 1991, Latvia has been an independent state with a democratically elected government. Al-

though Latvia developed an industrial economy during the
Soviet period, much of the
population, one third of whom
reside in rural areas, still depends on agriculture for sustenance.

Latvia has an ethnically
mixed population: 57.9 percent
Latvian and 29.4 percent Russian. Other ethnic groups include Belarusians, Ukrainians,
Poles, Lithuanians, and Jews.
Women comprise 54 percent of Latvia's population and men, 46 percent
in part because women's average life span is 76, considerably longer than
the male life expectancy of 65. Despite a spike in the middle 1990s, the
infant mortality rate declined to 11.0 per 1,000 births in 2001.[2] The maternal mortality rate was 41 per 100,000 births in 1999. Latvia has a total
fertility rate of 1.2, one of the lowest in the world.[3]

OVERVIEW OF WOMEN'S ISSUES

The transition to democracy and capitalism in the 1990s brought dramatic changes. Women and men have benefited from the expansion of
rights of free speech and assembly. Opportunities for travel, study, entre-

preneurship, and the acquisition of consumer goods have grown. At the same time, unemployment, poverty, discrimination in the labor market, and sexual exploitation have also increased. These negative phenomena have disproportionately affected women, a fact that has received little government attention. Women are underrepresented in elected bodies, though parliament in 1999 elected Eastern Europe's first female president. Despite women's difficulties, common wisdom in Latvia suggests that women have borne the dislocations of the transition period better than men: it is widely held that although many men have responded to crises with drinking and despair, women have largely responded with resolve and resiliency.

EDUCATION

Opportunities

Compulsory education for girls between six and sixteen years of age was accepted by the independent state in 1919: women's education in general has a long tradition of acceptance.[4] Universal education continued in the Soviet period, and women made further gains in higher and professional education. An educational gap favoring women opens in the 45–54 age group. In the postcommunist period, more women continue to graduate from high school and go on to higher education.[5]

There has been a rise in the number of early school leavers due in part to the independent state's 1991 decision to drop the mandatory high school education of the Soviet period. Data from 1999 show that although 12 percent of males ages 16–17 had left school, only 5.1 percent of females had done so.[6] There is also a notable difference between men and women in enrollment in institutions of higher education: 61 percent of students are female.[7]

Although women are more educated than men, their gains from this advantage are limited. Women are more likely to take degrees in fields such as medicine and teaching, which have traditionally been accorded low status and pay: for instance, in 2001–2002, women made up 78 percent of students at the Latvian Academy of Medicine and 87 percent of students enrolled at the Riga College of Pedagogy and Education. By contrast, they were just 36 percent of students at the Riga College of Economics.[8] The implications of such educational differences become apparent as graduates move into occupations: men are more likely to be managers and work in the more remunerative private sector and women tend to be employed by lower-paying state institutions like schools and hospitals.

Literacy

Literacy rates for both men and women are about 99 percent.

EMPLOYMENT AND THE ECONOMY

Job/Career Opportunities

Women's history of economic activity predates the Soviet period. In 1934, more than 56 percent of women worked for wages, which was Europe's second-highest rate.[9] In the postcommunist period, most women work and continue to make up close to half of the work force.[10] Women also make up about 57 percent of the unemployed[11] and a larger share of the long-term unemployed.

Pay

As in most of the rest of the world, women workers suffer a pay gap. In the state sector, women earn about 79.7 percent of men's salaries. A gap also exists in the private sector, where men are three times more likely than women to be employers.[12] Gender occupational segregation explains part of the gap. However, even women working in the same occupation as men experience a pay gap.[13]

Working Conditions

The Constitution of Latvia prohibits discrimination on the basis of sex and age, but women's difficulty in finding work is compounded by gender bias. Employers have placed job advertisements calling for "young, pretty, female worker[s]," some even stipulated that the applicant be under thirty. At the behest of nongovernmental organizations (NGOs), Latvia's largest newspaper has banned such ads. Some women experience employment discrimination based on their status as mothers, a problem that is serious in a context in which women with children are especially vulnerable to poverty.[14]

Support for Mothers/Caretakers

The pro-natalist state has attempted to create conditions favorable to motherhood. Among the provisions designed to help working mothers is a law stipulating that women with children under three should be entitled to full wages while working thirty rather than forty hours per week. The practical application of this policy, however, has been limited by a lack of information among mothers and fear of job loss.[15]

Social/Government Programs

The Labor Code focuses on *women* as caregivers, reinforcing stereotypes of women as primary parents and marginalizing men's role in the family.

The state has also continued programs of support like universal child allowances, though in the context of rapidly rising living costs, the value of state social welfare payments is paltry.[16]

FAMILY AND SEXUALITY

Gender Roles

Although the *Latvia Human Development Report 1995* argues for equal rights and opportunities for women, it also tacitly reinforces traditional gender roles and norms. It notes that a "good portion of a woman's life is occupied by bearing and raising children, caring for the home and family. For men, raising children and caring for children do not require leaving work. This division of labor is natural and acceptable to all."[17] This notion highlights stereotypical images of women and men. Consequently, in spite of the fact that most women are economically active, women's role in the family remains that of the primary domestic worker.

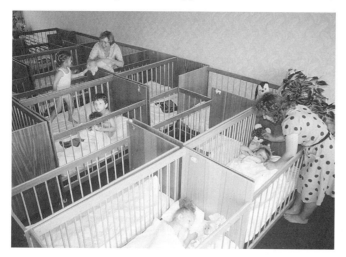

Nursery in Liepaja, Latvia. Photo © TRIP/V. Kolpakov.

Marriage

Although most people believe that marriage is a vital social institution,[18] the marriage rate has declined in the last several decades. From a rate of 10.1 per 1,000 in 1970, the marriage rate inched downward to 8.8 in 1990. From 1992 to 1995, the crude marriage rate dropped dramatically from 7.2 to just 4.4, bottoming out at about 3.9 per 1,000 in 2000.[19]

In the first postcommunist decade, divorce spiked and then fell to a postwar low. In 1990, the divorce rate per 1,000 was 4.0. By 1992, it had climbed to 5.5, but, just 4 years later it stabilized at about 2.4 where it remains.[20] The fall of the divorce rate is linked to the decline of marriage, but the state has also sought to discourage divorce by making it lengthier and more costly than during the Soviet period.

Reproduction

During the 1990s, fertility in Latvia fell precipitously. The age-specific fertility rate per 1,000 women 15–49 was 58.5 in 1990. By 2001, it had dropped to 33.2, which represented a rebound from the historical low of 1998: 30.4.[21] The total fertility rate, the average number of children born to a woman in her lifetime, has fallen to 1.2.

Growth in the proportion of nonmarital births was slow until the end of the 1980s, accelerated in the 1990s and does not appear to have leveled off yet: in 2000, nearly 40 percent of births were outside of marriage. This increase is the product of the growth of births outside of marriage, as well as the decline of births within marriage. The increase in nonmarital births cannot be characterized as an adolescent phenomenon, though in the age group 13–19, the majority of births (over 70 percent) are nonmarital. In the next age category, 20–24, the proportion in 2000 was 47.9 percent, and for those women ages 25–29, it was 33.2 percent.[22]

Contraception and Abortion

The availability of effective and safe contraception was limited in the Soviet period. In the decade after communism, nongovernmental organizations in Latvia have taken steps to facilitate access to contraception. In the past decade, there has been an increase in the use of hormonal contraceptives, such as the birth control pill.[23] The IUD and condoms remain, however, the most commonly used forms of contraception.[24]

Though there has been political debate about abortion, the state has not put legal restrictions on the procedure. Women's access may, however, be limited by an inability to pay, as a growing number of health services go uncovered by the state. The number of abortions fell in the past decade. In 2000, there were 17,240 induced abortions. There were slightly more births than abortions that year (1000:854), a reversal of the trend that held through most of the 1990s.[25] The rise in the use of contraception may be implicated in the falling number of abortions, which, in the near absence of other effective means, was used as a form of birth control in Soviet Latvia.[26]

HEALTH

Health Care Access

A study conducted by *Healthcare Europe* in thirty-five countries placed Latvia second to last, trailed only by Russia, in the health of its inhabitants.[27] Although the Soviet health care system was plagued by problems, it was universally accessible and provided basic services, including those critical to public health, such as vaccinations. Despite the postcommunist government's attempt to retain some semblance of the socialist-style universal health care system, the shift to a market-based economy has affected public access to physicians: a 1999 study found that many inhabitants did not seek out needed care because of a lack of money or insurance.[28] The number of hospitals has also fallen in the past decade.[29] Although ambulatory clinics have multiplied over the same period, some of those are private and accessible only to those with the means to pay.

A positive development in a decade characterized by negative health trends has been the improvement of birthing conditions. For instance, in the Soviet period fathers were frequently prohibited from attending births or handling newborns, but now many birthing facilities encourage fathers' participation. The dissemination of accurate information about what to expect during pregnancy and birth has also improved.

Diseases and Disorders

The greatest killer of women is cardiovascular disease. This disease takes the lives of more women than men, though most fatalities occur in women over seventy-five, an age the average man never reaches.

Alcohol is a leading contributor to health problems. The problem of alcoholism has become acute in the postcommunist period. A Ministry of Welfare study notes, "Alcoholism is associated with work and road accidents, birth defects, premature death of working age people, especially among men, broken families, and abandoned children."[30]

AIDS

The registered number of AIDS cases in Latvia has been low by world standards. In 1990, Latvia had just eight registered persons with HIV and only two known instances of HIV-positive persons who had developed AIDS. By 2000, the number of known HIV cases had risen to 466: 354 registered men and 112 registered women.[31] Although the number of sufferers is still low, the rise of problems like intravenous drug use and prostitution makes the country vulnerable to a further spread of the disease.

Cancer

The second major killer of women is cancer.[32] The most common cancers among Latvia's women are breast, skin, and uterine cancer. Early diagnosis of cancer in women lags behind that in Western countries.[33]

Depression

Available data suggest that women are twice as likely as men to report being depressed "often" or "very often."[34] In spite of the higher incidence of depression, women's suicide rates are far lower than those of men: the male suicide rate in 2000 was 56.5 per 100,000, compared to a rate of 11.9 for women.[35]

POLITICS AND LAW

Suffrage

In 1918, Latvian women were among the first in Europe to secure the franchise to vote.

Political Participation

Women's political status in the interwar period of independence was relatively high. The 1922 Constitution also enshrined equal political rights for men and women. Despite this, few women had the opportunity to participate in political decision making.[36]

Under Soviet rule, women retained equal citizenship rights and gained positions in legislative bodies: in the early postwar period, women comprised about 30 percent of the Supreme Soviet of the Latvian Soviet Socialist Republic.[37] Despite this, higher rungs of power like the Central Committees of the USSR and the republics continued to be ruled by men, and the political power conferred on women was more symbolic than substantial in the context of a single-party dictatorship.

Postcommunism has brought more democracy but less representation for women. In the seventh national parliament (*Saeima*), elected in 1998, women made up 17 percent of deputies.[38] Women have, however, made inroads into politics at the local level: in 1997, fully 38.7 percent of elected deputies were women.[39] As well, Latvia's first woman president, Vaira Vike-Freiberga, was elected by the parliament in 1999.

Women's Rights

Feminist Movements

It has been said that feminism in postcommunist Eastern Europe is a dirty word and, indeed, the similarity in the vocabulary of rights and equality embraced by liberal feminists and that of the reviled communist state may impede the development of feminist ideas and movements in Latvia. In spite of this, women's organizations are active. For instance, the Latvian Women's Organization Cooperation Council was formed in 1992 and encompasses a variety of women's groups built around common interests and backgrounds in business, religion, sports, social welfare, and education.[40] Women's groups are also increasingly active in the political sphere. In 1998, the first all-women's party, the Social Democratic Women's Organization of Latvia, was listed on the parliamentary ballot. The party did not receive enough votes to win seats in the *Saeima*.[41]

Military Service

Latvia has a military draft, from which women are exempt. Women have not been an active part of Latvia's military. The Latvian military's participation in internal peacekeeping missions, in Bosnia for instance, has been limited to male soldiers and officers. There is no notable pressure in society to increase women's role in the military.

RELIGION AND SPIRITUALITY

Despite its constitutional commitment to religious freedom, the atheist Soviet state actively discouraged public participation in organized religion. In the period after communism, however, the number of congregations in Latvia has grown considerably. Lutherans claim 302 congregations, though Roman Catholics are close behind with 243. Latvia has smaller numbers of Orthodox, Baptist, Pentecostal, Old Believer, and Seventh-Day Adventist congregations.[42] Many Latvians also participate in *dievturiba*, an ancient pre-Christian "religion" that has long been an important part of Latvian culture.

Women's Roles

Although Roman Catholicism prohibits the ordination of women, the Latvian Lutheran Church has a small number of female pastors. There has been debate within the Latvian Lutheran Church about the ordination of women, and although the practice is common in the émigré churches of the West, it has been prohibited by the sitting archbishop in Latvia. In contrast to many Christian denominations, *dievturiba* holds female figures in high esteem: nature, the object of worship, is densely populated with female goddesses.

VIOLENCE

Violence against women is difficult to assess because of the absence of comprehensive statistics on the problem.[43] Large-scale data seem to reflect a serious problem of underreporting: in a 1997 study, 9.4 percent of women reported being victims of physical violence, 18.7 percent of psychological violence, and 6.6 percent of sexual violence. In 1999, there were 7.7 reported rapes per 100,000 females.[44] Smaller surveys and informal data gathered by nongovernmental organizations, however, have yielded results that more closely reflect global trends, which suggest that between a quarter and a half of women may be victims of gender-based violence.[45]

Domestic Violence

The insufficiency of data is part of a larger picture characterized by a failure to embrace the seriousness of gender-based violence and a tendency to cast women as complicit in their own victimization. For instance, a study of press accounts of violence against women found that domestic battering was presented as a phenomenon only in "problem families," the product of female provocation, and a form of violence as likely to victimize men as women.[46]

Trafficking in Women and Children

In the postcommunist period, prostitution, which was illegal in the Soviet period, has grown into a massive business: in 1995, in Riga (the capital) alone, there were over 500 known establishments offering a range of sexual services. The "export" of women to neighboring countries has also become common. The processes of entry into the sex trade are complex. Some women choose to sell sexual services, though this "choice" is often driven by economic hardship. In other instances, women are lured into prostitution by advertisements claiming to match young women with jobs as dancers, waitresses, or nannies in the West. Upon arrival at their destination, these women are "sold" into the sex trade.[47] Greater press attention may reduce the problem over time, though the profitability of sex trafficking makes its demise unlikely.

OUTLOOK FOR THE TWENTY-FIRST CENTURY

The outlook for women in the twenty-first century cannot be characterized with any single adjective. In some respects, it looks bleak: women are underrepresented in elected bodies and the upper echelons of the economy and overrepresented among those who are poor, unemployed, and sexually exploited. In other respects, it is potentially bright: full rights to speech and organization mean that women are free to organize around their own issues, the election of a woman president offers a valuable political role model, and the expansion of the free market provides opportunities for women to bypass the discriminatory labor market and pursue their own entrepreneurial dreams. The fact that women are well represented among the highly educated suggests that, especially in an economy ever more dependent on the production of knowledge and services, women are in a position to make important contributions. Although traditional gender stereotypes abound in society, Latvian history, folk culture, and literature are also full of powerful female figures that highlight the broad, expansive array of roles women can and will play in the future.

NOTES

1. Central Statistical Bureau of Latvia (CSBL), *Latvian Women and Men* (Riga: Author, 2001), 30.

2. CSBL, *Latvia: Statistics in Brief* (Riga: Author, 2002), 7–8.

3. United Nations Development Programme (UNDP), *Human Development Report 2000/2001* (2000–2001), http://ano.deac.lv/html_1/undp_02.htm.

4. Inna Zariņa, *News about Women in Latvia* (Riga: Latvian Women's Studies and Information Center, 1994), 8–9.

5. Ritma Rungule, "Education," in *Dzīves apstākli Latvijā 1999* (Riga: CSBL, 2001), 65.

6. Rungule, 2001, 64–65.

7. CSBL, *Izglītības iestādes* (Riga: Author, 2002), 13.

8. I am grateful to Ritma Rungule for passing on to me this unpublished information from the Central Statistical Bureau of Latvia.

9. Koroleva and Trapenciere, 1992, 232–55.

10. UNDP, 2000–2001, 149.

11. CSBL, "Aprīlī nedaudz," press release, May 17, 2002, www.csb.lv.

12. UNDP, 1998, 13; and UNDP, 2000–2001, 148.

13. UNDP, 1998, 13.

14. UNDP, *Gender and Human Development in Latvia*, 1998, http://ano.deac.lv/html_1/undp_02.htm.

15. UNDP, 1998, 14–15.

16. Daina Stukuls, "Body of the Nation," *Slavic Review* 58 (1999): 535–58.

17. UNDP, *Latvian Human Development Report*, 1995, http://ano.deac.lv/html_1/undp_02.htm.

18. Pēteris Zvidriņš et al., *Fertility and Family Surveys* (New York: United Nations, 1998).

19. CSBL, *Latvijas demogrāfija gadagrāmata* (Riga: Author, 2002), 186.

20. CSBL, 2000, 47.

21. CSBL, 2002, 85.

22. Unpublished data provided in 2000 to the author by the Central Statistical Bureau of Latvia Population Data section.

23. UNDP, 1998, 23.

24. Zvidriņš et al., 1998, 38–39.

25. CSBL, 2000.

26. UNDP, 1998, 22.

27. Zigrīda Gosa, "Viriesu ekonomiskā loma gimenē," in *Man's Role in the Family, Proceedings of the International Conference*, November 19–20, 1998, Riga, Latvia.

28. Institute for Applied Social Science, *Dzīves Apstāklu Apsekojums Latvijā 1999* (Riga: CSBL, 2000).

29. CSBL, 2000, 106.

30. Nora Dudwick et al., *Nabadzīgo cilvēku viedokļi* (Riga: Institute of Philosophy and Sociology, 1998).

31. Statistics Lithuania, *Women and Men in the Baltic Countries* (Vilnius: Author, 2002), 35.

32. UNDP, 1998, 21.

33. Gosa, 1999, 119.

34. UNDP, 1998, 22.

35. Statistics Lithuania, 2002.

36. Zariņa, 1994, 10–11.

37. Zariņa, 1994, 10–12.

38. UNDP, 2000–2001, 149.

39. UNDP, 1998, 28.

40. Zariņa, 1994, 36–39.

41. UNDP, 1998, 30.

42. CSBL, 2000, 194.

43. Ieva Zaķe, "The Latvian Press and Violence against Women," in *Invitation to Dialogue* (Riga: Institute of Philosophy, 1997), 56–68.

44. UNDP, 2000–2001, 152.

45. UNDP, 1998, 25.

46. Zake, 1997, 58–65.

47. Stukuls, 1999.

RESOURCE GUIDE

Suggested Reading

Central Statistical Bureau of Latvia (CSBL). *Latvian Women and Men: A Statistical Portrait*. Riga: Central Statistical Bureau of Latvia, 1997. Data covering the early to mid-1990s including statistics on sex ratios; demographic events; comparisons of income, education, and employment; and some sociological surveys.

Kirss, Tiina, ed. Special issue of the *Journal of Baltic Studies*: *Women in the Baltics*. A multidisciplinary overview of historical and contemporary women's issues in the three Baltic countries. Forthcoming in 2003.

Statistics Lithuania. *Women and Men in the Baltic Countries*. Vilnias: Author, 2002.

Stukuls, Daina. "Body of the Nation: Mothering, and Prostitution, and the Place of Women in Postcommunist Latvia." *Slavic Review* 58, no. 3 (1999): 537–58. An analysis of the position of women in postcommunist Latvia, using the prism of the sex trade and social welfare policies.

United Nations Development Project (UNDP). *Gender and Human Development in Latvia*. 1998. http://ano.deac.lv/html_1/undp_02.htm. A good statistical and analytical overview of gender issues authored by local researchers.

Web Sites

Central Statistical Bureau of Latvia, www.csb.lv.
Has a good selection of statistical data relating to gender and other economic and social issues.

United Nations Development Project, http://gender.undp.sk/index.cfm.
Contains a "Gender Virtual Library" with fruitful links to information about Latvia as well as other countries in East Europe and the CIS.

Organizations

Gender Studies Center at the University of Latvia
Raina boulevard 19, Room 133
Riga LV 1586, Latvia

Phone: (371-7) 034-327
Fax: (371-7) 034-422
Email: dzsc@lanet.lv

Offers information about gender studies, feminism, and conferences and workshops about gender studies in Latvia and elsewhere. The center also houses a library with pertinent resources.

Latvian Women Studies and Information Center
Akademijas laukums 1, Room 805
1050 Riga, Latvia
Phone: (371-7) 224-040, 227-474
Fax: (371-7) 820-608
Email: spiceina@lza.lv

Gathers, analyzes, and disseminates data about the women of Latvia, especially regarding economic and family activities.

SELECTED BIBLIOGRAPHY

Central Statistical Bureau of Latvia (CSBL). *Latvia: Statistics in Brief.* Riga: Central Statistical Bureau of Latvia, 2002.

Gosa, Zigrīda. "Women's Health at the Turn of the 20th Century." *Humanities and Social Sciences Latvia* 24 (1999): 114–24.

Koroļeva, Ilze, and Ilze Trapenciere. "Women in Latvia: Some Significant Historical Data and Figures." In *Fragments of Reality: Insights on Women in a Changing Society,* edited by Ilze Trapenciere and Sandra Kalnina. Riga: VAGA, 1992.

Kristapsone, Silvija. "Mortality Caused by External Reasons of Death in Latvia in the 1990s." *Humanities and Social Sciences Latvia* 24 (1999): 97–113.

Ostrovska, Ilze. "Barriers to Political Mobilization of Women." In *Invitation to Dialogue: Beyond Gender (In)equality,* 34–44. Riga: Institute of Philosophy, Latvian Academy of Sciences, 1997.

Stukuls, Daina. "Body of the Nation: Mothering, Prostitution, and the Place of Women in Post-Communist Latvia." *Slavic Review* 58 (1999): 535–58.

United Nations Development Project (UNDP). *Gender and Human Development in Latvia.* 1998. http://ano.deac.lv/html_l/undp_02.htm.

———. *Human Development Report 2000/2001: The Public Policy Process in Latvia.* 2000–2001. http://ano.deac.lv/html_l/undp_02.htm.

———. *Latvia Human Development Report.* 1995. http://ano.deac.lv/html_l/undp_02.htm.

Zaķe, Ieva. "The Latvian Press and Violence against Women in the Context of Gender Inequality." In *Invitation to Dialogue: Beyond Gender (In)equality,* 58–68. Riga: Institute of Philosophy, Latvian Academy of Sciences, 1997.

Zarina, Inna, ed. *News about Women in Latvia.* Riga: Latvian Women Studies and Information Center, 1994.

Zvidriņš, Pēteris, Ligita Ezera, and Aigars Greitāns. *Fertility and Family Surveys in Countries of the ECE Region Standard Country Report: Latvia.* New York: United Nations, 1998.

Selected Latvian Bibliography

Central Statistical Bureau of Latvia (CSBL). *Aprīlī nedaudz samazinājās bezdarba līmenis (In April the unemployment rate fell somewhat)*. Press release, May 17, 2002. www.csb.lv.

———. *Grūtniecība, aborti, zīdaiņu barošana (Pregnancy, Abortion, Nursing)*. 2002. Health statistics at www.csb.lv/Satr/rad/P09.cfm?kurs03=P09.

———. *Izglītības iestādes Latvijā 2001./2002. mācību gadu sākumā (Educational Institutions in Latvia at the Beginning of the School Year 2001/2002)*. Riga: Central Statistical Bureau of Latvia, 2002.

———. *Latvijas Statistikas gadagramata 1999 (Latvia's Statistical Yearbook 1999)*. Riga: Central Statistical Bureau of Latvia, 1999.

———. *Latvijas Statistikas gadagrāmata 1999/2000 (Latvia's Statistical Yearbook 2000)*. Riga: Central Statistical Bureau of Latvia, 2000.

———. *Reģistrēta bezdarba līmenis pilsētās un rajonos 2002. gada jūnijā. (Registered Unemployment in Cities and Districts in June 2002)*. July 15, 2002. www.csb.lv.

———. *2000. gada Tautas skaitīšanas provizōriskie rezultāti (Provisional Results of the 2000 National Census)*. Riga: Central Statistical Bureau of Latvia, 2001.

Central Statistical Bureau of Latvia and Fafo Institute for Applied Social Science. *Dzīves apstākļu apsekojums Latvijā 1999. gadā (The Survey of Living Conditions in Latvia in 1999)*. Riga: Central Statistical Bureau of Latvia, 2000.

Dudwick, Nora, and Ilze Trapenciere, Ritma Rungule, Maruta Pranka, and Taņa Lāce. *Nabadzīgo cilvēku viedokļi: Nabadzības sociālais vērtējums Latvijā (Perspectives of the Poor: A Social Analysis of Poverty in Latvia)*. Riga: Institute of Philosophy and Sociology, 1998.

Gosa, Zigrīda. "Vīriešu ekonomiskā loma ģimenē" ("Men's Economic Role in the Family"). In *Man's Role in the Family, Proceedings of the International Conference*, November 19–20, 1998, Riga, Latvia.

Rungule, Ritma. "Izglītība" (Education). In *Dzīves apstākli Latvijā 1999. gadā*. Riga: Central Statistical Bureau of Latvia, 2001.

23

LITHUANIA

Vicki L. Hesli, Alexis Bushnell, and Rasa Alisauskiene

PROFILE OF LITHUANIA

The elected representatives of the Lithuanian people demonstrated their courage and their self-determination when they were first among all the peoples of the Union of Soviet Socialist Republics (USSR) to declare their independence on March 11, 1990, in the midst of Mikhail Gorbachev's democratizing reforms. This declaration of independence was recognized by the world community of states over a year later in September 1991 in the aftermath of the abortive attempt to overthrow USSR President Mikhail Gorbachev by hardliners within the Communist Party of the Soviet Union. The failed coup of August 1991 cemented the delegitimization processes that eventually led to the full dissolution of the Soviet Union in December 1991.

Lithuania was well positioned to establish independent statehood given its relative autonomy within the federal structure of the USSR, its independence between World War I and World War II, its relatively homogenous population (81 percent Lithuanian, 9 percent Russian, and 7 percent Polish by nationality, and primarily Roman Catholic by religion), and its relative proximity to the European Union. Lithuania moved quickly to adopt a new constitution in October 1992 and applied for membership in Western European institutions, most notably NATO and the European Union (EU). In 2001, Lithuania became a member of the World Trade Organization. In spite of its European leanings, relations with Moscow remain good, in part because of the relative lack of discrimination experienced by Lithuania's Russian-speaking minority.

Lithuania's national economy is tightly tied to its trade with Russia and Germany. The 1998 Russian financial crisis therefore had a severe negative impact on the economy of Lithuania. GDP growth rates returned to approximately 3 percent for 2000 and 2001. GDP per capita was estimated for 2000 at US$7,300 (purchasing power parity). A serious and continuing challenge facing the economy of Lithuania is the environmental pollution, that remains a legacy of Soviet rule.

Geographically, Lithuania shares borders with Russia, Belarus, Poland, and Latvia, and borders as well on the Baltic Sea. The capital city is Vilnius. The land area measures 65,200 square kilometers, which is slightly larger than the U.S. state of West Virginia.

The estimated population of the country (as of mid-2001) was 3,610,535.[1] Although the total fertility rate was positive at 1.37 children born per woman, out-migration of the population has created negative population growth rate of–0.27 percent (2001 estimate). Females constituted 53.2 percent of the overall population in 2001. The proportion of males in the population is greater than females for age cohorts under twenty-four years. For all other age cohorts, females outnumber males. The estimated infant mortality rate for 2001 was 14.5 deaths/1,000 live births, and the maternal mortality rate was 27 per 100,000 live births in 1995. Life expectancy at birth in 2001 was 66 years for males and 77 years for females.

OVERVIEW OF WOMEN'S ISSUES

In comparison with other states in the world, one can argue comfortably that women in Lithuania enjoy legal rights equal to those of men. With regard to norms of behavior in the home, the workplace, and society as a whole, the lives of women, although marked by traditional divisions of labor, are not as significantly burdened as is the case in so many other countries. As early as 1529, women's rights to an inheritance and to attend meetings were confirmed in the First Lithuanian Statute, which included a chapter on protecting women against violence. This was the first law in Europe to define the rights of women as human beings and not simply as mothers or as potential mothers. In 1905, the first women's organization, Unification of Lithuanian Women for the Protection of Women's Rights, was founded in Vilnius. The First Congress of Lithuanian Women (meeting in Kaunus in 1907) discussed women's problems and addressed the question of women's equality.

Under the oversight of the Communist Party, and while Lithuania was part of the Soviet Union, women's republic-level congresses were held in 1946, 1966, 1968, 1977, 1982, and 1987. In November 1996, the government of Lithuania approved an Action Plan for the Advancement of Women in Lithuania (Resolution No. 1299). This plan may be considered to be an outline of the major issues of concern to women in Lithuania today.[2] The Action Plan envisions support programs for small businesses and for large families, improvements in the public transportation system, programs to promote healthy lifestyles and family planning, efforts to improve living conditions in rural areas, as well as a government commitment to improve programs, training, shelters, and legal codes dealing with violence against women and to improve images of women in the mass media. In 1998, the parliament adopted a Law on Equal Opportunities for Men and Women.

EDUCATION

Opportunities

Women outnumber men at all levels of education, except for in general schools and vocational schools.[3] When looking at the type of degrees earned, however, we see more men than women in doctoral studies, while women outnumber men in master's degree programs and in bachelor degree programs at the university level.

When men are enrolled in professional colleges and universities, they tend to be concentrated in engineering, transportation and security services, architecture and building, and computing. Women, on the other hand, most frequently study educational sciences (teacher training), social services, health care, humanities, business, and administration. These differences are significant because in terms of professional status and in terms of salary, areas such as transportation and engineering are more prestigious than those of nursing and education. This is not to say that women never obtain prestigious or high-paying careers, yet in general they go into jobs that are seen as "appropriate for women" by the culture in which they live. Therefore, even though women are well educated in Lithuania, they often end up with less prestigious and lower-paying careers than men upon graduation.

The field of education itself is a good example of this phenomenon. Whereas women often make up the majority of the enrollment in schools, they do not make up the majority of administrators or top-level positions in the education field. Recognizing this, Vilnius University decided to allow women extended academic leave, allow women to publish their research readily and even decided to give them head positions over men when their achievements are equal. Some people are opposed to these provisions, stating that they contradict the Law on Equal Opportunities.[4]

Literacy

It is estimated that between 98 percent and 99 percent of women and men in Lithuania over the age of fifteen can read and write.[5]

EMPLOYMENT AND THE ECONOMY

Job/Career Opportunities

Clerk in privatized state store, Vilnius, Lithuania. Photo © TRIP/ J. Greenberg.

In terms of comparative rankings, regarding the position and status of women within the country, Lithuania receives a "five star" rating (the best possible rating).[6] This rating implies that professionals and workers are nearly equal in gender terms. Employers are required to treat men and women equally in the workplace. Legally, employers must "set the same employment standards for both (men and women), provide equal opportunities for training, and allow men and women to fill the same positions at the same salary levels."[7]

Both men and women work in a variety of occupations. In 2000, females constituted 48 percent of the total labor force. Nonetheless, patterns of gender separation by occupation may be observed. In Lithuania, women more frequently work in the public sector (65 percent of public sector employees are women and 35 percent are men), whereas men more frequently work in the private sector (43 percent of private sector employees are women and 57 percent are men).[8]

In Lithuania, services employ the largest percentage of the workforce (56 percent in services, 37 percent in industry and construction, and 16 percent in agriculture, hunting, forestry, and fishing). The male labor force is divided almost equally between agriculture, industry, and services, although a slightly larger proportion of the male labor force is employed in industry (36 percent). The female labor force, however, tends to be concentrated in services (63 percent), with smaller proportions of the female labor force in industry (21 percent) and agriculture (17 percent).[9] Most of those working in health care, social work, education, and hotel and restaurant services are women, while the majority of those working in construction; agriculture, hunting, forestry, and fishing; utility supply; and transport, storage, and communication are men. Self-employment tends to be higher among men (20 percent of males employed in 2000 were self-employed) than among women (12 percent of females employed in 2000 were self-employed), while wage and salary employees are more frequently female (76 percent of males and 83 percent of females are wage and salary employees).[10]

The World Bank Group reported an unemployment rate for the male labor force of 17.3 percent for 2000, and an unemployment rate within the female labor force that was slightly lower at 13.3 percent. Figures for 2001 place the unemployment rate for men at 20 percent and for women at 14 percent.[11] Labor Survey data confirm this with an overall unemployment rate among those aged 15–64 reported at 17.2 percent in 2001.[12]

Pay

Women on average are paid less than men. The pay difference, however, is not as large as is found in most other countries of the world. Across Lithuania's entire economy, women on average earn 81 percent of what men earn. In the public sector, women's earnings average 77 percent of men's earnings. In the private sector, women earnings are 83 percent of men's.[13] Although men and women fairly equally fill full-time positions, the part-time positions are filled somewhat more frequently with women (59 percent of part-time employees are women, and 41 percent of part-time employees are men).

Working Conditions

Sexual Harassment

Sexual harassment became illegal as of 1999. Women and men are both protected against sexual harassment in places of work and education. Men and women both have the right to report harassment and are legally protected from repercussions that might result from such a report. If harassment is proven, the perpetrator is subject to punishment. A recent study reported that "71.4% of Lithuanian women older than sixteen have been victims of sexual harassment at least once by a stranger, and 34.8% at least once by a known man."[14]

Support for Mothers/Caretakers

Lithuanian laws for women in the workplace are generally very supportive. Unfortunately, many women feel uncomfortable in taking leave to care for their children and are afraid to report their employers. Oftentimes, employers will not hire or are not supportive of pregnant women and women with children.

Maternal Leave

Women are allowed a shortened workday or week if they are pregnant. They may also choose between working part- or full-time and are not required to do anything that may be potentially harmful to their child's health. Women are allowed maternity leave for seventy days before and fifty-six days after giving birth. In addition, women who are pregnant or mothers of children less than three years of age are not permitted to work overtime.[15]

A family may designate any one of its members to stay at home and provide care for the child. The person chosen to stay with the child is guaranteed their job upon returning to work. The family may receive monetary support from the state for childcare until the child is three years old. The state offers numerous benefit programs, including benefits for pregnancy and childbirth, pregnancy benefits for mothers who are studying, foster family benefits, military family benefits, orphan scholarships, extraordinary benefits for children without parental support, and benefits for families with three or more children.

Daycare

Only 15 percent of children under three years of age were attending preschool establishments (institutional daycare) in 2001; but for children aged three through six years, 56 percent were attending preschool establishments.[16] Attendance at preschool establishments is significantly higher in urban as compared with rural areas.

Inheritance and Property Rights

When women from the Christian Democrat faction in Lithuania's 1922 parliament recommended that an amendment be made to the Civil Code that would reinstate women's rights to property and inheritance equal to men's, the recommendation was adopted by the parliament. In 1937 a Lithuanian Women's Congress demanded that the constitutional guarantees of equality for women be implemented in daily life and not be narrowed by government laws and decrees. In the Soviet Constitutions, and in Lithuania's postindependence constitution, equal rights of men and women to inheritance and to property have been formally guaranteed.

FAMILY AND SEXUALITY

Gender Roles

The roles of men and women in the family have seen few changes since Lithuania was part of the Soviet Union. Women and men both need to work to support their families. Women also have the primary responsibility for care of the children, therefore in terms of overall working hours at work and at home and doing errands, women do work longer hours than men. A widely held perception within the society (among both men and women) is that men should work and women should stay home and raise the family. The perception is that both children and the family as a whole suffer when the mother works full-time. Economic hardship, however, prevents most mothers from staying at home with their children. Rather, both males and females work outside the home, and in most couples the woman takes on the majority of the child-raising and household chores (although in younger families there is evidence of a trend toward more of a partnership with regard to household duties).[17]

Marriage

Marriage rates have been lower since Lithuania's independence in 1991 than they were during the Soviet era. People are no longer getting married in large numbers or at as young of an age. As of 2001, the average age of first marriage for women was 24 years and for men 26 years. At the same time, divorce rates have increased. The total divorce rate in 2001 per 100 marriages was 41 percent.[18] Divorce rates among both men and women are highest in the age cohort between 25 and 34. In 2001, 52 percent of women (fifteen years and older) were married. Among men, 61 percent were married.[19] Widowed rates are higher among women (17 percent) than among men (3 percent), and single rates are higher among men (28 percent) than among women (21 percent).

Reproduction

The drop in marriage rates and increase in divorce have had a negative effect on reproduction in Lithuania. A significant decrease is demonstrated by looking at the number of births in 1990 compared to 1999. In 1999, the birthrate was 34 percent less than in 1990.[20] Many people in Lithuania feel that for true happiness, a married couple needs at least one child. Therefore, the emphasis put on childbearing is still great. Single motherhood even has wide acceptance because of this strong emphasis on childbearing.[21] With more and more people living together and having children out of wedlock, and given divorce and economic strife, marriage and a mother and father both living together with children are not as common as during the Soviet era.

Sex Education

Sex education is taught in Lithuanian schools as part of the curriculum in other courses, such as health. Nonetheless, educators often feel uncomfortable teaching sex education in their classes and instead require students to read about it. Programs that focus specifically on sexual education are very few and far between, and individuals have to take it upon themselves to attend a program.[22]

Contraception and Abortion

Abortion is the number one means of birth control in Lithuania. Abortion is legal in the first twelve weeks of conception. Anything beyond that requires the consent of a physician. Although abortion is legal, it is not socially supported. Women will go to great lengths to hide their abortions, and illegal abortions do take place as well. In 2001, there were forty-four legally induced abortions for every 100 live births.[23]

Contraceptives are not widely used in Lithuania. Although individuals do have access to contraceptives, they are expensive and inspire concerns about the health consequences associated with their use. For example, many women worry that hormonal contraceptives compromise their health. Most women go to their regular doctor rather than family practice specialists for information about birth control. It is rather expensive to provide mass literature about contraceptives, and many individuals do not seek information from a family planning provider. The most widely used and offered forms of contraceptives are condoms and intrauterine contraceptives; contraceptive implants are not offered.[24]

Teen Pregnancy

Teenagers, like adults, are allowed to purchase contraceptives with or without prescriptions, depending on what birth control method the individual chooses. Teen sexuality is looked down upon in Lithuanian society, and subsequently, only limited information about it is available. In 1997, 7.1 percent of abortions were performed on women under the age of nineteen, and this number has been on the rise. Girls under the age of sixteen are required to prove consent from a parent before they can have an abortion.[25]

HEALTH

Health Care Access

The availability of universal access to free health care was a hallmark of the Soviet system. Through a system organized and managed by the government, the Soviet Union provided hospital beds for a greater percentage of its population than any other country in the world. Often factories and universities had their own medical clinics. The system also provided specialized clinics and facilities for women's and children's care.

Although the system provided health care for large numbers of people, the Ministry of Public Health's obsession with predetermined quotas and limits constrained possibilities for quality, personalized care. Because the legacy of the Soviet system remains, most physicians are women and most are paid low salaries. Women are likely to be general practitioners providing basic care in polyclinics, whereas men are likely to teach medicine, to work in the prestigious hospitals, and to specialize and thus receive higher pay than women.[26]

In general, the medical and health care systems are not highly regarded in Lithuania. Private (nonstate) clinics are being established, but state-run facilities still provide most care for most people. In 1996 and in the two previous years, only a minority of Lithuanian residents had either visited a private clinic (22 percent) or had consulted a private physician (29 percent).[27] An overall perception does exist that either physicians do not care or that they are unqualified. Shortages of medical supplies are not a major reason for dissatisfaction with medical care, even though the media tends to give more attention to shortages than to standards of medical training or to doctor–patient relations.

Women are provided medical services during and after pregnancy. Women in Lithuania do have ready access to health care. Health care is nationally funded and available to all citizens. Survey data from Lithuania confirms that health services are assumed to be free, and this is what the people continue to expect. Extra fees are frequently paid for medications and for some needed supplies, like syringes and dressings, but fees for examination or treatment are rare. The practice of giving gifts or extra payments for medical services, however, is reported by a fair number of people. Men give gifts for medical services less frequently than do women. Thus, even though free services are taken for granted, the idea of extra payments, whether it be in the form of a gift or a monetary exchange, is not unusual in Lithuania or in other post-Soviet settings.

Diseases and Disorders

Out of all diseases, circulatory system diseases are the most common causes of death among women in Lithuania. In 2001, 65 percent of all female deaths were caused by circulatory diseases. The abuse of alcohol is more common among men than among women. In 2001, nearly eight times as many men as women suffered from chronic alcoholism. Smoking is also significantly more prevalent among men: 45 percent of men smoke every day, whereas 7 percent of women are everyday smokers.[28]

Sexually transmitted diseases also exist in Lithuania, due primarily to the limited education in this area and to prostitution. The most common sexually transmitted disease among women is syphilis. "In 1997, there were 84.9 cases of syphilis per 100,000 inhabitants, 1.47 times higher than 1994 figures and 17.7 times higher than in 1991."[29] Although STDs are a problem, the number of reported cases has been declining since the early 1990s.

AIDS

AIDS is present in Lithuania but not to the extent as in many of the other former Soviet countries. Compared to worldwide statistics, AIDS is much less prevalent in Lithuania. Lithuania had its first registered AIDS patient in 1988. Although the number of people infected with AIDS is small, infection rates are higher among men than among women. At the end of 2001, the number of confirmed new cases of HIV among women was twenty-three and the number of confirmed new cases of HIV among men was forty-nine.[30] Only five people died from HIV-related complications in Lithuania in 2001.

National STD and AIDS prevention programs have been implemented in Lithuania to help minimize HIV infections. These programs focus on education, testing, and treatment. It has also been suggested that AIDS patients should all receive care funded through the national budget.[31]

Cancer

Cancer is also a leading cause of death among women. Breast and skin cancer are the two most common cancers among women in Lithuania. Ovarian cancer and cancer of the body of the uterus are also very common in Lithuanian women.[32]

Depression

A stigma is often associated with mental disorders. This stigma still exists from the Soviet era, when people who suffered these disorders were outcasts. Individuals now seek medical attention when suffering mental disorders, but many people avoid it if possible. In 1997, females made up 44.4 percent of all people suffering from mental disorders. Most common among women with disorders was temporary insanity.[33]

POLITICS AND LAW

Suffrage

When elections were held in 1920 to Lithuania's Founding Parliament, ten of the 112 delegates were women, and when the Provisional Lithuanian Constitution was adopted in the same year, it declared equal rights for men and women. In 1922, women's right to vote was confirmed in the Lithuanian State Constitution. Today in Lithuania, all citizens eighteen years of age have the right to vote (except those declared legally incompetent by a court).

Political Participation

Lithuania is a parliamentary democracy that has earned the ranking of "Free" by Freedom House, Inc. Freedom House uses the designations Free, Partly Free, or Not Free, as determined by a combination of the political rights and civil liberties ratings, to indicate the general state of freedom in a country or territory. Only eighty-five of 192 countries evaluated in 2002 received the designation of "Free."

The president of Lithuania is elected by popular vote for a five-year term. Lithuania's unicameral parliament (the *Seimas*) is partly elected through single member districts (seventy-one seats) and partly elected through a proportional party-list system (seventy seats) on an electoral cycle of every four years.[34] Political participation in these elections has declined since independence: turnout in the 1992 parliamentary elections was 75 percent, but only 53 percent in 1996 and 59 percent in 2000. In the 1996 parliamentary elections, men and women turned out to vote in roughly equal proportions.

Men and women are similar as well with regard to modes of participation other than voting in elections. According to public opinion data, other modes of political participation are very low among both men and women.[35] Only 7.6 percent and 6.0 percent of males and females respectively had contacted (by letter or phone) a newspaper, magazine, or television station in 1996, the year prior to the survey. Just 10 percent and 6.8 percent of males and females respectively had contacted a deputy or other public official. Fourteen percent of males and 18 percent of women had signed a collective letter or petition, and 20 percent of both men and women had participated in a rally or demonstration. Thus, levels of political participation are remarkably similar (low) among men and women, with the minor exceptions that women are somewhat more likely than men to sign petitions, whereas men are more likely than women to contact a public official.[36]

Women saw a significant increase in representation in Lithuania's national parliament between 1993 and 1997, but they experienced a relative decline in 2000. The proportion of female members increased from 7.1 percent (of 141 members) in 1993 to 18 percent of members in 1996, and it decreased to 11 percent of members in 2000. In 2000, only 18 percent of candidates for a seat in parliament were women. This means that in Lithuania's 2000 national parliament, fifteen of 141 members are women. These women do represent both liberal and conservative viewpoints, and at least one woman does serve on each of the major committees in the parliament (in 2001). Three of thirteen members of the XII Cabinet Council were women (as of 2001).[37]

Women serve in somewhat larger proportions of the councils of Lithuania's municipalities. Eighteen percent of members of the municipalities' councils were women as of 2001. Fifty-two percent of judges, 42 percent of prosecutors, and 37 percent of lawyers were women in January 2002. Only two of Lithuania's sixty mayors, however, were women as of May 2003.[38]

Women's Rights

In 1994 (after Lithuania had once again been recognized as an independent country), a government position was created titled Consultant to the Government on Women's Questions. The position, after being renamed in 1997, was abolished when a new position with jurisdiction over questions of women's equality was created titled State Consultant with Abroad and with Non-Governmental Organizations. In 1995, Lithuania's parliament ratified the UN General Assembly Convention on the Abolition of All Forms of Discrimination against Women (CEDAW). Also in 1995, the Lithuanian Women's Party was founded.

An Action Plan for the Advancement of Women in Lithuania (Resolution No. 1299) was approved in November 1996.[39] In 1998, the parliament of Lithuania adopted a Law on Equal Opportunities for Men and Women and, as a follow-up, a Parliamentary Ombudsman for Equal Opportunities was established in 1999 to guarantee equal rights for women and men. In 2000, an Inter-Ministerial Commission of Equal Opportunities for Men and Women was established. Also in 2000, the Third Congress of Lithuanian Women was held in Vilnius.

Lesbian Rights

Under the Penal Code of the Soviet Union, sexual relations between men were a criminal offense. Lithuania abolished its severe penalties for consensual gay male sexual acts in the early 1990s, but protections for lesbians and gay men against discrimination or targeted "instigation" attacks did not appear in legal codes until the last few years. Discrimination in employment on the grounds of sexual orientation is now explicitly prohibited in two legal acts that went into force in January 2003. Article 2 of the (new) Labor Code (adopted by the Lithuanian Parliament in June 2002) defines legal equality in employment and includes sexual orientation as prohibited grounds for discrimination and as prohibited grounds for dismissal. Also, a new Law on Health and Safety of Workers was adopted in November 2001 that specifies working time as well as preventive measures for the health of young people and for pregnant workers. Included in this law is a requirement for equal working conditions for all sexual orientations. The new Penal Code (adopted in September 2000) also explicitly mentions sexual orientation as punishable grounds for discrimination.

In general, negative attitudes toward lesbians and gay men are strong in Lithuania. Lithuania has among the lowest indices of homosexuality in Europe. Catholic Church officials condemned a symbolic marriage ceremony of two gay men in Vilnius in 1997, and gay men have been subject to violent harassment. Thus, it has fallen in most cases to international organizations to advocate for the rights of homosexuals in Lithuania. For example, as part of the European Initiative for Democracy Rights, a seminar was held in Vilnius in September 2001 on human rights for lesbians and gay men. This was part of the project *EU Anti-Discrimination Policy*.

RELIGION AND SPIRITUALITY

Lithuania is a predominantly Catholic nation. In a nationwide survey, conducted in 1997, 80 percent of the Lithuanian population identified themselves as believers. Among women, 88 percent are believers; among men, 73 percent are believers. Among these believers, 87 percent (of men and women combined) are Roman Catholic and 5 percent are Russian Orthodox. Women are somewhat more inclined to participate in religious services, but, on average, both men and women attend service less than twice per month.[40]

Roman Catholicism has played a critical role in Lithuanian politics and society. During the Soviet period and into the present, Catholic priests represent themselves as guardians of Lithuanian traditions and culture. Catholic priests are particularly known for having maintained an underground publication (*samizdat*) titled the *Chronicle of the Lithuanian Catholic Church* during the height of Soviet repression. This publication criticized Soviet policies, such as controls over seminaries and textbooks, but it also provided an independent source of information for the population on a variety of topics.

In the early 1990s there was a preoccupation with overcoming fifty years of repression.[41] Thus, in the postindependence period, the Lithuanian Catholic Church has shown a more conservative character, being slow, for example, to implement Vatican II reforms. The Catholic Church, of course, opposes abortion, although surveys show a majority of the people disagree with the pro-life agenda of the Catholic Church. The church has also been in the forefront of the fight against alcoholism.

VIOLENCE

All forms of crime are perpetrated by men more frequently than by women. Of persons charged with crimes in 2001 in Lithuania, 91 percent were men. Men are also more likely to be victims of violent crime than are women (this includes murder, murder attempts, and serious bodily injuries). The only exception is that women are more frequently victims of rape and rape attempts. The prison population in Lithuania is 96 percent male.

Domestic Violence

Domestic violence is a problem in Lithuania, and victims face difficult challenges. Women must report the crime in order for any legal action to occur, and many women are too afraid to take that step. Many Lithuanians believe that domestic violence should be taken care of privately by the family. One study showed that over half of all women interviewed who had lived with a significant other had been victims of domestic violence or threats.[42] Another study organized at Vilnius University showed that out of 200 women, 48 percent of them had been victims of abuse.[43]

Rape/Sexual Assault

Laws do exist in Lithuania for incarcerating rapists or perpetrators of sexual assault. Again, sexual assault often goes unreported due to embarrassing court trials, feelings of doubt in women, and even threats.[44] Studies show an alarming trend of women increasingly subjected to this crime. One study showed that 20 percent of adult women had been victims of attempted rape.[45] In terms of registered rape (or rape attempts), the number peaked in 1999 and declined in both 2000 and 2001. The assistance available for rape or sexual assault victims is limited. The assistance they do receive comes from general domestic violence programs or hotlines.

Trafficking in Women and Children

Prostitution is illegal in Lithuania. Punishment for prostitution is carried out with fines, unless the individual is a repeat offender, in which case incarceration may also result. Lithuanian women are sometimes brought to surrounding countries for prostitution. Many times, women are conned into prostitution under false pretenses of legitimate work in other countries. The traffickers then steal the women's travel identification so they cannot return home, forcing them to stay in the business. Incarceration is also the punishment for trafficking women and for the trafficking and prostitution of children. Because of the activities in which they are engaged, the women who are being trafficked can be held legally responsible for prostitution or for crossing international borders without required documentation. Therefore, the women themselves are often subject to punishment as are traffickers.[46]

OUTLOOK FOR THE TWENTY-FIRST CENTURY

Although there is room for improvement when considering the status of women in Lithuania, Lithuania is a good place for women to live and work in comparison to most other places in the world. Wage differentials between men and women are not large. Women have access to advanced education, although most career opportunities are found in lower-status jobs. The workplace does show occupational segregation by gender, and the problem of domestic violence has not been adequately addressed. The government and the economy are unquestionably directed and managed by men, but there are no legal obstacles to the participation of women in the commanding heights, and sanctions are enforced against serious discrimination or abuse.

Societal attitudes need to change about the role and proper place of women and men in the society if further strides are to be made toward full equality between the sexes—but neither men nor a majority of women in Lithuania are pushing for or advocating such a radical restructuring of relations between the sexes. The Catholic Church remains a moral force whose agenda conflicts with the women's right to self-determination. Women's organizations, however, are active, and many women academicians are doing research on women's issues. Major political parties, such as the LDLP, do have references to male and female equality and to support for the family in their party election programs. Movement can be seen in the society as it becomes more aware of and more responsive to women's needs.

NOTES

1. CIA, *World Factbook*, 2001, www.odci.gov/cia/publications/factbook/geos/lh. html.

2. See the "Mission" statement on the Women's Issues Information Centre homepage, www.wgsact.net/lithuania/lt-wiic.html.

3. "Women and Men in Lithuania, 2002," statistical pocketbook published by the Women's Issues Information Centre (P.O. Box 1218, Vilnius—2000), www.wgsact. net/lithuania/lt-wiic.html.

4. Giedrçe Purvaneckiençe, *Women in the Education System* (Women's Issues Information Center, 1999).

5. World Bank, World Development Indicators Database (April 2003).

6. Andrew Meier, "Country Profile: Lithuania," *New Internationalist*, 311 (April 1999): 31, www.newint.org.

7. Center for Reproductive Law and Policy, "Lithuania," in *Women of the World: Laws and Policies Affecting Their Reproductive Lives. East Central Europe*, 2000, Center for Reproductive Law and Policy, 78–100, www.crlp.org/pdf/Lithuania.pdf. See also: "Women's Reproductive Rights in Lithuania: A Shadow Report," published by the Center for Reproductive Law and Policy, 120 Wall Street, New York, New York 10005 (2000).

8. "Women and Men in Lithuania, 2002."

9. Figures are for 1995. World Bank, Gender Statistics.

10. World Bank, Gender Statistics.

11. The unemployment rate is for ages 15–64. "Women and Men in Lithuania, 2001."

12. Figures are for 2001. From Statistikos departamentas prie Lietuvos Respublikos Vyriausybes, www.std.lt/STATISTIKA/Socialine/uzimtumas/uzimtum_tyrimas_e.htm.

13. "Women and Men in Lithuania, 2002."

14. Center for Reproductive Law and Policy, 32.

15. Center for Reproductive Law and Policy, 31.

16. "Women and Men in Lithuania, 2002."

17. Giedrçe Purvaneckiençe, "Women in the Domestic Domain," in *Women in Transition: Voices from Lithuania*, ed. Suzanne La Font (Albany: State University of New York Press, 1998).

18. "Women and Men in Lithuania, 2002."

19. "Women and Men in Lithuania, 2002."

20. Victoria Eidukiene quoted in "Global Family Planning," *The Ryan Report* (October 2002), STOPP International.

21. Purvaneckiençe, 1998.

22. Center for Reproductive Law and Policy, 29–30.

23. "Women and Men in Lithuania, 2002."

24. Center for Reproductive Law and Policy, 11–12.

25. Center for Reproductive Law and Policy, 16–17.

26. D.A. Barr, "The Professional Structure of Soviet Medical Care," *American Journal of Public Health*, 85, no. 5 (1995): 373–78.

27. Vicki Hesli and Rasa Alisauskiene, "Attitudes on Health Care Reform in the Former Soviet Union," in *Medical Issues and Health Care Reform in Russia*, ed. Vicki Hesli and Margaret Mills (New York: Edwin Mellen, 1999), 65–112.

28. "Women and Men in Lithuania, 2001."

29. Center for Reproductive Law and Policy, 16.

30. "Women and Men in Lithuania, 2002."

31. Center for Reproductive Law and Policy, 14–15.

32. Eidukiene and Litvinavieiene, "Health and Social Welfare" (Women's Issues Information Center), 1999.

33. Women's Issues Information Center.

34. The first directly elected president of Lithuania, Algirdas Brazauskas (elected in 1993), had served previously as head of the Lithuanian Communist Party and therefore as de facto ruler of the Lithuanian republic during the last years of the Soviet rule. The successor to the Lithuanian Communist Party, the Lithuanian Democratic Labor Party (LDDP), also won the majority of the seats in the first postindependence (1992) parliamentary election. This majority was defeated in the 1996 parliamentary elections by the Homeland Union/Lithuanian Conservatives (HU/LC), which formed a center-right coalition government. Valdas Adamkus was elected president of Lithuania in February 1998. Given the public's dissatisfaction with the economy, the HU/LC experienced defeat in the October 2000 parliamentary vote. Although the Social Democratic Coalition, which united four leftist parties, secured the most votes, the government was formed from a centrist bloc of other parties whose combined electoral strength yielded a bare majority of parliamentary deputies. This ruling coalition collapsed in June 2001, and a new government and ruling coalition was organized under the leadership of Brazauskas as head of the Lithuanian Social Democratic Coalition (which includes the LDDP). Brazauskas became prime minister in July 2001. The presidential elections held in December 2002 were won by Rolandas Parkas of the Liberal Democratic Party (a new party) who ran a populist campaign for change.

35. Research supervised by Arthur Miller, Vicki Hesli, William Reisinger, and Rasa Alisauskieni.

36. Research supported by the National Science Foundation, United States.

37. "Women and Men in Lithuania, 2001."

38. "Women's Specific Situation in Lithuania," *European Network of the Adult Education Organizations Working on Women's Employment Issues*, produced under the support of the European Commission within the framework of the Socrates Programme 1999–2003 www.women-employment.lt/lithuani.htm. See also www.isa.lt/english/.

39. "Mission" Statement, *Women's Issues Information Centre* homepage, www.wgsact.net/lithuania/lt-wiic.html.

40. The survey was conducted with funding from the National Science Foundation for research on political change in post-Soviet societies. Project directors are Arthur Miller, William Reisinger and Vicki Hesli, www.undp.lt/wiic/women_in_lithuania/paz_progr.html.

41. Robert F. Goeckel, "The Baltic Churches and the Democratization Process" In *The Politics of Religion in Russia and the New States of Eurasia*, ed. Michael Bourdeaux (Armonk, NY: M.E. Sharp, 1995), 202–25.

42. Center for Reproductive Law and Policy, 26.

43. Giedrçe Purvaneckiençe. "Violence against Women" (Women's Issues Information Center).

44. Center for Reproductive Law and Policy, 23–24.

45. Purvaneckiençe, "Violence Against Women."

46. Center for Reproductive Law and Policy, 25–26.

RESOURCE GUIDE

Suggested Reading

La Font, Suzanne, ed. *Women in Transition: Voices from Lithuania*. Albany: State University of New York Press, 1998.

"Women and Men in Lithuania 2002," statistical pocketbook published by the Women's Issues Information Centre (P.O. Box 1218, Vilnius—2000) www.wgsact.net/lithuania/lt-wiic.html, ISSN 1648-052X (90 pages). The publication presents data on gender statistics. This covers information on the number of men and women, their participation in public administration, vital statistics, education, health care and social protection, employment and unemployment, wages and salaries, crime, etc.

Videos/Films

All Different, All Equal. 2000. 24 minutes. Color. Directed by Di Tatham. Produced by Television Trust for the Environment. Executive Producer, Jenny Richards. Series Editor, Robert Lamb. Series Producer, Luke Gawin. Grade Level: 7–12, college, adult. ISBN: 1–56029–850–2.

The Bathhouse (Pirtis) (Lithuania). 1997. 10 minutes. Directed by Rimantas Gruodis. (U.S. Premiere at the 1998 Margaret Mead Film & Video Festival.) On alternate days of the week, elderly men and women take refuge in the oldest and last active public bathhouse in Vilnius. In its timeless space, the visitor's musings about the hardships of daily life and an uncertain future are tempered with birch branches and the ritual bath.

Web Sites

Department of Statistics to the Government of the Republic of Lithuania (Statistics Lithuania), http://www.std.lt/web/main.php.

Equal Opportunities for Men and Women in Lithuania, 2002, Open Society Institute, http://www.eonet.ro/pdf/Lithuania.pdf.

Lithuania, www.asg.physik.uni-erlangen.de/europa/lit/lit1e.htm.

Women's Issues Information Center, www.undp.lt/wiic/women_in_lithuania/ and http://www.wgsact.net/lithuania/lt-wiic.html.

Organizations

Lithuanian Association of Women
Jaksto 9-22
2001 Vilnius
Email: kaprun@rc.lrs.lt

Women's Centre "Ievos namai"
Utenio a. 2
4910 Utena
Email: med.mok@utena.omitel.net

Women's Issues Information Center
Jakoto 9-303,315
2001 Vilnius
Web site: www.undp.lt/wiic

SELECTED BIBLIOGRAPHY

Alisauskiene, Rasa. "Women in Politics." In *Lithuania: Women in the Changing Society*, report presented at the UN 4th Women's World Conference 1995, Vilnius: Pradel, 13–14, 207–12. New York: Routledge, 1995.

Barr, D.A. "The Professional Structure of Soviet Medical Care: The Relationship between Personal Characteristics, Medical Education, and Occupational Setting for Estonian Physicians." *American Journal of Public Health* 85, no. 5 (1995): 373–78.

Buckley, Mary, ed. *Post Soviet Women: from the Baltic to Central Asia*. Cambridge: Cambridge University Press, 1997.

Eidukiene, Virginia, and Litvinavieiene. "Demography and Health." Women's Issues Information Center, 1999.

———. "Health and Social Welfare." Women's Issues Information Center, 1999.

Funk, Nanette and Magna Mueller, eds. *Gender Politics and Post Communism*. New York: Routledge, 1993.

Goeckel, Robert F. "The Baltic Churches and the Democratization Process." In *The Politics of Religion in Russia and the New States of Eurasia*, edited by Michael Bourdeaux. Armonk, NY: M.E. Sharpe, 1995.

Hesli, Vicki, and Rasa Alisauskiene. "Attitudes on Health Care Reform in the Former Soviet Union." In *Medical Issues and Health Care Reform in Russia*, edited by Vicki Hesli and Margaret Mills, 65–112. New York: Edwin Mellen, 1999.

Katzive, Laura, and Mindy Jane Roseman, eds. *Women's Reproductive Rights in Lithuania: A Shadow Report*. New York: Center for Reproductive Law and Policy, 2000. www.reproductiverights.org.

Lithuania: Women in the Changing Society. Pradal.

Purvaneckiençe, Giedrçe. "Violence against Women," Women's Issues Information Center.

———. *Women in Lithuanian Society; Project Report*. United Nations Development Programme.

———. "Women in the Domestic Domain." In *Women in Transition: Voices from Lithuania*, edited by Suzanne La Font. Albany: State University of New York Press, 1998.

———. *Women in the Education System*. Women's Issues Information Center, 1999.

24

MACEDONIA

Galina Schneider

PROFILE OF MACEDONIA

The Republic of Macedonia,[1] the "Pearl of the Balkans," is a 25,713-square-kilometer[2] emerging democracy of 2,031,112 Macedonians (66 percent), Albanians (23 percent), Turks (4 percent), Roma (2 percent), Serbs (2 percent), and Vlachs (0.5 percent).[3] Its spectacular mountains, ancient lakes, and river valleys are dotted with Roman, Byzantine, and Ottoman monuments. A unicameral Parliament of 120 members (twenty-one women), a president, and a prime minister manage Macedonia's 90 percent privatized economy.

Women comprise slightly less than half of the population, enjoy a life expectancy of 76.7 years (compared to 71.6 years for men), and are 37 percent of a shrinking work force. Infant mortality is 134 per 1,000 live births,[4] the maternal mortality rate .01 percent, and the total fertility rate is 1.82. In the period 1948–2001, the average age of Macedonians has risen from 26.1 to 34.2 with the elderly (over 65) rising from 8.7 to 14.3 percent of the population.[5]

Macedonia's economy has declined in the past decade from United Nations sanctions on Yugoslavia (1992–1998), Greek economic sanctions and embargoes

against the country (1992–1995), delayed and provisional memberships in key international institutions, war in its regional theatre, the housing of 360,000 refugees from Kosovo in 1999, and the takeover of 18 percent of its territory by a paramilitary incursion in 2001.

Although Macedonia is the only country from the former Yugoslavia to form a state through demilitarization, multiethnicity, and tolerance, today it has thousands of internally displaced citizens and a large number of destroyed houses, schools, and churches needing reconstruction. Divisiveness among groups of differing heritages has increased because Kosovar paramilitaries were successful in recruiting Albanian Macedonian mercenaries and because international organizations have not prevented further terrorism. The international community imposed a new "civic model" of government[6] and greater than equal constitutional rights for the Albanian minority.[7] This has rendered traditional multiethnicity and tolerance difficult and has earmarked a larger percentage of the budget for defense.

OVERVIEW OF WOMEN'S ISSUES

Macedonian women are challenged by their low percentage of high positions in government, academe, and business. Also, a nationwide unemployment rate of over 40 percent in a shrinking economy with devalued markets has rendered new hires unlikely.[8] Twenty-two percent of the population lives in poverty. Discrimination in hiring women over the age of thirty exists in advertisements for positions. Women's value to greater society is declining with the increasing absence of middle-aged and elderly women in public life, through an increase in sexist billboards and other public media campaigns, and from the presence of women trafficked for prostitution. A sense is developing that women are cheap, are expendable, and should conform to certain unattainable beauty standards.

Macedonia has over 100 women's organizations with many members of a strong umbrella union, The Union of Women's Organizations of the Republic of Macedonia (SOZM/*Sojuz na Organizacite na Zhenite na Makedonija*). The union includes numerous mixed-heritage groups and an increasing number of political organizations. Also notable are both the fifty-eight-year-old group, Organizations of Women in Macedonia (OOZhM/*Organizacija na Organizatcite na Zhenite na Makedonija*) with 65,000 women members, and the Union of Albanian Women of Macedonia.

Many Albanian women remain virtually isolated from society in patriarchal family structures, disenfranchised by family bloc voting by male patriarchs, discouraged from attending school beyond primary grades, and subjected to early arranged marriages, all contrary to Macedonian law that mandates school through age fifteen, marriage not before age eighteen, and equal voting rights.

Displaced citizens from the paramilitary takeovers last year and the presence of some refugees from the Kosovo war still in the republic are mostly housed in private homes, further straining family resources.

EDUCATION

Opportunities

Girl-to-boy ratios are 93:100 at the primary school level, 92:100 at the secondary level, and an astounding 123:100 at the tertiary level, meaning that a much larger percentage of women than men attain higher education. However, these women are disproportionately of Macedonian heritage since only 37.3 percent of Albanians, 32 percent of Roma, and 30.4 percent of Turkish girls complete high school, and only a few dozen Albanian women attend university despite positive admissions incentives that have been in place for a decade.[9]

There are significant efforts to encourage minority education, educational inclusion, and multiheritage education. However, after the recent paramilitary conflict, families are reluctant to return their children to bilingual schools, which were popular only a year ago. It is hoped that enrollment of Albanian women will increase at a new internationally funded Albanian-speaking university.

Literacy

Illiteracy of the population over age 15 is 5 percent.[10]

EMPLOYMENT AND THE ECONOMY

Job/Career Opportunities

Although job and career opportunities are legally the same for both sexes, disparities exist at higher levels of position and income, and are currently being addressed by women's groups in the country.

Women hold 43.5 percent of all teaching and 58 percent of all science positions but are only 8 percent of college deans and 11 percent of full professors, occupying lower positions in both fields. The media is the only industry dominated by women, who work as reporters and announcers, especially in television, newspapers, and magazines. Ironically, there are no well-known female filmmakers.

The most pervasive problem is the sequestering of women in the Albanian community as stay-at-home mothers and daughters, together with their arranged marriages, lower school attainment, and ethnic isolation.

Pay

Pay is legally equal for both sexes within the same occupation, but women still hold lower-paid positions overall.

Working Conditions

Working conditions are relatively good with few environmental and physical hazards. Pregnant women are exempted from heavy lifting.

Sexual Harassment

Sexual harassment is not statistically significant.

Support for Mothers/Caretakers

Maternal Leave

Maternity, disabled child, and first-year childcare leaves are generous— nine consecutive months for one child and a year for twins. Women have greater child leave rights than men, who can only take paternal leave on the death or illness of the mother.

Daycare

Daycare is available but is less frequently used, as unemployment continues to strain resources. Family members are often available for daycare, since all heritage communities have healthy extended family structures.

Inheritance and Property Rights

Inheritance and property rights are equal, but women in some of the traditional communities are prevented from availing themselves of legal resourses to their inheritances.

Social/Government Programs

Welfare

Welfare follows very liberal European norms. A comparison of the percent of the total population to the percent of welfare recipients shows that Macedonians are 66 percent of the total population and 43 percent of welfare recipients. Albanians, who are 23 percent of the population, are 30 percent of the welfare recipients; and Turks are 4 percent of the population and 8 percent of the welfare recipients. The respective percentages for

Roma are 2 percent and 13 percent, Serbs are 2 percent and 1.1 percent, and Vlachs are 0.5 percent and .07 percent.

FAMILY AND SEXUALITY

Gender Roles

Macedonia has one of the lowest divorce rates in the world at 5 percent of all marriages.[11] Except for patriarchal roles within part of the Albanian community, gender roles can be considered egalitarian in terms of occupations but traditional in terms of women and girls providing nurturing. Both men and women are equally seen in public and maintain conservative public deportment. Women do the majority of cooking in the kitchen as well as cleaning, washing, ironing, and grocery shopping, but men do outdoor grilling and some grocery shopping. Although women assume traditional family roles, Macedonians tend to be a well-educated population, proud of female professional accomplishments. It is common for men to publicly praise their wives' educational and professional accomplishments, and women tend to express self-confidence.

Reproduction

Contraception and Abortion

Education about contraception is introduced late in secondary school. One successful anti-AIDS contraception program is run by the Soros Open Society Institute. Four in twenty Macedonians (but only one in twenty Albanian Macedonians) under seventeen years of age are taught about contraception by their parents. Only 42 percent of childbearing-age Macedonians, 21 percent of Albanian, and 36 percent of other heritage Macedonains use any contraception.[12]

Teen Pregnancy

A 10 percent teen pregnancy rate mostly pertains to rural and minority communities.

HEALTH

Health Care Access

With the exception of rising costs for prescription drugs, health care access remains affordable and available.

Diseases and Disorders

Macedonia has one of the lowest HIV/AIDS rates in the world, moderate cancer rates, rising depression rates due to the dual stresses of unemployment and war, but good overall health partly due to the fact that people walk a lot and generally maintain a healthy diet. One alarming statistic, however, shows that 7 percent of Macedonians overall and 6 percent of children are undernourished.

POLITICS AND LAW

Suffrage

All women vote, but certain Albanian women have reduced suffrage.

Political Participation

Women's political participation is much lower than it should be. A concerted effort is being made by indigenous women's organizations and national initiatives to remedy this. Nevertheless, males are entrenched in political power. One important Albanian Macedonian female political leader is Teuta Arifi, who is also well known for her book *Existential Feminism*, her essays on Macedonian constitutional law and on legal and minority issues, and her short stories and poetry.

Macedonian women cast their ballots, September 2002, in Skopje during parliamentary elections. AP/ Wide World Photos.

In the 2002 elections, twenty women were elected to Parliament from ballots that were encouraged to increase the number of women candidates to one third of candidates. Teuta Arifi was recently elected to Parliament and slated for a ministerial position. In the 2002 elections, 21 women were elected to Parliament from ballots that by law had to include a minimum of 30 percent women candidates for each party.[13] Ganka Samoilova-Cvetanova, the extremely popular, hardworking, and competent head of the Ministry of Culture in the previous administration, was elected to Parliament but lost her previous ministerial position to an actor. Radmila Sekerinska became vice president of European Integration. Mirjana Lazarova-Trajkovska remains head of the State Election Commission and spearheads an effort to increase women's participation in government. Ilenka Mitreva remains a respected foreign minister in the new government. In all, the new government has a 12 female member increase in the Parliament and has maintained several ministerial positions.[14]

Women's capacity building is especially supported by initiatives of the Open Society Institute, which alone has a capacity building program, a fund for dialogue development and understanding among women, information and oral histories centers, a WEB for Women program to teach Internet skills, the Community Coordinated Response to Violence Against Women program, and a special Roma women's initiative, among others. Soros is also responsible for developing the Research Center for Gender Studies in 1999 to promote studies in this field, resulting in the state university's School of Gender and Politics.[15]

Women's Rights

Article 9 of the Macedonian Constitution mandates equal rights and freedoms to women, Article 42 affords special protection to mothers, and gender discrimination is punishable by Article 139 of the Penal Code. A male ombudsperson monitors human and civil rights abuses.[16] Macedonia ratified the CEDAW[17] in 2000, and a Ministry of Labor and Social Policy was established to advance women's positions.

Women prisoners enjoy better conditions than men—better hygienic conditions, adequate heat, unrestricted telephone access, and regular physician visits in prison. They may raise their infants to age one in prison, but prisons lack special educational and leisure programs.

Feminist Movements

The numerous local and national women's organizations typically follow a similar list of initiatives including increasing women's participation in local, regional, and national political life; increasing literacy for minority women; pursuing peaceful alternatives to national and international conflict; and protecting the environment.[18]

Lesbian Rights

Lesbians do not experience legal discrimination but are shunned by society.

Military Service

Women are not subject to mandatory military service and hold few military and police positions. However, one of the most respected military strategists, Biljana Vankovska, is female. Women can join officer and non-commissioned officer corps as well as choose to enlist.

RELIGION AND SPIRITUALITY

Women's Roles

There are a number of interesting female folklore characters in ancient Macedonian pagan songs and epics, including the unique *Samovila*,[19] as well as other women figures in heroic as well as nurturing roles in folk literature.[20] In Orthodox religious society, women are treated as equal except in terms of priestly functions. Women are equal at the monastic level, and the word "monk" can be either masculinized or feminized. There are several Igumena (women monastic leaders) and prominent women religious writers and leaders. And women are encouraged to study at theological institutions.

Among the various Islamic groups, it is notable that the first female *imams*, or religious leaders, in the Balkans were trained and ordained and then practiced in Macedonia. Traditionally, Muslim women in the Balkans do not veil themselves, and most Macedonian Islamic women wear Western or traditional dress without head coverings, with the exception of certain Albanian Muslim communities where the women wear large headscarves and floor-length raincoats in public even in high heat.

VIOLENCE

Domestic Violence

The only study of domestic violence was short term with a small, unrepresentative sample and no follow-up study.[21] This 1998 study has been accepted as true and has been repeated in several publications. Some of its findings are relevant such as showing the majority of victims at the Trauma Center of Skopje to be middle-aged women. Marital rape is difficult to report and can only be prosecuted as a civil suit.

Rape/Sexual Assault

Rape and sexual assault are uncommon in the society but are becoming more frequent with the rise of human trafficking to service international troops and personnel in Kosovo. Rape is punishable by prison terms gauged to the degree of injury.

Trafficking in Women and Children

Trafficked women, chiefly from Eastern Europe, began appearing in large numbers in the country in 1999 consequent to the presence of international troops in Kosovo. Although the country is vigilant against prostitution and trafficking, there is little control over elements of society that traffick in drugs, weapons, and persons in crisis regions. Initial difficulties in identifying and protecting trafficked women have been rectified with cooperation with U.N. antitrafficking programs.[22]

War and Military Repression

The recent war resulted in local Albanian Macedonian women being subjected to martial law by paramilitaries and Macedonian women being displaced. Several men and women were raped during the crisis.[23]

OUTLOOK FOR THE TWENTY-FIRST CENTURY

A firmer control over paramilitary elements in Kosovo and Albania and an international commitment to the integrity of Macedonia's borders and nation are necessary to its sustainable future. Macedonian women, already playing a prominent role in society, could continue to consolidate and improve their roles if stability is actualized. However, internationally mandated changes to the Constitution and local laws have further isolated minority women from greater social and political participation.

NOTES

1. The Republic of Macedonia (Republika Makedonija) is the constitutional name of the country; its short form is Macedonia, its acronyms are RM and MK, and .mk is its Internet delimiter.

2. One kilometer equals 0.6 miles.

3. Vlachs are indigenous Balkans who speak several related endangered romance languages. On various types of Vlachs, see the explanation by Society Farsarotul at www.farsarotul.org/nl2_3.htm. It's five-year-old online newsletter, at www.farsarotul.org/newslett.htm, comprises the best information in English on this cultural heritage.

4. World Bank, *ICT at a Glance. Macedonia, FYR*, www.worldbank.org/data/countrydata/ict/mkd_ict.pdf (accessed September 19, 2002).

5. This is according to a National Statistical Office study in 2000. The majority of statistics in this chapter are taken from official statistics of the Republic of Macedonia as of July 2002. The Statistical Office is online in English at www.stat.gov.mk/english/index_eng.htm. Certain statistics, particularly those differentiating women, have not been calculated since a large statistical analysis released in 1997, which is also available at the same web site.

6. The civic model imposed on Macedonia is in place in no other country in the world. It provides for key institutions to be run locally rather than nationally, for key legal issues to be subject to veto by a "majority of the minority" that exceeds 20 percent, i.e. only the Albanian population, and thus not only provides greater than equal rights to one minority but also decreases the voices of other minorities, makes geographic separatism in the best ruling interest of that minority and, through isolation

of some functions, takes an already self-isolated part of a citizenry and provides a negative incentive for integration with the majority population. New efforts at multiethnic policing are hoped to decrease violence in crisis areas.

7. The "civil model" mandated greater than equal rights for a minority exceeding 20 percent. The Albanian Macedonian population claimed they comprised at least a third of the populace. An internationally conducted census costing approximately 9 million € in November 2002, updating an internationally conducted census of 1994, determined that only 19 percent of the populace is Albanian. The census has not been published as the international community continues to insist on imposed constitutional provisions mandated for a minority over 20 percent.

8. Macedonia determines unemployment by ILO standards. A clearer look at unemployment is difficult to accomplish. An unemployment rate of 30 percent for a labor force of 673,000 in 1995 has become a 35 percent rate for a work force newly recalculated numerically as 539,762 out of a 2.2 million population. Thus, in 1995, 32.1 percent of the population was the work force while in 2002 the work force dropped to 24.53 percent. Assuming the willing work force is the same percentage of the population as in 1995, a not unreasonable assumption, then the real work force would comprise 705,047 persons and raise the number of unemployed by 165,285 to 354,200 or indicate a more realistic unemployment rate of 50.2 percent.

9. Macedonia has tough testing and grade standards for college admissions, which are lowered to encourage participation of minorities (male and female).

10. World Bank 2002.

11. Gulnar Nugman, *World Divorce Rates* (Heritage Foundation, 2002).

12. Ljubica Balaban, "School Girls Get Pregnant before They Reach the Lesson on Contraception," *Dnevnik* (May 17, 2003), www.realitymacedonia.org.mk/web/news_page.asp?nid=2574.

13. For an analysis of women elected to Parliament, see Natenane's translation of the *Dnevnik* no. 1925, August 18, 2002 article "Dami vo Parlamento" ("Women in the Parliament"), retitled "Not Enough Ladies in Macedonian Parliament," www.realitymacedonia.org.mk/web/news_page.asp?nid=2231.

14. For women who ran in the 2002 elections, see (in Macedonian) the map of electoral disricts, www.sobranie.mk/Izbori2002/kandidati.htm.

15. See *Open Society Institute Macedonia*, www.soros.org.mk.

16. A woman is presently deputy ombudsperson.

17. Convention on the Elimination of All Forms of Discrimination against Women.

18. The *Menada* Association of Women, of Tetovo, Macedonia, has a typical list of goals: "to monitor legal provisions concerning women and support women in all spheres of decision making and activity; to follow, study and initiate questions concerning the status of women; to promote and to profess inalienability of women's dignity and civil rights; to expose civil, moral and ethical abuse of women on the individual to the national level; to protect women's dignity and integrity; to eliminate all kinds of violence against women; to create conditions for better participation by women in all spheres of life; to organize peaceful and ecologically sensitive activities and demonstrations; to develop pro family policies including medical and social protection of women, including individual reproductive rights; to support peace, pacifism, nonviolence and the elimination of all kinds of ethnic, religious, age, national and sexual discrimination." www.geocities.com/TheTropics/Cove/6064/menada.htm.

19. *Samovili* are wind-associated, beautiful, and beguiling mythological beings that have ultimate power over men.

20. Several large publications glorify literally every Macedonian woman who served in the country's liberation and antifascist struggles and in the Balkan Wars.

21. Minnesota Advocates for Human Rights, *Domestic Violence in Macedonia* (Minneapolis: Minnesota Advocates for Human Rights, 1998). Their mailing address is 310 Fourth Avenue South, Suite 1000, Minneapolis, MN. Their web site is www.mnadvocates.org/Publications/Women%20Publications/macedon.htm.

22. On human trafficking and sex slaves, see David Binder and Preston Mendenhall, *Sex, Drugs and Guns in the Balkans. Ethnic Albanian Rebels Benefit from Sex Slavery. Ethnic Albanian Rebels in Macedonia Are One of the Many Groups to Profit from the Smuggling of Women, Guns and Drugs*, MSNBC, www.msnbc.com/news/667790.asp?osp=v3b5&cp1=1. See especially the sidebar story, *Sex Slaves*, which chronicles the sex trade in Veleshta, and the crisis region of Macedonia and the association of human trafficking with the arms trade.

23. Rapes of women at the village of Radusha are reported in a *Dnevnik* editorial, "Pod nosot na KAFOR se grapiraat stotici albanski" ("Under the Noses of KAFOR, Hundreds of Albanians are Massing"), no. 1630, August 20, 2001. On some of the male rapes and torture, see Human Rights Watch www.hrw.org/press/2001/08/macedonia-0811.htm (accessed June 26, 2003).

RESOURCE GUIDE

Suggested Reading

There are few nonpartisan, unbiased, agenda-free, and reliable general sources on Macedonia available in English. However, a considerable number are available online.

Arifi, Teuta. *Existential Feminism*. Skopje: Skupi Press, 1997. A book on feminism published in Albanian by a prominent Albanian Macedonian politician and professor. This is presently unavailable in English, but see an online interview with Teuta Arifi on the role of Albanian Macedonian women in politics at www.pressonline.com.mk/en/default.asp?pBroj=100&stID=687.

Zhelyazkova, Antonina. *Macedonia and Kosovo after the Military Operations*, translated from Bulgarian by Violeta Angelova. www.omda.bg/imir/mk_social2.html. Presents a picture of the area today.

Videos/Films

Across the Lake (Preku Ezeroto). 1997. A true story about a Macedonian and an Albanian who fall in love and survive separation.

Preku Dozhdot (Before the Rain). 1994. Filmed in England and Macedonia, *Before the Rain* is writer and director Milcho Manchevski's masterpiece concerning intercommunal distancing and violence between the Macedonian and Albanian communities.

Web Sites

Blesok/Shine, www.blesok.com.mk/.
A journal with a large number of contributions in various media by contemporary Macedonian women, in English and Macedonian.

History of Macedonia, www.historyofmacedonia.org/.

Macedonia Frequently Asked Questions Website, http://faq.macedonia.org/. Numerous resources on Macedonia.

Reality Macedonia, www.realitymacedonia.org.mk/. The best current news source in English, and one with a nonsexist policy often covering women's events.

Sun Music, www.sunmusic.com. Macedonian music in all genres, including folk, religious, popular, and rock and roll, can be sampled and purchased through this English-language web site, which also features some online videos of traditional activities.

United States Institute of Peace's Library's Web Links on Macedonia, www.usip.org/ library/regions/macedonia.html. Contains many useful documents and links.

Virtual Macedonia, www.vmacedonia.com/. Another comprehensive web site.

Women's Political Participation in Macedonia, www.widtech.org/Publications/ Womens%20Political%20Participation%20in%20the%20Republic%20of%20Macedonia. pdf.

Organizations

OOZhM (Organizacija na Organizatcite na Zhenite na Makedonija)
Web site: www.oozm.org.mk/index-e.html.

Union of Albanian Women of Macedonia
Web site: www.sazm.org.mk/index-e.html.

Union of Women's Organization of Republic of Macedonia
Web site: www.sozm.org.mk/index-e.html.

SELECTED BIBLIOGRAPHY

Gelevska, Irina. *Reality Macedonia*. 2002. www.realitymacedonia.org.mk/web/news_ page.asp?nid=2375.
International Labor Organization (ILO). www.sztaki.hu/providers/ilo/, www.ilo.org/ public/english/employment/gems/eeo/links/macedoni.htm.
IOM Press Briefing Notes. "Trafficking in Women to Macedonia." March 23, 2001. www.uri.edu/artsci/wms/hughes/ukraine/trafmac.htm.
Macedonian Information Agency. www.mpa.gr/abna/mia/.
Menada Association of Women. Tetovo, Macedonia. www.geocities.com/TheTropics/ Cove/6064/menada.htm.
Republic of Macedonia, Statistical Office. In English. www.stat.gov.mk/english/ index_eng.htm.

25

MALTA

JosAnn Cutajar

PROFILE OF MALTA

Malta comprises the Maltese Islands which lie in the middle of the Mediterranean Sea, ninety kilometers south of Italy. Malta is one of the smallest countries in Europe with a total population in 2000 of 382,525 living in an area of 316 square kilometers. Standing at the crossroads of Europe and Africa and of eastern and western Mediterranean cultures, this archipelago is a meeting ground between orient and occident.

The Maltese Islands are a resource-poor limestone outcropping. Nevertheless, their strategic location together with their deep and sheltered harbors have attracted the attention of world powers. The country has experienced the domination of, among others, the Romans, Byzantines, the Arabs, the Knights of St. John, and the British, until they gained their independence from the latter in 1964 and became a republic in 1974.

With independence, Maltese politicians adapted the liberal political structures and discourses prevalent in Western Europe. The head of state is the president, who is the executive authority of the country. The House of Representatives, which comes under the general direction and control

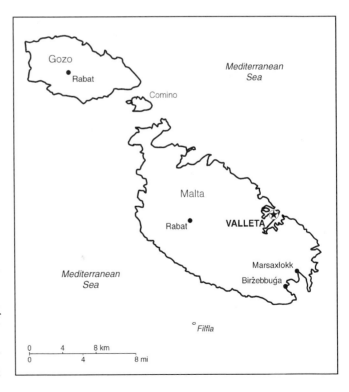

of the prime minister, is elected upon the principle of proportional representation by means of the single transferable vote.

The economy started developing with the departure of the British. Until the late 1950s, the Maltese economy depended on fishing, agriculture, stone quarrying, and British military spending. Since the 1960s, the economy has depended on manufactured exports such as microchips and service industries such as tourism. The 1990s saw a shift in the economy toward private services that has increased the job opportunities for women. This era has also heralded the dismantling of a centralist economic policy with the deregulation and liberalization of state-owned assets.

Emigration in the past together with the higher mortality rate of male babies and the lower life expectancy of males mean that the population is skewed in favor of women (50.4 percent) rather than men (49.6 percent). Total mortality rates among infants under one year of age was 7.2 per 1,000 live births in 1999, and maternal mortality was calculated at 11.2 per 100,000 live births within the period of 1990–1996. In 1999 the crude birthrate was 11.3 per 1,000 population, and the crude death rate was 8.2 per 1,000. The total fertility rate in 1999 was 1.8 among females of childbearing age. In 1998 the life expectancy at birth was calculated to be 80.1 for females and 74.4 for males.

OVERVIEW OF WOMEN'S ISSUES

Caring responsibilities are keeping women out of the labor market. Since Maltese citizenship rights are based on an individual's participation in the public sphere, women's low participation in this sphere means that their rights are derived through their relationship to men and/or the state. Nongovernmental organizations and political leaders are concerned at women's low representational level in the labor market and trying to envisage ways of ensuring that more women participate in this sphere.

EDUCATION

Opportunities

The British government reigning in the Maltese Islands in the nineteenth century introduced the policy of universal state elementary education in 1836. The first state educational services were first directed at males, and gradually extended to their female counterparts. The same gendered pattern was maintained with regards to access to secondary and tertiary education. The University of Malta, founded in 1592, opened its doors to women in the mid-1920s when the first Maltese woman graduated in 1926. One needs to underline that prior to the 1970s education in the Maltese Islands was the prerogative of the propertied class, especially where secondary and postsecondary education was concerned. Parents with little means were more likely to invest in their son's education, to the detriment of their female siblings.

Since the 1970s, Maltese students have had access to a free education, including tertiary education. To encourage students to continue their education beyond compulsory school age, students who qualify for entry into postsecondary and tertiary educational institutions are given a stipend. The number of female students at secondary (11–16 years), postsecondary (16–18), as well as tertiary level has increased in the last decade. In fact, the number of female students at tertiary level started surpassing that of their male counterparts at the end of the 1990s. Although female university students represent 52 percent of the students, they are still taking courses in health, education, and social issues and are less likely to be found in gender-atypical fields such as architecture, engineering, and science. Female students are also less likely to take vocational courses.

Literacy

The educational facilities available in the twenty-first century did not always exist. In fact, the illiteracy rate in the Maltese Islands is quite high. The 1995 census found that 9 percent of the working age population is illiterate. The rate for males (11.6 percent) is higher than that for females (7.2 percent).

EMPLOYMENT AND THE ECONOMY

Job/Career Opportunities

The Labour Force Survey maintains that 66.6 percent of men and 26.6 percent of women were in paid employment in 2001.[1] Women's activity rate within the labor market has not risen above 33 percent, which is one of the lowest rates in Europe, in the last two decades. Women are inactive rather than unemployed, since women's unemployment rate lies at 1.7 percent whereas men's is 4.3 percent.

The labor market is still gender segregated and segmented. Women are more likely to be found working within the manufacturing, wholesale, retail, education, health, and social work sectors rather than in agriculture, fishing, quarrying, or construction. And as late as 2000, women were invisible in the highest

Office worker, Malta. Photo © TRIP/D. Ellul.

echelons of the public service. Statistics on women's presence in the various occupational rungs within the private sector are harder to come by.

Women's rate of participation within the labor market starts decreasing when they reach their late twenties and early thirties and become mothers. They tend to drop out of the labor market but take up part-time jobs as their primary jobs when their caring responsibilities become lighter. The percentage of women who have a part-time job as their main occupation starts picking up within the 25–34 age bracket and remains stable until retirement age.

Pay

The Maltese Constitution deems that women should have the right to equal pay. In reality women still make 80 percent of the average gross salary that a male colleague takes home.

Support for Mothers/Caretakers

Women and men working within the public sector have access to several measures that enable them to reconcile work and family responsibilities. These consist of maternal and parental as well as responsibility leave, which entitles civil servants with dependents to twelve months' unpaid responsibility leave.

Maternal and Parental Leave

In 2002, female employees were entitled to thirteen weeks of maternity leave with full pay. Employees working within the public sector were entitled to unpaid parental leave for a period of twelve months after the birth of each child. Both parents could avail themselves of this leave. Parents are entitled to a one-time career break of three years to take care of children under five.

Daycare

Women tend to drop out of the labor market because of the lack of childcare facilities as well as because of the stigma connected with putting their career before the well-being of their children. In October 2001 there were approximately 15 state subsidized daycare centers or nurseries registered in Malta. Private provisions also exist, although there is no fiscal policy that aids the parents who make use of these policies.

Inheritance and Property Rights

According to Maltese law, married spouses can bequeath their property to each other in ownership or usufruct, which is the legal right to use the profits or materials belonging to someone else. In real fact, however, legitimate children have the right to one third of the property of the deceased parent. The surviving spouse who has children, own or adopted, cannot receive more than one fourth ownership of the deceased's property and is entitled to the usufruct of the rest of the deceased's estate. When the spouse dies intestate, remaining spouses are entitled to their part of the community of acquisitions and usufruct of the house of residence. Children of the deceased succeed their parents without distinction of their gender.

FAMILY AND SEXUALITY

Gender Roles

Although research demonstrates that men are participating in household chores more than they did in the past, domestic and caring chores are still seen as women's responsibilities.

Marriage

The structure and morality of the family are changing as well. The family is smaller in size, and people are more tolerant of divorce, single parenthood, homosexuality, and family planning.

Reproduction

A sign of increasing secularization is the mean number of live births within marriage, which was 7.1 in 1920 but had decreased to 1.9 by 1995.

Contraception and Abortion

Family planning in the Maltese Islands has been gaining ground since the 1960s. This is evident from the fact that the ban on the advertisement of contraceptives was abolished in the 1974 Press Law, and the prohibition on the importation of contraceptives was repealed the following year. The Roman Catholic Church tends to promote natural family planning over other forms of contraception. The state, on the other hand, only provides indirect support for family planning activities.

Abortion is prohibited under all circumstances under the Criminal Code of Malta. Individuals who perform or consent to its performance are subject to imprisonment.

Teen Pregnancy

Secularization is further substantiated by figures that demonstrate that there has been an increase in the number of pregnancies among teenage single women. In fact, 16.6 percent of the children born in 1999 were born to mothers aged 15–19 years of age. Between 1995 and 1999, 46.1 percent of these children were born to unmarried mothers under twenty, an eight-fold increase over the previous decade.

HEALTH

Health Care Access

The Maltese government provides a free comprehensive health service funded from general taxation to all those residing in Malta. Individuals who suffer from one or more of a list of specified chronic diseases are entitled to receive free treatment for their ailments. Those with a low income can also benefit from free pharmaceuticals if they pass a means test.

Diseases and Disorders

The main causes of death are noncommunicable diseases, mainly circulatory disease and cancer.

AIDS

There were only forty-one cases of AIDS and thirty-seven deaths in Malta from 1985 to 1996.

Cancer

The main causes of mortality among women are breast cancer and coronary artery disease. In 1996, cancer accounted for 25 percent of all mortality. The rates of gastrointestinal cancer, lung cancer, and cancer of the cervix are among the lowest in Europe, and those of the breast, the uterus, and lymphomata are among the highest.

POLITICS AND LAW

Suffrage

Maltese women were given the right to vote and stand for elections in 1947. This came about through the instigation of the first Maltese women's movement, The Women of Malta Association, which was set up in 1944 with the intention of attaining the right for women to vote and be elected. This group dissolved once it obtained its objective.

Political Participation

Since 1947, a number of women participated and were elected in the general elections. Total female representation at parliamentary level is quite low. In 2002, only 9.2 percent of the members of parliament were female. The percentage of women who participate and are elected within the local councils elections is higher at 17.3 percent.

Women's Rights

Feminist Movements

Other women's groups have come after the dissolution of The Women of Malta Association, although they all had the tendency to disband after a couple of years. The only group that has withstood the tests of time is the National Council of Women, founded in 1964. This group adopts a moderate tone and rarely touches on issues that are anathema to the Maltese Catholic Church, namely divorce and contraception. This might explain why this group is still functioning whereas others no longer exist.

RELIGION AND SPIRITUALITY

Religion is still important for the Maltese, especially the Roman Catholic religion that is constitutionally recognized as the religion of the nation. Even though church and state have been formally separated, the church is still powerful and is consulted when social policies relating to family and marriage are being devised. Both church and state start from the premise that women are the biological reproducers and nurturers of the future generations, which in turn affects policies and official statements.

VIOLENCE

Domestic Violence

Although women are becoming more assertive and conscious of their rights, violent incidents against women seem to be escalating as men feel that they are losing their control over their previously accommodating partners.

OUTLOOK FOR THE TWENTY-FIRST CENTURY

Although legally women have the same rights as men within the Maltese Islands, more work needs to be done before they can have access to the same resources and privileges. As long as caring responsibilities are socially relegated to women, women cannot partake on the same level as men within the social structure.

NOTE

1. Labour Force Survey, www.nso.gov.mt/labourforcesurvey.

RESOURCE GUIDE

Video/Film

Sustainability Indicators for Malta. 2002. Sustainability Indicators Malta Observatory, Old University, St. Paul Street, Valletta, Malta.

Web Sites

Health in Malta, www.health.gov.mt/information/hom.htm.

Labour Force Survey, www.nso.gov.mt/labourforcesurvey.

Ministry for Social Policy, www.msp.gov.mt/.

Social Statistics on Family Values, www.discern-malta.org/domestic.htm.

Organizations

Grace Attard (President)
New Centre
Mountbatten Street
Blata l-Bajda, HMR 02, Malta

Lorraine, Mercieca
Snowdrop, Triq il-Ferrovija
Santa Venera, Malta

National Council of Women
Web site: ncwmalta@camline.net.mt

Women's Study Group
Web site: wsg@um.edu.mt

An informal women's group.

SELECTED BIBLIOGRAPHY

Abela, A. M. *Women's Welfare in Society*. Valletta: Commission for the Advancement of Women, Ministry for Social Policy, 2002.

Abela, A. M., ed. *Gender Issues and Statistics*. Valletta: Department for Women's Rights, Ministry for Social Policy, 1998.

Deguara, A. *Life on the Line. A Sociological Investigation of Women Working in a Clothing Factory in Malta*. Msida: Malta University Press, 2002.

International Labor Organization. "Library and Information Services: Malta." www.ilo.org/public/english/support/lib/contact/mlt.htm.

Vassallo, M., L. Sciriha, and M. Miljanic Brinkworth. *The Unequal Half: The Underused Female Potential in Malta*. Valletta: Commission for the Advancement of Women, Ministry for Social Policy, 2002.

26

THE NETHERLANDS

Benjamin F. Shearer

PROFILE OF THE NETHERLANDS

The Netherlands, whose first constitution came in 1814 and was significantly revised in 1848 and many times thereafter until 1983, is a constitutional monarchy currently ruled by Queen Beatrix. Royal succession, mandated constitutionally, passes the throne to the sovereign's legitimate descendants without regard for gender. The queen as titular head of state and the Cabinet ministers constitute the government, which is answerable to the parliament, or States General, for legislation. The States

General consists of two chambers. The seventy-five members of the First Chamber enjoy four-year terms and are elected by the twelve provincial legislatures. Bills may not be initiated or amended by the First Chamber, but its approval is required on bills coming from the Second Chamber. The 150 members of the Second Chamber also enjoy four-year terms unless the government falls before the term's end. They are elected directly on a proportional party basis, and because there is no minimum percentage a party must achieve for representation, small parties may proliferate and coalition building becomes a necessity in governing. There is universal suffrage at eighteen years of age.

The Dutch themselves constitute the nation's largest ethnic group at 83 percent. Nine percent of the remaining 17 percent are of non-Western origins. After World War II, immigrants from the Netherlands' former colony of Indonesia (Dutch East Indies) streamed into the country. When the Dutch labor force was depleted in the 1960s, corporations brought in workers from Turkey and Morocco. In 1975, the former Dutch colony of Surinam became independent, thus causing another influx into the country. 1996 estimates of minority populations include 288,800 Surinamese, 264,100 Turks, 224,900 Moroccans, and 151,470 others. Most immigrants congregate around the large cities. The religious orientation of the population has diversified with these immigrations. Roman Catholics total 31 percent of the population; Protestants (primarily Dutch Reformed Church), 21 percent; Muslim, 4.4 percent; other, 3.6 percent; and unaffiliated, 40 percent.

The Netherlands is very densely populated with approximately 382 persons per square kilometer. Estimated 2002 total population was 16,067,754, with .98 male to each female. Of the population, 18.3 percent was 0–14 years old, 67.9 percent was 15–64 years old, and 13.8 percent was sixty-five years old and over. Females predominate only in the last group with 1,304,306 versus only 913,020 males. In 2002, there were 11.58 births, 8.67 deaths, and 2.35 net migrations per 1,000 population and a population growth rate of 0.53 percent. The maternal mortality ratio was 10 per 100,000 in 1995. The infant mortality rate in 2002 was 4.31 deaths per 1,000 live births. The 2002 total fertility rate was 1.65. Dutch citizens have a high life expectancy at birth of 78.58 years. Life expectancy for females is 81.59 years, and for males it is 75.7 years.

The Netherlands created a comprehensive welfare state with its successful economic development after the Second World War. Now a member of the European Union and a consistent proponent of European integration, the Netherlands exports 78 percent of its goods to European Union members and imports 56 percent of its goods from Union members. Seventy-three percent of the nation's 7.2 million work force is employed in services, 23 percent in industry, and 4 percent in agriculture. The 2001 unemployment rate was 2.4 percent, and the per capita purchasing power was US$25,800.[1]

OVERVIEW OF WOMEN'S ISSUES

Social policy in the Netherlands had long served to define and safeguard traditional gender roles. And for centuries, cultural representations portrayed the Dutch woman as a stereotypically dutiful housewife. Thus the emancipation of women began more slowly than in some other Western countries. However, in the 1960s and 1970s feminists began to challenge Dutch policy and culture as limiting women's opportunities for equal participation in public life and for personal fulfillment. When the welfare state

based on a strong male breadwinner–female caregiver model of family began to make way for a welfare state based on the individual, a key element
in that journey would be women's participation in the labor force. The
evolving story of women in the Netherlands is one in which the government now actively roots out discriminatory laws and regulations, encourages women to work, and seeks to protect the equality of men and women
in all phases of life. This activism has led the Netherlands further than
many countries as, for example, in legalizing same-sex marriages, at the
same time that mothers continue to leave the work force to care for their
children at home and fathers remain the breadwinners.

EDUCATION

Opportunities

Freedom of education in the Netherlands allows any group or denomination to found a school. If governmental regulations are followed, the
schools become eligible for state funding, but they retain the right to follow and teach their own traditions. Thus public and private schools provide common educational objectives and parents may choose the school
they want their children to attend. Free education is provided until age
sixteen.[2]

In the 16–18 age group, full-time education participation in 1988 for
males was 77.7 percent and for females 75.7 percent, up from 53.7 percent
and 36.7 percent in 1971 respectively. In the 19–23 age group, full-time
education participation in 1988 for males was 31.6 percent and for females
23.6 percent, up from 18.1 percent and 7.1 percent in 1971.[3]

Although educational attainment has continued to rise in the Netherlands for women and men, persistent patterns remain in female and male
choices of fields of study throughout the educational system. In pre-
vocational secondary education, for example, 43,467 full-time students
were pursuing technical training in the 2000–2001 school year, but only
1,245 were female. On the other hand, 30,971 full-time students were in
health and beauty care, but only 2,683 were male.[4] In senior vocational
secondary education, 75,798 full-time students were pursuing technical
training, but only 13,262 were female. Of the 78,965 full-time students in
health care, only 9,794 were male.[5] At the vocational college level in 2000–
2001, full-time female students outnumbered male students three to one
in teacher training, and 4.5 to one in health care, whereas full-time male
students in technical areas outnumbered females nearly six to one.[6]

Total enrollment in universities on December 1, 2000, included 86,584
men and 80,364 women. In the first-year class, however, there were 16,527
women and 15,777 men. The field of study patterns seen in vocational education translate also to university education. Twice as many men as
women were science majors, and nearly five times as many men as women

were engineering majors. For every nineteen male economics majors there were only eight females, and for every eight male science majors there were four females. Women predominated 4:3 in health majors, 2:1 in behavioral and social sciences, and almost 2:1 in language and culture fields.[7]

In 1988 the government attempted to tackle this issue, among others, in a memorandum, *Social Position of Girls and Young Women*. With the ultimate objective of increasing women's presence in the labor force, a media campaign was launched to help girls make educational choices for their working future that involved their following male-dominated educational and career tracks. The campaign was not effective as the data above suggest. The government had in fact blamed girls for making educational choices that diminished their prospects in the labor market, and it was unwilling, in the best Dutch tradition, of keeping the government outside of household decision-making to cross the line that demarcates public and private life. The government had no intention of telling parents how to raise their children in their own homes even though parents often encouraged traditional female and male educational choices at early ages. Nor was the government willing to take on the issue of the meaning of equality in work life and care life.[8]

Literacy

The literacy rate in the Netherlands was estimated at 99 percent in 2000.[9] Since the early twentieth century, school attendance has been mandated. Children are now required by law to go to school full-time between five and sixteen years of age, although most begin at four. Between sixteen and eighteen, part-time attendance is required, which allows for work-study programs.

EMPLOYMENT AND THE ECONOMY

Job/Career Opportunities

The year 2000 participation rate in the labor force was 67 percent overall, with 79 percent of working men and 55 percent of working women. The unemployment rate was 2 percent for men and 3 percent for women.[10] In 2001, with women constituting 40 percent of the total work force, women's participation rates by sector approximated 79 percent in health and welfare, 54 percent in culture and other services, 53 percent in education, 38 percent in government, and 30 percent in the private sector. Twenty-six percent of women across all sectors held management positions, but in the health and welfare sector, women managers predominated.[11]

Pay

The gross income per hour of men in 2000 was 38.79 dfl, and of women, 26.87. The annual gross income of men was more than twice that of women. Men worked 1,558 paid hours per year and women, 1,1000.[12] For many years, about two thirds of working women have held part-time paying jobs. By 1994, 24.2 percent of working women held part-time jobs of fewer than twelve hours per week and 43.5 percent held part-time jobs of 12–32 hours per week. Analysis of these data for men and women over time has led to these conclusions: married women are less likely to be employed, women with children are less likely to be employed for more than twelve hours per week, and women experience significant wage penalties when combining childcare and work.[13]

Woman working in cheese store, Alkmaar, The Netherlands. Photo © Dave Bartruff/CORBIS.

When A.E. Verstand-Bogaert, Secretary of State for Social Affairs and Employment of the Netherlands, introduced her report on compliance with the UN Convention on Elimination of Discrimination against Women (CEDAW) to a panel of experts in June 2001, she noted that the government had set the goal of 65 percent women participation in the work force by 2010. Another objective was to employ 60 percent of women, most currently part-time workers, "in a way that would give them economic independence." She described labor participation as "the spearhead of the emancipation policy" and "paid employment . . . a prerequisite for economic independence." But achieving greater participation of women in the labor force, she said, "could only be achieved in tandem with a reallocation of care tasks between men and women."[14]

In regard to the 25 percent gap in pay between men and women, Verstand-Bogaerts noted that it was "not as bad as it seemed . . . given that part of the pay gap was caused by the lower education of women, their relative lack of experience, earlier retirement owing to children, and later re-entry into the labour market." When these differences were factored out, however, the gap was 7 percent. She went on to say that the Equal Treatment Commission was studying the issue and the government was actively considering ways to address the pay gap.[15]

Working Conditions

Sexual Harassment

Dutch law prohibits sexual harassment and places the burden on those in charge of the place where harassment has occurred to take appropriate action to correct it. The 1998 Act on Working Conditions defines sexual harassment as

> unwanted sexual advances, request for sexual favours or other verbal or non-verbal or physical behaviour on the following circumstances: 1. submission to such behaviour is implicit or explicit a condition for employing a person; 2. decisions that affect the work of the person concerned are based on submission to or rejection of such behaviour; 3. such behaviour is intended to affect the performance at work of the person concerned and/or is intended to create an intimidating, hostile or uncomfortable working environment, or has the effect that the performance at work is affected and/or an intimidating, hostile or uncomfortable working environment is created.

The Equal Treatment Commission has ruled that this definition would not be limited to the workplace and may have a universal application.[16] In spite of governmental efforts to increase awareness of the problem and address it legislatively, 245,000 women (6.6 percent of the female work force) are harassed every year in the workplace.[17]

Support for Mothers/Caretakers

Maternal Leave

The maternity leave regulations permit mothers to take off work for sixteen weeks with full pay. The Parental Leave Law permits parents three months of leave without pay with an extension of more than six months to take care of children up to eight years old. Part-time workers (less than twenty hours' work per week) are also eligible for parental leaves. Yet a third of women leave the work force after their first child is born.[18] Daycare unavailability is seen as a major factor hindering an increase in female labor participation. In 1990 and still in 1993, there was a waiting list of 40,000 children for daycare. The government responded to this need and as a result of subsidizing the growth of daycare, the number of full-time places for 0–4-year-olds grew from 20,395 in 1989 to 70,981 in 1995. Again in 1994, the government intervened with a measure to add another 10,000 spaces. But the beneficiaries of these policies have been higher-paid, better educated women who are more likely to return to work after giving birth.[19]

Daycare

Most childcare actually takes place as undeclared work by relatives and neighbors. It is estimated that 500,000 children are cared for in this way. The government acted again in 1998 to get the number of daycare spaces to 150,000, in part to formalize the informal work going on throughout the childcare business. But in fact the tremendous growth of daycare had not kept up with the explosive demand created by the increasing number of women with young children who were working. Waiting lists persisted. And in June 1999, the government wished to add another 71,000 places and make childcare less expensive for lower-income families.[20]

Social/Government Programs

Welfare

The Dutch social security system is extensive. All people are entitled to a pension at age sixty-five. Married and cohabiting couples get a net pension of approximately 50 percent for each person of the net minimum wage, the statutory minimum wage less local charges when applicable. Single persons receive about 70 percent of the net minimum wage, the minimum wage less any special subsidies. Dependents and orphans receive pensions under certain conditions. Working people are protected against exceptional medical costs. The General Child Benefits Act provides insured quarterly child allowances for children under sixteen living at home, children unemployed who are sixteen or seventeen in certain conditions, and children from eighteen to twenty if unemployed after finishing training or education. Unemployment benefits may extend to 3.5 years, the first year at 70 percent of pay up to a maximum. When sickness prevents workers from working, they are entitled to 70 percent of gross pay up to fifty-two weeks, but most receive 100 percent. Disabled workers are protected from loss of income. There are both national health insurance and private health insurance schemes.[21]

All Dutch nationals and lawfully resident foreigners over eighteen (with exclusions for prisoners, students, and so on) are entitled to benefits under the National Assistance Act (1996) if their resources do not cover basic needs. There is a means test that exempts a portion of home investment and capital. Between 1995 and 1998, the number of claimants declined 19 percent, from 489,200 to 397,100. In 1998, 18 percent of claimants were married couples, 56 percent were single persons, and 26 percent were lone parents. Also in 1998, if married couples are considered separately rather than as one application for assistance, 40 percent of claimants were male and 60 percent female. Eighty-four percent of Dutch nationals made claims, but only 14 percent of non-Dutch nationals made claims.[22]

FAMILY AND SEXUALITY

Gender Roles

The Dutch welfare state that developed after World War II was built around the husband at work as breadwinner and the wife at home as caregiver. In 1947, the joint parental control of children was recognized in law. In 1955, the ban on married women working in the civil service was lifted, and in 1956 married women attained full rights in regard to legal contracts. By the 1980s, women finally attained most social entitlements.[23] In 1990, with the publication of the Scientific Council for Government Policy's report "A Working Perspective," formal work was directly associated with social integration and full citizenship. Only through formal work would citizens enjoy all the economic and social benefits of the welfare state.[24]

Marriage

At midnight on April 1, 2001, three gay couples and one lesbian couple were married at city hall by the mayor of Amsterdam. These two women and six men were the first to take advantage of the new law allowing same-sex marriage. Thus marriage in Dutch law is no longer defined as a union between a man and a woman. The culmination of sixteen years of gay rights activism, the new law went beyond the 1998 law allowing registered partnerships. Now gay and lesbian couples could enjoy all the rights and privileges in law of male–female married people. In addition, same-sex married couples could now adopt Dutch children.[25] For 2002, male–female marriages are expected to total 85,500 and same-sex marriages 1,900. Male–female partnerships are expected to increase to 6,900 from 3,300 in 2001, and same-sex partnerships to 900 from 600. About 66 percent of the new partnerships are married couples changing their legal status from marriages to partnerships. This is done in order to take advantage of a fast divorce process without the courts.[26]

Reproduction

Dutch women gave birth to their first child at the mean age of 28.9 years in 1996. In 1970 the mean age was 24.3 years. The vast majority of men and women aged 18–42 want to have children.[27] Yet the birth rate has declined over time.

Sex Education

Sex education takes place in the context of health education. Teenagers learn about safe sex and have easy access to form of birth control.

Contraception and Abortion

Of Dutch teens, 85 percent use some form of birth control at first intercourse, 46 percent use condoms only, and 24 percent use both condoms and birth control pills. Seventy-four percent of married women were using some form of contraception in 1999.[28]

Teen Pregnancy

In 1990–1995, the teen birthrate was 7 per 1,000 girls in the Netherlands compared to 64 per 1,000 in the United States. Teen abortion rates per 1,000 were 5.2 in the Netherlands as against 17 in the United States. The national health service provides easy access to sexual health care. Dutch parents tend not to set strict rules for teenage sexual behavior but are supportive of their children from a distance. Only 1 percent of parents wanted their children to abstain from sex.[29]

HEALTH

Health Care Access

The Dutch health care system provides everyone with access to health care through a tiered system of mandatory insurance. Sixty-two percent of the people who have incomes below a certain threshold are insured through sixty sickness funds, which are funded by employee and employer contributions, as well as through retirement and unemployment funds. Thirty percent of the population buys private insurance with the help of an employer contribution, 6 percent are insured through the public employees insurance program, and 2 percent are able to pay without assistance. The Dutch have a high satisfaction rate with their health care.[30] Long-term care costs for qualified populations are paid by a universal catastrophic insurance fund, which is financed by personal income tax receipts.[31]

Diseases and Disorders

All births in the Netherlands are attended by skilled personnel, which may include midwives. There are 10 maternal deaths per 100,000 live births.[32] Women's health care in the Netherlands is supported by self-help organizations that receive government subsidies. They arose in the 1970s because women were dissatisfied with the health care they were receiving. The Dutch Federation of Women's Self-Help organizations includes five groups that support women's health beyond the medical establishment. The Foundation for Women and Medication aims to prevent women's addiction to tranquilizers and stimulants through self-help groups and educational programs. The Mastopathy Foundation helps doctors deal with fear of cancer and provides women with information about benign lumps in the breast and treatment options. The Foundation for Women of Menopausal Age provides information about changing lifestyles and bodies. The Foundation for Women with Post Partum Depression and PMS provides group interactions and information to women as well as midwives and doctors. The Foundation for Women with Gynecological Problems has been successful in preventing unneeded hysterectomies and continues programs for childless women and women with vaginal disorders. Three affiliated organizations work with women who have silicone breast implants, victims of anorexia and bulimia, and women who want to change their lives radically but find that the health care system does not meet their needs. Women's self-help has become part of the women's health care movement.[33]

AIDS

From 1996 to 2000, total AIDS deaths have decreased markedly from 327 to 132 owing to extensive media campaigns and health education programs by the government and nongovernmental organizations. Deaths of women from AIDS likewise declined over the same period from thirty-one to twenty-six. The adult incident rate was projected at .1970 in 1999.[34]

Eating Disorders

Eating disorders have a low prevalence rate. Two percent of women reported having anorexia at some time in their lives, and 1.1 percent reported having bulimia.[35]

Cancer

Breast cancer is the most frequently discovered cancer in Dutch women as it is in other developed countries. Between 1980 and 1996, deaths from breast cancer have steadily risen from 2,690 to 3,577. However, the survival rate after five years is 70 percent.[36]

Depression

The percentage of persons with psychosocial symptoms has remained steady between 1989 and 2000. These symptoms are defined as loneliness, restlessness, boredom, depression, or feeling upset. Respondents to the Affect Balance Scale who reply that they have experienced one or more symptom often or very often are counted in the survey. In 2000, 15.5 percent of women and 9.2 percent of men reported having psychosocial symptoms. The 1989 data were 15.0 percent and 9.6 percent respectively.[37]

POLITICS AND LAW

Suffrage

Women received the right to vote in 1919. The struggle for suffrage began at least symbolically on March 22, 1883, when physician Aletta Jacobs wrote a letter to the mayor and councilmen of Amsterdam asking that her name be included on the voter registration list "since I fulfilled the legally stipulated conditions for enfranchisement." At that time, the Dutch constitution did not specifically exclude women from voting. At the council meeting the next day, the letter "was read aloud to the general mirth of all." She received a letter more than a week later explaining that the spirit of the constitution does not allow for woman's suffrage. The Amsterdam District Court, hearing Dr. Jacob's appeal, ruled that " 'it could never have been the intention of the Dutch legislature to allow women suffrage.' " On May 18, 1883, the Dutch Supreme Court declared among other things that women don't have voting rights because " 'they do not have full citizenship or civil rights' " because " 'they lack the right to vote.' " In 1887, the new constitution specifically gave men suffrage. When the woman's suffrage bill finally became law on September 19, 1919, Dr. Jacobs described her initial happiness "as a sense of delicious relief."[38]

Having won the vote and over time some other new rights, the belief was prevalent that welfare state policies had completed the emancipation of women. Social security entitlements were different for men and women not because they were "regarded as pointing to any 'natural' inequality between the sexes, but rather as recognizing natural differences in abilities, talents, and tasks." Social policy defined citizenship differently for men and women, thereby segregating breadwinners from caregivers. As a result, the Netherlands "showed a low level of stratification in terms of families, although it showed (and still shows) much more stratification in terms of gender."[39] Families across the pillarized society tended to look very much alike, but the differences between men and women maintained.

Political Participation

Women have made tremendous strides in political participation, and old strictures have been lifted. From 1970 to 1999, the percentage of women in parliament increased from 8.7 percent to 36 percent.[40] In 2000, the percentage of women in government was 31 percent. Although the government set quotas to increase the number of women in government, the parties are not penalized if they fail to meet them. The main national effort now is to increase the women participating in local-level politics.[41]

Women's Rights

Feminist Movements

Radical feminist groups arose out of student protests in the 1960s. By 1982, there were about 160 such groups, which had concentrated their efforts "strongly at grassroots level, campaigning to establish rape crisis centers, women's health groups and adult education centers." They also succeeded in redefining abortion as a women's issue.[42] An article by Joke Smit in 1967, "The Discomfort of Women," is commonly pointed to as the beginning of the second wave of feminism. She "turned the vocabulary of 'completed emancipation' into a guidebook for women's liberation." The recognition of what were considered natural differences between men and women earlier "was now regarded as perpetuating inequality, discrimination, and injustice to women."[43] Giving women the vote and perpetuating traditional female roles through welfare state policy had not completed the process of women's emancipation.

Since signing the Convention on the Elimination of Discrimination against Women in 1991, the government has pursued an emancipation policy at three intertwined levels. At the first level, the government has had to ensure that women and men have equality under the law and in public life. These structural measures have largely been accomplished and continue as any discriminatory laws or regulations are uncovered. At the second level, legal equality has to translate into practice. The government remains actively involved in promoting diversity, ending workplace segregation by sex, increasing women's labor force participation, and promoting women's equal participation in education. At the third level, in an evolving policy, the government will promote cultural change that eliminates stereotypes and misperceptions about masculinity and femininity.[44]

The Equal Treatment Act of 1994 established the Equal Treatment Commission, which oversees enforcement of the act in a semijudicial function. The act forbids discrimination "on the grounds of religion, belief, political orientation, race, gender, nationality, sexual preference, marital status, part-time or full-time work" in "employment relationships . . . in offering goods and services," and "in receiving advice about educational or career opportunities."[45] Since the commission began issuing opinions on discrimination cases in 1994–1995, sex discrimination has been found to be the leading grounds of discrimination, followed by race discrimination. In 2001 seventy (or 41 percent) of the commission's opinions involved sex discrimination.[46]

Lesbian Rights

Lesbian couples were permitted to marry and adopt children on April 1, 2001. Full legal adoption became possible not only for married same-sex couples but also for couples who have been living together for three years and have cared for the child together for a year.[47]

Military Service

Women have served in the Royal Netherlands Armed Forces since 1944. Three separate Women's Corps developed—army, navy, and air force. The corps were integrated into the three services in 1979 and then disbanded by January 1982. The Positive Plan of Action for the Integration of Women into the Armed Forces was initiated in 1988 and called for "enhancing female recruitment, selection, training, part-time work, maternity leave and child care." In 1993 the military became an all-volunteer organization. The 4,170 women in the military now account for 9.2 percent of the navy, 7.2 percent of the army, 8 percent of the air force, and 8.7 percent of the military police. Employment in the marines and the Submarine Service is "closed to women on the grounds of combat effectiveness and practical reasons," but all other opportunities are open to women. The goal for recruitment by 2010 calls for a female force of 12 percent.[48]

RELIGION AND SPIRITUALITY

In the Pacification of 1917, the important Dutch political parties accepted a constitution that provided the same state funding for denominational and public schools. This effectively marked the rise of denominational parties, albeit in coalition with other parties, into power until 1994 and ushered in the period known as Pillarization. Communication and consensus across party lines became necessary for governing, and it was assumed that agreement at the top of these various pillars would trickle down to lower levels and maintain peaceful coexistence in a pluralistic society. With state subsidies, social and political organizations developed that were worlds unto themselves, permitting their members a cradle-to-grave existence.[49] Thus, for example, a young Catholic girl might be born in a Catholic hospital, schooled in Catholic schools, join a Catholic social club and a Catholic athletic league, join a Catholic political party, join a Catholic union, and eventually be buried in a Catholic cemetery, all with state assistance.

The walls that separated people's social and cultural lives began to fall apart in the 1960s. Political parties merged, organizations combined, and secularization began to take hold. The effect on the churches has been remarkable. The total number of Catholic priests dropped 44 percent, and the number of religious women dropped 50 percent in the space of 1980–2001.[50] The Netherlands Reformed Church has lost 66 percent of its membership in the last fifty years. Between 1955 and 1995, denominational membership in the Netherlands fell from 80 percent to 60 percent. Church attendance, which was 54 percent for those twelve or older in 1954–1955, dropped to 24 percent for those eighteen or older in 1995. From 1970 to 1991 to 1999, the percentage attending church at least once every two weeks fell from 71 percent to 30 percent to 14 percent for Catholics; from 50 percent to 43 percent to 30 percent for Netherlands Reformed churchgoers; and from 89 percent to 73 percent to 51 percent for Calvinists. This drop in church attendance crossed all age groups. Among 17–30-year-olds, attendance dropped from 62 percent to 39 percent; 31–50-year-old attendance dropped from 68 percent to 36 percent; and 51–70-year-old attendance dropped from 72 percent to 51 percent. In 1995, Roman Catholics made up 33 percent of the population eighteen and older. Members of the Netherlands Reformed Church were 14 percent of the population, followed by Calvinists at 7 percent, Muslims at 4 percent, "other" at 3 percent, and "none" at 40 percent. Thus, although freedom of religion is a guaranteed right of everyone in the Netherlands, 40 percent claimed no religion.[51]

Even though about 20 percent of those leaving traditional religious denominations seek truth and spiritual succor in nonorthodox movements from Theosophy to Hare Krishna, they may not necessarily join those movements. Islam is the only denomination that is actually growing. Fueled by increased numbers of migrant workers from Turkey and Morocco and asylum seekers from Iran, Somalia, Iraq, and Bosnia, Islam is expected to be the second largest denomination by 2010.[52]

VIOLENCE

Domestic Violence

Two hundred thousand women each year are victimized by violence from spouses or partners, current or former. Ethnic minorities are particularly vulnerable. Fifty thousand women each year become victims of serious violent crime, including sexual violence, mental or physical abuse, manslaughter, and battering. Sixty to eighty women die each year, from domestic violence. It is estimated that fewer than 10 percent of domestic violence incidents are even reported to authorities.[53] Victims surveys in 1998 revealed that "2 percent of women had been victims of sexual offence, and 1 percent victims of abuse." Yet surveys and police statistics seemed to minimize the problem. In 1999, women's shelters took in more than 25,000 women and children.[54] There is a subsidized system of forty-eight shelters and various nongovernmental organizations for victims of violence, who become eligible for social benefits if they leave their spouses. The government conducts an awareness campaign on these issues.[55]

Rape/Sexual Assault

Rape occurred at the rate of 15 per 100,000 inhabitants aged 12–79 in 1999, and other sexual offenses occurred at the rate of 17 per 100,000.[56]

Trafficking in Women and Children

The trafficking of girls and women for the purpose of prostitution is a significant issue in the Netherlands. In spite of specific laws forbidding trafficking, special police task forces, and, as of 2000, the establishment of the Bureau of the National Rapporteur on Trafficking in Persons, estimates are that 3,000 girls and women are illegally trafficked into the Netherlands each year for prostitution. In 2000, sixty-eight trafficking cases were prosecuted and thirty-four convictions attained.[57]

The controversial legalization of brothels on October 1, 2000, was an effort by the Dutch government to control voluntary prostitution. Not only would legalization of the sex business create a windfall of new tax money, but health issues could also be addressed.

The number of people employed in prostitution is believed to be 20,000 to 30,000. About half of the prostitutes are not western Europeans and reside illegally in the Netherlands. They are trafficked primarily from Nigeria, China, the Philippines, Thailand, Colombia, and the Dominican Republic. Many others come from Central Europe.[58]

OUTLOOK FOR THE TWENTY-FIRST CENTURY

Women and men are now equal in the eyes of the law, but gender segregation remains in education and the workplace, and traditional gender roles stubbornly carry on in everyday life. Equal pay for equal work is mandated by law, but women continue to make less than men. Most jobs in the military are open to women, but women are woefully underrepresented in the armed services. Violence against women at home and harassment in the workplace continue, and no good solution has yet been found to end the trafficking of girls and women into the Netherlands.

The government, however, is actively addressing all these issues. Given the dramatic increases in women's political and workforce participation as the emancipation policy has unfolded, there is certainly evidence that the full emancipation of women is possible. Clearly, the third tier of the policy—changing the culture—is the most difficult and ambitious. Building more daycare centers may bring more women into the workforce, but it does little to change attitudes or gender roles. Dutch society as a whole has not determined how to deal with caregiving and paid work. One possible solution may be to take caregiving out of the category of informal, undeclared work and recognize it in some way as a paid contribution to society. Dutch society, however, continues to cherish the distinction between public and private matters.

NOTES

1. CIA, *The World Fact Book 2002*, www.cia.gov; U.S. Department of State, Bureau of European and Eurasian Affairs, "Background Note: The Netherlands," June 2000, www.state.gov; *Cultural Policy in the Netherlands*, a Publication of the Ministry of Education, Culture and Science, www.minocw.nl; Dutch Royal House, "The Monarchy: Constitution," www.koninklijhuis.nl; and Dutch Royal House, "The Monarchy: Nassau and Orange."

2. *Cultural Policy in the Netherlands.*

3. Annemieke van Drenth, "Citizenship, Participation and the Social Policy on

Girls in the Netherlands," in *Gender, Participation and Citizenship in the Netherlands*, ed. Jet Bussemaker and Rian Voet (Aldershot, UK: Ashgate, 1998), 86.

4. Statistics Netherlands, "Figures, Key Figures: Pupils in Secondary Education, by Type of School, 2000/01," www.cbs.nl.

5. Statistics Netherlands, "Figures, Key Figures: Schools and Pupils in Senior Vocational Secondary Education by Sector, Fulltime, Education, 2000/01," www.cbs.nl.

6. Statistics Netherlands, "Figures, Key Figures: Institutes and Students in Vocational Colleges by Field of Study, 2000/01. Provisional Figures." www.cbs.nl.

7. Statistics Netherlands, "Figures, Key Figures: Enrolment [*sic*] in University Education by Field of Study and University," December 1, 2000, www.cbs.nl.

8. See van Drenth, 1998, 81–83.

9. CIA, 2002.

10. Statistics Netherlands, "Figures, Key Figures: Labor Force by Some Features," www.cbs.nl.

11. Statistics Netherlands, "Webmagazine—More Women Managers," November 20, 2002, www.cbs.nl.

12. Statistics Netherlands, "Figures, Key Figures: Income, Wage Rates, Labour Costs, and Working Hours of Employees," www.cbs.nl.

13. Ronald Dekker et al., "A Longitudinal Analysis of Part-time Work by Women and Men in the Netherlands," in *Gender and the Labor Market*, ed. Siv S. Gustafsson and Danièle E. Meulders (New York: St. Martin's Press, 2000), 266, 280–81.

14. United Nations (UN), "Netherlands Claims Progress in Improving Situation of Women; Conceding Further Positive Changes Needed," UN press release WOM/1288, www.un.org.

15. UN, "Netherlands."

16. Marcel Zwamborn, "Anti-discrimination Legislation in EU Member States; A Comparison of National Anti-discrimination Legislation on the Grounds of Racial or Ethnic Origin, Religion or Belief with the Council Directives: The Netherlands," ed. Jan Niessen and Isabelle Chopin (Vienna: European Monitoring Centre on Racism and Xenophobia, 2002), 16–17.

17. U.S. Department of State, Bureau of Democracy, Human Rights, and Labor, "The Netherlands, Country Reports on Human Rights Practices," March 4, 2002, 5, www.state.gov.

18. U.S. Department of State, 2002, 5.

19. Trudie Knijn, "Social Care in the Netherlands," in *Gender Social Care and Welfare State Restructuring in Europe*, ed. Jane Lewis (Aldershot, UK: Ashgate, 1998), 92–93.

20. K. Tidjens, *Employment, Family and Community Activities: A New Balance for Women and Men—The Netherlands* (Amsterdam: European Foundation for the Improvement of Living and Working Conditions, 2000), 9, www.eurofound.ie.

21. F. de Haan and F. Verboon, *Integrated Approaches to Active Welfare and Employment Policies: The Netherlands* (Dublin: European Foundation for the Improvement of Living and Working Conditions, 2002), www.eurofound.eu.int.

22. de Haan and Verboon, 2002.

23. Jet Bussemaker, "Gender and the Separation of Spheres in Twentieth Century Dutch Society: Pillarisation, Welfare State Formation and Individualization," in Lewis, 1998, 31–32, 36.

24. Janneke Plantenga, "Double Lives: Labour Market Participation, Citizenship and Gender," in Lewis, 1998, 57.

25. Arjan Schippers, "Wedding Bells for Dutch Gay Couples," by Radio Netherlands, August 15, 2001, www.rnw.nl.

26. Statistics Netherlands, "Press Release: More Marriages and More Partnerships," November 27, 2002, press release PB02-244.

27. Cécile Wetzels, *Squeezing Birth into Working Life* (Aldershot, UK: Ashgate, 2001), 129–31.

28. "2002 Women of Our World — Reproductive Health — Europe," www.prb.org.

29. Maureen A. Kelly and Michael McGee, "Report from a Study Tour — Teen Sexuality Education in the Netherlands, France, and Germany," *SIECUS Report* 27, no. 2 (1998): 11–14.

30. Jeffrey L. Jackson, MD, "The Dutch Health Care System: Lessons for Reform in the United States," *Southern Medical Journal* (June 1996), www.sma.org/smj/96jun3.htm.

31. Yvonne Erdmann and Renate Wilson, "Managed Care: A View from Europe," *Annual Review of Public Health* (2001): 278.

32. "2002 Women of Our World — Reproductive Health — Europe."

33. Statistics Netherlands, "Figures, Key Figures: Health and Welfare, Deaths by Important Causes of Death," www.cbs.nl.; and M. Sant et al., "Survival of Women with Breast Cancer in Europe: Variation with Age, Year of Diagnosis and Country: The EUROCARE Working Group," *International Journal of Cancer* 77 (August 31, 1998): 679–83.

34. Statistics Netherlands, "Statline: Deaths by Main Primary Cause of Death, Sex and Age"; and Statistics Netherlands, "Statline: Deaths by Main Primary Cause of Death, Sex and Age, Females," both December 7, 2002, http://statline.cbs.nl; World Fact Book 2002, www.bartleby.com

35. Statistics Netherlands, "Statline: State of Health of the Dutch Population — Psychosocial Symptoms," December 7, 2002, statline-cbs.nl.

36. R.V. Bijl et al., "Prevalence of Psychiatric Disorder in the General Population: Results of the Netherlands Mental Health Survey and Incidence Study (NEMESIS)," *Social Psychiatry and Psychiatric Epidemiology* 33 (1998): 588–89.

37. Marlies Bosch, "Stronger Together: The Federation of Women's Self-Help Organizations of the Netherlands," *Women Wise* 19 (January 31, 1998): 4.

38. Aletta Jacobs, *Memories*, ed. Harriet Feinberg, trans. Annie Wright (New York: The Feminist Press at the City of New York University, 1996), 54–55, 170.

39. Bussemaker, 1998, 32.

40. Ruth Henig and Simon Henig, *Women and Political Power: Europe since 1945* (London: Routledge, 2001), 105.

41. "European Database: Women in Decision-making: Report from the Netherlands by Our Transnational Partner, Milja A.C Bos," www.db-decision.de.

42. Henig and Henig, 2001, 30.

43. Bussemaker, 1998, 32–33.

44. UN, Press Release WOM/1288.

45. Equal Treatment Commission, "Legislation: Short (and Simplified) Description of the Equal Treatment Law."

46. "Equal Treatment Commission Fact Sheet, 2000–2001," www.cgb.nl.

47. Netherlands, Department of Justice, "Fact Sheets: Same-sex Marriages," April 2001, www.minjust.nl; and Netherlands, Department of Justice, "Fact Sheets: Adoption of a Child in the Netherlands," April 2001, www.minjust.nl.

48. NATO, International Military Staff: Committee on Women in the NATO Forces, "The Netherlands," www.nato.int.

49. Bussemaker, 1998, 26–29.

50. "Catholic Hierarchy: Netherlands, Statistics by Diocese," www.catholic-hierarchy.org.

51. "Cultural Policy in the Netherlands," 7; and U.S. Department of State, "The Netherlands: International Religious Freedom Report 2002," www.state.gov.

52. "Cultural Policy in the Netherlands," 7; and U.S. Department of State, "The Netherlands: International Religious Freedom Report 2002."

53. U.S. Department of State, "The Netherlands: Country Reports on Human Rights Practices, 2001."

54. UN, Press Release WOM/1288.

55. UN, Press Release WOM/1288.

56. Statistics Netherlands, "Figures, Key Figures, Justice and Public Safety," March 9, 2001, www.cbs.nl.

57. U.S. Department of State, "The Netherlands: Country Reports on Human Rights Practices, 2001."

58. U.S. Department of State, "The Netherlands: Country Reports on Human Rights Practices, 2001."

RESOURCE GUIDE

Suggested Reading

Altink, Sietske. *Stolen Lives: Trading Women into Sex and Slavery*. London: Scarlet Press; New York: Harrington Park Press, 1995.

Bussemaker, Jet, and Rian Voet, eds. *Gender, Participation and Citizenship in the Netherlands*. Aldershot, UK: Ashgate, 1998.

Drew, Eileen, et al., eds. *Women, Work and the Family in Europe*. London: Routledge, 1998.

Jacobs, Aletta. *Memories*. Edited by Harriet Feinburg, translated by Annie Wright. New York: The Feminist Press at the City University of New York, 1996.

Web Sites

International Information Centre and Archives for the Women's Movement, www.iiav.nl.
This is the site of the national library, documentation center and archives of the women's movement, past and present, in the Netherlands.

Transact—Dutch Center for Gender Issues in Healthcare and Prevention of Sexual Violence, www.transact.nl.
Transact tries to prevent sexual abuse and improve social aid to men and women.

Organization

Netherlands Council of Women
Louise de Colignystraat 44
2595 SR Den Haag
The Netherlands
Email: nvr@vrouwen.net
Web site: www.vrouwen.net

SELECTED BIBLIOGRAPHY

Baker, Susan, and Anneke van Doorne-Huiskes, eds. *Women and Public Policy: The Shifting Boundaries Between the Public and Private Spheres*. Aldershot, UK: Ashgate, 1999.

de Haan, F., and F. Verboon. *Integrated Approaches to Active Welfare and Employment Policies: The Netherlands*. Dublin: European Foundation for the Improvement of Living and Working Conditions, 2002. www.eurofound.eu.int.

Gustafsson, Siv S., and Danièle E. Meulders, eds. *Gender and the Labor Market*. New York: St. Martin's Press, 2000.

Henig, Ruth, and Simon Henig. *Women and Political Power: Europe since 1945*. London: Routledge, 2001.

Lewis, Jane. *Gender, Social Care and Welfare State Restructuring in Europe*. Aldershot, UK: Ashgate, 1998.

Tidjens, K. *Employment, Family and Community Activities: A New Balance for Women and Men—The Netherlands*. Amsterdam: European Foundation for the Improvement of Living and Working Conditions, 2000. www.eurofound.ie.

Wetzels, Cécile. *Squeezing Birth into Working Life: Household Panel Analyses Comparing Germany, Great Britain, Sweden and The Netherlands*. Aldershot, UK: Ashgate, 2001.

27

NORWAY

Jill M. Bystydzienski

PROFILE OF NORWAY

Norway is one of the Scandinavian or Nordic countries,[1] covering nearly 150,000 square miles of land on the western half of the Scandinavian Peninsula, the Svalbard Archipelago, and numerous islands in the North and Arctic Seas. Its 4,478,000 people are distributed unevenly over the land, mostly in settlements along the coast and some in inland communities.[2] Although Norway has been inhabited for more than 10,000 years, only 1 percent of its land is developed, as the pressures of a convoluted coastline (deeply cut by narrow fjords that extend over 12,000 linear miles) and barren mountain ranges limit human settlement. Consequently, historically small and isolated Norwegian communities produced a diversity of styles of clothing, architecture, farming methods, and linguistic dialects and such regional differences, with their roots in geographic barriers, have persisted even until the present day.[3] Norway also has a minority Sami population that resides in the northern part of the country and is self-governing and largely autonomous.

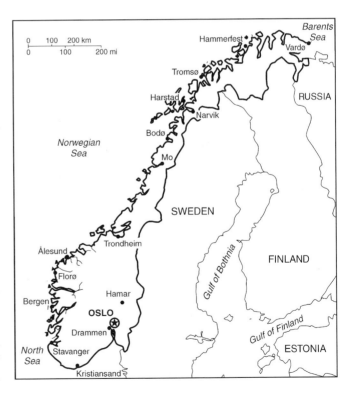

Norway is a constitutional monarchy with executive power formally vested in the king. In practice, however, political power in this liberal democratic state is controlled by the 165-member Parliament (*Storting*), the Council of State (cabinet), and the head of state—the prime minister. Norway's economy is capitalist but is tempered by substantial welfare provisions and trade union activity. Norway's per capita income is the third highest in the world.[4] In 2000, women constituted 51 percent of the Norwegian population and had a life expectancy of 81.1 years as compared to that of 75.6 years for men. The infant mortality rate was 7 per 1,000 live births, and the maternal mortality rate was 4 per 100,000 births. The total fertility (average number of births per woman) was 1.8.[5]

OVERVIEW OF WOMEN'S ISSUES

Compared to most countries in the West, women's situation in Norway appears enviable. Norwegian women have substantial political representation, access to free education and health care, expanding employment opportunities, one of the world's best maternity leave provisions, ability to control their reproduction through access to contraception and free abortions, a legacy of strong women's movements, and many feminist organizations that are active on their behalf. However, women have not achieved equality with men in Norway. Women still remain mostly responsible for housework and childcare, they constitute the majority of lower-level workers in a largely sex-segregated labor market, and their pay lags behind that of men. Although the proportion of women politicians is reaching close to 40 percent, they still operate within a largely male-defined political system. As more immigrants from non-Western countries settle in Norway, race and ethnicity as well as gender and class become important dimensions of inequality. Women are continuing to address these issues within the major Norwegian institutions and as members of independent women's organizations.

EDUCATION

Norwegian women attained access to all levels of education during the nineteenth century. In 1876, the Ministry of Education declared that women could take entrance examinations to secondary and vocational schools, and in the early 1880s women were first granted the right to take university entrance exams and then the final examinations at all the faculties of the universities, as well as to practice in such professions as law and medicine.[6] Almost 100 years later, in 1970, a report on the status of women in Norway found that women who completed upper-level secondary schools (graduation from which is required for entrance to tertiary education) constituted 43 percent of all students. The percentage of women who completed higher education was considerably below that of men at every age level, the majority of young women chose traditionally feminine fields of specialization, and most undertook shorter training than men.[7] In 1967, only 24.9 percent of all students enrolled in higher education were female, and they tended to cluster in relatively few fields like languages, pharmacy, and psychology. Only 0.3 percent of all women aged 24–64 had earned a university degree or the equivalent in the late 1960s, approximately 10 percent of all such degrees.[8]

Although Norwegian women have made some significant gains in education during the last thirty years, they have not achieved educational parity with men. While women students outnumbered men in secondary schools as well as institutions of higher learning by 1998, they obtained most of their university degrees in the humanities and social sciences. Men obtained twice as many degrees in the natural sciences and engineering as women did, and women constituted the majority of students enrolled in the fields of health and social services and in the humanities.[9] Even though women now obtain about one third of all degrees at the tertiary level of education, the pattern of their being clustered in traditionally feminine fields, observed earlier, has continued. Moreover, even in such areas as health and social services where women students outnumber men by two to one, men hold the majority of graduate degrees.[10]

In 1983, a private Women's University was established in Norway by a group of feminist activists and academics. The university's main objective is to improve women's opportunities for learning and development so that they can enter and transform many of the fields and organizations dominated by men. In recent years, the university has focused its curriculum on management and information technology.[11]

The pressure of students seeking admission to Norwegian universities and higher vocational colleges has been great during the last several decades, and although the higher education system has expanded, it has not been able to accommodate the increasing demand. Consequently, a growing number of Norwegian students has pursued study abroad. The majority of those studying in other countries are women (58 percent), most of whom are enrolled in European universities outside Scandinavia.[12]

Literacy

At the end of the twentieth century, women's literacy rate (99 percent) was equivalent to that of men.[13]

EMPLOYMENT AND THE ECONOMY

Job/Career Opportunities

Norwegian women's labor force participation was relatively low until recent years. For instance, in 1960 women made up only 23 percent of the labor force, a 2.2 percent decline from the 1950 figure.[14] Only 23.8 percent of women between the ages of sixteen and sixty-four were gainfully employed in 1960.[15] This low rate has been explained by a combination of factors, including an increase after World War II in the frequency of marriage, increased participation of younger women in higher education, lack of childcare facilities, the persistence of traditional sex roles, a substantial number of women occupied in unpaid farm work, and improved social security provisions for older women.[16]

Since 1960, the numbers of women in paid employment have increased steadily. By 1999, 76.2 percent of all women aged 16–64 were in the formal economy, comprising 42 percent of the labor force.[17] This substantial growth in about forty years can be attributed largely to the expansion of the Norwegian welfare state following the discovery of oil in the North Sea in the 1960s. With the growth of social services, especially in the areas of health, family care, and education, women were drawn in large numbers into paid work in state institutions such as the civil service, public hospitals, daycare centers, and schools.[18] By the late 1970s, more than 50 percent of all state employees were women,[19] and in 1999 54 percent of all employed women, as compared to 19 percent of men, were engaged in public services.[20]

In recent years, Norwegian women have also found employment opportunities in the wholesale and retail trade sector, and in restaurants and hotels, where 17 percent of all working women are employed. Other sectors of the economy where women comprise about 11 percent are finance, insurance, real estate, and business services, as well as mining, manufacturing, electricity, and water, where another 11 percent are employed.[21] Although women hold about 40 percent of supervisory and managerial positions in the public sector, they comprise only 25 percent of all administrative and managerial workers in the private sector.[22] Women thus fare much worse in the private economy than in the state institutions.

An important feature of Norwegian women's labor force participation is that a significant proportion (about 35 percent) of employed women hold part-time jobs.[23] These jobs are typically held by women with younger children who either prefer to divide their time between paid employment and taking care of children or cannot afford or are unable to find childcare.

Although unemployment in Norway has risen in recent years, it was around 4 percent at the end of the 1990s and women's unemployment rate has been consistently somewhat lower than men's. In 1999, 3 percent of working-age women were unemployed as compared to 3.4 percent of men.[24] The lower rate for women can be attributed to greater job security in the public sector where most women are employed.

Pay

In 1959, Norway ratified the International Labor Organization's Convention 100 on equal pay and established the Equal Pay council. The Council, consisting of representatives of employers, employees, and the government, was to investigate comparative pay rates for women and men, encourage improved job possibilities for women who wished to enter gainful employment, and promote the principle of equal pay for work of equal value.[25] In 1961 the Norwegian trade unions agreed on a framework for a plan to implement by stages the principle of equal pay. Wage agreements were no longer to set rates of pay separately for men and women but rather to set them according to the type of work done. The new system was implemented by 1967.[26]

In 1967, the average hourly pay rate for women employees in the manufacturing industries was 74 percent of that of men. In other occupations such as office work, sales work in retail trade, banking, and insurance, women received on average 65 percent of men's pay. However, a comparison of women's and men's pay on the same occupational level showed a much smaller difference—women made about 87 percent of men's wages in the same category.[27]

By 1998, although Norwegian women's average pay as compared to men's increased over the 1960s level, the gender wage gap still was approximately 15 percent when controlled for years of education, expertise, and seniority.[28] The continuing income differences between men and women can be explained by women's concentration in the more "feminized" sectors of the economy, their greater turnover than men's, and their lower representation in the upper rungs of all occupations. Even though Norway makes available extensive family leave provisions to both women and men, women use such provisions much more extensively than men and often opt for part-time work when raising children.

Support for Mothers/Caretakers

Even though the Norwegian childcare and family provisions are formally gender neutral (i.e., intended to benefit parents and not just mothers of small children), in practice they help women with children to establish and maintain participation in the paid labor force. Childcare centers make it possible for women to work outside the home;[29] parental leave provides temporary retreat from the labor force, but a retreat with a guarantee of reentry; and reduced working hours help women cope with pressures from combined employment and care responsibilities. Although the number of men receiving parental leave benefits increased in the 1990s, women still received more than 70 percent of these benefits in 1998.[30] Despite changes in gender relations, women continue to be primary caretakers of children and families.

Maternal Leave

Norway has one of the world's best parental leave provisions. As early as 1936, the Workers' Protection Act gave mothers the right to a leave of absence from work for six weeks before and six weeks after birth and stipulated that they could return to their jobs after taking the leave. In 1977, the National Insurance Act was amended to give mothers eighteen weeks of paid leave. In the 1980s, paid maternity leave was extended first to twenty and then to twenty-four weeks, and in 1990 the leave became available to both parents and was extended to thirty-two weeks with full pay, or an alternative fifty-two weeks with 80 percent pay, and up to three years of unpaid leave without the loss of a job.[31] To encourage men to take part in childrearing, four weeks of paid parental leave are reserved for fathers.[32] Additionally, working women and men have been entitled since 1987 to ten days of paid leave a year in case of children's illnesses or other family emergencies.[33]

Daycare

In the 1980s, the Norwegian government developed childcare policies whose goal was to increase the number of places in daycare centers as well as provide direct childcare payments to families.

Social/Government Programs

Legislation also was enacted to allow working parents of small children to reduce their daily hours over a period of time and for breastfeeding women by one hour per day.[34] Norway also provides generous child allowances to parents of small children. In 1998 the average annual child allowance in Norway, 1,200 euro, was the highest when compared to the other four Nordic countries.[35] During the economic recession of the early 1990s, the central government had on several occasions decreased funding to municipal social services, and these reductions were felt first by women who worked in the social service area and/or were the recipients of the benefits. The cuts in childcare and family programs resulted in increased responsibilities for women whose benefits were reduced.[36]

FAMILY AND SEXUALITY

Gender Roles

Norway has been characterized by a split between "official egalitarianism and private traditionalism."[37] On the one hand, ideals of justice and equality have been integral to the country's historical heritage, but on the other, practices and attitudes that treat and regard women as different from and inferior to men have been common.[38] Thus, despite women having formal equal rights for many decades, traditional gender roles have persisted in Norway. These roles are particularly visible in the economy, where the labor market continues to be largely sex segregated, and in the family, where women are still the primary caretakers of children.

Although Norwegian men have assumed more responsibilities within families and households in recent decades, by the late 1990s women were still spending more time than their male partners performing household tasks such as cooking and cleaning, and women still did most of the family care tasks. In 2000, women spent on average 3 hours 56 minutes per day on household work and 42 minutes

Norwegian mother and child playing chess, Oslo. Photo © TRIP/ J. Isachsen.

on family care (including childcare), while men spent on average 2 hours and 41 minutes per day on household work and 33 minutes on family care.[39] The gender gap in housework and childcare in Norway, however, was smaller than in most countries and has been decreasing over time, especially among the younger population (25–35 years of age).[40]

Marriage

In 2000, 49 percent of Norwegian women over the age of fifteen were married. The number of marriages increased during the 1990s and the number of divorces dropped slightly.[41] This can be explained by more women entering marriage at an older age than previously (twenty-five years on average) and fewer couples are cohabiting for long periods of time without marriage.[42]

Reproduction

Norwegian women's birthrates decreased significantly during the 1990s. The most dramatic drop has been among younger women, especially those under twenty years of age.[43] The trend toward smaller and more stable Norwegian families in recent years is no doubt a consequence of more egalitarian gender relations, which are, in turn, related to increased opportunities for women in the economy and politics.[44]

Contraception and Abortion

Seventy-six percent of all women over fifteen years of age use some form of contraception.[45] In 1978, Norway passed a law allowing abortion on demand. The law allows women to make their own choices regarding whether to have an abortion during the first twelve weeks of pregnancy without a physician's or institution's interference.[46] In 1998 there were 240 abortions per 1,000 live births in Norway, a slight decrease from the average of 250 per 1,000 live births between 1991 and 1995.[47] The rate of women's deaths from abortions is one of the lowest in the world—one per 8,333.[48]

HEALTH

Health Care Access

Norway has a public health service with a well-established system of primary health care. In addition to general practice, there are preventive services for mothers and children, school medical and dental care for children and adolescents, and occupational health services.

Diseases and Disorders

Despite access to medical care and the emphasis on prevention, the percentage of women diagnosed with major diseases such as cardiovascular, musculoskeletal, and cancerous ones has risen substantially from 1985 to 1995. More women than men are diagnosed with musculoskeletal and cardiovascular diseases, but more men than women fall victim to cancer. However, the mortality rate for both women and men from cardiovascular diseases as well as accidents (two major causes of death in Norway) decreased from 1985 to 1995.[49]

AIDS

The number of new HIV-positive women has risen significantly in the 1990s over the 1980s figure. In 1989, there were twenty-eight new cases reported of HIV-infected women; in 1997, that figure rose to forty cases. Although the numbers for men overall have been much higher, the trend has been for fewer new cases of men with HIV reported each year during the last decade (from 105 in 1989 to seventy-one in 1997).[50]

POLITICS AND LAW

Suffrage

Norwegian women obtained the right to vote in local elections and became eligible for public office in 1910, and to vote in general elections in 1913.

Political Participation

Norway has one of the world's highest female political representations at the national and local levels.[51] In 2000, 36 percent of Parliamentary seats were occupied by women and 40 percent of the ruling cabinet was female.[52] At the municipal level, women constituted 34 percent of local councilors by 1998.[53] However, women did not achieve significant political representation in Norway until relatively recently.

Starting in the 1970s, women's representation began to grow as a result of election campaigns organized by mainly female activists that included the mobilization of women to run for political office and to vote for candidates of their own sex. In a period of about two decades, women's political representation tripled.[54] Fueled by an active women's movement, the campaigns made use of Norway's relatively open election structure (proportional representation, multiparty system, and preference voting rules) and were able to appeal to the country's ideals of justice and equality.[55] The adoption of gender quotas by Norway's leading political parties (that at least 40 percent of either sex be represented on all election ballots, in party committees, and in all other party organs and levels) became an important means for increasing women's political representation.[56]

In recent years, women have also made substantial progress in representation on the public boards, committees, and councils of the Norwegian corporate sector.[57] In 1988, the government passed a law that there should be 40 percent representation of either sex on all public boards and committees.[58] In 1989, women constituted 35 percent of all representatives in the corporate sector and by the mid-1990s they were 39.8 percent; however, the proportion of women chairing the corporate bodies was much lower, around 20 percent.[59]

The substantially increased female political representation has had important consequences for politics and public policy in Norway. Since the 1970s, women representatives have brought new issues (e.g., childcare, parental leave, and sexual harassment in the workplace) into political party agendas and into discussions and debates. More social policies and legislation favorable to women and families have been promulgated, and the norms of conduct in politics have changed somewhat (e.g., meetings have become less formal).[60] Nevertheless, the structure of government and politics remains gendered, that is, dominated by masculine values and practices,[61] and the attainment of full gender equality in politics remains problematic.[62]

Women's Rights

Despite the Norwegian Constitution guaranteeing equal rights to all citizens and Norwegian residents regardless of their sex, and an impressive earlier history of women's attainment of rights under the law,[63] women have not achieved equal status with men. In 1972, the Norwegian government established the Equal Status Council,[64] which took over the tasks of the Equal Pay Council (founded in 1959) as well as being charged with new responsibilities to develop measures to promote equal status in families, education, business, and community life. The council is a liaison for organizations and the public in all equality matters, to initiate studies of gender inequality, and to seek remedies to rectify inequalities.[65] As a result of the council's first major study of women's status, the Norwegian Gender Equality Act (or Equal Status Act) was passed by Parliament in 1978, including the establishment of an Equal Status Ombud and an Appeals Board. The act is comprehensive, aiming to promote equality between the sexes in all sectors of society and in particular to improve the position of women.[66]

Due to the existence of the Equal Status Council and the Gender Equality Act, many policies and regulations aimed at achieving equal status between men and women have been enacted and implemented in Norway. These have included an Action Plan to Promote Equal Status adopted by Parliament and implemented in all governmental ministries and organizations, the gender quota provision mandating 40 percent representation of either sex on all public boards and committees, and a Local Government Act promoting gender balance in municipal and county councils.[67]

Despite the Equal Status Act's language that suggests affirmative action to remedy the subordinate status of women, the act has been largely interpreted in a gender-neutral way, and as Norwegian feminists have argued, it has not been used effectively especially to address the discrimination against women in the sex-segregated labor market and to close the gender gap in the economic sphere.[68] The gender-neutral interpretation has prevailed as a result of the merging of organized interests of trade unions and private employers as against those of the women's movement.[69]

Feminist Movements

Norway has had a long history of women's organizing and feminist activism. The first broad wave of feminism began in the mid-nineteenth century when an organized movement emerged primarily in the cities where upper- and middle-class female intellectuals began to express their discontent. Later, formal organizations were established, first among middle-class and then by working-class women. Middle-class women formed women's rights organizations like the Norwegian Association for Rights of Women (*Norsk Kvinnesaksforening*) established in 1884, which demanded political rights, the right to education, and access to employment for women;[70] and the Women's Public Health Organization (*Kvinnesanitetsforeningen*), founded in 1896, which focused on women's access to health care and initiated public health campaigns.[71] Working-class women struggled to improve their working conditions and to create trade unions. Some of these early organizations and efforts have continued until the present.

In the 1950s and 1960s, a critical debate concerning sex roles arose in Norway. Since by then most of the formal, legal restrictions on the activities of women were abolished, many Norwegians believed that problems of gender inequality were solved. However, several reports on the status of women in Norway published during the 1950s and 1960s indicated that significant gaps existed between women and men in most areas of life.[72] Thus some of the older and established women's organizations began to mobilize once again to address issues of gender inequality and to improve the status of women by pressuring the government to develop better policies and legislation.

The late 1960s and early 1970s, like in many other countries, also produced a new women's movement, known in Norway as the New Feminists (*Nyfeministene*). This strand of the feminist movement was radical and often militant; developed small consciousness-raising groups and nonhierarchical, participatory organizations; and used highly visible forms of protest. The New Feminists preferred to work "outside the system," creating, for example, alternative economic opportunities for women in work cooperatives and crisis centers for abused women and children. Although the more established feminists and the New Feminists at first worked separately, by the end of the 1970s their efforts began to converge as the more radical women increasingly began to accept the notion that change can be brought about through existing institutions and the older organizations became revitalized and radicalized by the new movement. The two groups thus started to cooperate in pre-election campaigns to get more women into public office, and many of the New Feminists began to join political parties, unions, university faculties, and the government administration.[73] Although this has resulted in a much less visible feminist movement, feminist activism continued, albeit in a more institutionalized form.

Today, numerous women's and feminist organizations exist in Norway. They include some of the oldest rights and humanitarian organizations that were established in the nineteenth century, women's chapters of political parties, a wide range of organizations that emerged out of the new feminist movement, and women's economic organizations such as women's trade unions, cooperatives, and countrywomen's associations. A recent development is the proliferation of women's organizations that focus on issues of importance to women of color and immigrant women. Another new type of women's organization is the international nongovernmental organization with ties to women's groups in other countries.

Lesbian Rights

While lesbian and gay rights are not guaranteed in the Norwegian Constitution, Norway has legislation that offers legal protections for homosexuals in its general civil penal code. The act relating to worker protection and working environment also offers legal protection for gay men and lesbians, prohibiting employers from taking homosexuality into consideration when persons apply for jobs.

In 1993, the Norwegian Parliament passed a Registered Partnerships Act, which has been enforced under the Ministry of Children and Family Affairs. This legislation allows two persons of the same sex to register their partnership with the same legal consequences as the contraction of a marriage with the exception of the provisions of the Adoption Act. However, one of the registered partners may adopt the other partner's children.[74]

VIOLENCE

Although Norway prides itself on being a peaceful country, its women are not immune to violence. However, the proportion of women reporting having experienced violence or threats of violence during recent years is relatively low (4 percent in 1982 as compared to 6 percent in 1997).[75] Nevertheless, the percentage of women who fear violence or threats is substantially higher: 14 percent in 1982 and 17 percent in 1997.[76]

Domestic Violence and Rape/Sexual Assault

Violence against women was an important issue taken up by the New Feminists in the 1970s who established Norway's first Crisis Centers. By the early 1990s, there were centers in all of Norway's nineteen counties.[77] These centers provide refuge to battered or raped women and children and offer women the opportunity to take an active part in the centers' work. Local (municipal) and national governments provide funding for the centers, but they depend mostly on voluntary help. Over the years, the organizational structure of the centers has become more hierarchical as increased funding by local authorities has lead to the establishment of representative boards, executive committees, managers, and staff.[78]

OUTLOOK FOR THE TWENTY-FIRST CENTURY

Women in Norway made great strides in the second half of the twentieth century. Today they have one of the world's highest female political representations at the national and local levels, extensive social provisioning programs that make it possible to combine family and employment responsibilities, still limited though expanding economic opportunities, and formal equality with men. On the other hand, in practice, gender inequality persists and is manifested in the unequal division of labor within families, in the subordinate status of women in most workplaces, in the gender gap in pay, and in higher education.

The prospects for women in Norway in the future are mixed. On the one hand, the economy is not likely to expand greatly, and recent cuts in funding to municipal social services that have affected women disproportionately may continue if the economy does not rebound. On the other hand, women's integration in the political system and in the welfare state bureaucracies will make it difficult for politicians to reverse the hard-won victories of the feminist movement.

NOTES

1. Other Scandinavian countries include Denmark, Finland, Iceland, Sweden, and the self-governing island communities of Greenland, Aland, and the Faroe Islands.

2. *Nordic Statistical Yearbook* (Copenhagen: Nordic Council of Ministers, 2000), 20.

3. Peter Reed and David Rothenberg, eds., *Wisdom in the Open Air* (Minneapolis: University of Minnesota Press, 1993), 5–6.

4. United Nations (UN), *The Worlds of Women 2000* (New York: United Nations, 2000), 146–47.

5. *Nordic Statistical Yearbook*, 2000, 22, 28, 59.

6. Equal Status Council, *Milestones in 150 Years' History of Norwegian Women* (Oslo: Likestillings radet, 1989), 1.

7. Betty Selid, *Women in Norway* (Oslo: Department of Cultural Affairs, 1970), 40.

8. Selid, 1970, 41–45.

9. *Nordic Statistical Yearbook*, 2000, 112–13.

10. *Nordic Statistical Yearbook*, 2000, 114.

11. Kvinneuniversitetet, 2002, www.kvu.hm.no/kueng.htm.

12. *Nordic Statistical Yearbook*, 2000, 116.

13. Shawn M. Burn, *Women across Cultures* (Mountain View, CA: Mayfield, 2000), 288.

14. Selid, 1970, 52.

15. Selid, 1970, 53.

16. Harriet Holter, ed., *Patriarchy in a Welfare Society* (Oslo: Universitetsforlaget, 1984).

17. *Nordic Statistical Yearbook*, 2000, 140.

18. Helga Maria Hernes, *Welfare State and Woman Power* (Oslo: Norwegian University Press, 1987).

19. Hernes, 1987, 39.

20. *Nordic Statistical Yearbook*, 2000, 157.

21. *Nordic Statistical Yearbook*, 2000, 157.

22. United Nations, 2000, 171.

23. Lauri Karvonen, "Trade Unions," in *Women in Nordic Politics*, ed. Lauri Karvonen and Per Selle (Aldershot, UK: Dartmouth Press, 1995), 136.

24. *Nordic Statistical Yearbook*, 2000, 140–41.

25. Selid, 1970, 67.

26. Equal Status Council, 1989, *Milestones*, 3.

27. Selid, 1970, 68–69.

28. Erling Barth, *Monopsonistic Discrimination* (Cambridge, MA: National Bureau of Economic Research, 1999).

29. By the end of the 1980s, there was still a substantial gap between the need for

childcare and the number of spaces in daycare centers that were available; see Anne Marie Berg et al., *Tid til Likestilling?* (Lysaker: Staten Institut for Forbruksfurskning, 1990).

30. *Nordic Statistical Yearbook*, 2000, 76.

31. Equal Status Council, 1989, *Milestones*, 2–3.

32. Janneke Van der Ros, "The State and Women," in *Women and Politics World-wide*, ed. Barbara T. Nelson and Najma Chowdhury (New Haven, CT: Yale University Press, 1994), 6.

33. Equal Status Council, *The Norwegian Equal Status Act* (Otta, Norway: Engers Boktrykkeri, 1989), 12.

34. Equal Status Council, 1989, *Milestones*, 12.

35. *Nordic Statistical Yearbook*, 2000, 77.

36. Van der Ros, 1994, 542–43.

37. Holter, 1970, 83.

38. Jill M. Bystydzienski, *Women in Electoral Politics* (Westport, CT: Praeger, 1995), 19.

39. *Statistics Norway*, 2002, Table 9, www.ssb.no/english/subjects/00/02/20tidsbruck_en/tab-2002-05-13-19-en.html.

40. Joni Seager, *The State of Women in the World* (New York: Penguin, 2000), 61; *Statistics Norway*, 2002, Table 9; and Anne Lise Ellingsaeter, "Dual Breadwinners between State and Market," in *Restructuring Gender Relations and Employment*, ed. Rosemary Crompton (New York: Oxford University Press, 1999), 45.

41. *Nordic Statistical Yearbook*, 2000, 52–53.

42. Burn, 2000, 288; and Rosemary Crompton and Fiona Harris, "Employment, Careers, and Families," in Crompton, 1999, 142.

43. *Nordic Statistical Yearbook*, 2000, 57.

44. Crompton, 1999; and Runa Haukaa, ed., *Nye Kvinner, Nye Menn* (Oslo: Ad Notam, 1991).

45. Burn, 2000, 288.

46. Like all medical care in Norway, abortion is free of charge, and the cost of abortion has never been an issue in the debates surrounding abortion (Van der Ros, 1994, 531).

47. *Nordic Statistical Yearbook*, 2000, 56.

48. Burn, 2000, 288.

49. Statistics Norway, 2002.

50. Ibid.

51. Burn, 2000, Appendix A.

52. *Nordic Statistical Yearbook*, 2000, 120–23.

53. Burn, 2000, 288.

54. Bystydzienski, 1995, 38.

55. Bystydzienski, 1995, 38.

56. Bystydzienski, 1995, 49–50.

57. The corporate system of boards, committees, and councils includes representation from organizations and institutions of the state, organized interests (like labor, industry, and professional associations), and technical expertise. These bodies manage, control, advise, coordinate, and formulate legislation in specific fields, and their members are nominated by governmental ministries or appointed directly by Parliament. Although this type of formalized access to the state exists in most Western countries, it is especially well developed in Nordic countries due to their extensive public welfare bureaucracies and wide-ranging policy planning functions.

58. Equal Status Council, 1989, *Milestones*, 3.

59. Christina Bergqvist et al., *Equal Democracies?* (Oslo: Scandinavian University Press, 1999), 40.

60. Bergqvist et al., 1999, Part II; and Bystydzienski, 1995, Ch. 4.

61. Joan Acker, "Hierarchies, Jobs, Bodies," *Gender and Society* 4, no. 2 (1990): 139–58.

62. Bergqvist et al., 1999, 277–89; and Bystydzienski, 1995, Conclusion.

63. For example, women achieved equal rights under family laws and the right to property ownership in 1888 in Norway.

64. In the mid-1990s, the English name of the council was changed to Gender Equality Council to better reflect its work.

65. Equal Status Council, 1989, *Norwegian*, 2–3.

66. Equal Status Council, 1989, *Norwegian*, 4.

67. Bergqvist et al., 1999, 213.

68. Beatrice Halsaa, *Policies and Strategies on Women in Norway* (Lillehamer, Norway: Oppland Regional College, 1989); Van der Ros, 1994.

69. Van der Ros, 1994, 538.

70. Torild Skard, "Women in the Political Life of Nordic Countries," in *Women in Contemporary Scandinavia*, ed. Torild Skard (Oslo: Norwegian University Press, 1987), 639.

71. Van der Ros, 1994, 529.

72. Selid, 1970.

73. Bystydzienski, 1995, 51.

74. Ministry of Children and Family Affairs, "Registered Partnership," www.dep.no/bfd/engelsh/publ/handbooks/004041-12003/index-dok000-b-n-a.html.

75. Other surveys of violence against women have estimated that about 25 percent of Norwegian women have suffered some form of abuse (Burn, 2000, 288).

76. *Statistics Norway*, 2002, 60.

77. Van der Ros, 1994, 539.

78. Van der Ros, 1994, 540.

RESOURCE GUIDE

Suggested Reading

Bergqvist, Christina, et al. *Equal Democracies? Gender and Politics in the Nordic Countries*. Oslo: Scandinavian University Press, 1999. A comparative review of gender equality in Norway, Sweden, Denmark, Finland, and Iceland; includes a good overview of family policy in Norway.

Bystydzienski, Jill M. *Women in Electoral Politics: Lessons from Norway*. Westport, CT: Praeger, 1995. A comprehensive study of why there are large numbers of women in politics in Norway, how women achieved high political representation, and what the effects of increasing numbers of women have been on the political system.

Ellingsaeter, Anne Lise. "Dual Breadwinners between State and Market." In *Restructuring Gender Relations and Employment*, edited by Rosemary Crompton, 40–59. New York: Oxford University Press, 1999. A description of reform policies regarding work and family care and how both motherhood and fatherhood have come to be placed on the political agenda in Norway.

Holter, Harriet, ed. *Patriarchy in a Welfare Society*. Oslo: Universitetsforlaget, 1984. A collection of articles focused on explaining how a highly developed welfare society like Norway, characterized by a commitment to equality between the sexes, maintains male-dominated institutions.

Nordic Statistical Yearbook. Copenhagen: Nordic Council of Ministers, 2000. Major statistical resource on Norway and other Scandinavian countries, published every year in English and available in many university and some public libraries.

Web Sites

Women's Organizations–Norway, www.2.euronet.nl/~fullmoon/womlist/countries/norway.html.
A site that provides current listing in English of women's groups and addresses in Norway.

Statistics Norway, www.ssb.no/english/.
A major source of statistical data on women.

Organizations

Forum for Women and Development (FOKUS)
Storgaten 33C
0184 Oslo, Norway
Phone: (0047) 22 20 95 70
Fax: (0047) 22 20 95 69
Email: fokuskvinner@online.no
Web site: www.focuswomen.org

A coalition of more than forty women's organizations in Norway with a focus on supporting women's projects in the Third World. Has an information center and a coordinating office. Its web site is both in Norwegian and English.

MIRA Center for Black, Migrant and Refugee Women
P.O. Box 1749
Vika, 0121 Oslo, Norway
Phone: (0047) 22 11 69 20
Fax: (0047) 22 36 40 19

An organization focused on issues of importance for women of color, immigrant women, and refugee women in Norway.

Nordic Institute for Women's Studies and Gender Research (NIKK)
University of Oslo
P.O. Box 1156 Blindern
N-0317 Oslo, Norway
Phone: (0047) 22 85 89 21 (34)
Fax: (0047) 22 85 89 50
Email: nikk@nikk.uio.no
Web site: www/uio/no/www-othernikk/english-index.html

A transnational, interdisciplinary research institute for the Nordic countries, the institute also provides information for and on women's studies and gender research in the region as well as women's NGOs.

Sami Nisson Forum
P.O. Box 110
N-9735 Karasjok, Norway
Email: lene@antonsen@c2i.net
Web site: http://home.c2inet/leneant/

A Sami women's network that works for local and regional development on women's premises. Publishes a magazine in English.

SELECTED BIBLIOGRAPHY

Acker, Joan. "Hierarchies, Jobs, Bodies: A Theory of Gendered Organizations." *Gender & Society* 4, no. 2 (1990): 139–58.

Barth, Erling. *Monopsonistic Discrimination and the Gender Wage Gap in Norway*. Cambridge, MA: National Bureau of Economic Research, 1999.

Berg, Anne Marie, Randi Lavik, and Inger Lise Solvang. *Tid til Likestilling? Likestillingspolitikk og Tidsorganiseting 1970–1990* (Time for Equality? Public Policy, Gender Equality and the Organization of Time 1970–1990). Lysaker: Staten Institutt for Forbruksforskning, 1990.

Burn, Shawn M. *Women across Cultures: A Global Perspective*. Mountain View, CA: Mayfield, 2000.

Crompton, Rosemary, and Fiona Harris. "Employment, Careers, and Families: The Significance of Choice and Constraint in Women's Lives." In *Restructuring Gender Relations and Employment*, edited by Rosemary Crompton, 128–49. New York: Oxford University Press, 1999.

Equal Status Council. *Milestones in 150 Years' History of Norwegian Women*. Oslo: Likestillingsradet, 1989.

———. *The Norwegian Equal Status Act*. Otta, Norway: Engers Boktrykkeri, 1989.

Halsaa, Beatrice. *Policies and Strategies on Women in Norway: The Roles of Women's Organizations, Political Parties and the Government*. Lillehamer: Oppland Regional College, 1989.

Haukaa, Runa, ed. *Nye Kvinner, Nye Menn* (New Women, New Men). Oslo: Ad Notam, 1991.

Hernes, Helga Maria. *Welfare State and Woman Power*. Oslo: Norwegian University Press, 1987.

Holter, Harriet. *Sex Roles and Social Structure*. Oslo: Norwegian University Press, 1970.

Karvonen, Lauri. "Trade Unions and the Feminization of the Labour Market in Scandinavia." In *Women in Nordic Politics: Closing the Gap*, edited by Lauri Karvonen and Per Selle, 133–54. Aldershot and Brookfield, VT: Dartmouth Press, 1995.

Kvinneuniversitetet. 2002. www.kvu.hm.no/kueng.htm.

Reed, Peter, and David Rothenberg, eds. *Wisdom in the Open Air*. Minneapolis: University of Minnesota Press, 1993.

Seager, Joni. *The State of Women in the World*. New York: Penguin Books, 2000.

Selid, Betty. *Women in Norway: Their Position in Family Life, Employment and Society*. Oslo: Department of Cultural Affairs, 1970.

Skard, Torild. "Women in the Political Life of the Nordic Countries." In *Women in Contemporary Scandinavia*, edited by Torild Skard, 639–55. Oslo: Norwegian University Press, 1987.

Statistics Norway. 2002, Table 9. www.ssb.no/english/subjects/00/02/20tidsbruk_en/tab-2002-05-13-09-en.html.

United Nations. *The Worlds of Women 2000: Trends and Statistics*. New York: United Nations, 2000.

Van der Ros, Janneke. "The State and Women: A Troubled Relationship in Norway." In *Women and Politics Worldwide*, edited by Barbara T. Nelson and Najma Chowdhury, 528–43. New Haven, CT: Yale University Press, 1994.

28

POLAND

Jill M. Bystydzienski

PROFILE OF POLAND

Poland is located in Eastern Europe, between Germany to its west and several Newly Independent States (NIS), including Belarus and Ukraine, on its eastern border. Its land consists chiefly of plains, with significant highlands in the southwest (Sudeten Mountains) and the southeast (Tatra Mountains), and a wide lake region above the central lowlands. Poland's northern boundary hugs the Baltic Sea. The country has had a long history of dramatic shifts that included changes of dynasties, realignments of frontiers, foreign invasions, occupations, and repeated partition by its neighbors. A new era emerged for Poland in 1989 when the communist regime, which began after the Second World War, was voted out of office and the Solidarity movement came into power. With the change in government from a one-party system to a parliamentary democracy came the beginning of the transition from a centrally planned economy to a capitalist market system.

Poland has approximately 39 million people, 51 percent of whom are women. About 98 percent of the population is ethnic Poles, with the largest minority groups being Ukrainians, Belarusians, and Germans. About 96 percent of the population is Roman Catholic. Currently, life expectancy is 77 years for women and 69 years for men. The infant mortality rate is 10.2 per 1,000 live births, and the maternal mortality rate is 19 per 100,000 live births. The total fertility (average number of births per woman) is 1.4.[1]

OVERVIEW OF WOMEN'S ISSUES

With the transition to a liberal democracy and market economy, Poland has been going through rapid changes. These changes have had both positive and negative effects on the status and experiences of women. With the privatization of the economy, many women are beginning to own and run businesses. However, the change to a market economy has brought about unemployment, which has affected women disproportionately. Although since World War II Polish women have had relatively high rates of labor force participation, there is a high degree of sex segregation and discrimination, with women dominating fields that have low prestige and provide lower pay. Benefits that women enjoyed under communism, such as subsidized childcare and paid maternity leave, are no longer guaranteed. Under communism, women had substantial representation in government, but since 1989 their numbers in political office have been reduced by more than one half. With the growing influence of the Catholic Church in politics, women have lost the right to abortion. Sex education in schools is not being offered, and periodic attempts have been made by religious groups to restrict methods of contraception. The opening up of borders and introduction of capitalist commodification of women's bodies have contributed to rapidly increasing prostitution and sex trafficking in women. On the other hand, the introduction of the right to freedom of association and free expression have resulted in a growing number of women's and feminist groups and organizations that are addressing the problems and issues faced by women in the transition.

EDUCATION

Access to education was considered to be the most important issue for women activists in Poland in the nineteenth century as well as during the period between the two world wars in the twentieth century. They fought for and gained entry for women into first primary and secondary, and later higher, education. Under the communist regime, the highly centralized and standardized educational system became an important vehicle for providing the state economy with an educated and vocationally trained labor force that included women. Thus women in Poland have had a long legacy of social acceptance and inclusion in the educational system.

The Polish educational system is organized such that after completion of primary school there are three different options: (1) basic vocational (incomplete secondary), (2) technical and vocational secondary, and (3) general secondary. In 1998–1999, 30 percent of primary school graduates went on to basic vocational schools, where they received training for a trade but not a secondary school diploma; among them, 34 percent were women. On the other hand, women constituted 49 percent of those enrolled in technical and vocational secondary and 63 percent of those in general secondary schools.[2] Thus, although men are more likely than women to have only basic vocational education, women are at least as or more likely than men to pursue vocational secondary and general secondary education. However, women and men in vocational schools still tend to choose traditionally gender-specific education, with women concentrating in fields that prepare them for work in personal services, semiskilled blue-collar jobs in light industries, lower management occupations, and auxiliary health care fields.

Secondary school enrollment ratio (F/100 M) in Poland is 103 and in 1998–1999, 98.1 percent of enrolled women graduated from secondary education institutions as compared to 96.6 percent of men.[3]

Women make up 65 percent of students in higher education in Poland; however, they are not equally represented in all higher education fields.[4] Although in 1998–1999 women were at least 50 percent of students in such areas as mathematics, computer science, the medical sciences, and architecture, they were 29 percent of students in technical universities, 28 percent in merchant marine academies, 17 percent in engineering, and 6 percent in transport and communications, but 74 percent in teacher education.[5] Women also received approximately one third of all graduate university degrees. Although women account for significantly more than half of all university students, they are not as well represented among the faculty. Women constituted 37 percent of all the teaching staff at Polish universities in 1998–1999 and only 17 percent of full professors.[6]

Even though gender gaps continue to exist at the higher education level, it is important to point out that less than two decades ago, most women in Poland had not completed secondary school. The gains in education are especially visible among younger adult women (aged 25–34) who now have higher levels of education than men. Among women employed in the public sector, over 75 percent have high school or higher education, compared to 50.6 percent of men.[7]

Literacy

Another consequence of the achievement in education for Polish women is their high literacy rate: 99 percent of women in Poland are literate.[8]

EMPLOYMENT AND THE ECONOMY

Job/Career Opportunities

One of the legacies of the communist era in Poland is that women have relatively high rates of labor force participation. Women as well as men were needed to rebuild the post–World War II economy, and they were actively recruited and trained to take part in the paid work force. As early as 1960, women accounted for 44 percent of the labor force in Poland; by 1988, they constituted nearly 47 percent, and they were 45.1 percent in 1998.[9] Despite longstanding female participation, the labor force in Poland is still sex segregated with women dominating occupations in such branches of the economy as health care, social welfare, hotel and restaurant service, public administration, and teaching at the primary and secondary level, whereas men are significantly more involved in industry, construction, agriculture and forestry, and transportation.[10] Men are also beginning to take over areas—such as finance—that were previously dominated by women but are now more important in a market economy. In 1988, 84.2 percent of workers in finances and insurance were women; by 1997, their share of the finance and insurance sector had dropped to 74 percent.[11]

Television factory, Warsaw, Poland. Photo © TRIP/Ask Images.

In all sectors of the economy, including those in which they outnumber men, women are clustered in the lower and middle levels of the occupational structure. Although few are in managerial and executive positions, the opportunities for women to obtain higher-level occupations have been increasing: from 1995 to 1998, the percentage of women managers grew from 18 to 28.[12] Also, more women are starting to own businesses. Whereas in 1989, 3.7 percent of all employed Polish women were owners or co-owners of businesses, by 1995 the figure increased to 11 percent. In 1998, 37 percent of all business owners were women.[13]

Unemployment

One of the negative aspects of the transition to a market economy is that unemployment, which was practically nonexistent prior to 1989, has become a problem affecting women disproportionately. Women, the lowest-paid and most expendable of workers, were the first to be let go as the economy began to privatize. Consequently, their rate of unemployment initially was higher than that of men, dropped some toward the mid-1990s, but then increased again. In 1998 women constituted 58.5 percent of all the registered unemployed while the total unemployment rate was 10 percent.[14] The percentage of unemployed increased to 18 by 2002.[15] In 2001, women constituted 59 percent of the unemployed.[16] The highest rates of women's unemployment are found in large towns and cities (Poznan, Katowice, and Warsaw) even though these cities offer many new jobs and have the highest percentages of women with higher education degrees; over 35 percent of unemployed women in these cities have college or university education. Moreover, the duration of unemployment is longer for women than for men. Among all unemployed women, 49.9 percent, as compared with 27.1 percent of men, were unable to find a job for over twelve months, and 31 percent of all unemployed women, compared to 12.7 percent of men, were unemployed longer than twenty-four months.[17]

Reasons for the higher rates and longer duration of unemployment of women are that the supply of new jobs does not meet the demand;[18] most of the job advertisements, particularly for more secure and better-paid positions, are directed to men;[19] and employers prefer to hire male employees. Despite their high levels of formal education, unemployed women do not generally know foreign languages (a requirement of many employers in the new economy), and their professional experience was most often gained under different economic conditions and is generally of little use currently.[20] However, even younger women who have received their education since 1989 are not faring well in the new market economy. Women's unemployment rates are highest among those 25–34 years of age, the group with the highest levels of education.[21]

Although women in Poland live on average eight years longer than men, they are forced to retire five years earlier as the mandatory retirement age for women is sixty, whereas it is sixty-five for men. Retirement income is low and relatively fixed, and the majority of the retired are women who find it increasingly difficult to survive. Many retired women do odd jobs for pay to supplement their meager pensions, and they generally do not report the extra income to avoid taxes.[22]

Pay

The Polish Constitution guarantees men and women equal pay for equal work, however women typically earn less than men. As already indicated, women tend to work in lower-paying sectors, and within fields, men tend to have the higher-level occupations. Between the years 1991 and 1994, the average pay for women remained at a relatively constant level of about 75 percent of the average income for men.[23] In 1998, women's average income was 80 percent of that of men's. The largest pay gaps were between men and women in the physical, mathematical, and engineering science professions (where women received on the average 71 percent of men's remuneration), life sciences and associate professions (69 percent), personal service providers and salespersons (69 percent) and craft and related trades (66 percent).[24]

Women's earnings as percentage of the remuneration of men have varied over the years since 1989, with greater variation between the private and public sectors. Generally, women's pay in the public sector has been more stable over time and closer to men's than in the private sector. Moreover, the fewer the women in a given occupational category, the less favorable to them are the differences in earnings. They are especially at a disadvantage in such occupations as industrial worker or medium-level technical officer, which are characterized by financial discrimination against women.[25]

Given fewer opportunities than men to obtain employment, women are more likely than men to accept lower than average pay even when they have higher education. Thus there is no direct correlation between the generally high level of women's formal education and their remuneration in the market economy.

Working Conditions

Women in Poland continue to be subjected to discrimination and sexual harassment in the workplace. Attitudes favoring paying men more than women and treating women as less competent and as sex objects continue to persist.

Women traditionally, even under communism, had been perceived as supplemental workers rather than as equal or main contributors to family income. This tendency has been exacerbated under new economic conditions since 1989. Women themselves report that the most important reason they are employed is because their husbands' earnings are not enough.[26] Without women's financial contributions, families would not be able to have adequate support, and in many cases women are the sole breadwinners, yet many Poles believe that women should stay home to take care of children and households, and that jobs requiring professional responsibility are incompatible with women's domestic duties. Employers often are reluctant to hire women, especially women who have young children or those of childbearing age, except for part-time, temporary, and low-paying jobs. Given women's higher unemployment rate than men's, women often are willing to accept low earnings in order to get any job available. All these factors work against women being paid on an equal footing with men. Employers thus continue to accept the notion that women attach less importance to pay and therefore are justified in paying a woman less even if she has the same qualifications as a man.[27]

Many Poles believe that women are not capable of functioning well in managerial and executive positions. A 1998 opinion poll found that 10 percent of men and 3.6 percent of women agreed with a statement that women managers' performance is inferior to that of men managers. Moreover, 62 percent of the respondents agreed that women executives are a threat to the family.[28]

Sexual Harassment

Sexual harassment in the workplace remains a largely ignored or hidden phenomenon.[29] Although there is enough anecdotal evidence to suggest that it exists and may be quite pervasive, to date no studies focusing specifically on sexual harassment have been done in Poland. A Polish observer noted that "it [sexual harassment] is characteristic in our culture. . . . No secretary will object to her boss for being patted on the behind, because she considers this as something normal. . . . Probably no one will regard it as unusual if a woman gets promoted by sleeping with her supervisor. In Polish legislation there is not even one paragraph referring to such violations, not even judicial precedence. A penalty for such acts remains unidentified."[30] Although there has been legislation passed since 1989 focused on improving conditions for workers, sexual harassment has not been addressed.

However, a 1999 report based on a survey conducted by the Office of National Labor Inspection documented unequal pay for women and men performing the same or similar types of work, unequal treatment of women and men seeking employment, and cases of sexual harassment.[31] This may be an indication that sexual harassment is starting to be noticed and taken more seriously.

Support for Mothers/Caretakers

Since 1989, access to welfare and social services in Poland has become greatly reduced.

Maternal Leave

One of the very first changes made by the new Solidarity government was to curtail maternity benefits. Under the communist system, women received full pay for the first six months of maternity leave, reduced pay for another six, and could have up to six years of unpaid leave. Currently, only in the public sector are women able to take up to six months leave with reduced pay; in the private sector, enterprises set their own policies and most do not provide paid maternity leave. There were 2.6 times fewer women taking maternity leave in 1994 than in 1989, and during the 1995–1997 period their number dropped by another 18 percent.[32]

Daycare

Although under the previous regime childcare services left much to be desired,[33] during the years 1989–1994, 59 percent of all daycare centers were closed and the number of places for children was reduced by approximately 50 percent. Funding for daycare shifted from central to local governments, which commanded few resources, and, consequently, conditions deteriorated in those centers that remained.[34] A few private, highly priced childcare centers have emerged, replacing some of the government-sponsored ones that have closed down due to lack of funding. Also, during the early transition years, 25 percent of kindergartens were closed. During the 1995–1997 period, there was a further 4 percent drop in the number of kindergartens.[35]

Who takes care of children now that there is a shortage of places for them in daycare centers and kindergartens? Some are cared for by mothers who are unable to find a job or have no other possibility of securing childcare, or by grandmothers who have taken early retirement as part of the policy of pushing older women out of the job market. Some women with young children opt for low-paying jobs that allow them to bring their children to work (e.g., weeding flower beds in a park), and others do part-time work at home that brings little money and excludes benefits.[36]

Inheritance and Property Rights

The Polish Constitution guarantees equal rights of women to inheritance and property, yet women are less likely to inherit and own property than are men.[37] This is largely due to the persistence of traditional gender roles within the family and in society.

Social/Government Programs

As increasing numbers of women become unemployed, they are forced to fall back on unemployment and welfare benefits that provide poverty income. Although social welfare benefits increased twentyfold during the period 1990–1998, on average unemployed women received less than 36 percent of their average monthly salary in unemployment benefits.[38] Under the communist system, the state created a number of provisions in the form of subsidies to women and families including a childbirth benefit, a subsidy to low-income families with several children, a benefit for families burdened with care of sick or disabled members, and a fund for single-parent families in difficult financial circumstances. Since 1989, these benefits have been substantially reduced.[39] In 1993, with the passage of anti-abortion legislation, the government established a fund to financially help pregnant women and women with small children whose family incomes were below the poverty line. The Ministry of Labor and Social Welfare estimated that about 10,000 women would take advantage of the provision in the year 1994. To their surprise, 80,000 women applied for the benefit in the first two months that the provision became available. Consequently, the government shortened the term of the provision from twelve to four months and gave the subsidy only to the most destitute women and families.[40]

FAMILY AND SEXUALITY

Gender Roles

Despite high levels of education and, until recently, labor force participation of women in Poland, traditional gender division of labor in the family and stereotypes of women and men continue. In national surveys, the majority of Poles indicate that they believe gender differences to be innate, and that women want above all to have a family and children, whereas for men having a family is equally as important as employment.[41]

Polish historical legacy, especially the long periods of external threat to national existence, has contributed to a strong emphasis on "the family" and the particular role and situation of women within it. As in many other countries under siege, where men were frequently absent due to wars, uprisings, or exile, women took on the responsibility for decision making regarding childrearing and households, as well as the preservation of cultural traditions, heritage, and language. Polish Catholicism, with its cult of the Madonna, on the one hand gave women an aura of "spiritual superiority," while on the other taught women to accept their fate and to be martyrs for their nation and the family.

Although after the Second World War women became paid workers as well as mothers, communist ideology did not challenge the traditional division of labor in the family and women were expected to reproduce the nation as well as to contribute to its economic growth. Women continued to be viewed as essentially different from men—for example, as naturally suited to take care of children—and were excluded by law from employment in about ninety specific jobs that were seen as dangerous to their reproductive health.[42]

Currently, although most Polish women are mothers, wives, and workers, their family roles are considered to be of greater importance than all others. Along with this has come increased family responsibility; hence even though men are still considered officially heads of households, women often make more of the important decisions regarding family expenditures and welfare of children.[43] As in many other countries, employed women in Poland typically work a double shift. In 1994, the average employed Polish woman spent six hours and twenty-three minutes on housework and childcare per day, whereas a man in a comparable family situation devoted only two hours and twenty minutes to household duties.[44] However, traditional gender roles and stereotypes seem to be diminishing among the younger generation, with both women and men 24–35 years old expressing more acceptance of women's employment for their individual needs and shared housework than their older counterparts.[45]

Marriage

Although marriage continues to be the desired norm for the majority of Poles, the number of marriages dropped in Poland between the years 1990 and 1997, from 6.7 to 5.3 per 1,000 population, and the number of divorces remained constant.[46] The drop in marriage can be explained partly by the fact that younger women are pursuing more years of education and delaying marriage and children. In 1995, women married on average at the age of 23 and men at age 26;[47] by 1999, the average age at marriage for women was 24 years.[48] The majority of married Polish women report being satisfied with their marriages, yet they indicate a higher degree of satisfaction with their children than with marriage. Sources of conflict in marriage as indicated by women include men's lack of participation in family responsibilities, alcoholism (often related to violence), and dissatisfaction with sexual relations.[49]

In comparison to other East European countries and Russia, Poland has a significantly lower divorce rate.[50] This is often attributed to Poland being a traditionally Catholic country, yet there are other reasons as well for this phenomenon. For one thing, in the past, and currently still for many people, it has been difficult to obtain new housing, thus women have had to, and continue to, remain in bad marriages because they are unable to move out. Moreover, the procedures for obtaining a divorce have become more complicated, and the cost of divorce has risen significantly since 1989.[51]

Reproduction

In Poland until recently, marriage, sexual relations, and reproduction were considered to be inextricably related. Young people were expected to enter marriage at a "reasonable" age (early twenties), which in turn signified sexual initiation and the subsequent birth of the first child, preferably within a year of the marriage. However, during the latter part of the twentieth century, norms concerning marriage, sex, and reproduction have liberalized significantly. A study conducted in 1994 found that only 22.6 percent of the population was against premarital sexual relations for young women and 13.5 percent opposed such relations for young men.[52] The same study also found that the majority of women and men did not see adultery as a necessary reason for divorce.

Sex Education

Despite the trend toward greater separation between marriage, sex, and procreation, the Polish government's health and educational institutions have not responded effectively to the changing norms. Due to increased involvement since 1989 of the Catholic Church in politics and policy making, sex education in schools is not taught and there are no family planning programs or clinics in Poland that could inform women about the options available to them.

Contraception and Abortion

Although women are more interested today in contraceptives, which have become more easily available in recent years, many barriers remain to their widespread use. According to a national sample of Polish women surveyed in 1995, women have limited access to contraceptives, their cost is too high for many, and not all types are available outside of large cities; moreover, 65 percent of respondents reported not having adequate sex education to be able to choose an appropriate contraceptive.[53] Although close to 75 percent of all Polish women support free access to contraceptives, almost half (45.2 percent) of sexually active women do not use any reliable method of contraception.[54] Hence, many Polish women risk unwanted pregnancies rather than controlling their reproduction. Meanwhile, beginning in 1990, access to abortion became increasingly restricted. Between 1956 and 1989, abortion was available on demand and by the 1970s was commonly used by Polish women to limit the number of children. Under the new, noncommunist government, with its strong link to the Solidarity movement and the Catholic Church, the Polish parliament, despite popular opposition, immediately began to whittle away at the abortion law.[55] First, in 1990, new regulations were passed allowing abortion to be performed only in public hospitals after a woman had acquired the agreement of three physicians and a psychologist. Then in 1992, a new medical code of ethics prohibited doctors from performing abortions under the threat of license revocation. Finally, in 1993, Parliament passed a family planning law for the protection of the unborn, prohibiting abortion with the exception of life- or health-endangering circumstances of the woman, the pregnancy being the result of a rape, or severe damage to the fetus.[56] At the same time, new restrictions were placed on women's access to fetal development examinations (e.g., amniocentesis), limiting access to women over thirty-five years of age who may have concerns due to genetic reasons. Although the law was overturned in 1995 with the election of President Aleksander Kwasniewski, a neocommunist who promised to change the anti-abortion law, when a right-wing and centrist church-allied majority was elected in 1997, the anti-abortion law was reinstated.

The number of officially registered abortions dropped significantly after 1993; however, hospitalization and death from complications due to pregnancy increased in the following years, suggesting the return of illegal and unsafe abortions.[57] In 1999, the official figure for deaths from abortions in Poland was 1 in 2,770.[58] According to a government report, in 1999 there were 151 legal abortions performed in public health institutions, but the Federation for Women and Family Planning, an NGO, estimated that a more accurate number of actual abortions could be anywhere between 80,000 to 200,000.[59] Since abortion remains legal in several neighboring countries, Polish women seeking abortions who can afford to travel abroad have been able to avail themselves of services provided by entrepreneurs who arrange trips to foreign abortion clinics.[60]

Teen Pregnancy

By 1988, 5.8 percent of all births in Poland were to unmarried mothers, most of whom were in their teens.[61] In 1994, 8 percent of all births were out of wedlock.[62] In 2003, 7 percent of children were born to unmarried teenage mothers.[63]

HEALTH

Health Care Access

Prior to 1989, health care in Poland was universal and free of charge. With the introduction of capitalist market economy, health care became increasingly privatized and a dual system of private and public health care, one for the rich and another for the poor, was created. Access to private health clinics and hospitals (usually providing better services) became restricted to those who were insured or could afford to pay for health care. Since women are generally paid less than men and many more are unemployed, their access to effective health care has been curtailed. Although the government provides some health benefits to families and women who require help taking care of a disabled or chronically ill family member and low-income women who are pregnant or raising young children, these benefits are very low and only available in the public health care sector, which has been shrinking rapidly. By 1994, public hospital and clinic personnel, including nurses, nursing assistants, and doctors, had been cut by 30,000, and many health care staff were forced to take early retirement.[64]

In 1999, the Polish government introduced a Health Fund system aimed at reforming the quality and scope of health care in Poland. The Health Fund, or general health insurance, is responsible for the collection of insurance contributions and payment of benefits. The funding for this system is to come from a 7.5 percent tax on personal income of those covered by the system. The fund then contracts medical services from both public and private health service providers.[65] It is still too early to tell whether this new system will improve access and health care for women.

Diseases and Disorders

The mortality rate of women in Poland is 4 percent higher than that of women in Western Europe.[66] More than half (57.7 percent) of deceased Polish women in 1997 died of heart disease or a related circulatory illness. As in many other countries, women in Poland are more likely than their male counterparts to seek medical care. In 1992 they constituted 53 percent of all patients in the public health care system; in 1995 and 1997, 52 percent.[67] Women also make use of medical leave more often than do men.[68] Although the public health care system was poorly funded during the 1990s and was not able to provide quality health care, nevertheless, a growing number of patients, female and male, used its services, indicating that the health of Poles had deteriorated during this period.[69]

AIDS

The Polish Central Statistical Office does not provide data regarding HIV/AIDS in Poland. Anecdotal evidence, however, suggests that the number of HIV-infected persons is increasing as travel abroad has become easier and many more foreigners are visiting Poland than in the past. In addition, prostitution and other forms of sex work are on the rise, and, as indicated above, sexual norms have become more liberal in recent years. Several of the new women's organizations, including PSF Women's Center—Feminist Foundation in Warsaw, have developed programs for prevention of HIV/AIDS targeting mainly prostitutes.[70]

Cancer

The second most common cause of death for women is breast and cervical cancer, and the third is brain tumors.[71]

Depression

Since 1990, observers also have noted a new wave of mental illnesses, particularly affecting women.[72] Women are twice as likely as men to be diagnosed with a mental disorder, especially depression and psychosis.[73] Although Polish men attempt or commit suicide more often than do women, the rate of suicide, especially for older women, is rising.[74] This can be related to the more difficult economic and social conditions of women as they age.

POLITICS AND LAW

Suffrage

Polish women obtained the right to vote and hold office in 1918.

Political Participation

Until the communist era, Polish women's political representation and public activity had been very low. Post 1918, women constituted only 2 percent of the elected deputies in the Sejm (lower house) and did not exceed that proportion between the two world wars. In the Senate (upper house), women's representation was slightly higher, rising to 5.2 percent by 1938.[75] A strong emphasis on women as mothers and guardians of the private sphere, while the public sphere was reserved for men, made it extremely difficult for women to run for political office and to be elected.[76]

Under the communist system, which actively recruited women into political positions, women's political representation increased considerably. By the mid-1980s, women constituted 23 percent of parliamentary members, 30 percent of officials at the provincial level, and 26 percent at the local (municipal) level. However, they did not exert much political power; they held low-level positions and were virtually absent from Central Party Committees and councils where most of the important decisions were made.[77] Also, women politicians had no independent associations, caucuses, or committees that could represent their interests and concerns as women.[78] Consequently, gender-specific agendas were absent from the political discourse, and only very limited working women's issues were addressed sporadically.

Beginning in the early 1980s, the Solidarity trade union movement mobilized many Poles to oppose communist party rule. Women participated in the movement in proportion to their representation in the labor force, or a little less than 50 percent.[79] Although they took part in demonstrations, strikes, and other activities, they did not assume leadership roles but rather were found within Solidarity organizations mostly in support positions. Only 7.8 percent of the delegates elected to the Solidarity Congress were women, only one woman was elected to Solidarity's National Executive Council, and when the Round-Table negotiations with the Communist government began in February 1989, not even one woman was a chief negotiator for any of the eleven subgroups.[80]

In the first open parliamentary election in 1989, women's representation decreased significantly. Although 200 women (out of a total of 2,500 candidates) ran in the election, they obtained only six of the 100 seats in the Senate and sixty-two of the 460 seats in the *Sejm*.[81] In the first local government elections in May 1990, women gained only 10.2 percent of the seats on local councils.[82] The 1991 parliamentary election brought even worse results for women: only 44 of the total 560 elected (in both houses), or 8 percent, were women. Women's parliamentary representation increased in 1993 to 13 percent and remained at this level until 2001.

Women also are not well represented in the different governmental ministries. However, those that are involved in the government now may have more political power than did past women members of parliament. They have more experience in politics and are more active than their predecessors.[83] The Women's Parliamentary Group, established in 1991, is a coalition of women Members of Parliament from different political parties working together to represent women's interests and protect women's rights. In 1998, it had forty-two Sejm deputies and seven senators out of a total of seventy-two female parliamentarians.[84] Although this group has been actively promoting a feminist agenda that includes the liberalization of the restrictive abortion law, sex education in schools, access to inexpensive contraceptives, and legislation that would liberalize the divorce law, the group has had limited influence, largely because it comprises less than 9 percent of all MPs.

In February 2001, a "Pre-Election Coalition of Women," consisting of about fifty women's organizations from all over Poland, was formed to elect to Parliament a larger number of women and to raise the awareness of politicians and the general public about issues of gender inequality. The coalition held a conference in May 2001 titled "Politics of Government for Women," which was attended by several hundred people, including representatives from over 100 women's organizations as well as leaders of the largest political parties. Each of the leaders was asked to discuss its party's program concerning gender equality. The coalition also has engaged a number of newspapers and other media in its campaign to get more women representatives into public office.[85] As a result of this campaign, female representation in the Polish parliament rose to 20.7 percent.[86]

Women's Rights

Articles 67 and 68 of the 1952 Polish Constitution guaranteed equal rights, irrespective of sex, for all citizens in public, political, economic, and social life. Article 71 affirmed the right to education for all citizens. Under the constitutional provision of "equal pay for equal work" women had the right to be compensated for their labor equally with men. In the early 1950s, gender discrimination was abolished in civil, family, and criminal law.[87] However, under the communist regime women were far from equal with men; although their participation in the labor force and public life was substantial, they remained burdened with family responsibilities, were paid less than men, and were underrepresented in top positions.

The current Polish Constitution, in Article 33 among others, also guarantees women equal rights with men in all spheres of life. In 1982, Poland ratified the United Nations Convention on the Elimination of All Forms of Discrimination against Women (CEDAW) and although in 1993 the Office of the Ombudsperson for Civil Rights (*Rzecznik Praw Obywatelskich*) found the legal provisions pertaining to women in Poland to be in compliance with the precepts of the U.N. convention, the ombudsperson's report also found widespread discrimination against women in the labor market and in public life.[88] Continuing traditions, customs, and stereotypes that feed discriminatory behaviors, as well as a lack of procedures for enforcement of CEDAW, are reasons most commonly cited for violations of women's rights.[89]

An example of how seemingly gender-neutral laws are used to discriminate against women in Poland comes from research that has found that offenses committed by girls were sexualized (i.e., linked to their sexual lives irrespective of the nature of the offense) and punished more severely by the law than offenses committed by boys.[90] The double standard is also used by judges in divorce cases. The model of marriage endorsed by the courts is traditional and patriarchal. Polish women, whether or not they are employed outside the home, are charged with all familial duties and are seen as responsible for building and maintaining family relationships, whereas men are expected only to be the providers and to abstain from certain behaviors such as physical abuse, alcoholism, and adultery.[91]

Those Poles who are committed to gender equality under the law place great hopes on Poland entering the European Union (EU). Before Poland becomes a member in 2004, it will need to comply with all laws and regulations of the EU concerning the abolition of discrimination against women and other disadvantaged groups. Recently, the European Commission increased the pressure on the Polish government to enforce gender equality laws, pointing to the country lagging behind the EU members' female participation in economic and political spheres.[92]

Feminist Movements

The development of a feminist movement in Poland has been slow. A long legacy of patriarchy reinforced by the threat of external forces and periods of foreign domination, in combination with a strong presence of the Catholic Church and customs that emphasized women's subordination to men, have made it extremely difficult for women activists to challenge gender inequality. Although a few feminist groups were active in Poland in the nineteenth century and during the period between the world wars, their influence was very limited.[93] Under communism, women could not establish independent organizations, and the regime has left a legacy of general distrust of feminism—it had discredited feminism as the pastime of bourgeois, disaffected Western women. Currently, the economic and political circumstances resulting from policies instituted by the Polish government have curtailed women's opportunities and pose serious obstacles to women's organizing.[94] Despite these barriers, however, a fledgling feminist movement has emerged in Poland.

The sweeping reforms of 1989, especially freedom to form associations, to demonstrate, and to publish and distribute information without fear of repression, gave impetus to feminist organizing. The threat to legal abortion posed by the new government in 1989 provided feminist groups with their first issue for mobilization. As soon as the law on organizations was liberalized, the Polish Feminist Association (a collection of activists who were active informally since 1980) was the first feminist group to legally register and to begin a campaign to preserve abortion rights; other organizations, similarly focused on the abortion issue, followed.[95]

By 1993, there were fifty-nine officially registered women's organizations in Poland and by 1995 the number rose to seventy.[96] In 2000, there were approximately 180 registered women's organizations.[97] The organizations are quite varied, including single issue and multi-issue groups, lobby groups, women's and gender studies programs, philanthropic organizations, self-help groups, nongovernmental organizations (NGOs), and federations that bring together several organizations. Not all are feminist (i.e., committed to gender equality). In recent years, a substantial number of conservative women's organizations has emerged, several of which are affiliated with the Catholic Church.

After the abortion fight was lost, some of the early feminist organizations, as well as new ones, began to focus on additional issues of concern to Polish women. Women's rights in the economic market and in politics; violence against women; sex education and access to contraceptives; sexual exploitation of women, including prostitution and trafficking in women; sexual harassment in the workplace; discrimination against women in the courts; and discrimination against lesbians—these are issues that have been addressed increasingly by Polish feminists during the 1990s.[98]

The feminist organizations have developed a variety of activities and actions to address the pressing issues they have identified. Some engage in political lobbying to change legislation and regulations affecting women, others provide counseling services to women ranging from information on reproduction and contraception to helping unemployed and abused women, and still others run workshops for retraining women for the economy or use the media to educate the public about violence against women.[99] A number of these organizations have formed links with feminist groups in other countries, which have sometimes helped them with funding needs and allowed for cross-national projects that have furthered international feminist networks and understanding.

Lesbian Rights

The emerging Polish feminist movement has only begun to address lesbian rights. The new Polish Constitution "protects motherhood and marriage as a union of a man and a woman," and homosexuality has been a taboo subject in Catholic Poland.[100] However, partly as a result of contacts with groups in other countries, several lesbian and gay organizations have been established in Poland. For example, *Emancypunx*, founded in Warsaw in 1996, is a small group of self-defined feminist-anarchist women that "aims to change the sexist mentality and homophobia of Polish society" and works with other organizations to improve conditions for lesbian and gay people.[101] Another organization, Polish Lesbian Archive, is even more explicit about its mission to support lesbians. It makes accessible lesbian archives and literature through its lesbian-feminist library, "creating a safe space in which women would be able to develop their social and cultural identity," and provides information on other feminist and lesbian organizations and initiatives.[102] Such groups, however, are considered marginal even among women activists in Poland.[103]

Military Service

Women in Poland are exempt from mandatory military service, but men are not. The number of women in the military is increasing: in 2000, 140 women graduated from military schools, which was four times as many as in 1999, and all military schools in Poland had admitted women by the year 2000.[104] However, women continue to be discriminated against in the military (e.g., not being allowed to serve in combat) and as the Central Headquarters of NATO[105] recently indicated, their overall numbers are still extremely small.[106]

RELIGION AND SPIRITUALITY

Women's Roles

The Catholic Church in Poland has greatly influenced the traditional division of labor in the family and the roles of women and men. As 95.5 percent of Poles are Catholic, women's roles in organized religion are restricted since women are barred from becoming priests.[107] The influence of the Catholic Church in everyday life and politics also has made the work of Polish feminists extremely difficult, particularly in areas of reproduction and sex education.

Polish Catholicism, although more church-oriented since the late 1980s, historically has been associated with Polish national identity. During 200 years of partitions and fifty years of communism, the church provided Poles the possibility of a civil society, a limited sphere of life outside the purview of the state. Both church and family were seen as areas of privacy that Poles could retreat to. Women, the upholders of family life, were the ones responsible also for preserving national values. The role of the "Polish Mother" (*Matka-Polka*) was socially recognized and supported by the church, thus encouraging women to subordinate their own personal development to family needs. The role of *Matka-Polka* "places woman on a pedestal while simultaneously chaining her to the family and the hearth. The Polish Mother is a figure of courage and great strength and at the same time an ideal of woman in which she is empty, with no meaning of her own."[108] This legacy accounts for Polish women's continuing insistence on prioritizing family responsibilities above all else.[109] Although there is tension between the increasing independence of Polish women and the patriarchal ideology of the Catholic Church, women's family role propagated by the church is still deeply rooted in Polish traditions and attitudes.

A study of Catholic women's attitudes in Poland and the United States concerning work and family issues found that on some of the issues Polish women were less traditional than their U.S. counterparts.[110] Although Polish women were more likely than U.S. women to view women's family roles as most important, they were more committed to work outside the home and more likely to accept divorce and abortion. It seems that in some respects, Polish women have turned away from religious orthodoxy, becoming more selective of religious beliefs.

Rituals and Religious Practices

Many women in Poland derive spiritual sustenance from religion. Women are more active church attendees than men and are more highly represented among the "faithful."[111] Women who live in rural areas are more religious than those residing in the cities, and they indicate that religion makes the hardships of rural life more bearable.[112] In recent years, some Polish women have turned to nontraditional ways of expressing their spirituality. New religious groups such as the Local Spiritual Assembly of the Bah'ais and Wicca are providing women with alternatives to Catholicism and other established faiths.

VIOLENCE

Currently, violence against women is the most important issue taken up by women's organizations in Poland. Until recently, the problem was officially unacknowledged,[113] however, due to extensive activities by feminist groups involving publications and media campaigns, there is much more awareness of the issue, especially about domestic violence, rape, and trafficking in women.[114] Some hotlines and shelters have recently come into existence as well.

Domestic Violence

Statistics regarding domestic violence are problematic in any country as they typically document the number of cases reported to the police, which leaves out all the unreported incidents. In Poland, the magnitude of the problem is even more difficult to assess as only the number of convictions is officially recorded. Nevertheless, even focusing only on the convictions, the data indicate a significant increase in domestic violence convictions from 1990 to 1995, from 8,999 to 12,459. Less than 3 percent of those convicted during this period were women. A 1993 survey conducted by the Center for the Study of Public Opinion found that 18 percent of Polish female married or divorced respondents were regularly or occasionally beaten by their husbands, and 41 percent reported personal knowledge of other women who are so abused.[115] Studies conducted in Poland on the extent to which alcoholism contributed to divorce indicate that "alcoholism" of the husband in virtually all cases was associated with physical and psychological abuse of wives and children.

There are reasons to believe that domestic violence is a widespread phenomenon in Poland. Although it is not endemic to the period since 1989, it is a problem exacerbated by the recent economic and political changes, which have resulted in high unemployment, a rising cost of living, and increasing challenges to male domination. A number of women's organizations focused on domestic violence have emerged in recent years, including the Association of Battered Wives, which has a support group for women and disseminates information about abuse of women through the newspaper *Gazeta Przymorska* in Bydgoszcz; and the *Promyk* Association against Violence in the Family in Krakow.[116] The Women's Parliamentary Group in 1997 introduced new legislation on evicting a person who is physically or emotionally abusive to family members, but the proposed legislation was not passed by Parliament. In 2002, the newly appointed Ombudswoman for Equal Status of Women and Men introduced similar legislation; it was voted down again.

Rape/Sexual Assault

The extent of rape of women also is difficult to assess, yet indications are that it is far from an isolated occurrence in Poland. A 1998 statistic provided by the *Promyk* Association Against Violence in the Family is that 1,894 rapes were reported that year.[117] Conviction data for 1990–1995 show that the number of rape convictions increased during this time and that men were convicted of rape in 99.7 percent of the cases.[118]

Trafficking in Women and Children

One of the contradictions brought about by the transition to democracy and market economy is associated with the opening up of Poland's borders. Many Poles enjoy the new freedom to travel abroad and to buy foreign goods. But open borders have also resulted in a significant increase in the traffic in women and children as sex workers. Due to high unemployment, especially of young women, many women and girls want to go to the West to find a job and earn money. Some respond to newspaper advertisements for young and attractive women to work as servers or au pairs, but when they arrive at their destinations they are forced to work as prostitutes. Some women know that they will work as prostitutes, but only later discover that they are expected to work fourteen-hour days, every day of the week. Often, their documents are taken away from them, making it difficult for them to leave.[119]

La Strada is an organization that, since 1995, has been working in Poland to stop the trafficking in women. It is part of an international network with chapters in the Netherlands, the Czech Republic, Ukraine, and Poland. La Strada's work in Poland focuses on three aspects: publicity, education and prevention, and providing help and support for victims. By making the problem visible in the media, the public has become more informed about trafficking in women and children. La Strada members also distribute leaflets at border checkpoints and give presentations in high schools, especially in small towns near the borders. They run anonymous hotlines for victims and provide shelter, legal and medical assistance, psychological counseling, and job training. The organization works with other NGOs that specialize in these areas. In 1996, La Strada organized the first international conference on trafficking in women in Central and Eastern Europe. The conference drew over 1,000 attendees to Warsaw, including members of the Polish Parliament.[120] Subsequently, the Women's Parliamentary Group began work on legislation aimed at addressing the issue.[121]

OUTLOOK FOR THE TWENTY-FIRST CENTURY

The current situation of women in Poland is complex. The transition to political democracy and market economy has created both problems and opportunities for women. Women have been hit harder than men by unemployment, reduced social services, and new barriers in politics. They have lost legal access to abortion and have become more frequent victims of battering and sex trafficking. At the same time, some women have become entrepreneurs, and others have established independent organizations that are addressing many of the problems created by the transition. The fledgling feminist movement in Poland offers hope as its growing number of organizations and groups increasingly challenge male-dominated institutions and seek to transform society into a more inclusive democracy.

NOTES

1. Central Statistical Office, *Concise Statistical Yearbook* (Warsaw: GUS, 1999), 104, 108, 128.
2. Central Statistical Office, 1999, *Concise*, 257.
3. Central Statistical Office, 1999, *Concise*, 251.

4. Central Statistical Office, 1999, *Concise*, 259.

5. Central Statistical Office, 1999, *Concise*, 264–65.

6. Maria Anna Knothe and Ewa Lisowska, *Women on the Labour Market* (Warsaw: Center for the Advancement of Women, 1999), 11.

7. Knothe and Lisowska, 1999, 11.

8. Shawn Meghan Burn, *Women across Cultures* (Mountain View, CA: Mayfield, 2000), 289.

9. Central Statistical Office, *Aktywnosc Ekonomiczna* (Warsaw: GUS, 1999), 21.

10. Barbara Lobodzinska, "Polish Women's Gender-segregated Education and Employment," *Women's Studies International Forum* 23 (2000): 49–71, esp. 57.

11. Lobodzinska, 2000, 57.

12. Lobodzinska, 2000, 64.

13. Knothe and Lisowska, 1999, 35.

14. Central Statistical Office, 1999, *Concise*, 142.

15. Fisher, Ian. 2002. "As Poland Endures Hard Times, Capitalism Comes Under Attack." *The New York Times* (June 12), A1, A8.

16. Central Statistical Office (Glowny Urzad Statystyczny), *Concise Statistical Yearbook* (MalyRocznik Statystyczny) (Warsaw: GUS, 2002), 49.

17. Knothe and Lisowska, 1999, 21.

18. An analysis of job advertisements in December 1998 in the Warsaw region found that in the most dynamic Polish job market, there were at least four unemployed persons for every job vacancy (Knothe and Lisowska, 1999, 24).

19. Most occupations have a feminine and a masculine form in the Polish language, and job advertisements use specific gender forms. Thus, male technician, male engineer, male driver, female hairdresser, female restaurant server, female receptionist, and so on are typically used. Often, employment ads addressed specifically to women call for attractive, young women to apply.

20. Knothe and Lisowska, 1999, 25–28.

21. Central Statistical Office, 1999, *Concise*, 143.

22. Jill M. Bystydzienski and Barbara Lobodzinska, "Poland: Gender Discrimination Unrecognized," *Humanity & Society* 22 (1998): 290–312, esp. 307.

23. Knothe and Lisowska, 1999, 13.

24. Central Statistical Office, 1999, *Concise*, 161.

25. Knothe and Lisowska, 1999, 14.

26. Knothe and Lisowska, 1999, 18.

27. Knothe and Lisowska, 1999, 17.

28. Aleksandra Wiktorow, "Bedzie nas coraz wiecej," *Rzeczpospolita Online* (February 24, 1994), www.rzeczpospolita.pi/PL-iso/dodatki/praca.html.

29. Bystydzienski and Lobodzinska, 1998, 304.

30. Agnieszka Sobotka, "Babski problem," *Zycie Warszawy* 252 (September 9, 1995): 9.

31. Iza Pur Rahnama, "Kobieta pracujaca," *Gazeta Wyborcza Online* (February 28, 2000), www.gazeta.pl/iso/praca/040.html.

32. Knothe and Lisowska, 1999, 17–18.

33. Childcare centers were often unavailable near parents' workplaces, and although there were usually enough places for children to meet the demand for childcare, the centers were of low quality.

34. Anna Kowalska, *Aktywnosc ekonomiczna Kobieti Ich Pozycja na Rynhu Pracy.* (Warsaw: Central Statistical Office, 1996).

35. Knothe and Lisowska, 1999, 17.

36. Jill M. Bystydzienski, "The Effects of the Economic and Political Transition," in *Women and Political Change*, ed. Sue Bridger (New York: St. Martin's Press, 1999), 91–109; and Anna M. Zacijek and Toni M. Calasanti, "The Impact of Socioeconomic Restructuring on Polish Women," in *Family, Women, and Employment in Central-Eastern Europe*, ed. Barbara Lobodzinska (Westport, CT: Greenwood, 1995), 179–91.

37. Matgorzara Fuszara, "Kobiety w sadach rodzinnych: Podwujne Standardy," in *Co To Znaczy, Byc Kobieta w Polsce*, ed. Anna Titkow and Henryk Domanski (Warsaw: Polish Academy of Sciences, 1995), 155–74.

38. Central Statistical Office, 1999, *Concise*, 294.

39. Bozena Klos, " 'Maciezynstwo i rodzina w systemie Swiadczen spolecznych panstwa,' " in *Kobiety o Kobietach*, ed. Jolanta Szymanczak (Warsaw: Women and Economics Global Working Group, 1995), 91–108.

40. Klos, 1995, 97–98.

41. Joanna Kowalczewska, "Kobieta wobiec zmiany rolw rodzinie," in Szymanczak, 1995, 25–36, esp. 25.

42. Joanna Regulska, "Women and Power in Poland," in *Women Transforming Politics*, ed. Jill M. Bystydzienski (Bloomington: Indiana University Press, 1992), 175–91, esp. 181.

43. Kowalczewska, 1995, 27.

44. Kowalczewska, 1995, 27.

45. Henryk Domanski, "Rownouprawnienie," in Titkow and Domanski, 1995, 65–87, esp. 86.

46. Danuta Duch-Krzystoszek, "Malzenstwo, seks, prokreacja," in Titkow and Domanski, 1995, 175–88; and Central Statistical Office, 1999, *Concise*, 613.

47. Victoria A. Velkoff, *Women in Poland* (Washington, DC: U.S. Department of Commerce, 1995), 2.

48. Central Statistical Office, Concise Statistical Yearbook (Warsaw: GUS, 2000), 405.

49. Kowalczewska, 1995, 31, 32.

50. Central Statistical Office, 1999, *Concise*, 613; and Velkoff, 1995, 2.

51. Kowalczewska, 1995, 34.

52. Duch-Krzystoszek, 1995, 180.

53. Luczak, 1995, 44.

54. The 1995 survey found that of those not using contraceptives, 55.9 percent practiced withdrawal, and the rest used some form of the rhythm method (Luczak, 1995, 44).

55. Bystydzienski, 1999, 97–101.

56. Luczak, 1995, 45.

57. Central Statistical Office, 1999, *Concise*, 282; and Lukzac, 1995, 39.

58. Burn, 2000, 289.

59. National Women's Information Center (OSKA), "Rzadowy raport," in *Kobiety i Ich Mezowie*, ed. Joanna Sikorska (Warsaw: IfiSPAN, 2001), 60.

60. Bystydzienski, 1999, 100.

61. Duch-Krzystoszek, 1995, 184.

62. Ewa Luczak, "Zdrowie Kobict," in Szymanczak, 1995, 37–46, esp. 44.

63. National Women's Information Center (OSKA), "Zeby dzieci nie mialy dzieci" (Children should not have children). 28 April 2003, www.oska.org.pl/wydarzania/krajo4–03.html, 1.

64. Bystydzienski, 1999, 97.

65. Chancellery of the Prime Minister of the Republic of Poland, *Effectiveness, Openness, Subsidiarity* (Warsaw: Government Plenipotentiary for the Systematic Reform of the State, 1999).

66. Luczak, 1995, 37.

67. Central Statistical Office, 1999, 282.

68. Luczak, 1995, 39.

69. Central Statistical Office, 1999, 282; and Luczak, 1995.

70. Center for the Advancement of Women, *Directory of Women's Organizations and Initiatives in Poland* (Warsaw: Author, 1998), 241.

71. Central Statistical Office, 1999, 282.

72. Jan Bejnarowicz, "Zmiany stanu zdrowia," *Nauki Spoleczne i Medycyna*, no. 1–2 (1994): 9–36; Luczak 1995; and Antonina Ostrowska, "Zdrowie is samopoczucie," in Sikorska, 1996.

73. Luczak, 1995, 42; Ostrowska, 1996, 50.

74. Central Statistical Office, 1999, 108.

75. Regulska, 1992, 177.

76. Barbara Post "Trudne wybory," in Szymanczak, 1995, 77–92.

77. Regulska, 1992, 180.

78. Renata Siemienska, "Women and Social Movements in Poland," *Women & Politics* 6, no. 4 (1986): 5–35.

79. Regulska, 1992, 185.

80. Regulska, 1992, 185–86.

81. Post, 1995, 80.

82. Regulska, 1992, 187.

83. Post, 1995, 81.

84. Center for the Advancement of Women, 1998, 277.

85. National Women's Information Center, "Przedwyborcza" (2001), www.oska.org.pl/Koalicja/onas.html.

86. National Women's Information Center (OSKA). 2003a, 1.

87. Bureau for Women's Affairs, *Sytuacja Prawna Kobiety* (Warsaw: Author, 1990).

88. Szymanczak, 1995, 111.

89. Post, 1995.

90. Fuszara, 1995.

91. Fuszara, 1995.

92. National Women's Information Center, Centrum Informacji Europejskiej 1999 "Komisja europejska," (April 2001), www.oska.org.pl/aska/rzad4.html.

93. Anna Reading, *Polish Women, Solidarity and Feminism* (London: Macmillan, 1992), 22; and Siemienska, 1986.

94. Jill M. Bystydzienski, "The Feminist Movement in Poland: Why So Slow?" *Women's Studies International Forum* 24, no. 5 (2001): 501–11.

95. Bishop, 1990, 20; and Bystydzienski, 2001.

96. Judy Root Aulette, "New Roads to Resistance," in *Democratization and Women's Grassroots Movements*, ed. Center for the Advancement of Women, *Directory of Women's Organizations and Initiatives in Poland* (Warsaw: Author, 1995).

97. Center for the Advancement of Women, *Directory of Women's Organizations and Initiatives in Poland* (Warsaw: Author, 2000).

98. Aulette, 1999; and Szymanczak, 1995, 111.

99. Aulette, 1999; and Bystydzienski, 2001.

100. Centrum Informacji Europejskiej, *Informator Unia Europejska—Kobiety* (Warsaw: Author, 1999), 36.

101. Center for the Advancement of Women, 2000, 41.

102. Center for the Advancement of Women, 2000, 145.

103. Centrum Informacji Europejskiej, 1999, 38.

104. National Women's Information Center 2000, "Rzadowy," 4.

105. Poland became a member of North Atlantic Treaty Organization (NATO) in 1999 and thus has been under pressure to conform to its standards and demands.

106. National Women's Information Center, "Co wolno Kobiecie," June 20, 2000, www.oska.org.pl/oska/rzad4.html, 3.

107. Central Statistical Office, 1999, 116.

108. Reading, 1992, 21.

109. Domanski, 1995.

110. Sandra L. Hanson and Kaja Gadowska, "Catholicism, Country, and the Construction of Gender," *Polish Sociological Review* 3 (1999): 353–76.

111. Central Statistical Office, 1999, 117.

112. Dorota Stankiewicz, "Waruki Zycia Kobiet," in Szymanczak, 1995, 65–76, esp. 75.

113. Bystydzienski, 1999, 102.

114. Aulette, 1999, 253–56.

115. Szymanczak, 1995, 115–16.

116. Center for the Advancement of Women, 1998.

117. Burn, 2000, 289.

118. Szymanczak, 1995, 115.

119. Aulette, 1999, 227.

120. Aulette, 1999, 226.

121. Center for the Advancement of Women, 1998, 279.

RESOURCE GUIDE

Suggested Reading

Aulette, Judy Root. "New Roads to Resistance: Polish Feminists in the Transition to Democracy." In *Democratization and Women's Grassroots Movements*, edited by Jill M. Bystydzienski and Joti Sekhon. Bloomington: Indiana University Press, (1999): 217–40. An overview of the different types of women's organizations in Poland, based on interviews with their members.

Bystydzienski, Jill M. "The Effects of the Economic and Political Transition on Women and Families in Poland." In *Women and Political Change: Perspectives from East—Central Europe*, edited by Sue Bridger, 91–109. New York: St. Martin's Press. Examines the consequences of the transition for women, including unemployment, the lack of substantial female political representation, erosion of social welfare, curtailment of reproductive rights, and lack of recognition of violence against women.

Bystydzienski, Jill M. "The Feminist Movement in Poland: Why So Slow?" *Women's Studies International Forum* 24, no. 5 (2001): 501–11. Focuses on historical, political, economic, and social conditions that pose obstacles to the formation of an effective feminist movement in Poland.

Bystydzienski, Jill M., and Barbara Lobodzinska. "Poland: Gender Discrimination Unrecognized." *Humanity & Society* 22 (1998): 290–312. Authors argue that current discrimination against women is a continuation of some patterns established under the communist system, whereas others originate much earlier. They also attempt to account for why these patterns are not recognized.

Central Statistical Office (*Glowny Urzad Statystyczny*). *Statistical Yearbook of Poland*. Warsaw: GUS, 2000. Major statistical resource on Poland, published every year and available in most university and some public libraries.

Gregory, Abigail, Mike Ingham, and Hilary Ingham. "Women's Employment in Transition: The Case of Poland." *Gender, Work and Organization* 5, no. 3 (1998): 133–47. Focus on the transitional economy and the decrease in women's employment.

Lobodzinska, Barbara. "Polish Women's Gender-Segregated Education and Employment." *Women's Studies International Forum* 23 (2000): 49–71. Explains why women in Poland continue to occupy lower positions and earn less pay than men.

Reading, Anna. *Polish Women, Solidarity and Feminism*. London: Macmillan, 1992. An insightful look at the early stage of the transition in Poland by an American feminist.

Zajicek, Anna M., and Toni M. Calasanti. "The Impact of Socioeconomic Restructuring on Polish Women." In *Family, Women, and Employment in Central–Eastern Europe*, edited by Barbara Lobodzinska, 179–91. Westport, CT: Greenwood Publishing Group. Focus on the social construction of gender under conditions of recent socioeconomic changes in Poland.

Web Sites

Centrum Praw Kobiet, the Women's Rights Center, http://free.ngo.pl/temida/spis.htm. Dedicated to promoting equal protection for women under Polish law.

Federation for Women and Family Planning (*Federacja na Rzecz Kobiety i Planowania Rodziny*), www.waw.pdi.net/~polfedwo/. Contains extensive information about abortion rights in Poland. Full text of their publications can be found here with many items available in both Polish and English.

Kobiety, www.kobiety.pl. A portal for women's information with articles on all topics of interest to women, from the more serious such as law, politics, and Catholicism to others such as fashion and fitness. The English version introduces the site and provides short summaries of articles.

National Women's Information Center (*Osrodek Informacji Srodowisk Kobiet*), www.oska.org.pl. Contains a wealth of information on many topics including politics, law, health, and culture. There is an English version of the site.

Onet, www.onet.pl/. Has a very detailed subject directory as well as search options for various parts of the Polish Internet.

Warsaw Voice, www.warsawvoice.com.pl/. An English language online news publication that deals with a variety of topics and frequently carries articles on women's issues.

Organizations

Association Women for Women (Stowarzyszenie Kobiety—Kobietom)
ul. 23 Lutego 4/6
61-741 Poznan, Poland
Phone/Fax: (0 61) 851 97 84

Information and educational center for women that provides legal and job employment
counseling, provides job training, and organizes promotional meetings and conferences. Part of a network of organizations with similar interests throughout Poland.

Center for the Advancement of Women (Centrum Promocji Kobiet)
ul. Lwowska 17/3
Warsaw 00-660, Poland
Phone: (48 22) 629 92 57
Fax: (48 22) 622 46 21
Email: cawp-cpk@ikp.atm.com.pl

A nonprofit, private foundation that provides information, education, and training to
women to help them in the transition. Produces a number of publications, including
a directory of women's organizations in Poland. Has chapters in several other cities.

PSF Women's Center—Feminist Foundation (PSF Centrum Kobiet—Fundacja Fem-
inistyczna)
ul. Mokotowska 55
Warsaw 00-542
Phone: (48 22) 629 4847
Fax: (48 22) 628 87 63
Email: psfwomen@it.com.pl

A foundation that promotes women's rights and gender equality through campaigns,
lobbying, and education. Focuses especially on eliminating violence against women.

Women's Defense Movement (Ruch Obrony Kobiet)
ul. Boltucia10/61
85-791 Bydgoszcz, Poland
Phone: (0 52) 43 44 36

A mass organization devoted to the support of women's equal status in all spheres of
life. Opposes anti-abortion legislation, promotes sex education and birth control,
and addresses issues of domestic violence through meetings and discussions, collection of data on discrimination against women, and dissemination of research on the
status of Polish women.

Women's Studies Center (Osrodek Naukowo-Badawczy Problematyki Kobiet)
University of Lodz
ul. Narutowicza 54/11
90-136 Lodz, Poland
Phone: (0 42) 31 97 60
Fax: (0 42) 31 95 82
Email: eoleksy@krysia.uni.lodz.pl

Promotes interdisciplinary research and the development of courses on women and gender, lectures for the general public, and professional and vocational training for women in Poland and abroad.

SELECTED BIBLIOGRAPHY

Aulette, Judy Root. "New Roads to Resistance: Polish Feminists in the Transition to Democracy." In *Democratization and Women's Grassroots Movements*, edited by Jill M. Bystydzienski and Joti Sekhon, 217–40. Bloomington: Indiana University Press, 1999.

Bishop, Brenda. "From Women's Rights to Feminist Politics: The Developing Struggle for Women's Liberation in Poland." *Monthly Review* (November 1990): 15–34.

Burn, Shawn Meghan. *Women across Cultures: A Global Perspective*. Mountain View, CA: Mayfield, 2000.

Bystydzienski, Jill M. "The Effects of the Economic and Political Transition on Women and Families in Poland." In *Women and Political Change: Perspectives from East–Central Europe*, edited by Sue Bridger, 91–109. New York: St. Martin's Press, 1999.

———. "The Feminist Movement in Poland: Why So Slow?" *Women's Studies International Forum* 24, no. 5 (2001): 501–11.

Bystydzienski, Jill M., and Barbara Lobodzinska. "Poland: Gender Discrimination Unrecognized." *Humanity & Society* 22 (1998): 290–312.

Center for the Advancement of Women. *Directory of Women's Organizations and Initiatives in Poland*. Warsaw: Author, 1995.

———. *Directory of Women's Organizations and Initiatives in Poland*. Warsaw: Author, 1998.

———. *Directory of Women's Organizations and Initiatives in Poland*. Warsaw: Author, 2000.

Central Statistical Office (*Glowny Urzad Statystyczny*). *Aktywnosc Ekonomiczna Ludnosci Polski w 1998 Roku (Economic Activity of the Population of Poland in 1998)*. Warsaw: GUS, 1999.

———. *Concise Statistical Yearbook (Maly Rocznik Statystyczny)*. Warsaw: GUS, 1999.

———. *Concise Statistical Yearbook (Maly Rocznik Statystyczny)*. Warsaw: GUS, 2000.

Centrum Informacji Europejskiej (Center for European Information). *Informator Unia Europejska—Kobiety (European Union Information—Women*. Warsaw: Author, 1999.

Chancellery of the Prime Minister of the Republic of Poland. *Effectiveness, Openness, Subsidiarity: A New Poland for New Challenges*. Warsaw: Government Plenipotentiary for the Systemic Reform of the State, 1999.

Domanski, Henryk. "Rownouprawnienie: Streotyp tradycyjnego podzialu rol" (Equality: Stereotype of the traditional division of roles). In *Co To Znaczy Byc Kobieta w Polsce (What It Means to Be a Woman in Poland)*, edited by Anna Titkow and Henryk Domanski, 65–87. Warsaw: Polish Academy of Sciences, 1995.

Duch-Krzystoszek, Danuta. "Malzenstwo, seks, prokreacja" (Marriage, sex, procreation). In *Co To Znaczy Byc Kobieta w Polsce (What It Means to Be a Woman in Poland)*, edited by Anna Titkow and Henryk Domanski, 175–88. Warsaw: Polish Academy of Sciences, 1995.

Fisher, Ian. "As Poland Endures Hard Times, Capitalism Comes Under Attack." *The New York Times* (June 12, 2002), A1, A8.

Fuszara, Matgorzata. "Kobiety w sadach rodzinnych: Podwujne standardy" ("Women in Family Courts: Double Standard"). In *Co To Znaczy Byc Kobieta w Polsce (What It Means to Be a Woman in Poland)*, edited by Anna Titkow and Henryk Domanski, 155–74. Warsaw: Polish Academy of Sciences, 1995.

Hanson, Sandra L., and Kaja Gadowska. "Catholicism, Country, and the Construction of Gender: Catholic Women in Poland and the U.S." *Polish Sociological Review* 3 (1999): 353–76.

Klos, Bozena. " 'Maciezynstwo i rodzina' w systemie swiadczen spolecznych panstwa" (" 'Marriage and Family' in the National Social Welfare System"). In *Kobiety o Kobietach (Women About Women)*, edited by Jolanta Szymanczak, 91–108. Warsaw: Women and Economics Global Working Group, 1995.

Knothe Maria Anna, and Ewa Lisowska. *Women on the Labour Market: Negative Changes and Entrepreneurship's Opportunities as the Consequences of Transition.* Warsaw: Center for the Advancement of Women, 1999.

Kowalczewska, Joanna. "Kobieta wobiec zmiany rol w rodzinie" ("Woman and Changing Roles in the Family"). In *Kobiety o Kobietach (Women About Women)*, edited by Jolanta Szymanczak, 25–36. Warsaw: Women and Economics Global Working Group, 1995.

Kowalska, Anna. *Aktywnosc ekonomiczna kobiet i ich pozycja na rynku pracy (The Economic Activity of Women and Their Position in the Labor Market).* Warsaw: Central Statistical Office, 1996.

Lobodzinska, Barbara. "Polish Women's Gender-Segregated Education and Employment." *Women's Studies International Forum* 23 (2000): 49–71.

Luczak, Ewa. "Zdrowie kobiet" ("Women's Health"). In *Kobiety o Kobietach (Women About Women)*, edited by Jolanta Szymanczak, 37–46. Warsaw: Women and Economics Global Working Group, 1995.

Ostrowska, Antonina. "Zdrowie is samopoczucie a spoleczna sytuacja kobiet" ("Health and Self-feeling and Social Situation of Women"). In *Kobiety i Ich Mezowie (Women and Their Husbands)*, edited by Joanna Sikorska, 63–85. Warsaw: IFiS PAN, 1996.

Post, Barbara. "Trudne wybory: Kobiety w zyciu publicznym" ("Difficult Elections: Women in Public Life"). In *Kobiety o Kobietach (Women About Women)*, edited by Jolanta Szymanczak, 77–92. Warsaw: Women and Economics Global Working Group, 1995.

Rahnama, Iza Pur. "Kobieta pracujaca" ("Working Woman"). *Gazeta Wyborcza Online.* February 28, 2000. www.gazeta.pl/iso/praca/040.html.

Reading, Anna. *Polish Women, Solidarity and Feminism.* London: Macmillan, 1992.

Regulska, Joanna. "Women and Power in Poland: Hopes or Reality?" In *Women Transforming Politics: Worldwide Strategies for Empowerment*, edited by Jill M. Bystydzienski, 175–91. Bloomington: Indiana University Press, 1992.

Siemienska, Renata. "Women and Social Movements in Poland." *Women & Politics* 6, no. 4 (1986): 5–35.

Sobotka, Agnieszka. "Babski problem: Seksims w pracy wciaz tabu" ("Women's Problem: Sexism at Work Still a Taboo Subject"). *Zycie Warszawy* 252 (September 9, 1995): 9.

Stankiewicz, Dorota. "Warunki zycia kobiet na wsi" ("Conditions of Life of Rural Women"). In *Kobiety o Kobietach (Women about Women)*, edited by Jolanta Szymanczak, 65–76. Warsaw: Women and Economics Global Working Group, 1995.

Sytuacja Kobiet w Polsce (The Situation of Women in Poland). Warsaw: Polish Committee of NGOs for Beijing, 1995.

Szymanczak, Jolanta. "O dyscryminacji i przemocy wobiec kobiet" ("About Discrimination and Violence against Women"). In *Kobiety o Kobietach (Women about Women)*, edited by Jolanta Szymanczak, 109–18. Warsaw: Women and Economics Global Working Group, 1995.

Velkoff, Victoria A. *Women in Poland*. Washington, DC: U.S. Department of Commerce, 1995.

Wiktorow, Aleksandra. "Bedzie nas coraz wiecej" ("There Will Be Many More of Us"). *Rzeczpospolita Online*, February 24, 1999. www.rzeczpospolita.pl/PL-iso/dodatki/praca.html.

Zajicek, Anna M., and Toni M. Calasanti. "The Impact of Socioeconomic Restructuring on Polish Women." In *Family, Women, and Employment in Central–Eastern Europe*, edited by Barbara Lobodzinska, 179–91. Westport, CT: Greenwood Publishing Group, 1995.

Selected Polish Bibliography

Graff, Agnieszka. *Swiat Bez Kobiet: Plec w Polskim Zyciu Publicznym* (World Without Women: Gender in Polish Public Life). Warsaw: Fundacja Friedrich Albert, 2001.

Kowalska, Anna. *Aktywnosc Ekonomiczna Kobiet i Ich Pozycje na Rynku Pracy* (The Economic Activity of Women and Their Position in the Labor Market). Warsaw: Central Statistical Office, 1996.

Siemenska, Renata. *Nie Moga, Nie Chca, Czy Nie Potrafia: O Postawach i Uczestnictwie Politicznym Kobiet w Polsce* (They Can't, They Don't Want To, or They Don't Know How: About Polish Women's Status and Political Participation). Warsaw: Scholar, 2000.

Sikorska, Joanna, ed. *Kobiety i Ich Mezowie* (Women and Their Husbands). Warsaw: IfiS PAN, 1996.

Szymanczak, Jolanta, ed. *Kobiety of Kobietach* (Women About Women). Warsaw: Women and Economics Global Working Group, 1995.

Titkow, Anna, and Henryk Domanski, eds. *Co To Znacy Byc Kobieta w Polsce* (What It Means to be a Woman in Poland). Warsaw: Polish Academy of Sciences, 1995.

Walczak, Renata. *Obraz Siebie u Kobietach Dlugotrwale Bezrobotczych* (Self-perceptions of Long Term Unemployed Women). Lublin: Towarzystwo Naukowe, 2000.

Zarnowska, Anna, and Andrzej Szwarca. *Rowne Prawa i Nierowne Szanse: Kobiety w Polsce Miedzywojennej* (Equal Rights But Unequal Chances: Women in Poland Between the Wars). Warsaw: DIG, 2000.

29

PORTUGAL

Kathryn Bishop-Sanchez

PROFILE OF PORTUGAL

Located at the southwestern edge of Europe, bordered to the north and east by Spain and to the west and south by the Atlantic, Portugal has traditionally turned its back on the hinterland and the mountains and privileged the sea. This geographic position has been one of the determining factors in shaping Portugal's past and present. It is along the fertile areas of the coastline that Portugal's major cities are situated in contrast to the less populated, inhospitable frontier zone with Spain. Portuguese territory today includes mainland Portugal and the Atlantic archipelagoes of Madeira and the Azores, yet during the height of the Age of Discoveries it boasted the mightiest seaborne empire that encompassed overseas lands as distant as South America, Africa, India, Indonesia, and Asia. As such, it is not surprising that a strong sense of history marks the Portuguese people and contributes to the intense patriotism of the nation.

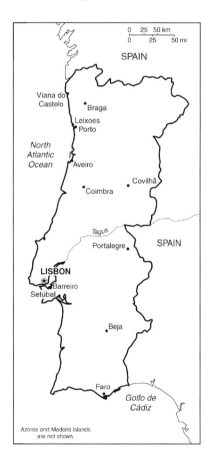

Following the Portuguese Revolution of 1974 that brought an end to fifty years of fascist reign, Portugal made the transition to democracy and became a member of the European Community (EU) in 1986. In the wake of this accession, the country faced many challenges and changes. On the economic front, farming became rapidly more modernized and nowadays continues to yield competitive products such as wine, fruit, vegetables, olive oil, and cheese. In the industrial sector, the country's traditional structure of manufacturing and industry that relied predominantly on textile, ceramics, footwear, cork, and naval repairs gave way to the increasing role of new sectors such as automotive parts, electronics, and pharmaceuticals. In line with the growth characteristic of developed countries, Portuguese economy has privileged the service sector in recent years and this dynamic sector of commerce, tourism, communications, and financial services provides more than half the nation's jobs. At the last census in 1997, the total population was reportedly 10,335 million, of which women represented 52 percent. Life expectancy for women reached 78.7 years, seven years more than that recorded for men. Portugal is among the countries with the lowest fertility rates in the world; nonetheless, having steadily increased since the 1980s to an average of 1.45 children per woman by the end of the twentieth century, in the future it is expected to assure the substitution of generations.[1]

OVERVIEW OF WOMEN'S ISSUES

In the twentieth century, the situation of women in Portugal was deeply marked by the fascist Salazar-Caetano regime, the repressive system of the New State (*Estado Novo*, 1933–1974), whereby women were primarily confined to their role as housewives, explicitly excluded from legal citizenship on account of their "natural sexual difference and for the good of the family."[2] Similar to the position of women in marriage in nineteenth-century bourgeois society, under Salazar women were assigned the role of domestic angels, relegated on a social and political front to a position of inferiority under the aegis of an archetypal patriarchal figure, a fascist dictator embodying the authoritarianism of the nation.[3] The New State banned several liberal measures (e.g., educational rights of women, the right to divorce, and the use of contraception) that first-wave feminism had successfully obtained before the dictatorship, thus turning back the legal clock of the Portuguese women's emancipatory movement.[4] Following the Revolution, the 1976 Socialist Constitution stimulated women's equal citizenship, legalizing divorce and contraception. Women became politically visible as they participated in public demonstrations and organized various lobbies within the overarching movement of second-wave feminism that hit Portugal in the early 1970s.

EDUCATION

Opportunities

In Portugal women's access to formal education has a relatively short history of just over 100 years. It was at the beginning of the twentieth century that the first schools for girls were opened at a time when schooling became compulsory for children of both sexes from the ages of seven to eleven. In the early 1920s the education of children was further modified as coed schooling was authorized throughout Portugal. During the New

State, women's (and men's) education suffered greatly as over 100 grade schools were closed and separate sex education was reinstated. Salazar insisted on the role of women as educators in the home, yet by the same token provided no educational rights for women.

Since the 1980s, there has been a constant increase of women obtaining university degrees and, in contrast to the 1960s when women were not the majority even in areas more traditionally associated with women (such as letters and arts), they now form the majority of university students in all areas other than architecture, engineering, forestry, and fishing. In line with this tendency, it is not incidental that in 1995 it was reported that more than 60 percent of Portuguese college graduates under the age of thirty were women. This clearly shows that within this renewed social context there is no longer the traditional investment that privileged men's education over that of women.

Literacy

Salazar viewed women's literacy as a threat to the nation. Illiteracy among women was widespread, as is still visible in the older generations today whereby the illiteracy rate increases with each age group. According to the 1991 census, women represented 60 percent of the total illiterate population and close to half of the women over the age of 65 did not know how to read or write. In 1995, it was reported that there are still more women than men with no education whatsoever, yet in secondary and higher education the proportion of women to men favors women.

EMPLOYMENT AND THE ECONOMY

The growing acceptance of women in the professional sphere stemmed from the economic need for women to enter the work force during the years of the colonial war (1961–1974) and the massive male emigration to other parts of Europe that ensued. Following April 1974, women fought to hold onto their jobs, and consequently the feminization of the labor force has continued to grow over the past few decades. In 1997, 42 percent of all women were employed, constituting a significant part of Portugal's work force. It is estimated that increasing the number of women in employment to 60 percent will be

Portuguese women with tomato harvest. Photo © Peter Turnley/CORBIS.

possible by 2010. These statistics include a high percentage of mothers who work for lack of social and family support infrastructure.[5] As is to be expected, per age group there is still a higher percentage of men employed than women.

Job/Career Opportunities

Most women are employed in agriculture (15.5 percent), followed by other activities and services (11.7 percent), teaching (11.2 percent), and textiles and footwear (11 percent). When considering the proportion of women to men per activity, women represent the vast majority of employees in the areas of teaching, health, and social services. Men and women have similar employment contracts with the great majority of their jobs secured with a permanent contract. Yet women still remain significantly absent from positions of management and responsibility, for these are traditionally perceived as male. Likewise, they are barely visible in the armed forces and the sector of law enforcement.

Over the past years, women have constantly registered a higher rate of unemployment in relation to men. Yet, when viewed in terms of age groups, after age fifty there are more men unemployed than women. Recently on the job market, there has been a significant decrease in women employed between the ages of fifteen and twenty-four: this is mostly due to a greater number of women entering the university for higher education. As women grow older, statistics show that they work fewer hours per week, the general pattern being a shift from full-time to part-time work. For example, in 1995 close to 94 percent of all women employed under the age of twenty-five worked full-time in comparison to those over sixty-five, of which only 62 percent worked full-time. Household obligations, including caring for children and other dependents, are reported as representing the main cause for Portuguese women working fewer than thirty hours a week, whereas for men the main causes for part-time employment were illnesses and disabilities.

In the future, as a higher proportion of qualified women is employed, it is hoped that the job market will be modified accordingly in order to achieve equality and equal opportunities for women. Although Portugal is barely starting to assimilate new job ethics including job sharing, flexible hours, and temporary jobs, these innovations are destined to have an impact on women and the role they will play in the job market.

Pay

Women's salaries per sector remain generally lower than those of men, and the gap between men's and women's wages in the private sector is worsening. Women generally occupy the most unqualified, intense labor and the worst-paid jobs, and there is especially a high concentration of women in jobs that present no possibility for career advancement.

Working Conditions

Sexual Harassment

There has been a greater awareness of issues concerning sexual harassment following the 1998 revision of the Portuguese Penal Code that made violence against women a public offense and criminalized it in the workplace. However, the crime of sexual harassment in Portugal is viewed as an "attack on modesty," and it is not rare for judges to maintain a biased attitude toward women.[6] In this area there is a persistence of stereotypes fueled mainly through the media that awareness campaigns and seminars aim to address as they concomitantly inform women of their legal rights. In practice, though sexual offenses have become a public issue, there remains a lot of progress still to be made before Portuguese women will take full advantage of such measures in a predominantly patriarchal society.

Support for Mothers/Caretakers

Maternal Leave

Maternity leave consists of four months of paid salary, and there are presently negotiations for a six-month paid maternity leave. The same law also provides fathers with five days of paid leave during the first month of the child's life and fifteen days of paid leave to be taken after the wife's maternity leave. In 1999, the law on maternity protection was amended to provide mothers the possibility of two hours of breastfeeding breaks daily, and it increased the penalties for employers who violated the maternity protective measures. Pregnant women are also permitted to attend doctor's appointments during work hours without the loss of any benefits.[7]

Daycare

In general, in line with Portuguese family traditions, women spend a greater proportion of time per week looking after children. Women are entitled to thirty days of sick leave to attend to childcare.[8] Grandparents continue to play a key role in looking after grandchildren and enabling women to return to work following their leave.[9]

Inheritance and Property Rights

In contrast to women's feeling that children are not an impediment to their careers, in certain areas of Portugal (the northern province of Minho, for example) the feminine task of taking care of the elderly is still a family matter, intimately linked to the pattern of female inheritance of houses and land.

FAMILY AND SEXUALITY

Gender Roles

In a predominantly Roman Catholic society that inherited national sexual ideologies from fifty years of fascist rule, it is not surprising that gender remains a sensitive issue at the heart of the debate concerning family structures and sexuality. Even towards the end of Salazar's dictatorship, the new 1967 Civil Code stipulated that the husband was the "head of the family and as such is to decide and direct all matters concerning marital life."[10] Women were essentially dependent on their husbands or fathers, deprived of economic independence and individual authority until the depletion of the male work force due to the war overseas and massive emigration.

Over the last few decades, with an increasing number of women seeking higher education and employment outside the home, the traditional gender divide of women in the home and men in the public sphere has been challenged. A recent survey shows that the general opinion is that women working outside the home make positive contributions to both self and family; on the other hand, the same majority considers the mother most capable of looking after the family and household.[11] Along these lines, it is interesting to note that the constitutional amendments adopted in 1997 recognized the right for women to reconcile professional and family life, promoting their active and direct participation in public affairs as a condition of the democratic system. Among the younger generations, stereotypical gendered roles within the family are much less pronounced than among couples over the age of forty.[12]

Marriage

The average age for women to marry is twenty-three; the equivalent for men is twenty-five. In 1997, it was estimated that 50 percent of Portuguese women were married despite the fact that over the past decade the divorce rate has doubled and on average one in every five marriages ends in divorce. As a direct consequence, there has been an increase in single-parent families, the majority composed of single mothers with children. In 1995 joint custody was established in Portugal, yet traditionally the children stay with the mother. It is not incidental, then, that men are reported to recuperate from divorce better than women and start new relationships. As such, there has been a feminization of poverty that accompanies these trends.[13]

Reproduction

The family structure has also been impacted by the increase of women pursuing higher education. Women are choosing to postpone having children until an average age of twenty-six, and this is proportional to the level of education of the woman.

Sex Education

Since the late 1970s and early 1980s, the Comissão da Condição Feminina has organized a series of informative and educational projects on family planning, but much more remains to be done.

Contraception and Abortion

Contraception was legalized soon after the 1974 revolution, and nowadays the pill is overall the preferred method of contraception, followed by the use of condoms and then the IUD. Condoms are preferred among the younger generation: over the age of thirty-five, more women choose the IUD. Women traditionally become sexually active at a later age than men, respectively at ages twenty and seventeen. A deeply marked divide persists whereby women are sexually submissive to men at all socioeconomic levels and young women continue to give in to the demands of boyfriends.[14]

Abortion is an ongoing issue among partisans for women's rights. A restrictive abortion act was passed in 1984 for cases of rape, fetal abnormality, or when the life of the mother is in danger. Because of the impact of illegal abortions on women's health and well-being, restrictive abortion laws were once again an issue brought up by the Committee on the Elimination of Discrimination against Women (CEDAW) in January 2002. It is estimated that there are 20,000 legal and illegal abortions per year, hence the urgent need for improved family planning services and a greater national dialogue on women's right to reproductive health.[15]

Teen Pregnancy

There is a high number of adolescent pregnancies that in 1994 were reported at 8,557 for women under the age of twenty, which corresponds to 7.8 percent of the total births for that year and situates Portugal far above the averages of the European Union.

HEALTH

Health Care Access

After April 1974, health care improved dramatically for both men and women, with improved facilities, technology, and medical training.[16] A National Health Service was included in the 1976 constitution that in 1979 implemented the creation of a network of health centers in which curative and preventive services were united. Maternal and infant mortality was considerably reduced, and free health care for pregnant women and infants became accessible to everyone.[17] The great majority of births takes place in hospitals, where there is a conscious ongoing effort to better accommodate the needs of mothers and their newborn children. Legalized contraception has had obvious repercussions in the lives of women in Portugal, permitting a greater distinction between sexual activity and reproduction.

Diseases and Disorders

Drug addiction among women is less frequent than among men but is still considered of great seriousness especially because of the repercussions on the children born from these mothers and from ones who suffer from mental and physical illnesses. A national organization was established in 1994 to assist women in effectively recuperating from drug abuse.[18]

The main causes of death in women are cardiovascular diseases (43 percent) and cancer.[19] Most importantly, the past decade has witnessed a significant new awareness of issues pertaining to women's health. This was partly fostered by the conferences organized by the United Nations in Cairo and Beijing, and it has become visible at a national level by specific governmental measures such as the project "Health Inequalities" (*Desigualdades em Saúde*) that since 2001 focuses on health issues of female ethnic minorities, prostitutes, the elderly, and the disabled.[20] The Ministry of Health recognizes the importance of three different subgroups of health issues pertaining to women: problems that are *prevalent* in women (such as eating disorders, osteoporosis, breast cancer, sexual abuse, and domestic violence), problems *specific* to women (reproduction and menopause), and problems that affect women *differently* than men (AIDS, STD, and heart diseases). It is in these three areas that Portugal hopes to make progress toward improving well-being and health for women throughout Portugal.

AIDS

AIDS is also the cause of modified relationships between the sexes. Over a period of fourteen years (1983–1997), 4,300 cases of AIDS were reported in Portugal, of which 15 percent were women. As with other European countries, successfully preventing the epidemic is a national priority and further justifies the need for a more widespread sex education that reinforces the importance of protected sex especially among teenage couples. As of 2002, the government has established nine mobile health units to reach out to the poorer rural communities and provide free reproductive health education.[21]

Cancer

One of the primary causes of death for women is cancer, predominantly breast, colorectal, and lung (26 percent), though since 1996 there has been a decrease in cancer-related deaths among women under the age of sixty-five.[22]

POLITICS AND LAW

Suffrage

It is well known that the first woman to vote from the twelve member countries that would later form the European Union by the end of the 1980s was Portuguese: Carolina Beatriz Angelo, a literate widow and mother and thus a "head of family," took the Portuguese juridical law literally and registered to vote in 1911. A year later, the Portuguese election law was made more specific to clearly exclude women: women would have to wait until 1976 to obtain that right. During the New State period, women were classified as subcitizens, deprived of any legal voice; juridical equality was out of the question. Virginia Ferreira sums up the era as follows: "The Estado Novo restricted or annulled previously recognized rights. In terms of rights and development, the Estado Novo was a glacial era of sorts, during which the few social conquests previously achieved were lost."[23] It is not surprising that women were an active part of the opposition to the regime, fighting for rights as citizens. After the revolution, legal changes were obtained without any opposition; it was clearly time for Portugal to move toward legal equality.

Political Participation

Since the 1980s women's involvement in politics has slightly increased, yet they remain but a very small percentage of political representatives. This is especially true in the case of positions to which one is elected, and once women are elected to office they are very rarely reelected, thus serving generally only one term. There are several factors that contribute to this unbalance: cultural preconceived ideas and traditions, gendered stereotypes, lack of motivation on behalf of the women, lack of political education, fear of not having enough credibility, and greater family obligations, to name but a few.[24] Since the mid-1980s, quotas stipulating the number of female deputies to be sent to the National Assembly and the European Parliament were established but as the 1994 elections clearly show, women represent an extremely small percentage of the elected candidates.[25] In the newly formed social-democratic government (March 2002), two of the seventeen ministers are women: Manuela Ferreira Leite as minister of finance and Celeste Cardona as minister of justice. To date, there has been one female prime minister, Maria de Lourdes Pinta Silgo, elected in 1978.

Women's Rights

Feminist Movements

In this postrevolutionary climate, several women's movements became more visible, notably the women's democratic movement (Movimento Democrático de Mulheres/MDM) and the autonomous movement for the liberation of women (Movimento de Libertação das Mulheres/MLM). The MDM was affiliated with the Portuguese Communist Party and was much larger than the MLM; it had existed since 1960 and its main focus was the fight against structural class inequalities. The MLM, which denounced the MDM's agenda, fought for sexual freedom, abortion rights, and the empowerment of women in the family, but collapsed in 1975 shortly after what is known as the "burning of the bras demonstration," a thwarted attempt to publicly celebrate the international year of the woman and women's right to sexual equality.[26] The limited scope of action of women's movements in Portugal, mainly due to a lack of funds and autonomy, speaks for itself. Abortion is the only "women's issue" that has caused any real debate at a national level; needless to say, there has not been a full-scale feminist movement in Portugal.[27]

Lesbian Rights

As of March 2001, couples who have lived together for over two years are legally recognized by the government regardless of sex or sexual orientation, and many of the heterosexual privileges of married couples are extended to these de facto relationships. This excludes the right of adoption and, in the case of lesbian couples, the right to artificial insemination. The INE (Instituto Nacional de Estatística) census does not account for sexual orientation, but it is estimated that 5 percent of the population is homosexual.[28] In July 2002 these issues were brought to the forefront during the "Pride Days" that were organized in Lisbon, where diverse topics such as improved sex education, discrimination in the workplace, and the omission of homosexuality from school manuals were also discussed.

RELIGION AND SPIRITUALITY

Portugal is predominantly a Roman Catholic country, and according to a recent survey, close to 90 percent of the population defined themselves as Catholic though a much smaller percentage are active churchgoers.[29] Traditionally women play a crucial role in the religious sphere in Portugal: women are the most fervent practitioners, especially the older and poorer female population of the suburbs and rural areas.

The younger generations on the whole have a different perspective toward religion; they are less fervent and more skeptical about miracles and certain popular beliefs such as Fátima. With the economic and social demands that these generations face, they often do not invest time in religious traditions other than in contexts that would otherwise offend close (and/or elderly) relatives: a family baptism, first communion, confirmation, wedding, or funeral. They are also more tolerant toward women's issues, different sexual orientations, and abortion.

Women's Roles

Official involvement in church ordinances is monopolized by men, although a survey conducted in 1998 that asked the question "Would you be in favor or against the next Pope authorizing women to receive priestly ordinances?" received an overwhelming positive response.[30]

Rituals and Religious Practices

It is only in certain rituals such as death-related practices in rural areas that women are bestowed with unofficial religious authority that in some respects parallels the authority of priests. In these contexts, the women who accompany the elderly and the sick as they approach death help prepare them spiritually by prayers and assist them in cleansing their souls through repentance. Likewise, it is mostly women who wash and dress the corpse.[31]

In both the private and public sphere, there is a clearly marked feminization of religious practices; and though these are concepts that cannot be qualified numerically, throughout Portugal women interlace religious themes and their domestic duties such as care for children, care of the elderly, giving birth, and contraception. The overarching cult of the Virgin Mary as the protector of female purity, fertility, and childbirth is directly evoked in connection to these "female" issues. As such, pilgrimages to the sanctuary at Fátima in the center of Portugal are a vital part of religious women's lives.[32] This is not unique to Portugal, yet here the lines of women walking on their knees visibly convey the women's roles as mediators with Mary on behalf of other family members or their responsibility to fulfill vows for themselves, both generally related to bodily health. It is also through these rituals that women demonstrate a form of religious autonomy outside the jurisdiction of the priest and the confessional booth.[33]

VIOLENCE

Domestic Violence

Over the past decade and predominantly since the beginning of the new millennium, domestic violence has acquired more visibility, becoming the focus of government agencies and nongovernment organizations. Progressively, domestic violence has been accepted and recognized as a public crime and is no longer considered a private family problem but regarded as a violation of human rights. As such, better informed professionals have been trained to develop a greater sensitivity to this problem in order to aptly identify, orient, and support the victim. Information manuals have been provided as a source of guidance and reference for professionals, and informative pamphlets are currently distributed in health centers for the information of the general public. In Portugal, approximately one out of every three women suffers from domestic violence, a rate that is significantly higher than the European Union average of one in five. In the year 2000 alone, 11,765 complaints of domestic violence were registered on a national level.[34] The by-products of domestic violence are also of great concern, given that the intergenerational impact on children who witness the crime or who are direct victims are most likely to use aggression in their own adult lives. It appears evident that domestic violence is directly related to gender issues whereby the woman is dependent on the man who abusively exercises his power over his wife.

Rape/Sexual Assault

Rape and sexual assault are penalized by law. However, as has been noted, the procedure that a woman has to go through is so complicated that it does not facilitate the victim's support, and the average delay between the crime and the hearing is twenty months.[35] Although it is hard to determine whether there are more rapes than before, what is certain is that nowadays more women are pressing charges. In 1994, 196 men were taken to court accused of rape and 124 accused of sexual assault.

Trafficking in Women and Children

Portuguese law penalizes neither the prostitute nor the client but only the pimp, with a sentence ranging from six months to five years; or, if violence is proven to have been used, from one to eight years. Trafficking in women and children is generally known to be associated with drug trafficking and abuse, and in Portugal that is certainly true. Since 1997 prostitution has increased mainly due to drug dependency and economic difficulties, and new forms such as the prostitution of children have also been reported. The AIDS threat and an increased sensitivity to gender inequality have intermittently brought prostitution to the forefront of political debates. This was the case, for example, concerning the reopening and legalization of brothels banned since 1991. Yet to this day no major improvement has been implemented nor measure adopted to eliminate prostitution, stemming in part from the widespread misconception that prostitution can be considered a profession like any other. Of particular concern is the trafficking of women and teenagers between Portugal and Spain. It is known that women between the ages of seventeen and twenty-five are frequently forced from the northern and central areas of Portugal across the border to Spain to provide sexual services.[36] Once again, gender inequality is at the root of the problem within these relationships of explicit sexual subordination and domination.

OUTLOOK FOR THE TWENTY-FIRST CENTURY

The Portuguese government has introduced a series of initiatives to promote aspects of equal opportunities and to end sex-based discrimination, yet there is still much to be done. If the areas of women's health and education have reached commendably high standards, the persistence of gender-based stereotypes, restrictive abortion laws, violence against women, prostitution, disproportionate female illiteracy, and low participation of women in political offices and the evidence of women's occupational segregation are among the women's issues that still need to be further addressed.

NOTES

1. Unless otherwise indicated, all statistics are from the official government report "A Situação da Mulher em Portugal" provided by the Instituto Nacional de Estatística (INE), March 1999, www.ine.pt.

2. The notorious Addendum to Article 5 (of the 1933 constitution) asserted that women not be afforded equal citizenship on account of "as diferenças resultantes da sua natureza e do bem da família." Comissão para a Igualdade e para os Direitos das Mulheres 1995. *Portugal Situação das Mulheres* (Lisboa: CIDM, 1995) 49, quoted in Hilary Owen, *Portuguese Women's Writing 1972–1983* (Lewiston, NY: Edwin Mellen Press, 2000), 4.

3. Ana Paula Ferreira, *Home Bound, Portuguese Studies*, no. 12 (1996): 133–44.

4. Virginia Ferreira, "Engendering Portugal," in *Modern Portugal*, ed. António Costa Pinto (Palo Alto, CA: Society for the Promotion of Science and Scholarship, 1998), 162–88, esp. 173.

5. V. Ferreira, 1998, 169.

6. V. Ferreira, 1998, 179.

7. V. Ferreira, 1998, 166.

8. V. Ferreira, 1998, 166.

9. Ana Vicente, *As mulheres em Portugal* (Lisboa: Multinova, 1998), 78.

10. Glória Fernandes, "Women in Contemporary Portuguese Society," in *Women, Literature and Culture in the Portuguese-speaking World*, ed. Cláudia Pazos Alonso (Lewiston, NY: Edwin Mellen Press, 1996), 39–50, esp. 42.

11. Vicente, 1998, 68.

12. Vicente, 1998, 29.

13. Vicente, 1998, 38–42.

14. V. Ferreira, 1998, 118.

15. Vicente, 1998, 112.

16. Vicente states that maternal mortality rates went from 42.9 for 100,000 deliveries in 1975 to 9 in 1995; for the same period, infant mortality rates dropped from 38.9 for 1,000 births to 7.4 (Vicente, 1998, 106).

17. It is estimated that during the New State, infant mortality rates reached nearly 50 percent (V. Ferreira, 1998, 173).

18. Reviver, Associação de Solidariedade Social e Reabilitação de Mulheres Toxicodependentes (Vicente, 1998, 114).

19. Ministério da Saúde, *Ganhos de saúde em Portugal* (Lisboa: Direcção-geral da Saúde, 2002).

20. The United Nations Fourth World Conference on Women: Action for Equality, Development and Peace, September 1995, Beijing, China; and the United Nations International Conference on Population and Development, September 5–13, 1994, Cairo, Egypt.

21. Ministério da Saúde, 2002.

22. Ministério da Saúde, 2002.

23. V. Ferreira, 1998, 173.

24. Vicente, 2002, 65–79.

25. In the 1994 elections, women represented 2 percent of the total local seats of government, five out of 305 mayores, 7 percent of the deputies elected to the National Assembly, and two out of the sixteen ministers (José Manuel Leite Viegas and Sérgio Faria), *As mulheres na política* (Oeiras, Portugal: Celta Editora, 2001).

26. The demonstration took place in the center of Lisbon on January 13, 1995, at the foot of the Parque Eduardo VII. Distorted by the press as a public burning of bras and brooms, it was met with misogynist opposition and was to be the last public demonstration of any women's movement.

27. In June 1998, there was a referendum concerning abortion, but the response was so weak (less than a 32 percent turnout) that it was unsuccessful. See Yves Léonard, "Le référendum au Portugal, quel avenir?" *Lusotopies* (1999): 37–54.

28. This is according to Opus Gay, a GLBT activist group in Portugal that provides a forum for discussion of such issues. At this time, Opus Gay and other activist groups post information about rights and other issues of interest at www.portugalgay.pt.

29. Since census questions do not include religion, it is difficult to determine the exact percentage of religious affiliation. Approximately 70 percent of all marriages are still performed through the church.

30. The survey polled a representative group of the population, and 71 percent answered affirmatively. The results of the survey were published in a national newspaper, *O Público*, on October, 3, 1998 (Vicente, 2002, 154).

31. Lena Gemzoe, *Feminine Matters: Women's Religious Practices* (Stockholm: Elanders Gotab, 2000).

32. The legend has it that the Virgin appeared to three shepherd children in 1917

on the outskirts of Fátima and delivered a message known as the Secrets of Fátima that included pleas for mankind to say the rosary, a vision of hell and the need for Russia to convert to Catholicism in order to obtain world peace (Gemzoe, 2000, 167–202).

33. Gemzoe, 2000, 89–96.
34. Ministério da Saúde, 2002, 36–38.
35. Vicente, 1998, 153.
36. Vicente, 1998, 167–70.

RESOURCE GUIDE

Suggested Reading

Klobucka, Anna, and Helen Kaufmann, eds. *After the Revolution: Twenty Years of Portuguese Literature 1974–1994*. Lewisburg, PA: Bucknell University Press, 1997. Though the main focus of the book is literature, the articles are couched in sociohistoric and political contexts. There are also entries on newspapers, censorship, and women's issues with an excellent introduction to the time period.

Owen, Hilary, ed. *Gender, Ethnicity and Class in Modern Portuguese-Speaking Culture*. Lewiston, NY: Edwin Mellen Press, 1996. An excellent introduction to issues of gender, ethnicity, and class from various standpoints. The chapter by Pat Odber de Baubeta, "Representations of Women in Portuguese Advertising Today," is particularly well worth consulting.

Pinto, António Costa, ed. *Modern Portugal*. Palo Alto, CA: The Society for the Promotion of Science and Scholarship, 1998. This collection of articles presents a wide scope of current issues in Portugal ranging from emigration to economics, literature, the development of Portuguese democracy, society, and values.

Sadlier, Darlene J. "Feminism in Portugal. A Brief History." Appendix to *The Question of How: Women Writers and New Portuguese Literature*. Westport, CT: Greenwood Press, 1989, 113–29. This concise history of feminism in Portugal pinpoints key aspects of women's issues from the second half of the nineteenth century to the 1980s. It provides an overview of women's rights, prominent feminist activists, and organizations.

Web Sites

Organizações do Conselho Consultivo da CIDM (Comissão para a Igualdade e para os Direitos das Mulheres, www.ongdm.org.pt.
The official web site for the council of nongovernmental women's organizations for the equality and rights of women. It encompasses over forty organizations with objectives as diverse as sports, violence, and feminist studies. Links to each organization are provided along with their contact information. Web site is in Portuguese, French, and English.

Portuguese Association of Women's Studies (Associação Portuguesa de Estudos sobre as Mulheres), www.apem.web.pt.
Aims to promote women's studies in all areas and facilitate contacts between researchers. Web site is in Portuguese and English.

Organizations

Associação para o planeamento da família (Association of Planned Parenthood)
Rua Artillaria Um, 38-2°. DTO
1250-040 Lisboa
Portugal
Phone: 213853993
Fax: 213887379
Email: national@apf.pt
Web site: www.apf.pt

Affiliated with International Planned Parenthood, the association is very active and
provides information, activities, projects, and legislative updates on parenthood and
related issues. There are regional offices throughout Portugal and the Azores.

Movimento Democrático das Mulheres (MDM)
Avenida Duque de Loulé, III-4°
1050-089 Lisboa
Portugal
Phone: 213527853
Fax: 21352667

With close to 5,000 members, this organization unites Portuguese women in defense
of their interests as citizens, employees, and mothers and promotes a greater awareness of women's social, economic, and political problems.

SELECTED BIBLIOGRAPHY

Committee on the Elimination of Discrimination against Women. "Portugal." In *Con-
siderations of Reports of States Parties*. January 23, 2002. www.ongdm.org.pt.
Fernandes, Glória. "Women in Contemporary Portuguese Society." In *Women, Liter-
ature and Culture in the Portuguese-Speaking World*, edited by Cláudia Pazos
Alonso, 39–50. Lewiston, NY: Edwin Mellen Press, 1996.
Ferreira, Ana Paula. "Home Bound: The Construct of Femininity in the Estado
Novo." In *Portuguese Studies*, no. 12 (1996): 133–44.
Ferreira, Virgínia. "Engendering Portugal: Social Change, State Politics, and Women's
Social Mobilization." In *Modern Portugal*, edited by António Costa Pinto, 162–
88. Palo Alto, CA: Society for the Promotion of Science and Scholarship, 1998.
Gemzoe, Lena. *Feminine Matters: Women's Religious Practices in a Portuguese Town*.
Stockholm: Elanders Gotab, 2000.
Owen, Hilary. *Portuguese Women's Writing 1972–1986. Reincarnations of a Revolution*.
Lewiston, NY: Edwin Mellen Press, 2000.

Selected Portuguese Bibliography

Léonard, Yves. "Le référendum au Portugal, quel avenir?" In *Dynamique religieuse en
lusephonie contemporaine, Lusotopies*. Paris: Editions Karthala, 1999. 37–54.
Ministério da saúde. *Ganhos de saúde em Portugal: ponto de situação*. Relatório do
Director-Geral da Saúde 2002. Lisboa: Direcção-Geral da saúde, 2002.

Vicente, Ana. *As mulheres em Portugal na transicão do milénio.* Lisboa: Multinova, 1998.
————. *Os poderes das mulheres, os poderes dos homens.* Lisboa: Gótica, 2002.
Viegas, José Manuel Leite, and Sérgio Faria. *As mulheres na política.* Oeiras: Celta Editora, 2001.

30

ROMANIA

Livia Popescu

PROFILE OF ROMANIA

Romania is situated in the southeastern part of Europe and has a territory of 92,043 square miles. The privatization of the economy has been distinctively slow compared with other Eastern European countries. The gross domestic product (GDP), which is created predominantly in services and industry, is among the lowest in the region: US \$5,533 purchase power parity (PPP) per inhabitant and US \$4,706 (PPP) for women.[1]

Romania is an emergent democracy with a mixed presidential–parliamentary system. As of January 2001, there were 22.43 million inhabitants, 54.6 percent of them urban residents. According to the 1992 census, 89.4 percent of the population is Romanian. The most important ethnic minorities are Hungarians (7.1 percent) and Roma (1.8 percent).[2] Women represent 51.1 percent of the total inhabitants, and the gender ratio is estimated to be 104 women to 100 men.[3] In the last decade, the fertility rate decreased to 40.3 live births per 1,000 women. Despite noticeable improvements in recent years, in 2000 both the maternal mortality rate (33 per 100,000 live births) and the infant mortality rate (18.6 per 1,000 live births) continue to

be among the highest in Europe. In 2000, women's average life expectancy was 74.2 years, seven years higher than men's.[4]

OVERVIEW OF WOMEN'S ISSUES

Although gender equity is stated in Romanian legislation, inequalities between men and women are pervasive both in public and in private realms. The labor market reproduces the gender hierarchy in job opportunities, wage policy, and career prospects. Women's emancipation in the domestic sphere is slowed down by patriarchal family relations. Many women have no control over their sexual lives, and their reproductive health is exposed to high risks. The legal framework on domestic violence, rape, and sexual harassment is rather permissive toward these violations of women's rights. Furthermore, women's voices in politics and decision-making processes are yet to be heard.

Woman using wood-burning cooker, Tigmandru, Romania. Photo © TRIP/J. Farmar.

EDUCATION

Opportunities

As stated in all the Romanian postwar constitutions, access to education is equal to both genders. Yet the educational gender gap has persisted over the years while changing its size and characteristics. It is considerably bigger in the case of Roma minority, where females without education are the majority of women.[5]

In recent years, the gross enrollment rate was higher for women than for men at all levels of education.[6] The relative increase of female students in 1992–1998 reduced the gender disparity and eventually evened the proportions of the two sexes among the university population. Nevertheless, the proportion of persons with university degrees is still lower for women (6 percent) than for men (8 percent).[7]

Literacy

The differences in literacy rates decreased between 1992 and 1998, but the female literacy rate is still lower than for men: 95.7 percent and 98.7 percent, respectively. Among the population aged seventy-five and above, women's illiteracy rate exceeds men's by 17.6 percent. Women represent 78 percent of the total illiterate rural inhabitants, the majority of them being elderly.[8]

EMPLOYMENT AND THE ECONOMY

Job/Career Opportunities

In 2000, the employment rate (of the population aged fifteen years and older) was lower for women than for men: 52.8 percent compared to 65.1 percent.[9] If the occupational status is considered, the data show that most females are employees (53.7 percent) and "non-paid family members" (29.4 percent). The most important group, about 44.1 percent of the employed female population, works in agriculture. The remaining women are employed in nonagricultural activities mostly as technical staff/clerical workers, skilled workers, and "specialists with intellectual and scientific occupations." The proportion of women with managerial and high administrative positions is less than half of the men's: 1.2 percent of the total number of employed females.[10] The gender composition of the labor force varies to a great extent by branch of economic activity. Women working in health care, social services and pre-university education represent more than 70 percent of the total employed population in the respective sectors.

Women's unemployment rate was constantly higher than men's from 1991 to 1998. Since then the opposite trend is in place, but women tend to remain unemployed longer than men.[11]

Pay

Both the Constitution (1991) and the Labor Code (1972) include provisions on equal pay for equal work. Nevertheless, women are paid less than their male coworkers for every category of nonagricultural economic activity. In 2000, their gross salary represented 83.5 percent of men's.[12] Excepting the banking and insurance sector, all other fields where women make up the majority of employees have average salaries below the national average. As a result, female workers constitute a larger share of the low-income categories, whereas men tend to be twice as numerous as women in high-income groups.[13]

Working Conditions

There are no legal provisions specific to women's general working conditions. The Labor Code entitles pregnant employees to claim their transfer from dangerous workplaces or to be exempted from night work.[14] In practice, these regulations are hardly enforced by authorities.

Sexual Harassment

Sanctions against sexual harassment were instituted for the first time by the 2002 Law on Equal Opportunities between Women and Men. Cases are settled according to the civil law provisions and subsequently punished by fines.[15] There are no official data about complaints on sexual harassment that have come to court yet. Authorities tend to overlook the problem in spite of evidence about its seriousness. A 1996 survey carried out by a UN research institute mentions that Romania had the highest prevalence of sexual incidents involving female workers (108 per 1,000 women) among eleven post–state socialist countries.[16]

Support for Mothers/Caretakers

There are three types of cash benefits, that are provided to mothers/caretakers: birthing allowance, state allowance for children, and supplementary family allowance. All of them are universal benefits financed by the state budget. Both the state allowance and the supplementary allowance have a rather minimal purchasing power.

Mothers are entitled to a birthing allowance, which is a one-time flat sum provided for each of the first four live births. The benefit can be paid to the child's legal representative only if the mother is unable to use it. The state allowance for children is actually provided as a universal right of the child. A flat amount of money is paid monthly to any child up to age sixteen (or eighteen if the child is enrolled in school or is disabled). The supplementary allowance for families with children is provided to families with two or more dependent children.

Maternal Leave

The paid maternity leave is insurance-based. Consequently, maternity benefits are provided to employed women who actually contribute to the public insurance scheme. It is cofinanced by the employer. The entitlement continues after the contribution period if the delivery occurs within nine months after the woman lost her insured status. Women receiving unemployment benefits are also covered for maternal leave. The maternal leave consists of sixty-three prenatal and sixty-three postnatal days that can be accumulated. The leave counts toward the employee's contribution period for purposes of social security calculations. The maternity benefit is 85 percent of the mother's income base. The insured mother, father, or legal caretaker is entitled, upon request, to an additional paid leave to extend until the child reaches age two, at the same benefit level.[17]

A significant number of mothers, which is not officially documented, do not get any financial support during the prenatal and postnatal period. They are the long-term unemployed or women working as "family members." Women who have temporary work contracts or who work without contract are not entitled to benefits, either.

Daycare

Preschool care comprises crèches, or nurseries (for ages 0–3), and kindergartens (for ages 3–6). They provide instruction, education, and medical assistance free of charge. The food provided in full-time care facilities is partially paid for by parents. The parents' contribution is a percentage of the family monthly income and also depends upon the number of children enrolled in care facilities. The highest level of parental contribution covers 75 percent of the cost of the food.

In the transitional period between 1989 and 1995, when Romania experienced its sharpest decline in enrollment, the number of children in public nurseries (two months to three years) decreased by half.[18] Besides parental unemployment, the extension of the leave period also contributed to the declining enrollment. The decrease in public kindergarten enrollment was less dramatic, and by 1999–2000 the net rate rose to 67.3 percent.[19] Placing children aged 3–6 in formal care is a common practice because it provides preschool education and allows mothers to work outside the home as well.[20]

Family and Medical Leave

According to the Law on the Public System for Pension and Other Social Insurance Rights, a parent (whether natural, foster, or adoptive) or legal tutor qualifies for a medical leave to care for a child up to age seven if the minimum six months' contribution has been paid. The benefit is granted for a maximum of fourteen days per year per child and amounts at 85 percent of the last six months' average salary.[21]

Inheritance and Property Rights

No legal provision discriminates on the basis of gender in the ownership, inheritance, or transfer of property. Unmarried partners living together have no rights to inheritance from each other. Women are likely to be disadvantaged in such situations if they cannot prove their contribution to the common property.[22]

Social/Government Programs

Welfare

During the 1990s, the welfare system inherited from the communist regime underwent substantial changes. Following the continental pattern, which is observable in most Eastern European countries, the welfare reform led to a system that "preserve(s) the current status hierarchies via insurance-based systems and intervenes in the provision of welfare only as a last resort."[23]

The gendered nature of the welfare regime is emphasized by some of the recent policy changes. The new pension law raised the minimum employment period to fifteen years and abolishes the so-called social aid pension, which was provided to people having less than the required minimum. It is quite likely that women will be more affected than men by these measures since women have shorter periods of paid work. The disadvantages of the old system have not been remedied either. Pensions established before 1990 have been adjusted very little due to the devastating inflation of the 1990s. Under these circumstances, the older you are, the smaller pension you get. Since women live longer, they are more likely to have low pensions and live in poverty.

FAMILY AND SEXUALITY

Gender Roles

At the beginning of the twenty-first century, 46.2 percent of the Romanian population lives in rural settings. Under these circumstances, it is not surprising that the patriarchal pattern of family life is perpetuated.[24] Industrialization brought about an increased participation of women on the labor market, which influenced the gender roles. However, the division of domestic work was not essentially modified, and women continued to perform their traditional activities of caretakers and housekeepers along with the paid work. A recent public opinion survey shows that 63 percent of the representative sample believes that domestic activities are mostly women's rather than men's duty. Moreover, both the majority of female and male respondents agreed that the "man is the head of the family." A similar strong support exists for other defining elements of the traditional gender representations.[25]

Marriage

Romanian Family Code considers a couple to be married if the office of the mayor recorded the marriage. Marriage is monogamous and is permitted only between male and female. Law bases it on free consent and full equality between spouses.[26]

The minimal age to marry is eighteen for a male and sixteen (or fifteen for "special reasons") for a female. In 2001, 5 percent of the women fifteen to nineteen years old were married, most of them in rural areas or ethnic Roma. As a result of a steady increase in the last decade, the average age for a first marriage in 2000 was 26.9 for men and 23.6 for women. The same year, the marriage rate was 6.1, the lowest recorded in postwar time.[27] Marriages last twenty-two years on average and the divorce rate is low (1.37), which indicates a high level of family stability.[28]

Reproduction

The fertility rate decreased by 10 percent during 1990–2000 and has stabilized at around forty live births per 1,000 women aged 15–49. Consequently, the birthrate has dropped to 10.5 newborn for 1,000 inhabitants. In 2000, the mother's age at her first birth was 23.7 years. A quarter of all children are born out of wedlock.[29]

Sex Education

According to a 1996 survey, 88 percent of females fifteen to twenty-four years old received some sex education in schools. However, only one third of them have been exposed to information on sexually transmitted diseases and AIDS prevention. Even fewer received education on birth control methods.[30] Over half of the young women took their specific information on contraception from a "friend" (27 percent), the media (17 percent) or a "colleague" (13 percent). Health providers accounted for 12 percent, mothers for 10 percent, and schools for only 4 percent.[31]

Contraception and Abortion

Although contraceptives are legal and relatively available, abortion remains the most commonly used method of fertility control. In 1999, 64 percent of married women used contraceptive methods, but the traditional ones, such as withdrawal and the rhythm method, are prevailing. Modern contraceptive methods accounted for only 27.5 percent.[32]

Abortion was liberalized immediately after December 1989. It is legal if requested within fourteen weeks from the presumed date of conception and performed by a licensed doctor. Induced abortion is not covered by the health insurance plan unless it is performed for therapeutic reasons. Most of the induced abortions are performed on women from rural areas, those with less education, and Roma women.[33] They have serious difficulties in controlling their pregnancies because they are not informed and have no access to family planning services.[34] Yet free abortions are available to students and low-income women.

The number of abortions performed immediately after their legalization increased tremendously. The absolute number recorded in 1990 was close to 1 million (about four abortions per each live birth) and the corresponding abortion rate—315 per 100 live births—was the highest in Europe. The rate has since steadily decreased, but is still at 110 per 100 live births.[35]

Teen Pregnancy

The reported rate of sexual activity among teenagers is relatively low. A 1999 survey shows that 88 percent of the female respondents aged 15–17 have not had a sexual experience.[36] Nevertheless, the fertility rate for the youngest age group (from fifteen to nineteen years old) is close to the total fertility rate. Live births by mothers aged fifteen to nineteen represent 13.5 percent of the total.[37] Campaigns and programs to prevent unwanted pregnancies among teenagers were not launched until recently, and they still lack efficiency, particularly among higher-risk groups such as teenagers from destitute families, homeless, and Roma.

HEALTH

Health Care Access

The shift from a universal system to health insurance was an essential component of health care reform. The health care sector is actually facing systemic problems that are caused mostly by the insufficient funding. Problems impact both the access to and the quality of health services, especially for the most vulnerable layers of the society.[38]

Services specifically addressing women's health problems other than reproductive health are underdeveloped. Preventive care, and particularly screening for female cancers, is overlooked. In 1996, 49 percent of urban sexually active women fifteen to twenty-four years old had a routine gynecological exam, and 18 percent of them had a cervical cancer screening. In the case of rural women, the proportions were much lower.[39]

Diseases and Disorders

Health statistics are rarely desegregated by gender. Estimations based on surveys indicate that cardiovascular diseases are prevalent among women. The reemergence of syphilis is likely to affect more women than men.[40] The main causes of women's mortality in Romania are cardiovascular diseases and cancer with incidence rates of 714 and 151 respectively per 100,000 women.[41]

AIDS

Romania still has a sad notoriety as being the country with the highest share of HIV-infected children in Europe. In 2000 there were thirty AIDS cases per 100,000 inhabitants. Females are reported as being 51 percent of the total AIDS cases among adults. Children up to nine years old (2,084 girls and 2,968 boys) accounted for 75 percent of the total cases, and the majority of them have been infected as a result of medical maneuvers with contaminated needles and blood. The most frequent transmission path of HIV infection among adult males and females is heterosexual sex, accounting for 58.8 percent of total registered cases.[42]

The prevalence of both children and adult HIV infections has increased since 1990. AIDS patients are entitled to free medication, and the National Program for AIDS should ensure access to prevention, diagnosis, and medical care. Still, for many years it has been underfunded.[43]

Cancer

Cancer has an incidence rate of 157.13 cases per 100,000 women. Breast cancer ranks first among the types of cancer that affect women with an incidence rate of 35.53. The second-highest type was cervical cancer (21.51). The same forms of cancer are the main causes of death by cancer, with a rate of 21.6 per 100,000 women in the case of breast cancer, and 14.7 in the case of cervical cancer.[44]

POLITICS AND LAW

Suffrage

Citizens eighteen years of age and older may vote.

Political Participation

Political equity between men and women was enacted in the 1991 Constitution, but Romanian female political participation is among the lowest in Europe. Women elected members of parliament in the year 2000 represent 9.7 percent of the total.[45] Three percent of elected mayors and 6 percent of local councilors are women. The present Cabinet includes five female ministers and several vice-ministers.

Women's Rights

Women are constitutionally entitled to equal treatment, including in marriage, paid work, and political participation.[46] The Law on the Prevention and Punishment of All Forms of Discrimination prohibits discrimination, including gender based, in all public life spheres. Discrimination is an administrative offense that is punishable by fine. If the woman, or anyone who has been discriminated against, goes to court, they will not be requested to pay the standard litigation tax.[47] A similar approach is reflected by the Law on Equal Opportunities between women and men. The law stipulates the obligation of employers to ensure equal opportunities and treatment and forbids gender discrimination in advertising, job-related examinations, and the like under the penalty of fines.[48]

Feminist Movements

Postsocialist transformations in Romania were not auspicious for the emergence of the feminist movements. On the contrary, gender became a "non-issue" and feminism is rather silent. Since both the "socialist emancipation" and the "Western feminism" ideologies failed in mobilizing a women's movement, a new legitimizing vision has yet to be found.[49] Yet, women's studies are institutionalized, and the gender perspective is gradually penetrating the public discourse. These developments, along with the embryonic feminist practice promoted by the few women's organizations, presumably raised the gender awareness. They will eventually prompt the emergence of feminism(s).

Lesbian Rights

Same-sex relations have been decriminalized since 2001 when the Parliament repealed Article 200 of the Criminal Code. The law on preventing and punishing all forms of discrimination is the first one to mention sexual orientation as a protected identity.[50]

Marriage. According to the Family Code, marriage's definition excludes same-sex unions.

Parenthood. There are no specific regulations on lesbian and gay parenthood rights.

Military Service

Military service is not compulsory for women. Military careers can be embraced by females, but the access is mostly confined to noncombatant jobs.

RELIGION AND SPIRITUALITY

Romania is a secular state, but the populace trust the church much more than the state institutions. In Romania, there are several denominations and churches. The majority of the population is Christian Orthodox, a religion that endorses the man's dominant role. Most of the respondents to a 2002 public opinion survey consider themselves religious persons.[51]

Women's Roles

Women and especially elderly peasants are religious to a higher proportion than men, and they observe more strictly the religious commandments and practices.

Religious Law

Women cannot become priests. However, the Orthodox Church permits and even requires that priests marry prior to their ordination.

VIOLENCE

Domestic Violence

More than half of all respondents to a 2000 survey knew of a man who beat his wife or partner, and 18 percent of the female respondents have been victims of domestic violence.[52] The national data about the incidence of physical and sexual violence inflicted on women within their families are either lacking or not entirely reliable. According to a study done by the Institute of Sociology, an average of 11,700 women (1.1 percent of women age sixteen and over from Bucharest and surroundings) who are beaten up and injured by their partners are registered yearly by legal medicine experts in Bucharest. Yet the real number of victims is likely to be two or three times higher. As of 1998, forty women were killed by either husbands or partners.[53]

There is no specific legislation pertaining to domestic violence, but other laws may apply to the respective crimes. Police investigation and prosecution cannot be initiated without the survivor's prior complaint unless the violence is very serious. The number of victims who report the violent act to police is lower than the actual number of women who have been beaten, especially in cases of simple battery. Economic dependency upon the perpetrator and a lack of alternative housing arrangements discourage women from following the legal procedures.[54] The dominant perception that domestic violence is a "private matter" is equally unfavorable to survivors.[55]

Rape/Sexual Assault

In 2000, there were five reported rape cases per 100,000 women.[56] Yet the real figure is much higher because many victims do not complain out of shame and fear of ruining their marriage prospects. The Romania legislation considers rape a crime that is punishable by a three- to ten-year prison term or even longer if the victim is under fourteen years old or other aggravated circumstances exist. As in the case of domestic violence, the criminal investigation requires the prior complaint of the victim. The criminal responsibility of the perpetrator is exempted if a "reparatory marriage" between him and the victim occurs. The criminality of rape within marriage is neither denied nor stated explicitly in the Criminal Code. However, jurisprudence considers that marriage implies a woman's "consented limitation of her sexual freedom," and therefore the provision pertaining to rape does not apply within marriage.[57]

Trafficking in Women and Children

Trafficking in women and children was overlooked until recently, but the growing international concern for this issue prompted Romanian authorities to enforce the laws on trafficking and recruiting for sexual exploitation. The extent of the problem is still unknown, but existent data suggest that Romania is both a source and a transit country for trafficked women and girls. Romanian prostitutes, including minors, are exploited in different European countries and in the Balkans by several domestic and international prostitution rings. Official records show that 726 women were registered by the authorities as being trafficked from Romania in 2001, and 167 of them were minors.[58]

OUTLOOK FOR THE TWENTY-FIRST CENTURY

New legislative and institutional arrangements to address gender issues at the workplace were recently put in place as part of preaccession to the European Union. Similarly, the requirements of the Beijing Platform increased the government responsiveness to women's issues. However much external pressure has prompted changes, gender inequalities cannot be addressed efficiently if local women's agency is lacking. In addition, female leaders and politicians are expected to tackle women's disadvantages consistently and to mainstream gender perspective into all policy areas.

NOTES

1. *National Human Development Report Romania 2001–2002* (NHDR), UNDP, 2002, www.undp.ro/publications/NHDR.pdf.

2. Comisia Nationala de Statistica (CNS), *Rezultate generale* (Bucharest: Author, 1994).

3. Institutul National de Statistica (INS), *Analize demographice* (Bucharest: Author, 2001): 1; and INS, 2001, 6–7.

4. INS, 2001, *Analize*, 38–41.

5. Gabriela Adamesteanu, "Statutul femeilor in Romania," 22, no. 6 (1998): 9.

6. NHDR, 2002.

7. Programul Natiunilor Unite pentru Dezvoltare in Romania PNUD Comisia Nationala de Statistica (CNS). *Femeile si barbatii in Romania (Women and Men in Romania)* (Bucuresti: PNUD, 2000), 35.

8. CNS, PNUD, 2000, 36.

9. INS, *Ancheta a supra forti de Munca* (Bucharest: Author, 2001), 24.

10. INS, 2001, *Ancheta*, 27.

11. CNS, PNUD, 2000; 24 INS, 2001.

12. NHDR, 2002.

13. CNS, PNUD, 2000, 27–29.

14. *Monitorul Oficial al Romaniei* (MOR), no. 140, December 1, 1972.

15. MOR, no. 301, May 8, 2002.

16. UNICEF, "Women in Transition," *Regional Monitoring Report*, no. 6 (1999): 84.

17. MOR, 2000.

18. Monica Fong and Michael Lokshin, *Child Care and Women's Labor Force Participation in Romania*, 2000, http://wbln0018.worldbank.org/research/workpapers/nsf.

19. INS, *Starea sociala si economia* (Bucharest: Author, 2001), 68.

20. Fong and Lokshin, 2000.

21. MOR, 2000.

22. *Women of the World*, 2000, www.crlp.org/pdf/Romania.pdf.

23. Tony Makkai, "Social Policy and Gender in Eastern Europe," in *Gendering Welfare States*, ed. D. Sainsbury (London: Sage Publications, 1994), 203.

24. Elena Zamfir, "Politica de protectie a copilului in Romania," in *Politici Sociale*, ed. E. Zamfir and C. Zamfir (Bucharest: Editura Alternative, 1995), 200–244.

25. *Baromentrul de gen* (Bucharest: Fundatia pentriuo Societate Deschisa, 2000); and Livia Popescu and Maria Roth, "Variabila gen," in *Prezente feminine*, ed. G. Cosma et al. (Cluj, Romania: Editura Fundatiei Desire, 2002), 453–77.

26. MOR, no. 1, January 4, 1954.

27. INS 2001, *Analize*, 60.

28. CNS, PNUD, 2000; 11 and INS, 2001, 60–69, *Analize*.

29. INS, 2001, *Analize*.

30. INS, 2001, *Analize*.

31. F. Serbanescu and Leo Morris, "Young Adult Reproductive Health Survey: Romania 1996" (Bucharest: National Institute of Mother and Child Care, 1998).

32. Survey on Reproductive Health, cited by *Women of the World*, 2000.

33. INS, 2001, *Analize*.

34. Popescu and Roth, 2002.

35. INS, 2001, *Analize*, 38.

36. Survey on Reproductive Health, 1999, cited by *Women of the World*, 2000.

37. INS, 2001, *Analize*.

38. NHDR, 2002.

39. Serbanescu and Morris, 1998.

40. UNICEF, 1999.

41. INS, 2001, *Analize*.

42. INS, Anuarul statistic al Romaniei (Bucharest: Author, 2001).

43. *Women of the World*, 2000.

44. Institute of Oncology Bucharest, *Epidemiological data recording cancer in Romania*, 1996, www.iob.ro/iob/3/eu_f.html.

45. NHDR, 2002.

46. *Constitutia Romaniei*, 1991, www.parlament.ro/pls.dic/.

47. MOR, 2002.

48. MOR, May 8, 2002.

49. E. Magyari-Vincze, "Despre femei si nu numai," in G. Cosma et al., 2002, 7–30.

50. MOR, 2002, *Ancheta*.

51. *Barometru de opinie publica* (Bucharest: Fundatia pentru o Societate Deschisa, 2002).

52. *Barometrul de gen*, 2000.

53. Ana Muntean et al., *Vietimele violentei domestice* (Timisoara, Romania: Editura Eurostampa, 2002).

54. Muntean et al., 2002.

55. Popescu and Roth, 2002.

56. NHDR, 2002.

57. *Codul Penal* cited by Muntean et al., 2002, 24.

58. *Women of the World*, 2002; and Ministry of Internal Affairs et al., 2001, cited by Sorina Bumbulut and Maria Roth, "Sexually Abused Children in Romania," in *Child Sexual Abuse in Europe*, ed. Corrine Wattam and Maria Herczog (2002).

RESOURCE GUIDE

Suggested Reading

Baban, Adriana. "Women's Sexuality and Reproductive Behavior in Post-Ceausescu Romania: A Psychological Approach." In *Reproducing Gender: Politics, Publics, and Everyday Life after Socialism*, ed. Susan Gal and Gail Kligman (Princeton, NJ: Princeton University Press, 2000): 225–56. Combines statistical and qualitative analysis on women's sexuality and reproductive behavior.

Fodor, Eva, Christy Glass, Janette Kawachi, and Livia Popescu. "Family Policies and Gender in Hungary, Poland and Romania." *Communist and Post-Communist Studies* 35 (2002): 475–90.

Gal, Susan, and Gail Kligman. *The Politics of Gender After Socialism*. Princeton, NJ: Princeton University Press, 2000. A comprehensive analysis of new forms of relations between men and women in the workplace, in families, and in politics, which emerged in postsocialist countries.

Grunberg, Laura. "Women's NGOs in Romania." In *Reproducing Gender, Politics and Everyday Life after Socialism*, edited by Susan Gal and Gail Kligman, 307–36. Princeton, NJ: Princeton University Press, 2000. Examines the characteristics of women's organizations and questions their contribution to the feminist movement.

Magyari, Nandor, Eniko Magyari-Vincze, Livia Popescu, and Traian Rotariu. "The Social Construction of Romanian Poverty: The Impact of Ethnic and Gender Distinctions." In *Poverty, Ethnicity, and Gender in Eastern Europe During the Market Transition*, edited by Rebecca J. Emeigh and Ivan Szelenyi, 123–56. Westport, CT: Praeger, 2001. Discusses poverty in Romania and argues that it is both racialized and feminized.

Web Sites

AnA Society for Feminist Analysis, www.anasaf.ro.
The web site provides access to research papers and to information on women in Romania.

Baza de date legislative (Legislative database), www.parlament.ro/pls/legis/legis_pck.
frame.
The collection of laws and government ordinances.

National Human Development Report Romania 2001–2002-NHDR, www.undp.ro/
publications/NHDR.pdf.
The 2002 report analyzes the transition process in Romania. A useful Statistical Annex
is provided.

UNICEF, "Women in Transition." *Regional Monitoring Report*. no. 6, 1999, www.
eurochild.gla.ac.uk/Documents/monee6/pdf.
A comprehensive analysis of women's issues in Eastern Europe.

*Women of the World: Laws and Policies Affecting Their Reproductive Lives: East-Central
Europe-Romania*, www.crlp.org/pdf/Romania/pdf.
A critical overview of legislation and policies on women's issues.

Organizations

AnA Society for Feminist Analysis
Laura Grunberg
24 Bd. Ferdinand, apt. 12
Bucharest, Romania
Email: ana_saf@anasaf.ro

The organization is committed to understanding and improving women's status in
Romania.

Asociatia femeilor rome din Romania (Roma Women's Association from Romania)
Violeta Dumitru
Aleea MS Buteica nr.2
bl.68, ap.1, sector 3
Bucuresti, Romania
Email: violeta@dnt.ro

The association runs projects for Roma women.

Asociatia pentru promovarea femeii din Romania (Association for Woman Promotion
in Romania)
Elena Francisc
Bd. Tineretii nr.19
ap.1, 1900
Timisoara, Romania
Email: apfr@mail.dnttm.ro

It runs projects on domestic violence and women's solidarity in politics.

SELECTED BIBLIOGRAPHY

Bumbulut, Sorina, and Maria Roth. "Sexually Abused Children in Romania." In *Child
Sexual Abuse in Europe*, edited by Corinne Wattam and Maria Herczog, manuscript, 2002.
Institute of Oncology, Bucharest. *Epidemiological Data Recording Cancer in Romania*.
1996. www.iob.ro/iob/3/eu_f.html.

Fong, Monica, and Michael Lokshin. *Child Care and Women's Labor Force Participation in Romania*. 2000. http://wbln0018.worldbank.org/research/workpapers/nsf.

Makkai, Tony. "Social Policy and Gender in Eastern Europe." In *Gendering Welfare States*, edited by D. Sainsbury. London: Sage Publications, 1994.

National Human Development Report Romania (NHDR). 2002. www.undp.ro/publications/NHDR.pdf.

Serbanescu, F., and Leo Morris. "Young Adult Reproductive Health Survey: Romania 1996." Bucharest: National Institute of Mother and Child Care, 1998.

UNICEF. "Women in Transition." *Regional Monitoring Report*, no. 6. Florence, Italy: UNICEF Innocenti Research Centre, 1999.

Women of the World: Laws and Policies Affecting Their Reproductive Lives: East-Central Europe — Romania. 2000. www.crlp.org/pdf/Romania.pdf.

Selected Romanian Bibliography

Comisia Nationala de Statistica (CNS, National Commission for Statistics). *Rezultate generale: Recensananal populatiei, gospodariilor si cladirilor din 7 ianuarie 1992* (General Results: The Census of Population, Households and Dwellings at January 7, 1992). Bucharest: Author, 1994.

Institul National de Statistica (National Institute for Statistic/INS). *Analize demografice. Situatia demografica a Romaniei in anul 2000* (Demographic Analyzes. Romania's Demographic Situation in 2000). Bucuresti: INS, 2001.

———. *Ancheta asupra fortei de munca in gospodarii in anul 2000 (AMIGO)* (Household Survey on the Labour Force in 2000). Bucuresti: INS, 2001.

———. *Anuarul statistic al Romaniei* (Romania's Statistical Yearbook). Bucuresti: INS, 2001.

———. *Starea sociala si economia Romaniei in perioada 1997–1999* (Social Situation and Economy in Romania within 1997–1999). Bucuresti: INS, 2001.

Magyari-Vincze, E. "Despre femei si nu numai. O introducere la studiile despre femei in Romania (About Women, but Not Exclusively. An Introduction to Women's Studies in Romania)." In *Prezente feminine: Studii despre femei in Romania* (Female Occurrences: Women's Studies in Romania), edited by G. Cosma, E. Magyari-Vincze, and O. Pecican, 7–30. Cluj: Editura Fundatiei Desire, 2002.

Monitorul Oficial al Romaniei/MOR (Official Gazette of Romania), No. 1, January 4, 1954.

———. No. 140, December 1, 1972.

———. No. 401, July 20, 2001.

———. No. 45, 2002.

———. No. 301, May 8, 2002.

Muntean, Ana, et al. *Victimele violentei domestice: copiii si femeile* (The Victims of Domestic Violence: Children and Women). Timisoara: Editura Eurostampa, 2002.

Popescu, Livia, and Maria Roth. "Variabila gen in analiza dezvoltarii umane din Romania" ("Gender variable in the human development analysis in Romania"). In *Prezente feminine: Studii despre femei in Romania* (Female Occurrences. Women's Studies in Romania), edited by G. Cosma, E. Magyari-Vincze, and O. Pecican, 453–77. Cluj: Editura Fundatiei Desire, 2002.

Programul Natiunilor Unite pentru Dezvoltare in Romania (PNUD), Comisia Nationala de Statistica — CNS. *Femeile si barbatii in Romania* (Women and Men in Romania). Bucuresti: PNUD, 2000.

Zamfir, Elena. "Politica de protectie a copilului in Romania" ("The Child Protection Policy in Romania"). In *Politici Sociale: Romania in Context European* (Social Policies: Romania in European Context), edited by E. Zamfir and C. Zamfir, 200–244. Bucuresti: Editura Alternative, 1995.

31

RUSSIA

Carol Nechemias

PROFILE OF RUSSIA

Russia is both an old and a new country, with schoolchildren tracing their history to the founding of Rus', as it was called in the eighth century. Yet the contemporary Russian state is of recent vintage, formed in 1991 as the result of the breakup of the USSR. This new Russian state faced daunting economic and political challenges: the dismantlement of a centralized, socialist economy coupled with the construction of a market economy; and the establishment of a pluralist, democratic political system after decades of communist rule. The collapse of communism was arguably the most significant political event that closed out the twentieth century, and the ongoing effort to build a market economy and a democratic state forms one of the major dramas of the new millennium.

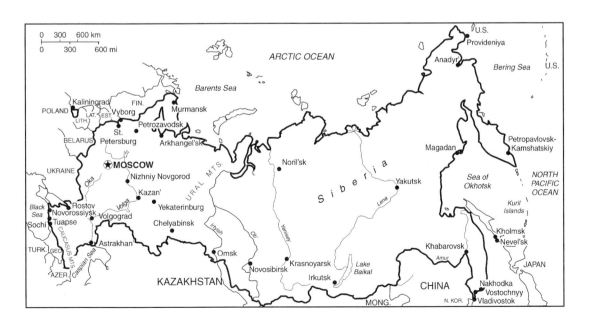

Ethnic Russians make up about 80 percent of the population of Russia, with no other nationality representing more than 4 percent of the population. Many of the smaller ethnic groups are Muslim, whereas Russians are overwhelmingly Russian Orthodox by tradition. Despite the greater ethnic homogeneity than in the former Soviet Union, nationality issues remain. Russia's form of government, a federation, formally recognizes ethnicity as an important organizing principle of statehood. The country's official name is the Russian Federation, and many of its subnational administrative units represent "homelands" for particular ethnic minorities.[1]

Russia is suffering a population decline unprecedented for an urbanized, literate population during peacetime: mortality rates soared in the 1990s, reaching 14.7 per 1,000 persons in 1999, and the birthrate was 8.4 per 1,000. Russia's population has consequently declined since the 1991 Soviet collapse from 148 million to 144 million in 2002. To sustain the population at current levels, fertility would need to reach 2.15 births per woman, but as of 1999 the fertility rate was only 1.17.[2] Demographic concerns reflect sharp gender differences: figures for 1999 show life expectancy for women at 72 years and 4 months and for men, 59 years and 9 months.[3] Mortality rates for men aged 40 to 44 climbed from 7.6 per 1,000 in 1990 to 15.2 in 1995. The fate of middle-aged men figured prominently in discussions of the health issues associated with the demographic crisis.

With the period of *glasnost* or greater openness that emerged under Gorbachev in the late 1980s came shocking revelations about high Soviet maternal and infant mortality rates. These issues have not disappeared: maternal mortality in 1996 was 49 per 100,000 births, eight to ten times higher than in developed European countries; and infant mortality in 1994 was 18.6 per 1,000 births, again far above average by Western European and U.S. standards.

OVERVIEW OF WOMEN'S ISSUES

The post-Soviet era ushered in sweeping change for women's lives. A backlash against communism led many to reject its conception of "women's emancipation" as part of a discredited past. Calls for a return to women's "natural mission" as wives and mothers became common.[4] Women's position in the economy deteriorated as women predominated in lower-paid, public sector positions and continue to make up roughly 70 percent of the officially unemployed. Public support systems like pensions, child allowances, free health care, daycare, and children's summer camps eroded and in many cases collapsed. In the political arena, women virtually disappeared and were excluded from high-level decision making. The road to capitalism included increased violence against women, the sexualization of women's images in advertising and the mass media, the trafficking of young women, and a flood of pornography. Reproductive rights were limited due to a lack of access to modern contraception; abortion has remained, as it was under communism, the primary mode of controlling fertility and spacing children.

On the other hand, after seventy years of communist rule women enjoyed the freedom to organize and to speak out, to form a plethora of organizations that allow women to act on behalf of women, and to pursue and defend women's rights. Thus a nascent women's movement emerged that promised to give a voice to women in Russian society.

EDUCATION

Opportunities

When the Bolsheviks came to power in 1917, they saw women's entrance into the work force as the key to women's equality. Education received a high priority as a means of preparing women for working lives and for raising their political consciousness. On the eve of World War II, women had increased their share of enrollments in higher education to 43 percent. By the mid-1970s, women constituted 50 percent of students in higher education; and by the mid-1990s women formed the majority, at 55 percent, of higher education students.

Whereas there are gender patterns with respect to type of degree, these patterns differ from those found in Western countries. The communist regime encouraged women to study technology and agronomy, to become skilled workers contributing to the building of a socialist state. Western observers often expressed surprise at women's educational attainment: by the close of the Soviet era, women were 33 percent of the country's engineers, 70 percent of the physicians, 38 percent of the agronomists and veterinarians, 40 percent of the academics, and 65 percent of the economists.[5] Yet stereotypical gender patterns do exist. For example, higher education enrollments for 1996–1997 show that women accounted for 87 percent of the students studying to become teachers, 74 percent of the students in culture and the arts, 30 percent of enrollees in the information sciences, and 16 percent in aviation and rocketry.[6]

Nearly 20 percent of Russian women between the ages of twenty and forty-nine have completed a higher education level and, more significantly, are better educated than their male peers.[7] In Russia boys are deemed the ones who are shortchanged and somewhat alienated from school. They receive lower grades than girls, in the sciences as well as the humanities, and they exhibit far more problems like dropping out, failing a grade, or violating behavioral norms like skipping school, smoking, and stealing. During the Soviet era, girls and young women were much more likely to hold leadership positions than their male counterparts in the Pioneers, a mass organization for children, and in Komsomol, the Young Communist

League. Some Russian scholars blame the school atmosphere for boys' problems, calling the educational system too "feminized" due to the heavy predominance of women teachers who, it is argued, favor girls because they are less trouble.

Although women achieved high levels of formal education, there are several features of Soviet and post-Soviet education of significance for women. First, the content of education stressed natural and immutable differences between men and women, reinforcing the traditional idea that the central feature of women's lives involved nurturing children and creating a cozy home.[8] The images of women in children's readers promoted the mother-worker: a woman who combined workplace participation with traditional homemaker roles. Secondly, from the late 1920s through the late 1980s, women (and men) were taught that women's emancipation counted among communism's accomplishments, and that the "woman question," as it had historically been referred to in Russia, was solved.

Women in Russia seized the educational opportunities available to them and succeeded in a wide variety of educational fields. Yet, educational advantage did not translate into pay equity or access to leading positions in the economy or political system. Since women had officially achieved equality with men, women attracted little attention as a scholarly category, with the important exception of demographic issues related to women's roles as producers and reproducers. Indeed, key feminist works like Simone de Beauvoir's *The Second Sex* were banned by state censorship. In post-Soviet Russia, women's studies with its potential to empower women slowly emerged and established a small foothold in the educational system. Although the educational system as a whole continued to offer women substantial opportunity for professional training, it also failed to offer a feminist critique of society.

Literacy

Thus, under communism educational opportunity for women dramatically improved. As the result of a government campaign to wipe out illiteracy and expand educational opportunity, the proportion of girls among secondary school students approached 50 percent in the 1930s. Literacy rates increased rapidly, and the gap between men and women closed: between 1926 and 1939, the literacy rates for males between the ages of nine and forty-nine rose from 71.5 percent to 93.5 percent, and for females the comparable figures are 42.7 percent and 81.6 percent.[9] Contemporary Russian women have literacy rates close to 100 percent and are strikingly well educated by international standards.

EMPLOYMENT AND THE ECONOMY

Job/Career Opportunities

The communist past remains a powerful influence on patterns of women's labor force participation in the postcommunist era. Women's current employment situation is rooted in the watershed years of the 1930s. That decade witnessed Stalin's rapid industrialization and the collectivization of agriculture, and a staunch government campaign calling on women to leave their homes and join the work force. In particular there was a demand, succinctly captured in the official slogan "Women to the factories," for industrial labor. World War II reenforced the demand for women's labor, not just during the war but afterwards: the loss of 20 million citizens,

disproportionately male, ensured an intense demand for women workers in a wide variety of fields. Moreover, the centrally planned economy relied on a large work force rather than on a high degree of labor productivity.

By the 1970s Soviet labor force participation rates for women ranked first in the world. Women formed over half the labor force, and 90 percent of working-age women either worked or were students. Employment meant full-time work, as part-time positions were vir-

Street sellers, Moscow, Russia. Photo © TRIP/B. Turner.

tually unknown under communism. Women on average took only 3.6 years off from work to have their families.[10] Thus the bulk of Russian women had no firsthand knowledge of being full-time housewives.

There was a strong stress on the moral obligation to work: a "good" Soviet citizen, male or female, was a member of the work force. High labor force participation rates were presented as a prime indicator of women's emancipation. This did not mean that men and women were considered identical or interchangeable. The image of the ideal woman was that of the mother-worker who took her place in the socialist economy without abandoning her traditional roles of mother and homemaker. The Soviet state developed social policies to assist women in combining their roles as mothers and workers. These included daycare, free health care, and children's summer camps. Only rarely were men called on to shoulder more of the burden on the home front.

This legacy of heavy work force participation separates the Russian experience from that of the West. The Russian context also produced distinctive patterns of work force participation. The 1930s drew women into many traditionally male fields of work in industry and in physical labor. These patterns linger: in 1989, 56 percent of working women in Russia were engaged in physical work compared to 11 percent of their U.S. counterparts.[11] Work that is frequently mechanized in the West, like milking cows, often involved laborious physical labor in Russia. In 1995 women constituted 40 percent of industrial workers; the comparable figures for agriculture and construction were, respectively, 34 percent and 23 percent.[12]

At the same time, however, other job categories grew increasingly feminized. By the 1990s, 80 percent of workers in trade and catering were female; the figures for education, health, credit and finance, and the state bureaucracy, were, respectively, 77, 85, 87, and 69 percent.[13] Nearly 100 percent of clerical workers were female. The medical profession became "feminized" in the 1930s as the Soviet Union built its system of socialized medicine, rapidly expanded opportunities for medical training, and lowered the pay relative to that of average wages. Although the high proportion of women physicians frequently was cited as an example of women's professional achievement, women doctors in Russia received relatively low salaries and ranked low with respect to prestige and prerogatives.

Pay

Sex segregation in the work force coupled with outright sex discrimination accounted for a familiar finding—a substantial gender gap in earnings. Both the Soviet Union and the Russian Federation embraced the principle of equal pay for equal work. But the greatest progress toward pay equity occurred during the 1920s, the first decade after the Bolshevik Revolution, when the gap between women's and men's earnings closed from less than 50 percent to 66 percent.[14] Further improvement occurred more slowly, with women earning roughly 70 percent as much as men by the close of the Soviet era.

That gap rested upon several factors, including women's lower skill levels, low relative pay for "women's work," and outright sex discrimination. In industry, men employed in manual work were more skilled and more highly paid, whereas women's physical labor remained heavy, low paid, and low status. The number of unskilled women workers was twice as high as that of men.[15] Women's skill grades were lower than men's in every branch of industry, women were far less likely to improve their skills due to the "double burden" of housework and childcare, and managers exhibited little interest in career development for their women employees. Within industry, the more female dominated the occupation, the lower were the average rates of pay.[16] Outside of industry, in feminized sectors like health, culture, and education, average wages ranged between 53 and 78 percent of average industrial earnings.

According to UN statistics, the gender gap in pay remained stable in the post-Soviet era, with women earning about 70 percent of men's earnings. It should be noted, however, that the Moscow Center for Gender Studies, established in the late 1980s as the first academic research unit focusing on gender issues, estimated that women's wages dropped to 40 percent of men's wages during the initial years of the post-Soviet transition. The reliability of economic statistics on phenomena like earnings and unemployment are difficult to assess due to the widespread hiding of income for tax purposes and of unreported, informal economic activities.

Working Conditions

Despite their formal educational credentials and high labor force participation, opportunities for upward mobility for women were limited during the Soviet era. A glass ceiling kept the numbers of women in leading economic positions low. At the close of the communist era, only 5.6 percent of USSR managers were female, while the figure for Russia was 6.5 percent. Even in female-dominated areas, men enjoyed an advantage. Although women made up 70 percent of doctors, they constituted only 6 percent of surgeons and 50 percent of chief physicians and executives of medical institutes. Similarly, in the field of education women made up 83 percent of teachers but only 39 percent of head teachers. Women particularly fared poorly in the largest political, economic, and cultural centers of the country, constituting only 3.5 percent of managers in St. Petersburg (formerly Leningrad) and 4.2 percent in Moscow.[17]

Fears of runaway unemployment proved unfounded as privatization of the economy proceeded. In January 1995, for example, unemployment reached 8.4 percent of the work force, with another 6 percent on compulsory unpaid leave or only partially paid leave.[18] But women bore the brunt of job loss: from 1990 to 1995, women lost 7 million jobs compared to 1–2 million for men. In big cities like Moscow and St. Petersburg, women made up 60–70 percent of the officially registered unemployed. Nonetheless, the high initial female employment rates meant that high labor force participation rates were maintained: 75 percent of women aged sixteen to fifty-four were economically active in 1996 compared to 80 percent of men, a relatively small gender gap.[19]

Yet there is reason to believe that women have not seized the new opportunities offered by the market economy to the same extent as their male counterparts. Labor force statistics showed that men were more likely to join cooperatives and work in the private sector. Women disproportionately remained in sectors of the economy funded by state budgets like education and health care, and they lagged behind in entrepreneurship. A survey of fourteen of Russia's eighty-nine regions revealed that women headed 18 percent of small enterprises, defined as employing between five and 100 people.[20] Women were particularly active in trade and catering, frequently operating small kiosks. As in the Soviet era, they have been shut out of top managerial positions in large-scale enterprises, a fact recognized by Russians who hold university degrees, 70 percent of whom consider that men enjoy a privileged position in pursuing careers.[21]

Controversy over women's labor force participation waned by the late 1990s as economic necessity rendered mute the idea that women could return home. Indeed, survey research demonstrated that women possessed similar commitments to work as men, although a substantial proportion would opt for part-time work if that were economically feasible.[22] The economic hardships of the 1990s apparently shifted public opinion toward an appreciation for the value of work in women's lives. A survey taken in 1995 and repeated in 2001 demonstrated that Russians from all demographic groups became significantly more likely to name a good job over a successful marriage as a priority for an actual or would-be teenage daughter. Over a six-year period, the respective priorities shifted from 46 percent to 27 percent favoring a successful marriage and from 36 percent to 64 percent mentioning a good job.[23] Greater support for women's careers thus emerged on the heels of a backlash against the "emancipated" woman.

Sexual Harassment

Women in postcommunist Russia faced new challenges in pursuing employment and careers. Although sexual harassment was a problem under communism, the issue intensified in the "anything goes" atmosphere that equated freedom with lawlessness, with the right to do anything you please. Advertisements sometimes included the term *bez kompleksov*, or "without inhibitions," meaning that sleeping with the boss is part of the job description.[24] Although Article 118 of the Russian Federation Criminal Code provides punishment of up to three years for taking advantage of job status to coerce someone into having sexual relations, it has been extraordinarily rare for charges to be brought. Moreover, the issue has been treated with silence or occasionally with ridicule, as a shining example of how political correctness and feminism have been carried to an extreme in the United States. Efforts to address sexual harassment have been fragmentary and dependent on the support of Western foundations. With the assistance of Western foundations, women's rights activists held a seminar in Moscow in 1995 on the topic of sexual harassment. That session resulted in the publication of a book, *Seksyal'nye domogatel'stva na rabota* (*Sexual Harassment at Work*), in an edition of 1,100 copies. This volume provided individuals and organizations committed to addressing the problem of sexual harassment with a key resource.

Support for Mothers/Caretakers

The postcommunist transition introduced new wrinkles in women's employment issues. First, the backlash against communism led to challenges to the longstanding communist assumption that "women's emancipation" was closely tied to women's work force participation. In 1987 then–General Secretary Mikhail Gorbachev expressed this "new thinking":

we failed to pay attention to women's specific rights and needs arising from their role as mother and home-maker, and their indispensable educational function as regards children. Engaged in scientific research, working on construction sites . . . women no longer have enough time to perform their everyday duties at home—housework, the upbringing of children and the creation of a good family atmosphere. We have discovered that many of our problems—in children's and young people's behavior, in our morals, culture and in production—are partially caused by the weakening of family ties and slack attitude to family responsibilities. This is a paradoxical result of our sincere and politically justified desire to make women equal with men in everything. Now, in the course of *perestroika*, we have begun to overcome this shortcoming. That is why we are now holding heated debates . . . about the question of what we should do to make it possible for women to return to their purely womanly mission.[25]

This "send the women back home" theme proved popular well into the 1990s. Politicians and journalists called for the removal of women from "unfeminine work," for paying men more so women could remain home, and for passing legislation to reduce the work week of mothers with children under age fourteen to thirty-five hours per week. This legislative measure would have cut women's earnings, and it ultimately failed to pass the Russian Supreme Soviet in 1992. Some democratic and reform-minded leaders noted that in "civilized" countries women's labor force participation rates were lower than in Russia, and they therefore believed that the process of joining the "civilized" world signaled the desirability of reducing women's labor force involvement. For nationalists, there was an emphasis on women renewing their traditional roles as wives and mothers. For many women, emancipation—the equal right to swing the hammer—represented a failed concept, exhaustion, and a life akin to that of a draft animal. For proponents of market reform, fear of high unemployment generated pressure to drive women from the work force. As Russia's Minister of Labor Gennady Melikian put it in a February 1993 press conference, "Why should we employ women when men are unemployed? It's better that men work and women take care of children."[26]

With the transition to a market economy, female labor force participation dropped, although the rates remained high by international standards. The decline in employment was concentrated among women in two distinct age categories, women aged fifty to fifty-five and women aged twenty to twenty-four. The legal age for retirement for women is fifty-five, and it appeared that the older age group took on greater childcare responsibilities for grandchildren as families coped with cutbacks in free or highly subsidized daycare. For women in the younger group, labor force participation rates declined by 12 percent from 1989 to 1996 compared to a 6 percent decline for young men. About one quarter of the decline for women could be explained by higher enrollment in education, but the rest reflected reduced opportunities for employment for young women, a problem accentuated by changes in social policy that discourage employers from hiring women of childbearing age.[27]

Maternal Leave

Russia inherited from the Soviet Union an array of policies designed to protect motherhood and ease the quandaries associated with combining traditional familial roles with work force. These policies typically became more generous over time. By 1998 the main features of maternity leave included 140 days of leave from work paid at 100 percent of the last wage. There are a series of "privileges" traditionally granted to mothers: women cannot be refused work or dismissed from work due to pregnancy, women with children up to age three cannot be fired from the workplace, women are guaranteed the right to return to their position after completing parental leave; women who are pregnant or have children under the age of fourteen can request part-time work, women with two or more children under the age of fourteen can receive an extra fourteen days of unpaid leave to look after their children, and pregnant women can request a transfer to easier work and are banned from night work. Many of these measures were made available to fathers beginning in 1999.

Parental leave, taken after maternity leave expires, was revised in 1991 to include members of the family other than just the mother—the father as well as a grandparent can exercise this right. Paid parental leave extends for a year and a half, with the option of an additional year and a half of unpaid leave. However, prevailing social attitudes and economic realities—on average, women earn 70 percent of men's wages—dictate that parental leave and other "privileges" are overwhelmingly taken by women. Fathers take less than 1 percent of parental leaves. There is considerable debate among Russian feminists concerning support for many of the "protections" granted working women. This debate centers on whether protective policies and privileges foster discrimination against women in the market economy and reflect patriarchal attitudes that treat women, along with children and the handicapped, as the special wards of state policy.

Russian policy traditionally promoted women's equality through differential or protective treatment. This approach includes pensions: the legal age of retirement for women is fifty-five, and for men, sixty. Moreover, men must work at least twenty-five years to receive a full retirement pension, and women only twenty years. The "separate but equal" retirement ages take into account women's unpaid labor within the household. Unfortunately, however, state income support, whether in the form of pensions, family allowances, or aid to single mothers, suffers from a severe lack of funds, with benefit levels falling below subsistence and the delivery of benefits falling behind schedule. This financial crisis spurred an as yet unresolved political debate over how to reform welfare policies, with a key issue involving whether scarce resources should be shifted away from universal programs toward a system based on need.

Daycare

The advent of privatization led to the demise of many of these benefits. Childcare became expensive: between 1989 and 1997, the percent of children aged 3–6 enrolled in kindergartens declined from 78 to 65 between 1989 and 1997; the comparable figures for children aged zero to two in nurseries were 37 and 20 percent.[28]

Social/Government Programs

Article 19 of the Russian Constitution guarantees, "Men and women shall have equal rights and freedoms and equal opportunities to exercise them." Women have achieved "declarative equality"—equality on paper—but, historically, legal guidelines did not play a central role in shaping Russian realities. Women thus face the challenge of promoting the implementation of laws that already exist, laws that guarantee social security in old age, free preschools and health care, and equal opportunity. Unless social consciousness undergoes a transformation, however, discrimination in the workplace will pass largely unrecognized, shrugged off as the "natural" result of women's preference for subordinating career goals to motherhood or for "women's" work that is painstaking and careful like catering and garment making.

Welfare

The key work-related issue for women involves the erosion of the Soviet social contract, the provision of extensive social and welfare services. Although workers often received low wages and encountered poor working conditions, labor force participation carried with it a number of perks: workplaces often provided housing, childcare, summer camps for children, health care, and opportunities to purchase items in short supply in Soviet society. In the new market economy, women appear as more expensive and therefore less attractive employees than men, and the cutbacks in work-related social services complicate women's ability to combine work with household responsibilities.

FAMILY AND SEXUALITY

Gender Roles

In the closing decades of communist rule, a variety of views about sex roles were expressed in the popular press and in academic literature. Overall, however, Soviet society increasingly emphasized biological distinctions and natural differences between men and women and drew attention to the idea that equality between the sexes did not mean identity. There were complaints about how Soviet society had "masculinized" women and "feminized" men, and how there was a need for a corrective. This discussion did not take place in a vacuum but stemmed from the desire to address the soaring divorce rates and falling birthrates among the European (Slavic and Baltic) nationalities of the Soviet Union.

In 1984 the Soviet Union introduced a new course, "The Ethics and Psychology of Family Life," designed to teach students about their special male and female roles.[29] The class targeted teenagers—ninth and tenth graders—and met for two hours per week. Pupils learned that boys should be "honest, responsible, intelligent, brave, decisive, noble; he should possess self-control, a love of work, a readiness to defend the weak and take on himself the most difficult and demanding jobs."[30] In contrast, girls received the message that women should be feminine—kind, soft, tender, thoughtful, modest, sensitive, loyal, intelligent, of high moral character, committed first and foremost to her family and home, and skilled housekeepers. Motherhood and family life were treated as women's great mission, and teachers were advised to inform pupils that the one-child family, so common to the European nationalities, did not constitute a true collective and resulted in anxiety-ridden parents and selfish children.[31]

In post-Soviet Russia, discourse about gender roles often reflects these more traditional emphases. There is a concern that communism distorted the "natural" roles of men and women and considerable lamentation that present socioeconomic conditions do not provide the conditions in which women are either able or willing to have children and thus fulfill their primary destiny in life. In addition, there are new images of women associated with the marketization of the economy. Sexual freedom became equated with freedom but in a manner that focused on male fantasies and male fulfillment rather than on women's needs. Femininity is more sexualized, with seductive images of women used widely to sell products and in the entertainment industry. Beauty contests boomed as well as new TV programs in which women demonstrated "feminine" skills like cooking. New versions of the Cinderella story appeared as many Russian women answered personal ads placed by foreigners looking for Russian wives, or dreamt of careers as models or even as prostitutes.[32]

Marriage

Under communism, marriage in Russia was nearly universal and occurred at a relatively young age. The average age of women at first marriage was 22–23 years of age and remained in that range through the 1990s. Childbearing took place among young couples, and the share of single-parent families stood at a stable 13 percent for the time period from the early 1970s to 1989,[33] in contrast to the steady growth of such households in the West. Divorce rates were among the highest in the world, but re-marriage rates after divorce were higher than in the West. Cohabitation was rare. Marriage codes stressed equality between husbands and wives, the ease of marriage and divorce, and the civil registration of marriage, and other policies encouraged marriage by providing a range of benefits from lower taxes to better access to housing.

Since 1989 several trends in family formation are evident. Birthrates have dropped sharply, marriage rates are down, divorce rates remain high, the share of teenage births and births outside of marriage increased, and the proportion of single-parent households rose. Nearly six out of ten marriages end in divorce, with one third of divorces requested by couples married less than five years. The primary cause of divorce involves male alcoholism. Custodial parents are overwhelmingly women, and more than half of children do not receive child support and average payments are in arrears. The percentage of single-parent (mother) households rose to 25 percent by 1997.[34]

It is unclear whether these emerging trends result from economic hardship and might be reversed by economic recovery, or whether a more fundamental change in lifestyles is occurring. In other areas, there is more continuity than change. Like the Soviet era, marriage codes—a new family code was adopted in 1995—stress equal rights for spouses. The new code approaches sex roles from a gender neutral perspective, noting that spouses must materially support one another and that each is free to choose work and decide where to live. The code emphasizes the principle that internal family matters should be decided on the basis of mutual consensus and equality between the spouses. However, as in the past declarative statements about equality are undermined by inequality within the private sphere. Women continue to perform the bulk of childcare and domestic chores, with time-budget studies demonstrating that men spend less time than women on housework and have more free time.

Reproduction

Terms like family planning (*planirovanie sem'i*) and reproductive rights (*reproduktivnye prava*) are new and poorly understood concepts in Russia.

Traditional rhetoric spoke of tireless concern for mother and child, and of the protection of motherhood.

Nonmarital births skyrocketed from 14 to 33 percent from 1989 to 2000.[35] Only about five percent of single mothers (divorced, widowed, or never married) live with a partner, a low figure by Western standards. Growing numbers of single mothers reside with their parents; and among children born outside of marriage, only about half of the fathers registered themselves as a parent of the child. These trends stem in part from the larger share of first-borns, who are more likely to be born to single mothers: from 1989 to 1997, the proportion of first-borns among all births rose from 46 to 59 percent.[36]

Sex Education

Fundamental aspects of reproductive rights like access to information did not exist during the Soviet era, and recent efforts to introduce sex education programs in the schools met stiff political opposition. Despite a $750,000 grant from the UN Population Fund to develop a sex education program for Russian schoolchildren, opposition from nationalist, communist, and Russian Orthodox forces succeeded in derailing plans to introduce sex education on a broad scale within the public school system. These groups do favor programs that discuss family life minus issues related to sexual intimacy, a position reminiscent of the Soviet era family life courses. As Alevtina Aparina, a Communist Party deputy and chair of the State Duma Committee on Women, Family, and Youth Affairs, put it, sex education programs that teach "safe sex" are "in reality aimed at destroying morality, corrupting children, and reducing birth rates in our country."[37]

Contraception and Abortion

The use of modern contraceptives remains low: the Russian Association of Family Planning (RAFP), founded in 1991, concludes that 23.5 percent of women use modern methods, with intrauterine devices accounting for 19.8 percent and oral contraceptives 3.7 percent.[38] A large proportion of women rely on the rhythm method and on withdrawal. For decades there has been one basic means of birth control available to Russian women—abortion. Russia's abortion rate is the highest in the world, standing at 69 per 1,000 women aged 15–49, a sharp contrast with that of Finland, 8 per 1,000 women, and Holland, 5 per 1,000 women.[39] In Russia two abortions occur for every live birth, and the average Russian woman has experienced five abortions in her lifetime.[40] Abortions in Russia frequently are done in crude, assembly-line fashion where modern medical equipment and hygienic conditions are substandard.

After briefly funding family planning efforts in the early to mid-1990s, the Russian government eliminated federal funding for that purpose as political opposition to such programs grew. Yet experts point to the multiple numbers of abortions undergone by a large proportion of Russian women as a leading factor behind chronic infections and widespread infertility. The pursuit of pro-natalist policies has fueled growing political opposition to the reproductive rights movement. This factor, along with a culture long used to regarding abortion as the fundamental means of birth control, and problems regarding the availability and the cost of modern contraception, generate a plethora of obstacles that cloud the future of women's reproductive rights.

Teen Pregnancy

The greater share of first-borns to single mothers (59 percent of all births in 1997) is associated with the growing perception that there is a teen pregnancy problem. Adolescent fertility declined in Russia from roughly fifty births per 1,000 women aged 15–19 in 1989 to thirty-five births per 1,000 in 1998. However, birthrates have fallen more rapidly among other groups, and thus the share of teen births has not only risen but also increasingly occurs outside of marriage.[41]

HEALTH

Health Care Access

Russia is facing a health care crisis. The severe underfunding of the state health care system, the failure to develop alternative ways of providing health care, and the poverty of the population led to an increased emphasis on private care service and to large segments of the population being denied even the most basic medical care. In Russia the percent of people reporting that they were unable to obtain prescribed medicines due to their high cost rose from 23 percent in 1994 to 48 percent in 1996.[42] "Poverty diseases" like diphtheria and tuberculosis that had largely disappeared under communism reemerged, the incidence of venereal diseases like syphilis increased sharply, and new diseases like HIV/AIDS pose challenges to an overburdened public health care system.

Diseases and Disorders

There are gender dimensions to health care issues in Russia. Put most succinctly, women get sick but men die. What has grabbed the most public attention is the surge in deaths among working-aged men: male life expectancy fell from sixty-four in 1989 to fifty-eight by 1993, an unheard-of development in modern times in the absence of a war. The increase in male mortality stems from rising levels of heart disease, alcohol poisoning, murder, suicide, and various types of accidents. Male rates of alcohol consumption and cigarette smoking are among the highest in the world. For women, health care issues focus on women as mothers, on maternal health and infant mortality. The maternal mortality rate is roughly fifty maternal deaths per 100,000 live births, a figure far higher than that of Western Europe. The percentage of births labeled "complicated" soared from 1989 to 1997: the most common problem involved anemia, which figured in 23 percent of births. Given the government's concern with low birthrates and a falling population, women's reproductive health constitutes a major priority in health care planning for the Putin administration.

It is unclear, however, whether targeting women's reproductive health will include a push to improve access to modern contraception. But political opposition to federally funded family planning efforts in the early to mid-1990s influenced the Russian government to eliminate the budget. The health of the large proportion of Russian women who have multiple numbers of abortions indicate it as a forceful cause of chronic infections and widespread infertility. Some Western aid is targeted on improving women's health and developing new, integrated models for women's health care that emphasize public education and disease prevention.

AIDS

Although the numbers of HIV/AIDS cases were officially regarded as rather low in the early 1990s, the incidence of HIV/AIDS has since skyrocketed in Russia. This swift expansion of HIV appears related primarily to intravenous drug users, a relatively rare problem before the early 1990s. These drug users are concentrated among youth aged 15–24. Efforts to promote safe sex and safe drug use are in their initial stages and are complicated by the absence of sex education in the schools.

Eating Disorders

Diseases that are prominent in the West, like eating disorders and cervical and breast cancer, receive far less attention in Russia. During the communist era, the "ideal" body type for girls and women reflected a more full-bodied image than the "thin is better" approach that has been characteristic of the West in recent decades. During the 1990s, however, Western-style advertising and the popularity of supermodels may introduce changes in the culture that ultimately generate more eating disorders. Ads for "body shaping" have emerged as a new type of capitalist enterprise; overall, marketing may well convince girls and women that everything about their bodies needs to be improved or fixed.

Cancer

Breast cancer rates appear much lower than in the United States, but most women are not diagnosed until the disease is at an advanced stage.

Western assistance efforts targeted on women's health frequently have focused on modern mammography equipment and teaching breast self-examination as means of reducing mortality from breast cancer.

Depression

Studies of mental health problems show marked gender differences. By their teenage years, girls are more likely than boys to self-report feelings and symptoms like depression and anxiety.[43] Mental health problems tend to differ for women and men: for women, depression, posttraumatic stress disorders, and Alzheimer's and other dementia loom large; for men, alcohol and drug dependence and self-inflicted injuries form the major categories of mental health problems. Although women traditionally have exhibited higher incidence rates of depressive disorder, there is nonetheless a widespread belief in Russian society that women have handled the stresses associated with the postcommunist transition better than men, who demonstrate a far greater tendency to engage in self-destructive forms of behavior.

POLITICS AND LAW

Suffrage

The Bolshevik Revolution of 1917 led to women gaining the right to vote and the right to hold elective office.

Political Participation

From 1919 to 1930, the Communist Party, operating through a special women's section (*Zhenotdel*) within the Party's Secretariat, sought to promote women's political consciousness and activism and draw more women into the party. In 1929, however, the party declared the "woman question" solved: for the rest of the Soviet era, the communist regime pointed to women's emancipation as one of its great achievements.

Women form a majority of the electorate, yet their distinctiveness as a voting bloc has faded with the 1995 decline in the electoral fortunes of the all-women electoral bloc, Women of Russia; the divisiveness among women's organizations; and the absence of a gender gap in voting behavior, especially in the 1999 parliamentary election. The major political parties, with the exception of Zhirinovsky's Liberal Democratic Party, an extreme nationalist group despite the name, all draw strong support among women. Major political figures and parties need not fear a "women's vote" and show little interest in developing platforms that address women's status in Russian society.[44]

Under communism, women's political participation served propaganda and symbolic purposes. Women's presence in the political arena was con-centrated in legislative bodies called *soviets* (councils). One third of the members of the last USSR Supreme Soviet, "elected" in 1984, were women; higher proportions of women served in lower-level legislatures. The large numbers of women's deputies serving in soviets did not mean that women walked the halls of power. The USSR Supreme Soviet was an institution that provided the façade but not the substance of democracy. Its members were nominated to run in noncompetitive elections in accor-dance with rough quotas established by the Communist Party for groups like workers, peasants, and women; it met only a few days a year; its members did not give up their full-time jobs; and the Supreme Soviet dutifully and unanimously passed decisions that had already been made elsewhere. The stereotypical woman deputy was a milkmaid or textile worker.

In the final decades of Soviet power, scholars utilized membership in the Central Committee of the Communist Party (CCCPSU) as a key in-dicator of having achieved elite status in the Soviet political system. Women never represented more than 3 to 4 percent of the CC member-ship, although they formed roughly one third of rank and file party mem-bers. Similarly, women rarely gained ministerial office, and when they did it was invariably in ministries connected with "women's sphere" like social security, culture, education, and health care.

After the fall of communism, the proportion of women deputies in the national legislature fell at the same moment that its power increased. In 1989 Mikhail Gorbachev introduced a new institution, the Congress of People's Deputies (CPD), designed to become a real, working parliament with considerable political clout[45] The bulk of its members were chosen through competitive elections. Women fared poorly, securing 17 percent of the seats compared to 33 percent in the old Supreme Soviet. Their num-bers sank to a dismal 4 percent in the 1990 Russian republic election, when the idea of reserving seats for public organizations, including the Soviet Women's Committee, was jettisoned. Women's representation temporarily rebounded to 13.5 percent in 1993, facilitated by a newly introduced national party list ballot and the surprising success of the all-women electoral bloc Women of Russia, which secured 8 percent of the party list vote.

Women of Russia emphasized the slogan "Women of Russia—for Rus-sia" and stressed the populist goal of restoring social benefits. Its primary organizational base involved the Union of Women of Russia, the direct successor of the old-line Soviet organization, the Soviet Women's Com-mittee. Its origins in the top-down politics of the communist past meant that it was regarded with suspicion by new, independent organizations, particularly the feminist ones that sprang up in post-Soviet Russia.

Failing to widen its support, Women of Russia did not clear the 5 per-cent barrier necessary to gain some of the 225 proportional representation seats available in the elections held in 1995 and 1999, and women's share of seats in the Duma fell from 13.5 percent to 10.2 percent and then to 7.5

percent. Following the 1995 election, Women of Russia ruptured into two groups, with the new organization taking on the strikingly similar name of the All-Russian Socio-Political Movement Women of Russia. The latter group placed greater emphasis on democratic reform and on advancing women's rights, although the label "feminist" is generally avoided.

As in the communist era, few women reach the top levels of the executive branch, estimated at 4 percent in the mid-1990s. And the few women who do achieve high positions remain clustered in areas connected with social policy, health care, and culture.[46]

Women's Rights

Under communism, there was no freedom of association, but state-sponsored mass organizations did exist. For women, there was the Soviet Women's Committee (SWC), an elite organization for most of its history with no links to rank and file Soviet women. In the wake of the break up of the Soviet Union, the SWC registered itself as a nongovernmental organization, the Union of Women of Russia (UWR). It has survived as one of the major networks of women's organizations. The UWR is headed by Alevtina Fedulova, who is regarded with suspicion by some independent women's groups due to her extensive background as a Communist Party functionary. The UWR pursues political activism as the key organization behind the electoral bloc Women of Russia. Tensions revolve around perceptions that the UWR represents a top-down organization that wishes to present itself as the manifestation of the women's movement in Russia.

A group of independent women's organizations came together at the First Independent Women's Forum held in Dubna, near Moscow, in 1991, and they ultimately formed a women's network that is more feminist in orientation and leery of hierarchical relationships. Other networks include the All-Russian Socio-Political Movement Women of Russia, RAFP, the Association of Crisis Centers, the Consortium of Women's Organizations, and the Committees of Soldiers' Mothers. Hundreds of women's organizations were founded, though many have ceased their activities due to a lack of key resources like a phone line and office space. Although some of these organizations are concerned with advancing women's rights and engaging in policy advocacy, many women's groups eschew women's rights rhetoric and focus on issues like helping families with many children, families headed by single parents, or families with handicapped children. There also are professional women's organizations involving women entrepreneurs, women journalists, and women police officers.

Feminist Movements

A diverse women's movement has emerged but remains rather weak, particularly with respect to women's consciousness. Most women do not perceive that women are discriminated against and reject feminism as an extreme position denoting hatred of men and/or lesbianism.

The Soviet Union was a signatory to the United Nations Convention on Elimination of All Forms of Discrimination against Women (CEDAW), an obligation the Russian Federation has assumed. The UN World Conference on Women held in Beijing in 1995 stimulated a series of valuable seminars and contacts among women's organizations and between women's groups and the Russian state.[47] Women activists employ UN documents to prod the Russian state to produce research on women's status and plans on how to advance gender equality. Implementation of these plans, however, remains another matter.

Finding domestic sources of financial support are difficult in contemporary Russian society. Moreover, there are concerns that aid from Western governments and foundations distorts the agendas of local women's organizations and rewards groups that possess the skills associated with grant writing and the ability to manipulate the rhetoric of the international women's movement.[48]

Lesbian Rights

Lesbian rights represent an aspect of the women's movement in the West that receives little attention from women's groups in Russia. A major victory for men was achieved in 1993 when a new legal code was adopted that dropped the article making gay male contact punishable by a prison term of up to five years. This was not the result of pressure from the gay community, which had no input into the legal discussion, but rather a consensus among legal experts that it was time to legalize consensual sex among adult males. Lesbian women traditionally had been punished in an entirely different manner: labeled mentally ill, lesbians risked commitment to mental institutions, forced treatment with mind-altering drugs, and permanent registration with local psychiatric clinics, where they had to check in on a regular basis. The numbers of these cases is unknown.

A gay rights movement dates back to 1990 and grew rapidly to include dozens of groups and several publications. The focus has been on overcoming social isolation by holding social gatherings and organizing discothèques, dating services, and hotlines. The movement has not been able to marshal political influence.[49]

Military Service

In the mid-1990s, about 8.5 percent of those serving in the Russian armed services were women. This statistic is surprising because women are not subject to the draft, which is the main basis for drawing people into service. Due to manpower shortages, however, Russia has been accepting volunteers who serve on a contract basis, and women have formed roughly half of this category. Women serve almost entirely in support units or do clerical work, and there are few women in the military leadership—four colonels and no generals. Many of the women who join the military are wives of soldiers and are seeking additional wages for their families.

RELIGION AND SPIRITUALITY

For decades, the Soviet state sought to obliterate religion. The numbers of working churches, synagogues, and mosques were severely reduced, and religious education (except for clergy) was banned, as was charitable work. Clergy did not speak out on social or political issues except when required to parrot Soviet propaganda about freedom of religion or the peace-loving nature of the Soviet state. In the late 1980s, religion underwent a revival as Gorbachev's program of *perestroika* began to loosen the restrictions on religious practice.

For Russians the religious revival overwhelmingly involved the Russian Orthodox Church, a faith closely identified with Russian history and ethnicity. During the communist era, churchgoers consisted largely of elderly, poorly educated women—*babushkas*—who had endured a hard life and found comfort in the flickering candles and beautiful liturgy. As atheism faded, new patterns developed. By 1991 one of every three Russians reported an affiliation with the Russian Orthodox Church, although only one out of ten said they has been raised in the church.[50] Survey research suggests that about 40 percent of the population by 1993 could be counted as religious believers, with the deeply religious still concentrated among poorly educated older women living in urban areas. However, believers in St. Petersburg and Moscow include a large group of young, well-educated women who may represent the leading edge of changing patterns of religious identification.[51]

Women's Roles

The Russian Orthodox Church often is regarded as a conservative force with respect to women's rights. And despite recognition of women's equality within the family and within society at large, the church cautions against the tendency to belittle women's roles as wives and mothers and warns that equality does not mean the abolition of natural, God-given differences between the sexes and their missions within the family and the larger society.

The influence of the Russian Orthodox Church is limited. Churchgoing remains at a low level; the services are conducted in Church Slavonic, a language that cannot be understood by the congregation; and the absence of religious education left its mark. Public opinion surveys carried out in Moscow revealed that there is just as much and often more belief in witchcraft, astrology, and hexes than in Christian beliefs like the resurrection of

Christ, eternal life through salvation, and so on. Orthodox believers embrace both sets of "doctrines," and women are much more likely to pursue these various spiritual outlets than men.[52]

Religious Law

This is a church that condemns abortion as a grave sin, opposes forms of contraception that prevent fertilized eggs from being implanted in the uterus, and is governed by celibate men (married priests, who serve largely as parish priests, are excluded from the church hierarchy).

VIOLENCE

According to Human Rights Watch, "Violence against women in Russia persists as a chronic and overwhelming problem."[53] During the Soviet era, there was silence regarding the issue of violence against women. In the 1990s Russian women, often inspired by their visits to and study of shelters for battered women in the West, formed the first crisis centers and hotlines in Russia. During the 1990s the trafficking of women and girls grew rapidly as a result of more open borders, naïveté, the presence of organized crime, a weak legal system, and women's economic desperation. In addition, the war in Chechnya spawned women's groups committed to promoting military reform and to protecting the rights of their draft-age sons or of sons serving in the military. The Chechen War also generated an outflow of refugees, among whom women and children figure prominently.

Domestic Violence

Official statistics severely underestimate the extent of domestic violence. In official crime data, the government groups violence within the home between families or people living together with other crimes caused by "everyday" motives like jealousy or arguments. Disputes involving neighbors or street fights, therefore, are included; moreover, there is no breakdown by gender. Activists staffing crisis center hotlines in Russia report that the majority of their callers who experience domestic violence do not go to the police, and even if they did, the police are unlikely to act or file an official complaint.[54]

In the 1990s, an estimated 14,000 women a year were killed by their husbands or lovers. Thirty to 40 percent of murders in Russia occur within families, and women and children are generally the victims. One of the strongest areas of activism within the women's movement involves the founding of the pioneering crisis centers in Moscow and in St. Petersburg, and the subsequent growth of centers and hotlines across Russia. In many cases, Russian women activists received training and inspiration from foreign travel that involved the study of women's crisis centers in the West.

International assistance has provided crucial funding, with the 1999 U.S. Agency for International Development (USAID) three-year grant of $500,000 to support women's crisis centers in Russia a prime example. At least thirty-five centers existed by the year 2000, and most of these centers, with the exception of those located in the two large cities of Moscow and St. Petersburg, serve both domestic violence and rape victims.[55]

These centers increasingly provide psychological and legal aid and engage in public advocacy, a process aided by the networking and coalition building associated with the founding of the Russian Association of Crisis Centers in 1994. The task of securing political influence is in its initial stages. There have been at least forty draft laws on domestic violence before the State Duma since the mid-1990s, none of which have passed. Russia lacks specific legal provisions addressing domestic violence or adequate social services for victims. The crisis centers conduct invaluable public awareness and education campaigns designed to raise public consciousness about domestic violence, to teach prevention, to convince the police and lawmakers of the value of criminal sanctions, and above all to demonstrate the seriousness and fundamental unacceptability of domestic violence.

Rape/Sexual Assault

As in the case of domestic violence, government statistics underreport rape with an estimated 5 to 10 percent of rape victims turning to the police for assistance. No records are kept on the numbers of women whose complaints are not accepted or officially recorded by the police, but by all accounts police and prosecutors view victims' complaints with hostility and skepticism. There is a strong tendency to blame women for provoking or fabricating attacks. Not surprisingly, investigations frequently are flawed, particularly with respect to the gathering of forensic evidence.

There is no legal recognition of rape within marriage, and other forms of sexual violence like acquaintance rape "are seen as idiosyncratic problems with no name or as the woman's fault."[56] But legal codes adopted in 1996 did introduce several changes. Before 1996 it was unclear whether rape laws included forms of sexual intercourse other than vaginal intercourse; new legal codes make other forms of forced sexual acts equally grievous crimes.[57] Moreover, rape law no longer specifies that rape must involve the use of physical force or the threat thereof; the adjective "physical" has been dropped before the use of force, opening the possibility that rape can stem from mental or psychological coercion.

During the 1990s, a small but growing movement emerged in Russia that has tackled the issue of violence against women. These activists established dozens of crisis centers and work with great energy and initiative to advance the principle that women have the "fundamental right to live free from bodily harm."[58]

Trafficking in Women and Children

In the ten years following the breakup of the Soviet Union, an estimated 500,000 Russian women have been lured by advertisements or recruiters who promise modeling lessons or jobs as nannies, waitresses, or maids in foreign countries. When arriving in the designated country, they are met by criminals who seize their passports and force them into a life of prostitution. For Russians, the main destinations for sex slaves are Germany, Italy, Greece, Belgium, China, and the Persian Gulf states. Young women in small towns and villages located in deeply depressed areas of Russia particularly fall prey to these promises of travel abroad and the chance to earn money.

A turning point in Russian activism on this issue occurred in November 1997 when an international conference, "The Trafficking of NIS (Newly Independent States) Women Abroad," was hosted by the Andrei Sakharov Foundation in Moscow. The conference was sponsored by the Global Survival Network (Washington, DC), the International League for Human Rights (New York), and *Syostri* (Moscow), a crisis center for victims of sexual assault. By 2001 about forty Russian nongovernmental organizations joined the Angel Coalition to campaign against human trafficking. The primary activities have involved education campaigns: leaflets, a media blitz made possible by free airtime on state-owned TV stations, conducting informational programs in schools, and newspaper articles in rural areas and small towns.

During the 1990s, Russian law enforcement exhibited little interest in the issue and regarded the women not as victims of a crime, but as having voluntarily agreed to engage in prostitution. Sex slavery is an incredibly lucrative aspect of global criminal enterprise—you can sell a woman over and over again as opposed to selling narcotics or weapons. There is widespread corruption among Russian officials, a factor that complicates the fight against trafficking. In addition, it is difficult to get victims to give evidence as they often are subject to threats and extortion even when they return home. Yet, as of June 2003, it appears that a strong law will soon pass the State Duma that outlaws human trafficking by adding new crimes to the criminal code. In addition, the bill calls on the government to conduct educational campaigns and to protect and rehabilitate victims. This pending victory stems from more than three years of work by the Angel Coalition and growing pressure from the international community. In June 2002, the U.S. State Department issued a report ranking anti-trafficking activism in 89 countries; Russia's position in the lowest category carried the possibility of economic sanctions. In addition, the Russian government's desire to ratify the UN Convention Against Transnational Organized Crime demanded a more aggressive stance vis-à-vis human trafficking. The current bill, which is expected to pass the State Duma, enjoys the support of the Putin government.

War and Military Repression

Perhaps the most visible women's organization in Russia during the 1990s was the Committee of Soldiers' Mothers (CSM), an organization founded in Moscow in 1989. CSM sought to stop human rights abuses in the military, end the war in Chechnya, and implement an alternative service bill.[59] Its early leaders especially included women whose sons had fought in Afghanistan. There are hundreds of local affiliates, groups that act fairly independently from the Moscow office. CSM offers advice to parents on their legal rights and conducts sessions on how to avoid the draft. In 1995 the organization's antiwar efforts landed it the Sean MacBride Peace Prize, awarded by the International Peace Bureau in Geneva.

CSM stresses motherhood and the maternal instinct to protect one's children, and utilizes the ideology of motherhood to justify their political activism. The organization won sympathetic press coverage when it sent groups of mothers across the front lines in Chechnya to secure the release of their sons who were being held by Chechen rebels. But events in 1999 transformed the political arena: terrorist attacks in Moscow killed hundreds of civilians, and, coupled with incidents elsewhere in Russia, generated widespread public support for Putin's policy of renewing the war in Chechnya. The CSM thus faces a political environment less receptive to messages critical of military service and of the Chechen War.

One of Russia's most effective regional women's groups, the Women of the Don Union, probably because of its proximity to Chechnya, has included in its activities citizen diplomacy, hosting international conferences on Women for Life without War or Violence, and interaction with Chechen women.

OUTLOOK FOR THE TWENTY-FIRST CENTURY

The modern Russian Federation has experienced barely ten years of independence, and that decade has proved tumultuous by any standard. Women have suffered setbacks, particularly with respect to the erosion of social benefits that assisted working mothers. Yet women are showing great initiative and creativity in forming hundreds of new women's organizations. These organizations pursue a wide array of interests, from environmental degradation to reproductive rights to schools of leadership for women. Networking activities have increased, providing clear evidence that an independent women's movement has not only emerged but also seeks a voice in Russian society. The road to democratization will be a long one, and the solution to Russia's economic woes will not come easily. The inclusion of women's voices surely would bring a positive contribution to this challenging process of building a new nation.

NOTES

1. Gail W. Lapidus, "State Building and State Breakdown in Russia," in *Contemporary Russian Politics: A Reader*, ed. Archie Brown (Oxford: Oxford University Press, 2001).

2. Murray Feshbach, "Russia's Population Meltdown," *The Wilson Quarterly* (September 7, 2001), http://wwics.si.edu/OUTREACH/WQ/WQSELECT/FESHB.HTM.

3. Russia, 2001.

4. Carol Nechemias, "The Prospects for a Soviet Women's Movement," in *Perestroika from Below*, ed. Judith B. Sedaitis and Jim Butterfield (Boulder, CO: Westview Press, 1991), 73–96.

5. Barbara Clements, *Daughters of Revolution* (Arlington Heights, IL: Harlan Davidson, 1994), 150.

6. *Zhenshchiny i muzhchiny Rossii 97* (Moscow: Gaskomstat Rossii, 1997), 41–42.

7. *Zhenshchiny*, 1997, 36.

8. Lynne Attwood, *The New Soviet Man and Woman* (Bloomington: Indiana University Press, 1990).

9. Gail Warshofsky Lapidus, *Women in Soviet Society* (Berkeley: University of California Press, 1978), 136.

10. Sue Bridger et al., *No More Heroines?* (New York: Routledge, 1996).

11. Khotkina, 1994, 92.

12. *Zhenshchiny*, 1997, 53.

13. *Zhenshchiny*, 1997, 52.

14. Clements, 1994, 62.

15. Khotkina, 1994, 94–96.

16. Bridger et al., 1996, 16.

17. Khotkina, 1994, 96.

18. "Unemployment continues to grow," *OMRI* 1, no. 35 (February 19, 1996).

19. *Zhenshchiny*, 1997, 50.

20. *Zhenshchiny*, 1997, 67.

21. "Public Opinion Foundation Presents Results of Polls Concerning Women," *Johnson's Russia List*, no. 5141 (March 9, 2001): www.cdi.org/russia/johnson/5141.html.

22. Sarah Ashwin and Elain Bowers, "Do Russian Women Want to Work?" In *Post-Soviet Women*, ed. Mary Buckley (Cambridge: Cambridge University Press, 1997).

23. "Public Opinion," 2001.

24. Alessandra Stanley, "Sexual Harassment Thrives in the New Russian Climate," *New York Times* (April 17, 1994), 1, 8.

25. General Secretary Mikhail Gorbachev, *Perestroika: New Thinking for Our Country and the World* (New York: Harper and Row, 1987), 117.

26. Bridger et al., 1996, 51.

27. UNICEF, "Women in Transition," *Regional Monitoring Report*, no. 6 (Florence, Italy: UNICEF International Child Development Centre, 1999), 26.

28. UNICEF, 1999, 55.

29. Attwood, 1990, 184–91.

30. Attwood, 1990, 186.

31. Attwood, 1990, 187.

32. Olga Lipovskaya, "The Mythology of Womanhood," in *Women in Russia*, ed. Anastasia Posadskaya, trans. Kate Clark (London: Verso, 1994), 123–34.

33. UNICEF, 1999, 43, 47.

34. "Russians Divorcing," *RFE/RL Newsline* 3, no. 101, pt. 1 (May 25, 1999): and Megan Twohey, "1 in 3 Babies Born to Unmarried Moms," *Moscow Times* (November 29, 2001).

35. "Russians Divorcing"; and Twohey, 2001.

36. UNICEF, 1999, 42–49.

37. "Duma Committee against Sex Education Program," *RFE/RL Newsline*, no. 152, pt. 1 (November 4, 1997).

38. Nadezhda Baklaenko, "Zakonodatel' stvo," paper presented at International Training Seminar, Moscow, March 17–21, 1996.

39. I.I. Grebesheva, "Shok! Ili kontratseptivnaia revoliutsiia," *Moskvichka* (November 1997): 8–9, esp. 8.

40. Tatyana Roshchina, "A Choice Based on Love or an 'Accident,' " *Current Digest of the Soviet Press* 45, no. 32 (September 8, 1997): 23.

41. UNICEF, "Young People in Changing Societies," *Regional Monitoring Report*, no. 7 (Florence, Italy: UNICEF International Child Development Centre, 2000), 33.

42. UNICEF, 1999, 69.

43. UNICEF, 1999, 73–74.

44. Carol Nechemias, "Politics in Post-Soviet Russia," *Demokratizatsiya* 8, no. 2 (2000): 199–218.

45. Carol Nechemias, "Democratization and Women's Access to Legislative Seats," *Women & Politics* 14, no. 3 (1994): 1–18.

46. Nechemias, 2000.

47. Valerie Sperling, *Organizing Women in Contemporary Russia* (Cambridge: Cambridge University Press, 1999), 249–54.

48. Patrice C. McMahon, "Building Civil Societies in East Central Europe," paper presented at the Annual Meeting of the American Political Science Association, Washington, DC, August 31–September 3, 2000.

49. Masha Gessen, *The Rights of Lesbians and Gay Men* (San Francisco: International Gay and Lesbian Human Rights Commission, 1994).

50. Peter Steinfels, "Atheism Is Said to Fade in Russia," *New York Times*, December 10, 1993, sec. A14.

51. Mark Rhodes, "Diversity of Political Views," *RFE/RL Research Report* 3, no. 11 (March 18, 1994): 44–50.

52. Tatyana Ivanovna Varzanova, "What Russia's People Believe In," *Current Digest of the Soviet Press* 44, no. 9 (February 27, 1997): 7.

53. Human Rights Watch, "Russia—Too Little, Too Late," *Human Rights Watch* 9, no. 13 (1997): 11.

54. Human Rights Watch, 1997.

55. Sarah Henderson, "Crisis Centers for Women," in *Encyclopedia of Russian Women's Movements*, ed. Norma C. Noonan and Carol Nechemias (Westport, CT: Greenwood Press, 2001), 224–26.

56. Janet Elise Johnson, "Sisterhood vs. the 'Moral' Russian State," paper presented at the Role of Women in Post-Communist Transitions Workshop III, February 7–8, 2002, Washington, DC.

57. Human Rights Watch, 1997, 17.

58. Johnson, 1997, 21–22.

59. Amy Caiazza, "Committee of Soldiers' Mothers of Russia," in Noonan and Nechemias, 2001, 218–20.

RESOURCE GUIDE

Suggested Reading

Bridger, Sue, et al. *No More Heroines? Russia, Women and the Market*. New York: Routledge, 1996.

Buckley, Mary. *Perestroika and Soviet Women*. Cambridge: Cambridge University Press, 1992.

Kay, Rebecca. *Russian Women and Their Organizations: Gender, Discrimination and Grassroots Women's Organizations, 1991–96*. New York: St. Martin's Press, 2000.

Lapidus, Gail Warshofsky. *Women in Soviet Society: Equality, Development, and Social Change*. Berkeley: University of California Press, 1978.

Noonan, Norma Corigliano, and Carol Nechemias, eds. *Encyclopedia of Russian Women's Movements*. Westport, CT: Greenwood Press, 2001.

Posadskaya, Anastasia, ed. *Women in Russia: A New Era in Russian Feminism*. Translated by Kate Clark. London: Verso Press, 1994.

Racioppi, Linda, and Katherine O'Sullivan See. *Women's Activism in Contemporary Russia*. Philadelphia: Temple University Press, 1997.

Rule, Wilma, and Norma C. Noonan, eds. *Russian Women in Politics and Society*. Westport, CT: Greenwood Press, 1996.

Sperling, Valerie. *Organizing Women in Contemporary Russia: Engendering Transition*. Cambridge: Cambridge University Press, 1999.

Stites, Richard. *The Women's Liberation Movement in Russia: Feminism, Nihilism and Bolshevism, 1860–1930*. Princeton, NJ: Princeton University Press, 1978.

Web Sites

Association of Women's Organizations, www.owl.ru/eng/women/aiwo/.

Charter of Women's Solidarity, www.owl.ru/eng/charter/.
Fifteen women's organizations developed the charter, which was endorsed in the Moscow Parliamentary Center by thirty-seven women's organizations, politicians, and public leaders.

Open Women Line, www.owl.ru.

Russian Feminism Resources, www.geocities.com/Athens/2533/russfem.html.

Organizations

Consortium of Women's Nongovernmental Organizations
Elena Ershova, Coordinator
Stolory per. 6, Str. 2, Office 215
Moscow 123999
Phone: (095) 290-47-08
Fax: (095) 203-08-07
Email: wcons@com2com.ru

The Gaia International Women's Center
Nadezhda Shvedova, president

2/3 Khlebny Pereulok
Moscow, 121814
Phone: 7 (095) 382-75-02
Fax: 7 (095) 200 12 07
Web site: www.owl.ru/eng/women/aiwo/gaia.htm

Information Center of the Independent Women's Forum
Elizaveta Bozhkova, co-director
P.O. Box 230
Moscow 121019
Phone/Fax: (095) 366-92-74
Email: iciwf@glas.apc.org

Women's Archives
Zoia Hotkina, director
Phone: (095) 305-15-39
Web site: www.owl.ru/eng/women/aiwo/arhive.htm

Women's Information Network (formal short name is *ZhenSet*)
Tatiana Troinova, director
P.O. Box 65, Moscow 121019
Phone/Fax: (095) 291-22-74
Email: tatiana@ttg.msk.su
Web site: www.womnet.ru/db/english/english.html

Women's Movement of Russia (WMR)
Web site: www.owl.ru/win/women/wmr/indexe.htm
Registered with the Ministry of Justice.

SELECTED BIBLIOGRAPHY

Ashwin, Sarah, and Elain Bowers. "Do Russian Women Want to Work?" In *Post-Soviet Women: From the Baltic to Central Asia*, edited by Mary Buckley, 21–37. Cambridge: Cambridge University Press, 1997.

Attwood, Lynne. *The New Soviet Man and Woman: Sex-Role Socialization in the USSR*. Bloomington: Indiana University Press, 1990.

Bridger, Sue, Rebecca Kay, and Kathryn Pinnick. *No More Heroines? Russia, Women, and the Market*. London: Routledge, 1996.

Caiazza, Amy. "Committee of Soldiers' Mothers of Russia (*Komitet soldatskikh materei Rossii*) (1989)." In *Encyclopedia of Russian Women's Movements*, edited by Norma Corigliano Noonan and Carol Nechemias, 218–20. Westport, CT: Greenwood Press, 2001.

Clements, Barbara Evans. *Daughters of Revolution: A History of Women in the U.S.S.R.* Arlington Heights, IL: Harlan Davidson, Inc., 1994.

"Duma Committee against Sex Education Program." *RFE/RL Newsline*, no. 152, part I (November 4, 1997). www.rferl.org/newsline.

Feshbach, Murray. "Russia's Population Meltdown." *The Wilson Quarterly* (September 7, 2001). http://wwwics.si.edu/OUTREACH/WQ/WQSELECT/FESHB.HTM.

Gessen, Masha. *The Rights of Lesbians and Gay Men in the Russian Federation*. San Francisco: International Gay and Lesbian Human Rights Commission, 1994.

Gorbachev, Mikhail. *Perestroika: New Thinking for Our Country and the World*. New York: Harper and Row, 1987.

Henderson, Sarah. "Crisis Centers for Women, Association of (*Assotsiatsiia krizichnykh tsentrov*) (1994–)." In *Encyclopedia of Russian Women's Movements*, edited by Norma Corigliano Noonan and Carol Nechemias, 224–26. Westport, CT: Greenwood Press, 2001.

Human Rights Watch. "Russia—Too Little, Too Late: State Response to Violence against Women." *Human Rights Watch* 9, no. 13 (1997).

Johnson, Janet Elise. "Sisterhood vs. the 'Moral' Russian State: The Post-Communist Politics of Rape." Paper presented at The Role of Women in Post-Communist Transitions, Workshop III, February 7–8, 2002, Kennan Institute, Washington, DC, 2002.

Khotkina, Zoya. "Women in the Labour Market: Yesterday, Today and Tomorrow." In *Women in Russia: A New Era in Russian Feminism*, edited by Anastasia Posadskaya, translated by Kate Clark, 85–108. London, UK: Verso, 1994.

Lapidus, Gail Warshofsky. "State Building and State Breakdown in Russia." In *Contemporary Russia Politics: A Reader*, edited by Archie Brown, 348–54. Oxford, UK: Oxford University Press.

———. *Women in Soviet Society: Equality, Development, and Social Change*. Berkeley: University of California Press, 1978.

Likhanov, Albert. "The Situation of Children in Russia." *The Current Digest of the Post-Soviet Press* 48, no. 48 (1996): 8–10; translated from *Nezavisimaia gazeta*, no. 8 (November 21, 1996): 6.

Lipovskaya, Olga. "The Mythology of Womanhood in Contemporary 'Soviet' Culture." In *Women in Russia: A New Era in Russian Feminism*, edited by Anastasia Posadskaya, translated by Kate Clark, 123–34. London: Verso Press, 1994.

McMahon, Patrice C. "Building Civil Societies in East Central Europe: The Effect of American NGOs on Women's Groups." Paper presented at the Annual Meeting of the American Political Science Association, Washington, DC, August 31–September 3, 2000.

Nechemias, Carol. "Democratization and Women's Access to Legislative Seats: The Soviet Case, 1989–1991." *Women & Politics*, 14, no. 3 (1994): 1–18.

———. "Politics in Post-Soviet Russia: Where Are the Women?" *Demokratizatsiya*, 8, no. 2 (2000): 199–218.

———. "The Prospects for a Soviet Women's Movement: Opportunities and Obstacles." In *Perestroika from Below: Social Movements in the Soviet Union*, edited by Judith B. Sedaitis and Jim Butterfield, 73–96. Boulder, CO: Westview Press, 1991.

"Public Opinion Foundation Presents Results of Polls Concerning Women." Johnson's Russia List, no. 5141 (March 9, 2001): www.cdi.org/russia/johnson/5141.html.

Rhodes, Mark. "Diversity of Political Views among Russia's Believers." *RFE/RL Research Report* 3, no. 11 (March 18, 1994): 44–50.

Roshchina, Tatyana. "A Choice Based on Love or an 'Accident'." *Current Digest of the Post-Soviet Press* 44, no. 7 (March 19, 1997): 23; translated from *Trud* (February 15, 1997): 2.

"Russians Divorcing." *RFE/RL Newsline* 3, no. 101, Part I (May 25, 1999): www.rferl.org/newsline.

Sazonov, Vadim. "Poll: A New Symbiosis." *Current Digest of the Post-Soviet Press* 45, no. 32 (September 8, 1993): 25; translated from *Nezavisimaya gazeta*, August 12: 1993, 5.

Sperling, Valerie. *Organizing Women in Contemporary Russia: Engendering Transition*. Cambridge: Cambridge University Press, 1999.

Stanley, Alessandra. "Sexual Harassment Thrives in the New Russian Climate." *New York Times*, April 17, 1994, 1, 8.

Steinfels, Peter. "Atheism Is Said to Fade in Russia," *New York Times*, December 10, 1993, A14.

Twohey, Megan. "1 in 3 Babies Born to Unmarried Moms." *Moscow Times*, November 29, 2001. *Johnson's Russia List*, no. 5571 (November 29, 2001). www.cdi.org/russia/johnson/5571.html.

"Unemployment Continues to Grow." OMRI, Part I, no. 35 (February 19, 1996).

UNICEF. "Women in Transition." *Regional Monitoring Report*, no. 6. Florence, Italy: UNICEF International Child Development Centre, 1999.

———. "Young People in Changing Societies." *Regional Monitoring Report*, no. 7. Florence, Italy: UNICEF International Child Development Centre, 2000.

Varzanova, Tatyana Ivanovna. "What Russia's People Believe In." *Current Digest of the Post-Soviet Press* 44, no. 9 (1997): 14–15; translated from *Nezavisimaya Gazeta, NG Religions, Monthly Supplement* (February 27, 1997): 7.

Selected Russian Bibliography

Baklaenko, Nadezhda. "Zakonodatel'stvo o reproduktivnykh pravakh zhenshchin" (Legislation on Women's Reproductive Rights). Paper presented at an International Training Seminar, *Ustanovlenie i monitoring prav zhenshchin v Rossii* (Establishing and Monitoring Women's Rights in Russia), Moscow, March 17–21, 1996.

Grebesheva, I.I. "*Shok!Ili kontratseptivnaia revoliutsiia, edinstvennaiia revolutsiia, kotoraia trebuetsia Rossii*" ("Shock! Or a Contraceptive Revolution, The Only Revolution Russia Needs"). *Moskvichka* (November 1997): 8–9.

Zhenshchiny i muzhchiny Rossii 97: kratkii statisticheskii sbornik ("Women and Men in Russia, 1997: A Short Statistical Handbook"). Moscow: Goskomstat Rossii, 1997.

32

SERBIA AND MONTENEGRO

Lilijana Cickaric

PROFILE OF SERBIA AND MONTENEGRO

On February 4, 2003, the Yugoslavian Parliament adopted the new constitution for Serbia and Montenegro. The new unicameral parliament of the federation will have 126 seats (Serbia: 91, Montenegro: 35), filled by nominees of the two state parliaments for the first two years until public elections take place. After three years, both states are allowed to unilaterally leave the federation based upon the outcome of a public referendum.

The former Federal Republic of Yugoslavia (FRY), consisting of the Republic of Serbia (population 10,213,000) and the Republic of Montenegro (population 654,000), was proclaimed by the Constitution on April 27, 1992. The legislative branch is entrusted to the bicameral federal parliament, the executive branch to the president of the republic, the prime minister, and to the federal government, and the judiciary to the federal prosecutor and federal court.

As the Socialist Federal Republic of Yugoslavia endorsed the end of the one-party state in 1990, nationalist ambitions, ethnic conflict, and war were fragmenting

its multiethnic, multistate federation. First Slovenia, then Croatia, Macedonia, and Bosnia and Herzegovina declared their independence; and when the Federal Republic of Yugoslavia was constituted in 1992, it consisted of Serbia and Montenegro. Conflicting ethnic and national aspirations sparked war in Slovenia, Croatia, Bosnia and Herzegovina, and the province of Kosovo. It was in Kosovo that nationalisms were expressed in their most virulent forms against the civilian population, and NATO reacted with air strikes against Serbia in 1999. Peace accords, monitored by United Nations and NATO troops and supported by the popular ouster of Milošević from power in Serbia in 2000, have created the space for reconstruction and refugee relocation to begin. After political and social changes in 2000, Serbia and Montenegro is in the first stage of economic and structural reforms.

In 2001 life expectancy was 76.67 for women and 70.57 for men. The total fertility rate was 1.75, the infant mortality rate was 17.42 per 1,000 live births, and the maternal mortality rate was 9.3 per 100,000 live births.[1]

OVERVIEW OF WOMEN'S ISSUES

The human trauma and infrastructural losses of war, the needs of large refugee populations, and the economic devastation that have plagued postcommunist Yugoslavia have concentrated women's goals on nonviolence, survival, and reconstruction. Women confront increased unemployment as well as declining incomes and social supports, all reinforcing patriarchal ideologies of gender roles in the family and public life. Women's inequality is manifest in their few numbers as heads of major companies and institutions, and in political offices, as well as in marriage, family relations, and employment practices.

EDUCATION

Opportunities

Legislation in Serbia and Montenegro does not contain any provisions that discriminate against women in terms of equal access to education. According to the Federal Statistical Office in 1997–1998, female college and university students comprised 54 percent of the total number of students and 53.4 percent were "regular" students, indicating that women in Serbia and Montenegro have equal access to college and university education (see Table 32.1). During the 1990s, women in Serbia faced various problems because they bore the burden of the social and economic crisis, doing most of the household tasks and trying to find an additional job in the gray economy.[2] As a result, women have gradually been moving away from the educational process as they have less and less time for training and the impoverished society cannot provide funding for women-oriented educational programs.

Table 32.1
Selected Gender Indicators (Federal Statistical Office, 1999)

	Year	Women	Men	Total
University degrees (%)	1998	60	40	100
Degrees in education (%)	1998	90	10	100
Degrees in engineering (%)	1998	35	65	100
Degrees in law (%)	1998	61	39	100
Working population (%)	1999	42	58	100
Labor force participation rates (%)	1999	40.9	46.0	86.9
Unemployment rates (%)	1999	22.5	15.7	38.2

Literacy

The general literacy rate rose for persons over the age of ten from 1961 to 1991 in FRY. However, this process is slower for women than for men. According to the last census in FRY in 1991, nearly 10 percent of women are illiterate.

EMPLOYMENT AND THE ECONOMY

Job/Career Opportunities

Women's unemployment has been constantly increasing faster than general unemployment: the rates for women and men in 1998 were 33.6 percent and 18.9 percent respectively. In 1998, more than half of all women in FRY (53.7 percent) waited between one and three years for a job, and women still comprise the majority of those waiting for a job. The so-called female professions are trade (55.5 percent), administrative workers, civil servants and similar (62.2 percent), and experts and artists (52.8 percent).

Women made up around 33–35 percent of all owners of enterprises in 1991. According to the Survey on the Work Force from 1997, the percentage of women private owners has decreased to 20 percent.

Pay

In 1997 women's average wage was lower than the average wage of men by 11 percent. According to a survey on the population's possibilities to meet economic needs carried out by the Economics Institute in Belgrade in 1998, about 1.2 million persons work in the gray market, and approximately one third of the participants in this market are women. Women's average wage in the gray market was 28 percent lower than men's average wage; and this disparity in salaries between the sexes implies a high degree of discrimination against women in the gray economy.

Sexual Harassment

Sexual harassment as a form of discrimination and violence against women finally entered the criminal law in Serbia. Fines and imprisonment for up to six months or one year for those who misuse their professional position for sexual abuse and harassment is predicted.

Support for Mothers/Caretakers

Maternal Leave

The basic right of employed women concerning pregnancy and birth is the right to maternity leave. A woman may choose to go on maternity leave forty-five days before delivery and must go on leave twenty-eight days before delivery. Maternity leave lasts at least until the child is one year old or until the third child reaches the age of two. During maternity leave, employed women have the right to compensation in the amount of the earnings they would have had in their workplace, on the condition that they have been employed for at least six months. The republics' regulations also prescribe that one parent—or only the mother in Montenegro—may be absent from work until the child reaches the age of three. During that period, the rights and obligations of that person are suspended; in Montenegro, mothers have the right to health and retirement insurance if they benefit from that right.

FAMILY AND SEXUALITY

Gender Roles

The 1991 census showed that 62.1 percent of households live in nuclear families, but the number of extended families has increased since there were three waves of refugees from Bosnia, Croatia, and Kosovo in the last ten years. The present social environment, especially wars, political and economical destruction, and moral deterioration during the 1990s, brought women back to patriarchal roles and expectations. Most women spend all their resources, health, energy, time, and knowledge on the activities of feeding and taking care of children and other members of family. The erosion of working conditions contributed to the aggravation of the social services, especially schools, medical institutions, kindergartens, and social protection. In that context, there is no real equality between men and women, despite the constitutional provisions and legislation.

Marriage

Marriage rates are down significantly. Most likely this reflects delays in family formation due to economic circumstances, although cohabitation is increasing. Over the last few years, the average age at first marriage has started to climb, but women are still marrying at a relatively younger age than are women in Western countries. Divorce initially increased. According to official statistics, the rate of divorce is 0.6 per 1,000 citizens in Serbia, and the average age of women seeking divorce is thirty-six. Where there have been rises in the number of family breakups, the reasons may include social stress, changes in lifestyles and social values, and streamlined divorce procedures.

Reproduction

Contraception and Abortion

Abortion has been the most common form of birth control in Serbia and Montenegro for many years. About 200,000 abortions are performed a year, or 90.5 abortions for every 1,000 women aged 15–44.[3] In this respect, there are no differences among women according to age, level of education, marital status, or other social, psychological, or cultural characteristics. Unfortunately, there is no regular statistical monitoring of contraceptive use.

Abortion was legalized in 1952 when regulations concerning permissible abortion were adopted. The Law on Abortion Procedures in Health Institutions, which was adopted in May 1995, with restrictive regulations marks the beginning of a new and conservative demographic policy. Although the 1995 law also provides that abortion may be performed only at the request of the pregnant woman, it states that abortion must be performed within ten weeks of pregnancy, with no particular legal exceptions. After this time, pregnancy can only be terminated if a doctor's consultation establishes the presence of legal preconditions, that is certain medical or criminal reasons (for example, if the woman's life is endangered, or the pregnancy poses a threat to her health, or she was raped).

HEALTH

Health Care Access

In Serbia, health care is funded by a social insurance system paid for by contributions from employees and employers up to a maximum of 9.7 percent of earnings or payroll. Regional pension associations and employment groups also contribute to health care insurance pools. The insurance funds are administered locally.[4] In 2000, total health expenditures were 5.6 percent of the gross domestic product.[5] There are 213.17 physicians and 540.63 hospital beds per 100,000 people.[6] In 1995, 90 percent of births were attended by skilled health staff.[7] The 1990s saw a dramatic decline in health care spending at the same time as needs increased with the influx of war refugees leading to a decline in health care access.[8]

Increased poverty and social stress, migration, changing social values, and growing criminality provides fertile ground for risk-taking behaviors. The population faces the declining access to medical services, including the availability of and ability to pay for medical treatments and drugs. This is being compounded by the fact that there is often a lack of awareness, education, infrastructure, and programs addressing the problems of health.

POLITICS AND LAW

Suffrage

All citizens may vote as of sixteen years of age if they are employed. Voting is a universal privilege when a citizen becomes eighteen years of age.

Political Participation

Elections in September 2000 for the Council of Citizens and the Council of Republics did not significantly improve the proportion of women's representation in parliament. Women won only ten (5.6 percent) of the combined total of 178 seats—nine in the Council of Citizens (6.5 percent) and one in the Council of Republics (2.5 percent). At this level Serbia and Montenegro remains among the lowest in Europe. Of the twenty seats in the Council of Republics that belong to Montenegro, none are held by women. However, in republic parliaments, both in Serbia and Montenegro, women's representation is somewhat better than it is in the federal parliament. Elections in spring of 2001 resulted in women winning eight (10.4 percent) of the 77 seats of the Parliament of the Republic of Montenegro. In the Parliament of Republic of Serbia, women hold only 27 (10.8 percent) of 250 seats.

Women were elected in proportion close to their numbers among the candidates. For example, the DOS (Democratic Opposition of Serbia) Coalition list, which has the highest numbers of women's representatives elected, nominated women as 14 percent of its candidates and elected 13.6 percent women.

Montenegrin woman casts her ballot in Montenegro's presidential elections, Podgorica, February 2003. AP/Wide World Photos.

At the level of the municipalities, women's representation is lower than it is in the republic parliaments. In Serbia, women average 6.5 percent of the representatives in all municipalities while the average for the municipalities of Montenegro is 4.8 percent.[9]

Women's Rights

Feminist Movements

There are more than 100 autonomous women's organizations in Serbia and Montenegro.[10] Most of them are oriented toward women's education and economic empowerment, the affirmation of women's human rights, the problem of violence against women, humanitarian activities and the publication of women's books.

Women head several large and influential NGOs; for example, the Centre for Cultural Decontamination, the Belgrade Open School, CESID, the European Movement in Serbia, the Helsinki Committee for Human Rights, the Humanitarian Law Centre, Yugoslav Lawyers for Human Rights—YUCOM, Centre for Anti-War Action, and the Women in Black, among others.

Lesbian Rights

Homosexuality is still a hidden and taboo issue in society and still has no place in public discussions among professionals, politicians, researchers, journalists, and so on. Voluntary sexual relations between adult homosexuals are not prohibited by law in Serbia and Montenegro. At present, there is no law that regulates lesbian and gay partnerships and families. General public perceptions are very negative, and psychiatrists still speak publicly about homosexuality as a type of deviation.

VIOLENCE

The political context in Serbia for the past ten years has had a great impact on the increase of violence against women and girls. Furthermore, nationalism and the growing traditionalism of gender roles have had a strong impact on common perceptions of the problem of violence in the home. The lack of legal and social protections, as well as the low level of public perceptions, directly affect women victims of violence. The only relevant resources on gender-based violence are the statistics and research of women's NGOs.

Domestic Violence

Research has shown that around 30 percent of court cases involving general violent crimes are domestic.[11] In 57.2 percent of these cases, the public or private prosecutor dropped the charges. In 47 percent of convictions, "being the father or family man" was the frequent justification for lowering the sentence of a perpetrator of domestic violence. The number of hidden cases of domestic violence is very high. Whether committed within the family or elsewhere, research shows that the majority of violent criminal acts result in light bodily injuries (accounting for 54.95 percent); 30 percent of all violent acts jeopardize personal security, 11.81 percent of all violent acts result in severe bodily injury; and 2.75 percent of all violent crimes involve the use of a weapon. There are only two shelters for women victims in Serbia, both located in Belgrade.

Trafficking in Women and Children

The increased presence of soldiers in the region and the sudden worsening of the economic situation make the risks of trafficking in women and girls greater than ever. Serbia is becoming primarily a country of transit for women and girls from Eastern Europe. A new draft on legal changes in the Criminal Code of Serbia and Montenegro is preparing to be introduced. There are media reports about foreign prostitutes and trafficked women from Serbia and Montenegro in the daily and weekly newspapers. Several women's NGOs are dealing with this issue, although there remains much confusion about the substance, meaning, and definition of trafficking, as well as ways to document, combat, and prevent it.

War and Military Repression

According to evidence of various international organizations, in all Balkan wars, almost 4,500,000 people were displaced and about 90 percent of refugees were women and children. During the wars, the rape of women from different ethnic groups was used as a weapon of "ethnic cleansing." Approximately 50,000 women were raped in wars in Croatia and Bosnia and Herzegovina. Most women refugees were raped during the wars. For the first time, mass rape in war became visible and a matter of inquiry in the international community and law. Rape of women has been well documented and brought to the world's attention through the effort of both local and international women's organizations to pursue the redefinition of internationally recognized human rights in women's favor.

The wars also created an atmosphere that led to increased levels of domestic physical, psychological, and sexual abuse.

OUTLOOK FOR THE TWENTY-FIRST CENTURY

Economic and structural reforms in the context of greater democracy and relative peace may provide the conditions for improving the economic picture of Serbia and Montenegro in general and of women in particular.

Members of autonomous women's organizations, who were among those criticizing war and nationalist and patriarchal ideologies, and who are creating nongovernmental supports for victims of violence, are participating in promoting interethnic conflict resolution and women's equal participation in politics, business, and civil society.

NOTES

1. Federal Statistical Office, *Summary Report, Statistical Yearbook* (Belgrade, 2001).

2. Today, the Serbia and Montenegro labor market is still divided into two sections: about three-quarters of the total work force are employed in the "regular" labor market, and about one-quarter are employed in the "hidden," "illegal," or "gray" labor market. According to the gross rate of occurrence, about one third of the total work force is absorbed by the illegal labor market.

3. National Action Plan for Women (Belgrade: Institute for Economy, Ministry of Family Care, 2000).

4. Social Security Administration, *Social Security Programs Throughout the World: Europe 2002*, www.ssa.gov/statistics/ssptw/2002/Europe/Serbia.html.

5. WHO (World Health Organization) Regional Office for Europe (2003), www.who.int/inf-fs/en/feature198.html.

6. World Bank, *GenderStats* (January 17, 2003), http://genderstats.worldbank.org.

7. WHO (World Health Organization) (January 18, 2003), *Yugoslavia*, www.who.int/country/yug/en/.

8. WHO (World Health Organization), "New Politicians, Old Vulnerabilities: Serbia's Health Crisis" (2000), www.who.int/inf-fs/en/feature198.html.

9. Milka Puzigaca, *Status and Challenges for Gender Equality in Yugoslavia* (2002), www.europeanforum.net/gender_issues/reports/140302milka.html.

10. Centre for Development of Non-profit Sector, 2001, www.crnps.org.yu.

11. Victimology Society of Serbia, *Domestic Violence in Serbia* (Belgrade: Author, 2002).

RESOURCE GUIDE

Suggested Reading

Blagojevic, Marina. "Gender and Survival: Serbia in the 1990's." In *Construction/Reconstruction: Women, Family, Politics in Central Europe, 1945–1998*, edited by A. Peto and B. Rasky. New York/Budapest: CEU, Budapest, Osterreichisches Ost- und Sudostteuropa-Institut, Aubenstell, Budapest, OSI Network Women's Program, 1999.

Corrin, Chris. *Gender and Identity in Central and Eastern Europe*. London: Frank Cass, 1999.

Nikolic-Ristanovic, V. *Women, Violence and War*. Budapest: CEU Press, 2000.

Web Sites and Organizations

Association for Women's Initiative
Web site: www.fly.to/awin

Campaign for Gender Equality Mechanisms
Web site: www.ravnopravno.org

Center for Development of Non-Profit Sector
Web site: www.crnps.org.yu

Center for Women's Studies
Web site: www.zenskestudie.edu.yu

Women's Movement in Yugoslavia
Web site: www.womenngo.org.yu

SELECTED BIBLIOGRAPHY

Cickaric, L. "Women's Advocacy in the Building of Civil Society in Serbia." Paper presented at Global Network Electronic Conference, Women's Organizations and the Building of Civil Society in the Twenty-First Century: An International Perspective, Binghamton, New York, 2000. www.philanthropy.org/GN.

Domestic Violence in Serbia. Belgrade: Victimology Society of Serbia, 2002.

Gender in Transition. Washington, DC: The World Bank Eastern Europe and Central Asia Region, Human Development Unit, 2002.

Krstic, G. *An Empirical Analysis of Formal and Informal Labour Markets in Yugoslavia, 1995–1998.* Mimeo: Sussex University, 2000.

Lukic, M. *Report on Violence against Women and Girls in FRY.* Commission on the Status of Women. New York, March, 2000.

Puzigaca, Milka. *Status and Challenges for Gender Equality in Yugoslavia.* 2002. www.europeanforum.net/gender_issues/reports/140302milka.html.

Social Security Administration. *Social Security Programs throughout the World: Europe 2002.* 2002. www.ssa.gov/statistics/ssptw/2002/Europe/Serbia.html.

WHO (World Health Organization). "New Politicians, Old Vulnerabilities: Serbia's Health Crisis." 2000. www.who.int/inf-fs/en/feature198.html.

———. Regional Office for Europe. 2003. www.who.int/inf-fs/en/feature198.html.

———. *Yugoslavia.* 2003. www.who.int/country/yug/en/ (accessed January 18, 2003).

World Bank. *GenderStats.* 2003. http://genderstats.worldbank.org (accessed January 17, 2003).

33

SLOVAKIA

Sharon L. Wolchik

PROFILE OF SLOVAKIA

Slovakia came into existence as an independent state on January 1, 1993, following the breakup of the Czechoslovak Federative Republic. Some 5.4 million people live in Slovakia. The majority (85.7 percent) are Slovaks. Hungarians account for approximately 11 percent of the population. There is also a small Ukrainian/Ruthenian minority and a sizeable Roma population.

The Slovak Republic is a parliamentary democracy. The president, elected by popular vote, has limited powers. The government, which is responsible to the 150-seat unicameral legislature, is the effective executive. Aside from a brief period from March to December 1994, political life was dominated by Vladimir Meciar and his Movement for a Democratic Slovakia from 1993 to 1998. Although popularly elected, Meciar's government engaged in numerous nondemocratic practices that delayed the re-creation of a market economy and derailed Slovakia's bid for NATO and EU membership. The 1998 elections brought in a center-right government. Under the leadership of Prime Minister Mikulas Dzurinda, Slovakia began energetic economic reforms and regained the ground it had lost under Meciar internationally. The 2002 elections resulted in the formation of another center-right government.

Slovakia's economy is largely in private hands. Growth in GDP began to decrease in 1996 and dropped again in 1999. Unemployment increased to 18.2 in 2000 and remained at that rate in 2002.

The Slovak population con-

sisted of 2,612,000 men and 2,767,000 women in 2001.[1] Women thus accounted for slightly over half (51.4 percent) of the population. Infant mortality was 89.7 per 1,000 live births.[2] The total fertility rate was estimated to be 1.25 children per woman in 2001.[3] In 2000, life expectancy was 77.2 years for women and 69.2 years for men.[4]

OVERVIEW OF WOMEN'S ISSUES

Women's lives and opportunities in Slovakia have been influenced profoundly by the end of communism. Before 1989, women's equality was in theory guaranteed by the constitution and protected by laws that prohibited discrimination in all areas. In reality, however, gender equality was a low priority goal that was often subordinated to other, higher-priority policy considerations. Women's roles changed unevenly in different spheres, and for many women, equality in theory meant the burden of double or triple roles as worker or employee, homemaker and parent, and citizen in practice.[5]

After the end of communism in 1989, women gained many new opportunities. They could once again exercise their political rights; they could also establish private businesses, travel abroad, or choose not to work if circumstances allowed. The impact of the transition to democracy and the market, however, has not been the same for all groups of women. It has been primarily younger, urban, educated women who have been able to take advantage of the new opportunities that are available. For other groups, including single mothers, older women, uneducated or less educated women, and those living in rural areas, the last decade has brought primarily uncertainty and hardship.[6] Many Roma women in particular continue to live in substandard conditions and remain marginalized from the rest of society.[7]

After 1989, women continued to experience many of the same problems they faced under socialism, such as occupational segregation, lower pay for equal work, sexual harassment, and the glass ceiling. They also faced new problems created by the end of state subsidies and the shift to the market. These included those that women face in many other market economies, including difficulties in finding childcare, decreases in public services, unemployment, and in some cases poverty. Women continued to play a very small role in the exercise of political and economic power. With the end of tight political control and the opening of borders, social pathologies such as violence in the family, crime, prostitution, drug and alcohol abuse, and trafficking in people have become subjects of public debate and political action. Gay and lesbian issues have also come into the open. Women have also faced challenges to their reproductive rights. The organization of political power and popular attitudes based on traditional ideas of gender roles have affected women's organizations and activists engaged in working for greater equality.[8]

EDUCATION

Opportunities

Women's educational opportunities expanded markedly in Slovakia under communism. By the second half of the communist era, women accounted for over half of all students in *gymnazia*, the general secondary schools that prepare students for university entrance. They also accounted for over half of all university students.

Women were somewhat less frequently students at technical or vocational secondary schools, but even here, their representation increased dramatically. However, girls and young women chose or were channeled into areas of education that differed from those of boys and young men. At the level of higher education, women were greatly overrepresented in faculties of medicine as well as in education.[9] These patterns have continued after the end of communism. In 2000, women accounted for 59.7 percent of all secondary students and 51.9 percent of all students in higher education. But many girls and boys continue to receive different educations and enter the labor force with different skills.[10]

Literacy

Most women as well as men (99.99 percent) in Slovakia are literate. The main exception to this pattern occurs among Roma women. Given the wide variation in estimates of the number of Roma in Slovakia, reliable data are not available to assess the extent of illiteracy among this group.[11]

EMPLOYMENT AND THE ECONOMY

Job/Career Opportunities

Women's participation in paid employment increased dramatically during the communist era and came to be an anticipated part of most women's lives. This trend has continued after the end of communism. Women accounted for 45.9 percent of the labor force in 2000. Women's percentage of the labor force was greatest in the areas of health and social work (82.2 percent), hotels and restaurants (61.1 percent), financial services (68.5 percent), and wholesale and retail trade (58.9 percent). They accounted for almost all (94.8 percent), of a new category of workers, those who worked in private households. Women were slightly less likely to be found in the area of manufacturing (41 percent), real estate (39.3 percent), and in community, social and personal services (47.4 percent), and far less likely to work in agriculture (29.4 percent), mining (12.5 percent), or construction (8.2 percent).[12]

A breakdown of the labor force by occupation also illustrates significant

Women working at Sumitomo Electric Wiring Systems, Topolcany, Slovakia. Photo © TRIP/J. Bartos.

differences in the concentrations of men and women. Women accounted for the highest proportions of administrative workers (77.2 percent) and workers in services and trade (66.5 percent). They were also overrepresented in comparison to their share of the labor force as scientists and other intellectuals (62.1 percent) and in technical, medical, pedagogical, and related professions (61.2 percent). By way of contrast, women accounted for 30.8 percent of those who were legislators, senior officials, or managers. Women comprised 48.7 percent of skilled workers in agriculture, forestry, and related fields; their share of supporting and unskilled workers and employees was approximately equal (49.7 percent). However, they were far less likely to be skilled craftsmen and qualified workers or repairmen (19.4 percent) or machine operators (20 percent).[13]

Unemployment has become an important issue for women. In 1999, when women accounted for 45.6 percent of those who were unemployed, the unemployment rate of women (16.4 percent) was somewhat higher than that of men (16.0 percent). In 2000, when women accounted for 44.4 percent of the unemployed, the rates were the same (18.6 percent) for both men and women.[14] There are sizeable regional differences in unemployment; in some regions, up to 30 percent of the labor force was unemployed in 2000. Unemployment is particularly high among the Roma.[15]

Pay

These patterns have been reflected in gender-related differences in wages and income. Women's wages have typically been from 25 to 30 percent less than those of men.[16] Women also face additional competition from men in those professions, such as law and banking, which used to have low salaries and limited earning potential, now that those occupations are potentially far more lucrative.[17]

Working Conditions

Since the end of communism, women have also faced greater pressure to perform well at the workplace and have faced the threat, if not the reality, of unemployment. The emphasis on efficiency and productivity in a market economy has had special implications for women, many of whom can no longer count on at least unofficial tolerance for the previously common practice of using part of the workday to run personal errands and take care of family business.

Sexual Harassment

Many women also face discrimination and sexual harassment in the workplace. These practices appear to have increased since the end of communism and are now more open. Small private businesses, in particular, often do not observe legal regulations prohibiting discrimination. Public opinion polls indicate that men and women feel that men have greater advantages than women in the workplace. A 1995 survey found that although more men than women (32.4 percent compared to 27.1 percent) indicated that they had experienced discrimination, far more women than men (39.2 percent compared to 2.5 percent) indicated that they had experienced discrimination based on gender.[18]

Support for Mothers/Caretakers

Maternal Leave

Maternity provisions from the communist era were maintained for the most part. Thus, women can take six months of paid leave at 90 percent of their salary, not to exceed a maximum of 370 Slovak crowns[19] per month. After that, mothers or fathers can take parental leave until the child is three years of age. The parent taking leave receives 3,700 crowns a month, which is below the minimum subsistence level. If the child goes to individual daycare (that is, in the care of a grandmother, neighbor, or the like), the parent can receive 1,200 crowns a month until the child is three years old.

Daycare

Under communism, women received a number of benefits related to childbearing and childrearing. Many of these were enacted in the 1970s to encourage young families to have more children. The state also attempted to provide public childcare for children, particularly those of working mothers.[20] As the result of the shift to the market and decreased funding for local governments, childcare places decreased precipitously, particularly for infants. The number of public nurseries declined from 618 to sixteen in the two years after 1991; the number of places for children decreased from 166,218 to 582.[21] Places for children in kindergartens also dropped.[22]

FAMILY AND SEXUALITY

Gender Roles

The legacy of the communist era, when women's equality was a goal imposed from above, discredited gender equality as a goal. Experience with the negative impact of the uneven pattern of gender role change that occurred under communism also led many women, as well as men, to reject the whole idea of gender equality. Many women, including women activists, either did not recognize women's issues as deserving of attention in their own right or felt that women needed to give more emphasis to their neglected roles as homemakers and mothers.[23]

Marriage

Marriage rates have fallen gradually since the late 1970s, reaching a rate of 4.4 per 1,000 inhabitants in 2000.[24] The average age at marriage has increased since the end of communism, as young couples postpone marriage. The average age of brides increased from 22.5 to 25.2 between 1990 and 2000; the average age of grooms increased from 24 to 28.2 during the same period.[25] Divorce continues to be common, particularly in urban areas. In 2000, there were 35.8 divorces per 100 marriages.[26]

Reproduction

Birthrates have fallen precipitously since the end of communism. There were 15.1 live births per 1,000 population in Slovakia in 1989.[27] By 2001, when there were 9.7 deaths per 1,000 inhabitants, there were 9.5 live births per 1,000 inhabitants.[28]

Contraception and Abortion

Use of contraception rather than abortion to control births increased from 1990 to 2000. A survey conducted in the mid-1990s, which asked women which form of contraception they would recommend to their friends, found that 83 percent would recommend condoms; 52 percent would recommend birth control pills; and 48 percent IUDs. However, 45 percent indicated that they would recommend coitus interruptus and 43 percent the rhythm method.[29] Experts estimated that under 6 percent of Slovak women used birth control pills in the mid-1990s.[30] Approximately 13 percent of all women in the fertile ages used the pill in 1998,[31] a low proportion compared to that in other industrialized countries.

Abortion rates also fell dramatically. In 1988, there were 51,000 artificially induced abortions, a rate of 45.8 per 1,000 women in the fertile ages. By

2000, there were 18,468 abortions, a rate of 16.3 abortions per 1,000 women in the fertile ages.[32]

HEALTH

Health Care Access

The privatization of the economy and problems in the state sector have led to increasing difficulties in the area of health care. Slovakia ranks well on standard indicators of access to health care, but decreased funding and the rising indebtedness of the health care sector have led to what many observers have termed a crisis in health care.[33]

Diseases and Disorders

Although women's life expectancy, in contrast to that of men, increased steadily over the last three decades, women face a number of critical health problems. There has been a dramatic increase in deaths among women due to heart disease; strokes and other vascular cerebral diseases are the second most common cause of death among women.[34]

AIDS

HIV and AIDS are increasing public health problems. Compared to the dramatic increase in HIV infection in parts of the former Soviet Union and many other countries, however, this problem is still relatively small in Slovakia, where there were thirty-six new cases diagnosed in 1999 and twenty-six in 2000.[35] Other sexually transmitted diseases decreased substantially from 1989 from 31.4 cases per 100,000 population to 8.5 in 2000.[36]

POLITICS AND LAW

Suffrage

Suffrage is universal at eighteen years of age.

Political Participation

The marginalization of women in positions of political power that existed during the communist era has continued. Women accounted for 11.5 percent of the members of the Slovak National Council in 1992 and 14 percent in 1994.[37] After the 1998 elections, there were twenty women among the 150 deputies in parliament; two of the eighteen ministers in the government were women. As the result of the elections in 2002, twenty-eight of 150 deputies of the national legislature are women (18.6 percent).[38] Since the end of the communist era, the educational levels and occupations of women deputies have been similar to those of their male counterparts.[39]

However, since women still are few in number and dependent upon party backing for election, cooperation across party lines on issues of particular interest to women has been difficult. Some women deputies have participated in a group of women legislators. In 2003, interest in establishing an equal opportunities subcommittee of the committee on human rights and minorities was established in parliament.[40]

Women's Rights

Previous governmental bodies set up to address women's issues have proved to be relatively powerless bodies that have not been consulted on issues of importance to women, such as a draft law proposed by the government in 1992 that would have seriously limited access to abortion.[41]

Feminist Movements

Numerous women's groups have formed since 1989 as part of the rapid expansion of nongovernmental organizations (NGOs) in Slovakia. Women also play an important role in the NGO sector and its leadership. However, few of these organizations have been explicitly devoted to fostering gender equality. Two notable exceptions include the Alliance of Women of Slovakia, founded in 1992 with financial support from the EU's PHARE program, and women affiliated with *ASPEKT*, an explicitly feminist journal published since the early 1990s.

Several new initiatives developed in the context of the 2002 election campaign. These included a campaign against violence, "Every Fifth Woman," organized by women's nongovernmental organizations. In 2002, a new nongovernmental organization, *Urobme* (Let's do it), focused on getting out the vote among women and on increasing women's role in public life.[42] The activities of these groups supplemented those of *Forum zien 2000* (Women's Forum 2000), a program of fifty nongovernmental organizations designed to increase the representation of women in decision-making posts in politics. The forum has called on political parties to include at least 30 percent women on their candidate lists, supported independent candidates in elections, and organized a campaign to amend the electoral law to require every third candidate to be of a different gender.[43] The activities and potential impact of these groups remain limited, however, by many women's lack of interest in taking part in politics and particularly in becoming party members or running for political office. Their role in policy making has also been limited by the relatively weak links that have existed to date between women's groups and political leaders.

Lesbian Rights

Groups have also formed to defend the rights of lesbians and gays since 1989. In 1990, a 1961 law that decriminalized consenting relations among heterosexual couples over fifteen years of age but among homosexual couples eighteen years and older was revised to put both on the same footing.

Marriage. Nongovernmental groups, such as those joined in *Iniciativa Inakost* (Initiative Difference), have held seminars on registration of same-sex partners and pressured political leaders to adopt laws giving gay and lesbian couples the same rights as heterosexual couples in marriage,[44] but to date such laws have not been adopted. Popular prejudices against homosexuality are reinforced by the position of the Catholic Church on this issue.[45]

RELIGION AND SPIRITUALITY

The Catholic Church continues to be the most influential church in Slovakia, although there is also a strong Protestant tradition. Although many people are observant, the church appears to have relatively little impact on many day-to-day decisions, including the use of birth control and attitudes toward abortion. Most Slovaks support the right of women to choose to abort a pregnancy.[46] In June 1992, the government led by Prime Minister Jan Carnogursky, leader of the Christian Democratic Movement, introduced a bill to restrict abortion. Since it was clear that his government would not be reelected, this effort caused little controversy. In 2003, different views on abortion threatened the unity of the center-right coalition.

VIOLENCE

Domestic Violence

Domestic violence has only been recognized as a serious problem in Slovakia in the recent past. The government has done little to deal with this problem in terms of increasing awareness among the public, training police to intervene effectively, or providing shelters for abused women.[47]

In late 2001, a number of women's groups began an Internet campaign against violence, "Every Fifth Woman." Their web site includes information about legislation and advice for women in need of help. Sponsored by outside donors, the campaign aims to increase public awareness of domestic abuse and bring about legal changes to protect women.[48]

Trafficking in Women and Children

Trafficking in women and children has received little official attention.[49]

OUTLOOK FOR THE TWENTY-FIRST CENTURY

After a decade of independence, women in Slovakia face many challenges. With the introduction of the market economy and decreased state role in providing employment and services, women face many of the same problems as women in other developed Western states. Thus, many women, including those who have benefitted most in the last decade, face issues related to balancing work and family, childcare, and discrimination in the workplace. Other groups of women face more serious threats to their well-being, including unemployment, poverty, and abuse. Women's ability to articulate their interests and press governmental leaders to take action on issues of particular concern to them has been limited by their low level of representation in positions of political power, as well as by the lack of significant pressure from women's groups outside parliament. Popular attitudes that have not been supportive of gender equality among both elites and ordinary citizens have complicated the picture.

In the recent past, several initiatives have developed that suggest that this picture may be changing. Gender issues have come to be seen as legitimate topics of discussion and investigation among certain groups of intellectuals, and women's groups have banded together to mount public campaigns to increase women's representation in politics. The aspirations of Slovakia's leaders to join the EU and the actions of international donors have also helped to bring gender issues into the public domain. The ability of women's advocates to use public resources to address women's issues in the future will depend on the country's economic future and on political trends. It will also depend on how successful NGO leaders and those who advocate more concerted action on these issues will be in mobilizing public opinion outside the framework of an election campaign in support of such initiatives.

NOTES

Thanks to Maya Serban and Sean Timmins for their help with research for this article, and to Zora Butorova, Iveta Radicova, Anna Okruhlicova, and Grigorij Meseznikov for help in providing materials.

1. Statistical Office of the Slovak Republic (2001), www.statistics.sk.

2. CIA, *World Factbook* (Brassey's Inc., 2001).

3. CIA, 2001.

4. Rudolf Zajac and Peter Pazitny, "Health Care," in *Slovakia 2001*, ed. Grigorij Meseznikov et al. (Bratislava: Institute for Public Affairs, 2002), 407.

5. Sharon L. Wolchik, "Elite Strategy toward Women in Czechoslovakia: Liberation or Mobilization?" *Studies in Comparative Communism* 14, no. 2–3 (Summer/Autumn 1981): 23–42; Hilda Scott, *Does Socialism Liberate Women?* (Boston: Beacon Press, 1974); Alena Heitlinger, *Women and State Socialism* (Montreal: McGill–Queen's University Press, 1979); and Barbara Jancar, *Women under Communism* (Baltimore: Johns Hopkins University Press, 1978).

6. Sharon L. Wolchik, "Women and the Politics of Transition," in *Women in the Politics of Postcommunist Eastern Europe*, ed. Marilyn Rueschemeyer (Armonk, NY: M.E. Sharpe, 1994), 3–28; and Sharon L. Wolchik, "Transition Politics in the Czech and Slovak Republics," in *Women and Democracy*, ed. Jane S. Jaquette and Sharon L. Wolchik (Baltimore: Johns Hopkins University Press, 1998), 153–84.

7. Michael Vasecka, "Roma," in Meseznikov et al., 2002, 149–64.

8. See Zora Butorova, *Ona a On na Slovensku* (Bratislava: Focus, 1996), for public opinion on gender roles.

9. See Jancar, 1978; Heitlinger, 1979; Wolchik, 1981; and Wolchik, 1994, "Women."

10. Statistical Office of the Slovak Republic, 2002, www.statistics.sk.

11. See Ol'ga Gyarfasova and Marian Velsic, "Public Opinion," in Meseznikov et al., 2002, 217–19; and Vaseceka, 2002.

12. Statistical Office of the Slovak Republic, 2002.

13. Statistical Office of the Slovak Republic, 2002.

14. International Labor Organization (ILO), 2002, www.ilo.laborstats.

15. Iveta Radicova, "Social Policy," in Meseznikov et al., 2002, 429–44, esp. 429.

16. Ministry of Foreign Affairs of the Slovak Republic, *The National Report on the Status of Women* (Bratislava: Center for Strategic Studies for the Slovak Republic, 1995); and "Women and Human Rights," *Women's International Network News* 22, no. 2 (Spring 1996): 2.

17. Liba Paukert, "The Changing Economic Status of Women," in *Democratic Reform*, ed. Valerie M. Moghadem (New York: Oxford University Press, 1993), 248–79; Jacqueline Heinen, "The Reintegration into Work of Unemployed Women," in *Transition Countries* (Paris: OECD, 1994), 311–33; and Sharon L. Wolchik, "Gender Issues during Transition," in *East-Central European Economies in Transition* (Washington, DC: GPO, 1994), 147–70.

18. Butorova, 1996, 80–82.

19. The Slovak crown exchange rate to the US dollar was on October 8, 2002.

20. Henry P. David and Robert J. McIntyre, *Reproductive Behavior* (New York: Springer, 1981); and Sharon L. Wolchik, "Reproductive Policies," in *Reproducing Gender*, ed. Susan Gal and Gail Kligman (New York: Springer, 2000).

21. *Federalni statisticky urad. Cesky statisticky urad, Slovensky statisticky urad* (Prague: SVET, 1992), 589.

22. Jan Pisut and Ivan Kraus, "Education and Science," in Meseznikov, 2002, 455–62, esp. 453.

23. Wolchik, 1994, "Women."

24. Statistical Office of the Slovak Republic, 2002.

25. Jarmila Filadelfiova, "Demographic Developments," in Meseznikov, 2002, 569–96, esp. 575.

26. Statistical Office of the Slovak Republic, 2002.

27. Wolchik, 2000, 62.

28. Statistical Office of the Slovak Republic, 2002.

29. Butorova, 1996, 44.

30. Butorova, 1996, 44.

31. Filadelfiova, 2002, 572.

32. Filadelfiova, 2002, 573–74.

33. Zajac and Pazitny, 2002, 407.

34. Zajac and Pazitny, 2002, 408.

35. UNICEF, *Social Monitor 2002* (Florence, Italy: Author, 2002), 110.

36. UNICEF, 2002, 110.
37. Wolchik, 1994, "Women," 121.
38. Anna Okhrulicova, "The Results of the General Election" (Bratislava, 2002).
39. Wolchik, 1994, "Women," Interview, member of Parliament, Dr. Lazslo Nagy, Slovak National Council Bratislava, May 2003.
40. Okrhulicova, 2002, "The Results," 1.
41. Wolchik, 1994, "Women."
42. See "Urobme to," 2002, www.urobmeto.sk/prisekumy.html.
43. Anna Okruhlicova, "New Programmes for Women in Slovakia," paper presented in Graz, Austria, April 2002, 2–4.
44. Iniciativa Inakost," *ASPEKT* 2 (2001): 215–16.
45. See Vladimir Pirosik, Margita Janisova, and Viola Suterova, "Marginalovane skupiny," in Meseznikov, 2002, 783–804, esp. 784–85.
46. Butorova, 1996, 41.
47. Miroslav Kusy, "Human Rights," in Meseznikov, 2002, 113–26, esp. 120.
48. Okruhlicova, 2002, "New Programmes," 1–2; see also www.stopnasiliu.sk.
49. Okruhlicova, 2002, "New Programmes," 1–2; www.stopnasiliu.sk.

RESOURCE GUIDE

Suggested Reading

Heitlinger, Alena. *Women and State Socialism: Sex Inequality in the Soviet Union and Czechoslovakia*. Montreal: McGill–Queen's University Press, 1979.
Jaquette, Jane S., and Sharon L. Wolchik, eds. *Women and Democracy: Latin America and Central and Eastern Europe*. Baltimore: Johns Hopkins University Press, 1999.
Scott, Hilda. *Does Socialism Liberate Women?* Boston: Beacon Press, 1974.

Web Sites and Organizations

Aliancia zien na Slovensko, www.changenet.sk.

ASPEKT, www.aspekt.sk.
Feminist journal.

"Every Fifth Woman," www.kazdapiatazena.sk/.
Internet campaign against domestic abuse.

Urobme, www.urobmeto.sk.
New women's umbrella group founded in 2002 to increase women's presence in public life.

SELECTED BIBLIOGRAPHY

Butorova, Zora. *Ona a On na Slovensku*. Bratislava: Focus, 1996.
Central Intelligence Agency. *The World Factbook*. Brasseys, Inc., 2001, 447–49.
David, Henry P., and Robert J. McIntyre, eds. *Reproductive Behavior: Central and Eastern European Experience*. New York: Springer, 1981.
Federalni statisticky urad, Cesky statisticky urad, Slovensky statisticky urad. *Statisticka rocenka Ceske a Slovenske Federativni Republiky*. Prague: SVET, 1992.

Filadelfiova, Jarmila. "Demographic Developments." In *Slovakia 2001: A Global Report on the State of Society*, edited by Grigorij Meseznikov, Miroslav Kollar, and Tom Nicholson, 569–96. Bratislava: Institute for Public Affairs, 2002.

Gyarfasova, Ol'ga, and Marian Velsic. "Public Opinion." In *Slovakia 2001: A Global Report on the State of Society*, edited by Grigorij Meseznikov, Miroslav Kollar, and Tom Nicholson, 201–30. Bratislava: Institute for Public Affairs, 2002.

Heinen, Jacqueline. "The Reintegration into Work of Unemployed Women: Issues and Policies." In *Transition Countries: Transient or Persistent*? Paris: Center for Cooperation with the Economies in Transition, OECD, 1994, 311–33.

"*Iniciativa Inakost.*" *ASPEKT* 2 (2001): 215–16.

International Labor Organization (ILO). 2002. www.ilo.laborstats.

Jancar, Barbara. *Women under Communism*. Baltimore: Johns Hopkins University Press, 1978.

Kusy, Miroslav. "Human Rights." In *Slovakia 2001: A Global Report on the State of Society*, edited by Grigorij Meseznikov, Miroslav Kollar, and Tom Nicholson, 113–26. Bratislava: Institute for Public Affairs, 2002.

Ministry of Foreign Affairs of the Slovak Republic. *The National Report on the Status of Women in the Slovak Republic to the Fourth UN Conference on Women in Beijing*. Bratislava: Center for Strategic Studies of the Slovak Republic, 1995.

Okhrulicova, Anna. "New programmes for women in Slovakia." Paper presented at international conference in Graz, Austria, April 4, 2002.

———. "The results of the general election in the Slovak Republic from the gender perspective." Bratislava, 2002.

Paukert, Liba. "The Changing Economic Status of Women in the Period of Transition to a Market Economy System: The Case of the Czech and Slovak Republics after 1989." In *Democratic Reform and the Position of Women in Transitional Economies*, edited by Valerie M. Moghadam, 248–79. New York: Oxford University Press, 1994.

Pirosek, Vladimir, Margita Janisova, and Viola Suterova. "Marginalovane skupiny." In *Slovakia 2000: Suhrnna sprava o stave spolocnosti*, edited by Grigorij Meseznikov and Miroslav Kollar, 783–804. Bratislava: Institut pre verejne otazky, 2001.

Pisut, Jan, and Ivan Kraus. "Education and Science." In *Slovakia 2001: A Global Report on the State of Society*, 445–62. Bratislava: Institute for Public Affairs, 2002.

Radicova, Iveta. "Social Policy." In *Slovakia 2001: A Global Report on the State of Society*, 429–44. Bratislava: Institute for Public Affairs, 2002.

Statistical Office of the Slovak Republic. 2002. www.statistics.sk.

UNICEF. Innocenti Research Centre. *Social Monitor 2002. The MONEE Project. CEE/CIS/Baltics*. Florence, Italy: UNICEF, 2002.

"Urobme to." 2002. www.urobmeto.sk/prisekumy.html.

Vasecka, Michael. "Roma." In *Slovakia 2001: A Global Report on the State of Society*, 149–66. Bratislava: Institute for Public Affairs, 2002.

Wolchik, Sharon L. "Elite Strategy toward Women in Czechoslovakia: Liberation or Mobilization?" *Studies in Comparative Communism* 14, no. 2–3 (Summer-Autumn 1981): 23–42.

———. "Gender Issues during Transition." In *East-Central European Economies in Transition: Study Papers Submitted to the Joint Economic Committee, Congress of the United States*. Washington, DC: GPO, 1994, 147–70.

———. "Reproductive Policies in the Czech and Slovak Republics." In *Reproducing Gender: Politics, Publics, and Everyday Life after Socialism*, edited by Susan Gal and Gail Kligman, 58–91. Princeton, NJ: Princeton University Press, 2000.

————. "Transition Politics in the Czech and Slovak Republics." In *Women and Democracy: Latin America and Central and Eastern Europe*, edited by Jane S. Jaquette and Sharon L. Wolchik, 153–84. Baltimore: Johns Hopkins University Press, 1998.

————. "Women and the Politics of Transition in the Czech and Slovak Republics." In *Women in the Politics of Postcommunist Eastern Europe*, edited by Marilyn Rueschemeyer, 3–28. Armonk, NY: M.E. Sharpe, 1994.

"Women and Human Rights." *Women's International Network News* 22 no. 2 (Spring 1996): 2.

Zajac, Rudolf, and Peter Pazitny. "Health Care." In *Slovakia 2001: A Global Report on the State of Society*, 407–28. Bratislava: Institute for Public Affairs, 2002.

34

SPAIN

Eva Martínez-Hernández

PROFILE OF SPAIN

Spain, a southern European, Mediterranean nation, has a population over 38 million. The 1978 constitution defines it as a welfare and democratic state governed by a parliamentary monarchy. However, from 1939 to 1975 the country lived under the dictatorship of General Francisco Franco, whose regime abolished rights and liberties for the entire population and impeded Spanish women's efforts to gain the same social achievements as other European women. After Franco's death, the new constitution granted statutes of autonomy to the seventeen regions (*Comunidades Autónomas*) in Spain. As a consequence of this regional autonomy, subnational governments and parliaments were established with their own party systems and limited jurisdictions over some political areas. Thus, some public policies are implemented at both national and regional level, and this process of implementation may vary slightly from one autonomous region to another. This also occurs in the case of gender equality policy, which shows different trends and results in the various parts of the country.

The living conditions for women in Spain improved dur-

ing the 1980s mainly due to the efforts of the women's movement and the sympathetic new political regime. In 1982 the Socialist Party won the general elections in Spain, and the new government developed a more open policy on women's issues.

More than half of the Spanish population (51.03 percent) is female. The average life span for women is 82.10 years, and 75.30 for men. Spanish women total fertility rate is 1.24. Moreover, Spain ranks among the lowest in Europe in infant mortality rate (6.1) and maternal mortality rate (3.2).[1]

OVERVIEW OF WOMEN'S ISSUES

During the Franco regime, women in Spain suffered political, economic, and social discrimination. The role of women was highly circumscribed, and topics like sexuality or any form of birth control were absolutely taboo. Feminist organizations were silenced by the regime; thus, much of the progress in women's lives achieved by women's movements elsewhere in Europe was not a reality in Spain until the early 1980s.

The 1978 Constitution granted women some basic legal rights. Because of its political history, radical legal reforms for women's equality that had taken more than four decades to realize in other European countries were achieved in fewer than ten years. However, as happened everywhere else, legal equality in Spain did not necessarily mean real and effective equality. Although women's living conditions have improved in Spain, some of the prevailing feminist goals are still unfulfilled. For example, women still rank highest in unemployment, they are underrepresented in the political sphere, they remain responsible for caregiving and housework even if they work outside the home, and they are often battered, raped, and even killed by their partners.

EDUCATION

Opportunities

Educational achievement is a necessary condition of economic independence for girls and women, especially because it increases their opportunities for paid employment, earning power, age at marriage, control over childbearing, and even their exercise of legal and political rights.[2] The Spanish educational system has traditionally relied on the many private schools associated with the Catholic Church and subsidized by public funds. Compulsory schooling free of charge for children six to fourteen years old was established relatively late—in 1970—and only expanded to sixteen-year-olds as recently as 1990. Today, private schools still enroll around 30 percent of the whole student population. The government continues to subsidize these schools in spite of the now widespread existence of public schools.

Although increasing numbers of both males and females are in school, Spain still ranks lowest in Europe in the percentage of 25–29-year-olds that have completed at least high school education. Specifically, the figure for Spain is 36 percent, compared to 51 percent in Ireland, 62 percent in France, 77 percent in Sweden, and the European average of 59.9 percent.[3]

Nonetheless, women have made great strides in education, and their participation rate is accelerating faster than

Teacher leads young children on an outing in Madrid. Photo © TRIP/H. Rogers.

men's. Women constitute 49.78 percent of those enrolled in all levels of education. There are slightly more women in secondary education (51.92 percent of the total), and they make up half of the students enrolled in postgraduate studies. For Spanish universities, the present overall enrollment of women is 53.8 percent compared to 32 percent in the early 1970s. However, figures differ according to the type of studies chosen by both sexes: the presence of women is higher in health studies (70.81 percent), humanities (63.86 percent), and social and law studies (60.58 percent). Surprisingly, and for the first time in Spanish university history, they are the majority in the experimental sciences (53.43 percent), but they are still underrepresented in technical degrees (26.05 percent).

Significantly, 59 percent of teachers in the Spanish educational system are women; and at the early childhood educational level, women account for 95 percent of the staff. Women teachers are more represented in all levels of education except at university, where they account for only 32.49 percent of the faculty. The common assumption that education is the one crucial and straightforward path to improved employment and economic independence for women is not always easy to uphold.[4] In the case of Spain, at the same time that women's educational attainments are rising, ever-increasing levels of education are required for the job market. Consequently, the access of women to all levels of education has not necessarily meant better working conditions. In fact, there may be enormous gender discrepancies in incomes, with women concentrated at the lowest wage and salary levels, working in part-time jobs, and confronting sexual harassment in the workplace.

Literacy

It is very significant that illiteracy rates in Spain have fallen over the last years for both men and women, although women still show a higher illiteracy percentage than men (4.22 percent of women as opposed to 1.81 percent of men). The biggest difference between women and men's rates is found among people over sixty.

EMPLOYMENT AND THE ECONOMY

The International Labor Organization (ILO) defines people as "economically active" if they work for pay or profits, or if they are seeking such work during a specific time period. Moreover, to fit the ILO parameters of "economically active," the job must be full-time. The economic activity of Spanish women often remains outside this definition, because they are frequently working on a part-time contract, or without a contract at all in the so-called informal economy. Still, 40.24 percent of all economically active people in Spain are female. Actually, Spanish women's working activity has grown during the last ten years, but it is still lower than the economic activity rate recorded by Spanish men and by women in other European countries.

Job/Career Opportunities

The labor market is clearly sex-segregated. Women mainly work in the service sector, where 48.3 percent of all the employees are women, and they are highly underrepresented in the construction sector, where they constitute 4.8 percent of the employees. Not surprisingly, given the less discriminatory recruitment and promotional policies of the civil service, women's numbers there have increased, with 48.5 percent of the civil service posts currently occupied by women.

Important differences exist between jobs held mainly by women and jobs where the participation rate of males and females is similar. These differences are mainly the requisite training and the type of contract and levels of pay, and they consequently affect career possibilities. For the first time, the national government has recently approved measures to encourage the entrance of women into the professions where they are clearly underrepresented.

Overall, Spanish women have a worse place in the labor market than men in terms of employment rates, length of employment, access to full-time jobs, and the like. Thus, the percentage of economically inactive people is obviously higher for women, who are 64.42 percent of the whole inactive population. As a consequence of this, the rate of unemployment for women was 19.76 percent versus 9.47 percent for men in 2000. Unemployment benefits are not granted to all unemployed people in Spain. A minimum of one year of paid work is required to get four months' unemployment benefit at 80 percent of the average of the last earned salary. Recent statistical data show that only a small percentage of unemployed people are getting this financial help: 33 percent of unemployed men but only 18 percent of unemployed women. The difference between the figures for men and women are based mainly on the relation of women to the labor force that makes it difficult for women to meet the necessary conditions to qualify for these unemployment benefits. For example, they are 80 percent of the part-time workers, and most of the contracts signed by women are temporary contracts. Frequently, women work with short-term contracts or without any contract at all; moreover, many of the women registered as unemployed have never worked under a legal contract in their entire lives.

Pay

Women earn less than men in all economic sectors, and these differences differ greatly from one autonomous region to another. Recent statistical data from the whole country reveal that women's salaries are approximately 25 percent lower than men's salaries in all economic sectors. Moreover, since retirement pension benefit levels are tied to the employee's employment and pay histories, inequities between sexes are carried over to the retirement pension: the average pension received by retired women in Spain is 20 percent lower than the average one received by men.

Working Conditions

Sexual Harassment

Most recent surveys on working conditions reveal that women and men have similar levels of job satisfaction.[5] However, as happens in other countries, the problem of sexual harassment at work is an unresolved problem. Although both men and women can suffer sexual harassment, the majority of victims are women, and most of those guilty of harassment are men.[6] The legal definition of "sexual harassment" was not developed in Spain until the late 1980s, when trade union campaigns began to recognize it as a problem deserving state intervention.[7] A 1989 labor law included a legal definition of sexual harassment, and the *Estatuto de los Trabajadores*[8] (Worker's Statute) had to be reformed. Recent research carried out by *Comisiones Obreras* (a major trade union in Spain)[9] revealed that 18.3 percent of women workers had suffered some kind of unwanted harassment and more than one half have experienced "slight episodes" of harassment including verbal and obscene comments.

However, both men and women reject the use of the term "sexual harassment" to identify their own experience; thus, only 6.6 percent of women and 2 percent of men answered affirmatively when they were asked directly whether they had ever suffered sexual harassment. In spite of data indicating the widespread nature of the problem of sexual harassment, the legal definition and treatment of this phenomenon are still extremely vague, and the decisions are normally left to the courts.

Support for Mothers/Caretakers

Maternal Leave

Inequalities in the labor market are also revealed by the maternity leave legislation. In the case of Spain, labor legislation has at least made some strides in giving rights to pregnant women. When the Workers Statute was first approved, women were allowed twelve weeks of maternity leave; by the mid-1980s this period was raised to sixteen weeks, during which time the woman could claim 75 percent of her last pay rate. Moreover, women with children up to the age of nine months were granted one hour off from work per working day for breastfeeding purposes. Differences between regional laws are again important, especially in relation to maternity leave benefits and fathers' access to parental leave. In any case, in 1995, the maternity leave system in Spain, like the one in Ireland, was considered one of the most precarious systems in Europe as the level of their provision of facilities for maternal leave was much lower than in the other European countries.[10]

Recently, the Spanish government approved a revolutionary law with the purpose of harmonizing family responsibilities and paid work. The so-called *Ley de Conciliación de la Vida Familiar y Laboral* (Law on Reconciliation of Work and Family Life), approved in November 1999, included new possibilities for maternity and paternity leave. According to this law, maternity leave remains at sixteen weeks, but only the first six weeks are compulsory for the mother and the other ten can be taken by either of the parents. In 2000, 192,449 maternity and paternity leaves were taken, 26,503 more than in 1999.[11] The legal provisions for unpaid parental leave have been reconsidered as well. Either mother or father, but only one of them, is allowed to leave work for a maximum of three years to take care of their children with a guarantee that their job will be reserved for them when they return to work. These new opportunities also apply to adoptive parents.

The breastfeeding permit was made more flexible, especially regarding the distribution of this time throughout the day or month. Moreover, the legal provisions designed to prohibit employers from dismissing pregnant employees were broadened, mainly in response to the more liberal European Union policies. At the same time, from now on the national government will subsidize contracts to substitute maternity leave so that when a woman or a man decides to take this leave, the employer will take charge only of some of the additional expenses of a substitution contract.

Daycare

Daycare centers for young children in Spain are scarce. Even though the birthrate has been falling during the last years, state daycare provision is still insufficient. Research based on data on the 1980s has showed that most childcare policies in Spain are preschool programs for children over four years old, and the proportion of children under three who attended state-funded centers was very low.[12] Both private and public centers are normally expensive, and their schedules do not always suit the needs of employed parents. As a consequence, many young couples rely on help from family members—mainly grandmothers—or part-time baby-sitters to take care of their children. The debate over childcare in Spain has recently raised the question of whether daycare versus education should be stressed. Daycare professionals advocate the inclusion of the care of children 0–3 years old in the formal educational system, since then they are not only being cared for but also educated.

Daycare is mainly provided for by local and regional governments. However, during the last national election campaign, the leader of the Conservative Party, now the president of the Spanish government, promised a coordinated national policy to ensure daycare for all children. That promise has yet to be fulfilled.

Social/Government Programs

Besides unemployment benefits, the national government provides little financial assistance. Benefits such as family allowance, housing assistance, or antipoverty funds are granted in some way in all the autonomous regions. Men receive both contributive benefits (such as old-age pensions or unemployment benefits) and welfare benefits (such as antipoverty aid or housing assistance) much more often than women do. Recent data show that 61 percent of unemployed women do not receive any kind of state financial help. In fact, some of these welfare benefits are granted to families in general and not to individuals, and men are the principal beneficiaries in accordance with their traditional roles as breadwinners, a tradition still alive in Spanish society.

FAMILY AND SEXUALITY

Gender Roles

The 1999 law, enacted to harmonize family and working life, has failed, at least in the matter of so-called domestic work. Although the law includes provisions that, to some extent, facilitate the care of young children, it makes no concrete reference to the participation of men in other family responsibilities such as housework or caring for adult members of the family. In fact, although women have achieved full legal status and almost half of them now work outside the home, the traditional sexual division of economic roles is still in force.

According to recent data of the *Instituto de la Mujer*, Spanish women spend seven times more hours doing housework than their male partners. In quantitative terms, women dedicate 4 hours 24 minutes a day to housework in contrast to the 37 minutes spent by men. Although these data are pessimistic, there has surely been an evolution in Spanish men's attitudes toward house and caring work during the last ten years. This is especially important as family and domestic duties may prevent women from having opportunities in every other sphere.

Marriage

The Spanish family can no longer be assumed to conform to the model of the traditional nuclear family. Changes not only in social structures but also in mentalities have permitted a new range of family forms. For example, the number of single-parent families has increased considerably during the last years; these families are mainly composed of women and their children.

Marriage has undergone some important changes since the establishment of democracy. The new constitution grants, for the first time in forty years, the equality of husband and wife and the equality of children born in or out of wedlock. Although the status of married women has improved, the number of unmarried people living together has risen, and the average number of children per family has dropped. In 1998, 207,041 marriages were celebrated in Spain, 46.54 percent of them between people 25–29 years old. The birthrate has been falling steadily in Spain since the early 1970s, and data from 2000 reveal a rate of 1.18 children per woman and an average age for first-time mothers of 30.39.

It was not until 1981 that a limited divorce bill was approved. During the 1980s, half of the divorce cases filed by women were on the grounds of domestic violence. Since then, although main causes have varied, divorce rates have been increasing. The number of divorces in 1982 was 21,463; and in 1999, there were 59,547 legal separations, 36,900 divorces, and 133 annulments.

Reproduction

The legal provisions that protect women in the areas of family and reproduction have been of dubious success. Most of this legislation has encountered opposition and many obstacles to its implementation. The few reproductive rights that have been achieved were accompanied by extensive feminist demonstrations, as was the case with the Bilbao trials in 1979,[13] in which nine women were put on trial for having had abortions.[14]

Contraception and Abortion

It was not until 1979 that the prohibition against information, diffusion, and sale of contraceptives was repealed, and health centers were set up all over the country to provide guidance on family problems. All contraceptives, without exception, were and still are paid for by the woman who uses them. Despite some advances in women's reproductive rights, the number of family planning centers that are public and free of charge has decreased during the last five years.

At the beginning of 2001, the debate on contraception entered once again the public agenda with the approval of the sale and use of the "morning-after" pill, *Norvelo*. The sides of debate went from more conservative positions that condemned the abortive results of the pill to the most progressive ones that sought the dispensation of the pill free of charge. Finally, the use of the controversial pill was approved and permitted as long as it is prescribed by a doctor; however, its cost is not covered at all by publicly funded social security. As happens with some other policy agreements, the different autonomous regional governments in Spain have not uniformly adopted this national government resolution. Thus, for example, the regional government in Andalusia decided to distribute the pill free of charge, whereas the government in Navarre prohibited the sale of the pill in the region.

Abortion was a crime punishable by law until 1985, with the exception of the 1931 law[15] during the Republic regime. Before 1985, abortions in Spain were either performed illegally or pregnant women traveled to England or Holland.[16] The abortion law of 1985 was, and still is, an extremely limited piece of legislation that allows abortion under three special cases: the mother's health being endangered, pregnancy resulting from rape, or the malformation of the fetus.

Although the law was very limited, there were massive demonstrations against the bill, mainly from Catholic groups and associations, but demonstrations for a more comprehensive abortion bill were rare.[17] When the first legal abortions took place in Spain, a great number of health workers refused to carry out their duties and perform abortions on the grounds of their moral objections. In any case, the limited abortions permitted were not covered by the health service at the time.

Since 1985, several attempts to reform the abortion laws have failed. The latest proposal on the matter was put forward in 1998 when there was a conservative majority in Parliament. The bill was defeated by only one vote. This projected reform would have permitted abortion when pregnancy causes some personal, family or social problem to the mother. The debate was followed by great expectation from the general population and mass media, but conservative views and probably pressure from church authorities and anti-abortion organizations did not allow broader legislation on abortion.

Abortions have increased in the last years. Recent data indicate that 58,399 abortions were performed in Spain during 1999 with teen abortions making up 14.57 percent of those. The real figures are probably much higher since most abortions are not easily recorded by statistics. Some estimates are that the number is more than 100,000 every year, though there are no reliable data. The abortions performed in Spain are mainly illegal ones, and the few legal abortions occur mainly in private clinics. The number of abortion clinics has grown; but private centers account for 96 percent of the total. The reason invoked by most of the women who abort is risk to the mother's physical or psychological health (97.79 percent), while 2.08 percent refer to fetus malformation and only 0.03 percent to rape. As a matter of fact, most of this 97.79 percent refers to psychological harm to mothers, which is actually the "legal disguise" that abortion has acquired in Spain.

HEALTH

Health Care Access

According to recent data, Spanish women attend the health service centers four times more often than men do. However, most of the time the patient is someone other than the woman—either a son or a daughter or a dependent relative. As for hospitalization rates, there are not great differences in frequency between the sexes. It is noteworthy that women's principal reason for staying in hospital is not a disease but pregnancy and childbirth.

Women are not only consumers of health services, but they are also major providers of health care, both unpaid and paid. In fact, in paid health care women are the majority of workers in Spain, as nurses are predominantly women and they do most of the caring work.

Diseases and Disorders

As happens in other societies in Europe, women in Spain report more illness, chronic disease, and distress than men, despite their generally greater longevity. Indeed, it is longer life itself that exposes women to more of the generative diseases of old age. Thus women are more likely to suffer from diseases such as arthritis, Alzheimer's, or osteoporosis. Women in Spain die principally because of disorders of the circulatory system (46.21 percent), tumors (20.52 percent), or diseases related to the respiratory system (7.65 percent).

AIDS

Women constitute only 20 percent of diagnosed cases of AIDS in the country.[18]

Eating Disorders

The number of women affected by eating disorders is growing, especially affecting teenagers. Recent data show that 1–4 percent of young women in Spain suffer from some kind of eating disorder, bulimia being much more frequent than anorexia.

Cancer

As for other typical female diseases, health authorities have lately been paying special attention to breast cancer. Almost all regional authorities are carrying out detection and prevention programs. These detection screenings are completely free for women between fifty and sixty-four years old, although recent debate has focused on the possibility of broadening the age eligibility.

POLITICS AND LAW

Suffrage

Spanish women got their right to vote for the first time in 1931[19] during the Second Republic.[20] Passive suffrage[21] had been conceded some years before so that at the beginning of 1931, the election system did not exclude women from running for election, even though they still lacked the right to vote. Thus, three women were elected to the 1931 Constituent Assembly, and two of them took the lead in the debate about the women's suffrage.

During the drafting of the 1931 constitution, there was bitter debate over women's right to vote. The high level of illiteracy among Spanish women, the close relationship they had with the Catholic Church, and the absence of a strong suffrage movement shaped this debate. The strongest defender of women's right to vote was Clara Campoamor, who had to face opposition from both left- and right-wing parties. Surprisingly, the Socialist Party members opposed women's suffrage, arguing that women were still not prepared for political life and that their conservative and Catholic political attitudes would give the election victory to the right. Finally, after a controversial debate, a constitution granting female suffrage and sexual equality was passed, and women voted for the first time in 1933.

The Second Republic ended with the Civil War won by Franco in 1939. From then until 1975 an authoritarian regime was set up in Spain, which abolished all the liberties and rights won by men, and especially by women, during the republic. After the death of Franco, the new political regime approved a constitution that reestablished some of these rights.

Political Participation

Women's entrance into political parties and institutions has occurred slowly from the democratic transition period to today. Women's participation in politics dropped off after the first election in 1977, and their presence in political parties has remained low. The presence of women in the Spanish parliament has increased from 1977 onwards. Women accounted for a mere 6.3 percent of the members of parliament at the time of the first parliamentary election, but for almost 30 percent by 2000.

This significant increase is due in part to the Socialist Party's use of the sex quota system and its determination to include more women at the executive level. Thus, the first woman minister since the second republic was appointed in 1981. Since then, women have occupied different posts in the Spanish cabinet, but they have never achieved more than 40 percent of the cabinet.

Women's Rights

The 1978 Spanish Constitution includes three concrete articles referring to equality: article 1.1 includes equality as one of the four principal values of the Spanish democratic constitution. Following this, article 9.2 states the duty to "promote the conditions for a real and effective equality and liberty . . . (and to) remove the obstacles to this equality and liberty." Finally, article 14 establishes, "All Spanish citizens are equal before the law regardless of race, sex, religion, etc." With these articles, in 1978 the Spanish Constitution underwrote women and men's equality before the law. However, although the constitution explicitly supported formal equality, the conditions for real equality had yet to appear; and there were indeed obstacles to be removed. As a matter of fact, there were very few references to women in the Spanish Constitution. The only articles that refer to women per se are related to motherhood, marriage, and equality within the civil service (art. 39.2, 32.1, and 23.2).

During the 1980s, several institutions with the objective of promoting equality between the sexes, the so-called femocracies (i.e., government agencies to address women's issues), were set up in Spain. As it happens with gender equality policy in general, these government agencies emerged in Spain at least fifteen years later than in other European countries. In fact, as a consequence of the political situation, these institutions were not necessarily established under pressure from society or social movements but rather as part of the general and rapid Europeanization that took place in Spain during the transition to democracy. Thus, in 1983, the Spanish Institute for Women's Rights (*Instituto de la Mujer*) was created; and some years later, almost all regional governments created some sort of femocracy. The importance of the creation of these institutions for the development of gender equality policy at all political levels is not to be doubted. However, femocracies in Spain tend to be assigned a very small budget, they normally lack executive authority, and their impact in the policy-making process never goes further than agenda setting.

Feminist Movements

Trends in women's political participation have varied significantly during the last thirty years. The new Spanish feminist movement emerged in the mid-1970s during the period of the transition to democracy. During Franco's dictatorship, feminism was necessarily a clandestine movement, which meant that it could not develop a mass base in the population. Thus, the Spanish feminist movement emerged some years later than in most other European countries. During the first years of transition, there were several national meetings of feminists that regularly involved over 3,000 women from all over the country. Because of its historical link with the transition to democracy, the fight for women's rights became inseparable from the fight for democracy and universal rights. As a consequence, left-wing parties adopted feminist demands, and the two positions (double versus single militancy)[22] became more polemical than in other countries. Autonomous feminist groups emerged around 1976 in Madrid, Barcelona, Valencia, and Bilbao and were opposed to collaboration with political parties. Thus, although Spanish feminism is generally regarded as being weak in comparison to that of other western European countries, this was certainly not true in the major cities.

At the beginning of the 1980s, once the new political framework was set up, the feminist movement was characterized by less political visibility. The movement was divided by disputes and established networks almost disappeared, uniting only to address very concrete issues such as sexual assault and abortion. During these years, the feminist movement notably diminished its presence in the streets. New feminist groups arose, a large number of women's associations was created, and women's issues arrived at the university. From then on, the action changed to other spheres such as the organizations of events, courses, conferences, and workshops for discussion.

Today Spanish feminism has reorganized and has strengthened its networks. Traditional feminist issues such as abortion, violence, and employment remain alive and share the feminist agenda with other concerns such as political representation, minority rights, or the relationship with so-called femocracies. Previous disputes among different positions in feminism have been dispelled, and contemporary feminist groups tend to unite in active networks all over the country. Recently, after more than a decade without any national meeting of feminist groups, in December 2000, the

State Women's Conference was held in Córdoba with more than 3,000 feminist women from all over Spain in attendance.

Lesbian Rights

Neither femocracies nor political parties nor feminist organizations in Spain have developed a visible discourse on lesbian rights. Although lesbians in Spain have been traditionally organized within the feminist movement, the general feminist discourse has ignored them for years, and only recently have their claims been incorporated into the feminist agenda. As for political parties, left-wing parties have recently included in their electoral programs the need for recognition of rights for sexual minorities, but no great advancement has taken place up until now.

Lesbian rights are slightly different in the various autonomous regions. There is no explicit consideration at the national level of legislation, so some regional governments have adopted concrete policies on the matter. Lesbians are not allowed to marry, but they can register as a civil union in some regional institutions. This does not necessarily give them inheritance rights, as that decision is normally left to the courts. As for parenthood, some regional governments allow lesbian women to adopt children, but again there is no national legislation that deals with the matter. In fact, recent debate on a law for so-called de facto couples (*parejas de hecho*) that would grant equal rights to unmarried couples (whatever the sex of the partners) and married ones has been refused by the Conservative Party currently in office.

RELIGION AND SPIRITUALITY

Spain is traditionally a predominantly Roman Catholic country. In 1998, 82 percent of the population considered themselves Catholic. The percentage is slightly higher for women, who declared themselves Catholic in 86.3 percent of the cases compared to 77.3 percent of men who considered themselves Catholic. Other religions are rare and constitute only 0.4 percent of the whole population, and 13.8 percent of Spanish people claimed that they were agnostic or atheistic.[23]

During the first years of the Franco regime, the Catholic Church was strongly allied with the ruling political forces; but from then on, the influence of the Spanish church in society has changed but remained prominent. In fact, the widespread existence of private Catholic schools and the lack of public school facilities before the 1970s enabled the Spanish church to play a definitive role in the socialization of new generations. Today Catholic schools continue to receive state financial aid and are a key element in the education network.

The Catholic Church is often seen as one of the parties responsible for delaying achievement by Spanish women of some of their rights, such as those related to reproduction. However, reasons for this delay must be placed in a broader context, which includes, apart from religion, aspects such as political history and the dominant political culture. In any case, the Catholic Church continues to play an important role as a pressure group when issues such as abortion, divorce, or contraceptive rights reach the political agenda.

Women's Roles

Despite the higher religiosity of women than men, they play a very subsidiary role in the Spanish Church, which has not modified its decision to exclude women from the priesthood and, consequently, from the church hierarchy. Recently, internal debate within the Spanish Catholic Church, together with the low number of young people choosing the priesthood as a vocation, have led to reconsideration of some of the limits on women in the church. As a consequence, women have been allowed to help in some religious ceremonies.

Rituals and Religious Practices

Religious practices such as attending church regularly are more rare among the Spanish population. However, women are again the ones who go to church more often, and the differences between men and women are greatest for people over sixty.

VIOLENCE

The first references to violence against women in Spain appeared at the beginning of the 1980s. Before this, cases of rape, sexual abuse, or domestic violence were often silenced: there were few official complaints, women ignored their own rights, and laws were intended more to prosecute runaway victims rather than to punish the guilty.

Public services for the care of women who have suffered gender violence have become widespread all over the country. There are, again, differences among the various autonomous regions, which each rely on their different social systems, but in general, only a few of these public centers have sufficient human and economic resources to accomplish their task. Shelters for battered women have been established throughout Spain; but in most of them women receive limited psychological care and can only stay for a limited period of time (normally less than three months).

Regional gender policies have improved, in some cases, the opportunities for women who are battered. Thus, for example, the Basque Autonomous Region approved financial aid for women in this situation, and the government of Castilla–La Mancha has proposed a highly criticized measure that allows the publication of the names of the aggressors. Even though there has undoubtedly been progress in addressing the needs of female victims and their children, there is still no comprehensive policy to prevent violence against women.

Domestic Violence

Domestic violence was not defined as an offense until the approval of the 1989 Penal Code, when "habituality" in battering a woman (i.e., at least three times) entered the offenses chapter of the code. However, most of the episodes of violence are typified as misdemeanors (*faltas*) rather than as offenses (*delitos*) and thus carry a lighter punishment.

Until the divorce bill was approved in 1981, women who were battered or raped by their own husbands could not officially complain. Moreover, wife abuse was not illegal, and there were no mechanisms in policy or law to help victims. The high incidence of violence in Spanish marriages did not end with the legalization of divorce, and figures show an alarming rate even today.

The issue of domestic violence was first given public importance as late as 1997, when a woman was burned alive by her former husband after she revealed his battering in a TV program. Mass media, government, and society in general suddenly realized the importance of this problem that had remained just a feminist issue for decades. Unfortunately, this case was not unique; but it shaped public opinion and helped to define a new political agenda around the matter. As a result, the government approved a plan against domestic violence, and some important changes were included in the legislation, such as the inclusion of psychological violence as a punishable offense and a prohibition against some men approaching their victims.

It is noteworthy that no data on violence against women were recorded until the early 1980s. Moreover, there are still no reliable figures on violence, since estimates are that only 10–30 percent of the women who are battered or raped file official charges. The limited data from official complaints to the police show around 30,000 cases of violence against women every year. Seventy-five percent of these complaints charge domestic violence, whereas the other 25 percent refer to sexual assault, sexual abuse, or sexual harassment. With the approval of the 1989 Penal Code, the legal concept of rape was broadened to include both oral and anal rape as well.

OUTLOOK FOR THE TWENTY-FIRST CENTURY

In the twentieth century, Spanish women made important advances in the struggle for their rights, and feminism as a political movement addressed many women's demands. However, problems remain. Spanish women, like women elsewhere in Europe, have broken out of the private sphere to enter public life; now it is time for men to enter the private realm.

NOTES

The author would like to thank the editor Lynn Walter for her understanding, patience, and suggestions for this chapter and Carrie Hamilton and Arantxa Elizondo for their valuable comments on earlier drafts.

1. Unless otherwise noted, all statistical data in this chapter are derived from *Instituto de la Mujer La Mujer en Cifras*, 2001, www.mtas.es/mujer/meifras.

2. Gisela Kaplan, *Contemporary Western European Feminism* (London: UCL Press, 1992).

3. *Instituto Nacional de Estadística, España en Cifras*, 2000, www.ine.es.

4. Kaplan, 1992, 23.

5. The most recent and complete research on this matter can be found in *Encuesta de Calidad de Vida en el Trabajo*, 2000, www.mtas.es/Estadisticas/ECTV/index.htm.

6. Celia Valiente, "The Regulation of Sexual Harassment in the Workplace in Spain," in *Crossing Borders*, ed. Barbara Hobson and Anne Marie Berggren (Stockholm: Forskningsradsnaamnden, 1997), 179–200.

7. Valente, 1997.

8. The *Estatuto de los Trabajadores* is the main Spanish legal text on workers' rights and duties.

9. The main results of this research had been compiled in Begoña Pernas and Josefina Olza et al., *El Alcance del Acoso Sexual en el Trabajo en España* (Madrid: Secretaría Confederal de la Mujer de Comisiones Obreras, 2000).

10. M. José Aubet, Democracias desiguales (Barcelona: Ed. El Serbal, 1995), 191.

11. Data about men's use of parental leave after the approval of the new law are not available. However, previous research, which was conducted at a time when men were allowed to enjoy only one month out of the sixteen weeks of parental leave, estimated that just a few men (less than 1 percent) would take the opportunity.

12. Celia Valiente, "Women in Segmented Labour Markets and Continental Welfare States: The Case of Spain," in *Comparing Families*, ed. Linda Hantrais and Marie-Therese Letablier (Leicestershire, UK: European Research Centre, 1996), 86–93, esp. 91.

13. The so-called Bilbao (or Basauri) trials had become a referent in the fight for abortion rights in Spain. The trials took place in Basauri (a city close to Bilbao, in the north of Spain) in 1979, and it was the first major episode related to abortion after the democracy was set up. The feminist movement of the whole country mobilized together against these trials.

14. Kaplan, 1992, 202.

15. The first abortion legislation in Spain was approved in 1931 during the Second Republic. In 1936 most of the revolutionary republican policies disappeared during the Civil War that lasted until 1939. The 1931 law on abortion was abolished by Franco's military regime, which ruled in Spain from 1939 to 1975.

16. In 1983 more than 23,000 Spanish women went to London for abortions (Kaplan, 1992, 203).

17. M. Angeles Duran and M. Teresa Gallego, "The Women's Movement and the New Spanish Democracy," in *The New Women's Movement*, ed. Drude Dahlerup (London: Sage, 1986), 200–226.

18. *Instituto Nacional de Estadística*, 2000.

19. Before 1931, women were granted the right to vote in 1924 during the General

Primo de Rivera dictatorship (1923–1930). At that time, women's suffrage was conceded only to either single or widowed women but not to married ones, "in order to prevent political disputes within marriage." However, elections were never held, and women could not exercise their right to vote.

20. The Second Republic was an important period for women's rights and liberties. During this time, women got not only their right to vote but also some important political measures related to divorce, the use of contraceptives, abortion, and so on. Most of these rights disappeared completely with Franco's regime.

21. "Passive suffrage" is the right of a person to run for a post in political elections whereas "active suffrage" is the right to vote. In most of the countries, women had achieved both passive and active suffrage at the same time. However, in the case of Spain, women were allowed to run for election earlier than they were allowed to vote.

22. "Single militancy" is the position that feminists should work solely within their own movement organizations, whereas "double militancy" means that feminists should work both within their autonomous organizations and within political parties.

23. Data on religiosity have been compiled from recent research carried out by the Spanish Center for Sociological Research (*CIS, Centro de Investigaciones Sociológicas*). More information is available at www.cis.es.

RESOURCE GUIDE

Suggested Reading

Astelarra, Judith. "Women's Political Culture and Empowerment in Spain." In *Women Transforming Politics: Worlwide Strategies for Empowerment*, edited by Jill M. Bystydzienski, 41–50. Bloomington: Indiana University Press, 1992.

Duran, M. Angeles, and M. Teresa Gallego. "The Women's Movement and the New Spanish Democracy." In *The New Women's Movement*, edited by Drude Dahlerup, 200–226. London: Sage, 1986.

Kaplan, Gisela. *Contemporary Western European Feminism*. London: UCL Press, 1992.

Martínez-Hdez, Eva, and Arantxa Elizondo. "Women in Politics: Are They Really Concerned about Equality? An Essay on the Basque Political System." In *European Journal of Women's Studies* 4, no. 4 (November 1997): 451–72.

Threlfall, Monica. "The Women's Movement in Spain." *New Left Review* 151 (1985): 44–73.

Valiente, Celia. "State Feminism and Gender Equality Policies: The Case of Spain (1983–95)." In *Sex Equality Policy in Gender Europe*, edited by Frances Gardiner. London: Routledge, 1997.

Web Sites

Federación Nacional de Mujeres Rurales, www.femur.es.

Instituto de la Mujer, www.mtas.es.

Librería de Mujeres, www.unapalabraotra.org/libreriamujeres.html.

Mujeres en Red, www.nodo50.org/mujeresred.

Periódico de Mujeres "Andra," www.andra-periodico.com.

Plataforma Política de Mujeres "Plazandreok," www.euskalnet.net/plazandreok.

Revista Fempress, www.fempress.cl.

Revista Prensa Mujer, www.prensamujer.com.

Voces de Mujer, www.vocesmujer.com.

Organizations

Asociación Univeristaria de Estudios de Mujeres (AUDEM)
Departamento de Filología Anglogermánica y Francesa
Campus de Humanidades—Universidad de Oviedo
E-33071-Oviedo
Email: info@audem.com
Web site: www.audem.com

Federación de Organizaciones Feministas del Estado Español
C/Barquillo, 44-2° izda
E-28004-Madrid
Phone/fax: (34) 91-308.12.33
Email: feministas@jet.es
Web site: www.nodo50.org/feministas

Instituto de la Mujer
C/Condesa de Venadito, 34
E-28027-Madrid
Phone: (34) 91-347.80.00
Email: inmujer@mtas.es
Web site: www.mtas.es/mujer

SELECTED BIBLIOGRAPHY

Duran, M. Angeles, and M. Teresa Gallego. "The Women's Movement and the New Spanish Democracy." In *The New Women's Movement*, edited by Drude Dahlerup, 200–216. London: Sage, 1986.

Gallego Mendez, M. Teresa. "Women's Political Engagement in Spain." In *Women and Politics Worldwide*, edited by Barbara J. Nelson and Najma Chowdhury, 661–73. New Haven: Yale University Press, 1994.

Kaplan, Gisela. *Contemporary Western European Feminism*. London: UCL Press, 1992.

Valiente, Celia. 1996. "Women in Segmented Labour Markets and Continental Welfare States: The Case of Spain." In *Comparing Families and Family Policies in Europe*, edited by Linda Hantrais and Marie-Therese Letablier, 86–93. Leicestershire: European Research Centre, 1996.

———. "The Regulation of Sexual Harassment in the Workplace in Spain." In *Crossing Borders: Gender and Citizenship in Transition*, edited by Barbara Hobson and Anne Marie Berggren, 179–200. Stockholm: Forskningsradsnaamnden, 1997.

Selected Spanish Bibliography

Aubet, M. José. *Democracias desiguales. Cultura política y paridad en la Unión Europea.* Barcelona: Ed. El Serbal, 1995.

Elizondo, Arantxa. *La Presencia de Mujeres en los Partidos Políticos de la Comunidad Autónoma del País Vasco.* Vitoria: Gobierno Vasco, 1999.

Instituto de la Mujer. *La Mujer en Cifras.* 2001. www.mtas.es/mujer/mcifras.

Instituto Nacional de Estadística. *España en Cifras 2000.* 2000. www.ine.es.

Martínez Hdez, Eva. "Políticas Públicas para la igualdad entre los sexos: reflexiones sobre el caso español (1975–1997)." In *Mujeres en Política: Análisis y Práctica,* edited by Edurne Uriarte and Arantxa Elizondo, 211–32. Barcelona: Ariel, 1997.

Pernas, Begoña, and Josefina Olza et al. *El Alcance del Acoso Sexual en el Trabajo en España.* Madrid: Secretaría Confederal de la Mujer de Comisiones Obreras, 2000.

Uriarte, Edurne, and Arantxa Elizondo. *Mujeres en Política: Análisis y Práctica.* Barcelona: Ariel, 1997.

35

SWEDEN

Linda Haas

PROFILE OF SWEDEN

Sweden lies in Scandinavia and is about the size of California. Women are 50 percent of the population of 8.9 million. Females born in 2001 were expected to live 82 years, compared to 77 for males. In 2002, the fertility rate was 1.6 children per woman. In 2002, 3.4 per 1,000 babies died in their first year. The maternal mortality rate is also very low, around 5 per 100,000 live births.[1] Since World War II, Sweden has offered sanctuary to many refugees. By 1999, one fifth of the population was foreign born or had at least one foreign-born parent.[2]

Sweden is a constitutional monarchy; policy making is the responsibility of a 350-member Parliament. The Social Democratic Party first won office in 1932, beginning a long era of buildup of the welfare state. According to political scientist Maud Eduards, "Equity and equality are probably the most basic values in Swedish—and Nordic—political culture. These conceptions have surely made it easier for women's demands to enter the political agenda."[3] Sweden has a capitalist economy, which in 2001 was strong, with low unemployment and inflation rates.[4]

OVERVIEW OF WOMEN'S ISSUES

Since the late 1960s, the government has been outspoken in its advocacy of gender equality (*jämställdhet*). In 1972, it set up a national commission on gender equality; based on its recommendations, a division for equality affairs was established at the cabinet level in

1982. By 2000, this division supervised a Council on Equality Issues, an Equal Opportunities Ombudsman, an Equal Opportunities Commission, and twenty-one regional experts on equality issues.[5] Sweden's vision of a gender equitable society was outlined in a recent government report:

> The over-all goal of gender equality policy [*jämställdhetspolitiken*] is a society where women and men have the same opportunities, rights and obligations within all important areas of social life. This means an equal division of power and influence, equal opportunities to become economic independent, equal conditions and benefits in regard to business ownership, employment, and workplace training. This also means equal access to education and opportunities to advance personal ambitions, interests and talents, shared responsibility for home and children, and freedom from gender-related violence.[6]

The government and all political parties promote gender equality "as an important strategic step on the path to justice, democracy, and the achievement of social parity."[7] By 1995, "The United Nations declared that Sweden had advanced further along the path to equality and equal opportunity than any other nation."[8] Historians consider the decision of the Swedish government to eliminate gender roles "a bloodless revolution," since resistance to change, especially among men, has been very strong.[9]

Policymakers did not develop this radical stance toward gender equality all on their own or overnight. They were pressed to do so over a long period of time by feminists inside and outside the traditional political system. Contemporary Swedish feminists are concerned about the remaining gender gap in pay, which undermines women's economic independence. They are increasingly concerned about male dominance, especially the low proportion of women in the management of work organizations, universities, and unions. There is strong interest in women's "bodily integrity," which includes issues related to sexual harassment in schools and workplaces, images of women in the media and advertising, the health and safety of employed women, and preventing rape and domestic violence. The division of labor in the family has also received close scrutiny, especially men's lack of equal sharing of responsibility for childcare and paid parental leave.

EDUCATION

Opportunities

Education is free at all levels in Sweden. As early as 1969, government guidelines portrayed education as "a powerful emancipatory instrument for social change, and equality between men and women was identified as one of the most important changes."[10] Despite government intentions, "There is no automatic awareness of equality issues at all levels in the educational system."[11]

Children begin mandatory "comprehensive" schooling at age seven. The national curriculum states that children should be taught the "equal value of all people, equality between women and men, and solidarity with the weak and vulnerable."[12] Both boys and girls are taught to be family bread-winners and share domestic responsibilities through classwork and appren-ticeships outside the classroom.

The majority of comprehensive schoolteachers were female in 2001 (73 percent). They receive training in equality issues, but many assume that they already treat girls and boys equally and that knowledge about women is well integrated into the curriculum. However, teachers still give males more time and attention than female students. Even with less attention, girls receive better grades than boys in languages and mathematics. One third of teachers report witnessing increasing problems with bullying and racism by boys, directed toward females and immigrants. In 1999, schools initiated programs to develop boys' "emotional intelligence," designed to improve their capacities for empathy and care.[13]

Youth complete comprehensive school at age sixteen. Most attend sec-ondary school to prepare for specific occupations or higher education. Al-though secondary school policy dictates that both sexes have equal access to education and opportunities to develop personal ambitions, interests, and talents, there is a distinct sex-typed distribution in students' choices of study subjects. In 1996–1997, girls were 87 percent of nursing students and 65 percent of social studies students, whereas 87 percent of engineering and technology students were male. Sociologist Gunilla Fürst reports, "The minority status of the female students has placed them in a vulnerable position. They are visibly deviant and are subjected to jibes and coarse jokes."[14]

Entrance to colleges and universities is competitive, based on past aca-demic performance (where women usually excel) and entrance exams (where men usually excel). Parents' financial status is not taken into ac-count in determining student financial aid, and overall women's average study assistance is the same amount as men's.[15] In 1998, women were a majority of students pursuing higher education (58 percent), up from 37 percent in 1972. This increase can partly be explained by the improved status of nursing and teacher training programs, which were recently added to the higher education system.[16]

According to a 1987 parliament resolution, colleges and universities must establish a minimum of 40 percent of each sex in all programs.[17] Admission standards and financial stipends should give females encouragement to en-ter science and technical fields and give males encouragement to enter teaching and caregiving professions.[18] Nevertheless, women are still more likely than men to study education, humanities, the arts, the social and behavioral sciences, and medicine. Men are more likely than women to pursue degrees in business, engineering, law, science, computer science, and mathematics.

Only 37 percent of college-level instructors are female.[19] In 1998, only 8 percent of full professors were women. Prompted by complaints about women's lack of power in the educational system, the government in 1998 set aside funds to triple the number of female professors in ten years' time.[20] Colleges and universities must also establish written action plans and procedures for combating and reporting sexual harassment, a problem estimated to affect 15 percent of students.[21]

In 1998, women completed 60 percent of all university degrees.[22] By 1997, women earned 22 percent of engineering degrees and 51 percent of business degrees.[23] Thirty percent of all Swedish women ages 20–64 have completed college, in comparison to 26 percent of men.[24] In 1997, women were 44 percent of graduate students, up from 28 percent in 1981. Women are more likely to pursue graduate studies in law, social sciences, and medicine, and men are more likely to pursue advanced degrees in natural and technological sciences.[25] In 1998, women earned 32 percent of all doctorates, up from 11 percent in 1972.[26]

Colleges and universities have decided to prepare students to analyze disciplinary knowledge from a gender perspective. To date, this occurs mainly in economics and law but is spreading to other disciplines (e.g., psychology). Gender research receives increasing support from public funding agencies. Centers for feminist research and women's studies courses exist at all large universities, and a National Secretariat for Gender Research was established in 1997. It has been noted that "gender-related research at colleges and universities has played a vital part in the development of Swedish equality policy."[27]

Literacy

Sweden was one of the first countries to establish 100 percent literacy, and nearly all citizens (98 percent) have completed some formal schooling.[28]

EMPLOYMENT AND THE ECONOMY

Job/Career Opportunities

Swedish women historically have been very involved in economically productive activities. As late as the end of the nineteenth century, over half still lived on farms, where they performed physically demanding outdoor work. Then, according to historian Lena Sommestad, "Women's status was tied to working capacity and physical strength, rather than to motherhood or domestic virtues."[29] In cities, households were often poor, which created pressure on women to bring in income. Women also outnumbered men

105 to 100, because immigrants to America tended to be disproportionately male. By 1920, 36 percent of city women were registered as employed for pay. Unknown numbers of women worked at "unregistered" jobs involving cleaning and laundry or home production of consumer goods such as textiles, clothes, and potatoes and other vegetables.

Swedish woman working in the Erickson Telephone plant in Stockholm. Photo © Jonathan Blair/CORBIS.

The idea that there should be separate spheres for men and women, based on work and family, never became popular in Sweden, since it was in conflict with the need for women's economic contributions. Women's importance as family breadwinners was symbolized in the 1920 Marriage Act, which stipulated that both spouses were obligated to provide for the family. However, according to Sommestad, "If the wife was not engaged in any gainful occupation, her domestic work was equated with male cash income as a contribution to family maintenance."[30]

As early as the 1930s, women's right to seek outside employment regardless of marital status was widely accepted.[31] The birthrate dipped well below replacement level during the Depression, so the government tried to encourage childbearing through marriage loans and free prenatal and maternity care. Some Social Democrats were concerned that pronatalist policies would negatively affect women's status. Noted social reformers Gunnar and Alva Myrdal argued "Higher birth rates must be accompanied by freedom of [reproductive] choice for women, and population policies must acknowledge employed mothers as a 'social fact.'"[32] Conservatives attempting to ban married women from employment made no headway; even male-dominated trade unions supported women's right to work.

Despite policymakers' intentions, by 1970, only 38 percent of married women worked outside the home. A million new jobs were created in the 1970s as the welfare state developed and public employment expanded.[33] New jobs in retail, service, and manufacturing were also created as the economy expanded. To deal with labor shortages, policymakers decided that married women needed incentives to enter the labor market. In 1971, the tax system was changed so that spouses' incomes were taxed individually, not jointly, which lowered taxes on dual-earner households. In 1980, the first equal employment opportunities legislation was passed, and by 1992, workplaces were required to develop annual "equality plans" covering recruitment, retention, promotion, pay, working conditions, and opportunities to balance employment and parenthood. Today, most companies have full-time staff devoted to the equality issue, linked by the government-sponsored Association for the Promotion of Equal Opportunity.[34]

In 2002, women made up 48 percent of the labor force with 79 percent of women ages 20–64 in paid employment, compared to 84 percent of men.[35] Native-born women have a higher employment rate than women born outside the country (80 percent vs. 64 percent).[36] The "dual-breadwinner" model has become the established norm. In 1975, one third of families with children involved a breadwinning husband and a wife who stayed home to care for children. By 1993, only 8 percent fitted this model. Women's contributions to families' disposable income increased from 31 percent in 1970 to 41 percent in 1994, and the percentage of women who earned more than their partners doubled from 10 percent to 20 percent between 1975 and 1995.[37]

Historically, women have been much more likely than men to work part-time, mainly because employers have offered reduced work hours to attract mothers into the labor market. Since the 1980s, all parents are entitled to request a six-hour workday (and less pay) to combine paid employment with parenting, and women have been much more likely than men to take advantage of this policy. Women's participation in part-time work has declined in recent years, however. In 1999, one third of employed females ages fifteen and older were employed less than thirty-five hours a week, down from two fifths in 1990.[38] Most part-time jobs average thirty hours a week and offer prorated benefits. Since the mid-1960s, feminists have campaigned for a thirty-hour workweek for all workers, to institutionalize a more family-friendly work schedule and eliminate the low status and gendered character of part-time work.

The labor market is distinctively sex-segregated. Half of women worked in the public sector in 2001, compared to less than one fourth of men (22 percent).[39] In 1999, almost half of all employed women (48 percent) worked in childcare, elder care, social work, health care, or education, compared to only 14 percent of men.[40] In 2001, women were as likely as men to work in professional and technical jobs, but much more likely than men to do clerical work. Men were much more likely than women to be craft and trade workers and machine operators.[41] Government efforts to break down job segregation have focused on encouraging young people to study nontraditional subjects and offering employers subsidies for nontraditional hiring. Sex segregation in occupations decreased slowly between 1960 and 1990, with the greatest changes taking place in the professions.[42]

In 2001, women were 24 percent of all managers.[43] The proportion of women in top management positions remained small—only 2 percent of chief executive officers of the 500 largest Swedish corporations.[44] Top managers typically come from male-dominated occupations such as engineering and economics. Traits that qualify a person for higher positions are the same ones that are associated with traditional masculinity (e.g., aggressiveness), and neither men nor women are comfortable with women acting masculine in order to get ahead. The expectations for management careers have also discouraged some women. Women in middle management tend to be younger than men in the same jobs, and they often report that they have turned down offers to move up the corporate ladder because such jobs involve more stress and work hours than they are interested in, especially during their children's early years.[45]

In 1995, the Leadership Academy was founded, developed by women representing employers and unionized workers and funded by the government to help prepare more women to become high-level managers. In two years' time, 350 women had attended the academy and over half had been promoted. The government has also sponsored seminars to increase employers' recognition of women's competence.[46] The lack of qualified women in upper management posts is increasingly described as an important issue of social justice as well as a waste of human resources.

Swedish unions play a very important role in determining the conditions and rewards of work. A higher proportion of women belong to unions than men (87 percent versus 83 percent), but central union leadership has remained male dominated. In 2001, women were half of the members of the confederation of blue-collar unions (LO), but only 33 percent of executive committee members. Women fare better in the white-collar union confederation (TCO), where they form the majority of the membership (62 percent) and 70 percent of executive committee members.[47] Women are more likely to take active political roles at the local level and have criticized unions for valuing central and top leadership work over local work. Union women have been reluctant to organize themselves into autonomous groups, but in 1991, 11,000 women from several blue-collar unions formed *Tjejligan* (The Gals' Team) to press unions and companies to reduce the gender gap in pay and increase women's share of top leadership positions.[48]

Pay

Looking at all women workers regardless of hours employed, women's annual income average was 79 percent of men's income in 1997.[49] This figure has risen from 67 percent in 1994 and 55 percent in 1975.[50] Female full-time workers earned an average income that was 85 percent of male full-time workers' income. Immigrant women earn lower wages than women born in Sweden. The gender wage gap is biggest in the private sector's most prestigious and well-paid occupations, whereas the smallest gap is in private sector blue-collar work, where women earn an average of 91 percent of men's pay.[51]

The Equality Ombud office has received an increasing number of complaints from women about unequal pay, but so far courts have been reluctant to penalize employers. The government has encouraged companies to voluntarily raise women's wages, sometimes in connection with a job evaluation system that establishes equal pay for comparable work.[52] Unions now have privileged access to lists of individuals' wages to help identify and eliminate wage inequities.

Working Conditions

Occupational injuries increased among women in the 1980s, leading to a government investigation and a feminist-driven debate about women's work environments. By 1998, women were still more likely than men to report working at jobs that caused them physical harm because of lifting or repetitive motion. They were, however, more likely than men to have their petitions for disability granted.[53]

Sexual Harassment

When the first equal employment opportunity law went into effect in 1992, no mention of sexual harassment was made. Over time, feminist concern for this practice has grown, and in 1998, a stiffer employment law mandated more serious penalties for violators. Sexual harassment is defined as "unwelcome advances of a sexual nature or other unwelcome advances based on sex which limits the employee's integrity at the workplace."[54] Employers must make clear that sexual harassment is unacceptable and establish procedures for reporting and investigating complaints. Employers are financially liable if a supervisor or a coworker harasses an employee.

Support for Mothers/Caretakers

Maternal Leave

In 1931, paid maternity leave was offered and a 1939 law prohibited firing women because of marriage, pregnancy, or childbearing. Since 1974, the Swedish parental leave system was designed to make it possible for both mothers and fathers to combine employment with parenthood.[55] Men and women have had the same right to take parental leave, which guarantees parents' return to their same or equivalent jobs and offers 80 percent income replacement (up to $2,349 a month in 1999). Financial compensation is dispensed through local social insurance offices but paid for by taxes on all employers. The well-compensated portion of the leave allows parents thirteen months away from work to be their children's primary caregivers. Parental leave can be taken in full, half, or quarter days until children reach school age.[56]

In 1995, a controversial change in parental leave was made, reserving one of the leave months for fathers and one month for mothers. Of children born in 1995, 70 percent had fathers who took parental leave before they reached the age of two, for an average of eight weeks.[57] This proportion was a dramatic increase from a year earlier, when the percentage of fathers who took leave for children was 50 percent. In 2002, an additional month was set aside for fathers, and one for mothers.

In 2002, fathers took only 16 percent of all regular parental leave days taken by parents (up from 9 percent in 1995).[58] Since 1974, several government-sponsored information campaigns have taken place to improve men's awareness of parental leave rights and the benefits to be gained from taking leave. These campaigns have targeted the mass media, unions, and employers. Recently, social insurance office workers have received extensive training on convincing fathers to take leave.[59] Several employers now offer fathers extra financial incentives to take leave, because they have found that men who take leave are better employees when they return to the job, having successfully faced a new challenge, learned ways to handle stress, developed the ability to engage in multiple tasks, and increased their ability to communicate with others.

Daycare

Daycare was rare before World War II, and public support for government-subsidized childcare developed slowly. Employed mothers worked odd hours so that relatives could care for their children; in the summer, some boarded children out to "summer parents" so they could work.[60] Childcare became an important part of family policy in the early 1970s for two main reasons: to make more mothers available to work and to "support and encourage children's development and learning."[61]

Demand for childcare exceeded supply through the early 1990s. In 1995, national childcare legislation required municipalities to provide subsidized care for all children, and the national government set aside special funds to help municipalities meet this goal. By 1999, waiting lists had almost disappeared.[62] In 1999, 74 percent of all children ages 1–6 attended government-managed childcare facilities or government-subsidized home daycare programs. This is a marked increase from 1990 when the proportion was 57 percent and from 1980 when it was 36 percent. In 1999, 63 percent of children ages 7–9 used government-subsidized after-school care, up from 50 percent in 1990 and 22 percent in 1980.[63]

Parents' costs for childcare are low, based on the number of children, the amount of time in care, and parental income, with the government subsidizing 85–90 percent of the total costs. In 2001, daycare fees were lowered to facilitate women's employment and encourage couples to have larger families. The maximum monthly fee is $137 for the first child, $92 for the second child, and $46 for a third.[64]

Family and Medical Leave

Both mothers and fathers may stay home with 80 percent pay with a sick child when the child's regular caregiver is sick, or to take a child to the doctor, up to sixty days per year (although the average actually used is five). In 2002, women took 57 percent of this type of leave.[65]

Although the vast majority of elders have relatives nearby willing and able to help when needed, the care of the elderly is considered a public responsibility in Sweden. The vast majority (89 percent) lives in their own homes instead of in institutions or with relatives.[66] Pensions are designed to keep the elderly above a certain modest income level. They can also rely on means-tested supplemental income and housing subsidies to help them maintain their independence. Independent living is also made possible by government-subsidized "home help" services, which provide personal care or housekeeping at low cost. In 1997, 8 percent of Swedes sixty-five and older, and 20 percent of those eighty and older, used this service for an average of thirty hours per month. Twice as many women than men get government-subsidized home help due to women's longer life span, greater chances of living alone, and receipt of less informal help from friends and relatives.[67]

Since 1998, relatives can be employed as personal assistants and home-help providers. Relatives are also entitled to take paid leaves of absence from work to care for a close relative or friend who is seriously ill or dying.[68] Family caregivers who receive financial compensation for caring for frail elders, sick family members, or handicapped children are disproportionately women (92 percent).[69]

The success of social policy in helping Swedish women combine family and work is evident in results of a recent study where most women (92 percent) rated their ability to combine employment with "everyday life" as "rather good" or "very good."[70]

Inheritance and Property Rights

Men and women have identical inheritance and property rights. Nevertheless, women have a slightly smaller proportion of private fortunes (47 percent) and disposable income (45 percent).[71]

Social/Government Programs

Swedish social policy is directed toward helping all households establish a high standard of living and giving special support to individuals and families in trying circumstances (involving chronic illness or handicap).

Welfare

Financial assistance is provided through child allowances paid to mothers ($1,000 per child per year). "Financially weak households" receive housing subsidies so they can "live in adequate and sufficiently spacious accommodation."[72] Single parents can count on regular financial support from a noncustodial parent, since the government guarantees payment even when the noncustodial parent fails to pay.[73]

Although their economic dependence on men has declined, Swedish women's economic dependence on the welfare state has increased. In 1997, the average proportion of women's income based on "public funds transfer" was 39 percent, up from 21 percent in 1975.[74] In contrast, 30 percent of men's income in 1997 came from welfare benefits, up from 8 percent in 1975.[75] There is no official measure of poverty in Sweden, but there is a level that is considered "low income" for the purposes of establishing eligibility for supplemental income assistance (*socialbidrag*). In 1975, Swedish women were more likely to be "poor" than men. By 1999, the same proportion of women and men fell under this threshold (6 percent).[76]

Sweden was one of the first societies that granted all individuals an old-age pension. Individuals typically get two pensions—a basic government pension available to everyone regardless of employment history and a secondary private pension related to employment history and earnings. In 1998, men received 57 percent of all retirement funds distributed from both sources. The gender gap in pensions is expected to decrease as more women spend more years in the labor force at higher wages. In 1999, the government increased the basic pension's amount to improve the economic situation of those elders (mostly women) who have no secondary pension.[77]

FAMILY AND SEXUALITY

Gender Roles

The aim of Swedish policy today is an egalitarian family in which both parents economically provide for the family and equally care for the home and children; both parents should also have the same opportunity to participate in public life and spend time in leisure pursuits or personal development. The vast majority of Swedes support this ideology of gender equality, although women are more likely to do so than men. Egalitarian attitudes are most common among younger people.

Men now perform chores they rarely did in the past, and the division of household labor has become more of a negotiated arrangement than a taken for granted gender-based pattern. When paid work hours and unpaid work hours are totaled, women and men work the same number of hours and consequently have the same amount of leisure time.[78]

Swedish men have made substantial progress in sharing childcare. In 1998, the vast majority of fathers (85 percent) were actively involved in caring for their young children, up dramatically from 1 percent in 1960.[79] Men's ties to children can no longer be taken for granted in a society such as Sweden's where women have reproductive choice and the ability to be economically independent. Most men recognize the importance of developing their own relationships with children, starting with infancy.

Despite the public acceptance of gender equality as an ideal, a traditional division of labor persists when it comes to household work. Partners without children tend to divide housework equitably, but when children arrive, there is a tendency to revert to traditional roles for women and men. Women are more likely to cook, clean, do laundry, and buy children's clothes, and men are more likely to look after the car and do home maintenance chores.[80] Men and women equally share responsibility for household work in only 10 percent of two-parent families.[81] About one fourth of couples practice a traditional division of labor, which puts the majority in a semishared arrangement.[82] A 1992 time-use study found that men were responsible for 34 percent of all the total time couples spent on household work, shopping, childcare, repair, care of others, and errands.[83] A 2001 time-use study found that men's share had increased to 42 percent.[84] Couples typically attribute the persistence of the traditional division of labor to women's lower contribution to the family economy, which in turn reflects inequality in the labor market. When women hold skilled jobs with high pay, the household division of labor is more equitable.[85]

Marriage

Less than half of Swedish women (43 percent) were married in 1998, one third were single, 11 percent were divorced, and 12 percent were widowed. The likelihood of marriage has decreased since the 1970s, especially among childless women. The average age of first marriage for women in 1997 was 30 (up from 26 in 1980). Cohabiting and married couples have identical legal rights and responsibilities. One fifth of couples in 1998 were cohabiting.[86] In the youngest age group (ages 20–24), over three fourths of women in unions were cohabiting (77 percent).[87]

Sweden has a relatively high divorce rate (fifty-one divorces per 100 marriages), which has been explained as "a manifestation of women's refusal to accept male power and male domination."[88] Since women can depend on government benefits if they cannot adequately support a family alone, it is easy for women who are dissatisfied with their marriages to declare their independence.

Reproduction

Although teen pregnancy is rare, out-of-wedlock births are commonplace, especially in the 25–29 age group. In 1997, over half of all children (55 percent) were born to unmarried parents sharing the same residence. Children born to unmarried parents suffer no social stigma or loss of rights, and nearly all unmarried fathers legally acknowledge paternity at the child's birth.[89]

Sex Education

Sexual attitudes are very permissive in Sweden and there is widespread acceptance of the government's involvement in sexual matters.[90] Sex education is a mandatory part of the school curriculum. It is assumed that teens will be sexually active and that education is needed to prevent unwanted pregnancies. Information on sexuality, reproduction, and contraception is offered children in stages, starting in the first grade. Psychological, social, and ethical aspects of sexuality are integrated into several school subjects.[91] The government also funds sex and contraceptive education provided by women's, youth, and immigrant organizations. A longitudinal study of 3,000 girls and women found that "providing teenagers with contraceptive information and supplies will not increase their level of sexual activity."[92]

Contraception and Abortion

Contraception has been widely accepted and practiced since the 1930s. Since 1974, birth control devices and medications have been provided free of charge. Secondary schools even offer students free condoms. About 70 percent of sexually active couples are reported to use contraception, usually the Pill and condoms before starting a family and the IUD after ideal family size has been attained.[93]

Abortions were allowed on medical and humanitarian grounds by 1938. In the early 1970s, women's groups lobbied heavily for greater access to legal abortion. In 1974, legislation allowed women to choose abortion up to the nineteenth week of pregnancy. Swedish abortion policy has been described as "enabling" (rather than "restrictive," "hindering," or "intrusive") because legislation grants women freedom of choice, the procedure requires no parental consent for minors and demands no waiting period, and services are accessible nationwide.[94] The abortion rate was 347 abortions per 1,000 live births in 1997, down from 359 in 1980.[95] The abortion rate for teens has also declined since the 1980s.[96]

Teen Pregnancy

Despite a high rate of sexual activity among teens, only 2 percent of births were to teen mothers in 1997, down from 5 percent in 1980.[97]

HEALTH

Health Care Access

All citizens, immigrants, visitors, and students on a year or longer visa have access to subsidized health care in Sweden. Although the general health status of women is high, there are gender differences in perception of health and use of health care services. In 1999, women ages 20–64 were less likely than men to report themselves as "completely healthy." Women averaged more sick days per year than men (fifty-two versus thirty-seven) and were also more likely to be hospitalized and take more medicines.[98] These gender differences may reflect women's lower health status or their greater likelihood of seeking help. Compared to women, men are more likely to be prescribed expensive medicines, attend expensive rehabilitation programs, and participate in medical research. These gender differences may reflect men's better treatment in the health care system.

Diseases and Disorders

Almost one-half of female deaths in 2000 (47 percent) were attributed to circulatory disease. Seven percent of female deaths were due to respiratory diseases and three percent to external causes (e.g., accidents and homicides).[99]

The average consumption of alcohol by men is more than double that of women's, although the gap is narrowing. An estimated 10 percent of men are considered to be alcoholics, with the percentage of women being rated as "much lower." In 1998, 26 percent of individuals in residential substance abuse programs were female.[100] Entrance into the European Union ended the government's monopoly on importation, production, and distribution of alcohol products, and increased alcohol use and abuse are expected.

Illegal drug use appears to be increasing. In 1998, 7 percent of females ages 15–75 said they had used illegal drugs at least once, compared to 13 percent of males. To discourage use of alcohol and narcotics, the government focuses on early prevention programs aimed at children.[101]

AIDS

The government has tried to prevent the spread of HIV/AIDS through education and advocacy of increased condom use. In 2001, a small number of individuals, ages 15–49, reported living with HIV/AIDS (.01 percent of the total population). Over one fourth of cases (28 percent) involved females.[102]

Eating Disorders

Anorexia nervosa is reported for about 1 percent of teens, and bulimia affects an additional 2 percent, nearly all of them girls.[103]

Cancer

In 2000, almost one fourth of female deaths (22 percent) were caused by cancer. Breast cancer is the most common cancer among women. Its incidence increased 1 percent per year between 1990 and 2000, but mortality rates remained unchanged.[104] Over one-third (36 percent) of ninth grade girls reported smoking cigarettes in 2001, compared to one-fourth (26 percent) of boys.

Mental Illness

Fifteen percent of the population has had a psychological problem or disease; this has remained unchanged since 1952. In 1998, one fourth of women but only 15 percent of men reported problems with anxiety, nervousness, or insomnia. Half of women, compared to one fourth of men, will have serious depression warranting treatment sometime during their lifetimes.[105] Women are more likely than men to attempt suicide, but men are more likely to succeed. Suicide rates, however, have dropped for both sexes and are now relatively low (20 cases per 100,000).

Foreign-born women have more problems with mental illness than native-born females. Government officials attribute women's greater problems with mental health to stressful work conditions and subordination in society.[106]

POLITICS AND LAW

Suffrage

Swedish women earned the right to vote in 1921.

Political Participation

Women are slightly more likely than men to vote. According to political scientist Agneta Stark, "Women voters are significantly more concerned than men with welfare issues, with the quality of child care and care of the elderly and with education. They are less concerned with reducing taxes. They put a lower priority on defense spending."[107]

Historically, women have been active members of political parties, at first in special "women's auxiliaries." These organizations, organized after suffrage to encourage women's participation in the political process, helped women gain leadership skills. Women's auxiliaries often raised political issues for the general public that the party leadership itself showed little interest in (e.g., the six-hour workday). Auxiliaries were mostly disbanded by the beginning of the twenty-first century, as parties made firmer commitments to integrate women and gender issues into regular party politics.

Sweden has an electoral system based on "proportional representation." Voters vote for a particular party. Parties gain representation in Parliament if they obtain at least 4 percent of the vote, which ensures that multiple political perspectives are represented. Parties determine which individuals from their party will serve in Parliament after the election. Until 1960, 90 percent of appointments were male. Women were forced to steadily lobby party leadership to place women on election lists. By 1987, women's proportion of Parliamentary membership had increased to 38 percent.[108]

When women's percentage of Parliamentary seats slipped to 33 percent after the 1991 election, a loosely organized network of feminist activists and politicians called *Stödstrumporna* (the Support Stockings) threatened to start their own Women's Party unless established parties made a stronger commitment to designate "every other seat for a woman." After discovering that a majority of women voters would consider voting for a Women's Party, all parties except the most conservative agreed to appoint more women. This led to women becoming 45 percent of elected members of Parliament in 2003.

Female members of Parliament are more likely to work on committees concerning education and social welfare than finances and technology.[109] When women want to get involved in policy-making areas that have traditionally been male dominated, they report feeling excluded, ignored, ridiculed, and left out of information networks.[110] Women members of Parliament have considerable contact with independent women's organizations and say it is personally very important for them to represent women's interests and concerns. They often feel conflict between loyalty to the party platform and loyalty to women's concerns.[111] Even though the days of separate women's auxiliaries are over, party women still meet separately to plot strategy. According to social scientist Gunnel Gustafsson, "They feel that only by acting through separate women's groups can they become strong enough to work against mainstream party perspectives and ideas."[112]

Women's Rights

Feminist Movements

Independent women's organizations in Sweden have maintained "a constant pressure for social change since the struggle for women's suffrage."[113] Such groups have helped to define the barriers to equality and to shape what political parties and government could do to promote equality.[114]

The oldest feminist organization in Sweden is the *Fredrika Bremer Förbundet*, established in 1884. This organization lobbied for suffrage and continues to encourage women to use regular democratic channels to gain rights for women. In the 1970s, young left-wing feminists doubted that gender equality could be realized through regular channels of democratic decision making. They formed an organization called *Grupp 8* to urge working-class women to strike for higher wages; they also organized abortion rights demonstrations, drew attention to male violence against women, and helped to develop the first support services for female victims of violence. They were the first to present arguments for men's increased involvement in childrearing. In the 1980s, a small group of intellectuals and politicians called *Grupp 222* met regularly to plot strategy in Parliament that would reduce the persistent gender gap in wages and increase the number of daycare places for children of employed parents.[115]

Some women's groups are now well established (e.g., the *Fredrika Bremer Förbundet*) whereas others have been short-lived or engage only in periodic collective actions (e.g., *Grupp 8*). By 2001, there were more national and local women's organizations and networks interested in improving the status of women than ever before.[116] Many new organizations devoted to promoting gender equality have been formed by order of the government, since each work organization, school, union, and government agency must establish an Equality Committee, that annually collects statistics, sets goals, and assesses the effectiveness of strategies designed to promote gender equality. These groups give almost every Swedish woman an important opportunity to press for change.

Today in Sweden there is a resurgent women's movement, which challenges "the toothlessness of the longstanding official approach to pursuing gender equality through gender-neutral reforms."[117] Historian Yvonne Hirdman is often credited for initiating an independent feminist discourse in Sweden through her writings on the concept of the gender system (*genussystemet*).[118] There are already signs that this independent feminist discourse is affecting policy making and visions for gender equality. A recent government study reported that much more attention should be paid to how inequality at home and in the workplace was an outcome of male dominance and male special interests. It concluded that progress toward gender equality would be limited if equality work focused only on changing outdated attitudes.[119]

Implied in most feminist action in Sweden is the assumption that gender equality can be reached through the influence of the ultimate political authority, the state. Nonetheless, most Swedish feminists agree that "feminist organizations, associations, and networks must become commonplace before male-dominated norms can be replaced by a more woman-friendly society."[120]

Lesbian Rights

Homosexual contact has never been illegal in Sweden. The Swedish Federation for Lesbian and Gay Rights, established in 1950, promotes gay and lesbian rights through twenty-six regional branches. A 1978 Parliamentary Commission recommended that the National Board of Health and Welfare be assigned the task of reducing prejudice and discrimination toward gays and lesbians. In 1987, a law prohibiting harassment and unequal treatment of women and ethnic minorities in public spaces was amended to include gay men and lesbians.[121] In 1992, responsibility for preventing discrimination was moved to the National Institute of Public Health, which funds research on hate crimes and gay issues and supports gay and lesbian studies at many universities.[122]

Marriage. Since 1995, a law permits same-sex couples to have "registered partnerships." Registered partners are treated just like heterosexual couples for national insurance and legal purposes. In 1999, the first ombudsman for gay and lesbian concerns was appointed and a new law was passed that banned labor market discrimination against gays and lesbians. By 2001, 2,487 individuals had registered partnerships.[123]

Parenthood. Until 2002, lesbian or gay couples could not adopt a child or share custody of a child of one of the partners.[124] In a society as child-friendly as Sweden's, denying official parenthood status to lesbians was a symbol of their lack of full citizenship rights. The Partnership Adoption Act became law on February 1, 2003 granting partners the right to adopt children.[125]

Military Service

Sweden remained neutral in the two world wars and has not actively engaged in war since the 1700s, but its proximity to countries with interests in foreign expansion has resulted in a fairly well-established military. Historically, all males aged eighteen were drafted and trained for one year to be the reserve army. Today, a lottery has replaced the draft and women as well as men can choose to join the military. Since 1997, active efforts have been undertaken to recruit women, promote women into higher levels, and encourage women officers to make the military a life-long career. Nevertheless, by 1998, women were only 4 percent of the armed forces. In 1998, half of female officers reported that they had experienced sexual harassment some time during the three previous years; this has led to the establishment of more training and report systems to prevent future harassment.[126]

RELIGION AND SPIRITUALITY

Christianity arrived late in Sweden because the country was divided into semi-independent provinces off the usual path of early missionaries. Pagan rituals and values connected to respect for the seasons and environment still have strong roots in Swedish culture. The first chieftain to be baptized as a Christian was Olof Skötkonung in 1000. Perhaps the most famous

Swedish religious figure is Birgitta of Vadsten (canonized in 1391), an early critic of the papacy who founded a religious order for women.

Sweden became an Evangelical Lutheran Kingdom in 1544. (The church only recently separated from the government in 2000.) Religious persecution was an important reason why some Swedes emigrated to America in the 1800s and early 1900s. During the first half of the nineteenth century, some women chose lives of celibacy and poverty in convents. In the 1960s, women's convents were converted into institutions serving local communities, and the requirements of celibacy and ties to a mother-house were dropped.

Swedes are generally not very religious. The vast majority officially belonged to the Lutheran Church in 1999 (85 percent), but this high proportion is mainly due to an old rule whereby children of Lutheran parents automatically became church members at birth. This rule has recently been eliminated, so church membership is predicted to sharply decline. Only 10 percent of Swedes attend church regularly, and only 7 percent consider themselves professing Christians.[127] Swedes' lack of allegiance to conservative religious traditions has been considered an important contributing factor in the improvement of the status of Swedish women.[128]

Women's Roles

Freedom of religion became law in 1951, and women became eligible to be ordained for the Lutheran priesthood in 1958. In 1999, 29 percent of employed priests were women.[129] Although Lutheranism dominates Sweden, other religions are practiced, involving 8,000 Jews, 8,800 Mormons, and 23,400 Jehovah's Witnesses. Immigrant groups have added to the mix 166,000 Catholics, 90,000 Muslims, 16,000 Hindus, and 16,000 Buddhists.[130]

VIOLENCE

Domestic Violence

Violence against women "appeared late on the political agenda."[131] Women interested in protecting women's "bodily integrity" organized the "shelter movement" in the late 1970s, which attracted 10,000 members.[132] The shelter movement created the first crisis line for victims of rape and domestic violence in 1978, two years before domestic violence became subject to public persecution. Sweden now has a network of 133 shelters and hotlines in all regions of the country. The National Organization of Battered Women's Shelters is an independent nonprofit agency coordinating the work of Sweden's shelters for women. Shelters began to receive government subsidies in 1984, and the amount of subsidies has increased over time.[133] On the whole, "women on municipal councils, boards and committees . . . have obtained government support for women's shelters."[134]

The emphasis of shelter programs is on protecting women's safety. Shelters advise victims of their rights, offer professional counseling, accompany victims to court for support, and educate the public about battering and sexual assault. In 1994, 40,000 women sought help at shelters for some kind of abuse.[135] Few women seek residence in shelters, however. Women are expected to rely upon their own wages and the support of friends and relatives to leave an abusive relationship.[136] These expectations can be too high for some women, especially immigrant women. In the 1980s, there was an increase in repeated incidences of violence against women and in the percentage of cases that were dropped because women refused to testify.[137]

Activists convinced authorities that professionals in contact with battered women needed to be trained in the legal aspects of domestic violence; such training was mandated for police, prosecutors, social workers, judges, and health and hospital workers.[138] Activists also insisted that some battered women were too frightened to cooperate in investigations, so authorities launched new efforts to ensure women's safety. Restraining orders were introduced in 1988, with transgressions punishable by up to six months in jail. Stalked women became eligible to carry personal alarms or have a twenty-four-hour bodyguard at public expense. No woman with such protective support was hurt, according to a police report for 1993.[139]

By the 1990s, women's shelters' supporters and staff were more openly feminist in their work. They encouraged the government to appoint a commission to study domestic violence and make recommendations for better prevention. The commission's 1995 report declared: "The most painful devaluation of women is the physical and psychological violence that stalks them from cradle to grave."[140] The wide dissemination of this report gave increased visibility to the problem of domestic violence. It set the stage for a new law in 1998 that made it easier to prosecute offenders, even when victims choose not to file a formal complaint. Stronger sanctions now face men found guilty of repeated violence against women. There is an increase in funding for violence prevention education and for restitution for victims.[141] By 2000, violence against women was viewed by authorities "as a serious situation affecting women's health":[142] According to Maude Eduards, "[P]oliticians and authorities at various levels in society have accepted a greater degree of institutional and professional responsibility for the situation of battered women."[143]

In 1999, there were about 20,000 reported cases of assault against women, up 30 percent from 1990.[144] The increase is attributed to lower tolerance of violence against women. The continued vulnerability of women is reflected in other statistics. Only one fourth of domestic violence reports (27 percent) resulted in formally charged cases in 1995.[145] About thirty women were murdered by domestic partners each year in the

1990s.[146] Ten percent of a random sample of 207 new mothers in Göteborg reported being victims of moderate or serious physical or sexual violence during their pregnancies.[147]

The 1998 law designed to protect women from violence has not punished many repeat offenders (only eighty men in one year's time).[148] In 1978, Sweden passed a law prohibiting physical punishment of children that seems to be a model for the 1998 violence against women law. Also, few parents have been prosecuted under this statute. In both cases, "The law is understood to articulate a consensus and generate social pressure against reprehensible behavior."[149]

The shelter movement now has allies in its efforts to prevent domestic violence. In 1999, a network of fourteen government agencies dealing with violence against women was formed, along with an advisory board made up of researchers, feminists, and union representatives. In 1996, men already active in promoting children's rights organized *Manliga Nätverk* (The Male Network) to raise men's awareness that violence against women and children is unethical. This group educates youth about violence, trains expectant fathers on violence prevention, and recruits men to work as advocates against gender-based violence.[150]

Rape/Sexual Assault

As with domestic violence, "Feminists found it very difficult to place sexual violence on the public agenda."[151] In 1976, a government commission recommended that rape be considered a "minor crime," which would reduce penalties for sexual assault, depending on victims' actions and attitudes. This proposal was strongly criticized by *Grupp 8*, who initiated a public protest. A network of women's and union organizations quickly formed, representing half a million women, to lobby for reconsideration of this issue. A new government commission proposed stronger penalties for rape, which were approved by Parliament in 1982.

The shelter movement's network of hotlines and shelters serves rape victims as well as victims of domestic violence. In the 1990s, feminists' efforts to raise public awareness of rape were renewed, resulting in the founding of a National Center for Raped and Battered Women in 1993, subsequently funded by the government.

In 1993, the number of reported rape cases was 2,153, up from 769 cases in 1975.[152] Three-tenths of one percent of men who were convicted for crimes against property or persons was convicted for rape in 1990. The conviction rate in rape cases was 50 percent higher than ten years earlier.[153]

Trafficking in Women and Children

In 1999, policymakers began to pay special attention to the importation of women into Sweden. Foreign partners of citizens may visit for up to two years, but women in these circumstances often become victims of domestic violence and exploitation. Consequently, the government limits the entrance of women who seem likely to land in these circumstances.

Forced prostitution is the most common form of trafficking in Europe. Sweden's generous social welfare benefits enable women to avoid prostitution as a form of livelihood, so prostitution has never been widespread. In the 1990s, the collapse of communism led to an influx of foreign prostitutes. By 1997, it was estimated that 2,500 women were selling sexual services, about one fourth of them on the street. An estimated 10–13 percent of men were presumed to have purchased sex from women prostitutes.[154]

A 1999 law strongly supported by feminists made it illegal to purchase a prostitute's services, punishable with a fine or up to six months of imprisonment. Prostitutes themselves face no criminal penalties. The reason why the buyer not the seller of sex is punished is outlined in a 1998 government report:

> Even if prostitution itself is not a desirable social activity, it is not reasonable to prosecute the party that, at least in most cases, is the weaker party, exploited by others to satisfy their sexual drive. This is also important if prostitutes are to be encouraged to get help to leave prostitution and can feel they will not have to worry about the consequences of having been prostitutes.[155]

A man active in the male network opposing violence against women summed up the significance of this new law: "We must give youth a new view of the world, a world where the citadels of power are held by 50 percent women and nobody is for sale on the streets."[156]

OUTLOOK FOR THE TWENTY-FIRST CENTURY

There is a fairly strong consensus in Sweden that gender equality is a desirable goal. The aim is to replace the traditional gender system based on the separation of the sexes and the primacy of male norms with a totally new social arrangement, in which men no longer dominate women and men and women both have the opportunity to realize their full potential in school, the labor market, families, and public life. According to political scientist Siv Gustafsson, "Representatives of the women's movement stress that there is strong reason to believe that democracy based on a new sexual contract in which men and women are of equal worth would be like entering an entirely new landscape."[157]

Swedish women have had extraordinary success in establishing economic independence and permanent positions in the labor market, aided by government programs that facilitate the balancing of work and family roles. Their high level of political participation promises to keep gender issues and concerns at the forefront of policy making. But formidable challenges remain. One stiff challenge is to dismantle the structures of male dominance that are still quite visible, reflected in women's low representation in positions of influence and in the persistence of sexual harassment and violence against women. An equally important challenge is to undermine the assumption that women are more responsible than men for reproductive work, by developing the expectation of men's equal sharing of housework and childcare and equal distributions of men and women in caring occupations. A final challenge is to pay more notice to improving the status and quality of life of ethnic women, who make up one fifth of the population of women in Sweden, so they can enjoy a life of economic independence, freed from exploitation and violence.

NOTES

1. Lene Mikkelsen, *Women and Men in Europe and North America* (New York: United Nations, 2000); and United Nations, *The World's Women, 2000* (New York: Author, 2000). Population Reference Bureau, "World Population Data Sheet" (Washington D.C.: Population Reference Bureau, 2002), www.prh.org.

2. Lars Jederlund, "From Immigrant Policy to Integration Policy," *Current Sweden*, no. 422 (1998).

3. Maud Eduards, "The Swedish Gender Model," *West European Politics* 14 (July 1991): 166–81.

4. Swedish Institute, "The Swedish Economy," *Fact Sheet on Sweden* (Stockholm: Author, 2001).

5. Gunilla Fürst, *Sweden—The Equal Way* (Stockholm: The Swedish Institute, 1999).

6. Näringsdepartementet, *Jämställdhetspolitiken*, National Government Report Series, no. 24 (1999–2000). The author's translation.

7. Fürst, 1999, 11.

8. Fürst, 1999, 8.

9. Christina Florin and Bengt Nilsson, "Something in the Nature," in *State Policy and Gender System*, ed. Rolf Torstendahl (Uppsala, Sweden: Uppsala University, 1999).

10. Rebecca Coulter and Inga Wernersson, "Education, Gender Equality, and Women's Organizing," in *Women's Organizing*, eds. Linda Briskin and Mona Eliasson (Montreal: McGill–Queen's University Press, 1999), 213–37, esp. 217.

11. Coulter and Wernersson, 219–20.

12. Elisabet Öhrne, "Changing Patterns?" *NORA–Nordic Journal of Women's Studies* 8 (2000): 128–36.

13. Näringsdepartementet, 1999; and Öhrne, 2000.

14. Fürst, 1999, 59.

15. Anita Nyberg, *Kvinnor, Män och Inkomster* (Stockholm: Arbetsmarknadsdepartementet, 1997).

16. Fürst, 1999.

17. Agnieszka Wojciechowska, "Education and Gender in Sweden?" *Women's Studies International Forum* 18, no. 1 (1995): 51–60.

18. Coulter and Wernersson, 1999.

19. Mikkelsen, 2000.

20. Fürst, 1999.

21. Högskoleverket, *Sexual Harassment of Students*, Report no. 17R (February 27, 2001), www.hsv.se (accessed July 22, 2001).

22. Fürst, 1999.

23. Mikkelsen, 2000.

24. Statistiska Centralbyrån, Jämställdhet (March 1, 2001), www.scb.se (accessed April 1, 2001).

25. Wojciechowska, 1995.

26. Fürst, 1999.

27. Fürst, 1999, 23.

28. Mikkelsen, 2000; and United Nations, 2000.

29. Lena Sommestad, "Welfare State Attitudes," *International Review of Social History* 42, supplement (1997): 153–74, esp. 165.

30. Sommestad, 1997, 168.

31. Fürst, 1999.

32. Reformers Gunnar and Alva Myrdal argued in Sommestad, 1997, 172.

33. Fürst, 1999.

34. Fürst, 1999.

35. Statistiska Centralbyrån, 2001.

36. Marina Calloni and Helma Lutz, "Gender, Migration and Social Inequalities," in *Gender, Economy and Culture*, ed. Simon Duncan and Birgit Pfau-Effinger (London: Routledge, 2000), 143–70.

37. Fürst, 1999.

38. Mikkelsen, 2000; and Näringsdepartementet, 1999.

39. Nyberg, 1997.

40. Statistiska Centralbyrån, 2001.

41. Mikkelsen, 2000.

42. Mariko Chang, "The Evolution of Sex Segregation Regimes," *American Journal of Sociology* 105, no. 6 (2000): 1658–1701.

43. Mikkelsen, 2000.

44. Näringsdepartementet, 1999.

45. Christina Hultbom, "Makt och Lederskap," in *Ledare, Makt och Kön*, ed. Anita Nyberg and Elisabeth Sundin (Stockholm: Arbetsmarknadsdepartementet, 1997); and Eva Meyerson and Trond Petersen, "Finns Det ett Glastak för Kvinner," in *Glastak och Glasväggar*, ed. Inga Persson and Eskil Wadensjö (Stockholm: Elander Gotab, 1997).

46. Näringsdepartementet, 1999.

47. Fürst, 1999.

48. Linda Briskin, "Union and Women's Organizing," in Briskin and Eliasson, 1999.

49. Mikkelsen, 2000.

50. Nyberg, 1997.

51. Näringsdepartementet, 1999.

52. Näringsdepartementet, 1999.

53. Fürst, 1999; and Näringsdepartementet, 1999.

54. Näringsdepartementet, 1999, 30.

55. Linda Haas, *Equal Parenthood and Social Policy* (Albany: State University of New York Press, 1992).

56. Riksförsäkringsverket, "Social Insurance in Sweden," 1999, www.rfv.se/englishpubli/index/html (accessed October 20, 2000).

57. Näringsdepartementet, 1999.

58. Statistiska Centralbyrån, 2002.

59. Näringsdepartementet, 1999.

60. Sommestad, 1997.

61. Swedish Institute, "Child Care," *Fact Sheets on Sweden* (Stockholm: Author, 1999), 1.

62. Swedish Institute, 1999, "Child Care," 1.

63. Statistiska Centralbyrån, 2001.

64. Swedish Institute, 1999, "Child Care."

65. Statistiska Centralbyrån, På Tal om Kvinnor och Män, www.scb.se (accessed May 3, 2003).

66. Swedish Institute, "The Care of the Elderly in Sweden," *Fact Sheets on Sweden* (Stockholm: Author, 1999).

67. Näringsdepartementet, 1999.

68. Swedish Institute, "Disability Policies in Sweden," *Fact Sheets on Sweden* (Stockholm: Author, 2000).

69. Riksförsäkringsverket, 1999.

70. Birgitta Eriksson, *Arbetet i Människors Liv* (Göteborg, Sweden: Göteborg University, 1998).

71. Nyberg, 1997; and Näringsdepartementet, 1999.

72. Riksförsäkringsverket, 1999, 56.

73. Näringsdepartementet, 1999.

74. Statistiska Centralbyrån, 2001.

75. Nyberg, 1997.

76. Statistiska Centralbyrån, 2001.

77. Näringsdepartementet, 1999.

78. Nyberg, 1997.

79. Fürst, 1999.

80. Fürst, 1999.

81. Näringsdepartementet, 1999.

82. Christine Roman, "Arbetsfördelning i Hemmet," *Social Forskning* 4, no. 2 (1999): 7–8.

83. Nyberg, 1997.

84. Statistiska Centralbyrån, 2002.

85. Näringsdepartementet, 1999; and Fürst, 1999.

86. Mikkelsen, 2000.

87. United Nations, 2000.

88. Fürst, 1999, 34.

89. Mikkelson, 2000; and Socialstyrelsen, *Social Services in Sweden* (Stockholm: Author, 1999).

90. Martin Weinberg, Ilsa Lottes, and Frances Shaver, "Sociocultural Correlates," *Journal of Sex Research* 37, no. 1 (2000): 44–52.

91. Swedish Institute, "Higher Education in Sweden," *Fact Sheets on Sweden* (Stockholm: Author, 1997).

92. G. Santow and M. Bracher, "Demography," in *The Joy of Demography*, ed. Anton Kuijsten et al. (Amsterdam: Netherlands Graduate School of Housing and Urban Research, 1999).

93. Swedish Institute, "Family Planning in Sweden," *Fact Sheets on Sweden* (Stockholm: Author, 1997).

94. Yael Yishai, "Public Ideas and Public Policy," *Comparative Politics* 25 (January 1993): 207–28.

95. Mikkelsen, 2000.

96. Swedish Institute, 1997, "Family Planning."

97. United Nations, 2000.

98. Mikkelsen, 2000; and Statistiska Centralbyrån, 2001.

99. Statistiska Centralbyrån, 2002.

100. Socialstyrelsen, 1999.

101. Socialstyrelsen, 1999; and Swedish Institute, 1995.

102. Mikkelsen, 2000.

103. Lene Lindberg, "Eating Disorders," 2001, www.cbu.dataphone.se (accessed July 19, 2001); and Socialstyrelsen, *Folkhälsorapport*, 2001, www.sos.se (accessed July 22, 2001).

104. Socialstyrelsen, 2001, *Folkhälsorapport*.

105. Socialstyrelsen, 2001, *Folkhälsorapport*.

106. Lindberg, 2001; and Socialstyrelsen, 2001, *Folkhälsorapport*.

107. Agneta Stark, "Combating the Backlash," in *Who's Afraid of Feminism?* ed. Ann Oakley and Juliet Mitchell (London: Hamish Hamilton, 1997), 241–42.

108. Chantal Maille and Lena Wängnerud, "Looking for New Opportunities in Politics," in *Women's Organizing and Public Policy in Canada and Sweden*, ed. Linda Briskin and Mona Eliasson (Montreal: McGill-Queens University Press, 1999), 184–209.

109. Yvonne Hirdman, "State Policy and Gender Contracts," in *Women, Work and the Family in Europe*, ed. Eileen Drew et al. (London: Routledge, 1998), 36–46.

110. Fürst, 1999.

111. Maille and Wängnerud, 1999.

112. Gunnel Gustafsson, "Sustainable Pressure," *Political Psychology* 19, no. 1 (1998): 43–61.

113. Gustafsson, 1998, 44.

114. Linda Briskin, "Mapping Women's Organizing in Sweden and Canada" in Briskin and Eliasson, 1999, 3–47.

115. Maud Eduards, "Interpreting Women's Organizing," in *Towards a New Democratic Order*, ed. Linda Briskin and Mona Eliasson (Stockholm: Publica, 1997), 12–25.

116. Eduards, 1997a.

117. Jennifer Curtin and Winton Higgins, "Feminism and Unionism in Sweden," *Politics and Society* 26, no. 1 (1998): 69–83, esp. 71.

118. Hirdman, 1990.

119. Fürst, 1999.

120. Gustafsson, 1998, 55.

121. International League of Gays and Lesbians, *World Legal Survey* (June 1998), www.ilga.org.

122. Jens Rydström, "Breaking the Ice," 1997, www.historia.su.se (assessed July 22, 2001).

123. Inga Marie Forman, "Two Parents of the Same Sex" (Stockholm: Swedish Institute, 2003) www.Sweden.se (accessed May 3, 2003).

124. International League of Gays and Lesbians, 1998.

125. Forman, 2003.

126. Näringsdepartementet, 1999.

127. Swedish Institute, "Religion in Sweden," *Fact Sheets on Sweden* (Stockholm: Author 1994, 1999).

128. Swedish Institute, 1994; and 1999, "Religion."

129. Swedish Institute, 1999, "Religion."

130. Swedish Institute, 1999, "Religion."

131. Maud Eduards, "The Women's Shelter Movement," in Briskin and Eliasson, 1997, 120–68, esp. 121.

132. Eduards, 1997, "The Women's," 121.

133. Carol Hagemann-White, "Male Violence and Control," in Duncan and Pfau-Effinger, 2000, 171–208; and Näringsdepartementet 1999.

134. Eduards, "The Women's," 1997, 166–67.

135. Mona Eliasson and Colleen Lundy, "Organizing to Stop Violence," in Briskin and Eliasson, 1999.

136. Hagemann-White, 2000, 201.

137. Socialdepartementet, *Kvinnofrid* (Stockholm: Author, 1995).

138. Näringsdepartementet, 1999.

139. Eliasson and Lundy, 1999.

140. Eduards, 1997, "The Women's," 123.

141. Eliasson and Lundy, 1999.

142. Lars Nylen and Gun Heimer, "Sweden's Response to Domestic Violence," Current Sweden, no. 428 (April 2000): 1–4, esp. 1.

143. Eduards, 1997, 148.

144. Socialstyrelsen, 2001, *Folkshälsorapport*.

145. Eliasson and Lundy, 1999.

146. Socialdepartmentet, 1995; and Socialstyrelsen, *Violence against Women*, 2001, www.sos.se (accessed July 22, 2001).

147. L.W. Hedin, H. Grimstad, A. Möller, B. Schei, and P. Janson, "Prevalence of Physical and Sexual Abuse," *Acta Obstetrica et Gynecologica Scandinavica* 78 (1999): 310–15.

148. Näringsdepartementet, 1999.

149. Hagemann-White, 2000, 190.

150. Gunnar Sandell, "Male Network for Men against Violence by Men," www.man-net.nu/engelsk/start.htm (accessed February 26, 2001).

151. Hagemann-White, 2000, 190.

152. Eduards, 1997, "The Women's."

153. Mikkelsen, 2000.

154. Maria Pia Boethius, "The End of Prostitution in Sweden," *Current Sweden*, no. 526 (October 1999).

155. Boethius, 1999, 1.

156. Boethius, 1999, 4.

157. Gustafsson, 1998, 56.

RESOURCE GUIDE

Suggested Reading

Briskin, Linda, and Mona Eliasson, eds. *Women's Organizing and Public Policy in Canada and Sweden*. Montreal: McGill–Queen's University Press, 1999.

Eduards, Maud. "The Swedish Gender Model." *West European Politics* 14 (July 1991): 166–81. Important early article by a well-known and influential feminist theorist.

Fürst, Gunilla. *Sweden—The Equal Way*. Stockholm: The Swedish Institute, 1999. (Order at order@si.se.) Summary of the history of change in gender roles in Sweden; emphasizes employment issues.

Genus [Gender]. A publication from the National Secretariat for Gender Research; available in hard copy for free in English (one issue a year). (Order at sekretariate@genus.se). The latest political debates and research on gender equality in Sweden.

Hirdman, Yvonne. "State Policy and Gender Contracts." In *Women, Work and the*

Family in Europe, edited by Eileen Drew, Ruth Emerek, and Evelyn Mahon, 36–46. London: Routledge, 1998. Recent piece by one of the best-known feminist theorists in Sweden.

Sommestad, Lena. "Welfare State Attitudes to the Male Breadwinning System." *International Review of Social History* 42, supplement 1997: 153–74. A historical and comparative perspective on the development of the dual-earner family in Sweden.

Web Sites and Organizations

Jämo
Web site: www.jamombud.se/eng/index.htm

Gender Equality Ombud office ensures compliance with Equal Opportunities legislation.

Male Network for Men against Violence by Men
Web site: www.man-net.nu/engelsk/searcht.htm

National Center for Battered and Raped Women
Web site: http://zebra.uas.se/lul/uas/kk/rkc/index.htm

National Organization of Battered Women's Shelters in Sweden
Web site: www.roks.se

National Secretariat for Gender Research
Web site: www.genus.gu.se/news.html

Swedish Central Bureau of Statistics
Web site:www.scb.se/eng/

Swedish Government
Web site: www.sweden.se

Swedish Institute
Web site: www.si.se

SELECTED BIBLIOGRAPHY

Boethius, Maria-Pia. "The End of Prostitution in Sweden?" *Current Sweden*, no. 526 (October 1999).

Briskin, Linda. "Unions and Women's Organizing in Canada and Sweden." In *Women's Organizing and Public Policy in Canada and Sweden*, edited by Linda Briskin and Mona Eliasson, 147–83. Montreal: McGill–Queen's University Press, 1999.

———. "Mapping Women's Organizing in Sweden and Canada." In *Women's Organizing and Public Policy in Canada and Sweden*, edited by Linda Briskin and Mona Eliasson, 3–47. Montreal: McGill–Queen's University Press, 1999.

Calloni, Marina, and Helma Lutz. "Gender, Migration and Social Inequalities." In

Gender, Economy and Culture in the European Union, edited by Simon Duncan and Birgit Pfau-Effinger, 143–70. London: Routledge, 2000.

Chang, Mariko. "The Evolution of Sex Segregation Regimes." *American Journal of Sociology* 105, no. 6 (2000):1658–1701.

Coulter, Rebecca, and Inga Wernersson. "Education, Gender Equality, and Women's Organizing in Canada and Sweden." In *Women's Organizing and Public Policy in Canada and Sweden*, edited by Linda Briskin and Mona Eliasson, 213–37. Montreal: McGill–Queen's University Press, 1999.

Curtin, Jennifer, and Winton Higgins. "Feminism and Unionism in Sweden." *Politics and Society* 26, no. 1 (1998): 69–83.

Eduards, Maud. "The Swedish Gender Model: Productivity, Pragmatism and Paternalism." *West European Politics* 14 (July 1991): 166–81.

———. "Interpreting Women's Organizing." In *Towards a New Democratic Order*, edited by Linda Briskin and Mona Eliasson, 12–25. Stockholm: Publica, 1997.

———. "The Women's Shelter Movement." In *Towards a New Democratic Order*, edited by Linda Briskin and Mona Eliasson, 120–68. Stockholm: Publica, 1997.

Eliasson, Mona, and Colleen Lundy. "Organizing to Stop Violence against Women in Canada and Sweden." In *Women's Organizing and Public Policy in Canada and Sweden*, edited by Linda Briskin and Mona Eliasson, 280–309. Montreal: McGill–Queen's University Press, 1999.

Florin, Christina, and Bengt Nilsson. "Something in the Nature of a Bloodless Revolution." In *State Policy and Gender System in the Two German States and Sweden 1945–1989*, edited by Rolf Torstendahl, 11–78. Uppsala, Sweden: Uppsala University, Department of History, 1999.

Forman, Ingamarie. "Two Parents of the Same Sex." Stockholm: The Swedish Institute, 2003. www.sweden.se.

Fürst, Gunilla. *Sweden—The Equal Way*. Stockholm: The Swedish Institute, 1999.

Gustafsson, Gunnel. "Sustainable Pressure for 'Women-Friendliness' in Sweden." *Political Psychology* 19, no. 1 (1998): 43–61.

Haas, Linda. *Equal Parenthood and Social Policy*. Albany: State University of New York Press, 1992.

Hagemann-White, Carol. "Male Violence and Control: Constructing a Comparative European Perspective." In *Gender, Economy and Culture in the European Union*, edited by Simon Duncan and Birgit Pfau-Effinger, 171–208. London: Routledge, 2000.

Hedin, L. W., H. Grimstand, A. Möller, B. Schei, and P. Janson. "Prevalence of Physical and Sexual Abuse Before and During Pregnancy among Swedish Couples." *Acta Obstetrica et Gynecologica Scandinavica* 78 (1999): 310–15.

Hirdman, Yvonne. "Genussystemet [The Gender System]." In *Demokrati och makt i Sverige* [Democracy and Power in Sweden], 73–116. Statens Offentliga Utredningar [Government Official Reports], no. 44. Stockholm: Arbetsmarknadsdepartementet [Ministry of Labor], 1990.

———. "State Policy and Gender Contracts." In *Women, Work and the Family in Europe*, edited by Eileen Drew, Ruth Emerek, and Evelyn Mahon, 36–46. London: Routledge, 1998.

Högskoleverket [National Agency for Higher Education]. *Sexual Harassment of Students*. Report no. 17R. February 27, 2001. www.hsv.se (accessed July 22, 2001).

International Lesbian and Gay Association. *World Legal Survey*. June 1998. www.ilga.org (accessed August 2, 2001).

Jederlund, Lars. "From Immigrant Policy to Integration Policy." *Current Sweden*, no. 422 (December 1998).

Lindberg, Lene. "Eating Disorders." Swedish Child and Adolescent Public Health Unit. www.cbu.dataphone.se (accessed July 19, 2001).

Maille, Chantal, and Lena Wängnerud. "Looking for New Opportunities in Politics." In *Women's Organizing and Public Policy in Canada and Sweden*, edited by Linda Briskin and Mona Eliasson, 184–209. Montreal: McGill–Queen's University Press, 1999.

Mikkelsen, Lene. *Women and Men in Europe and North America*. New York: United Nations, 2000.

Nylen, Lars, and Gun Heimer. "Sweden's Response to Domestic Violence." *Current Sweden*, no. 428 (April 2000): 1–4.

Population Reference Bureau. "World Population Data Sheet." Washington, DC: Population Reference Bureau, 2002. www.prb.org.

Riksförsäkringsverket [The National Social Insurance Board]. "Social Insurance in Sweden." 1999. www.rfv.se/englishpubli/index/html (accessed October 20, 2000).

Rydström, Jens. "Breaking the Ice—Lesbian and Gay Studies in Sweden." 1997. www.historia.su.se (accessed July 22, 2001).

Sandell, Gunnar. 2001. "Male Network for Men against Violence by Men." February 26, 2001. www.man-net.nu/engelsk/start.htm. (accessed July 22, 2001).

Santow, G., and M. Bracher. "Demography, Serendipity and Teenage Pregnancy in Sweden." In *The Joy of Demography and Other Disciplines*, edited by Anton Kuijsten, Henk de Gans, and Henke de Fejter, 361–67. Amsterdam: Netherlands Graduate School of Housing and Urban Research, 1999.

Socialstyrelsen [Swedish National Board of Health and Welfare]. *Social Services in Sweden*. Stockholm: Author, 1999. www.sos.se (accessed July 19, 2001).

———. *Violence against Women*. 2001. www.sos.se (accessed July 22, 2001).

Sommestad, Lena. "Welfare State Attitudes to the Male Breadwinning System." *International Review of Social History* 42, supplement (1997): 153–74.

Stark, Agneta. "Combating the Backlash." In *Who's Afraid of Feminism?* edited by Ann Oakley and Juliet Mitchell, 224–88. London: Hamish Hamilton, 1997.

Swedish Institute. "Religion in Sweden." *Fact Sheets on Sweden*. Stockholm: Author, 1994.

———. "Alcohol and Narcotics in Sweden." *Fact Sheets on Sweden*. Stockholm: Author, 1995.

———. "Family Planning in Sweden." *Fact Sheets on Sweden*. Stockholm: Author, 1997.

———. "Higher Education in Sweden." *Fact Sheets on Sweden*. Stockholm: Author, 1997.

———. "The Care of the Elderly in Sweden." *Fact Sheets on Sweden*. Stockholm: Author, 1999.

———. "Child Care." *Fact Sheets on Sweden*. Stockholm: Author, 1999.

———. "The Health Care System in Sweden." *Fact Sheets on Sweden*. Stockholm: Author, 1999.

———. "Religion in Sweden." *Fact Sheets on Sweden*. Stockholm: Author, 1999.

———. "Disability Policies in Sweden." *Fact Sheets on Sweden*. Stockholm: Author, 2000.

———. "The Swedish Economy." *Fact Sheets on Sweden*. Stockholm: Author, 2001.

———. "Financial Circumstances of Swedish Households." United Nations. Stockholm, May 2002. www.Sweden.se.

United Nations. *The World's Women 2000*. Social Statistics and Indicators Series K No. 16. New York: United Nations, 2000.

Weinberg, Martin, Ilsa Lottes, and Frances Shaver. "Sociocultural Correlates of Permissive Sexual Attitudes." *Journal of Sex Research* 37, no. 1 (2000): 44–52.

Wojciechowska, Agnieszka. "Education and Gender in Sweden?" *Women's Studies International Forum* 18, no. 1 (1995): 51–60.

Yishai, Yael. "Public Ideas and Public Policy." *Comparative Politics* 25 (January 1993): 207–28.

Selected Swedish Bibliography

Eriksson, Birgitta. *Arbetet i Människors Liv [Work in People's Lives]*. Department of Sociology Monograph No. 66, Göteborg, Sweden: Göteborg University, 1998.

Hultbom, Christina. "Makt och Ledarskap i Börsbolagen [Power and Leadership in Joint Stock Companies]." In *Ledare, Makt och Kön [Leadership, Power, and Gender]*, edited by Anita Nyberg and Elisabeth Sundin, 46–67. Statens Offentliga Utredningar No. 35. Stockholm: Arbetsmarknadsdepartementet, 1997.

Meyerson, Eva, and Trond Petersen. "Finns Det ett Glastak för Kvinnor? [Is There a Glass Ceiling for Women?]." In *Glastak och Glasväggar [Glass Ceilings and Glass Walls]*, edited by Inga Persson and Eskil Wadensjö, 109–35. Statens Offentliga Utredningar No.137. Stockholm: Elander Gotab, 1997.

Näringsdepartementet [Department of Trade and Industry]. *Jämställdhetspolitiken inför 2000-Talet [Equality Policy for the 21st Century]*. Regeringens Skrivelse [National Government Report Series] No. 24 (1999/2000).

Nyberg, Anita. *Kvinnor, Män och Inkomster [Women, Men, and Income]*. Statens Offentliga Utredningar, no. 87. Stockholm: Arbetsmarknadsdepartementet, 1997.

Öhrne, Elisabet. "Changing Patterns?" *NORA—Nordic Journal of Women's Studies* 8 (2000): 128–36.

Roman, Christine. "Arbetsfördelning i Hemmet [Division of Household Labor]." *Social Forskning [Social Research]* 4, no. 2 (1999): 7–8.

Socialdepartementet [Ministry for Health and Social Affairs]. *Kvinnofrid [Peace for Women]* Statens Offentliga Utredningar No. 60. Stockholm: Socialdepartementet, 1995.

Socialstyrelsen. *Folkhälsorapport 200 [Health report]* 1. www.sos.se. (accessed July 22, 2001).

Statistiska Centralbyrån [Central Bureau of Statistics]. *Jämställdhet [Gender Equality]*. March 8, 2001. www.scb.se (accessed April 1, 2001).

———. *På Tal om Kvinnor och Män [Talking about Women and Men]*. March 27, 2003. www.scb.se (accessed May 3, 2003).

36

Switzerland

Joy Charnley

PROFILE OF SWITZERLAND

Switzerland traces its origins back to 1291, when three German-speaking districts gained their independence from the Habsburg Empire. The country now consists of twenty full cantons and six half cantons with a total population of 7,200,000, approximately 20 percent of whom do not have Swiss nationality.[1] There are four national languages: German (spoken by 73.4 percent of Swiss), French (20.5 percent), Italian (4.1 percent), and Romansch (0.7 percent), and traditionally schoolchildren have learned at least one of the other languages spoken in Switzerland (although this is beginning to change with the increasing emphasis on English). The country is a federal republic, which means that each canton retains a high level of autonomy and has its own government that has jurisdiction over areas such as taxation and education. Switzerland is neutral (a tradition dating back to the sixteenth century and reaffirmed in the nineteenth) and is not a member of either the European Union or the Eurozone, although bilateral discussions with the EU are ongoing. Membership of the United Nations was accepted by the population in March 2002, and the country finally became a full member in September 2002.

The federal government has seven members known as federal councilors (two of whom are currently women), composed according to what is known as a "magic formula," which involves balancing political parties (Socialist, Radical, Christian Democrat, and Democratic Center Party), cantons, religions and, more recently, gender. Government therefore

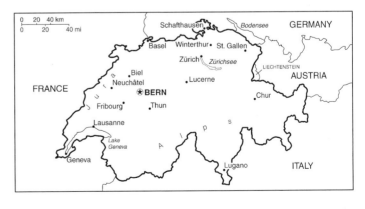

works on the basis of consensus: when a minister resigns (they are rarely if ever voted out or forced to resign), the party whose "turn" it is to propose a new member puts forward a candidate whose appointment is normally rubber stamped by the Parliament (although there have twice been exceptions to this tradition in the case of women!). The role of president is symbolic and confers no extra power since the position is simply occupied by a new member of the government each year. The Parliament is divided into an Upper House, which has forty-six members known as councilors of state (two members for each full canton, one per half canton), and a Lower House composed of 200 members (national councilors), where each canton is represented in proportion to its population.

Elections have taken place on the basis of proportional representation since 1919. Like the army, the Parliament functions on a "militia" system and only meets four times a year, which means that those elected to Parliament continue to pursue a career in addition to politics. In addition to electing members of Parliament, the population has the opportunity to vote on issues put to them several times a year in referendums and popular initiatives; and, in a few cantons in German-speaking Switzerland, *Landsgemeinde*, where the population meets, often in the town square, to vote in a public show of hands, continue to function.[2]

Unemployment was 1.9 percent in 2001 (1.6 percent for men and 2.3 percent for women) and in May 2002 the rate was running at 2.5 percent with inflation at 0.6 percent. In 1998 life expectancy was 82 for women and 76 for men, and in 1999 1.48 children were born per woman (although the rate falls to 1.3 if only Swiss women are considered). In 1999 infant mortality was estimated to be 3.5 per 1,000, and an ongoing study at the University of Zurich is looking at maternal mortality, which from 1985 to 1994 is reported to have been 5.4 per 100,000, although researchers also indicate a high level of underreporting.[3]

OVERVIEW OF WOMEN'S ISSUES

Swiss women live in a prosperous country that has been at peace for over 150 years and neutral for even longer and where they enjoy high levels of education and public services. Steady progress is being made in improving women's rights but in the eyes of many, women are still the main caretakers for the family with the consequent impact on pay and career progression. These conservative views were perhaps illustrated by the fact that Ruth Metzler, a member of the federal government who is in her thirties, declared she would not have a child while in office, reflecting the commonly held view that motherhood and career are not compatible. It remains very much the case that although rights have progressed, mentalities still need to change radically.

EDUCATION

Opportunities

Compulsory schooling lasts nine years, generally from the age of six or seven to fifteen or sixteen, but the organization of schools is not dealt with federally and can vary considerably from one canton to another (with regard to the age at which children move from primary to secondary school for instance, or begin a second language).

Women first entered Swiss universities as early as the 1860s, and although it was often foreigners who initially took the opportunity to study, it was a Swiss woman, Emilie Kempin-Spyri, who was the first woman in the world to ever undertake law studies.[4] In 1994 about 17 percent of young people took the school-leaving exam, which provides qualification for university entry, and by 1999 52.8 percent of them were women. In comparison to other countries there is a relatively low level of participation in higher education (in 1995, 8 percent of people under twenty-seven had a degree), one of the reasons for this being that there is in fact a good system of apprenticeships. Here

Elderly Swiss woman waits for a train in Basel. Photo © Painet.

too, though, there are gender differences, as in 1993 53 percent of twenty year-old women did an apprenticeship as opposed to 72 percent of men, the professions chosen by women tend to be limited, and they often opt for shorter studies whenever possible.[5] In 2000 about 14 percent of women and 34 percent of men had studied to higher educational levels, but as 46 percent of university students were female during the 2001–2002 academic year, this situation looks set to change.

Literacy

Illiteracy is currently considered to be negligible, although according to an Organization for Economic Cooperation and Development (OECD) report 11–19 percent of the population (6–11 percent of those born in Switzerland) experience difficulty with basic reading and writing skills.

EMPLOYMENT AND THE ECONOMY

Job/Career Opportunities

Swiss workers work on average a forty-two-hour week, with four weeks of annual holiday, having voted against both a move to a forty-hour week in 1976 and a fifth week of holiday in 1986. In 1999 54.7 percent of women were in part-time work, as opposed to 9.5 percent of men, and by 2000 44 percent of the work force were women.[6] Contrary to practice in neighboring France, where the masculine is often used to refer to both men and women, feminine forms of job titles are routinely used in all linguistic areas of Switzerland, meaning that the "feminine" is very much in evidence in the public arena, symbolizing equality of the genders and equal access to all jobs.[7]

Pay

Although women are extending the areas in which they work and there are measures in place to promote their careers in various domains, they still earn on average 20–30 percent less than men and wide disparities remain.

Working Conditions

Sexual Harassment

Sexual harassment was made illegal in 1996.

Support for Mothers/Caretakers

Maternal Leave

Switzerland was one of the first countries (in 1877) to introduce legislation preventing women from working for six weeks after giving birth. However, the legislation's effect was limited as it failed to make provision for any payment during this period, which meant that many women had no choice but to continue to work secretly at home. To some extent a similar approach still pertains, as women are not allowed to work for eight weeks after the birth and are protected against being fired during pregnancy and for sixteen weeks following it, but there is still no state maternity benefit (although some women may have a right to maternity benefit via their employer). The federal government has been committed to introducing one since 1945, but in recent years there have been three failures to convince the population to agree to fund it.

In June 1999, propositions that offered women fourteen weeks at 80 percent pay as well as payments for nonworking mothers were turned down by voters. In the absence of a universal benefit, certain liberal cantons, such as Geneva, are looking at introducing a cantonal benefit.

Daycare

There remain considerable differences from one canton to another as far as daycare is concerned, and the issue continues to pose problems for many women due to the fact that provision for it is erratic, especially in German-speaking Switzerland. It continues to be assumed that women are the main caretakers for children, and the organization of the school day (the necessity for children to return home to eat at midday, for example) has made it difficult or even impossible for some to combine family and career.[8]

Social/Government Programs

Women can now retire at sixty-four (as opposed to sixty-two previously) and men at sixty-five and retirement benefits (complemented by occupational insurance and personal savings) were introduced in 1948, followed by invalidity benefit in 1960. The legislation that introduced retirement payments initially assumed that women were either single or married and not working; therefore, the divorced were not covered. But the laws have been revised several times, and since 1997 benefits are calculated separately for couples. However, the system remains firmly based on the model of the heterosexual married couple, and alternative lifestyles are not taken into account.

FAMILY AND SEXUALITY

Gender Roles

On the whole (and in spite of cantonal differences, which can make it difficult to generalize), Switzerland remains a fairly conservative country. Despite the inclusion of the concept of equality in the Federal Constitution in 1981, a new marriage law in 1988, the passage of a law on equal legal status in 1995, and the creation of federal and cantonal Equality Offices, in practice women in Switzerland still encounter difficulty attaining true equality. For many years and until relatively recently, some less academically inclined girls attended secondary schools that specialized in the teaching of housekeeping skills, and the general assumption still is that mothers will be the main caregivers and will take on responsibility for childcare. A survey conducted in 2000, for instance, discovered that women bore the main responsibility for household duties in 87 percent of families with children under fifteen years of age. Although increasing numbers of women return to work after the birth of children (albeit often part-time), in many cantons school timetables are still organized on the assumption that women are full-time homemakers and able to organize their days around children. Many Swiss tended traditionally to return home to eat at midday, which obviously implied that someone (generally the woman) had to prepare a meal, although this is now changing, especially in urban areas. Another problem often faced by women who want to pursue a career is the difficulty of getting access to childcare, again due to the traditional view that young children are best looked after by the mother. A slightly different approach has been taken by women who argue for the economic and social recognition of housework and the payment of a "salary" to women not working full-time outside the home.

There is an increasing awareness of the importance of gender balance in politics and the professions, although girls are still tending to go into a restricted number of careers (e.g., office work, sales, hairdressing, and childcare) and choose shorter courses than boys, and there are areas where the percentage of women employed remains very low. In December 2002, when a new member of the federal government, Micheline Calmy-Rey, was elected, it was felt important that the post should go to a woman (which is a sign of progress) but on the other hand her "feminine" qualities, the fact that she had combined a career with motherhood and would be the first grandmother to join the federal government, were made much of by the media. It is probably the case now in Switzerland that although many gains have been made in the legal domain, much still remains to be done both practically and in terms of changing mentalities; when asked their views on gender roles and equality within the couple, many Swiss will respond positively, but these attitudes are unfortunately not always confirmed in practice.

Marriage

Switzerland has a higher number of both marriages and divorces than other European countries, although the number of marriages declined by almost 10 percent in 2001. Increasing numbers of couples choose to cohabit without marrying before having children (this is estimated to be the case of three quarters of women in the 20–24 age bracket), but once children are born, the tendency is to marry, with the result that 70 percent of 35–44-year-olds live in a "traditional" family and in 2001 only 11.4 percent of infants were born to unmarried parents. These new patterns mean that women are delaying the birth of children (fewer and fewer women are having their first child before the age of twenty-five) and marrying later than they used to (the average is now twenty-eight for women and thirty for men). On marriage, it is impossible for both members of a couple to simply retain their own name and the man's name automatically becomes the family's name, although women are now allowed to add their own if they wish. In June 2001, Parliament voted against a proposition to liberalize the choosing of the family name to ensure equality between the sexes, the arguments of opponents including the transparency of family histories and the supposed psychological impact on children.[9]

Over a third of marriages (38.5 percent in 2001) now end in divorce, increasingly at the request of the woman, and no-fault divorce has been an option since 1998, although if one partner does not agree to the divorce there is a waiting period of four years.

Reproduction

Contraception and Abortion

Access to contraception (the Pill being the most popular method) and gynecological care (Pap smear tests and the like) is widespread, but abortion has only been legal since June 2002, when voters agreed to decriminalize it up to twelve weeks. Before 2002, abortion had theoretically been illegal, according to the Penal Code of 1942, which was still in force, except in very strict circumstances such as serious risk to the mother's health. In practice, however, there were a number of "liberal" cantons, where abortions were available, and "conservative" cantons, where it was generally more difficult to obtain them. This led to what was known as "gynecological tourism," with women traveling to see a doctor in another canton if necessary. Thanks to improved information, access to contraception, and the introduction of the morning-after pill (available without a prescription as of 2002), the number of abortions has fallen considerably (there were about 12,000 in 1994 versus 70,000, most of them illegal, in 1966) and "backstreet" abortions have all but disappeared. In 1998 there were 8.3 terminations per 1,000 women and (in 1999) about 10 percent of babies were born to unmarried couples in a proportion of 100 girls for 105.5 boys.

Teen Pregnancy

Sex between minors is acceptable if the age difference between the two people concerned is not greater than three years.

In 1994 Switzerland had the lowest rate of teenage pregnancy in Western Europe (4.6 per 1,000), due to the availability of contraception, a long history of sex education in schools, and effective AIDS campaigns that inform about the use of condoms. It seems, however, that the fertility rate for non-Swiss teenagers is approximately 5–10 times higher than for Swiss ones; and due to the cantonal differences that pertained until 2002, there are no uniform statistics on the numbers of teenagers who may have terminated a pregnancy.[10]

HEALTH

Health Care Access

Health insurance, which is compulsory, is administered by private companies, and in 1998 10.5 percent of GNP was spent on health. Access to health care is excellent, and there is financial support from the state for those who may have difficulty paying for insurance. Although contraception is widely available and used by an estimated 78 percent of women, its cost is not reimbursed as it is deemed to be "preventive" medicine, and the same goes for voluntary sterilization.

Diseases and Disorders

AIDS

For a number of years, there have been serious problems with drug addiction in Switzerland, especially in urban areas, and one consequence of this has been the incidence of HIV and AIDS among addicts. To try to reduce the risks taken by addicts and combat the transmission of the illness, there are various schemes in operation throughout the country that offer needle exchanges and a safe environment in which to inject drugs, and some cantons have experimented with the provision of heroin on prescription. Thanks to the development of new treatments, the number of cases of HIV and AIDS has been falling since 1995. On the other hand, heterosexual transmission, now responsible for over 50 percent of HIV cases, has been rising, with an evident impact on women. Figures for cases up to March 2001 indicated that almost a quarter of AIDS sufferers were women, whereas about a third of those with HIV were female.

Cancer

There is no national program of screening for breast cancer, but some cantons are taking the lead in this area, including Geneva, where the incidence of cancers was reported in 2002 to be higher than both the Swiss and European averages. Since January 2001 in Geneva, screening for breast cancer has been free. A recent study of women diagnosed with breast cancer (covering the period 1978–1985) found a survival rate of 76 percent after five years.[11]

POLITICS AND LAW

Suffrage

Men acquired suffrage in 1848, but it was 1971 before women gained equality in this area. Several cantons did, however, begin to accord cantonal suffrage from 1959, the first being the French-speaking canton of Vaud. In contrast, in the half canton of Appenzell Innerrhoden (a German-speaking canton in Eastern Switzerland), there was considerable resistance (from both women and men) to according women the cantonal vote, and it was 1990 before they gained this right following pressure from the federal authorities.[12]

Political Participation

By October 1999, the most recent federal elections, 23.5 percent of members of the Lower House and 15.2 percent of the Upper House were women. Some Swiss feminists have, however, questioned to what extent this represents progress, pointing out that given the part-time nature of Swiss politics, which possibly makes a seat in Parliament less prized, it could be said that "power" has simply moved elsewhere, making men more prepared to make room for women. The first women to join the seven-member federal government were Elisabeth Kopp (1984–1989), and Ruth Dreifuss (1993–2000) in 1993. There are currently two women: Ruth Metzler (Ministry of Justice) since 1999, and Micheline Calmy-Rey (Ministry of Foreign Affairs) since 2002. Dreifuss was also the first woman (and the first person of Jewish origin) to ever become president of Switzerland (in 1999). She joined the government following an extraordinary nationwide campaign by women who were scandalized at a smear campaign against Christiane Brunner, the Socialist Party's initial candidate. This successful campaign stood in strong contrast to events of 1983, when the candidacy of Lilian Uchtenhagen was blocked and the Socialist Party withdrew its support, allowing a man to be elected in her place.[13]

Women's Rights

Unmarried women gained civil rights in 1882 with married women achieving very limited civil rights in 1912. In 1978 parental authority replaced paternal authority; and when a couple is unmarried, the mother now has authority over the children. In 1981 equality between the sexes was inscribed in the Constitution, a gain whose widespread nonapplication (for example, with regard to pay) was marked in June 1991 by a nationwide women's strike, in which half a million women participated. In 1988 a new marriage law was introduced and the Federal Office for Equality between Women and Men was set up; since then, similar offices have been established in some cantons.

Rights with regard to the acquisition of nationality were revised in 1992 and equalized. Previously a Swiss woman who married a foreign man gained her husband's nationality but could not transmit her Swiss nationality (unlike a Swiss man). Now neither women nor men lose their nationality if they marry a foreigner, and in both cases the foreign partner is accorded accelerated naturalization rather than automatic citizenship. In Switzerland, everyone has a "place of origin" that figures on official papers and is passed down patrilineally. Before 1988 women lost their "place of origin" on marriage and assumed their husband's, but they now have the right to retain their place of origin (while also automatically gaining their husband's, so the situation is still not entirely equal).

Feminist Movements

Traditionally, there have always been two sorts of women's groups in Switzerland—on the one hand the more traditional ones that sought to work within existing structures, and on the other the more radical ones that questioned them—and substantive disagreement between them on issues such as abortion and military service for women. The 1980s saw the big public demonstrations of the past being replaced by the steady notching-up of small successes as well as a move into new areas such as working with refugee women. Since the late 1980s, the two strands of the movement have tended to move closer together, and at the same time there has been increasing integration of feminist concerns into the mainstream. The attacks on Christiane Brunner in 1993 paradoxically served to reenergize many women and create a new desire to collaborate. This led in the late 1990s to the creation of the Feminist Coalition, which aims to coordinate the different feminist demands and which played a prominent role in the ultimately successful campaign for the decriminalization of abortion. There continue to be groups that campaign on specific issues, and the main cities, such as Geneva and Zurich, have women's centers where groups meet.

Lesbian Rights

Homosexuality and lesbianism have been legal since 1992, with the age of consent sixteen years, and discrimination on the grounds of "way of life" was outlawed in 1999.

Marriage. Although the Swiss authorities have proved slow to fully recognize alternative lifestyles, there were discussions in autumn 2002 on the introduction of a civil pact for gay couples, a version of which already exists in the cantons of Geneva and Zurich. This pact will not be available to heterosexuals unwilling for whatever reason to marry. The proposed law will not provide complete parity with married couples, and groups representing lesbians and homosexuals continue to lobby for legislation that would equalize rights to residence, pensions, and inheritance for same-sex couples. This is particularly important as the legislation around residence and work permits in Switzerland is strict, and obviously same-sex couples do not have the option of marriage to facilitate this.

Parenthood. Although cantonal differences are considerable and some cantons continue to take a very conservative view, lesbian mothers are generally able to retain custody of their children. On the other hand, homosexual and lesbian couples cannot adopt children and nonbiological partners cannot gain parenting rights.[14]

Military Service

Unless they are exempted for medical, religious, or psychological reasons (in which case they pay a military tax), all Swiss men have to complete a twenty-one-week military training course after the age of eighteen and then return for six refresher courses until at least thirty (recently reduced from forty-two with a more concentrated series of training sessions, in order to make army commitments more compatible with work). Homosexual and lesbian activity is not discriminated against in the army, in line with antidiscrimination legislation passed in 1999.

Currently women have the option of being included in this militia army.[15] The federal government discussed incorporating women into the army more formally in the 1980s, an idea that was supported by some for whom it was a symbol of equality but that was opposed by many feminist groups from a pacifist/antimilitaristic stance.

RELIGION AND SPIRITUALITY

In 2000 it was estimated that 40 percent of the population of Switzerland was Protestant, 46 percent Catholic, 2 percent Moslem, 5 percent of other faiths, and the remainder of no faith. Religious freedom is assured by the Constitution and although religious education is taught in schools, children can opt out of these classes. Christian churches traditionally have the right to levy a "church tax" on residents of the canton registered as members of a particular church, but in recent decades increasing numbers of people have been opting out of this tax.

Women's Roles

Women have begun to play a role in Protestant churches as pastors; and although their roles in the Catholic religion are more limited, opinions within the Catholic Church have evolved. Many were surprised, for example, in 1997 when women members of the Christian Democrat Party (traditionally profamily and antichoice) supported women's right to choose abortion, as did the Swiss Federation of Protestant Churches. In the late 1990s, the acrimonious debate around Switzerland's actions during the Second World War reignited feelings of anti-Semitism, which are latent in the country, but on the whole it can be asserted that the different faiths present in Switzerland coexist relatively peacefully.

VIOLENCE

Domestic Violence

Refuges for women abused by their partners have existed in the main towns since 1979 (although, as everywhere, more space is always needed), and in 1991 a center where victims of sexual violence could get help and counseling opened in Zurich. Since 1992 rape within marriage can be investigated if the woman goes to the police (although feminist groups are still lobbying for the legislation to be extended so the police can prosecute even if the woman concerned does not press charges); and in 1993 new measures were introduced to help women victims of violence, including the right to deal with a female police officer and female judge. A 1997 study estimated that around a fifth of women in Switzerland suffered physical or sexual violence from their partner, but about only 10 percent of cases actually reached the courts. A law to make domestic violence a crime is currently being studied by Parliament and it is possible that the police may gain the right to prosecute.[16]

Rape/Sexual Assault

According to the statistics available, the incidence of rape does not appear to be increasing significantly; 447 were reported in 1999, and in 2000 there were 404 reports of rape. It is obviously difficult, though, to estimate the level of nonreporting. The Swiss Penal Code, which defines rape exclusively as a male on female crime, establishes that those convicted can be sentenced to prison for up to ten years, with a minimum of three years if the victim was threatened with a weapon. Since the 1980s the main cities have had hotlines, known as "Viol Secours" in French-speaking Switzerland, which provide help and support for victims of rape.[17]

Trafficking in Women and Children

Hard pornography has been banned since 1992 but prostitution is legal, as are brothels (since 1992), although practice can vary from one canton to another (i.e., some local authorities ban street prostitution and fine "curb-crawlers" [men looking for prostitutes]. Foreign women are not allowed to work in prostitution (although in 2000 it was estimated that between 5,000 and 10,000 were clandestinely involved), which means that many of them come into the country as strippers and "dancers" and are vulnerable to exploitation. Often from countries such as Thailand or the Dominican Republic, they generally do not speak the language of the canton they end up in and all too often are obliged to work off debts incurred to bring them to Switzerland.

Given that Switzerland is a comparatively wealthy country, there is a certain tradition of Swiss men being involved in sex tourism or going abroad to look for wives in countries where women are perceived as more "pliable" and less "demanding."[18] Such women (or women working as "dancers" who contract marriages of convenience) can be very vulnerable, as they need to remain in a marriage for five years before qualifying for permanent residence, and if divorce occurs before this time they are likely to be deported. Many therefore feel pressured into remaining in unsuccessful or even violent marriages.

OUTLOOK FOR THE TWENTY-FIRST CENTURY

Although women in Switzerland have only had suffrage at the federal level since 1971, progress in the political arena has been rapid and the percentages of women in local, cantonal, and federal assemblies have steadily increased over the last thirty years. Although the blocking of Christiane Brunner's nomination to the government in 1993 and the attempt to conduct a smear campaign against her were depressing signals, the strong reaction from women across the country was encouraging, as it indicated that it was simply no longer possible to treat women this way and ignore the gender dimension. As a sign of the progress made, when one of the two women federal councilors recently left the government, she was replaced by another woman. Progress is also being made in terms of access to education, but there are still not enough women at the highest levels, and combining a high-level career and a family is still not considered entirely normal.

In the late 1990s and the early years of the twenty-first century, there have been many gains for women in Switzerland, not least concerning divorce, abortion, and political representation, but in the future they will need not only to defend the status quo (the raising of the retirement age for women to sixty-four was perceived by many as a failure, for instance) but also continue to press to expand rights. One notable area in which much remains to be done concerns the legal status of same-sex couples as well as unmarried heterosexual couples, where the prevailing models remain extremely conservative, and discussions on the civil pact in late 2002 were an important indication of current attitudes. Swiss women can be pleased that in June 2001 a report by the charity Save the Children rated Switzerland sixth in the world in terms of its investment in mothers and eighteenth for its investment in girls, but complacency would be misplaced and feminists in Switzerland will continue to push for still more improvement.

NOTES

1. There are a variety of reasons for the high number of foreigners in Switzerland, including the traditional need for foreign labor, the complex system for obtaining

nationality (involving payment in some cantons, a citizenship exam in others, and in a few the need to be voted in by one's fellow citizens), and the fact that some residents already hold an EU passport and do not see the need for Swiss nationality. The percentage of foreigners in the population varies from below 10 percent in some cantons to well over 30 percent in others (such as Geneva).

2. If a lobby group can collect 50,000 signatures, it can force a referendum on a law proposed by the government; and if a group wishes to propose a new law and collects at least 100,000 signatures, it can have a popular initiative voted on. Popular initiatives have included proposals such as the abolition of the army (1989), and referendums have included membership of the European Economic Area (1992), both of which were rejected by voters.

3. For further details, see www.research-projects.unizh.ch/med/unit41300/area181/ p610.htm.

4. See Thérèse Bielander, "La muraille universitaire," in *Le guide des femmes disparues* (Geneva: Metropolis, 1993), 169–83, esp. 171; and Claudia Crotti and Charlotte Müller, " 'Die Galanterie wich dem Kampf,' " in *Intellectual Emancipation*, ed. Joy Charnley and Malcolm Pender (Bern: Peter Lang, 2001), 29–49. On Kempin-Spyri, see Anne-Marie Käppeli, "Scènes féministe," in *Histoire de femmes en Occident*, vol. 4, ed. Geneviève Fraise and Michelle Perrot (Paris: Perrin, 2002), 575–613, esp. 607.

5. See Annelies Debrunner, "Career Opportunities for Women," in Charnley and Pender, 2001, 101–2, where the most popular careers chosen by male and female apprentices are listed.

6. Debrunner, 2002, 101–2, 104.

7. To get an idea of the scale of the problem in France, see Anne-Marie Houdebine-Gravaud, "La féminisation," in *Un siècle d'anti féminisme* (Paris: Fayard, 1999), 431–48.

8. Debrunner, 2002, 108; and Rosemarie Simmen, "Women in Switzerland since 1971," in Joy Charnley et al., *25 years of Emancipation?* (Bern: Lang, 1998), 13–23, esp. 18.

9. Bernard Wuthrich, "Putsch sous la Coupole: la loi sur les noms de famille passe à la trappe," *Le Temps* (23 juin 2001), 19.

10. See the details at www.agi-usa.org/pubs/journals/2823296.html.

11. See details at http://news.bbc.co.uk and http://breast-cancer-research.com.

12. For further background on the reasons why suffrage was only gained in 1971, see Regina Wecker, "The Oldest Democracy," and Brigitte Studer, "The Rise of 'Public Woman,' " both in Charnley et al., 1998, 25–40, 41–56.

13. Although she was the Socialist Party's official candidate, Christiane Brunner was opposed by many male politicians who considered her "too left-wing" and "too feminist"; not content with voting against her in Parliament, some resorted to spreading rumors about her private life (including the suggestion that she had had an illegal abortion), which were intended to tarnish her reputation. The events around Brunner's failure to be elected and Dreifuss's subsequent election are described by Catherine Duttweiler (1993).

14. For further information, see www.ilga.org/Information/legal-survey/europe/ switzerland.htm.region.

15. See the army's website at www.vbs.admin.ch/internet/e/armee/index.htm.

16. See the article on this subject (in English) dated April 28, 2003 and published at www.nzz.ch.

17. See the details at www.span.ch/violsecours.

18. This situation is depicted in Alain Tanner's film, *La femme de Rose Hill*, in which the man concerned is a farmer who has not managed to find a Swiss wife. For further details on sexual exploitation in Switzerland, see www.uri.edu/artsci/wms/hughes/switzer.htm.

RESOURCE GUIDE

Suggested Reading

Anderson, Bonnie S., and Judith P. Zinsser. *A History of Their Own: Women in Europe from Prehistory to the Present*, 2 vols. London: Penguin, 1990.

Charnley, Joy, Malcolm Pender, and Andrew Wilkin, eds. *25 Years of Emancipation?: Women in Switzerland 1971–1996*. Bern: Peter Lang, 1998. Chapters on the fight for female suffrage in Switzerland and the situation of Swiss women at the end of the twentieth century.

Steinberg, Jonathan, *Why Switzerland?* 2nd ed. Cambridge: Cambridge University Press, 1996. General coverage of history, politics, language, religion, and economics in Switzerland.

Film

La femme de Rose Hill. 1989. Directed by Alain Tanner.

Web Sites

Federal Commission for Women's Issues, www.frauenkommission.ch.
The federal department that collates and disseminates information concerning women in Switzerland; Eigerplatz 5, 3003 Bern.

Feminist Coalition, www.femco.org.

Femmes, Féminisme, Recherche/Verein Feministische Wissenschaft Schweiz, www.femwiss.ch/.
Promotes feminist research in universities.

Frauenzeitung, http://fraz.fembit.ch/frames/fraframe.htm.
Feminist press, in German.

L'Emilie, www.lemilie.org/.
Feminist press, in French.

Statistics and facts about women in Switzerland, www.statistik.admin.ch.

Various women's groups, www.unil.ch/liege/liens/liensfemCH.html.

Organizations

Autonomes Frauenzentrum, Mattengass 27
8005 Zurich
Email: frauenzentrum@fembit.ch

Women's center.

Espace Femmes International
2 rue de la Tannerie
1227 Carouge
Email: efi.geneve@worldcom.ch

Women's center.

Femco (Coalition Féministe/Feministische Koalition)
32 avenue Sévelin
1004 Lausanne
Email: femco@equal.ch

Campaigning coalition.

Femmes, Féminisme, Recherche/Verein Feministische Wissenschaft Schweiz, Lothrin-
    gerstr 93
4056 Basel
Email: femwiss@femwiss.ch

Group that works to support women and promote feminist research in universities.

SELECTED BIBLIOGRAPHY

Charnley, Joy, and Malcolm Pender, eds. *Intellectual Emancipation: Swiss Women and Education*. Occasional Papers in Swiss Studies, vol. 4. Bern: Peter Lang, 2001.
Debrunner, Annelies. "Career Opportunities for Women—New Possibilities at Swiss Colleges?" In *Intellectual Emancipation: Swiss Women and Education*, edited by Joy Charnley and Malcolm Pender, 99–120. Occasional Papers in Swiss Studies, 4. Bern: Peter Lang, 2001.
Lewis, Jane, ed. *Before the Vote Was Won: Arguments for and against Women's Suffrage*. London: Routledge and Kegan Paul, 1987.
Simmen, Rosemarie. "Women in Switzerland since 1971: Major Achievement—Minor Changes?" In *25 Years of Emancipation? Women in Switzerland 1971–1996*, edited by Joy Charnley, Malcolm Pender, and Andrew Wilkin, 13–23, esp. 18. Bern: Lang, 1998.
Wecker, Regina. "The Oldest Democracy and Women's Suffrage: The History of a Swiss Paradox" and Brigitte Studer, "The Rise of 'Public Woman': Politics, Citizenship and Gender in the Swiss Debate on Female Suffrage after World War Two." In Joy Charnley, Malcolm Pender, and Andrew Wilkin, 1998, 25–40, 41–56.

Selected French and German Bibliography

Bard, Christine, ed. *Un siècle d'antiféminisme*. Paris: Fayard, 1999.

Bielander, Thérèse. "La muraille universitaire." In *Le guide des femmes disparues*, edited by Anne-Marie Käppeli, 169–83, esp. 171. Geneva: Metropolis, 1993.

Cairolo, Alberto, Giovanni Chiaberto, and Sabina Engel. *Le déclin des maisons closes. La prostitution à Genève à la fin du XIXe siècle*. Geneva: Zoé, 1987.

Chaponnière, Martine. *Devenir ou redevenir femme*. Paris: Champion, 1992.

Commission fédérale pour les questions féminines. *Femmes. Pouvoir. Histoire. Evénements de l'histoire des femmes et de l'égalité des sexes en Suisse de 1848 à 1998*. Bern: Author, 1998.

Crotti, Claudia, and Charlotte Müller. " 'Die Galanterie wich dem Kampf': Women at Swiss Universities in the 19th Century." In *Intellectual Emancipation: Swiss Women and Education*, edited by Joy Charnley and Malcolm Pender, 29–49. Occasional Papers in Swiss Studies, 4. Bern: Peter Lang, 2001.

Duby, Georges, and Michelle Perrot, eds. *Histoire des femmes en Occident*, 5 volumes, 2nd ed. Paris: Perrin, 2002.

Duttweiler, Catherine. *Kopp, Madame et Monsieur*. Lausanne: Payot, 1990.

———. *Pardon Monsieur: Chronique d'une élection turbulente au Conseil fédéral*. Geneva: Zoé, 1993.

L'Exploitée. Geneva: Editions Noir, 1977.

Gaillard, Ursula, and Annik Mahaim. *Retards de règles: Attitudes devant le contrôle des naissances et l'avortement en Suisse du début du siècle aux années vingt*. Lausanne: Editions d'en bas, 1983.

Houdebine-Gravaud, Anne-Marie. "La féminisation des noms de métiers." In *Un siècle d'antiféminisme*, edited by Christine Bard, 431–48. Paris: Fayard, 1999.

Käppeli, Anne-Marie. "Scènes féministes." In *Histoire des femmes en Occident*, volume 4, edited by Geneviève Fraisse and Michelle Perrot, 575–613, esp. 607. Paris: Perrin, 2002.

Käppeli, Anne-Marie, ed. *Sublime croisade: Ethique et politique du féminisme protestant (1875–1928)*. Geneva: Zoé, 1990.

———. *Le guide des femmes disparues*. Geneva: Metropolis, 1993.

Montreynaud, Florence. *Le XXe siècle des femmes*, 2nd ed. Paris: Nathan, 1999.

Office fédéral de la statistique. *La difficile conquête du mandat de députée: Les femmes et les élections au Conseil national de 1971 à 1991*. Bern: Author, 1994.

Ruckstuhl, Lotti. *Vers la majorité politique: Histoire du suffrage féminin en Suisse*. Bonstetten: Association des droits de la femme et Interfeminas, 1991.

Woodtli, Susanna. *Du féminisme à l'égalité politique: Un siècle de luttes en Suisse 1868–1971*. Lausanne: Payot, 1977.

Wuthrich, Bernard. "Putsch sous la Coupole: la loi sur les noms de famille passe à la trappe." *Le Temps*, June 23, 2001, 19.

37

TURKEY

Tahire Erman

PROFILE OF TURKEY

Turkey is a rapidly urbanizing society. In 1955, only 28.8 percent of the population lived in cities, whereas in 1997 65.1 percent did. Its population is 56,473,035,[1] and the country occupies 779,452 square kilometers.[2] Turkey's population consists predominantly of Muslims with a small number of Jewish, Armenian Christian, and Greek Orthodox people. The Muslim population has different religious sects, such as the Alevi and the Sunni.[3] The official and majority language is Turkish, although for some people Kurdish, Laz, or Arabic serves as their mother tongue.

Turkey has been a parliamentary democracy since the establishment of the Turkish Republic in 1923, after the fall of the Ottoman Empire. Modernization has been the major goal of the founders of the Republic, who aimed at its secularization and democratization. A multiparty system was established in 1946, in the same period during which Turkey began to incorporate into the world capitalist economy.

Of the total population, 27,865,988 are female and 28,607,047 are male.[4] In 1996 the infant mortality rate was 67 (per 1,000 live births), and maternal mortality rate was 54.2[5] (out of 100,000 live births), down from 207 in 1974.[6] The total fertility rate is 2.65, and of the 3.7 children per woman, 3.14 survive to adulthood.[7] Life expectancy is 71.5 for women and 66.9 for men.[8]

OVERVIEW OF WOMEN'S ISSUES

Turkey is one of the countries in "the belt of classic patriarchy."[9] Classic patriarchy can be "characterized by extremely restricted codes of behavior for women, rigid gender segregation, and a powerful ideology linking family honor to female virtue."[10] Although this description holds true for many women in Turkish society, particularly those living in rural areas, it ignores the diversity among women and fails to inform us about women's attempts to open up spaces for themselves or even to challenge patriarchy.[11]

Upon the establishment of the Turkish Republic as a modern nation-state in 1923, the founder Mustafa Kemal Atatürk had on his agenda the modernization of women, who would symbolize the modern Turkey in the international arena and would raise children who could carry the Republic forward to catch up with the advanced societies. Elite women residing in large cities were to be the model of modern women for rural women to emulate.

Opportunities in education and employment began to be provided to women, and in the case of elite women, higher education and careers were even demanded. However, women living in rural areas, particularly those in rural eastern and southeastern Anatolia, lacked the opportunity to participate in modernizing Turkey. Despite the efforts of some educated women, who took the "missionary" role of educating women in the more isolated regions, the gap between the educated, modernized, professional women living in big cities and the illiterate women living in villages has widened.

Not surprisingly, many rural women prefer the city to the village.[12] They say city women are freed from the tiring, dirty work of the village as well as from its strict social control. Rural women want to move to the city to become housewives in their nuclear families. However, many such migrant women have limited educations and work in unskilled, low-paid jobs without job security.[13] Thus, although employment has brought a degree of autonomy and power to some, the majority of migrant women have not seen improvement in their status in the family.[14] Their economic contributions to their families remain largely invisible and unacknowledged. In addition, as the people from the same region cluster in the same urban neighborhoods, they recreate the patriarchal village culture in the city, as well as the social control of relatives and neighbors over "their" women.[15] In both the Alevi and Sunni migrant families living in urban squatter settlements, patriarchy prevails, and the husband is seen as the "head of the family." However, in Alevi families, there are fewer restrictions imposed on women, and Alevi women can more easily engage in paid work[16] or interact with the city than can their Sunni counterparts. Alevis emphasize their egalitarian approach to gender relations and their liberal attitudes toward women to distinguish themselves from Sunnis. On the other hand, Sunni migrants, especially those from eastern Anatolia and the Black Sea, emphasize the importance of women's *namus* (family honor) in their public life.

Born and raised in the city, the daughters of rural migrant women are more aware of their disadvantaged positions in the city, since they tend to take other urban young people as their comparison group. Although they are usually more educated than their mothers and find work as secretaries, sales assistants, and caregiving personnel, they are not educated enough to compete for higher positions. Some question patriarchy, but many accept it as part of their reality, arranging their lives and hopes within the constraints of the patriarchal family.[17]

The forced migration from eastern and southeastern Anatolia in the state's fight against the Kurdistan Workers Party's (PKK) terrorism in the region dislocated many families to the larger cities of western Turkey, mainly Istanbul and Izmir. The forced nature of their migration to cities distinguishes them from other migrants who moved to cities mostly in order to improve their economic positions and to take advantage of the facilities and services of the city. Lacking the necessary support networks in the city and living with the potential stigma of being seen as "terrorists who want to divide Turkey," the newcomers face social exclusion and economic suffering.[18] Since many do not speak Turkish, women in these families are more isolated inside their homes. Their large families, unemployment, and poverty spare them only enough for crowded, dilapidated housing in the most impoverished neighborhoods. Some have started working in the least desirable jobs for very low wages, thereby curtailing the bargaining power of women already in those jobs or even replacing them.

With the emergence in the 1980s of claims for recognition by the nationalist Kurds, the Alevis, and the radical Islamists,[19] Islamist women appeared as a group and became visible in their demonstrations, protesting against the state's ban on wearing the headscarf (the *türban*) in official places, especially in universities. Such protests have enabled these mostly traditional, lower-middle-class women to become active in the public realm, previously closed to them and defined as men's sphere. However, breaking into the public sphere has not always meant breaking away from patriarchy; and their being female has not brought women from different classes and ideologies together to defend the cause of women. The "secular" women in society have taken different positions vis-à-vis the Islamist women. Although some have supported them for their rights to decide about their own clothing styles, others have criticized them for acting as a political tool used by Islamist men to destroy the secular state.

The Turkish state is at a very different point now than in 1923, when it claimed to be the sole agent of the modernization of women and the improvement of women's status and conditions. Especially since the 1980s, civic organizations, including women's organizations, have brought a new dynamism to society. They organize the March 8 World Women's Day celebrations every year. Nearly 1,000 women walked from Istanbul to the Turkish capital Ankara in the "Women's March 2000 to Fight Poverty, War, Violence, Sexual Harassment and Rape." The women's nongovernmental organizations (NGOs) today criticize the state's top-down paternal approach to women and believe in women's emancipation through their own efforts in autonomous women's movements.

In terms of women's rights and conditions, Turkey is in a better position today when compared to the past. The government signed the Convention on the Elimination of All Forms of Discrimination against Women in 1985, and within this framework, the Directorate General on the Status and Problems of Women was established in 1990. Since then, women's divisions have been formed in municipalities and unions. Thirteen Research Centers on Women have been opened in universities along with graduate programs in women's studies in three universities. The Foundation for Women's Library and Information Center was established in 1990 as the outcome of women's volunteer movement and initiative. Turkey participated in the UN International Conference on Population and Development held in Cairo in 1994 and in the Fourth World Conference on Women held in Beijing in 1995. And, importantly, amendments to the Civil Code regarding women's rights have generated heated debates. Still, there is much to be done, especially when we consider the significant inequalities between the different groups of women in terms of social class, regional differences, rural/urban differences, and political positioning.

EDUCATION

Opportunities

In 1859, during the later period of the Ottoman Empire, middle school education for girls began, followed by high school education for girls in 1913 and the first university for women in 1915.[20] However, women and men attended different schools with different educational programs, which reproduced traditional gender roles. In contrast, the new Republic founded coeducational schools, based on the law on the unity of education and teaching, which was enacted in 1924 and whose goal was to put an end to the differential practices in education, including those based on gender. Primary school education for girls became obligatory nationwide. Nevertheless, women's education in traditional gender roles continued to be encouraged by the state. For example, the Girls' Institutes, which provided advanced study for women graduates of vocational schools, were established in 1945 to improve their skills in cooking, sewing, and the like and to prepare them for their roles as wives and mothers in the modern world.[21] Furthermore, the effects of these reforms were mostly limited to upper- and middle-class women living in large cities.

Disparities between the urban centers and rural areas, between the developed western and the undeveloped eastern regions, and between the social classes still determine women's educational opportunities. For example, attendance in junior high for girls living in cities is 38.71 percent, whereas for those living in villages, it is 29.64 percent.[22] Furthermore, in the academic year 1981–1982, women constituted 27.48 percent of the students in higher education, but their percentage increased to 34.05 percent for the 1991–1992 academic year.[23]

However, women's participation in the educational system still lags far behind men's. More girls than boys tend to stop their education after they complete the obligatory primary school education (41.9 percent and 23.9 percent respectively). Among those between the ages 6–14, 15.9 percent of the girls and 9.9 percent of the boys fail to attend school, and this reaches 40 percent for girls and 27.3 percent for boys at the age of fourteen.[24] This female-to-male ratio of 0.97 in primary school (51.5 percent and 53.2 percent respectively) drops to 0.6 in junior high, 0.68 in high school, and 0.51 in university (8.7 percent and 14.4 percent; 7.8 percent and 11.5 percent; and 2.8 percent and 5.5 percent respectively).[25] In universities, men tend to study engineering and law (the female-to-male ratio is 0.31 and 0.43 respectively), and women tend to study arts, humanities, educational sciences, and medicine and health (the female-to-male ratio is 1.15, 0.81, 0.76, 0.76 respectively).

Because education is viewed as a means to social, as opposed to purely economic, mobility, women's education is generally supported, including by many rural migrants. There is, however, an emerging opposition among radical Islamists who do not like the idea of sending their children to so-called secular schools but want them to attend religious schools, which are against the law. They are particularly opposed to sending their daughters to coeducational schools. Some political Islamist women university students attend the university together with men students, yet they have demanded recognition of their rights to cover their hair (the *türban/* headscarf issue). This issue, along with the extension of the obligatory primary school education from five to eight years and, related to this, the restrictions on the *Imam Hatip* Schools,[26] have created much controversy in public, contributing to the polarization of the society into "secularists" and "Islamists." There are also differences between Alevi and Sunni migrant families in their attitudes toward women's education. Although Alevis, who have been strong defenders of the secular Turkish Republic since its establishment in 1923, believe in formal (secular) education for both their sons and daughters, some conservative Sunni families (not necessarily radical Islamists) do not want to send their daughters to school, particularly after they reach the age of puberty.

Literacy

There have been significant improvements in the education of women in general. The women's literacy rate rose from 9.8 percent in 1935 to 50.5 percent in 1975 and to 72 percent in 1990.[27] There are adult literacy programs organized by the state. In 1996–1997, thirteen provinces in eastern and southeastern Anatolia opened 395 literacy courses.[28] Recently, municipalities and civil society organizations have opened an increasing number of literacy courses, mostly in poor squatter neighborhoods.[29] The five-year obligatory primary school education was extended to eight years in 1997. The percent of illiterate women is three times that of illiterate men (27.17 percent and 8.94 percent respectively).

EMPLOYMENT AND THE ECONOMY

Women's entrance into the labor force dates to 1897. Over 100 years later in 1998, only 34 percent of the female population participated in the labor force versus 75.3 percent of men. Of those women, 15.2 percent of city dwellers and 44.4 percent of rural residents were in the labor force.[30] However, we should approach these figures with caution. Women's work,

Turkish woman attends to a spinning machine in a textile mill in Tarsus. Photo © Abbas/Magnum Photos.

particularly in the lower classes living in the city, remains largely invisible and unrecognized, since many women work in the informal sector (the sector of the economy that includes work that is irregular or temporary, without a contract, and conforms to the "big sister" image of the employer in the case of domestic workers). Also, the traditional patriarchal culture defines women's work as insignificant and temporary while it emphasizes women's status as mothers and wives. Thus, some women state that they are housewives, even if they are engaged in paid work. Until 1990 when the Constitutional Court annulled it, the law required the permission of their husbands for women to do paid work.

Educational level is another important factor in women's participation in the labor force. In 1997, in the cities 10.6 percent of the primary school graduates participated in the labor force, whereas 72.2 percent of university graduates do.[31]

Job/Career Opportunities

Women work mostly in agriculture (70 percent), followed by services (19.4 percent) and industry (10.6 percent).[32] In rural areas, 79.3 percent of women in the labor force work as unpaid family laborers in the fields;[33] however, their economic contributions are not acknowledged. The cities offer women more opportunities and more variety in the types of jobs they can obtain. Educated, professional women tend to work as professors, doctors, lawyers, pharmacists, and middle managers in the private sector, and men still primarily occupy the top decision-making positions. Women's participation in the professions is higher than many of that of their counterparts in Western societies.[34] This may be because the modernizing male elite recruit "their women" to the new positions in the developing economy instead of opening them to lower-class men.

In the middle and lower social strata, being a housewife is a prestigious status for women, one that denotes that the husband earns enough money to keep his wife at home, where she supposedly belongs. Thus, the number of women who define themselves as housewives is high in cities, including among those living in squatter settlements,[35] who generally do piecework at home or work cleaning the houses of the upper classes. The irregular, temporary, and noncontractual character of these jobs contributes to women not defining themselves as employed. On the other hand, the rising inflation, declining wages, and increasing unemployment in the formal sector (as a result of the neoliberal policies adopted since the 1980s) is pushing lower-class women, many of whom are rural-to-urban migrants, into the labor market, usually in a highly disadvantaged way. Left to them are the low-paying, low-status, temporary positions in the informal sector without job security or retirement benefits.

Women generally prefer to work in the public sector where, in 1994, the 483,656 female state employees constituted 34.3 percent of the total public sector work force. The women working in the public sector are usually high school graduates concentrated in the middle-level service jobs with little chance of promotion. The limited number of women in the higher ranks of the bureaucracy indicates women's relative powerlessness in the decision-making processes of the state. Nevertheless, in 1992, for the first time, women were appointed as chief executive in three counties (*kaymakam*); and a woman ambassador was appointed in 1985.

Pay

The principle "equal pay for equal work" was legislated in 1971. However, "Sex discrimination in wages (is possible) by enforcing wage differentials through changes in job descriptions."[36] Results of a comprehensive study found that women's pay was lower than men's by 33.2 percent; 23.6 percent of this difference was attributable to the nature of jobs women and men did, and 76.4 percent was due to gender discrimination.[37] Since the pay difference between men and women decreased as the educational level of women increased, women with less education were more strongly discriminated against. Adding to their burden is the type of work less-educated women do, sometimes working at home doing piecework and sometimes working for small subcontracting firms, which easily leads to women's exploitation. The study also disclosed that the highest pay difference in terms of gender existed in agriculture, where female laborers received only as much as 37.1 percent of male wages.

Significant pay differences exist not only between women and men but also among women. In cities, 7.4 percent of the women were employed in the highest-paying bracket and received 51.1 percent of the money paid to working women, whereas the 39.2 percent of the women employed in the lowest-paying bracket received only 4.0 percent of the money paid to women.[38] In the latter group, the number of women exceeded the number of men. Thus, extremely low pay is the common experience of women in the lower classes.

Working Conditions

Sexual Harassment

The issue of sexual harassment in the workplace has recently come to the public's attention through the efforts of women's groups. Yet, the "male culture" is still largely protected against challenges. A project sponsored by the Directorate General on the Status and Problems of Women on women clerical and sales workers discovered that "women experience sexual harassment in different degrees, yet they lack formal and institutional facilities to turn to."[39] Women reported various forms of sexual harassment, such as derogatory and indecent talk, curses containing sexual expressions, and compliments (e.g., about women's "revealing" dresses, which made the women feel like sex objects) as well as touching. The victims used various coping strategies such as making excuses, leaving the scene, pretending that they did not notice it, and unashamedly challenging the person. In the long run, women facing sexual harassment may isolate themselves in the workplace, especially if they feel guilty about such approaches toward them, which is quite common. They usually do not take collective action. Women may not perceive such behavior as sexual harassment; because of the dominant patriarchal ideology, they may regard it as just the way men are.

Support for Mothers/Caretakers

Support for mothers, including maternity leave and daycare, are important issues in women's employment. Many women are employed in the informal sector, which means they have no social security rights, and specifically neither maternal leave nor daycare. Women are only 10 percent of the total work force with social security rights,[40] and 79.6 percent of the female work force are not registered in any social security institution.[41] In brief, women's employment after marriage is discouraged by the prevailing practices and supported by the patriarchal ideology. It reduces the pressure on the employers to provide social benefits, such as maternity leave and childcare.

Maternal Leave

First regulated in 1930, maternity leave law gives forty-two days' paid leave and a maximum of six months of unpaid leave upon giving birth. Although the rights of working women are defined in labor and social security laws, no reliable data exist on whether these laws are enforced. It is clear, however, that the economic system and the dominant culture work hand-in-hand to exploit women in the labor force. Praising the housewife status and motherhood reinforces the tendency of women to leave their jobs after they get married to be "the ladies of their homes." Thus, employers who benefit from young women's labor power avoid providing maternity leave and daycare services to their women employees. Those women who choose not to leave their jobs when they get married or pregnant may easily be fired, since they may have been hired on the condition that they would leave their jobs upon their marriage or pregnancy.

Daycare

An enterprise is required to provide daycare services if it employs more than 150 women. This creates a tendency in small establishments to employ fewer than this number to avoid this legal requirement.

Inheritance and Property Rights

In the Ottoman era, the status of women was based on the Quran, the Islamic holy book, and such matters as marriage, divorce, and inheritance were under Islamic Law (the Shari'at). An example of the disadvantages to women was that women could inherit only one half, one quarter, one seventh, or one eighth of the property, depending on their relation to the deceased.[42]

Aimed at secularizing the legal system and conforming to Western standards, the Turkish Republic adopted the Swiss Civil Code in 1926, which granted equal rights to women and men in matters of inheritance and property ownership. However, the potential emancipation of women in these legal reforms confronted a prevailing culture, shaped to varying degrees by Islam, which continues to affect the decisions about women's inheritance and property ownership in many parts of society.

Although the urban educated women, and particularly professional women, are aware of their legal rights, women in rural Turkey, especially those in eastern and southeastern Anatolia where feudal relations and local traditional structures dominate, are highly disadvantaged in inheritance practices. The women themselves tend to give up their legal inheritance rights, believing that their male relatives traditionally own the property. They would likely not change their minds even when they were informed of their legal rights, saying that they would not (or could not) stand against their tradition. Although many women in the rural villages work the hardest, they usually do not own any property. Values that define them as unpaid family laborers and primarily as wives, mothers, and daughters-in-law play a significant role in restricting women's property rights.

Although paid employment potentially promises women some property rights, including the right to retain their wages, the common practice is to own "family property" instead of "personal property"; and, as the "head of the family," the husband usually becomes the legal owner. Although true of both the upper and lower classes, since the early 1990s, educated, upper-class women increasingly own property in their names as a result of heightened gender awareness developed under the influence of the women's movement. The rural migrant women in the cities, on the other hand, tend to hand their earnings over to their husbands who decide how to spend them.[43]

Migrant women may sell the golden bracelets given to them by their relatives at their marriage and/or work at jobs they find highly unpleasant in order to save money to buy a house. Even so, it is almost always the husband who holds title to it. Recently, the Civil Code has been amended. Among the changes, there is a new "marriage regime" in which the wife and the husband exist as equal marriage partners, and, in the case of divorce, both partners will have equal shares of the properties owned during the marriage. And this happened despite the conservative groups on the committee trying hard to "tone down" the proposal so as not to make it a "threat to the unity of the family." However, they succeeded in limiting its practice to the families formed after the amendment became effective in 2001.

Social/Government Programs

Sustainable Development

The Directorate General on the Status and Problems of Women, established in 1990, initiated several programs in collaboration with international organizations, such as the United Nations and the World Bank, to improve women's legal, employment, and social status and to increase their participation in the economy. The projects, including some on entrepreneurship, development, national childcare, and professional orientation and training, have been mostly targeted to the most marginalized women. The programs include everything from helping women to produce and market goods such as needlework, handmade sweaters and carpets, and foodstuffs, mostly by using their traditional skills, to providing bank credit to set up their own businesses; and from teaching vocations, such as hairdressing, glass engraving, and toymaking, as well as literacy; placing graduates in appropriate jobs; and financing research on women's employment in various sectors, such as tourism and clothing and textile.

The NGOs also have projects for women. For example, the Development Foundation in Turkey seeks to improve rural women's life chances by providing them credit and insuring that the women (not their husbands) retain the money. Yet to be established are projects that move beyond women's traditional roles.

The emphasis of international organizations, such as the World Bank and the United Nations, on sustainability has brought this issue to the attention of social and governmental programs. However, sustainability remains largely outside of the public consciousness and without concrete political actions to back it up. Especially the relationship between sustainability and its gender implications has not yet received the attention it deserves.

FAMILY AND SEXUALITY

In the face of the socioeconomic changes the society has been experiencing, including urbanization and industrialization, the Turkish family has undergone changes, such as the increase in the number of separate households. However, family continues to play a significant role in the lives of all social classes in rural and urban areas alike, and family ties are generally very strong. The family usually takes on the roles of providing welfare and security in the face of the state's failure to do so. The nuclear family is the predominant family type,[44] although elderly parents may be living in the same residence since Turkish social norms assign eldercare to the family. Today about 60 percent of all families are nuclear as opposed to 20 percent that are joint patriarchal.[45] Patriarchal extended families, in which three generations (the man who is the head of the household, his wife, and their married sons and wives with their children) live together, are also found, especially in eastern and southeastern Anatolia, and more commonly in rural than in urban areas. In patriarchal extended families, the most disadvantaged are women who reside in the husband's parental home upon their marriage. As daughters-in-law (*gelin*, literally, "those who come in"), they live under the order and control of the husbands' parents. In some families, they are not even given the permission to talk to their husbands or to show affection to their children in the presence of their in-laws. This is one reason why village women want to move to cities in hopes of establishing nuclear families.[46] In urban families, although gender relations that favor men prevail, women are not usually as powerless as the young women in rural extended families are.

The important role family plays in society has different implications for women and men. Women trade their submission for security and protection, whereas men consolidate their power and authority through acting as family heads. Furthermore, since in Turkey, like in other Mediterranean and Middle Eastern societies, family honor is linked to women's sexuality, women's sexual conduct comes under the control of the male family members. Thus, the family is likely to oppose women's liberation, supporting patriarchal relations and reproducing patriarchal ideology.

Gender Roles

In general, there are strictly separate gender roles for women and men. The majority of the women acquire their identities through the family as wives, mothers, daughters, and daughters-in-law. Only a very small group of achievement-oriented professional women in big cities define themselves mainly in terms of their careers.

As a rule, men are socially, and until very recently legally,[47] defined as "the head of the family," and as such are responsible for the provision of the family's material needs, control of family resources, and family decision making. On the other hand, women's responsibilities in the family are defined as housekeeping and caregiving to family members.

Although the increasing participation of women in the work force has the potential to challenge this gender division of labor within the family, the reality is that women typically end up with the double burden of working outside and inside the home while men are spared housekeeping responsibilities. Under international influences, some husbands in upper-income urban families are willing to "help" their wives but not to take responsibility for housekeeping. In lower-income families in which both women and men work, necessity may push men to take on some housekeeping duties when their wives work long hours. In such cases, their doing "women's work" is kept a secret to protect their male image.[48]

A 1993 study found that 65.3 percent of the employed women between ages fifteen and forty-nine did all the cooking and 58.2 percent did all the cleaning, yet none of the husbands did all the cooking by themselves and only 0.1 percent of the husbands did all the cleaning. In the rest of the sample, women got help from their relatives. On the other hand, 23.9 percent of the women did the shopping and only 8.7 percent kept the family budget, while the respective figures for the husbands were 34.6 percent and 50.4 percent. In the case of the unemployed housewives, none of the husbands did any cooking or cleaning, but they were the sole decision-makers in budget matters in 55 percent of the families. Women also mainly shoulder responsibilities for children, and, if help is needed, female relatives, not the husbands, tend to provide it.[49]

Marriage

In accordance with the major goal of the Turkish Republic to secularize the legal system, when the Turkish Civil Code was adopted in 1926, important changes were made regarding marriage. Polygamy, which had been supported by Islamic principles in the Ottoman Empire, was made illegal. Civil marriage performed by a state official was declared as the legal marriage; and accordingly, marriage by religious law, which had been the dominant form, was declared to be illegal. Furthermore, "(M)arriage, in order to be valid, had to take place in the presence of the bride, which meant the abolition of marriage by proxy." In the past, the father could offer his daughter in marriage to someone of his own choice against her will, sometimes even without telling her.[50] Although these legal changes were quickly adopted among the upper classes living in cities, religious marriage and polygamy continued to be practiced in the rest of the society, although at a declining rate. The outcome of the struggle between the secular state and religion (and tradition) over marriage has been a sort of reconciliation. The common practice among the majority (except for a small group of modern secularists) is to have both types of marriages, first marrying by religious law and then by civil law. In 1993, 89 percent of the Turkish people had both civil and religious marriages, 3.2 percent only civil marriage, and 7.5 percent only religious marriage. Only 0.3 percent of couples cohabitated without any nuptial contract.[51] During this process of national integration, some groups of women may be pushed into highly vulnerable positions. For example, rural women in southeastern Turkey, many of whom do not speak Turkish and are married by religious law, may easily become marginalized and may even fail to be recognized by the state as citizens when they cannot provide the necessary documents, such as birth certificates.[52]

The practice of paying bridewealth (*başlık parası*), which disadvantages women by creating an image of women as a commodity bought and sold between families, has not fully disappeared. In 1993, in 28.6 percent of the marriages, bridewealth was paid to the bride's family by the bridegroom's.[53] Especially in southeastern rural Turkey, when a family pays bridewealth, they expect the bride to work obediently at home and in the fields, and to pay unconditional respect and loyalty to her "new" family.

Endogamy (in-group marriage) is practiced in some groups. For example, the Alevis' tradition of endogamy has its roots in their concern, as a minority religious sect, to insure their continued existence. On the other hand, rural-to-urban migration has brought different social groups into contact, resulting in an increase in the number of "mixed marriages." Nevertheless, marriage within the extended kinship group continues, constituting 22.6 percent of the marriages in 1993. It should be emphasized that in the predominant, modernized sections of society, civil marriages and monogamy are the rule, and women are recognized as individual citizens by the law.

A common problem that Turkish women still face today is the "virginity question," the norm that women should preserve their virginity until married. This emphasis on women's virginity is leading to psychological and sexual problems in women,[54] as well as to their seeking medical help to repair their hymen if it is broken.[55] In some cases, the termination of the marriage or even the murder of the bride (more frequent in traditional circles) is the result of doubts about the bride's virginity. The husband has the legal right to appeal to the court for divorce if the wife was not a virgin bride.

Reproduction

The fertility rate varies by region, urban or rural residence, social class, and level of education. The eastern provinces have a high total fertility rate of 4.2, whereas this number drops to 2.0 in western provinces.[56] The traditional cultural disapproval of contraceptives and abortion; the economic underdevelopment of the regional economy, which requires the labor of children; as well as lack of adequate family planning information and services all account for the high fertility rate in eastern Anatolia. Furthermore, whereas the total fertility rate was 2.4 in urban areas, it was 3.1 in rural areas.[57] The different types of economic activities in the city and the village, the higher cost of raising (and educating) children in the city, and the different social norms about children and childhood prevailing in the city and the village are important factors in the different rates. The education of women also makes a difference: the fertility rate of women without formal schooling was 4.2, whereas it was 1.7 for women who received education beyond middle school.[58]

"Family planning," which sounds like a neutral concept, has clear political implications in the Turkish context. The sharpening political conflict between the Turkish state and the Kurdish-nationalist PKK in eastern and southeastern Turkey since the 1980s has politicized family planning on both sides. Although the state supports the policy of family planning by identifying rapid population growth as an important factor impeding the country's economic development, some Kurdish (male) militants interpret this as a deliberate policy of the state to control the Kurdish population. The European-supported family-planning NGOs have developed various strategies to reach women in traditional families with many children. Kurdish families may easily become the target of such family planning groups, since they are the ones with many children. The increased number of radical Islamists since the 1980s, who also oppose birth control, further politicizes family planning issues.

Sex Education

The Ministry of Education has introduced sex education to schools. In the late 1990s, an experimental campaign was initiated, which aimed at providing students with scientific information on health, reproduction, and safe sex through interactive lectures in schools. However, the campaign has been short-lived, and under severe criticism from different social groups, it has lost its impetus.

Contraception and Abortion

In the early years of the Republic, the government supported pronatalist policies (ones favoring higher birthrates) in order to recover the population loss during the War of Independence[59] and the high rates of infant mortality thereafter. The government outlawed the import of birth control devices and abortion.

In the mid-1960s, when the steady improvements in health services led to a rapid growth in population, and when rural-to-urban migration increased the urban population and unemployment, the government began to change its policies to antinatalist ones. The 1965 law on family planning declared some limited birth control methods to be legal and abortion to be free (but only as a medical emergency). In 1985, this law was liberalized, and the right to abortion within the first ten weeks of pregnancy was recognized. Again, these legal changes mainly benefited upper- and middle-class women and, to some degree, migrant women in cities. Rural women, particularly those in eastern Anatolia, remained largely outside of the effects of the law. Especially in the traditional circles, cultural norms and practices oppose abortion and family planning. Today 36.1 percent of women do not use any birth control methods (58 percent in eastern Anatolia and 29.5 percent in western Anatolia), whereas the rest use modern or traditional methods (37.5 percent and 25.5 percent respectively).[60]

Teen Pregnancy

Teen pregnancy occurs in the context of marriages at a young age, practiced mostly in eastern and southeastern Anatolia. The unwed teenage mothers of Western societies are virtually nonexistent in Turkey. In the Turkish Civil Code, the legal minimum age for marriage was prescribed as eighteen for men and seventeen for women in 1926; but in 1938, it was reduced to seventeen and fifteen respectively; and with the recent amendments in 2001, it has become seventeen for both women and men. However, this legal standard only holds true for civil marriages, and religious marriage is also practiced.[61] Fathers or other close male relatives may decide that their girls should marry as young as twelve or thirteen in a religious ceremony. This practice is mostly observed in rural Eastern Turkey where it accompanies high fertility along with high infant and maternal mortality.

HEALTH

Health Care Access

In 1952 the Ministry of Health, which has been the major institution in the country responsible for developing and implementing health policies, began to offer mother–child health services. Since the 1980s, influenced by women's movements in the world and in Turkey, increasing attention has been given to women's health concerns. In 1994, following the International Conference on Population and Development held in Cairo, a national action plan was prepared. And following the Beijing Conference held in 1995, seventeen Turkish women's NGOs formed a commission (KA-SAKOM/National Voluntary Organizations' Health Commission for Women). It initiated projects in the least developed regions of the country, aimed at improving the quality of health care services for women and women's access to health care services, as well as educating women and girls and their families about women's health issues. There are also projects jointly supported by national and international agencies, for example, the Women/Family Health and Education Project in southeastern Anatolia, which is supported by the United Nations Development Program (UNDP) and the General Directorate of Women's Status and Problems as part of the larger National Project of Increasing Women's Participation in Development.

Despite these recent improvements in women's health care, the services fall short of what is needed both quantitatively and qualitatively. In 1997, there were only forty-five hospitals for women and children. Also, a gap exists with regard to women's health care services between the western and eastern regions of the country, as well as between different social classes. The increasing numbers of high-tech private hospitals along with the deterioration of services in public health institutions since the 1990s are widening the gap between social classes.

The tendency to define women's health issues solely in relation to women's sexuality and reproduction creates problems for women who need access to health services of all types. This emphasis on reproduction in women's health care also renders invisible the health problems of older women in menopause or who are postmenopausal.

Diseases and Disorders

Although the women from upper-income families living in big cities display a tendency to suffer from similar diseases as their Western counterparts, such as depression and eating disorders, the women from lower-income families living in cities (i.e., rural-to-urban migrant women) suffer mostly from such diseases as rheumatism, joint infections, and back pain, due to their substandard living and working conditions and domestic violence.

And in the case of women from traditional families living in rural eastern Anatolia, in addition to these health threats, high fertility rates constitute a serious danger. The persistent tradition of very young women marrying and giving birth to many children,[62] usually outside of a hospital or health clinic,[63] leads to health problems. Diseases caused by malnutrition are also common among women in this group, many of whom suffer from ane-mia.[64] In many families in this part of the country, it is the tradition to have men eat their meals first, and then women eat the leftovers; this significantly contributes to women's malnutrition. Abortion under unsan-itary conditions, which is induced by the women themselves, also carries important health risks for women.

Despite the availability of much information on women's health prob-lems with regard to fertility, there are no adequate statistical data and qual-itative information on women's other health problems, including breast and cervical cancer, osteoporosis, eating disorders, and depression. Women's depression may also be common in traditional families. It may end with the woman's suicide (usually hanging herself) about which we read in the newspapers.

Related to sexual intercourse, women in Turkish society confront other health problems, for example, vaginismus, that is "an involuntary spasm of the muscles surrounding the vaginal entrance whenever penetration is at-tempted."[65] The frequency of vaginismus cases in Turkey is alarming, and the significance given to women's virginity, which is seen as the prereq-uisite of marriage, is defined as the major factor causing it.

AIDS

AIDS is increasingly becoming a serious health problem in Turkish so-ciety. It is mostly transmitted through sexual intercourse, and wives may easily become the victims. Men's having sexual intercourse with prostitutes is generally socially accepted (although new generations of women social-ized in the idea of gender equality question it), and using condoms is still not widely practiced, which put wives as well as the men and women engaged in prostitution at high risk. In 1998, 829 AIDS cases were re-ported, and of those, 209 were women.[66] The media, women's NGOs, and public institutions all have campaigns to increase people's awareness about the risk of AIDS and the need to use condoms.

POLITICS AND LAW

Suffrage

Suffrage was not automatically given to women with the establishment of the Republic in 1923. Women obtained the right to vote in local elections and be elected for the local government in 1930, and they were enfranchised for national elections in 1934. Atatürk's sudden move toward women's po-litical rights in the 1930s has been interpreted as a response to criticisms of his single-party rule and as a way to dissociate himself from the Nazi re-gime in Germany in which women were defined entirely within the con-fines of the home as mothers and wives.[67]

Political Participation

Unlike their Western counterparts, women in Turkey did not fight for their political rights; they were given to them by the state to present a modern image to the outside world rather than to promote gender equality. Thus, "Women's rights were means to an end rather than ends in themselves."[68] This is why Turkish women remain "emancipated but unliberated."[69]

Despite the fact that Turkish women obtained the right to participate in political elections earlier than the women in some other European countries, their active political participation has remained limited. In 1935, in the first parliamentary elections in which women participated, they won 4.5 percent of the seats in the parliament (eighteen women Member of Parliaments, or MPs), which is still the highest percentage elected up to now.

In the 1990s, women's representation in the parliament remained low. In the 1991 national elections only 1.8 percent of the MPs, and in the 1995 national elections 2.4 percent of the MPs, were women.[70] In 1971 a woman minister was appointed for the first time, and in 1986 a woman MP was chosen as a cabinet minister. In 1994, for the first and only time, a woman, Tansu Çiller, became the prime minister. Although this might seem to signify an important step for women's political gains, during her time in office, no serious attempts to improve women's position in society were observed.

In March 4, 1997, the Association for the Support and Education of Women Political Candidates (KA-DER) was established as a nonpartisan, civil society organization to promote women's participation in politics through offering advice, organizing seminars, and putting pressure on political parties to establish quotas for women. Despite its public visibility during its establishment, it has lost its impetus in recent years.

Women's Rights

Feminist Movements

In the Ottoman Empire, the women's movement emerged in the mid-nineteenth century when the Empire's capital (Istanbul) became increasingly open to the West under the influence of the reforms carried out "to catch up with the West." There were forty women's magazines and newspapers,[71] and many women's associations in the Ottoman period.[72] The women's associations at the time articulated their demands in terms of the right of divorce for women, the prohibition of polygamous and arranged marriages, the right of women to work, and their right to education. Women activists, who were mainly from well-educated, middle-class families, used various strategies to put their demands into practice, sometimes making compromises so as not to create a public backlash, as happened in the case of their demand for a "national dress code for women" to replace the Islamic dress code.[73] In their struggle to improve women's status, they were restrained by Islam, which was the state's dominant ideology.

Following the dissolution of the Ottoman Empire, the grassroots women's movement came under the control of the newly founded Turkish state, which opposed the development of an autonomous feminist movement.[74] This period was one of "state feminism."[75] Women obtained rights through "the reforms made [by] the state 'from above' . . . [as a result of which] women's status certainly progressed a great deal compared to the Ottoman era."[76]

In the 1970s, leftist groups challenging the status quo and questioning inequality and social injustice regarded "the woman question" as a Western issue, inviting all women to join their men comrades in a fight against class exploitation and imperialism.[77] In this regard, they were antifeminist. After the 1980 military intervention,[78] women made a strong appearance on the public scene in March 1986 when "a group of women delivered a petition signed by 7,000 women demanding the implementation of the United Nations Declaration of Women's Rights which Turkey had officially signed."[79] This was followed by various activities to draw public attention to women's conditions in the society, including marches against the battering of women and protests against sexual harassment in public places.

Although the military government suppressed political ideas and actions, the feminist movement was initially perceived as having nothing to do with politics. This attitude created the opportunity for the women's organizations to mobilize around such issues as domestic violence and sexual harassment. However, feminist movement soon began to challenge the prevailing social and political arrangements by voicing more "radical demands."

Unlike women in other Middle Eastern countries, feminists in Turkey have not had to confront conflict between women's issues as defined universally and culturally specific traditions and identities.[80] Turkish nationalism, stripped of the Islamic identity and heritage, and Turkish "state feminism" both promote universal notions of women's rights. Leftist ideology, with its emphasis on universal values, also contributed. Feminists are also generally in agreement on the need for autonomous women's movements to insure and strengthen the state's commitment to women's rights.[81]

Feminists differ with regard to their affiliation with leftist politics. Although some adopt leftist ideology, others criticize the Marxist approach to the woman question for defining women's issues as subordinate to the class-based struggle against capitalism.[82] Feminists also differ on their definitions of feminism: some emphasize the importance of legal and social reforms; others focus on women's control over their bodies and emphasize the political nature of the personal.

Although feminist groups mostly have secular and modernist stances, Islamist women's groups have emerged since the mid-1980s, some of whom, the so-called turbaned feminists, adopt varying degrees of feminist ideology and discourse, although they usually do not acknowledge feminism overtly. On the other hand, there is a stricter approach to feminist groups in which they are distinguished from other groups that are interested in women's issues. For example, in a study of women's organizations,[83] three categories were identified: feminist (with an emphasis on empowerment, consciousness-raising as a goal, and commitment to secularism); Kemalist (with an emphasis on emancipation and women's participation in the public sphere, and with goals of promoting nationalist and secularist ideas)—the word is based on the middle name of Atatürk, the founder of the Republic; and Islamist (with an emphasis on welfare and the family, women defined as wives and mothers, and a commitment to religious/nonsecularist ideology). Furthermore, after the 1990s some Kurdish feminist groups were established who criticize Turkish feminists for their neglect of ethnic diversity.

In recent years, feminists have begun to collaborate with other progressive political groups to reach out to economically and politically disadvantaged women, countering the criticism that the feminist action and ideas are limited to the middle and upper classes.

Lesbian Rights

Lesbians' social and legal rights are nonexistent in Turkish society. Social norms and values render lesbian relations invisible, despite the fact that the majority of women in Turkish society spend most of their time with other women, developing intimate and emotional relations with them. Recently, some westernized women in their emulation of their Western counterparts have adopted a lesbian identity, and hence it remains largely a Western-imported identity in the Turkish context.

Military Service

Military service in Turkey is not compulsory for women. On the other hand, women are represented in the armed forces, although in limited numbers compared to other NATO countries, namely 0.1 percent. Turkish women were active in the War of Liberation (1919–1923), and Atatürk supported the presence of women in the military following the establishment of the Republic. Sabiha Gökçen became the first female pilot in the 1930s. Women officers were accepted into military schools for the first time in 1955 and graduated in 1957 as lieutenants. However, this practice was ended in the 1960s. Only in 1982 did the Turkish Armed Forces open their ranks to women, and they were recruited mostly as nurses, doctors, teachers, biologists, pharmacists, dieticians, and physiotherapists. Although the criteria for their admission somewhat vary from those for their male counterparts (e.g., a 1,600-meter run for women compared to 3,000 meters for men in testing physical strength), women's terms of work and promotion in the military are defined the same as men's, hence equity and conditions of equal treatment between women and men in the military are legally ensured. There are no rank restrictions for women officers.

However, in practice women officers face some problems. In a questionnaire administered to 119 women officers working in the hospitals of the Military Medical Academy,[84] 68.6 percent of the respondents said that they did not experience problems in their jobs because of their sex, but 22.4 percent said they did. Although 22.4 percent said they did not have difficulties in their work life in the military, 77.6 percent said they did. Having too limited authority and responsibility, doing tasks that were not their own specialties, working with conservative people who were closed to new ideas, as well as interpersonal relations, too heavy workload, and a lack of legal power were among the complaints of the respondents. To solve these problems, they suggested that duties, power, and responsibilities should be rearranged according to official rank. They also stressed the importance of having childcare facilities at the workplace. And when asked how they envisioned their future roles in the Armed Forces, the majority (56.5 percent) said that they could handle all the responsibilities and roles men did, some said that they wanted to work in their own branch (21.2 percent), and some others said that they did not want to undertake passive roles such as office work (16.5 percent).

When it comes to women in combat, women officers participate in domestic and overseas military exercises on equal terms with their male counterparts.[85]

RELIGION AND SPIRITUALITY

Women's Roles

Women position themselves differently vis-à-vis political Islam and the secular state, guarded by the military. Although some women defend the cause of Islam by defining themselves as the commanders of Allah (God), others defend Atatürk's secular Republic in which religion was seen as a serious obstacle to the progress of the society. In both cases, women take on active political and social roles. The organized protests of some women university students to defend their right to wear headscarves, which is seen as a requirement of their Islamic faith (the *türban* demonstrations), have been especially important in making Islamist women publicly visible.

The question of whether Islam oppresses or liberates women has been much debated since the 1980s.[86] Studies conducted mostly of turbaned women university students and graduates point to their attempt to open up spaces for themselves in the public sphere through reinterpreting both Islam and modernity, challenging the state's monopoly on modernist norms about women's presence in the public space.[87] Paradoxically, the experiences women gain in their active participation in the Islamist movement may have an empowering effect on them, despite the conservative Islamic ideology that confines women to the private realm.[88]

Rituals and Religious Practices

Many ordinary Muslim women find meaning in their lives through their belief in Allah and their religious practices. For example, they (mostly Sunni Muslims) join women's *mevlüt* groups in which hymns are sung. They seek remedies from spiritual healers; they place candles in the tombs of spiritual leaders in order for their wishes to come true. The secularized modern groups for whom religion is a private matter between God and the person criticize such practices. While keeping their faith in Allah, some people, especially city dwellers, do not observe the obligatory acts of Islam. Their demanding living conditions and busy schedules, and in some cases their secular ideas, lead them to neglect religious practice. To them, the increasing pull of ordinary women into radical Islamist groups is alarming.

It is also important to acknowledge the different experiences of women within orthodox Sunni Islam and Alevism. Among the orthodox Sunni group, religion limits women to the private sphere and demands strict gender segregation. Thus, Sunni women's religious practices are usually carried out in women's groups. In contrast, Alevi women's religious practices involve performing ritual dances (*semah*) together with men.

Religious Law

Religious law, which dominated the Ottoman society, has been outlawed in Turkish society since the establishment of the Turkish Republic in 1923.

VIOLENCE

Violence against women becomes more alarming in the honor crimes (*namus/töre cinayetleri*) mostly practiced in southeastern Anatolia. The traditional cultural norms dictate that the male members of the family should kill a woman in their family if she is suspected of any "disapproved" relation with a man. By reducing the penalty given to the man by defining the case as a murder committed under the influence of cultural rules, the law supports such violent behavior against women. Thus, women's organizations have been trying to change the law. They are, however, aware of the fact that it may take time to make changes in the Criminal Law. They are pushing for a special law that discourages such violence against women in the name of family honor. In the attempts of Turkish government to make Turkey a full member of the European Union, such changes in the law may soon become inevitable. A new Criminal Law draft, in which honor is no longer treated as a reason to reduce penalty, is under way.

Turkish women's organizations are also active in the international arena. In the Pekin+ 5 International Conference held in 2000 in New York under the leadership of the United Nations, they succeeded in adding an article that said, "Honor crimes violate human rights," despite the objections of Arab countries and the Vatican. In spite of these optimistic changes, honor crimes continue to happen. As reported by the Human Rights Association in Turkey, in January–March 2003, five women were killed in honor murders.

Domestic Violence

Domestic violence is an important issue in the lives of Turkish women and a critical topic among women scholars and advocates. Traditional norms and values support male violence against women. It is seen as a legitimate means to keep women under control, since women are traditionally portrayed as overly emotional and irrational beings who lack the intellectual capacity to decide and act on their own. The law supports this tendency by defining domestic violence as a family matter. The state intervenes only when there is a complaint filed by the victim, and this requires the victim's going to the local police station and being sent to a public hospital to receive an official document proving her injuries. Those who are found guilty of violence against family members are given up to thirty months of confinement, which in practice usually means only seven days in prison, not enough to discourage husbands from beating their wives.

On the other hand, the rise of the women's movement since the 1980s has brought the issue of violence against women onto the national agenda. Women's groups organized demonstrations against domestic violence. The Foundation of the Purple Roof Women's Shelter was established in Istanbul and has offered free consultation and shelter to battered women since 1995. In 1991, the Foundation for Women's Solidarity was established, again in Istanbul, and opened the first independent shelter for women in 1993. The foundation carried out projects to raise women's consciousness about domestic violence, such as the "Women's Human Rights" project, supported by the European Union.

The national and local states have also become sensitive to domestic violence. It was a municipality in Istanbul that established the first battered women's shelter in the country in 1990, followed by municipalities in other parts of Turkey. And in 1991, for the first time, a women's consultation center was opened in collaboration with a private organization (i.e., the Foundation for Women's Solidarity) and local government. In 1994, a data bank was established within the Directorate General on the Status and Problems of Women to provide consultancy and guidance for women's protection against violence. In 1998, the law on the Protection of the Family was enacted, which regulated measures for the protection of women and children against violence.

Despite these positive changes, as right-wing political parties with conservative religious tendencies have come to power in the local governments, they have directly closed down some women's shelters or indirectly done so by cutting their economic support and services. As of 1999, there were eleven women's houses/shelters in Turkey, as well as six consultation centers. In addition, the Child Protection and Social Services Agency provided services to women suffering from domestic violence through its nineteen social centers.

There are obvious difficulties in discovering what is really going on in the everyday lives of families regarding the use of violence against women, and the research provides us with only a rough picture of male violence. In research conducted by the Hacettepe University Institute of Population Studies in 1988, 44.9 percent of the men believed that men had the right to beat their wives when the wives failed to obey them; and 64 percent believed that women should accept their husbands' opinions without any confrontation. Another study found that 31.7 percent of the men and 20 percent of the women approved men's beating their wives. The number of people who approved of women being beaten was greater with age and fewer with higher levels of education. Fully 35 percent of the people stated that women sometimes act in ways that warrant their being beaten. In other research in 1990, 61 percent of the women said that they argued with their husbands, and 18 percent were beaten by their husbands during the argument. Of the women who were beaten by their husbands, 51 percent said that they did nothing in return, and 29 percent said that they tried to protect themselves.[89] Based on the data collected in field research on domestic violence, the authors concluded that "men expected to be respected, obeyed and tolerated in their families, particularly by their wives [and t]hey thought that when men were disrespected or disobeyed, they might have a 'legitimate right to turn to [a] violent act.' "[90] On the other hand, women mentioned, more often than men did, women's irresponsible and disobedient behavior, family honor (*namus*), husbands' job frustration and stress, and poverty and economic hardship as the causes of domestic violence. The authors interpreted this as women's strong internalization of the dominant male values of society. But the tendency observed by the researchers among the respondents to hide violence occurring in their families points to people's belief that such behavior is disapproved of, particularly by modernized women such as the researchers. Furthermore, in an in-depth study of 140 married women patients in a psychiatric clinic, eighty had a history of being victimized by repeated incidents of domestic violence (and a quarter of them had attempted suicide).[91] The educational level of the women did not make a difference in the incidence of their being beaten by their husbands.

Rape/Sexual Assault

Turkish women's consciousness about rape is quite low. The idea that married women could be raped by their husbands is a strange notion for many women, except for a very small group of educated women. In general, women believe it is their wifely duty to have intercourse at their husbands' desire. The Turkish Criminal Law, moreover, fails to recognize spousal rape.

The law favors men against women in rape cases in general. For example, whether the woman raped was a virgin determines whether the act will be defined as criminal. Until recently, when the sentencing differential was abolished, whether the victim was married or single, or was a prostitute, affected the convicted rapist punishment.

In traditional circles, male relatives strictly protect women's honor. It is they who punish, usually very violently, both the man and the woman involved in rape, completely ignoring the fact that the woman might have nothing to do with initiating the rape. In modern circles, the family still plays a significant role in "protecting their girls" against sexual assault, which usually means constricting their daughters' activities to "safe places" and "safe times." Thus, official rape rates are quite low, and the incidence of incest remains a taboo subject. Additionally, the practice of having women's virginity examined before marriage, although without legal grounds, puts women in a very helpless position, endangering their dignity.

Trafficking in Women and Children

Although until the collapse of the former Soviet Union trafficking women in Turkey was not an issue, it has become increasingly so, especially since the 1990s. Women from Russia and Ukraine are trafficked to Turkey, many of them working as prostitutes, and they are regarded by the native women of Turkey as a serious threat to their families. Sometimes women from the former Soviet Union themselves want to come to escape the economic problems of their own country, and sometimes they are forced to come. Because of their Russian origin, they are commonly referred to as "Natashas." The term has become a stigma on Russian women in Turkey, covering wrongly not only prostitutes but also those who have come to Turkey for trade. Natashas face continuous hardship and their lives even may be in jeopardy; their illegal presence and hence their "invisibility" are major factors in this. Because of their illegal status, they often face deportation from the country. The dramatic events portraying the resistance of the women to the police during their deportation appear frequently in the media. Yet no comprehensive research exists that investigates this important issue.

OUTLOOK FOR THE TWENTY-FIRST CENTURY

Into the twenty-first century, two paradoxical forces dominate the woman question in the Turkish context, one dividing and the other uniting women. A significant dividing force is the increasing social and economic distance between the women in different classes. The burden of economic globalization rests more than ever on the shoulders of poor women in the cities. The economy demands their cheap, unorganized, and potentially exploited labor, and their families' poverty requires them to find new ways to economize, thereby increasing their housework. On the other hand, the educated professional women have the chance to improve their social and economic positions by becoming more a part of the Western world. The social and political polarization of different groups, such as the Islamist and secularist women, is another axis that divides women.

On the other hand, democratization carries with it the potential to unite the women in an autonomous women's movement independent of any male-dominated ideology. The colorful picture of women from different cultural and ethnic backgrounds, economic standings, and religious orientations has a strong theme: the theme of women's solidarity.

NOTES

1. State Institute of Statistics (SIS), *Statistical Yearbook of Turkey* (Ankara: SIS Printing Division, 1996).

2. One kilometer equals 0.6 miles.

3. The Sunni form the major orthodox religious sect, followed by the Alevi, who range from at least 10 percent to over a quarter of the total population. Alevis have been the strong supporters of secularism. They are known for their social democratic and leftist tendencies.

4. SIS, 1996.

5. This was found in research conducted by the Ministry of Health in fifty-three provinces.

6. DGSPW, *Türkiye'de* (Ankara: Tatar Publishing, 1998).

7. SIS, 1996, *Statistical*.

8. The life expectancy of women was 69.0 years and that of men was 64.4 years in 1990. The average life expectancy varies from region to region. It is about 75 in the western regions of Turkey, but it is about 61 in the eastern regions; State Planning Organization (SPO), *Program for 1999* (Ankara: Prime Ministry Printing Division, 1997).

9. Deniz Kandiyoti, "Bargaining with Patriarchy," *Gender & Society* 2, no. 3 (1988): 274–90; and Deniz Kandiyoti, "Islam and Patriarchy," in *Women in Middle Eastern History*, ed. N.R. Keddie and B. Baron (New Haven, CT: Yale University Press, 1991), 23–42.

10. Valentine Moghadam, *Modernizing Women* (Boulder, CO: Lynne Rienner, 1993).

11. Tahire Erman, "Rural Migrants," *International Journal of Urban and Regional Research* 25, no. 1 (2001): 118–33.

12. Tahire Erman, "The Meaning of City Living," *Women's Studies International Forum* 20, no. 2 (1997): 263–73.

13. World Bank, "Migrant Women's Participation" (Washington, DC: World Bank, 1999).

14. Erman, 2001.

15. Tahire Erman, "The Impact of Migration," *Gender & Society* 12, no. 2 (1998): 146–67.

16. Sibel Kalaycıoğlu and Helga Rittersberger-Tılıç, *Evlerimizdeki* (Ankara: Su, 2001).

17. Erman, 2001.

18. Semá Erder, *Kentsel Gerilim* (Ankara: Uğur Mumcu, 1997).

19. Ayşe Ayata, "The Emergence," *New Perspectives on Turkey* 17 (1997): 59–73.

20. Yeşim Arat, *The Patriarchal Paradox* (London: Associated University Press, 1989).

21. Şule Toktaş, "Gender Awareness," master's thesis, Middle East Technical University, 1997.

22. SPO, *The Report* (Ankara: Prime Ministry Printing Division, 1994).

23. SIS, *Women in Statistics* (Ankara: SIS Printing Division, 1995).

24. The lack of attendance of girls in primary school is attributed to the girl's "disinterest" in school (24.7 percent), the family's not being able to pay for school expenses (17.2 percent), the family's being against the education of girls (14.0 percent), the family's needing the girl's contribution to housework (11.3 percent), and the family's needing the girl's labor in the household economic activities (7.5 percent); SIS, *Child Labor Survey* (Ankara: SIS Printing Division, 1994); and SIS, Child Labor Statistics (Ankara: SIS Printing Division, 1997).

25. SIS, 1995.

26. *Imam Hatip* Schools are high schools that were initially founded to educate religious clergy but later were politicized and used as a springboard to university education by the radical/political Islamists.

27. These numbers for men are 29.4 percent, 76.2 percent, and 88.8 percent respectively (SIS, 1995).

28. TESEV, *Insani Gelisme Raporu* (Ankara: Boyat, 1998).

29. Women may not attend these courses because of lack of time and childcare and/or because of family control. However, women's attendance increases when they are offered some economic gain, such as free coal or food. This legitimizes poor women's attendance at the courses, and they may then more easily get their husbands' approval.

30. SIS, *Household Laborforce Survey* (Ankara: SIS Printing Division, 1998).

31. SIS, 1998.

32. SIS, *Household Laborforce Survey* (Ankara: SIS Printing Division, 1996).

33. SIS, "Women in the 1990s," SIS Printing Division, Ankara, 1996.

34. Ayşe Öncü, "Turkish Women in the Professions," in *Women in Turkish Society*, ed. N. Abadan-Unat (Leiden: E.J. Brill, 1981), 181–93.

35. Jenny B. White, *Money Makes Us Relatives* (Austin: University of Texas Press, 1994).

36. Yıldız Ecevit, "The Status and Changing Forms," in *Women in Modern Turkish Society*, ed. S. Tekeli (London: Zed, 1995), 81–88.

37. SIS, 1996, "Women."

38. This was 22.8 percent and 15.8 percent for men respectively (SIS, 1996, "Women").

39. Dilek Cindoğlu and Ayşe Durakbaşa, "Discrimination at the Workplace," un-published manuscript, 1995.

40. SSI, *Statistics Yearbook* (Ankara: SSI Printing Division, 1991).

41. This number is 42.8 percent for men (SIS, *1996 Employment Statistics*, Ankara: SIS Printing Division, 1997).

42. Nermin Abadan-Unat, "Social Change and Turkish Women," in Abadan-Unat, 1981, 5–31.

43. World Bank, 1999.

44. There is a debate about whether the typical rural family is "patriarchally ex-tended" and whether the urban family is typically "nuclear." Indeed, some assert that most rural families have always been nuclear in form (Duben 1982) and that urban families living in separate households might better be conceptualized as "functionally extended families" (Kağıtçıbaşı 1982, 5), based upon the closed relations among and reliance upon kin, especially during times of crisis. See Çiğdem Kağıtçıbaşı, ed., *Sex Roles, Family and Community in Turkey* (Bloomington: Indiana University Press, 1982).

45. Arat, 1989, 39.

46. Erman, 1997.

47. The amendment to the Civil Code has brought equal rights and responsibilities to the wife and husband.

48. Erman, 2001.

49. SIS, *1990 Census of Population* (Ankara: SIS Printing Division, 1993).

50. Abadan-Unat, 1981, 14.

51. SIS, 1993.

52. Yakın Ertürk, "Rural Women and Modernization," in Tekeli, 1995, 141–52.

53. SIS, 1993.

54. Arsalus Kayır, "Women and Their Sexual Problems in Turkey," in Tekeli, 1995, 288–305.

55. Dilek Cindoğlu, "Virginity Tests," *Women's Studies International Forum* 20, no. 2 (1997) 253–61.

56. HUIPS, *Population and Health Survey* (Ankara: Hacettepe University, 1998).

57. HUIPS, 1998.

58. HUIPS, 1998.

59. The War of Independence, which took place following World War I (1914–1918), was a people's war under the leadership of Mustafa Kemal (Atatürk) to defend their land against the imperial Western forces, which proceeded to occupy what was left of the Ottoman Empire. Women, who also participated in the war, are remembered today for their courage and strong determination, and mostly portrayed as pulling the cow-driven carts that carried cannons to the battlefields. The war ended with the vic-tory for the people, and upon long and intense discussions and serious negotiations with the Western powers, the present territory of the Turkish state was drawn.

60. HUIPS, 1998.

61. In 1996, the average age at first marriage was 22.3 for women and 26.2 for men in cities, and 21.7 for women and 25.2 for men in villages. However, the continuing practice of marrying by religious law, which is illegal and hence not officially recorded, challenges the official data. Directorate General on the Status and Problems of Women, *Women in Turkey* (Ankara: Takar Publishing, 1999).

62. In western Turkey, the fertility rate is 4.1; in eastern Turkey, it is 7.9.

63. In rural areas, 39.2 percent of the women, and in rural eastern Anatolia 54.5 percent of the women, deliver at home without any authorized health personnel (HUIPS, 1998); a local midwife sometimes assists the birth.

64. Ayşe Baysal, "Nutritional Problems of Turkish Women," in Abadan-Unat, 1981, 107–21.

65. "Vaginismus" refers to the failure of the penetration of the penis into the vagina when the physical state of the vaginal muscles prevents it. Behind this physical problem are psychological causes. It commonly occurs when women are under stress or are scared of sexual intercourse, usually when they do not know what to expect or when they are horrified by the stories they have heard from other women about the "first night" (*gerdek gecesi*). Because of vaginismus, a woman may remain a virgin for many years of her marriage, and her husband will probably blame her for frigidity, which is a quite different state than vaginismus (Kayır, 1995, 290).

66. DGWSP, 1998, 22.

67. Şirin Tekeli, "Women in Turkish Politics," in Abadan-Unat, 1981, 292–310.

68. Arat, 1989, 30.

69. Deniz Kandiyoti, "Emancipated but Unliberated?" *Feminist Studies* 13, no. 2 (1987): 317–38.

70. SIS, *Women in Statistics 1927–1992* (Ankara: SIS Printing Division, 1995).

71. Some of them were *Terakki* (Progress), published in 1868; *Hanımlara Mahsus Gazete* (Newspaper for Woman), published in 1895; and *Mahasin* (Magazine) and *Kadın* (Woman), published in 1908 (Arat, 1989, 27).

72. Serpil Çakır, *Osmanlı Kadın Hareketi* (Istanbul: Metis, 1994); and Tekeli, 1995.

73. Pınar İlkkaracan, *Women's Movements in Turkey* (Istanbul: Metis, 1997).

74. This happened despite the fact that many women were very active during the War of Independence (Arat, 1989, 28).

75. Şirin Tekeli, "Emergence of the New Feminist Movement in Turkey," in *The New Women's Movement*, ed. D. Dahlerup (London: Sage, 1986), 179–99.

76. Tekeli, 1995, 12.

77. Fatmagül Berktay, "Has anything changed," in Tekeli, 1995, 250–62.

78. The increasing politicization of society in the late 1970s and violent clashes between "rightists" and "leftists," leading to many deaths, along with escalating economic problems, paved the way for a military intervention in September 1980. During its three years in power, the military emphasized religion (Sunni Islam) as the unifying element and tried to depoliticize society by putting restrictions on political participation and organizing. It tended to support neoliberal policies, which opened a new stage for the society in the coming years. The coup dissolved itself in 1983 after creating a new and conservative Constitution.

79. Nükhet Sirman, "Feminism in Turkey," *New Perspectives on Turkey* 3, no. 1 (1989): 1–34.

80. Nilüfer Çağatay and Yasemin Nuhoğlu-Soysal, "Comparative Observations," in Tekeli, 1995, 263–72, esp. 270.

81. Tekeli, 1982, in Çağatay & Nuhoğlu-Soysal, 1995, 270.

82. Sirman, 1989.

83. Simel Esim and Dilek Cindoğlu, "Women's Organizations in 1990s Turkey, *Middle Eastern Studies*" 35, no. 1 (1999): 178–88.

84. Nur İnanç and Sevgi Hatipoğlu, "GATA Komutanlığı," in *20 Yüzyılın*, ed. O. Çitçi (Ankara: TODAIE, 1998), 311–22.

85. Serhan Göltekin and Ayşegül Özdemir, "Kadın Subayların Türk," in Çitçi, 1998, 323–25.

86. Ayşe Kadıoğlu, "Women's Subordination in Turkey," *Middle East Journal* 48, no. 4 (1994): 645–60.

87. Ahu Tatlı, "Islamist Women," Master's thesis, Bilkent University, 2001; Elisa-

beth Özdalga, *The Veiling Issue* (Surrey: Curzon, 1998); Nilüfer Göle, "The Quest for the Islamic Self," in *Rethinking Modernity*, ed. S. Bozdoğan and R. Kasaba (London: University of Washington Press, 1997), 81–94; and Aynur İlyasoğlu, *Örtülü Kimlik* (Istanbul: Metis, 1994).

88. Yeşim Arat, "Feminism and Islam," in Tekeli, 1995, 66–78.

89. SPO, 1994, 87.

90. Helga Rittersberger-Tılıç and Sibel Kalaycıoğlu, Legitimating and Reproduction of Domestic Violence," *Zeitschrift für Turkeisstudien* 12, no. 2 (1999): 225–40.

91. Şahika Yüksel, "A Comparison," in Tekeli, 1995, 275–87.

RESOURCE GUIDE

Suggested Reading

Abadan-Unat, Nermin, ed. *Women in Turkish Society*. Leiden: E.J. Brill, 1981. This is the first comprehensive book published about women in Turkish society. The contributors are all Turkish women.

Arat, Yeşim. *The Patriarchal Paradox: Women Politicians in Turkey*. London: Associated University Press, 1989. This book is about women's participation in politics.

Bozdoğan, Sibel, and Reşat Kasaba, eds. *Rethinking Modernity and National Identity in Turkey*. London: University of Washington Press, 1997. This book mainly discusses the project and discourse of modernity in Turkey from the perspective of recent experiences, and hence it provides a good background to understand "the woman question" in the Turkish context.

Delaney, Carol. *The Seed and the Soil: Gender and Cosmology in Turkish Village Society*. Berkeley: University of California Press, 1992. An ethnographic study carried out by an American scholar in a village of western Anatolia.

Erman, Tahire. "The Impact of Migration on Turkish Rural Women: Four Emergent Patterns." *Gender & Society* 12, no. 2 (1998): 146–67. This article explores the diverse experiences of rural migrant women in the city and draws on data collected in an ethnographic study of migrants in Ankara.

———. "Rural Migrants and Patriarchy in the City." *International Journal of Urban and Regional Research* 25, no. 1 (2001): 118–33. This article investigates patriarchy in the context of rural migrant women living in the city.

Kağıtçıbaşı, Çiğdem, ed. *Sex Roles, Family and Community in Turkey*. Bloomington: Indiana University Press, 1982. Presents issues regarding women in the broader context of family and community. The majority of the contributors are Turkish women, with a couple of men and/or foreign scholars.

Kandiyoti, Deniz, ed. *Women, Islam and the State*. London: MacMillan, 1991. A comparative analysis of the Muslim societies in the Middle East and South Asia, including Turkey.

Tekeli, Şirin, ed. *Women in Modern Turkish Society: A Reader*. London: Zed, 1995. About women in Turkish society and written by Turkish women scholars based on original investigation.

White, Jenny B. *Money Makes Us Relatives: Women's Labor in Urban Turkey*. Austin: University of Texas Press, 1994. An ethnographic study conducted by an American scholar in a squatter settlement in Istanbul.

Videos/Films

Adı Vasfiye (Her name is Vasfiye). Directed by Atıf Yılmaz. A movie about a working woman.

Artık Dur Demenin Zamanı Geldi (It is the Time to Say, "Stop It"). 31 minutes. Directed by Pınar İlkkaracan and Asuman Şanver. A documentary about three women who experienced domestic violence and whose children were sexually harassed.

Bez Bebek (Fabric doll, i.e., stuffed doll). Directed by Engin Ayca. A movie about a woman living in a shantytown.

Kadınlar Vardır (There Are Women). Directed by Hale Sözmen. A documentary about the transformation of Turkish Women from the Tanzimat in the Ottoman times up to today. The film was shown at the Fourth Women's Conference in Pekin.

On Kadın (Ten Women). Directed by Şerif Gören. A movie shot in the late 1980s in which an actress plays the role of ten different women in Turkish society.

Ötekinin Sesi: Yeşilçam'ın Görünmeyen İlk Kadınları (The Voice of the Other: The Invisible Pioneer Women in *Yeşilçam* [i.e., the Turkish Hollywood]). Documentary. Can be obtained from Ankara University, the Faculty of Communications.

Üç Kuşak Kadın: Ben Annemin Kızıyım (Women of Three Generations: I am My Mother's Daughter). Directed by Seyhan Derin. It is about three generations of women in an immigrant Turkish family in Germany; the grandmother lives in Turkey, the mother migrated to Germany, and the daughter was born in Germany.

Yılanı Öldürseler (Wishing them to kill the snake). Directed by Türkan Şoray. A movie about a village woman.

Web Sites

Directorate General on the Status and Problems of Women, www.kssgm.gov.tr/.
Kadının Statüsü ve Sorunları Genel Müdürlüğü.

Flying Broom, www.ucansupurge.org/.
Uçan Süpürge.

Foundation for the Support of Women's Work, www.kedv.org.tr/.
Kadın Emeğini Değerlendirme Vakfı.

Gender & Women's Studies Graduate Program, Middle East Technical University, www.metu.edu.tr/home/www810.
Orta Doğu Teknik Üniversitesi, Kadın Çalışmaları Yüksek Lisans Program.

Kadın Sorunları Merkezi, www.istanbul.edu.tr/merkezler/kadinsorunlari.htm.

Kadın 2000, Kadının İnsan Hakları Bilgi Belge Merkezi, www.kadin2000.gen.tr/.

Kadının İnsan Hakları Bilgi Belge, www.comlink.de/info-ist/kihp.

METU, www.metu.edu.tr/home/www810.
In Turkish.

Mor Çatı, www.welcome.to/morcati.
English version; web site on domestic violence.

Photo Archive: A Visual Testimony on Women, www.kssgm.gov.tr/arsiv/en-index.
htm.
Consists of more than a thousand photographs documenting the lives of Turkish
women. It is the first archive of photography on Turkish women. The photographs
have been documented as life histories, working, learning, relaxing, getting married,
men, and portraits.

Women for Women's Human Rights—New Ways (WWHR), www.wwhr.org.

Organizations

Ankara University
KASAUM
Women's Studies Center
Cebeci 06590
Ankara, Turkey
Phone: 90 312 320 55 95
Fax: 90 312 363 59 04
Email: kasaum@media.ankara.edu.tr
Web site: http://kasaum.ankara.edu.tr

Center for Gender and Women's Studies
Middle East Technical University
Ankara
Phone/fax: 90 312 210 30 19
Email: gws@metu.edu.tr
Web site: www.metu.edu.tr/home/www810

Directorate General on the Status and Problems of Women
Ankara
Phone: 90 312 419 29 79
Email: info@merian.kssgm.gov.tr
Web site: www.kssgm.gov.tr

The Flying Broom ("Uçan Süpürge")
Ankara
Phone: 90 312 427 00 20
Fax: 90 312 426 97 12
Email: ucan.supurge@ucansupurge.org
Web site: www.ucansupurge.org

KA-DER (Kadın Adayları Destekleme ve Eğitim Derneği/The Organization to Support and Train Women Candidates)
Ankara and Istanbul
Phone: 90 312 467 88 16 in Ankara
90 212 273 25 35 and 90 212 267 17 21 in Istanbul

Fax: 90 312 427 39 79 in Ankara
90 212 273 25 36 in Istanbul
Web site: www.ada.net.tr/kader

Women's Library and Information Center Foundation (founded in 1990)
Istanbul
Phone: 0212 534 95 50
Fax: 0212 523 74 08
Email: kadineserleri@cihannet.com.
Web site: www.ARCHIMAC MAARUN.edu.tr

SELECTED BIBLIOGRAPHY

Abadan-Unat, Nermin. "Social Change and Turkish Women." In *Women in Turkish Society*, edited by N. Abadan-Unat, 5–31. Leiden: E.J. Brill, 1981.

Acar, Feride. "Women and Islam in Turkey." In *Women in Modern Turkish Society: A Reader*, edited by Ş. Tekeli, 46–65. London: Zed, 1995.

Arat, Yeşim. *The Patriarchal Paradox: Women Politicians in Turkey*. London: Associated University Press, 1989.

———. "Feminism and Islam: Considerations on the Journal 'Kadın ve Aile." In *Women in Modern Turkish Society: A Reader*, edited by Ş. Tekeli, 66–78. London: Zed, 1995.

Ayata, Ayşe. "The Emergence of Identity Politics." *New Perspectives on Turkey*, 17 (1997): 59–73.

Baysal, Ayşe. "Nutritional Problems of Turkish Women." In *Women in Turkish Society*, edited by N. Abadan-Unat, 107–21. Leiden: E.J. Brill, 1981.

Berktay, Fatmagül. "Has Anything Changed in the Outlook of the Turkish Left on Women?" In *Women in Modern Turkish Society: A Reader*, edited by Ş. Tekeli, 250–62. London: Zed, 1995.

Çağatay, Nilüfer, and Nuhoğlu-Soysal, Yasemin. "Comparative Observations on Feminism and the Nation-building Process." In *Women in Modern Turkish Society: A Reader*, edited by Ş. Tekeli, 263–72. London: Zed, 1995.

Cindoğlu, Dilek. "Virginity Tests and Artificial Virginity in Modern Turkish Medicine." *Women's Studies International Forum* 20, no. 2 (1997): 253–61.

Cindoğlu, Dilek, and Ayşe Durakbaşa. "Discrimination at the Workplace: An In-depth Approach to Women Clerical and Sales Workers." Report for the General Directorate of Women's Status and Problems. Unpublished manuscript, 1995.

Delaney, Carol. *The Seed and the Soil*. Berkeley: University of California Press, 1992.

Ecevit, Yıldız. "The Status and Changing Forms of Women's Labor in the Urban Economy." In *Women in Modern Turkish Society: A Reader*, edited by Ş. Tekeli, 81–88. London: Zed, 1995.

Erman, Tahire. "The Meaning of City Living for Rural Migrant Women and Their Role in Migration: The Case of Turkey." *Women's Studies International Forum* 20, no. 2 (1997): 263–73.

———. "The Impact of Migration on Turkish Rural Women: Four Emergent Patterns." *Gender & Society* 12, no. 2 (1998): 146–67.

———. "Rural Migrants and Patriarchy in the City." *International Journal of Urban and Regional Research* 25, no. 1 (2001): 118–33.

Ertürk, Yakın. "Rural Women and Modernization in South-eastern Anatolia." In *Women in Modern Turkish Society: A Reader*, edited by Ş. Tekeli, 141–52. London: Zed, 1995.

Esim, Simel, and Dilek Cindoğlu. "Women's Organizations in 1990s Turkey: Predicaments and Prospects." *Middle Eastern Studies* 35, no. 1 (1999): 178–88.

Göle, Nilüfer. "The Quest for the Islamic Self within the Context of Modernity." In *Rethinking Modernity and National Identity in Turkey*, edited by S. Bozdoğan and R. Kasaba, 81–94. London: University of Washington Press, 1997.

Göltekin, Serhan, and Ayşegül Özdemir. "Kadın subayların Türk Deniz Kuvvetlerindeki Yeri ve Görevleri" (The place and tasks of women officers in the Turkish Navy). In *20. Yüzyılın Sonunda Kadınlar ve Gelecek* (Women and the Future at the End of the 20th Century), edited by O. Çitçi, 323–25. Ankara: TODAIE, 1998.

Hacettepe University, Institute of Population Studies (HUIPS). *Population and Health Survey*. Ankara, 1998.

İlkkaracan, Pınar. *Women's Movement(s) in Turkey: A Brief Overview*. Report for Women for Women's Human Rights (WWHR), no. 2. Istanbul: WWHR, 1997.

İnanç, Nur, and Sevgi Hatipoğlu. "GATA Komutanlığı bünyesinde görev yapmakta olan kadın subaylar" ("The Women officers in the *Gülhane* Military Medical Academy"). In *20. Yüzyılın Sonunda Kadınlar ve Gelecek* (Women and the Future at the End of the 20th Century), edited by O. Çitçi, 311–22. Ankara: TODAIE, 1998.

Kadıoğlu, Ayşe. "Women's Subordination in Turkey: Is Islam Really the Villain?" *Middle East Journal* 48, no. 4 (1994): 645–60.

Kağıtçıbaşı, Çiğdem. "Introduction." In *Sex Roles, Family and Community in Turkey*, edited by Ç. Kağıtçıbaşı, 1–32. Bloomington: Indiana University Press, 1982.

Kandiyoti, Deniz. "Emancipated but Unliberated? Reflections on the Turkish Case." *Feminist Studies* 13, no. 2 (1987): 317–38.

———. "Bargaining with Patriarchy." *Gender & Society* 2, no. 3 (1988): 274–90.

———. "Islam and Patriarchy: A Comparative Perspective." In *Women in Middle Eastern History*, edited by N.R. Keddie and B. Baron, 23–42. New Haven, CT: Yale University Press, 1991.

Kayır, Arsalus. "Women and Their Sexual Problems in Turkey." In *Women in Modern Turkish Society: A Reader*, edited by Ş. Tekeli, 288–305. London: Zed, 1995.

Moghadam, Valentine. *Modernizing Women: Gender and Social Change in the Middle East*. Boulder, CO: Lynne Rienner, 1993.

Olson, Emelie A. "Muslim Identity and Secularism in Contemporary Turkey: 'The Headscarf Dispute.'" *Anthropological Quarterly* 58, no. 4 (1985): 161–69.

Öncü, Ayşe. "Turkish Women in the Professions: Why So Many?" In *Women in Turkish Society*, edited by N. Abadan-Unat, 181–93. Leiden: E.J. Brill, 1981.

Özdalga, Elisabeth. *The Veiling Issue: Official Secularism and Popular Islam in Modern Turkey*. Surrey: Curzon, 1998.

Rittersberg-Tılıç, Helga, and Sibel Kalaycıoğlu. "Legitimating and Re-production of Domestic Violence in Turkish Families." *Zeitschrift fur Turkeisstudien* 12, no. 2 (1999): 225–40.

Şenyapılı, Tansı. "Economic Change and the Gecekondu Family." In *Sex Roles, Family and Community in Turkey*, edited by Ç. Kağıtçıbaşı, 237–48. Bloomington: Indiana University Press, 1982.

Sirman, Nükhet. "Feminism in Turkey: A Short History." *New Perspectives on Turkey* 3, no. 3 (1989): 1–34.

Social Security Institute (SSI). *1991 Statistics Yearbook*. Ankara: Social Security Institute Printing Division, 1991.

————. *Household Laborforce Survey*. Ankara: State Institute of Statistics Printing Division, 1998.

State Institute of Statistics (SIS). *1990 Census of Population*. Publication no. 1616. Ankara: State Institute of Statistics Printing Division, 1993.

————. *1994 Child Labor Survey*. Ankara: State Institute of Statistics Printing Division, 1994.

————. *Women in Statistics: 1927–1992*. Publication no. 1712. Ankara: State Institute of Statistics Printing Division, 1995.

————. *Household Laborforce Survey*. Ankara: State Institute of Statistics Printing Division, 1996.

————. *Statistical Yearbook of Turkey*. Publication no. 1985. Ankara: State Institute of Statistics Printing Division, 1996.

————. *Women in the 1990s*. Unpublished manuscript. Ankara: State Institute of Statistics Printing Division, 1996.

————. *Child Labor Statistics*. Ankara: State Institute of Statistics Printing Division, 1997.

————. *1996 Employment Statistics*. Ankara: State Institute of Statistics Printing Division, 1997.

State Planning Organization. *The Report of the Committee on Women*. Publication no. 2358-OIK 426. Ankara: Prime Ministry Printing Division, 1994.

————. *Program for 1998*. Ankara: Prime Ministry Printing Division, 1997.

————. *Program for 1999*. Ankara: Prime Ministry Printing Division, 1998.

Tatlı, Ahu. "Emergence of the New Feminist Movement in Turkey." In *The New Women's Movement*, edited by D. Dahlerup, 179–99. London: Sage, 1986.

————. "Islamist Women in the Post-1980s Modern Turkey: Ambivalent Resistance." Master's thesis, Bilkent University, Ankara, Turkey, 2001.

Tekeli, Şirin. "Women in Turkish Politics." In *Women in Turkish Society*, edited by N. Abadan-Unat, 292–310. Leiden: E.J. Brill, 1981.

Toktaş, Şule. "Gender Awareness: A Study of Women Teachers and Academicians Who Are Graduates of Girls Institutes 1960–1970." Master's thesis, Middle East Technical University, Ankara, Turkey, 1997.

White, Jenny B. *Money Makes Us Relatives: Women's Labor in Urban Turkey*. Austin: University of Texas Press, 1994.

World Bank. *Migrant Women's Participation in the Laborforce in Urban Turkey*. Report prepared for the World Bank. Washington, DC: World Bank, 1999.

Yüksel, Şahika. "A Comparison of Violent and Non-violent Families." In *Women in Modern Turkish Society: A Reader*, edited by Ş. Tekeli, 275–87. London: Zed, 1995.

Selected Turkish Bibliography

Çakır, Serpil. *Osmanlı Kadın Hareketi* (The Ottoman Women's Movement). Istanbul: Metis, 1994.

Directorate General on the Status and Problems of Women (DGSPW). *Türkiye'de Kadının Durumu* (The Condition of Women in Turkish Society). Ankara: Takar Publishing, 1998.

Erder, Sema. *Kentsel Gerilim* (The Urban Tension). Ankara: Uğur Mumcu Foundation Publications, 1997.

Göle, Nilüfer. *Modern Mahrem: Medeniyet ve Örtünme* (The Private Modern: Civilization and Veiling). Istanbul: Metis, 1993.

İlyasoğlu, Aynur. *Örtülü Kimlik: İslamcı Kadının Oluşum Öğeleri* (The Covered Identity: Constitutive Components of Islamist Women). Istanbul: Metis, 1994.

Kalaycıoğlu, Sibel, and Helga Rittersberger-Tılıç. *Evlerimizdeki Gündelikçi Kadınlar* (Domestic Workers in Our Homes). Ankara: Su, 2001.

TESEV (The Foundation of Economic and Social Analyses in Turkey). *Insani Gelisme Raporu: Turkiye* (The Human Development Report: Turkey). Report for the United Nations Development Program (UNDP). Ankara: Boyut, 1998.

38

UKRAINE

Lyudmyla Smolyar

PROFILE OF UKRAINE

Ukraine, a former Soviet territory, is a densely populated and highly developed state with a total area of 603,700 square kilometers.[1] It is a sovereign, independent, and democratic republic with a president who is the head of state and acts in its name. State power is divided into legislative, executive, and judicial power with guarantees on the functioning of local self-government. Having gained independence in 1991, Ukraine took the road of market reform and the building of a democratic society. The transition to a market economy was supposed to assist the economy and society's ability to function.

As of January 1, 2002, the population of Ukraine was 48,416,000, of whom 25,941,000 (54.0 percent) were females and 22,475,000 (46.0 percent) were males. Unfavorable demographic trends, which exist to some extent in a number of countries, have acquired a crisis-like character in Ukraine. There has been a sharp decrease in the birthrate and a deterioration of people's health, particularly among women and children, which have resulted in the shortening of life spans of the population. Since the mid-1990s, the population has been decreasing by approximately 400,000 annually. Steadily decreasing birthrates have increased the proportion of population that is pension-aged from 380 to 409 persons per 1,000.

The average life expectancy of women is higher than that of men by 11.2 years. The overall mortality rate has been increasing for the last few years (from 12.9 percent in 1991 to 15.3 percent in 2000). How-

ever, a number of motherhood and childhood protection activities carried out in response to the Fourth World Conference on Women led to a decrease in the infant mortality rate from 14.7 per 1,000 live births in 1995 to 11.9 in 2000.

OVERVIEW OF WOMEN'S ISSUES

The parliament of Ukraine (*Verkhovna Rada*) has adopted the Declaration of General Principles of Ukraine's Governmental Policy Concerning Family and Women as well as the Concept of Governmental Family Policy. The government has also approved the National Plan of Actions for 2001–2005. The goals are to: refine the state mechanisms for improving women's status in society; ensure women's participation in decision-making at all levels of power; eliminate the feminization of poverty, tied to the inequality between women and men in all spheres of production activities; protect the health of women and adolescent girls; provide access to family planning knowledge and communicate women's and men's responsibility for sexual behavior and its consequences; develop the education system, taking full account of its gendered aspects; prevent all forms of violence against women in families and society; and end the trafficking of women.

EDUCATION

Opportunities

Women in Ukraine have the same rights as men to an education. The right to receive an education is reflected in the law "On Education" (Article 3) and in the respective laws "On Vocational Education" and "On General Secondary Education," which meet the requirements of Article 10 of the UN Convention on the Elimination of All Forms of Discrimination against Women (CEDAW).

In spite of the economic decline that has been taking place over the last few years, the state has managed to maintain basic conditions for people to obtain general secondary education. At present, 22,000 schools, lyceums, gymnasiums, and colleges provide education to 78 percent of the total population 6–17 years old. The female proportion of students is 49.7 percent (1999–2000 academic year).

At the beginning of the 1999–2000 academic year, higher educational programs enrolled 52.9 percent of the female and 46.1 percent of the male population aged 18–22. Among all students in institutions of higher education, 53 percent are female, mostly studying economy, law, medicine, teaching, art, and cinematography. The female proportion among the postgraduate students was 45 percent in 1995 and 48 percent in 2000; among the doctoral students, this figure was 26 percent and 31 percent, respectively.

Literacy

Ninety-eight percent of the total population is literate, breaking down to 100 percent of the male population and 97 percent of females.

EMPLOYMENT AND THE ECONOMY

Job/Career Opportunities

The equality of rights between women and men to work is guaranteed by the Basic Law, that is, the Constitution of Ukraine (Article 43). Women are exposed to the same possibilities as men to earn their own livelihood. They are guaranteed equal opportunities in the choice of profession and type of labor activity. The Labor Code of Ukraine and employment legislation regulate the creation of conditions for citizens to fully exercise their rights to labor, remuneration, and so on.

Ukranian laboratory workers. Photo © TRIP/L. Padrul.

Economic decline, competition, and closure of enterprises brought about a reduction in the number of jobs, which hit women harder than men. Women's employment level decreased from 60 percent in 1995 to 51.7 percent in 2000 and, by average indices, was lower in 2000 than men's employment by 9.2 percent.

The employment picture is characterized by trends toward a high concentration of women working in nonmanufacturing, light manufacturing, food, and medical industries (from 51.8 percent in the food industry to 86.6 percent in social welfare); a high proportion of female workers at jobs that require extensive qualifications; and a prevalence of females among the unemployed able-bodied (employable) population (62.1 percent). In all regions of the country, women's registered unemployment levels are higher than men's. As of January 1, 2000, women constituted 62.1 percent among officially registered unemployed persons.

Pay

In spite of the fact that, legislatively, women have rights on par with men to equal labor and remuneration, and that their educational level is higher than that of men, women's average wages in Ukraine are much lower than men's. Over the past few years, however, there has emerged a noticeable trend toward reducing gender imbalances in the level of remuneration. In 1995, the average pay of women was 68.6 percent of men's, whereas at the end of 2000 this went up to 72.4 percent. In 1999, the average monthly wage for women amounted to 148.89 UAH (about US$36).

Working Conditions

Sexual Harassment

Results of independent surveys conducted by public organizations suggest that 50 percent of women have been sexually harassed, 8 percent of them repeatedly.[2]

Support for Mothers/Caretakers

Maternal Leave

Ukrainian legislation guarantees women protection as mothers. To protect their reproductive rights and to create the conditions for safe maternity in Ukraine, women get seventy days leave before the birth and fifty-six afterward.[3] During this time, women receive their full wage. On the basis of the Labor Code, women have the right to three years unpaid leave to care for a child up to age six, with her position assured at her return and with her leave time counted in her years of work force experience. Employed women with infants are guaranteed special breaks for nursing.[4] Article 178 provides that pregnant women and mothers with children up to age three be transferred to work that has no negative effect on the health of the mother or her child. In this same spirit, the mother's wages are kept at the level of her former job. Article 176 and 176 Labor Code forbid night shift employment to this group of women.

Daycare

Daycare becomes increasingly difficult to obtain because there has been a reduction in the number of childcare centers, kindergartens, and nursery schools as well as an increase in the fees charged.

Social/Government Programs

The Ministry of Labor and Social Policy pays considerable attention to providing opportunities for people to launch their own businesses, particularly businesses with women's participation.

FAMILY AND SEXUALITY

Gender Roles

The growth and development of a market economy, difficulties in the transition, and deep economic and demographic crises result in an enhanced role for the family in the lives of individuals and society. Changes in the structure and functions of the family feature contradictory trends that affect changes in, and the development of, gender relations in society in general.

Marriage

The relatively high marriage rate in the precrisis period turned into a sharp decrease in the transitional period. The marriage rate per 1,000 persons decreased from 9.5 in 1989 to 5.5 in 2000; the divorce rate per 1,000 stabilized at an increased level of 4.0 in 2000 versus 3.6 in 1985.

Matrimonial problems are aggravated by societal concerns including low income and consumption levels and particularly low nutritional levels. Couples also have difficulties related to providing housing and obtaining a satisfactory standard of living; this includes problems of employment and the aggravation of gender asymmetry in the workload. There is an inefficient system of providing social services to families for maternity, paternity, and childhood issues as well as limited and expensive access to childcare centers, kindergartens, and nursery schools, all of which serve to increase stress on a marriage.

Reproduction

The average birthrate per 1,000 decreased from 13.3 in 1989 to 7.8 in 2000. The trend to postpone the birth of children until later in life implicates a decrease in family size to 3.1 or 3.0, or an even lower level, for the period throughout 2000–2005.

About 4,000 cases of male sterility and 40,000 cases of female sterility are registered in Ukraine. The most widespread cause for female sterility is inflammation, but the main reason for inflammation is abortion.

Sex Education

Sex education in Ukraine is part of the Nation Program "Children of Ukraine" and National Program on Family Planning. Special seminars are held for teachers and social workers with extensive coverage on sex education and the preparation of young people for married life.

Contraception and Abortion

Contraceptive use is limited due to the lack of Ukrainian providers, the high price of imported contraceptives, as well as a prejudiced attitude among women. Only 16.9 percent of women use contraceptives and within that number, only 3.4 percent use oral contraception.

The number of abortions still annually exceeds 600,000. The largest percentage of abortions are to women between the ages of eighteen and thirty-four (79.6 percent), of which 17.5 percent is for the 35–49 age group, 2.9 percent for teenage girls between fifteen and seventeen, and 0.047 percent for girls under fourteen years old. Due to complications from abortions, women of reproductive age suffer not only from sterility but also from premature birth. The frequency of abortions, the age of women getting abortions, and other factors led to the creation of the National Program on Family Planning in 1995. The Program's main objectives are: to form a family planning network and institutions; to prepare medical and teaching personnel for work in family planning; to make family planning services more accessible; to satisfy people's contraceptive needs; to prevent unwanted pregnancy, if there is a high risk of the mother's death; to establish institutions to cure infertility (barrenness); to raise people's knowledge of family planning issues, sexual education, and development of responsible sexual behavior.

Several years of implementing the National Program on Family Planning resulted in the organization and operation of the Main Ukrainian Center for Family Planning at Research Institute of Pediatrics, Obstetrics, and Gynecology, twenty-five provincial centers, Kiev and Sevastopol city centers for family planning, 495 doctor's consulting rooms, the preparation of twenty national experts, and more than 4,000 doctors, including 3,000 obstetrician-gynecologists specializing in family planning. Under implementation are a number of joint projects with international organizations and foreign countries, which contribute to the fulfillment of the National Program. Cooperation with the World Health Organization, the Population Foundation, and the US Agency for International Development has enabled Ukraine to attract investments and to equip family planning centers with projectors, video and cinema products, as well as to prepare national trainers and more than 3,000 obstetrician-gynecologists specializing in family planning.

HEALTH

Health Care Access

The transition to a market economy is characterized not only by social and economic hardships but also by the worsening of the quality of the public health system. The creation of a new model of the public health system that would meet today's requirements is occurring at a very slow pace.

Diseases and Disorders

Today one can observe cases of the so-called social diseases, especially tuberculosis. Annually, 20,000–23,000 people are affected by tuberculosis (29,800 in 2000).

The Chernobyl disaster not only damaged the environment but also caused a number of problems for the health of the population. The worsening of health is seen at almost every age group among both men and women. Among those 15–100 years of age, the morbidity rate is higher for women than men by 6.4 percent and the spread of disease by 7.7 percent.

AIDS

Over the last few years, the rate of sexually transmitted diseases has been growing both among the population as a whole and among women. However, beginning in 1995 the state enacted measures to reduce the rate of sexually contractible diseases, and there has been a trend toward a decrease in this rate. For example, the number of syphilis cases among women in 1996 was 144.8 per 100,000 people; and in 1999 it was 111.9.

As of January 1, 2000, more than 30,000 HIV cases had been registered among Ukrainian citizens (of whom 70 percent are injection drug abusers) and 283 among noncitizens. HIV infection is still spreading in all regions. The majority of those infected are persons 20–39 years old. Registration statistics also show a growing number of people infected through heterosexual contacts and of children infected in the birthing process. In 1996 there were ninety-two such children, and in 1999 more than 500.

Nutrition

Over 1995–2001, the living standard of the prevailing majority of families decreased dramatically. According to state statistics, the share of the family income going to food expenses is two thirds, twice as much as it was in 1989, which is evidence of the public's paucity of material resources. Only one in ten families assesses its nutrition as good and balanced.

Cancer

Diseases related to malignant tumors are especially worrisome. In 1999 as compared to 1990, they increased by 2.7 percent. In 2000, there were 77,700 cases among women and 78,900 among men. There are certain peculiarities in the morbidity rates of men and women. For instance, men are more affected by cancer of the trachea, bronchial tubes and lungs, stomach, skin, prostate gland, lymph glands, and rectum. Women are more affected by breast, skin, stomach, uterus, and cervical cancer.

POLITICS AND LAW

Political Participation

Since 1996, Ukraine has made perceptible shifts in attitudes in favor of women occupying higher positions in ministries, state committees, and other central bodies of executive power. The number of civil servants within central bodies of executive power is characterized by gender balance and even a prevalence of female civil servants. Women constitute 68 percent of state civil service employees. Nonetheless, one cannot fail to notice that the higher the body of executive power, the lower the proportion of female executive employees on staff.

In 2002, 24 women were elected to the Verkhovna Rada (the national parliament) of Ukraine (5.1 percent of all national deputies of Ukraine), as compared to 1998 when thirty-seven women (8 percent) sat in the VR. There are no women among chairpersons of oblast[5] councils and oblast state administrations in independent Ukraine. This is evidence that there is still no balance between women and men in the political sphere of Ukraine.

Women's Rights

The equality of rights and liberties of a person and a citizen, regardless of sex, is guaranteed by the Constitution of Ukraine and other legislative acts. The guarantees established in law, however, are not enforced to the full extent. The legal system protecting women's rights is largely inconsistent with the existing economic reality, making it difficult to implement. Women's relatively large percentage among the officially unemployed, along with difficulties creating new jobs for women released from jobs with working conditions harmful to pregnant women and mothers of young children, all reduce women's competitiveness in the labor market. For these and other reasons, women, under conditions of the economic reforms taking place in Ukraine, do not start on a par with men in the process of social development.

The level of income of almost one-third of women does not exceed the poverty line. Most of working women with wages lower than the poverty line are employed in public services, where women make up the majority of the work force. Job segregation and the related inequality between women's and men's wages lead to the feminization of poverty and push women to search for additional sources of income, impeding their integration into all spheres of life. Furthermore, the practices of management and administration historically developed in Ukraine are oriented mostly toward men. They do not support gender balanced social forces that would strengthen women's influence on the development of society, the state, and the family, nor do they further the development of the civil society and its democratization.

Women's Organizations and Feminist Movements

Ukraine currently has over 900 women's organizations (thirty-one have the status of international and national). Every year the number of women's organizations significantly increases. Women's organizations can be divided into four groups—historical or traditional women's organizations, socially oriented women's organizations, businesswomen's associations, and feminist organizations. Feminist organizations emerged only in the 1990s and make up one fourth of all women's organizations. Initial attempts to enter the international arena were by means of international branches of women's organizations in Ukraine established by contacts with foreign women's organizations.

RELIGION AND SPIRITUALITY

Conditions for the free development of all denominations without exception have been created in Ukraine after the collapse of the Soviet Union. This is especially important in view of the fact that there are almost 23,400 religious communities representing 100 denominations, beliefs, and sects. Most believers in Ukraine are women. Under conditions of religious freedom, the majority of women demonstrate a respectful attitude to the national religious tradition, specifically to Christianity. It is anticipated that Ukrainian women will become more religious in the future.

VIOLENCE

The problem of violence against women is extremely pressing. Various types of violence against women and teenage girls remain, for the most part, hidden, particularly when it concerns physical and psychological violence in families. However, even according to the Ministry of Internal Affairs of Ukraine, 1999 alone saw the detection of nearly 9,000 persons suspected of 11,100 crimes committed against the life, health, will, and dignity of female persons, 10,800 women having been victimized.

Trafficking in Women and Children

Sexual exploitation is another serious problem. And, according to the Ministry of Internal Affairs, in 1999 the number of persons brought to account for prostitution was 1.4 times greater than in 1998 and constituted 1,400, of whom 1,200 were not employed or studying.

OUTLOOK FOR THE TWENTY-FIRST CENTURY

Without individual democratic development, regardless of gender, it is impossible to prepare a society for democracy. There must be a system that defines for both sexes what will be the basis for equal rights for men and women, which in turn must be approved by legislation. The development of state, social, and private enterprises should comply with the equality principle, which is the basis for the existence of society in this millennium.

In the twenty-first century, achieving equality between men and women, as well as human development, must be based on a complex approach that includes "mainstreaming" gender equality and women's development into all societal institutions. The progress of mainstreaming depends upon constructive dialogue between women of different countries. The women of Ukraine are ready to be a part of the dialogue.

NOTES

1. One kilometer equals 0.6 miles.
2. *On the Implementation of the Beijing Declaration and Program of Action approved by the Fourth World Conference on Women* (Kiev: UNDP, 2001): 73
3. "Oblast" is the administrative and territorial province. Ukraine's administrative and territorial structure is composed of the Autonomous Republic of Crimea; twenty-four oblasts (provinces); 490 *raions* (districts); 448 cities (including those of state, republican, and oblast significance); 121 city *raions* (districts); 894 urban-type settlements (essentially towns); and 10,253 villages.
4. Labor Code, Art. 179.
5. Labor Code, Art. 183.

RESOURCE GUIDE

Suggested Reading

Analytical Report on the Project. *The Street Children*. Kyiv: UNICEF-Kyiv, 1998. *Children, Females and Family in Ukraine*. Kyiv: State Statistics Committee of Ukraine, 2000. *Information Campaign against Trafficking in Women from Ukraine*: Research Report.
Geneva: International Organization for Migration, 1998. *Statistical Yearbook of Ukraine for 2000*. Kyiv: State Statistics Committee of Ukraine, 2001. "Ukraine." *Human Right and Human Development*. Report. Kyiv: UNDP, 1998.

Web Sites

Bibo.Gender.Org, www.bibo.gender.org.ua and www.news.gender.org.ua. In Ukrainian.

Brama: Gateway Ukrainenews, www.brama.com/.

Innovation and Development Center, www.idc.org.ua.
In Ukrainian. Information on women's organizations.

Project Gender Education in Ukraine, www.bank.gender.org.ua.

State Statistics Committee of Ukraine, www.minstat.kiev.ua.

Ukraine Country Report on Human Rights Practice for 1997, www.state.gov/www/global/human_rights/1997_hrp_report/ukraine.html.

Ukraine Country Report on Human Rights Practice for 1998, www.un.kiev.ua.

Organizations

All-Ukrainian Women's Center of Information and Social-Economical Adaptation
Email: Loblud@mail.ru; Loblud@uninet.kiev.ua

The goal of the organization is to develop gender research, implement a national mechanism providing equal rights for men and women in society, and develop parity democracy in the Ukraine.

La Strada-Ukraine
P.O. Box 246, 01030 Kyiv
Ukraine
Phone/Fax: (380-44) 224-04-46
Email: lastrada@ukrpack.net
Web site: www.brama.com/lastrada

International women's rights center that works to prevent the trafficking in women in Central and Eastern Europe program.

Odessa Scientific Center of Women's Studies
Email: ocws@tekom.odessa.ua

The goal of the organization is to protect the rights and interests of women: the organization provides women with juridical education and develops gender research.

World Federation of Ukrainian Women's Organizations
Web site: www.wfuwo.org/

SELECTED BIBLIOGRAPHY

"About a Situation of Families in Ukraine." Report. Kyiv: Ukrainian Institute of Social Researches, 2000.
Gender Analysis of Ukrainian Society. Kyiv: The UNDP Gender in Development Program, 1999.
Marsh, R., ed. *Women in Russia and Ukraine*. Cambridge: Cambridge University Press, 1996.
"On the Implementation of the Beijing Declaration and the Program of Actions Approved by the Fourth World Conference on Women." Report. Kyiv: UNDP, 2000.

Pavlychko, S. "Progress on Hold: The Conservative Faces of Women in Ukraine." In *Post-Soviet Women: From the Baltic to Central Asia*, edited by Mary Buckley, 219–34. Cambridge: Cambridge University Press, 1997.

Smolyar, L. "The Women's Movement as Factor of Gender Equality and Democracy in Ukrainian Society." In *Ukrainian Women's Non-Profit Organizations*, 27–53. Kyiv: Innovation and Development Center, 2001.

———, ed. *Women's Studies in Ukraine: Women in History and Today*. Odessa: Odessa Scientific Center of Women's Studies, 1999.

Vlasenko, N.S., Z.D. Vinogradova, and I.V. Kalachova. *Gender Statistics for Monitoring the Progress in the Area of Equality between Women and Men*. Kyiv: V.M. Koretsky Institute of NAS of Ukraine, 2002.

Zhurzhenko, T. *Social Reproduction and Gender Politics in Ukraine*. Kharkov: Folio, 2001.

39

UNITED KINGDOM

Gillian Pascall

PROFILE OF THE UNITED KINGDOM

The United Kingdom's population is 59.5 million, of which 50 million are in England, 3 million in Wales, 5 million in Scotland, and 1.5 million in Northern Ireland. Social policies have generally been made at the central parliament at Westminster for the whole of the United Kingdom, but devolved government has brought some power to parliaments in Cardiff (Wales), Edinburgh (Scotland), and Stormont (Northern Ireland) with some resulting differences. For example, Scotland now has more collectivist policies than England for the cost of personal care in old age and for the support of undergraduate students. Through most of this chapter, "policy" will refer to the United Kingdom as a whole and "Great Britain" refers to England, Wales, and Scotland only. The power of the English monarchy is purely ceremonial and that of the parliamentary democracy decreasing: power lies in central government, increasingly with the prime minister rather than the cabinet. Membership in the European Union has implications for social policy. Citizens have the right to appeal directly to the European Court of Justice, and UK governments have been pushed into proactive policies for women as a result of European directives on equal pay, equal treatment at work, working time, parental leave, and part-time work.

There are slightly more women than men in the population, but the gap opens among 75+ age group, where there are over 9 million women and 5 million men. Female life expectancy is 79.8, male 74.9. One person in fifteen is from an ethnic minority. Infant mortality is 5.8 and fertility is at 57 live births per 1,000 women.[1]

OVERVIEW OF WOMEN'S ISSUES

What has happened to women's position in the British welfare state? The post-war era saw the establishment in the United Kingdom of a set of institutions designed to protect men and women from Beveridge's five giant evils of Want, Disease, Ignorance, Squalor, and Idleness. There were to be social insurance services to protect against the interruptions of earning through sickness, unemployment, and old age; family allowances to support all children in full-time education: and comprehensive health and rehabilitation programs, underpinned by Keynesian policies for maintaining full employment.[2] These were inclusive and comprehensive, intended to erase the damage of war and limit the damage of class. The consensus that underpinned these institutions unraveled in the 1970s giving way to Thatcherite governments that pushed neoliberal[3] agendas of free markets. Overall there has been a shift from a nearly social democratic model of welfare — comparable to a much later model in Scandinavian countries, though at a more basic level — toward a liberal model more like the United States. But how far has this process gone, how unequal are its consequences, and what are its implications for women?

A second transformation also begins from the Beveridge welfare state of the 1940s. Although the universalism of the Beveridge model had many advantages for women — by underpinning family work through its systems for health and education — it also embedded assumptions about men as breadwinners and women's roles as wives and mothers, which led to their treatment as second-class citizens. The system assumed that married women would not be in paid employment, that they would be full-time mothers, and that they could rely upon men to support them. In social security, entitlement to key benefits was through male partners. Nurseries, which had enabled women to do war work, were closed, giving many women little choice but full-time motherhood and dependency on male partners. Social transformations in the family (especially increasing divorce), economic transformations in the labor market (especially women's increasing participation in paid work), and political transformation wrought by the women's movement have all challenged the Beveridge model of women's lifetime dependence on a husband. How much have welfare systems changed in response? Is the male breadwinner model of gender relations still in place?

These transformations can be thought of as changes in the nature of welfare regimes, from nearly social democratic toward liberal and from male breadwinner toward dual earner. Through study of a range of welfare institutions, this chapter will examine the impact of the combination of these movements on gender relations in the United Kingdom.

EDUCATION

Opportunities

Access to education was a key post–world war promise and apparently was offered—through state schools and public universities—equally to boys and girls, men and women. In practice, the expectations of girls in the postwar era were of domesticity rather than university. Girls did well at primary school, but their achievements fell away as they reached national examinations and school leaving.

The educational participation and achievements of girls and women at all levels rose steeply during the 1980s and 1990s. For example in national examinations, the proportion of 17- and 18-year-old girls passing two or more Advanced levels subjects doubled between the mid-1970s and mid-1980s.[4] Boys' achievements increased, too, but more slowly, with the result that girls' achievements overtook boys' in 1988–1989, and the gap is now widening in favor of girls. A similar picture follows at university: the numbers of men entering university more than doubled between 1970–1971 and 1998–1999. But the increase for women was much larger: nearly five times as many women entered undergraduate courses in higher educational institutions in 1998–1999 as in the early 1970s. At the same time, the number of women postgraduates increased thirteenfold, more than three times the increase among men.[5] Concerns about the poorer educational achievements of boys have increasingly come to dominate policy debates.

This is a transformation of lives and opportunities as women have had access to education itself and to a labor market that has increasingly demanded higher skills. At the beginning of the twentieth century, women were still fighting for access to higher education and the right to professional jobs that went with it. In the middle of the century, they were embedded in a system of gender relations that made the choice of motherhood and domesticity difficult to avoid and undermined educational investment and achievement. At the beginning of the twenty-first century, women's educational transformation in the United Kingdom is a major part of the transformation of gender relations: it brings much fuller expectations of participation in public life, paid work, and politics. By their increasing educational achievements, girls and women have shredded the theory that their lack of abilities and human capital were to blame for their poorer access to jobs and lower incomes.

Gendered differences in education remain. The Sex Discrimination Act (SDA; 1975) promises equal access to educational resources, and the National Curriculum, designed after the SDA and within its terms, implements a core of common subjects for young people up to the age of sixteen. The traditional division of subjects by gender is narrowing as girls do better at school in science and mathematics as well as in English. But in vocational qualifications as well as in university departments, the traditional gender divide is still marked. Among young people training in modern apprenticeships, young women are the majority of those in hairdressing, health and social care, business administration, and retailing, whereas young men predominate in construction, engineering, the motor industry, and information technology.[6] In higher education there have been changes of access, with more women than men now entering medicine, but men still dominate in the physical sciences and architecture, whereas women are to be found in languages, education, and subjects allied to medicine.[7]

The expansions of educational opportunities, access to universities, and girls' and women's educational achievement have happened alongside a Thatcherite agenda of public sector retrenchment and market liberalization. This has implications for the terms on which educational services are provided, the character of the education offered, and the relation between educational services and the diverse populations of pupils and students. This agenda has not been substantially changed under the Blair governments. Higher education, for example, although more widely available, especially to women, is now offered on terms that bring costs to students and their parents and leave graduates in debt: these may increasingly deter poorer students and women whose expectations of earnings are still lower than men's. Public ideals of education have narrowed to a vocational agenda with the needs of industry and employment foremost: this may entrench the gendering of subjects at the higher levels of training and education as people look to a gendered labor market. The development of an educational marketplace within state education—in its management and allocation of places to pupils—has fostered diversity: the increasing standards shown by increasing achievements are not shared everywhere. Private sector growth, in education and elsewhere, has been accompanied by public sector poverty that leaves services in the United Kingdom underfunded by comparison with comparable countries in Europe. New Labour has been reluctant to address these problems with more public funding—preferring to see problems as located in management rather than in money. But debates about support for public sector services are now intense as even the government's friends argue that the country cannot have a European standard of public services with an American level of taxation.

Literacy

Boys' performance in England is lower than girls' in all literacy-related tasks and tests. Government tests for reading, writing, and spelling show that 88 percent, 89 percent, and 77 percent of seven-year-old girls achieved the official targets in England compared with 79 percent, 80 percent, and 67 percent of boys. The gap in reading test scores between boys and girls aged nine in England and Wales is more than twice that of the United States and Switzerland.[8] Current data show that 15-year-old UK children ranked second for Math and Science and third for Reading amongst European countries.[9]

EMPLOYMENT AND THE ECONOMY

Job/Career Opportunities

In the four decades from 1959 to 1999, women's employment rate (full- and part-time) rose from 47 percent to 69 percent and is now behind only Denmark, Finland, and Sweden among EU countries. Women's economic activity is now sustained at much higher rates through the childrearing years (76 percent of 25- to 44-year-olds in 2000 compared with 54 percent in 1971). Mothers of children under five years of age are now more likely than not to be employed, with 21 percent working full-time and 39 percent working part-time in the spring of 2000. These figures represent a growth, for better-off women, of a more continuous working pattern, shrinking the employment gaps associated with motherhood and using maternity entitlements to return to jobs after maternity leave.

Job segregation remains a problem. Equal opportunities legislation in the 1970s helped to establish women as workers, to assure their rights to equal treatment and equal pay, and to loosen men's hold on the better jobs. The professions have opened their doors: medicine and law now admit men and women broadly equally. But access to top positions is still difficult for women: men are 79 percent of hospital consultants, 95 percent of consultant surgeons, and 90 percent of professors in universities.[10] Women are still concentrated in a limited range of occupations where the work is often part-time and almost always low paid. Ten occupational groups occupy 60 percent of women employees: work as sales assistants and check-out operators, other sales and service occupations, numerical clerks and cashiers, teaching professionals, health occupations, secretaries, health associate professionals, clerks, childcare, and catering.[11]

Pay

Women's earnings have increased but not reached parity, with full-time workers' average hourly rate now at 82 percent of men's. There are great variations between women by qualifications, age, care responsibilities, and hours in paid work. Full-time work has been increasing but so has part-time, with nearly 5 million women in short part-time jobs and hourly earnings 58 percent of male full-timers', where they have stuck since the early 1980s. Part-time work and gender-segregated work carry a particularly heavy pay penalty in the United Kingdom and are a major part of the reason why the gender pay gap in Britain remains high by European standards.[12] The National Minimum Wage came into force in April 1999 and may improve these figures, but it has been set at a modest level, with no built-in plans to raise it to levels that will lessen the gender gap.

Women graduates can now be mothers and sustain their earnings at levels comparable to nonmothers', a pattern of work that has been spreading down the skill levels. But women without qualifications face big earnings losses if they have children: an unskilled married mother with two children has half the lifetime earnings of an unskilled woman without children. Lone mothers[13] have not entered the labor market on the Scandinavian model, despite the New Deal (see below). Typical marriages/partnerships still have men as higher earners, women adopting more flexible and accommodating work patterns, and women's responsibility for care virtually untouched. Only 3 percent of men aged 35–44 had part-time employment in 2000 compared with 48 percent of women.[14] In couples with children, men's average weekly income is £352, whereas women's is £147. The average pattern is not of dual worker/citizens but of one-and-a-half-wage-earner partnerships, with incomes coming into households very unequally.

Working Conditions

Sexual Harassment

A number of studies see sexuality as a central feature of women's work, not only for sex workers but also for women who work in a wide range of occupations from schools and hospitals to the tourism and leisure industry. Studies describe a routine expectation of harassment from colleagues and customers, which may compel women to carry out various forms of sexual work in employment situations, such as responding to sexual jokes, with women's sexuality an essential part of customer relations. Employment may make women into sex objects at work to the advantage of their male colleagues. Although there is a growing tendency for workplaces to have policies against sexual harassment, the growth of service industries and women's employment in these areas may make this an issue of increasing salience in the gender division of work and in understanding how men keep their positions of power.[15]

Support for Mothers/Caretakers

The Beveridge model of the family assumed that men would be breadwinners and that mothers would put care work, especially childcare work, before paid employment. It was not up to governments to support women's work through day nurseries or paid leave. Conservative administrations held broadly to these ideas almost to the end of the century. Women, then, as they joined the labor force, managed their own work—

life balance, often through part-time work with short hours, which cost them access to good pay and better jobs.

Maternal Leave

UK provisions to support working parents have been weak, fitting with a Beveridge style care model in which men were primarily breadwinners, and women primarily mothers. Changes in the reality of working parenthood—and pressures from organizations concerned with equal opportunities and children—have raised the standards of leave, as they have raised the provision of childcare. As of April 2003, mothers in Britain have a statutory right to up to 52 weeks' postpartum maternity leave, half paid and half unpaid, compared with 36 months on reduced pay in France, Germany, Spain and Finland. While new entitlements improve the situation of UK parents, leave entitlements are still low by European standards. New fathers are now entitled to two weeks' paternity leave, paid at 100 pounds per week, but they are not entitled to share the leave due to mothers. Again, the UK government has been very reluctant to bring measures to encourage men to share childcare, responding to pressure rather than seeking to change gender roles.

Daycare

Mothers also paid for childcare, as the increasing demand was met by a growing supply of private nurseries. Differences between women grew, as those with better qualifications got better jobs, which made childcare affordable and worthwhile. Those with poorer qualifications had less choice and were more likely to combine motherhood with low-paid part-time work. New Labour now tends to assume that women are paid workers and that responsibility and opportunity are expressed through doing paid work rather than unpaid care work. The *National Childcare Strategy* "welcomes women's greater involvement and equality in the workplace" and offers some improvement in access to childcare places with state support.[16] But access to childcare is still a problem for parents at work, especially those on low incomes, and provision lags well behind European countries. Early education is moving toward two years' part-time provision, whereas most European countries seek three years full-time. There is no entitlement to a publicly funded place for children under three, and the childcare work force, unlike that in the rest of Europe, is split between trained teachers in nursery schools and kindergartens with a more marginalized sector for daycare centers.[17]

Family and Medical Leave

It has been noted that "the United Kingdom was the last [European] country to introduce parental leave, and has the weakest measure in Europe: unpaid, inflexible and minimal in length with just three months per parent only available to be taken in four week periods per year."[18] Parental leave entitlement has been improved—mainly through the acceptance of European Directives. New regulations taking effect from April 1 2003 include paternity leave. There is as yet no right to work reduced or flexible hours to accommodate family responsibilities although there is a new right to ask employers for flexible working hours. Although the assumptions about women's role in paid employment have been changed rapidly and radically under New Labour, the United Kingdom creeps rather slowly toward a standard of state support for parents with care responsibilities that can be assumed in many other European countries. It is also well behind Scandinavian countries that have pioneered efforts to change gender roles in the family through paid "Daddy leave."[19] The concept of flexible working hours for mothers and for firms is higher up the current government agenda than is the long-hours culture for men or the unequal division of family work that underlies women's disadvantage in the labor market.[20]

Social/Government Programs

Welfare and Welfare Reform

Contemporary welfare reform in the United Kingdom owes a lot to ideas from U.S. models, though it is less stringent. Ideas about correcting the balance between rights and responsibility and about the importance of independence through paid work are central to Labour thinking.[21] There are New Deals designed to enable, encourage, and sometimes coerce people to join the labor market rather than live on benefits. These are aimed at people on job-seekers' allowance and disability benefits as well as lone parents.

The United Kingdom has very high rates of lone parenthood—mainly lone motherhood—compared with the rest of Europe. In 1996, lone-parent families were 23 percent of families with children compared with an average of 13 percent across Europe.[22] Under Conservative governments of the 1980s and 1990s, they were treated first as mothers, entitled to draw means-tested benefits; but it was particularly difficult for them to join the labor market, with poor access to childcare and a high risk of low wages. Lone mothers had a high rate of dependence on benefits rather than on paid work with trends away from paid employment, in contrast to the rest of Europe.[23] New Labour, then, has a New Deal for Lone Parents (95 percent of whose participants are mothers) to enable and encourage their employment through advice, training, and support for childcare. Current policy is that they may choose to be caretakers, but when their children reach school age they can expect encouragement to support themselves, through interviews about jobs and incentives. Labour has also restructured the benefit system through tax credits to encourage paid employment. The risks of this policy are that care needs for the children of lone mothers are insufficiently accounted for: lone mothers want and need paid work, but they also need confidence in the care of their children.

FAMILY AND SEXUALITY

Gender Roles

The division of unpaid work is profoundly gendered. A widespread transformation in UK peoples' views about who ought to do unpaid work is reflected in responses to attitude surveys. Couples act this out in terms of public appearances of equal partnerships. But the practice of unequal division of domestic labor and responsibility adapts only slowly, leaving women with responsibilities for household work, childcare and elder care that are in no way matched by their male partners.[24]

Men's long hours in paid work are a crucial ingredient in gender relations in the United Kingdom, as fathers lead Europe with their forty-seven-hour weeks while mothers often work short part-time hours that do not preserve their labor market position or sustain their economic autonomy. Europe's Working Time Directive is the first attack on long working hours in the interests of care work and families. But its implementation is hedged with restrictions. UK government concern with flexible working centers on the gains to business rather than the gains to parents, and current policy is for encouraging businesses to become flexible rather than for giving rights to people to make their own decisions about working time. Patricia Hewitt, the new minister for women at the beginning of New Labour's second term, has written *About Time: The Revolution in Work and Family Life* and may be positioned to enable people to make their own choices about "how much of our time, and when, will be 'consumed' by work."[25]

Marriage

Most people still get married, but marriage has declined, as people are more likely to cohabit and more likely to divorce. Among nonmarried women aged under sixty, cohabitation nearly doubled (increasing from 13 percent to 25 percent) between 1986 and 1998–1989, and now just under a third of women cohabit before marriage. Cohabitation tends to be a prelude to marriage rather than a substitute, with women now marrying at later ages (now twenty-seven). The major increase in rates of divorce happened between the 1960s and 1980s and was partly associated with changing legislation. Current annual figures are now 12 percent lower than their peak in 1993: 70 percent of divorce petitions are granted to wives.

The family has become much more diverse. The traditional marriage—male breadwinner, female caretaker, two-child family—has given way to lone mothers and stepparents. The meaning of these changes is debated.

Arguments for a return to "traditional" families have counted the risks to children of growing up in nontraditional households. But lone parent families' problems lie in poverty as well as in change and insecurity. Traditional marriage had largely hidden costs to women, in terms of violence and male dominance. And defendants of the new families argue that the negotiation of new relationships is not obviously less moral than the more rule-bound assumptions of older ones.[26] Lone parents emerge out of research studies, too, as moral agents for their children rather than as the feckless individuals described by critics.

Reproduction

Sex Education

Sex education in the United Kingdom has been highly politicized, with debates between health campaigners wanting a more open policy, which acknowledges young peoples' sexual activity, versus moral campaigners who have fought hard to constrain schools. The outcome has been a changing stream of legislation, compromise, diversity, and some uncertainty in schools about how to keep sex education within the law. Under the Conservative administration, sex education was compulsory in secondary schools, within a framework of "moral considerations and the value of family life," while section 28 of the Local Government Act prevented local authorities from promoting "the teaching in any maintained school of the acceptability of homosexuality as a pretended family relationship." Current policy continues to ensure that pupils learn about sex within a framework of teaching about the nature of marriage, family life, and the bringing up of children. It also requires that children should be protected from teaching and materials that are inappropriate to their age and religious and cultural background. In comparison with educational authorities, health authorities are rather freer to make their own decisions about the kind of services they provide, and some authorities have offered accessible and practical advice and services.[27]

Contraception and Abortion

Key demands of the women's movement in the 1970s were for free contraception and for abortion on demand. Free contraception is now available under the National Health Service (NHS), though services do not always reach young people when they need them. Abortion is more complicated. Since 1861 abortion had been entirely criminalized, and the 1967 Abortion Act represented a great relaxation of control. Under the 1967 Act abortion has, in effect, been made a medical situation, with the requirement for two medical practitioners to certify that continuing the pregnancy would be dangerous to the woman's physical or social well-being or that there is fetal abnormality. The law does not amount to abortion on demand, but it appears to have been implemented more liberally over time. There have been debates in the United Kingdom posing the right to choose against the right to life, but these have been more muted than in the United States. The Abortion Act has been defended in feminist campaigns and has undergone only minor amendment since 1967.

Teen Pregnancy

Births outside marriage have been rising since the 1960s. Now nearly two in five births take place outside marriage, mainly to cohabiting couples. In general women have been giving birth later, and the average age at childbirth is now twenty-nine. But teenage births in the United Kingdom are high. Throughout most of Western Europe, teenage birthrates fell during the 1970s, 1980s, and 1990s, but the United Kingdom rates have stuck at the early 1980s level or above. The United Kingdom, with an average live birthrate of around 30 per 1,000 women aged under twenty, had the highest rate of live births to teenage women in the European Union. This compares with just under twenty for the nearest rival, Portugal; just under ten for France; and just over five for the Netherlands. The United Kingdom was the only country in Europe not to have had teenage birthrates falling during the 1980s and 1990s.[28] These high rates are a serious policy concern, because of the problems of health and poverty that often go with teenage motherhood.

Free contraception and accessible family planning clinics where anonymity is assured have not brought the same success as has been achieved by the Dutch. Perhaps the best explanation lies in the lack of alternative opportunities faced by more disadvantaged young women in the United Kingdom. Teenagers may not actively choose motherhood, but those with fewer expectations have less incentive to protect themselves and are less likely to choose abortion. Rising teenage birthrates in the 1980s and 1990s are likely to have been part of the growth of social inequality, poverty, and social exclusion that belonged with Thatcherite policies for free markets. More recently, the New Labour government has set up a social exclusion unit within the cabinet office, which has taken teenage births as a key target.

The most recent data show little, if any, fall with twenty-nine live births per 1,000 girls aged 15 to 19 in the year 2000.[29]

HEALTH

Health Care Access

Socialized medicine, along with socialized education, was part of the postwar compact and was promised through the 1946 National Health

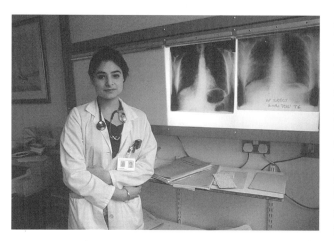

Physician, United Kingdom. Photo © TRIP/H. Rogers.

Service Act. In July 1948 a National Health Service was established that promised health care that would be free at the time of use to citizens on a universal basis. It would be paid for through taxation. The legislation bore the stamp of the Labour government that was in power, with its collectivist approach to the provision of services—though the services themselves were dominated by an individual model of medical care rather than by a social model of public or environmental health. And there has been "considerable disquiet" about the way that services have treated women.[30]

The principle of universal access has been particularly beneficial to women. Earlier systems of health insurance dating from 1911 had started from the needs of paid labor and tended to favor men. From the point of view of unpaid care work, too, the promise of health care without charge at the time of use has been a significant support to people with care responsibilities for children or older relatives. Women are still frontline caregivers and gain from the accessibility of primary health care services through general medical practitioners as well as the wider range of acute medical and preventive services.

How much has changed in the promises and delivery of health care? Early tensions over costs resulted in some charges for services since the 1940s, beginning with prescription charges, and continuing with charges for dentistry, optical services, and others. But many people are exempt, and charges remain a small part of the NHS budget. There have also been tensions over universal coverage, as fears of abuse by people coming to the United Kingdom have led to some restrictions. There have been continued tensions between the ideals of universal provision and the ideals of some governments committed to low public spending. But even Conservative governments have appreciated that the NHS brings health care at much lower cost than services funded through insurance: reforms have tended to introduce market principles of operation and management rather than to bring fully marketized health care. Some treatments have been cut or excluded from the NHS to contain rising costs. And the low levels of spending adversely affect the quality of buildings and maintenance and lead to perennial staffing crises. But there remains a National Health Service and a strong commitment to the principles of a universal and taxation-based service—from governments, from the NHS work force of a million or so people, and from people as voters and responders to opinion polls.

Diseases and Disorders

Although the NHS has broadly retained its essential postwar principles of comprehensive coverage, universal access, and freedom from charges, health itself is less egalitarian and has become steadily more unequal since the 1970s. The NHS offered a medical response to disease more than it offered health: egalitarian services have not produced equal health. Also, the social and economic conditions that underlie health became much more unequal in the last three decades of the twentieth century. There are gender differences in health and mortality—men having higher death rates while women suffer more ill health—but social class differences between women are more important in determining their health and life chances.

AIDS

By March 2000, 41,000 diagnoses of HIV infection had been reported in the United Kingdom and the numbers of cases reported by the Public Health Laboratory Service had reached 2,900 in 1999. But the pattern of transmission has been changing: whereas until 1998, the prime route of transmission was sex between men, these numbers have been falling. The number of infections through injected drugs has also been falling, more than halved since 1993 to under 100 cases. But in 1999, the numbers of those who contracted the virus through heterosexual sex had overtaken those contracted as a result of sex between men. The overall result of these changes is, of course, women's increasing vulnerability to HIV through heterosexual intercourse.

Eating Disorders

The National Diet and Nutrition Survey indicates that among fifteen- to eighteen-year-olds, 16 percent of girls and 3 percent of boys reported that they were dieting to lose weight. Eating disorders share with other mental health problems clear gender divisions.

Cancer

As other causes of death have fallen—especially those from respiratory and infectious diseases—the significance of cancer as a cause of disease and death has increased. Around a third of women will get cancer during their lifetime, and nearly a quarter of women currently die from it. In 1983, cancer overtook circulatory disease as the main cause of death among women in the United Kingdom. Breast cancer rates in the United Kingdom are high, though they have fallen a little since their peak in 1992. Nearly a third of cancer cases and a fifth of cancer deaths in women are due to breast cancer,[31] and death rates are above the European average.

The class gradients of deaths from cervical cancer and breast cancer are opposite, with better-off women suffering more deaths from breast cancer than poorer women.

Depression

Mental health problems are strongly linked to social inequality. Gender inequality is represented in data about the prevalence of treated depression from 1994 to 1998, which show a rate for women of 61 per 1,000 (two and a half times the rate for men). But these rates also show social class inequality, with women in deprived industrial areas showing 77 per 1,000 compared with 55 and 56 respectively in suburbia and rural fringe areas.

The United Kingdom has thus retained an egalitarian principle of provision for medical care while allowing the development of great inequalities in mortality and in physical and mental health. Gender is a factor in these, but the differences between women are also critical to understanding health in the United Kingdom.

POLITICS AND LAW

Suffrage

UK parliamentary institutions have been highly resistant to the effective participation of women. It took fifty years—and bloody campaigns—from the first debates about women's suffrage in the House of Commons in 1867 to the achievement of limited suffrage through the Representation of the People Act in 1918, which gave the vote to women over thirty who were householders or wives of householders, and sixty years to bring voting rights for women to the same basis—at age twenty-one—as those for men through the Representation of the People (Equal Franchise) Act in 1928. The voting age for both men and women is now 18.

Political Participation

Eligibility for election to the House of Commons was introduced in 1918. But representation of women has been low. Between 1918 and 1983, fewer than 5 percent of Members of Parliament (MPs) were women, rising to 9 percent before the 1997 general election. Now women are 17.9 percent of MPs at Westminster. The proportions are higher in other parliaments, with 24 percent in the European Parliament, 37 percent in the Scottish Parliament at Edinburgh, and 42 percent in the Welsh National Assembly in Cardiff. The first-past-the-post system,[32] which operates in Westminster, is unfavorable to women's election and does not look likely to be changed toward proportional representation in the near future.

The 1997 general election brought the biggest increase in women's membership of the House of Commons, doubling the number of women MPs from sixty to 120, 101 of whom were Labour. The Labour Party has been at the center of attempts to increase women's representation, and from 1990 adopted as official policy that half their membership in the House of Commons should be women within three elections. The strategy to achieve this has been controversial and changing. The strongest policy of positive discrimination,[33] which occurred between 1993 and 1996, was to have all-women shortlists for selected seats. The policy was dropped after legal challenges on the basis that it discriminated against men under the Sex Discrimination Act. There was little enthusiasm at the top for the all-women shortlist policy, and less radical strategies were substituted. Women's representation in parliament then took a step back in the election of June 2001, when thirty-six new Members of Parliament were elected, only four of them women. So women still work and wait for a system that will give them effective participation at Westminster. Current analysis shows that the policy of positive discrimination through all women short-lists had a considerable impact but will need to operate over a much longer timescale if it is to achieve a radical change in the numbers and culture in Parliament. New Legislation in 2002 puts these procedures outside the Sex Discrimination Act and makes it legal for parties to pursue strategies to enhance the election of women.

Women's membership of the government and the cabinet has increased with their increasing presence in the House of Commons. There are now 30.4 percent women in the Cabinet and slightly more among ministers in the wider government. These figures are much higher than in previous administrations. But government has become more centralized in Downing Street, with the chancellor of the exchequer and prime minister as key male figures. As women have gained the House of Commons, the influence of parliament itself is in decline.

Another strategy for improving the representation of women's concerns in government was the establishment of the women's unit in the Cabinet Office, now known as the Women and Equality Unit in the Department of Trade and Industry. Labour had promised a Ministry for Women, but in practice it has created a cross-departmental unit to coordinate the impact of policies on women and the representation of women's interests. The unit is an important source of research and policy for women. But although it appears to be at the heart of government, it is in practice only moderately influential. The Blair government's communitarian ideology has put a tra-ditional family policy into conflict with an agenda for women. There is some disenchantment among women voters with New Labour.[34]

Women's Rights

Feminist Movements

The women's movement is often characterized as having two waves. The first, starting from the middle of the nineteenth century, is mainly known for its fight for the vote, with a women's suffrage movement opposed through "Cat and Mouse" legislation, under which women were imprisoned and force-fed, released when near to death, and then reimprisoned for their political activities. But this first wave went wider and deeper than is often supposed in terms of mass support and in terms of its concerns with issues including access to equal pay for equal work, equality in family law and parenthood, pensions for widows with dependent children, and Suffragist Christabel Pankhurst's "votes for women, chastity for men."[35]

The women's movement's second wave is usually located in the 1970s, when a women's liberation movement demanded equal pay, equal education and opportunity, childcare, free contraception, a woman's right to choose her own sexuality, and freedom from intimidation by threat or use of violence or sexual coercion. Legislation for equal pay and protecting women against violence followed this second wave of political action. But the women's movement has also operated beyond formal politics through an "alternative political practice" involving a deliberate challenge to traditional welfare state traditions, with the development of women's aid and rape crisis centers run by women and for women. Women as workers are also now an active force in developing equal opportunity practice within employment and welfare agencies.[36]

The women's movement has been thought of as a new social movement. But it can also be argued that feminist action has been much more deeply rooted historically than this implies, with political activities around sexuality, prostitution, child sexual abuse, marriage, education, employment, and health dating back at least to the 1850s. It is also argued that the women's movement has never gone as underground as the account of the two waves implies.

Lesbian Rights

Because governments have until very recently supported a male breadwinner/female caretaker model of the family, it will not be surprising to find legislation discouraging lesbian relationships and motherhood. The broad picture is of legislation enlarging sexual and reproductive freedoms since the 1960s, but legal provisions governing heterosexual marriage and cohabitation do not apply to homosexual partners.[37] New reproductive technologies are controlled under the Human Fertilization and Embryology Act of 1990, which stipulates the need to take account of the welfare of a child who may be born as a result of treatment, "including the need of that child for a father." Although this does not amount to outright prohibition of artificial insemination, lesbian mothers may find it difficult to get treatment in clinics.

The Child Support Act of 1991 attempted to reconstitute the breadwinning function of fathers, and the Child Support Agency has required lesbian mothers to disclose the name of the biological father so that he can provide financial support for the child.[38] The UK government has shifted from the positions of its predecessors in some respects and the law has recently been amended to allow lesbian, homosexual, and unmarried heterosexual couples to adopt children.[39] But a more liberal position about homosexuality conflicts with government support for traditional families: therefore, lesbian mothers exist within a broadly disabling framework.

RELIGION AND SPIRITUALITY

Women's Roles

It has been noted that "very few religions or religious movements would even profess to treat women and men equally."[40] Quakers and Unitarians have been exceptions with a deep-rooted commitment to equality for men and women and some significant women reformers, for example Mary Wollstonecraft, whose feminist tract on the *Vindication of the Rights of Women* was published in 1792, and Elizabeth Fry, who campaigned in the nineteenth century for penal reform.[41] The Church of England has followed later, the Synod voting for the ordination of women to the priesthood in 1992, with the first women ordained in 1994 following a great debate within the church.

Gender is a highly significant variable in religious practice and belief, in quantitative and qualitative terms. Women predominate in the pews, and the differences between women and men increase with age and are increasing over time. The mainline churches in particular have experienced the greatest decline in men's attendance. Women are also more likely to count themselves as believers, whether practicing or not, and less likely to count themselves as unbelievers.[42]

Rituals and Religious Practices

The exclusion of women from ordination to the priesthood in the Church of England means that only for the past seven years have women been allowed to perform the rites of the church. It was argued that the sacramental function of priesthood as an icon of Christ meant that priests had to be men like Christ. On the other side of this debate, the culture of religion that excluded women was seen as manmade and changing, and it was argued that the laws of the church should be changed to reflect the spirit of Christianity in a modern world.[43] Changed they have been, and women's priesthood now helps to address the problem of declining numbers of men in the Church of England ministry.

Women's position in the rituals and practices of Christian churches beyond the Church of England and the other major religious groups is still largely of exclusion from priestly office. Latent membership of the Church of England is the most prevalent form of religious adherence in England.

Active membership declined rapidly in the latter part of the twentieth century to around 2 million members, although as many as half the population would regard themselves as latent members of the Church of England. Around 11 percent of the adult population of England and Wales is Roman Catholic, and there are smaller communities of Orthodox and free churches. The largest non-Christian population is Muslims, with perhaps 1.1 million mainly originating from the Indian subcontinent, notably Pakistan and Bangladesh, and smaller populations of Hindus and Sikhs.

Religious Law

Laws that have privileged the established churches—the Church of England and the Church of Scotland—have also privileged the men who were entitled to hold holy office. In England, the Archbishop of Canterbury is the highest-ranking nonroyal person. The sovereign is head of the church and must be a member of the Church of England. Although she can be a woman, until recently the bishops she appoints had to be men, and they have held privileged positions within government through the House of Lords. Although the church takes the leading role in national and civic occasions, the privileged position of the established church in law is giving way in practice to a more ecumenical representation of Christian churches and religious communities in public events. As active church membership has declined and the diversity of religious affiliation and practice has grown, the establishment of the Church of England has become less taken for granted. Blasphemy laws, which continue to protect the Christian religion without protecting other faiths, are a source of debate too, fired especially by the Rushdie affair, which brought the different status of different religions to public attention and controversy.[44] Although the established churches have been bastions of men's privilege, that will be transformed by women's ordination, the wider trends toward multiculturalism and diversity of religious practice make women's position in religions a much more complicated subject.

VIOLENCE

Domestic Violence

Feminists argue that men's physical and sexual violence against women tends to be ignored by the law and criminal justice system. These have historically sanctioned men's control of women through violence. For example, rape in marriage was legal until 1991. Domestic violence may now be treated as violence by the police and courts, but it is not always recorded as crime, and women are often in practice unprotected against violent partners or ex-partners. Counting men's violence against women is especially problematic, as it does not all appear in official statistics. The British Crime

Survey is a government-sponsored national crime survey conducted at intervals since 1982, and it is a major source of data for policymakers. It attempts to uncover the social experience of crime, going beyond the figures of crimes known to the police. In 1996 it recorded that 23 percent of women respondents aged between sixteen and fifty-nine said that a current or former partner had assaulted them at some time in their lives.[45] But feminist surveys have recorded much higher figures and argue that the experience of violence for women can be pervasive. The Wandsworth Violence against Women Survey found that 89 percent of respondents had experienced some form of violence during the past twelve months: 44 percent experienced violent attacks, 38 percent sexual harassment at work, and 12 percent threatened or attacked by the men they were living with.[46]

The women's movement in the 1970s established violence against women as rooted in gendered social structures. Women's Aid was established in 1971 to provide temporary refuges for women experiencing domestic violence, and there are now national networks across England, Wales, and Scotland. The ideals on which it has operated have been about mutual support rather than charity, self-determination rather than hierarchy, and open access rather than bureaucratic gate-keeping. Women's Aid has also campaigned vigorously for legislation to protect women from violence and enable them to establish themselves independently through access to social housing. There has indeed been legislation recognizing the needs of women trapped in violent relationships, especially the Housing (Homeless Persons) Act of 1977, now part of the Housing Act of 1996. These acts have identified women's need for a solution to their crisis as one of homelessness and have acknowledged their need for a long-term structural solution.

The research evidence has consistently pointed to women's need for a safe place, both at the point of crisis and in the longer term. This literature also documents women's difficulties in accessing safe long-term housing, showing that the lack of somewhere safe to go is a key reason for women returning to violent partners. There is a strong case that housing is a key resource, if not the key resource, that enables women to protect themselves against violence. Any erosion of housing access for women experiencing domestic violence exposes them to risk and makes them more vulnerable in relationships. But women's housing access has competed with other priorities—most involving reducing the public sector, but also some involving hostility to lone parent families and asylum-seekers—and real access to social housing has been reduced since the women's movement first fought these issues.[47]

Women's Aid has worked to change policy in law enforcement as well as in housing, with involvement in development violence forum and training work. A widespread recognition of women's experience of domestic violence has been achieved, and policies against it have been adopted in central and local government and in local police forces. But it will be a while before the legal and criminal justice systems, which have long protected men's interests, can be relied on to protect women's interests against men's violence.

Rape/Sexual Assault

Action against rape and sexual assault has also stemmed from women's groups outside the state, from informal and flexibly organized rape crisis centers. The difficulties in bringing women face-to-face in prosecutions against rapists have become much clearer, with the issue of consent at the heart of the difficulties of successful prosecutions.

Violence against women has become much more visible as a consequence of the work of women's groups in providing services to women, acting politically to change the law about housing and rape, and influencing policy implementation within the criminal justice system. The movement against violence has largely been based outside the state. It has achieved a large measure of cultural change, making men's violence unacceptable. Structural improvements in women's position will be needed to reduce women's vulnerability to men's violence.

OUTLOOK FOR THE TWENTY-FIRST CENTURY

The end of the twentieth century showed some clear trends that look likely to persist and underpin the development of gender relations in the United Kingdom into the twenty-first century. The enormous gains in women's educational achievement are the strongest support for their increasing equality in public and private life. Women's participation in the labor market has also developed in ways that will support a dual-earner model of gender relations for more advantaged women. The women's movement has been a crucial element in the politics of social welfare, in which the desirability of more equal gender relations is a taken for granted assumption. The male-breadwinner/female dependent model of the family is giving way to assumptions of more equal gender roles. But changes in commitments to collective services and public expenditure have made much greater social inequalities than existed within the postwar framework. These social inequalities mean that the services that might support women's equality—for example, childcare, health, and education—have often been limited and drained of resources. The breadth of Beveridge's attack on the five giants has reduced as some aspects of housing and social security have been privatized. The broad consequence of these trends for gender relations is that better-educated women have more equality with men and are likely to go on catching up. But poorer women suffer low wages and inadequate support from state childcare and other services—they risk falling further behind. Women's political action is still needed to entrench their position in formal politics, to support unpaid care work and share it more equally between men and women, and to make more widespread the gains that have come to better-off women.

NOTES

1. Unless otherwise noted, statistics are from the Office of National Statistics, (ONS) *Social Trends No 31*. London: The Stationery Office, 2001.

2. W. Beveridge, *Social Insurance and Allied Services cmnd 6404* (London: HMSO, 1942).

3. "Liberal" is used here in the standard historical and European sense of an ideology of free markets and a limited role for government in the political economy; as such, it is similar in meaning to what in the United States would be popularly labeled "conservative."

4. In the UK, students who wish to attend a university or an advanced technological institute must pass national examinations at the advanced level in at least two or more subjects.

5. Women's Unit, *Women and Men in the UK* (London: Stationery Office, 2000), 27.

6. Women's Unit, 2000, 23.

7. EOC, *Facts about Men and Women* (London: Office of National Statistics, 2001), 6.

8. The National Literacy Trust, www.literacytrust.org.uk/database/stats/keystatistics.html.

9. ONS, 2003, 6.

10. EOC, 2001, 5.

11. D. Grimshaw and R. Rubery, *The Gender Pay Gap* (Manchester: Equal Opportunities Commission, 2001).

12. Grimshaw and Rubery, 2001.

13. "Lone mother" is the preferred term in Europe for a single mother.

14. EOC, 2001, 7.

15. L. Adkins, *Gendered Work* (Buckingham: Open University Press, 1995).

16. DFEE, *Meeting the Childcare Challenge* (London: Author, 1998).

17. P. Moss, *The UK at the Crossroads* (London: Daycare Trust, 2001).

18. Moss, 2001, 4.

19. P. Moss and F. Deven, *Parental Leave* (Brussels: NIDI/CBGS, 1999).

20. G. Pascall and J. Lewis, "Care Work beyond Beveridge," *Benefits* (2001).

21. E. Heron and D. Dwyer, "Doing the Right Thing," *Social Policy and Administration* 33, no. 1 (1999): 91–104.

22. European Commission, *The Social Situation in Europe* (Luxembourg: Office for Official Publications of the EC, 2000), 103.

23. K. Kiernan, H. Land, and J. Lewis, *Lone Motherhood* (Oxford: Oxford University Press, 1998).

24. J. Gershuny, *Changing Times* (Oxford: Oxford University Press, 2000), 180–92.

25. P. Hewitt, *About Time* (London: IPPR/Rivers Oram Press, 1993), 168.

26. J. Lewis, *The End of Marriage?* (Aldershot: Edward Elgar, 2001).

27. D. Monk, "New Guidance/Old Problems," *Journal of Social Welfare and Family Law* 23, no. 3 (2001): 271–92.

28. J. Micklewright and K. Stewart, *Is Child Welfare Converging* (Florence, Italy: UNICEF, 1999).

29. *Teenage Pregnancy* (London: Stationery Office, 1999), www.cabinet-office.gov.uk/seu/index/whats_it_all_about.htm.

30. L. Doyal, *Women and Health Services* (Buckingham: Open University Press, 1998), 3.

31. Women's Unit, 2000, 7.

32. The "first-past-the-post" system is similar to the U.S. "winner-take-all" system of elections for Congress as opposed to a system of successful candidates being chosen from political party lists in proportion to their party's percent of the total vote in a district.

33. "Positive discrimination" is a commonly used term for affirmative action.

34. J. Squires and M. Wickham-Jones, *Women in Parliament* (Manchester: Equal Opportunities Commission, 2001).

35. S. Walby, *Gender Transformations* (London: Routledge, 1997).

36. J. Lovenduski and V. Randall, *Contemporary Feminist Politics* (Oxford: Oxford University Press, 1993).

37. Lorraine Fox Harding, *Family, State and Social Policy* (London: Macmillan, 1996), 125.

38. Nickie Charles, *Feminism* (London: Macmillan, 2000), 87–193.

39. In 2003 new legislation has been promised on official registration of same-sex relationships, bringing important new rights to lesbian couples.

40. A. Aldridge, *Religion in the Contemporary World* (Cambridge: Polity Press, 2000), 1999.

41. Aldridge, 2000.

42. G. Davie, *Religion in Britain since 1945* (Oxford: Blackwell, 1994), 118–19.

43. Aldridge, 2000, 202–3.

44. K. Boyle and J. Sheen, *Freedom of Religion and Belief* (London: Routledge, 1997).

45. Women's Unit, 2000.

46. T. Eadie and R. Morley, "Crime, Justice and Punishment," in *Social Policy*, ed. J. Baldock et al. (Oxford: Oxford University Press, 1999), 445.

47. G. Pascall et al., "Changing Housing Policy," *Journal of Social Welfare and Family Law* 23, no. 3 (2001): 1–17.

RESOURCE GUIDE

Suggested Reading

Charles, Nickie. *Feminism: The State and Social Policy*. London: Macmillan, 2000.

Equal Opportunities Commission. *Facts about Women and Men in Great Britain*. Manchester: Equal Opportunities Commission, 2003.

European Commission. *The Social Situation in the European Union 2000*. Luxembourg: Office for Official Publications of the European Communities, 2000.

Hallett, Christine. *Women and Social Policy: An Introduction*. Hemel Hempstead: Harvester Wheatsheaf, 1996.

Harding, Lorraine Fox. *Family, State and Social Policy*. London: Macmillan, 1996.

Office of National Statistics. *Social Trends No 33*. London: The Stationery Office, 2003.

Pascall, Gillian. *Social Policy: A New Feminist Analysis*. London: Routledge, 1997.

Pilcher, Jane. *Women in Contemporary Britain*. London: Routledge, 1999.

Salisbury, Jane, and Sheila Riddell. *Gender, Policy and Educational Change*. London: Routledge, 2000.

Watson, Sophie, and Lesley Doyal. *Engendering Social Policy*. Buckingham: Open University Press, 1999.
Women and Equality Unit. *Key Indicators of Women's Position in Britain*. London: Department of Trade and Industry, 2002.

Web Sites

Equal Opportunities Commission, www.eoc.org.uk.

European Database: Women in Decision-making, www.db-decision.de.

The Fawcett Society, www.fawcettsociety.org.uk.

National Statistics, www.statistics.gov.uk.

UNECE Gender Statistics, www.unece.org/stats/gender.

Women and Equality Unit, www.cabinet-office.gov.uk/womens-unit.

Organizations

Equal Opportunities Commission
Arndale Centre, Arndale House
Manchester M4 3EQ, UK
Email: info@eoc.org.uk

The Fawcett Society
Fifth Floor, 45 Beech Street
London EC2Y 8AD, UK
Web site: www.fawcettsociety.org.uk

Women and Equality Unit
10 Great George Street
London SW1P 3AE, UK
Web site: www.womenandequalityunit.gov.uk

SELECTED BIBLIOGRAPHY

Adkins, L. *Gendered Work: Sexuality, Family and the Labour Market*. Buckingham: Open University Press, 1995.
Aldridge, A. *Religion in the Contemporary World: A Sociological Introduction*. Cambridge: Polity Press, 2000.
Beveridge, W. *Social Insurance and Allied Services cmnd 6404*. London: HMSO, 1942.
Boyle, K., and J. Sheen. *Freedom of Religion and Belief: A World Report*. London and New York: Routledge, 1997.
Davie, G. *Religion in Britain since 1945*. Oxford: Blackwell, 1994.
Department for Education and Employment (DFEE)/Department of Social Security cm 3959. *Meeting the Childcare Challenge*. London: Department for Education and Employment/Department of Social Security, 1998.
Doyal, L. *Women and Health Services*. Buckingham: Open University Press, 1998.

Eadie, T., and R. Morley. "Crime, Justice and Punishment." In *Social Policy*, 2nd edition, edited by J. Baldock et al., 437–68. Oxford: Oxford University Press, 1999.

Equal Opportunities Commission. *Facts about Women and Men in Great Britain 2001*. London: Office of National Statistics, 2001.

European Commission. *The Social Situation in the European Union 2000*. Luxembourg: Office for Official Publications of the European Communities, 2000.

Gershuny, J. *Changing Times: Work and Leisure in Post-Industrial Society*. Oxford: Oxford University Press, 2000.

Grimshaw, D., and J. Rubery. *The Gender Pay Gap: A Research Review*. Manchester: Equal Opportunities Commission, 2001.

Heron, E., and P. Dwyer. "Doing the Right Thing: Labour's Attempt to Forge a New Welfare Deal between the Individual and the State." *Social Policy and Administration* 33, no. 1 (1999): 91–104.

Hewitt, P. *About Time: The Revolution in Work and Family Life*. London: IPPR/Rivers Oram Press, 1993.

Kiernan, K., H. Land, and J. Lewis. *Lone Motherhood in Twentieth Century Britain*. Oxford: Oxford University Press, 1998.

Lewis, J. "Work and Care." In *Social Policy Review 12*, edited by H. Dean, R. Sykes, and R. Woods, 48–67. Newcastle: Social Policy Association, 2000.

———. *The End of Marriage? Individualism and Intimate Relationships*. Aldershot: Edward Elgar, 2001.

Lovenduski, J., and V. Randall. *Contemporary Feminist Politics: Women and Power in Britain*. Oxford: Oxford University Press, 1993.

Micklewright, J., and K. Stewart. *Is Child Welfare Converging in the European Union?* Florence, Italy: Unicef International Child Development Centre, 1999.

Monk, D. "New Guidance/Old Problems: Recent Developments in Sex Education." *Journal of Social Welfare and Family Law* 23, no. 3 (2001): 271–92.

Moss, P. *The UK at the Crossroads: Towards an Early Years European Partnership*. London: Daycare Trust, 2001.

Moss, P., and F. Deven. *Parental Leave: Progress or Pitfall? Research and Policy Issues in Europe*. Brussels: NIDI/CBGS Publications, 1999.

Office of National Statistics. *Social Trends No 31*. London: The Stationery Office, 2001.

Pascall, G., S.-J. Lee, R. Morley, and S. Parker. "Changing Housing Policy: Women Escaping Domestic Violence," *Journal of Social Welfare and Family Law* 23, no. 3 (2001): 1–17.

Pascall, G., and J. Lewis, "Care Work Beyond Beveridge." *Benefits* 32 (September/October): 1–6, 2001.

Social Exclusion Unit. *Teenage Pregnancy*. London: The Stationery Office cm 4324, 1999.

Squires, J., and M. Wickham-Jones. *Women in Parliament: A Comparative Analysis*. Manchester: Equal Opportunities Commission, 2001.

Walby, S. *Gender Transformations*. London: Routledge, 1997.

Women's Unit. *Women and Men in the UK: Facts & Figures 2000*. London: Stationery Office, 2000.

INDEX
